YEAR	NAME OF LEGISLATION	PURPOSE AND EXPLANATION OF LEGISLATION
1997	IDEA (PL 105-17) Amendments *(continued)*	An IEP must include a statement of any modifications that are required to enable a student to participate in an assessment. A student's IEP must establish benchmarks or short-term objectives. The IDEA's triennial reevaluation requirement has been modified to allow evaluation teams to forgo testing where new information is not needed to assist in placement decision. The 1997 Amendments require state and local educational agencies receiving IDEA assistance to offer parents voluntary mediation, with the states being required to establish an informal mediation procedure and to make mediation available whenever a due process hearing is requested. Some of the most important sections of the IDEA Amendments of 1997 concern student discipline and the requirement that a free and appropriate education be made available to all student with disabilities, including those who have been suspended or expelled from school (certain students with disabilities can be removed from the classroom and placed in an alternative educational setting for an additional 45 days over the 10-day limit for carrying or possessing firearms or for having, using, or selling medication or illegal drugs at school or school functions). The IEP team is required to review whether the student's inappropriate action was a manifestation of the disability. Students with disabilities may properly be disciplined in the same manner as students without disabilities if the behavior is not a manifestation of the student's disability.
2002	No Child Left Behind Act (PL 110-107)	Includes children with special needs in legislation stressing accountability and testing
2004	IDEA Amendments	The new amendments focus on defining "qualified" for special education in the terms of qualified personnel in the basic legislation. Amends the earlier version of alternative placements for children with behavior problems to a maximum of 45 school days Authorizes earmarking up to 15% of IDEA funds to states for students who wish to continue under Part C instead of transferring at age 3 to Part B Proposes state pilot studies designed to reduce paperwork and extend IEPs that are apparently working to 3 years

Educating Exceptional Children

EDUCATING EXCEPTIONAL CHILDREN

ELEVENTH EDITION

Samuel A. Kirk
Late of University of Arizona

James J. Gallagher
University of North Carolina at Chapel Hill

Nicholas J. Anastasiow
Emeritus, Hunter College, City University of New York

Mary Ruth Coleman
University of North Carolina at Chapel Hill

HOUGHTON MIFFLIN COMPANY
Boston   New York

Publisher: Patricia A. Coryell
Senior sponsoring editor: Sue Pulvermacher-Alt
Senior development editor: Lisa Mafrici
Editorial assistant: Dayna Pell
Senior project editor: Rosemary Winfield
Editorial assistant: Jake Perry
Art and design coordinator: Jill Haber
Photo editor: Jennifer Meyer Dare
Composition buyer: Sarah Ambrose
Manufacturing coordinator: Chuck Dutton
Marketing manager: Nicola Poser
Marketing associate: Wendy Thayer

Cover: © Benjamin Shearn / Getty Images

Part and chapter opener photographs   *Part 1:* © Robin Sachs/PhotoEdit;
Chapter 1: © Bob Daemmrich Photography, Inc.; *Chapter 2:* © Susie Fitzhugh;
Part 2: © Myrleen Ferguson Cate/PhotoEdit; *Chapter 3:* © Dan McCoy/ Rainbow;
Chapter 4: © Elizabeth Crews; *Chapter 5:* © Photo courtesy of the Fragile X
Foundation, www.fragilex.org; *Chapter 6:* © Getty Images; *Chapter 7:* © Susie
Fitzhugh; *Chapter 8:* © Jeff Greenberg/The Image Works; *Chapter 9:* © Susie
Fitzhugh; *Part 3:* Jeff Greenberg/PhotoEdit; *Chapter 10:* © Susie Fitzhugh;
Chapter 11: © Peter Byron/PhotoEdit; *Chapter 12:* © Susie Fitzhugh; *Chapter 13:*
© Phyllis Picardi/Stock Boston.

Chapter 1, pages 23–24: From Frank Warren, Call them liars who would say all is
well, in H. Turnbull & A. Turnbull (Eds.), *Parents speak out: Then and now*
(Columbus, OH: Merrill, 1985). Reprinted with the permission of Pearson Education.

Printed in the U.S.A.

Library of Congress Catalog Card Number: 2004105490

ISBN: 0-618-473-890

23456789-DOW-09 08 07 06 05

CONTENTS

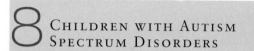

For the past four decades, the field of special education has operated as a major agent of change for the general field of education. Through the use of the four major engines of change in our society—legislation, court decisions, administrative rule making, and professional initiatives—special education and its advocates have actively changed the educational landscape.

▶ **Legislation**   The passage of a law guarantees that attention will be paid to the content of that law. Some of the most important advances for children with special needs have come through federal legislation that is over thirty years old (P.L. 94-142 Education for All Handicapped Children Act) but continues to be updated, revised, and renamed as we discover how to make the law serve us better. It is now called the Individuals with Disabilities Education Act, and the latest revisions in this text address the *2004 Reauthorization of IDEA*.

▶ **Court decisions**   Court decisions at both the state and federal levels have confirmed the basic right of children with disabilities to a free and appropriate public education.

▶ **Administrative rule making**   Administrative rule making has been important in bringing legislation and court decisions to a practical level. Administrative rules provide local educators with guidance on how broad general principles can be carried out in the school and the classroom.

▶ **Professional initiatives**   Professional initiatives have been made by several generations of special educators and researchers who design new technologies for educating exceptional children, organize alternative teaching approaches, and construct differentiated curriculum so that the basic purposes of educating exceptional children are carried out.

The result of all of these efforts has been an educational setting in the first decade of the twenty-first century that would not be recognized by educators of the 1950s. It has not been easy for educational personnel and parents to make these changes to accommodate exceptional children. It has taken large measures of cooperation and good will to reach our current state. Changes continue to be made even as we read this text. We believe that the majority of these changes have brought education to a more effective level, not only for exceptional children but for all children.

■ Target Audience

Past editions of this text have had as a target audience a wide range of students and teachers, cutting across professional disciplines and introducing the students to a multidisciplinary perspective that can be helpful in later professional careers. This edition stresses even more the importance of the *general education teacher*, since the broadening concept of *inclusion* has made the teacher a focal point for the programming for exceptional children. It does little good to announce that most exceptional children should be based in the regular classroom if, at the same time, we cannot find ways to prepare teachers for new responsibilities that require cooperative relationships with various professionals and the ability to talk several different professional languages. We hope this text will be one tool that can be helpful in this regard.

■ Themes

A number of themes flow through the various chapters and discussions of this text.

▶ **Ecology of the Child**   We emphasize the ecological approach to special education. There is an increasing awareness that the exceptional child swims in a rich cultural sea that includes families, peers, school, culture, and community that will determine much of the child's response to the world. We perceive the family as a central force in the education of the child, and resolving family needs and conflicts is critical to successful educational adaptation for the exceptional child. The ecological theme is addressed most heavily in Chapter 3, on early childhood intervention. It also is reinforced in each chapter's "Ecology of the Child" feature. This special feature allows us to highlight an exceptional individual's interactions with family, school, culture, or community and address issues that go beyond the classroom.

▶ **Genetic-Environment Interaction**   One of the continuing themes in this edition is the complex interactions between the child with exceptionalities and the ecological seas in which they swim. Although we have noted in the past the importance of the environment on the child, the power of the interaction effects between genetics and environment has become ever more evident. In part, the advancement of genetic understanding through the Human Genome Project has helped us to this conclusion, but we spend much time in this edition looking at the impact of this interaction on the developing child. The long-term genetic consequences of a condition such as autism or of situations such as low birth weight no longer seem clear, particularly if we can introduce positive elements in the child's environment early on. It becomes even more important to intervene now that we know that failure to intervene early may condemn the child to a negative development that could have been lessened or avoided.

▶ **Inclusion**   The increasing use of the educational principle of *inclusion* (the practice of establishing the child with exceptionality within the general education classroom as a base) has generated new techniques that such placement makes necessary. The universal design for learning (UDL) calls for the presentation of key ideas in many different modes and not merely in the standard verbal mode that is used for the regular student. Mathematics can be taught with a textbook—and also with computer software that visually presents figures as they are rotated in space. As in many different examples in this text, an instructional device used for children with special needs turns out to be effective for the average student as well.

▶ **Special Environments**   We now know that not every exceptional child can be comfortably housed in the general education classroom, even though that environment is recommended by the doctrine of inclusion. The least restrictive environment to maximize education for the child with special needs sometimes will be a resource room for a part of the day or even a special class designed for this child's special needs. The importance of thinking of one child at a time, instead of broad groups, becomes even more important for special education as the child's special problems create unique issues for the educator.

▶ **Policy** Because these exceptional children need special resources, one of the continuing questions is where these resources will come from. If we accept the definition of policy as "the allocation of scarce resources to almost unlimited needs," then it follows that somebody is going to be left out when these scarce resources are doled out. So our special education concern has to be not only classrooms or teacher-child interactions but also those halls in which policy decisions are made about the allocation of our scarce resources.

■ Organization of the Book

In Part One, "Introduction, History, and Social Forces in Special Education," we offer two chapters that discuss the general issues faced by all exceptional children. The first chapter, "Educating the Exceptional Child," introduces the reader to exceptional children and discusses why they present an educational challenge. It also addresses the *child and the family*, which clearly has great importance in determining the child's development and responses to the environment. The child's peer group and cultural background also play major roles in that development. The extraordinary diversity in cultural backgrounds in this country complicates the job of the professionals whose own understanding of diversity may be limited.

The second chapter, "Exceptional Children and Social Institutions: Schools, Government, and the Courts," deals with *major social institutions* that play important roles in the resources needed for special education. Schools, government, and the courts have played significant roles in the past and will continue to do so in the future of exceptional children. As with the discussion of the family in Chapter 1, our descriptions of key social institutions in Chapter 2 lay the groundwork for the rest of the text.

Part Two, "High-Incidence Exceptionalities" begins with Chapter 3, "Early Intervention: Priorities and Programs," which covers some of the common adaptation problems for the young exceptional child. This period from birth to age 5 is such an important part of the life of the child, particularly a child with special needs, that we have felt that it deserved a chapter of its own, again preparing the way for later educational program discussions.

The remainder of the chapters in Part Two and in Part Three, "Low-Incidence Exceptionalities," focus on a particular group of exceptional children (such as learning disabilities, autism, or hearing impairments) and discuss the differentiated programs that are needed to take into account the unique aspects of that condition. In each chapter, we discuss the identification and definition of each condition; its causes and characteristics; and intervention, assessment, assistive and instructional technology, transition, and lifespan and family issues. A major section on current educational adaptations for these children is offered as well.

■ Revisions in This Edition

We are delighted to have Dr. Mary Ruth Coleman join us for this eleventh edition of *Educating Exceptional Children*. Her years of classroom experience and her work enhancing the preparation of special and general education teachers allow her to bring a special sense of practical instruction to our discussions. In addition, her leadership with professional associations such as the Council for Exceptional Children enhances the text's discussion of the development and design of necessary policy for these children.

We have thoroughly updated each chapter in the eleventh edition, with up-to-date references and coverage. Highlights of new content in each chapter include:

Chapter 1, "Educating the Exceptional Child," introduces the Human Genome Project, a remarkable adventure in genetic discovery, with influences that are felt throughout the text. Also discussed is the universal design for learning (UDL) by which exceptional children can access the regular curriculum. The important role played by the family is emphasized.

Chapter 2, "Exceptional Children and Social Institutions: Schools, Government, and the Courts," presents the new emphasis on accountability in the schools and its implications for exceptional children. It also looks at the growing power of the inclusion movement, which has placed many exceptional children in the regular classroom. The role played by legislation and court decisions in the development of programming is noted.

Chapter 3, "Early Intervention: Priorities and Programs," emphasizes the young child as an active participant in learning. The family-centered approach is described, and the effectiveness of early intervention presented. Evidence is presented for the utility of well-designed early intervention programs and for the important role played by transition planning to help exceptional children move from preschool to school programs.

Chapter 4, "Children with Specific Learning Disabilities," introduces new concepts (such as responsiveness to instruction) that are designed to modify the definition and measure learning disabilities. The goal is to separate children whose poor performance has been due to environmental factors and children with true learning disabilities. The reasons for the sharp increase in the prevalence of these conditions are discussed.

Chapter 5, "Children with Mental Retardation and Developmental Disabilities," extends the role of adaptive behavior in definition and programming. The chapter focuses on strengths of the child and the role played by identifying needed supports. Fragile X syndrome is an important focus of attention. The rapidly increasing transition programming to help community adjustment following school is described.

Chapter 6, "Children with Emotional and Behavior Disorders," details the origins and consistency of aggressive behavior. The importance of functional behavior analysis in identifying positive behaviors and strengths to be worked with is presented. The uses of behavior contracts are noted.

Chapter 7, "Children with Communication Disorders in Speech and Language," stresses the importance of emerging literacy skills and its nurturance in young children, along with the growing issues of cultural differences in language development, particularly with children who have English as a second language.

Chapter 8, "Children with Autism Spectrum Disorders," describes children with Asperger's syndrome in particular as well as the genetic origins of autism in general. The politics of autism as it influences public policy is noted as is the use of relationship-focused (RF) intervention to help parents cope with these children with many differences.

Chapter 9, "Children Who Are Gifted and Talented," details the conflicts behind the dual societal goals of equity and excellence. Gender differences are presented. Arguments for multiple intelligences are stressed. The chapter also focuses on the importance of curriculum design for gifted students from low-income families along with observational methods for finding children with gifts and talents from culturally diverse families. The uses of problem-based learning for teachers of gifted students are described.

Chapter 10, "Children Who Are Deaf or Hard of Hearing," stresses the importance of early identification and treatment. The difficulties that children with severe hearing losses have in fitting into the general education classroom are pointed out, as is the need for social constructivism in the building of meaningful knowledge for the student in interactions with the teacher and peers, regardless of the particular method of communication.

Chapter 11, "Children with Visual Impairments," presents suggestions for early interventions. The expanded core curriculum for children with visual impairments—including orientation and mobility, independent living skills, recreation and leisure skills—is discussed. The importance of the universal design for learning and listening skills is pointed out, and the uses of assistive technology are noted.

Chapter 12, "Children with Multiple and Severe Disabilities," discusses the importance of literacy skills. The design of an ecological inventory is presented, including personnel resources and institutions that are available (such as malls, religious groups, recreational facilities, and so forth). Such an inventory can help educators design a realistic individualized educational plan. The uses of technology are stressed with these children.

Chapter 13, "Children with Physical Disabilities and Health Impairments," describes a wide range of various conditions, including the relatively new category of traumatic brain injury. The need for an ecological inventory as a prelude to planning for these children is noted. It is also pointed out that Section 504 of the Rehabilitation Act can supplement IDEA in preserving the rights of these children to an appropriate educational experience.

■ Special Learning Features in the Eleventh Edition

▶ **A new chapter structure** better accommodates the increasing number of courses that are cross-categorical in structure. Chapters are now divided between high-incidence and low-incidence disabilities to better define this new reorganization.

▶ A **new full-color design** improves the format and presentation of material, giving a thoroughly modern look and feel to the text.

▶ The **Introduction** presents significant history in special education and changes that have occurred during recent decades. This section prepares the reader for the content of the text and for critical thinking about the future of special education

▶ **Focus Questions** help readers set goals and establish purposes for their reading of each important topic.

▶ **Education Adaptations** features offer extensive suggestions for teaching to the strength of exceptional children by varying the learning environment, the content, or the teaching approach. The color background screens make these special pages easy to locate. This feature offers an abundance of bulleted lists, as well as boxes containing practical suggestions.

▶ An **Inclusion in Context** portion of each "Educational Adaptation" feature appears in the Adapting the Learning Environment section and takes a balanced approach to the dilemma of appropriate placement.

▶ An **Ecology of the Child** feature appears once per chapter. These features focus on the family, schools, peers, culture, or community in relation to the exceptional child.

▶ **Family and Lifespan Issues** sections appear near the end of every chapter. They allow students to view the individual throughout the lifespan and focus on issues such as the role of the family, work and higher-education opportunities, social adjustments in adulthood, and integration into the community.

▶ **Margin Notes** highlight important points and material. These are particularly useful for general education teachers. Many provide web addresses for further investigation of critical topics.

▶ **Summary** sections conclude each chapter and highlight in a clear, point-by-point format the major concepts presented in the chapter.

▶ **Future Challenges** sections encourage student to discuss and propose solutions for problems that are still being debated in the field of special education.

▶ **Key Terms** listed at the end of each chapter are cross-referenced to where in the text the terms are boldfaced and discussed.

▶ **Resources** sections tie together three types of resources: *References of Special Interest, Journals,* and *Professional Organizations.*

▶ A **Glossary** at the end of the text defines all key terms.

We hope that the instructors who use the eleventh edition of the text will let us know what works and what does not so that continuing adjustments can be made.

■ Additional Student and Instructor Support

▶ **Instructor's Resource Manual**   The *Instructor's Resource Manual*, prepared by Robert Zuckerman of Kent State University, is an all-purpose tool for reference and ideas when teaching this book. This manual provides instructor support from sample syllabi to assessment materials. The chapter-by-chapter resources include chapter outlines, learning objectives, focus questions, key terms, lecture topics, student activities and assignments, key concept review, and supplementary lists of professional publications and films. The assessment materials include both essay and multiple-choice questions.

▶ **Houghton Mifflin Testing Computerized Test Bank**   The assessment materials provided in the *Instructor's Resource Manual* are also available in electronic format for ease of use. This bank of test questions is compatible with both PC and Macintosh computers.

▶ **Website for Students**   The students' website is developed to help students practice and better absorb the learning they get from their book and classroom experiences. To this end, we offer chapter outlines, web links, questions for thought, and interactive flashcards of key terms with definitions. Students may also test their own learning with multiple-choice self-assessment quizzes for each chapter.

▶ **Website for Instructors**   The instructor's website includes materials in the *Instructor's Resource Manual*, in addition to content designed for a digital environment. PowerPoint slides for each chapter, web links, and a look at the student self-assessment quizzes help round out the website.

■ Acknowledgments

We are grateful to many of our colleagues and specialists in various exceptionalities for their criticisms and suggestions during the revision of this edition:

Heather L. Ball, University of Maine at Machias
Lawrence A. Beard, Jacksonville State University
Sherwood J. Best, California State University, Los Angeles
Laurence Coleman, University of Toledo
Maria D. Cox, Columbia University
Jean B. Crockett, Virginia Polytechnic Institute and State University
Carl Dunst, Orelena Hawks Puckett Institute
Dale C. Farran, Vanderbilt University
Herbert Goldstein, Emeritus, New York University
Carol Gothelf, The Shields Institute, New York
Timothy Lackaye, Hunter College of the City University of New York
John L. Luckner, University of Northern Colorado
James D. Persinger, Emporia State University
Lynne A. Rocklage, Eastern Michigan University
Robert B. Rutherford, Arizona State University
Rosanne K. Silberman, Hunter College of the City University of New York
Judith Smitheran, St. Vincent Hospital, Santa Fe
Janet W. Stack, University of Virginia
Robert Zuckerman, Kent State University

The authors also wish to acknowledge with gratitude the fine editorial work done by Kristen LeFevre, developmental editor, and Rosemary Winfield, production editor. Their work has made the work of the authors much more lucid and responsible. We also wish to note the contributions of senior Houghton Mifflin staff: Lisa Mafrici, senior development editor, who has been with several editions of this volume, and Sue Pulvermacher-Alt, senior sponsoring editor, who has been helpful on a variety of publication issues. Special thanks to Don Braswell, Tonya Gabrielle, and Raymond McKenzie for their unique contributions.

Finally, we wish to acknowledge the senior author of this work, Sam Kirk. Sam was a true giant in the field of education—scholar, teacher, writer, mentor, policy maker, colleague, and friend. Thousands of children and families who never knew his name have benefited from his insightful work.

James Gallagher
Nicholas Anastasiow
Mary Ruth Coleman

INTRODUCTION TO THE ELEVENTH EDITION

■ Special Education in the Twenty-First Century

Special education started the twenty-first century vigorously. A strong state and federal legislative base and a history of favorable court decisions supporting a "free and appropriate public education" for all citizens have resulted in several decades of established special educational practice.

It was not always so. A half-century ago, parents had to take their chances in finding help for their exceptional child. They sometimes even had to change neighborhoods or communities to locate and become eligible for special education services.

■ Changing Established Educational Practice

Four major mechanisms of change appear to drive modifications of standard educational practice:

▶ **Legislation**   The latest of the federal laws, the Individuals with Disabilities Education Act (IDEA 2004), continues a series of federal laws beginning in 1967 that ensure the presence of special education services for children with disabilities regardless of their communities or states.

▶ **Court decisions**   A broad series of decisions at state and federal levels confirmed the rights of children and families and forbade school districts from refusing enrollment to any children on the grounds that the district had no resources available to care for them. The courts essentially said that if resources are not there, then the districts must provide them.

▶ **Administrative rules**   Most people underestimate the power of rule making by the local, state, and federal governments. Detailed rules for creating individual education plans for each exceptional child guide local educators in implementing legislative and court decisions.

▶ **Professional initiatives**   One great benefit of the early laws was that they supported the preparation of special educators in higher education. This support has produced several generations of specialists who have generated important research and advances in the education of exceptional children.

All of these mechanisms of change have been involved in the important goal of parent involvement. The key legislation comments on the importance of parents, the courts have protected the rights of parents within the school setting, the administrative rules detail how parents are to be included in the development of the individual education program (IEP), and numerous research projects (professional initiatives) have examined the importance of parental influence. The critical role of the family is without question.

There is a single exception to these engines of change. Gifted students are not included in the federal legislation on exceptional children, although we include them in our definition of exceptional children, and about half of the states include them in their exceptional child programs.

The authors have seen many developments in special education that will make the twenty-first century different from the twentieth, and these develop ments need to be noted if we are to understand where we actually are and where we are most likely headed. We believe the old philosopher who said, "You can't know where you are going if you don't know where you've been."

In the early years of special education, a child's disability was narrowly perceived of as a medical diagnosis of an abnormality caused by nature. This disability was seen as a deficit, and often the child was segregated from nondisabled family, peers, and community. But today we use a developmental interactional model to replace the medical model. Today we take into account both nature and nurture. And today we see the whole child and the ecology of the child. Instead of viewing the exceptional child as deficient, we build on strengths. We strive for inclusion of the child in the school and society, not exclusion or isolation. In addition, this culture has moved away from an ethnocentric framework to a culturally and linguistically diverse view. Each of these concepts is discussed in more detail in the following sections.

■ The Developmental-Interactional Model

For good reasons, the medical profession was the first to become interested in the children that we refer to as exceptional. Many of those children had physical and health problems that brought them to the attention of physicians. The terminology relating to such problems was dominated by medical labels such as phenylketinuria, Down syndrome, mental deficiency, blindness, and deafness.

The medical community is still deeply involved in prevention and the discovery of causes. However, even though a disability might have a medical cause, we in education have gradually realized that we are concerned with the unusual and atypical development of the child that may have resulted from that cause. Those developmental patterns are more the province of educators, social scientists, and therapists than of medical practitioners. So the atypical development of the child in cognition, language and communication, social and behavioral processes, and so forth is our primary concern here. Each chapter of *Educating Exceptional Children* discusses the child's development, regardless of the category of disability.

Nature and Nurture

Historically, much of the dialogue about child development dealt with whether the conditions of the children that we identified as "exceptional" were caused by heredity (nature) or by environment (nurture). This was hardly just an intellectual or scientific discussion. Consider the consequences if either one of the two explanations was judged correct. If the child's behavior and performance are indeed determined by his or her genetic makeup, then our energies should be directed toward discovering the causes of these conditions to prevent disabilities or enhance giftedness. In other words, if nature is responsible, we should encourage epidemiologists, geneticists, and biologists to become more involved. If, on the other hand, the child's behavior should be viewed as being caused largely by his or her environment, then educators, psychologists, and sociologists would be involved. Much energy ought to be expended on designing that responsive environment and on the nature of the instruction that the child receives to maximize that environment.

We have concluded that *both* arguments have merit. In fact, nature and nurture are closely intertwined. While much of what we see in children with special needs is often related to their genetic makeup, the environment can play a significant role even in the development of conditions such as learning disabilities or behavioral disturbance. Nurture certainly plays a major role in determining how the child responds to the condition itself. So the complexity of the interactions of nature and nurture will surely challenge our next generation of professionals, on both sides of the issue.

In each chapter of the book, we focus on the causes and characteristics of the condition in question, and a feature section called "Educational Adaptations" examines how the design of the educational environment can maximize and nurture the growth of the individual child.

■ Interactions with Educators, Family, Peers, and Community

Most special education in the twentieth century was based on the assumption that since the condition was within the child, or intraindividual, the teacher or therapist should deal directly with the child. Other factors that might have been related to the condition, such as family or community, were often put aside. Gradually, we have realized that *many* other factors influence our ability to help the child with special needs to develop. Family members are important, but so is the school, the peer environment, the community, and the overarching culture. And we refer to all this as the ecology or the context of the child.

■ Building on Developmental Strengths

Children with learning problems used to be presented as having widely varying developmental patterns of strengths and weaknesses, and the weaknesses became the focal point of special education efforts to try to make the developmental patterns more even. Focus was, to a large extent, on correcting the deficit or what was "wrong with the child." So if a deaf child didn't talk, an enormous effort was made to help him or her to talk, and other developmental areas such as cognition and social processes were ignored or downplayed.

We now realize that it may be more effective to analyze a child's strengths and to focus a therapeutic program around them. For the child who is deaf, this might mean using good social skills to enhance communication or finding alternative ways of communicating, such as American Sign Language. Therefore, in the twenty-first century, increased efforts are being made to find the child's and his or her family's strengths and build a program around them, hoping that they can offset the deficit.

Our current chapter on learning problems stresses building on strengths, and special education for the child who is deaf no longer emphasizes the serious lack of speech development. Instead, alternative means of communication are encouraged by using the child's ability to learn symbolic language through signs and symbols and then helping speech develop through what is referred to as total communication.

■ Placement: Separated or Included?

In the nineteenth and early twentieth centuries, large state schools and institutions were constructed, often in rural areas of the state, and they were places where children who were deaf, blind, or mentally retarded were educated.

Much of the early twentieth century saw many exceptional children isolated and separated from typically developing children and often from their families. Only gradually was the child with special needs brought back to the core of society, first from institutions, then from special schools, then from special classrooms. Now many exceptional children are in general classrooms with a variety of special aids and assistance. A determination was made that such children should be "a part of," not "apart from," the schooling of other children. All of these moves from social isolation to inclusion have been and remain controversial, but current public sentiment has little doubt that these children deserve a chance to grow up in and experience the same educational system as their more typical peers. Accomplishing that objective, however, requires a multidisciplinary team.

The commitment to meeting the individual needs of each child means that a variety of educational strategies and placements may be necessary to accommodate the diversity of students with special needs. Although some professionals who are involved in special education are proponents of full inclusion under all circumstances, we feel that special education is moving toward the most favorable placement of each child: in other words, the child should be placed wherever he or she is most likely to learn. This may mean that the child spends part of the day in a resource room and part in the general education classroom. Professionals in each category of disability have their own views on inclusion for particular exceptionalities. These views are represented in this text.

■ Toward Cultural and Linguistic Diversity

One striking change that began during the twentieth century was the gradual demographic shift in our population. The number of exceptional children who come from a variety of cultures has increased. Their families have often felt distant or alienated from the ethnocentric traditions that have shaped American businesses, politics, and public schools.

We can see the effect of such a demographic shift in our cuisine, our art, and, of course, our schools. For children with special needs who come from a variety of cultural and linguistic backgrounds, special adaptations need to be made. Conflicts that formerly were assumed to be merely between family and school may now be recognized as between culture and school. And like the other types of changes we have just discussed, this realignment creates special challenges for educating exceptional children, particularly for those children for whom English is a second language.

All of these trends are like intertwining threads that comprise the new fabric of American society, of American education, and of our special interest in the education of exceptional children. One challenge for the next generation of special educators is to adapt to these changing trends in a way that can bring the maximum growth to these children and their families.

We cannot assume that the resources for providing special education services will always be available. Public policy ebbs and flows around topics, and scarce resources will always be needed for other priorities. If we work to make visible the needs of families of exceptional children, it will help to maintain their place in our nation's priorities.

Finally, the message that the authors wish to deliver to those who read this text is that we have no reason to be complacent. Each chapter in this book lists "future challenges" as a way of reminding us how much more needs to be done for exceptional children and their families. We have come far, it is true, but there is much more to be done.

EDUCATING EXCEPTIONAL CHILDREN

PART ONE

INTRODUCTION, HISTORY, AND SOCIAL FORCES IN SPECIAL EDUCATION

The book begins with a look at the rich history of special education over the past four decades and at the social forces that have played a significant role in establishing special education in the schools. In Chapters 1 and 2, we take a look at the old saying that "You can't know where you are going unless you know where you've been" through the lens of the field of special education.

EDUCATING THE EXCEPTIONAL CHILD

FOCUS QUESTIONS

► Who are children with exceptionalities?

► How have approaches to treating individuals with special needs changed over time?

► What is the ecological approach?

► How do parents and siblings respond to the presence of a child with disabilities in the family?

► How does cultural diversity affect the future of exceptional children?

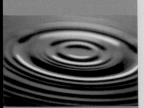

I t's not easy to be different. We've all felt the sting of not belonging, of not feeling a part of the group. We've all felt overwhelmed when asked to do things beyond our skills and capabilities, or bored when asked to do simple things that do not challenge us. Of course, being different is not always negative: It is what makes us interesting. But it also forces us to adapt to meet social expectations. When being different means that a child is not able to receive information through the normal senses, is not able to express himself or herself, or processes information too slowly or too quickly, special adaptations in the education program are necessary.

Despite the philosophical commitment to individualization in our education system, classrooms all too often are filled with grade-level textbooks, grade-level lessons, and grade-level expectations that assume that students deviate very little from their age norm—that is, they are "normal." What happens when students are different, when they cannot adapt to the standard education program because of their exceptionalities? The consequences are serious and have lifelong implications.

Adapting to educational programs is precisely the problem that exceptional children face, and some form of special education is necessary for these children to reach their potential. In this book we focus on the specific educational needs resulting from exceptionalities among different groups of children and the range of educational programs developed especially for them.

Council for Exceptional Children www.cec.sped.org

■ THE EXCEPTIONAL CHILD

Our focus is the individual exceptional child and his or her development, including how the forces around that child (family, school, peer culture, and community) adapt to meet his or her needs. We discuss in some detail the family and its adaptations, the school and special education, and other external forces, always with the goal of understanding and helping the special child to cope effectively with the outside world.

Who Is an Exceptional Child?

We consider a child to be exceptional when his or her differences or disabilities occur to such a degree that school practices must be modified to serve the child's needs.

The term *exceptional child* is generally accepted to include both the child with developmental disabilities and the child who is exceptionally able. Here we define an **exceptional child** as a child who differs from the average or normal child in (1) mental characteristics, (2) sensory abilities, (3) communication abilities, (4) behavior and emotional development, or (5) physical characteristics. These differences must occur to such an extent that the child requires either a modification of school practices or special educational services to develop his or her unique capabilities.

Of course, this definition is general and raises several questions. What is *average* or *normal*? How extensive must the difference be for the child to require special education? What is special education? What role does the child's environment play in the definition? We ask these questions in different forms throughout this text as we discuss each group or category of exceptional children.

Exceptional individuals tell us something important about human development. By studying and teaching children who are remarkably different from the norm, we learn about the many ways children develop and learn, inform ourselves more thoroughly about the developmental processes of all children, and develop our teaching skills and strategies for all children.

Categories of Exceptional Children

Internet Resources
for Special Children
www.irsc.org

If we define an exceptional child as one who differs in some way from a group norm, then many children are exceptional. A child with red hair is "exceptional" if all the other children in the class have brown or blond hair. But that difference, though interesting to a geneticist, is of little concern to the teacher. Educationally speaking, a child with red hair is not an exceptional child, because the educational program does not have to be modified to serve the child's needs. Children are considered educationally exceptional only when it is necessary to alter the educational program—for example, if their exceptionality leaves them unable to read or to master learning in the traditional way or places them so far ahead that they are bored by what is being taught.

The following groupings of exceptional children are typical:

▶ Intellectual differences, including children who are intellectually superior and children who are slow to learn (such as giftedness and mental retardation)

▶ Communication differences, including children with learning disabilities or speech and language disabilities

▶ Sensory differences, including children with auditory or visual impairments

▶ Behavioral differences, including children who are emotionally disturbed or socially maladjusted

There are many types of exceptionalities. Some of the categories of exceptionality include mental retardation, giftedness, communication disorders, learning disabilities, visual and hearing impairments, emotional and behavior disorders, and physical and health disabilities.

▶ Multiple and severe handicapping conditions, including children with combinations of impairments (such as cerebral palsy and mental retardation, or deafness and blindness)

▶ Physical differences, including children with nonsensory impairments that impede mobility and physical vitality

The Interaction of Heredity and Environment

Few topics stimulate more fascination than the question of how we become who and what we are. What forces shape our development and sequentially create a confident and complex adult from an apparently helpless infant? For many decades, we have been aware of the effects that both heredity and environment have on the developing child. Because it is the educators' role to change the environment of the child through instruction, it has been tempting to ignore the role of heredity. It is as though we have concluded that we, as educators, don't know much about heredity, so it can't be very important to us.

But the recent dramatic progress in the fields of genetics makes heredity impossible to ignore. Actually we have been through three major stages in our belief systems about the relative influence of heredity and environment, and each stage has had a profound effect on how we behaved as educators. Up until about 1960, it was strongly believed that heredity drove and determined various conditions related to intelligence, such as *familial* mental retardation (retardation without obvious neurological insult), giftedness, or mental illness. Those beliefs led us to consider it more or less impossible to change such conditions, and the role of educators was to help individuals adapt as well as possible to their hereditary roll of the dice (Plomin & Petrill, 1997).

Starting around 1960, there was a major movement to discover the important role played by environment and to suggest that many exceptionalities can be created by various environmental conditions. It was reasoned that mild mental retardation could be caused by lack of early stimulation or that giftedness emerged only because the environment for some children was incredibly favorable. Educators were encouraged to try to find ways to reverse unfavorable effects through education.

Around 1990, a similar shift in the view of the relative roles of heredity and environment took place. Now the emphasis is on the progressive interaction of heredity and environment and the resulting effects of those interactions. Gottlieb (1997) proposed that by changing the environmental conditions of early childhood we can activate different patterns of genes, which then can result in behavioral changes.

> The present viewpoint takes advantage of the well-accepted fact that only a very small proportion of an individual's genotype participates in the developmental process. . . . In our view, a change in developmental conditions activates heretofore quiescent genes thus changing the usual developmental process and resulting in an altered behavioral or morphological phenotype. (pp. 158–159)

The growing capabilities for genetic research, however, have made it clear that many conditions that result in special needs are linked to an intertwining of genetics and environment. Conditions such as fragile X syndrome, mental retardation, attention-deficit hyperactivity disorder (ADHD), and dyslexia all have seemed to have genetic components (McGuffin, Riley, & Plomin, 2001).

One of the most dramatic recent scientific breakthroughs has been the Human Genome Project (http://www.ornl.gov/hgmis). The goals of this international project were to determine the complete sequence of the three billion DNA subunits (bases) to identify all human genes and make them accessible for further biological study. The U.S. Department of Energy and the National Institutes of Health were the U.S. sponsors. The goals were reached in 2003. The many research projects fanning out from these basic discoveries include a number that relate to exceptional children (Coughlin, 1999).

What is important is that the complex interaction between heredity and environment urges the educator to seek out the most stimulating environmental conditions to apply, but always with an eye toward the contributions of heredity.

There is a trend toward identifying increased numbers of students as learning disabled.

Prevalence

Educational policy makers, those who make the decisions about how we should spend societal resources on education, want to know just how many exceptional children there are. Those numbers will tell us how big an issue this is and how much we, as a society, will have to spend on it.

A reasonable estimate is that about four to five million children can be classified in categories of exceptional children. This means that approximately one out of every ten to twelve children can be labeled *exceptional,* which is one reason for the extensive attention given to exceptional children in our school systems today.

There are many more than ten different categories in which a child can be placed as exceptional, but children are not distributed equally in these categories—far from it. Figure 1.1 gives a breakdown of the four leading categories of disabilities. The prevalence of children in the gifted category is given in Chapter 9.

The category of learning disability far outnumbers the other categories, with 50 percent of all children called exceptional currently being identified as learning disabled (*Twenty-fourth Annual Report to Congress,* Office of Special Education Programs, 2003). Children with speech and language disorders make up the next-highest category, at about 20 percent; children with mental retardation, about 10 percent; and behaviorally or emotionally disturbed at about 8 percent. Various reasons for this disparity in categories are discussed in more detail in subsequent chapters.

FIGURE 1.1
High-Incidence Disabilities Percentage of Students Served in Category

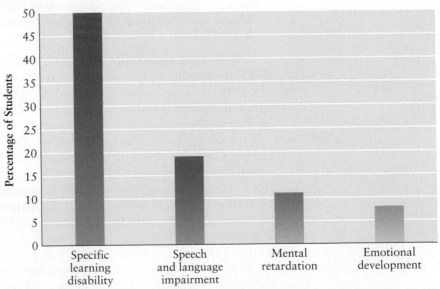

Source: U.S. Department of Education (2003). *Twenty-fourth Annual Report to Congress.* Washington, DC: Office of Special Education Programs.

The remaining categories make up about 1 percent or less of the total, including children with hearing impairments, children with visual impairments, children with autism, children with orthopedic impairments, and children with multiple disabilities. Separate chapters discuss the characteristics of these children and the educational adaptations made for them.

As we learn more about children, there is a tendency to establish more categories. Children with "traumatic brain injuries" and children with "attention-deficit hyperactivity disorders" (ADHD) are two relatively new categories for special educators and general educators to cope with.

Is there an epidemic of learning disabilities in this country affecting schoolchildren, or is something else happening? Obviously, there has been some important change in our perceptions of these students (MacMillan & Forness, 1998). (Chapter 4 discusses this trend and its implications.) The other categories of high-incidence disabilities seem to have been relatively stable over the same time period.

Children with attention-deficit hyperactivity disorder (ADHD) have many similarities with other groups of exceptional children, notably children with learning disabilities or behavior disorders, and so appear in a number of chapters in this text.

Students with attention-deficit hyperactivity disorder (ADHD) have difficulty maintaining attention, which can affect their academic success.

Yes I Can! Foundation
for Exceptional Children
http://yesican.sped.org

Intraindividual Differences

By definition, exceptional children are different from children of the same life age. The differences present educators with many challenges. What sometimes goes unnoticed is that some students differ substantially from others not only along key dimensions of development (interindividual differences) but also within their own abilities (intraindividual differences). A child may have the intelligence of an 11-year-old but the social behavior of a 6-year-old. Both interindividual and intraindividual differences are the concern of special educators.

Understanding a child's **intraindividual differences**—the differences in abilities *within* the same child—can help us develop individualized programs of instruction. These programs are tailored to the strengths and weaknesses of the individual child. They do not necessarily consider how that child compares with other children.

Intraindividual differences can show up in any area: intellectual, psychological, physical, or social. A child may be very bright but unable to see or hear. Or a child may be developing normally physically but be unable to relate socially to his or her agemates. It is just as important for teachers to know the child's unique pattern of strengths and weaknesses as it is to know how the child compares with other children.

One reason for the development of the Individualized Education Program (IEP), of which much will be said throughout this text, is that these intraindividual differences pose unique problems for educators to solve. The important legislation, the Individuals with Disabilities Education Act (IDEA), includes a requirement that the child with disabilities have "access to the general education curriculum."

One way to provide such access is by utilizing the major advances in technology that allow us to create a Universal Design for Learning (UDL). This means that there are different instructional avenues by which a teacher or a team of teachers can help the student gain access to the general education curriculum. If a child with disabilities cannot read material, perhaps a visual presentation can enable him or her to master the basic curriculum.

In this book, each chapter dealing with children with special needs or exceptionalities offers an Educational Adaptations feature describing specific educational strategies for specific exceptionalities.

■ The Context of the Exceptional Child

When discussing the child as learner, it's important to paint a complete portrait of the child, including the social and family context in which he or she lives. Even as the lead actor on the stage captures our attention, we are aware of the importance of the supporting players and the sets to the play itself. Once we recognize the individuality of each child and the complex and unique forces and circumstances that act on and surround him or her, it is easier to choose or create the most appropriate instructional strategies and the most suitable learning environment.

Interaction between the child and his or her surroundings begins at birth and continues and increases as time passes. Figure 1.2 provides a schematic showing the major components that are in continual interaction. For example, Paul was born with limited cognitive abilities. That, in turn, has caused the family some concern, which results in their anxiously trying to stimulate him to greater performance.

FIGURE 1.2
The Context/Ecology of the Exceptional Child

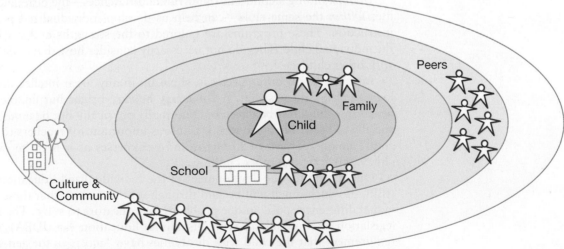

Source: U.S. Department of Education (2003). *Twenty-fourth Annual Report to Congress.* Washington, DC: Office of Special Education Programs.

Paul can sense the family's lack of approval, and this can translate into his being less confident in his own abilities and less likely to perform well. As Paul gets older and interacts with peers in the neighborhood and at school, he can receive further feedback on his limited cognitive abilities, which results in even more loss of self-confidence and affects his performance in school and in the neighborhood. Paul's performance is not the result of genetics. It is the result of the multitude of interactions that his genetic capabilities have experienced with his surroundings. So we must pay attention to these early interactions with family and peers and the society in which he lives (see Chapter 3).

Similarly, Ellen may have been born with some hyperactive tendencies that result in her always interacting with family members, whether they want her to or not. Depending on how easily these hyperactive tendencies are accepted or rejected by significant others in her life, Ellen's personality and her social and emotional development are shaped by the reactions of the family and the larger world. Her tendencies to hyperactivity, while clearly genetic, will be shaped in later years, positively or negatively, depending on the reactions of those around her.

The Influence of Family and Peers

When we first meet a child with disabilities at age 4 or 8 or 9, there is a tendency to believe his or her unusual or atypical behavior to be the result of whatever disability the child possesses. However, such behaviors could well be the cumulative response of the child to the reactions of peers, family, and neighborhood to the disability. If the child is aggressive, hyperactive, and noncommunicative, the chances are strong that such behavior will be met with counteraggression and hostility, which will tend to make the original behaviors of the child with disabilities worse! If we can change or modify these responses of peers and family members in a constructive way, we may be able to substantially reduce the atypical behavior of the child with disabilities (Rutter, Galler, & Hagell, 1998).

> Environment, or ecology, plays a major role in the initial development of an exceptional child. Some atypical behaviors are a response to the reactions of family and friends.

There is a natural tendency in families who are reacting to a child with disabilities to respond in a nonproductive way to the manifest behaviors being shown by that child. That is, parents tend to reduce or eliminate speaking to the child who does not speak back, or they will respond to the child's aggression with aggression of their own. Such reactions tend to compound and extend the original problem, and this means that families need to be educated in more productive responses to the original behavior of their child. Increasingly, the approach that educators are taking to cope with the milder forms of exceptionality is to try to aid the child's adjustment by modifying the life circles around the child (see Figure 1.2), in addition to attempting to attack the child's developmental delay problem.

Emotional Development and the Family

We have become increasingly aware that the emotional repertoire of the child is not a natural consequence of constitutional makeup, but instead is socially constructed (Shonkoff & Phillips, 2000). One of the main terms being used to describe the emotional development of the child is *theory of mind*. This term refers to children's becoming aware of the feelings and attitudes of others around them. They are aware of when their parents are angry or disapproving or when their peers are not anxious to play with them. Children with autism, in particular, have a strong delay in the development of **theory of mind,** but this is also true of many children with a variety of disabilities. The inability to grasp and interpret the behavior and communication of others can create long-term social problems (Flavell and Miller, 1998). But since the emotional repertoire of the child is socially constructed, it can be socially modified, and that is one of the major objectives of special education.

> Resources for People
> with Disabilities:
> A National Directory
> www.fergpubco.com

> The ecological approach seeks to modify the child's behavior directly by improving the context in which the child lives, learns, and plays.

The Ecological Approach

Perhaps the most dramatic change in educators' view of how to teach young children has resulted from the adoption of the ecological approach to child development (Bronfenbrenner, 1989). With this recognition of the role of the environment, the field moved from a **medical model** of exceptionality, which assumes that the physical condition or disease exists within the patient, to an **ecological model,** in which we see the exceptional child in complex interaction with many environmental forces.

The ecological approach tries not only to modify the exceptional child's learning and behavior through direct contact with the child but also to improve the environment surrounding the child, including the family and the neighborhood—the entire context of the child. This ecological approach became the strategy of Head Start and other programs targeted at children from economically disadvantaged families. Head Start pays much attention to the family in addition to the child (Zigler, Kagan, & Hall, 1996). The ecological model also helps us understand what we can realistically expect to accomplish through intervention programs.

The Unique Influence of the Family

One of the major forces that influence the exceptional child, or any child, is the family system. As it is a system, we expect that anything that happens to one member of that family will have an impact on all the other members of the family (Cox & Paley, 1997). If we expect to be effective in special education, we have to work with the family system in which the child lives, not just with the child. The trend toward early intervention (before the age of 5) increases the importance of the family. Much of the intervention with young children is directed toward changing the family environment and preparing the parent or parents to care for and teach their child. At the very least, intervention tries to generate more constructive parent-child interactions. (Chapter 3 focuses specifically on early childhood intervention from a variety of perspectives.)

The increasing interest in the family can be attributed to a series of basic assumptions about the exceptional child and his or her family (Bailey, Buysee, Edmondson, & Smith, 1994):

Families of exceptional children play an important role in early intervention. Parents can teach their children some of the skills and learning tools that will later be reinforced in a school setting.
© Peter Hvizdak/The Image Works

1. Children and families are inextricably intertwined. Intentional or not, intervention with children almost invariably influences families; likewise, intervention and support with families almost invariably influence children.
2. Involving and supporting families is likely to be a more powerful intervention than one that focuses exclusively on the child.
3. Family members should be able to choose their level of involvement in program planning, decision making, and service delivery.
4. Professionals should attend to family priorities for goals and services, even when those priorities differ substantially from professional priorities.

The purpose of this **family-focused approach** is to help parents become more autonomous and less dependent on professionals, to be able to form their own support networks as appropriate instead of being told by "experts" how to raise their children.

Whenever the helping professions (such as medicine, education, and social work) make a major shift from an almost exclusive emphasis on the child to an emphasis on the family, a lot of professionals find themselves in unfamiliar territory. These are the teachers, psychologists, occupational therapists, and others who have been trained under the old "treat the child" model. They now have to change their accustomed practices if the family-focused approach is to become a reality. Many professionals have not felt adequately prepared for this shift (Bailey, Palsha, & Simeonsson, 1991).

PROFILES

DEVELOPMENTAL

How can educators monitor and explore inter-individual and intraindividual differences? Developmental profiles provide one way to track the range of an individual's differences. The graph below shows the developmental profiles of three children.

Joan: Joan is an intellectually gifted 10-year-old. Her mental ability tests at age 14; her achievement in reading and arithmetic tests at

from one to four grades beyond her fifth-grade classmates. These are the interindividual differences between Joan and her classmates. But notice that Joan's performance shows many intraindividual differences. Although mentally she has the ability of a 14-year-old, her physical development is about average for a girl her age, and her social maturity is only slightly higher. If her parents or teachers expect her to behave like a 14-year-old in every dimension of

Profiles of a Child with Intellectual Gifts, a Child with Mental Retardation, and a Child from a Different Cultural Background

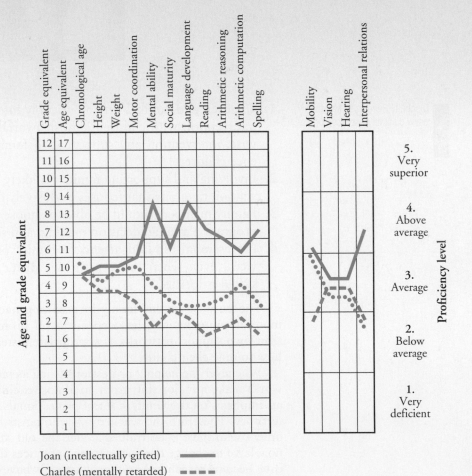

Joan (intellectually gifted) ———
Charles (mentally retarded) – – – –
Juan (culturally different) ••••••

development because her mental development is at that level, they are going to be disappointed.

Charles: The second profile in the figure is of Charles, a child with mental retardation. His profile shows him to be behind in development and performance in almost every dimension. Although he is 10 years old, his mental ability and academic performance are at first- and second-grade levels. These interindividual differences distinguish Charles from his classmates. In addition, Charles shows substantial intraindividual differences, ranging from the 6- and 7-year-old level in academic achievement to the 9- and 10-year-old levels in physical development and life age.

Joan and Charles have very different exceptionalities. Yet both present similar problems for their teachers and schools: Their inter- and intraindividual differences set them apart from their classmates and require special educational attention.

Juan: There has been a marked increase in children from culturally different backgrounds in U.S. schools in the past decade. Juan comes from a family that has been in the United States for four years, and they are having serious problems adapting to American schools and procedures.

His developmental profile may be seen in the graph on page 12, along with Charles's and Joan's. One can see that Juan is not performing at grade level in language development, reading, arithmetic, and spelling. Since his profile roughly parallels that of Charles, we must be especially cautious in reaching conclusions about Juan's cognitive abilities. We may underestimate his abilities because the different culture Juan has lived in has not given him the experiences that other American children his age have had. Actually, his measured mental ability seems to be in the normal range. While special adaptations should be made for him in the school program, he should *not* be considered a candidate for special education.

Teachers should be alert to procedures for assessing students as exceptional. Note whether any one gender or ethnic or racial group is overidentified as needing special education.

Child-Family Interaction

We stress the importance of viewing the child in the *context* of family and societal forces. Although less easily measured than interindividual and intraindividual characteristics, these contextual forces nevertheless have a powerful impact on a child's development.

Let us think of two youngsters, Dan and Roger, each of whom has been born with a moderate case of cerebral palsy, a disorder caused by damage to the parts of the central nervous system that control motor movements. This condition is certain to cause mobility and communications problems for both children. Each will surely find his way into some form of special services that exist in practically all school systems in the United States.

Dan's family viewed his arrival as a true disaster. Dan's mother sees his disability as a serious hindrance to her pursuing her own career goals. Despite her efforts to put such feelings aside, the resentment of what Dan's presence means to her and her interests is hard to submerge entirely. Similarly, Dan's father, struggling in his own career, sees Dan as a heavy and continuing burden of special expenses and needed therapies and, in the end, perhaps continued dependence on the family far into the future. These feelings, too, are hard to contain.

The relationship between an exceptional child and his or her family is lifelong and complex. Basic family responsibilities include economics, domestic and health care, recreation, self-identity, affection, socialization, and educational and vocational choices.
(© Richard Hutchings/PhotoEdit)

In Roger's family, however, after the initial disappointment of the diagnosis of cerebral palsy, his arrival was accepted as a special challenge. His mother and father told Roger's siblings that he will have some problems developing and that it is the responsibility of everyone in the family to help him develop as best he can. Both his mother and his father have felt the sting of social rejection in the past, and they are determined to do whatever they can to make sure that Roger is accepted as a normal child.

Now think about Dan and Roger at age 6: Which child do you think is more likely to be responsive to peers and teachers, and which child will become more quickly discouraged by failure and need more external support?

Differences in family attitudes, actions, and support result in variations in how children with special developmental problems such as cerebral palsy adjust to education or cope with their special condition. Thus, it is essential to consider familial and societal variables, in addition to assessing children's developmental profiles, to better understand what has happened to them in their family life before they entered school or even what is happening in their life now beyond the school environment. Interviews can provide important information about the context of the child.

It is important to consider the values of the culture and community as a major factor in how the exceptional child will adjust to education.

Parental Response

As the example of Dan and Roger shows, parents often react strongly (positively or negatively) to the birth of an exceptional child. And it is important to consider those responses, because they happen to every parent, regardless of his or her educational background or socioeconomic level.

Most parents who must cope with a child with serious disabilities face two major crises. The first is the "symbolic death" of the child who was to be. When their child is first diagnosed as having a serious disability, most parents feel shock and then denial, guilt, anger, and sadness before they finally adjust (Peterson, 1987). A few parents react with severe depression (Bristol, Gallagher, & Schopler, 1988). Members of groups composed of parents of children with similar disabilities are quite effective in helping new parents by sharing how they have coped with these problems.

The second, quite different crisis that many parents of exceptional children face is the problem of providing daily care for the child. The child who has cerebral palsy or is emotionally disturbed is often difficult to feed, dress, and put to bed. It is the continual, day-by-day responsibilities for care that often weigh families down and require sympathetic professional attention. The realization that their child may not go through the normal developmental process or may never become an independent adult often weighs heavily on the parents.

Parents of a child with serious disabilities must face two crises: the symbolic death at birth of the child-who-could-have-been and the difficulty of providing daily care for the child-who-is.

Family Responsibilities

The relationship between an exceptional child and his or her family is lifelong and complex, beginning with the disclosure of the exceptionality. When a child with disabilities is added to the family, the daily responsibilities grow larger. There is the additional expense, the time, and the energy needed to care for the child; the extra concern for the child's safety; the difficulty of helping the child develop a good self-image and social skills; and the problems of seeing that the child receives an appropriate education. Many ordinary tasks become more difficult and more stressful. Consider Roger's care:

Case Study: Roger's Family

The responsibilities of two-parent working families are awesome enough without adding the special condition of a child with disabilities. Roger's father and mother are awakened at 6:30 in the morning by the cries of Roger's sister. Roger has to be washed and dressed, a task of considerable difficulty because of his cerebral palsy. Meanwhile Roger's mother is setting out breakfast while beginning to think about her own workday as a teacher at a local school.

Roger's father gets Roger washed and dressed and down to the breakfast table and then begins to think about a shower and shave before going to the construction company where he works. Before work, he must deliver Roger to the developmental day-care program, where he is in an integrated program with his age peers. The family is fortunate in that Roger's sister goes to school where the mother teaches, so one transportation problem is solved.

Breakfast is a wild round robin with no one sitting down at the same time. Roger needs extra help from one of the adults because of his inability to totally control the tools needed to bring cereal and milk to the proper resting place. Mother puts the breakfast dishes in the dishwasher, and father is off with Roger while mother makes the beds before going off to school.

In the late afternoon and evening, the same procedure is reversed. This time mother has to pick up Roger because father is at a construction site on the other side of town. She is delayed further by the teacher describing an incident at the day-care center that involved Roger's conflict with another child over possession of some toy. Then is still dinner to prepare and baths to give and stories to read before the children are tucked in. Is it any wonder that the parents are weary at the end of the day and are not looking forward to tomorrow when Roger is to receive a medical checkup on top of the normal daily activities? Which parent is going to take Roger to the doctor's office?

Imagine, first of all, this type of routine with only one parent present to do all the tasks required. How much more harried and tired such a mother (most of the time the "one parent") is at the end of the day. Imagine further what would happen if there was not some tacit agreement between the parents about who was supposed to do what, or if there were interpersonal tensions between mother and father because they cannot agree about the proper way to discipline Roger or just because their own personal needs continually take second place to the requirements of the children. It is not hard to see that this family is key to positive experiences for the exceptional child or why all family members need understanding and support from time to time.

When considering basic family responsibilities, it is important to realize the enormous diversity of families. There has been a substantial increase in single-parent families. Because many single mothers live in poverty, their children are less likely to receive good prenatal and postnatal care, which increases the chances of the children having physical, academic, and emotional problems.

The perception that each partner in a two-parent family is taking responsibility for the family in an acceptable way determines family harmony (Bristol, Gallagher, & Schopler, 1988). The important factor for family harmony is whether the mother and father come to an understanding about the roles and responsibilities that each will hold in the family. The specific actions of one or the other parent are less important than the understanding that those behaviors have been agreed upon as appropriate at a particular stage in the family life cycle.

There are many stresses in the lives of families who have children with disabilities, but their lives are also filled with joy, laughter, and fun. These children can light up your heart with a smile just as any child can, and parents of children with disabilities, just like other parents, have their favorite stories of their young child's adventures in development. The child is always a child first and a child with problems second. The task of the professional is to allow that child to bloom and grow to the limit of his or her capabilities.

> Only when both parents understand and accept what each person's role and responsibilities will be in caring for a child with disabilities will there be family harmony.

Family-Professional Relationships

Continuous shifting of the relationship between professionals and families in the field of exceptional children has been taking place over the past few decades. Originally, the professionals' role was to interpret the special needs of the child to the parents and to give them directions or training for the proper treatment of the child. The mother was the traditional contact, with other family members playing a lesser role.

Now, those family members are being encouraged to assume a more significant role in the planning and execution of a program for their own child. Further, the child is viewed as part of a larger society, and professionals believe that successful treatment consists of their trying to modify those ecological elements in the life of the child, doing so in concert with the family.

Turnbull and Turnbull (2002) have described the **family-centered model** as the latest of the various family-professional models.

> First, the *family-centered model* primarily attempted to honor family choice by changing the power relationship between professionals and family.
> Second, the *family-centered model* abandoned a pathology orientation and adopted a strengths orientation.
> Third, the entire family is the unit of support, not just the child with a disability and the child's mother (p. 92).

These three principles can change dramatically the relationship between family and professional, particularly by motivating special educators to look for the strengths in the child and family instead of focusing on the shortcomings of both.

Working Mothers

Perhaps the greatest change in family roles has been in the movement of women into the work force. In 1948, fewer than 11 percent of mothers with children younger than age 6 worked outside the home. Now, over 60 percent of mothers with children under the age of 5 are in the work force (Bureau of Labor Statistics, 2002).

When we spoke in the past of family-professional relationships, we were really speaking mainly of mother-professional relationships. Traditionally, fathers have not played a large role in continuous relationships with professionals. Only recently have fathers become a source of study in the families of children with disabilities. This increase in working mothers reflects the way in which families must adapt to the necessity and reality of dual careers.

Parent Empowerment

To help empower parents, teachers might refer parents to any one of the many parent support groups for children with disabilities.

Parent empowerment refers to the parents taking action to get what their child needs. Parents are no longer expected to unthinkingly take advice from a professional or team of professionals about the treatment of their child with special needs. Parents of exceptional children are now expected to play a major and determining role in their child's care, and the professionals are to provide needed counsel and specialized advice.

There is general agreement on the need to form partnerships with parents, but the real question is how that partnership is forged and how that changes the traditional professional-parent relationship (Roberts, Rules, & Innocenti, 1998). Teaching the professional to respect the family as an equal partner and helping parents carry out an action plan for their child requires a different kind of training than has been the style in education or special education.

The current approach has the family actively seeking and collecting information from many different sources, particularly other parents of children with disabilities who have had experiences similar to their own. In this approach, the parents draw on the expertise of the professional community but make many of their own decisions about what is best for their child.

ECOLOGY OF THE CHILD

FAMILY   ## Deidre's Parents Encourage Her Success

Deidre Davis attributes her current success to her parents, Bernice and Hilton, and her unique experience in growing up as a child with a disability.

"My parents gave me confidence and the ability to get to know different people. They instilled in me their appreciation for differences. They also gave me the knowledge that I could set any goal I wanted and that I would have their support. Because of them, I never had any sense of fear or failure," Davis confides.

Davis is the deputy assistant secretary of state for equal employment opportunity and civil rights for the U.S. Department of State. Davis who has T-3 paraplegia (a thoracic-level spinal cord injury), was appointed to her current position by President Clinton in November 1994. . . .

Growing Up

When Davis was 6 years old, she woke up one morning and found she could not walk. Davis says of the event, "I remember thinking, 'Hmm, maybe I'm still asleep. Let me try that again.'" Only Davis was not asleep; a tumor on her spinal cord had temporarily paralyzed her. The tumor was removed, but doctors emphasized she would not walk again.

However, after nine months of intensive rehabilitation, Davis was able to walk with braces. Mrs. Davis remembers, "Deidre never seemed to be afraid, she never cried, and I think we took our strength from her. When she was very young, I remember she said, 'This is my life, and I'm going to make the best of it.' I think she really has."

During Davis's rehabilitation, she had been home-schooled. Davis remembers, "When I was ready to go back to school, my parents decided that it was not conducive for me to go back to the neighborhood school because it was four stories high, with many steps." In other words, accessibility would be a problem. Davis's parents approached the school board and petitioned them to reassign their daughter to a different school. Davis remembers, "They told my parents that they 'shipped all of their handicapped kids' to another city. It didn't matter what your disability was, or your academic prowess, that was where they went." Davis's parents were against this educational homogenization and instead set out to find an accessible full-inclusion school. . . .

School Days

Davis notes that the first few months at her new school were far from easy. She was relentlessly teased and her classmates had plenty of ammunition. Not only was she a minority as a black child at the school, but having a disability set her apart as well. Davis points out some of these children definitely

Parents as Collaborators

Many intervention programs for children with disabilities are developed and monitored by a multidisciplinary team. The team may include the child's teacher, special educators, doctors, therapists, and parents. Parents serve three primary functions as collaborators in the child's education program. First, their observations of the child are a valuable source of information to the professionals. This information becomes part of the basis for the child's educational program and the evaluation of that program. Second, parents—especially the

came from racist families, but for others, it was simply a lack of exposure. Davis emphasizes, "My parents and I knew that this school was the best for me academically and physically, so I wasn't going to go home and plead my case, saying, 'Let me out of this' because I knew what the alternative was."

Davis notes that eventually these same children who had been giving her a tough time grew to respect her because she proved herself as a good student and a regular kid. She showed them that she also enjoyed jokes, conversation, and playing. . . .

Davis declares, "My parents taught me to fight for myself. They never went the 'overprotective route' saying things like, 'Don't do that' or 'You're going to hurt yourself.' Their attitude was, 'Whatever you want to do, go ahead and try.'" And she did. . . . Davis excelled at tennis, gaining national ranking as a wheelchair tennis player. Her grandmother had been a professional tennis player in the Black American Tennis League, and her father had taught her how to play the net. Davis remembers, "I couldn't walk well, so I used the tennis racket as a cane, and I'd hit the ball, fall down, get up again, and do the same thing."

Aside from the constant encouragement and determination they had instilled in their daughter, Hilton and Bernice Davis also made a point not to protect or hide Deidre from other children who had special needs. "My parents sent me to a camp where there were other children like myself, and I think that this was a very proactive thing to do," Davis explains. . . . "Although I am not a parent, my own parents have taught me that you have to give a child self-esteem, an opportunity to be his or her own individual, and not to be overprotective. My parents did this for me, and I am truly grateful."

Source: Jennifer C. Stolting, "Acting Civil," *Exceptional Parent*, (September 1998): 74. Reprinted with permission.

WHAT IS THE CONTEXT?

The proactive approach taken by Deidre and her parents provided Deidre with the confidence she needed to achieve her goals. Now an adult, Deidre has a professional position in the U.S. Department of State. At the time Deidre went to school, her parents had to work hard to find her a full-inclusion school that was also wheelchair accessible. But they were determined to provide Deidre with a good education.

PIVOTAL ISSUES FOR TEACHERS

- What characteristics made Deidre an exceptional child?
- What are Deidre's strengths?
- How did Deidre's parents respond to their child's disability?
- How did Deidre's parents act as advocates for her?
- How did Deidre's peers influence her?
- How did she influence them?
- What was it like for Deidre to fit in at a new school?

Teachers can find support from parents by viewing them as collaborators in the child's education and by paying attention to the information parents provide about their exceptional child.

parents of preschoolers—often take an active part in the teaching process. They may be trained by team members to teach specific skills (such as living skills, preacademic skills, mobility skills, and communication skills) to their child. Third, with training, parents are able to reinforce learning. They are able to see that the functional skills the child learns in school are applied in the home. The shift over time has been to move the parent closer to the decision-maker role in each of these areas, or at least to encourage the parents to share their child's interests and capabilities with other parents.

Parents are active members of the multidisciplinary intervention team for children with disabilities. They can make valuable observations of the child, teach specific skills, and reinforce learning.
© Jerry Howard/Positive Images

Parents as Advocates

The recognition that culture and community, as well as schools, have a responsibility for exceptional children stemmed in large measure from the activities of some of those children's parents. Parents who were unable to get help for their children from local governments created their own programs in church basements, vacant stores, and any place that would house them. These informal groups, loosely formed around the common needs of the children, often provided important information to new parents struggling to find help for their children with disabilities. They were also a source of emotional support for parents, a means of sharing and solving the problems of accepting and living with exceptional children.

www.thearc.org
www.ldaamerica.org

These groups quickly realized that fundamental changes were needed in the allocation of educational resources at local, state, and federal levels. A casual, haphazard approach was not going to provide the kind of help that parents or their exceptional children needed. Accordingly, large parents' groups, such as the National Association of Retarded Citizens—now the Association of Retarded Citizens (ARC)—and the United Cerebral Palsy Association in the 1940s and 1950s and the Association for Children with Learning Disabilities in the 1960s—now the Learning Disabilities Association of America (LDA)—began to form. Parents of children with Down syndrome, autism, and other specific conditions have also formed groups to ensure attention to their children's special needs. These parent organizations have successfully stimulated legislation at the state and federal levels providing for additional trained personnel, research, and other programs that have brought children with disabilities to the attention of the general public and have attracted more qualified people into the field.

Organized parents' groups for children who are gifted have not yet had the same political influence as the national organizations for children with disabilities. Still, these groups are helping the parents of children who are gifted cope with the problems of precocious development (Gallagher & Gallagher, 1994).

Siblings

We now know enough about the family environment to dismiss the proposition that two children experience the *same* environment when they are growing up merely because they live in the same household. Obviously the home environment is not the same for a child with disabilities as it is for his or her nondisabled sibling or for an older daughter as it is for a younger daughter.

We should study the home environment through the eyes of the particular child with whom we are concerned. It is less important to know how much income the family has, or how many siblings, than it is to know how each family member perceives other family members (McCall, 1987).

Parents often worry about the effect that the child with disabilities has upon siblings. Will they grow resentful of the child with special needs or of the attention that the parents inevitably have to spend on him or her? When the parents grow old and are no longer able to take care of the child (now an adult) with disabilities, will the siblings pitch in and help, or will they turn their backs on the affected sibling?

Obviously, each of these situations is different from one family to another, but there are some trends to be noted. There does not seem to be any tendency for the siblings of children with disabilities to be more disturbed or stressful than the siblings of children without disabilities (Hannah & Midlarsky, 1987).

The goal of most American parents is for their child with disabilities to become an independent and self-sufficient adult living away from home, but many siblings appear willing to assume the role of protector if that is necessary (Krauss, Seltzer, Gordon, & Friedman, 1996). As noted earlier, there can be substantial cultural differences in such a decision.

Assumptions often made about families with a child with a disability are that the nondisabled sibling is inevitably neglected because the parents must pay so much attention to the child with disabilities, and that as a result, the sibling becomes resentful of the child with disabilities. It is now clear that although this set of events may happen, it certainly doesn't have to happen, particularly when the parents are sensitive to sibling rivalry and the needs for attention for the siblings as well as for the child with disabilities (McHale & Gamble, 1987).

As Harris and McHale (1989) point out, siblings of the child with a disability spend at least the same amount of time with their mothers and receive the same type of discipline as their brother or sister with disabilities receives, although they do perform a greater amount of household tasks. The sibling who appears most vulnerable for special adjustment problems seems to be the older sibling to whom the parents have given special child-care responsibilities. As in other family situations, it is not so much the actions of the parents that count as how the sibling interprets those actions. If the sibling is sure of being loved and cared for by the parent, then being given additional responsibilities for the child with disabilities does not seem to matter (Powell & Gallagher, 1993).

Family friends.
© Michael Newman/Photo Edit

Answering the siblings' questions is an important part of the parents' responsibilities. For example, consider the following questions, which are examples of what lies just below the surface in the concerns of siblings (Powell & Gallagher, 1993):

▶ Why does he behave so strangely?

▶ Can she grow out of this?

▶ Will other brothers and sisters also have disabilities?

▶ Will he ever be able to live on his own?

▶ Will I be expected to take care of her as an adult?

▶ Am I loved as much as my brother?

▶ How can I tell my best friends about my sister?

▶ What am I supposed to do when other children tease my brother?

▶ Will my own children be more likely to have a disability?

The fact that a sibling doesn't verbalize such questions doesn't mean that he or she is not thinking about them. It is the parents' responsibility to try to answer even unverbalized questions that the brother or sister may have about the child with disabilities and how that special child is affecting, and will affect, the family system.

The number of questions that the sibling has does not diminish over time, and the content of and the concerns evident in the questions reflect developmental changes. For example, an illness or death of one of the parents may heighten the sibling's concern about his or her own responsibilities. If the parents are gone or no longer able to care for the special child, will the sibling be expected to share in the care of the child with disabilities throughout his or her lifetime? Each family has to answer those questions in its own way, but the answers must be clear and unambiguous for all family members. What kind of questions would you have if your brother or sister was a child with disabilities?

Case Study: George's Sister

What happens when a younger sibling begins to surpass an older brother or sister with disabilities or begins to be ashamed of his or her deviant behavior? One sister described the guilt and love like this:

> I have a short story to tell. It is one of many stories of happiness and sorrow. It is a story of which I am not very proud, and one I have never told my parents. I will tell it now because it is time, and I have learned from my mistakes, as all people can.
>
> George is 21 years old today. He is a frequently happy, often troubled young man who has grown up in a society reluctant to accept and care for him even though he cannot fare for himself.
>
> I am very lucky. My crime was easily forgiven by someone who loved me very much, without reservation. George and I were very young. I was his frequent babysitter. As an older sister more interested in ponies and playing outdoors, I felt a great deal of resentment toward George and, of course, toward my persecutors, my mother and father. It was a day like any other day when I had been told to take care of George. They always seemed the same, those days, because I had no choice in the matter, and if I had one, I would have refused. It was that simple for me. I had better things to do.
>
> We were waiting in the car for our mother to come with the groceries. The recurring memory breaks my heart every time I think of it. He was antagonizing me again. Those unbearable, unreal sounds that haunted and humiliated me. They were the nonsense noises that made the neighborhood children speculate he was from Mars. I could hear their taunts, and rage welled up in me. How could I have a brother like this? He was not right at all. He was a curse. I screamed at him to "shut up." He kept on. He wouldn't stop. My suppressed anger exploded. I raised my hand and slapped him again and again across his soft, round baby face. George began to cry, low, mournful whimpers. He never once raised a hand to protect himself. Shaking with fear and anger, [unable to think clearly,] I just looked at him. In that swift instance I felt more shame and revulsion for myself than I have ever felt toward anyone. The rude ugliness of it will never leave me. I hugged him to me, begging for forgiveness. And he gave it to me unconditionally. I shall never forget his sweet, sad face as he accepted my hugs.

In that instance I learned something of human nature and the nature of those who would reject people like George. I had been one of them: sullen, uncaring, unwilling to care for someone who came into the world with fewer advantages than I myself had. Today, I am a better person for having lived through both the good times and the bad times that our family experienced as a result of my brother's autism. I have a sense of understanding and compassion that I learned from growing up with George. Best of all, I have my brother, who loves me with all the goodness in his heart.

My message is simple. Look into your hearts and into the hearts of all people to see what is real, what makes them real people. For we are all the same. Accept people for what they are and work to make the world a receptive place—not just for those who are perceived as normal. (Warren, 1985, p. 227)

Peer Influences

As we continue to look for influences that occur beyond children with exceptionalities and that shape their behavior, the peer group is a natural center for investigation. One device for such investigations has been sociometric studies in which the students in the classroom are asked whom they have as friends or whom they would like as friends.

A series of studies have shown that, in general, children with disabilities have relatively low levels of sociometric status—are not popular with the other students in the class. These studies showed that children with emotional and behavioral disorders, children with learning disabilities, and children with mental retardation all show limited peer relations with their classmates (Farmer & Farmer, 1996).

More detailed analysis of the social structure of classrooms, however, has shown that such a finding is too simplistic and does not characterize the individual child or the individual classroom. Within the classroom various subgroups can be discovered that can be characterized as *prosocial, antisocial, shy*, and so on (Cairns & Cairns, 1994). The various characteristics of the students and the classroom can determine which group a student belongs to, although there is a tendency among children to choose students who have perceived similarities to the chooser.

In most instances the child with disabilities is a member of a social subgroup in the class; however, this is not necessarily a cause for rejoicing, since he or she may well be a member of a disruptive or antisocial classroom group. With the expansion of inclusion as a key element in the education of children with disabilities, it becomes important to be sensitive to the social structure of the classroom since "the composition of classroom social networks can influence whether the students with special needs make positive social gains or become entrenched in a social system that supports and maintains their problematic or deficient social characteristics" (Farmer & Farmer, 1996, p. 432).

The twenty-first century teacher and educator may well add social structure to the items needing special attention in the classroom, and the composition of the classroom can become a matter of some concern and strategic decision making.

The support of the family in caring for the child continues to be important as the child grows, but it is joined by other factors, especially the school, peers, and the community.
© Robin Sachs/Photo Edit

■ The Influence of Culture and Community

Cultural differences are often apparent in religious views, child rearing, and attitudes toward authority.

Culture refers to the attitudes, values, customs, and language that family and friends transmit to children. These attitudes, values, customs, and language have been passed down from generations of ancestors and have formed an identifiable pattern or heritage. The child is embedded in the family, its habits, and its traditions; this is as true for the child with special needs as for one who does not show special needs. Although the child may be only dimly aware of these cultural influences, it makes a world of difference to the child's experiences if his or her family is fourth-generation American or first-generation Italian, Nigerian, or Taiwanese.

We can easily assume that the differences between school and family are due to family idiosyncrasies, when in fact it reflects the long history of that family in the cultural background of parents and grandparents. Families' religious beliefs, child-rearing practices, attitudes toward authority, and so forth, can often be traced to their cultural identity. Therefore, the schools must understand that background in order to form good relationships with the families of exceptional children. Children from diverse cultural backgrounds often encounter conflicting expectations and values in the home and in the school. Teachers can help these children by becoming aware of the wide range of norms represented in their classrooms. When values honored by the school, such as competitiveness and willingness to work at a desk with a minimum of talking, conflict with a minority subculture's preference for cooperation and for lively discussion about problems, then tensions arise between families and school. Such tensions are often increased by the presence of an exceptional child.

The strength of environmental forces varies as the child grows: Initially the family is predominant in caring for the child and acts as a link between the child and the larger environment. Children from diverse cultural backgrounds may be confused by differences between family values and school or societal values, an issue that the child often confronts for the first time when entering school. The support of the family continues to be important but is joined by other factors as the child grows.

As the child grows older, the peer group becomes a major force. Adolescence, with its focus on social development and career orientation, is a special challenge for the exceptional child. Potential rejection by the peer group can have a powerful influence on the adaptation of the child with disabilities or the child with special talents, as it can on any vulnerable and self-conscious adolescent.

Finally, society, which includes the culture and community along with the work environment, influences the adult who is trying to make the transition to a relatively independent lifestyle. Throughout their lives, many exceptional adults will be in contact with a support system that includes advocates, educators, friends, and service providers. In addition, representatives of the larger society (such as government leaders) often make rules that determine whether the exceptional child gets needed resources or is given an opportunity to succeed at some level of independence. (We discuss these environments further in Chapter 2.) All these forces contribute to the full picture of the exceptional individual.

Families from Diverse Cultures

Respect for the breadwinner, attitudes toward religion, child-rearing practices, and even political choices or tendencies may reflect the attitudes of the cultural group to which the family belongs. So it is important to consider cultural factors as one more dimension needing study and understanding if we as teachers are to be effective in helping these children fulfill their capabilities.

Here are some examples of how cultural values might affect the child with special needs: If a family comes from a culture that emphasizes a dominant masculine role, how will the father of a child with disabilities respond to a female professional? Will he reject her advice and suggestions just to maintain his own masculine self-image? And what does he feel about his son who has disabilities that are so serious that the father despairs of the boy ever being able to play that masculine role? Such issues are not talked about easily but can rest at the heart of parental concerns for many years.

The United States has long been proud of its role of accepting people from cultures around the world. Over the years, immigrants and their children have adapted but not without some pain and difficulty.

Correctly identifying children from diverse cultures as exceptional is an ongoing challenge.
© Tony Freeman/Photo Edit

One of the first challenges that children from diverse cultures present to educators is whether they can be correctly identified as exceptional children in the first place. Obviously, giving a child who doesn't speak English, an IQ test in English is a bad idea. But the problem is more complicated than that.

It appears that children who have had essentially little or no schooling do not even think in the same way as is assumed by intelligence tests (Rogoff & Chavajay, 1995). It apparently takes some schooling to teach them to categorize objects or use logical reasoning and inference. Nonschooled individuals seem to prefer to come to conclusions on the basis of experience rather than relying on the information in the problem alone.

How, then, can we determine if immigrant children are learning disabled, mentally retarded, or merely developing in a typical way for their cultural background? All too often, immigrant or minority children are inappropriately referred to special education services when, in fact, they need a very different set of experiences and grounding in the cognitive nature of the school program (Harry, 1992).

The term *minority* in our society traditionally has been reserved for persons who are "not white." The federal government recognizes six classifications based on race and ethnicity: Native American or Alaskan Native, Asian or Pacific Islander, Hispanic, African American, Caucasian, and multiracial. But even with those categories there are major differences. Under Hispanic is included Mexican, Puerto Rican, Cuban, Central American, and South American, cultures that are obviously very different from one another. Thus, the term *minority* means little beyond the possibility of adjustment problems for the families and for the child in fitting into a dominant white, European culture, on top of the problem of adapting as an exceptional child.

The following quotation from Harry (1992) gives a flavor of family adjustments that have to be made.

> In our countries, when children get spanked, they do not think their parents don't love them. I knew my parents did it because they loved me. They taught me manners and to be obedient. That's the way they see it. But here it's a whole different ballgame and the parents feel like they're in a system that is very fearful because if you behave like a parent should behave, you might lose your children. And the kids use the system. I know kids who have turned their parents in. The kid learns the system right away. So the parents feel helpless. . . . It's not that they hit all the time—it's a last alternative, but you use it and there is a case worker at your door. So the parents are frightened, they feel they're losing control of their children. Child Protective Services—Children's Division! That's the most feared word on the whole West Side!

Harry has called for a type of **cultural reciprocity** between the professional and families with a different view of life and society (Harry, Rueda, & Kalyanpur, 1999). This will require the professional to learn about the cultural expectations and goals that the family has for the child with disabilities. These expectations and goals can be quite different from those of the professional who comes from mainstream America.

For example, the most desirable long-term goal for many professionals is to see the youth with disabilities becoming independent in his living arrangements as a young adult and being self-sufficient. But many Latino and African American families believe in *family interdependence* and would be offended to think that the youth with disabilities would not be cared for by his siblings, if the parents were unable to care for him. The family members' interdependence plays a large role in such cultures, and the professional's view of independence (and perhaps loneliness) strikes them as rather strange, representing a rejection from the rest of the family.

The goal of cultural reciprocity is to find a meeting place between the two values so that the family can understand mainstream America better and the professional can adapt to the wishes and desires of the family.

One of the responsibilities of teachers and teachers-to-be trying to be culturally aware is self-awareness (Turnbull & Turnbull, 1997). It is important that teachers are aware what factors shape their own cultural views, in particular, to know that their cultural beliefs and traditions may work well for them but not necessarily for others. Cultural differences change and modify the special education for individual exceptional children, and adjustments have to be made in each instance.

It is easy—sometimes tempting—to focus on the differences between yourself as a teacher and the families. A useful task is to identify the strengths of the culture of the family. Whatever the immediate problems the family and the exceptional child may come with, it is a rarity that they do not also come with strengths, such as making the child feel loved and accepted, a willingness to seek support from friends and counselors, a strong religious faith, and a caring extended family (Turnbull & Turnbull, 1997). Such strengths are to be respected and used as a foundation on which to build an educational strategy for the child.

A professional's view of independence may seem inappropriate to people of some cultures who prefer to be interdependent and rely on each other.

It is important for teachers to identify the strengths of students and their families who are from diverse cultures.

Culture and Assessment

In each of the succeeding chapters there will be discussion of how a child who has disabilities *and* comes from another culture can be properly assessed. It is not too difficult to see that a child who does not have English as a first language can be poorly assessed with an achievement test written in English. In the Peabody Picture Vocabulary Test a child may be asked to identify which of four pictures shows a *wiener*. The child may know very well what a hot dog is yet never have heard the term *wiener*. What are we testing in such a situation, his vocabulary or his cultural experience (Salvia & Ysseldyke, 2004)?

There have been a number of attempts to promote a nonbiased assessment for children from different cultures, including the use of interpreters, "culture fair" tests, separate norms, and so on, all of which have their drawbacks. There has been a trend toward replacing standardized tests with informal procedures or using a mix of formal and informal measures to try to capture the child's range of abilities. The real problem may lie not in the tests themselves but in their interpretations (McLaughlin & Lewis, 2001).

Consider Jorge, a 10-year-old Hispanic child with learning disabilities that prevent him from grasping the reading process. Jorge comes from a rich tradition of a close-knit family with common interests and loyalty. The family is wary about the Anglo schools that Jorge is attending. When teachers and psychologists who are of a culture different from that of the family tell the family that something is wrong with Jorge's approach to school, are they reflecting a prejudice against Jorge because of his Hispanic background and his bilingual family? Are they going to help Jorge, or is this a way to prevent Jorge from getting a proper education? Will Jorge's father, misunderstanding the school's message, put even *more* pressure on Jorge to do well in school, assuming that his son is not giving proper effort to his school lessons? The opportunities for misunderstanding from one culture to another are great and can substantially complicate the original learning problems faced by the exceptional child.

Observers of special education programs have long pointed to a disproportionately large number of minority students in them, except in programs for gifted students, where the number of minority students has been proportionately smaller than expected.

Such observations came to the attention of the Office of Civil Rights (OCR) in the U.S. Department of Education, and OCR mounted a major national survey to determine whether such observations were true (Donovan & Cross, 2002). Figure 1.3 provides a summary of the results in three categories of exceptional children: mental retardation, learning disabilities, and emotional disturbance. In the area of mental retardation, the percentage of black students is more than twice that of white students in those programs, while the percentages of Hispanic and Asian students are somewhat less.

In contrast, in the learning disabilities category there are high percentages (6 percent or more) of white, black, and Hispanic students, but the unusual figure is the small percentage of Asian students. Perhaps the strong emphasis in the Asian populations on education has lessened the number of students in academic trouble.

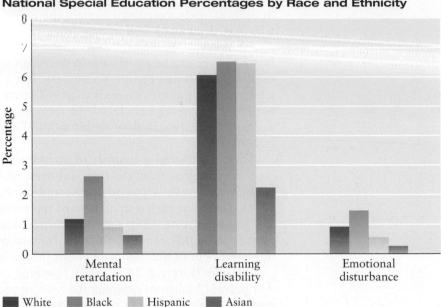

FIGURE 1.3
National Special Education Percentages by Race and Ethnicity

■ White   ■ Black   ■ Hispanic   ■ Asian

Source: U.S. Department of Education (2002). *Fall 1998 Elementary and Secondary School Civil Rights Compliance Report.* Washington, DC: Office for Civil Rights.

Finally, in the category of emotional disturbance, there again appear to be more black students than white and Hispanic, while the Asian population is very small. But finding disproportion in these programs by race does not explain why such disproportion exists. There are at least three possible explanations.

1. The tests and measurements employed in diagnosing the conditions are biased against the minority students and provide inaccurate information about them.
2. In many minority family situations there are unfavorable ecological conditions that can cause the inadequate development of abilities in early life. This can be seen in the lower performance of their school-age children.
3. The schools are discriminating against minority students by removing them from the regular classes and placing them in special programs away from the other students.

The third possibility has energized the Office of Civil Rights to look at many individual school districts where disproportionate membership in special education programs has occurred, in order to determine whether the third possibility is true in those schools.

Summary

► The exceptional child differs from the average child to the extent that he or she needs special educational services to reach full potential.

► The major categories of exceptionality include children with intellectual differences, communication differences, learning disabilities, sensory differences, behavioral differences, multiple and severe disabilities, physical and health differences, attention-deficit hyperactivity disorder (ADHD), and autism.

► Special educators have moved from a medical model, which stresses that the physical condition exists within the child, to an ecological model, which focuses on the individual's interaction with the environment. Genetics research suggests that environmental changes can activate previously inactive genes, creating new heredity-environment interactions and affecting behavior.

► Exceptional children show both interindividual (among children) and intraindividual (within a child) differences. Both kinds of differences require special adaptation by the teacher at school.

► The success of a family-focused approach depends on its acceptance by professionals. Families from diverse cultures may have differing values and child-rearing practices, which compound the issues of adaptation for the child with special needs.

► The adjustment of siblings of children with disabilities depends in large measure on parental sensitivities to those siblings' needs.

► Parent empowerment gives parents more influence on the special programs established for their child and requires rethinking of the traditional roles played by professionals.

► Cultural attitudes, values, customs, and language are often embedded in a family and must be taken into account when educators and other professionals work with exceptional children from a variety of cultural backgrounds.

Future Challenges

Every generation leaves, as its legacy to the next generation, certain problems for which solutions have not been found. There are many issues in the field of special education that today's professionals have been either unable or unwilling to resolve. The end-of-chapter sections entitled "Future Challenges" briefly describe widely debated topics as a beginning agenda for the current generation of students, who will face these issues in their professional or private lives.

1. Who is identified as exceptional?

The boundary line separating exceptional children from nonexceptional children has become blurred where children with mild disabilities are concerned. Yet legislation and the courts call for eligibility standards to clearly separate those who should receive special education from those who should not. How do we distinguish, for example, between the child who is emotionally disturbed and the child who is experiencing a temporary behavior problem?

2. What is the impact of the family system?

For many years, special educators focused only on the exceptional child and excluded the child's environment. Increasingly we have become aware that the child is only one component in a complex family system and that many elements within that system can have a positive or negative impact on the child. Interacting constructively with the family system is a new objective of special education that has yet to be incorporated fully in our personnel preparation or educational programs.

3. How to develop a comprehensive program for young children with special needs?

There are no public school programs against which to plan adaptations for preschool-age children with special needs. Are we to model our programs after Head Start or various prekindergarten programs? Should we take a developmental approach from child psychology? How will people be recruited to become professionals in the early childhood field—and where will they be trained? We have made a start on these issues, but much more remains to be done.

Key Terms

cultural reciprocity   *p. 28*

culture   *p. 25*

ecological model   *p. 10*

exceptional child   *p. 3*

family-centered model   *p. 17*

family-focused approach   *p. 11*

intraindividual differences   *p. 7*

medical model   *p. 10*

parent empowerment   *p. 17*

theory of mind   *p. 10*

Resources

References of Special Interest

Cross, C., & Donovan, M. (2002). *Minority Students in Special and Gifted Education.* Washington, DC: National Research Council. *A report from a special panel brought together by the National Academy of Sciences to address the disproportion of minority students in special education programs for children with disabilities and also for children who are gifted. The panel explores whether such a disproportion in fact exists, why the disproportions exist, and what can be done about this issue. The panel concludes that such disproportions do exist and proposes better-integrated general education and special education programs, increased teacher training in sensitivity to cultural differences, high-quality early childhood intervention programs, and increased research.*

Gottlieb, G. (1997). *Synthesizing nature-nurture: Prenatal roots of instinctive behavior.* Mahwah, NJ: Lawrence Erlbaum Associates. *A fascinating look into the rapidly developing field of genetics and its possible influence on education. In this volume, the author proposes that one can change the behavior of animals and humans through changes in the environment, triggering different sets of genes and changing the developmental process without the long wait for evolution to take place.*

Roberts, R., Rule, S., & Innocenti, M. (1998). *Strengthening the family-professional partnership in services for young children.* Baltimore, MD: Paul H. Brookes. *A text that explores in great detail the new relationship between professional and parent and presents some of the procedures necessary for making the parent a more active participant in the plans for his or her own child. It also presents what is needed in the educational system to allow such a result to occur.*

Salvia, J., & Ysseldyke, J. (2004) *Assessment* (9th ed.). Boston: Houghton Mifflin. *One of the problems in identifying children with special needs is the lack of knowledge about acceptable measuring instruments. This volume provides a wide variety of informal and formal methods of assessment and several chapters discussing the broad topic of general assessment itself. The authors include developmental appraisals of infants, toddlers, and preschoolers. Also included is a chapter on outcomes-based accountability assessment, which is a topic of growing interest in education.*

Shonkoff, J., & Phillips, D. (Eds.). (2000). *From neurons to neighborhoods.* Washington, DC: National Academy Press. *An update from the National Academy of Sciences on the current state of the science of early childhood development, by a distinguished multidisciplinary panel. The book includes the latest information on nature versus nurture, the developing brain, and the latest trend toward studying the ecology of the developing child. A series of recommendations for scientists and public policy makers is provided, based upon current knowledge.*

Journals

Exceptional Children
Council for Exceptional Children (CEC)
www.cec.sped.org

Journal of Special Education
www.proedinc.com

Teaching Exceptional Children
www.cec.sped.org

Disability Resources Monthly
www.disabilityresources.org

Professional Organizations

Council for Exceptional Children (CEC)
www.cec.sped.org

Please visit the book's website at http://education.college.hmco.com/students for new and updated information on websites listed here and for the mailing addresses of the journals and organizations.

EXCEPTIONAL CHILDREN AND SOCIAL INSTITUTIONS

SCHOOLS, GOVERNMENT, AND THE COURTS

2

FOCUS QUESTIONS

► How has the educational reform movement affected exceptional children?

► What are some of the learning environments being used today for exceptional children?

► What types of government legislation support students with disabilities?

► How are special educators using technology to teach exceptional students?

► How have the courts influenced the development of educational services for exceptional children?

In Chapter 1, we discussed the nature of exceptional children and their surrounding ecology of family, peers, and culture. In this chapter, we look at the responses of three major social institutions—schools, government, and the courts—to the needs of exceptional children.

How a society feels about its diverse membership, particularly about citizens who are different, is expressed through such institutions.

Council for
Exceptional Children
www.cec.sped.org

▶ The *schools* design programs to prepare these students for a productive and satisfying adult life.

▶ The *government* provides the money and authority for the special arrangements necessary to meet the special needs of these students.

▶ The *courts* rule on what is fair, just, and equitable with regard to these exceptional students.

Schools, government, and courts are social institutions that have a major impact on the education of children with special needs.

Each of these social institutions has its own rules and traditions that influence how decisions are made and how conclusions are reached in its domain. This chapter touches briefly on how each of them affects the child who is exceptional in our society. Take, for example, Sam.

Sam is a 5-year-old with Down syndrome, a genetic condition that will affect his entire life. He has mental retardation and other problems caused by this genetic accident. Yet how Sam will fare in life will depend to a large degree on the environmental circumstances around him.

Will Sam do better in a loving, rather than a rejecting, family? Will he do better in a neighborhood with some comfort and resources than he would do in an urban ghetto? Will Sam do better in a school program that recognizes his problems and adapts the program to his needs instead of unfairly expecting him to meet some kind of "normal" standard? Of course!

The ecology of the child refers to the influence of outside factors—family, school, peers, and community.

No matter what the degree of exceptionality, how the child will eventually adapt to life is determined in large measure by how the environmental forces outside the child facilitate or inhibit his or her development. That is why we spend so much time studying these outside forces, which we refer to as the **ecology of the child,** or the **context of the child.**

Each child's responses to outside forces is very individual.

How the exceptional child adjusts to adulthood is determined in large measure by his or her interactions with these social institutions and the way in which they are mediated by family and by the child's unique characteristics. It is difficult, if not impossible, to predict the outcome of special education services for a specific individual because of the range of each child's response and potential.

We begin with an overview of society's attitudes toward the education of exceptional individuals. By looking at how society has viewed exceptional students and directed its resources to them, we can better understand how schools treat these youngsters and what is expected from them.

■ A Historical Perspective

During the last century, there have been enormous changes in the way society treats exceptional children, moving from rejection and the charitable isolation of children with disabilities to acceptance of them as contributing members of society. The current level of acceptance has few precedents, representing a much more enlightened view than was evident even in the immediate past.

The notion of educating *every* child to achieve his or her greatest potential is a relatively new idea. The current use of the term *exceptional* is itself a reflection of radical change in society's view of people who differ from the norm. The journey toward public acceptance has been slow, moving from neglect and maltreatment, to pity and overprotection, and finally to acceptance for students into society to the fullest extent possible.

Residential Schools

Nineteenth-century reformers such as Horace Mann, Samuel Gridley Howe, and Dorothea Dix gave impetus to the establishment of residential schools for children with disabilities. From 1817 to the beginning of the Civil War, a span of more than forty years, many states established residential schools for children who were deaf, blind, mentally retarded, or orphaned, patterning them after similar schools in Europe. In 1817, the American Asylum for the Education and Instruction of the Deaf, a residential institution, was opened in Hartford, Connecticut. In 1829, the New England Asylum for the Blind—later renamed the Perkins School—was founded in Watertown, Massachusetts. Thirty years later, a residential school for the mentally retarded, the Massachusetts School for Idiotic and Feebleminded Youth, was established in South Boston. This school is now called the Fernald Developmental Center. These schools offered training, but equally important they provided an environment that often protected the individual throughout life (Smith, Boone, & Higgins, 1998).

The first special class for deaf children in a public school was held in Boston in 1869. Not until 1896 was the first special class for children who were mentally retarded organized, in Providence, Rhode Island. It was followed in 1899 by a class for children with physical impairments and, in 1900, by a class in

The exceptional child's adjustment to adulthood is determined in large measure by his or her interactions with the school, the culture, and the society and by the way in which these interactions are mediated by the family and the child's unique characteristics.
© Susie Fitzhugh

Chicago for children who were blind. Since 1900, special programs and services for exceptional children have been organized in the majority of public schools throughout the nation (Safford & Safford, 1996).

■ The Exceptional Child and the School

Certainly one of the most significant of all our social institutions is the schools. Schools in large measure are a mirror of our society as a whole. Most of the values taught there reflect the values of the dominant sectors of society. Many of the problems encountered in the schools, such as lack of motivation, drug use, and violence, are part of the larger societal fabric.

In the last part of the twentieth century, there was constant discussion within the education field as to where the exceptional child should be placed and what relationship should exist between general education and special education. The struggle for special services and special programming for exceptional children has consumed much of the attention of special educators during that time.

Also, exceptional children are affected by major trends in the general field of education, just as are all other students. The trend toward *accountability,* a term used to determine whether educators have done what they said they would do for their students, has forced special education to demonstrate not only that exceptional children are receiving special services, but also whether the students have learned from a special program as expected.

The emphasis on accountability has raised the question of which of two seemingly contradictory purposes should be emphasized. The Individuals with Disabilities Education Act (IDEA) of 2004 proposed the need for specially designed instruction (meaning shaping or creating lessons to meet the special needs of the individual who has those needs). This is to be spelled out in the individualized education program (IEP), but IDEA also wishes to ensure the exceptional child access to the general curriculum. This would seem to mean that the exceptional child will be included in regular class activities to the extent that he or she can master the basic facts and types of knowledge that all the other students are expected to master. The fact that the vast majority of exceptional children are to be included in statewide testing programs indicates that the schools are expected to attain *both* of these desirable goals, and it is the responsibility of the schools to achieve this result in individual circumstances.

The changing social environment of exceptional children has spawned a new and different vocabulary. Two terms that are in common use today are *inclusion* and *continuum of services.* These terms reflect the interest of society in trying to integrate exceptional children and adults more effectively into the school and the community at large.

▶ **Inclusion** is the process of bringing all, or nearly all, exceptional children into the general classroom for their education with special educational support.

▶ **Continuum of services** refers to the range of placements that may constitute the least restrictive environment where the exceptional child learns best.

Special educational services in a school system are responsible for five major tasks.

1. Find children who need special help.
2. Assess the developmental strengths and weaknesses of that child.
3. Design an individual program of education to meet the needs of that child in concert with the child's family.
4. See to it that this special program is implemented within the framework of the overall education program of the school.
5. Periodically assess the progress that child is making and adapt the program accordingly.

Finding the Child with Special Needs

A child may be referred for special education services for any of a variety of reasons, but mainly because of observations by school staff that this child differs from same-age children in a significant way that is affecting his or her learning in school.

Sometimes the school will administer screening tests in reading or arithmetic in the early grades in an effort to discover children who need special help before they have identified themselves to their teacher through either school failure or extraordinary success. For example, Paul, age 8, has been referred for special education services because his third-grade teacher, Mrs. Parker, claims he is insolent, talks back to her, isn't mastering his reading and math skills, and is constantly disturbing the other children. Maybe Paul acts that way because he has a serious learning or behavioral disability, but maybe he and the teacher have started off on the wrong foot. He may be reacting in a predictable way to his inability to do the schoolwork (which may seem uninteresting to him anyway), and Mrs. Parker doesn't know how to cope with Paul's frustrations.

In such a situation, many school systems establish a prereferral committee to find ways of coping with a child's behavior short of a referral for special education services. In this case, the assistant principal, a master teacher, and a psychologist met with Mrs. Parker to see what she might be able to do. Not every child having trouble adjusting to school is a candidate for special education. In Paul's case, several months went by with no appreciable improvement in his behavior, so a full referral was made, calling for a full assessment of Paul and consideration for special education.

■ Ecology of the Child

The Role of Assessment

Assessment is a process of collecting data for the purpose of making decisions about individuals and groups (Salvia & Ysseldyke, 2001). It tries to answer the following questions:

1. Does a serious school performance problem exist?
2. What are the student's strengths and weaknesses?

ECOLOGY OF THE CHILD

SCHOOL   **Inclusion for Katie**

If you saw my 14-year-old daughter Katie enter the middle school lunchroom you would notice that she bobs the top half of her body a little to one side to gain momentum. You would hear Katie's open-mouth hums and Peter Pan-like "crows" join the cafeteria chaos followed by, "Hi, Katie" from several of her schoolmates.

Included from the Start

Katie has been in inclusive environments since she was an infant. We lived in a small Rocky Mountain resort community where large city "segregated" programs were unavailable; Katie was "included" as another member of the community in daycare and school services.

Katie was in daycare right alongside the babies who sat up and crawled, though she remained stationary. When she was not in daycare I took her for private therapy, as therapy in "natural environments" had not yet evolved.

When Katie started kindergarten, the transportation director installed a seat belt with a harness so she could ride the big yellow school bus with the rest of the neighborhood children. Each morning the children greeted her, and some even volunteered to sit beside her. However, one blue-eyed boy with rebellious strands of blond hair used to customize his greeting each morning.

"Hi, slobber mouth," he would say, always careful to give his friends a glance before chuckling his way to a seat in the back. Katie would respond with her usual glistening grin, enjoying the laughter.

Time Changes Attitudes

That was at the beginning of the school year. By spring, I noticed a metamorphosis: this bully turned into a peer. He was reading books to Katie in library period and bringing her pictures he made in art marked "TO KATIE" in crayon. The teachers said while he was discreet about his goodwill, he also stopped making fun of her.

That was also the year Katie used a special wooden chair on wheels with a tray clipped to the front for eating and fine motor skills. The chair helped her support the trunk of her body. The children in school nicknamed Katie's chair "the Ferrari," and would run up alongside it in the hallways like a devoted pit crew, their backpacks bouncing in unison.

Dealing with Doubts

Later in the school year Katie's teacher said, "Let's put Katie in the Christmas music production." At first I was pleased to have her included in the festivities, but eventually reality became painful to watch. She would sit or stand when physically prompted by a teacher or an older schoolmate. The spotlight would shine on the children as they waved their hands like pine boughs and sang "Jingle Bells." But the bright beam of light seemed to magnify the contrast of Katie's lack of focus and participation. People would say to me, "It's great to see Katie up there." I just blinked back tears, swallowed the lump in my throat, and quit trying to include her in extracurricular activities.

Rather than the typical fifth-grade curriculum of Math, Geography, and English, Katie's individualized education plan (IEP) included self-help skills like feeding herself, dressing herself, and learning to use the toilet. I wondered if she belonged, if her experience was one-sided, if she contributed to the class.

When I discussed this with her teachers they told me how good it is for the rest of the kids to have Katie in school with them. "It's good for their self-esteem," they said. "Katie always has lots of classmates volunteering to help her, to read to her, or to do the cooking projects with her." It seems to me like inclusive education naturally promotes what the national movement in schools proposes to teach: universal values.

As I walked through the school hallway one day, a boy said something to me as I passed. "Katie's a lot easier once you get to know her," he commented, not quite looking at me. Initially, I was surprised an 11-year-old boy would strike up a conversation with someone's mother. Then I realized that he felt he "knew" Katie. "Oh you know Katie?" I asked. He is still walking, but he does a half turn into a backward stride to face me. "Yeah," he said, casually pleased. "I'm in a cooking class with her." I grinned.

Adjusting to Meet the Future

I have learned to look past the loss of "normal," grin through the grief, and notice the way children are with Katie. I see it in her smile, when she does a little circle dance around the driveway as the bus comes to pick her up and when I visit the classrooms.

Each fall as I go to Katie's class and talk about Katie, I try to answer their questions—try to eliminate some of the fear-of-the-different factor. "What happened to her?" they ask. "Does Katie have any pets? If she can't talk, can she hear?"

I tell them a little about Katie, how she can hear you say "hello" but she cannot say "hi" back. I tell them she was born with a "hurt" brain. "Doctors gave her lots of tests," I always say. "But she is undiagnosed. We don't know what happened or how she'll be when she grows up." I tell them incoming messages get scrambled, or have to take detours around the "hurt" parts and sometimes get lost.

When Katie reached fifth grade, we played the same "Fun Game." I start the game by asking the class, "What about Katie is the same as you?" A few children raise their hands.

"She likes to swim," volunteered one little girl.

"She likes horses," said another.

"She dresses the same!"

Suddenly hands were clamoring faster than a recess bell stampede. Then a boy with thick brown hair, who sits across the aisle from Katie and her sometimes-vacant desk, raised his hand. "She's a human being," he said.

I guess different really is the same.

Source: Jodi Buchan, "When Different Is the Same," *Exceptional Parent Magazine* (September 2000). Reprinted with permission.

WHAT IS THE CONTEXT?

Katie has always been included in the general education classroom. Her classmates learned to accept the ways she is different from them and the ways she is like them. Katie's mother played an active role in her daughter's adjustment to school.

PIVOTAL ISSUES FOR TEACHERS

- What kind of preparation do teachers need to successfully work in an inclusive setting?

- As a new teacher, what skills would enable you to work with students with disabilities in your general education classroom?

- What kind of support would you need from parents and professionals?

3. What relationship does the school problem have to the student's environment and to his or her family, peers, and neighborhood?
4. What type of goals and objectives seem appropriate?
5. How would we evaluate the effectiveness of our plans?

Answering these questions calls for a complex process of reviewing the development of the individual child and his or her ecology.

An assessment starts with the general issue of whether a school performance problem exists and then moves on to the child's strengths and weaknesses, the content areas affected, and the relationship of any academic problems to the child's learning environment. We finish with a prescription of educational goals and objectives and with strategies to help us meet them. Ongoing evaluation (for example, asking, "How effective is the educational program?") gives us the necessary information to revise the educational program.

It is important to realize that a child develops on many different physical and psychological dimensions at once. To understand a child's problems, we must keep track of individual differences in a number of dimensions. The task of determining how an individual child is different, and along which dimensions, has become a major step in identifying and educating exceptional children. Such assessment serves two purposes. First, it identifies which children are eligible for special services. Second, it may provide information by which an individualized plan to meet the child's particular needs can be formulated.

Teachers and other staff members can use five general approaches to provide an assessment of a child: norm-referenced tests, diagnostic achievement tests, interviews, observations, and informal assessments. We summarize these approaches in Table 2.1. Generally, a combination of tests and procedures is used to detect and thoroughly evaluate a child's interindividual and intraindividual differences. Each method has advantages and disadvantages.

Interindividual Differences

Areas of interindividual differences include academic aptitude, academic performance, language development, and psychosocial development.

Interindividual differences are substantial differences among children of a similar life age along key dimensions of development. Special educators and school psychologists assess interindividual differences along key dimensions such as academic aptitude, academic performance, language development, psychomotor skills, and psychosocial development.

Academic Aptitude   One area in which interindividual differences appear is **academic aptitude.** The measure of children's aptitudes can tell teachers and schools a great deal about their student population and how students are performing in relationship to their potential.

For decades, the standard measure of academic aptitude has been the intelligence test. These tests measure the development of memory, association, reasoning, evaluation, and classification—the mental operations so important to school performance. In fact, intelligence tests are accurate predictors of academic performance: Those who score high on intelligence tests generally do well in school; those who score low generally do poorly.

TABLE 2.1
Assessment Strategies: Strengths and Weaknesses

STRATEGY	ADVANTAGES	DISADVANTAGES
NORM-REFERENCED TEST	It provides a comparison of a particular child's performance against the performance of a reference group of children, as in intelligence and achievement tests.	It does not provide reasons for the results; for culturally diverse children, the reference groups used for comparison may be inappropriate.
DIAGNOSTIC ACHIEVEMENT TEST	It is designed to provide a profile of strengths and weaknesses, analyses of errors, etc., in arithmetic or reading to pinpoint specific academic problems of the student for remediation.	The scores generated by such instruments often have limited or suspect reliability; consequently, the profiles may not be very valuable.
INTERVIEW	Information from the child, parent, teacher, or others can provide perspective and insight into the reasons for the child's current performance.	All interviewees see the child through personal perspectives that may be limited by scope of experience, personal bias, or, in particular, reference to themselves.
OBSERVATION	It can provide information based on the child's spontaneous behavior in natural settings and a basis for intervention planning.	The child may not reveal significant behaviors during the observation; the meaning of the child's behavior may be unclear.
INFORMAL ASSESSMENT	Information from teacher-made tests, particular language samples, or descriptions of significant events in the life of the child may yield valuable insights leading to effective educational planning.	It is rarely possible to match a particular child's performance with the performance of others on these measures or observatons. Such measures should be used with caution.
PORTFOLIO ASSESSMENT	The student collects items of quality about his work. This allows a more direct assessment of student performance and affords the student a chance to show higher-order thinking.	A problem of rater bias is always possible: Did the student create the work included? Also, portfolio assessment is labor-intensive.

Any serious problem with or developmental delay in the mental operations that these tests evaluate can create major difficulties in school. Intelligence tests assume a common experience base for most children (and the desire of the child to do well). We must be cautious in our interpretation and use of test results for individuals whose language or experience or both differ from the normative and native-born group. This is particularly true for students whose primary language is not English.

Intelligence tests have come under severe attack in recent years. One reason is that there is strong disagreement over the use and meaning of intelligence quotient (IQ) scores. In the past, those scores have been used (1) to indicate

Intelligence tests are not pure measures of intellectual potential; rather, they are valuable predictors and indicators of academic ability and performance.

innate intellectual potential, (2) to predict future academic performance, and (3) to indicate a child's present rate of mental development compared with that of same-age children. The sharpest criticism has been raised over the use of IQ scores to indicate intellectual potential. Intelligence tests are not pure measures of intellectual potential and never should be used to try to demonstrate the innate superiority of one sex or ethnic or racial group over another. They are valuable predictors of academic performance and indicators of current academic aptitude. They are useful when employed for those purposes.

Many people now believe that intelligence is multidimensional. Gardner's theory of multiple intelligences (1993) is the best-known proposal of a multifaceted view of intelligence. Gardner has proposed seven major dimensions of intelligence: *linguistic, musical, logical-mathematical, spatial, bodily-kinesthetic, social awareness,* and *self-awareness.* These dimensions provide some basis for differentiating curriculum, and there are continuing efforts to design programming based on Gardner's model of intelligence.

Executive Function Another important dimension of intelligence not covered by these tests is the *executive function* or *executive processes* (Sternberg, 1997). This function regulates thinking processes, behaviors, and performance. It is a type of traffic manager that monitors and controls. The executive function may be referred to as *metacognition* or *self-regulation* and must be activated by the learner. If you are planning what you will do tomorrow or deciding which things in your environment to pay attention to or how to respond to a task, you are using your *executive function.* Some of the serious learning problems faced by exceptional children appear to occur through the individual's inability to use the executive function properly.

Academic Performance Two well-accepted approaches to describing interindividual differences in academic performance are standard (norm-referenced) achievement tests and diagnostic achievement tests. **Standard (norm-referenced) achievement tests** measure a student's level of achievement compared with that of students of similar age or grade. These tests tell whether the student is achieving at expected levels of performance, but usually they do not tell *why* the student is not performing as well as he or she might. **Diagnostic achievement tests** help determine the process a student is using to solve a problem or decode a reading passage so we can understand why a particular student is not mastering some aspect of the school curriculum, that is, why he or she is not performing at the level of other students.

Language Development Language, one of the most complex of human functions, is particularly vulnerable to problems that affect the development of children. Because using language effectively is one of the keys to academic success, it must be carefully analyzed, particularly when a student is not performing well.

The assessment of an individual child's overall language development should be completed in his or her primary language and dialect. But for students acquiring English, it is also appropriate to assess language functioning in English to assist with the appropriate educational programming. The assessment of language competence should include evaluation of a student's ability to process in comprehension and expression in a spoken and written format. There are four major communication processes: oral comprehension (listening and comprehending speech), written comprehension (reading), oral expression (speaking), and written expression (writing). A wide variety of instruments are available to measure one or more of these language components (Salvia & Ysseldyke, 2004).

Psychomotor Development Many children with special needs have associated problems in coordination or mobility, which adds to their basic exceptionality. Obviously, children with cerebral palsy and other conditions that clearly impair the ability to physically move around and that interfere with fine motor control need exercises and practice in motor skills. However, they are not the only candidates for special psychomotor exercise. Some children with learning disabilities, autism, or mental retardation also have problems in the psychomotor areas that need attention. For many children, the individualized education program should have improved motor performance as one of the objectives and should detail how such improvements will be brought about.

Psychosocial Development Another area of interindividual difference is the individual child's ability to respond to the social environment, or how well the child is able to adapt. Does the child show aggressive tendencies when frustrated? Is he or she able to work cooperatively with others? How does the child react when things don't go right? How well the child is able to do these things when faced with increasingly complex social interactions (for example, with teachers or peers) strongly influences how well he or she will adapt as an adult.

Social adaptation also greatly influences how the exceptional child responds to remediation. Many children who fail to respond to special programs have behavioral and social problems, not academic ones. It is difficult to remediate a reading disability if a child has a severe attention problem or becomes aggressive when frustrated. For that reason, special educators often focus on behavioral and social problems at the same time they tackle academic difficulties.

To assess psychosocial development, we often rely on the observations of others—parents, teachers, and caregivers—for information on how the child behaves in different settings. Ratings scales can be used to bring some order to those judgments.

Another strategy is to systematically observe the child at home or school so that we can catalog the child's typical patterns of behavior. When children are able to articulate, we can ask them about their feelings or perceptions of themselves. These self-reports can be very revealing. They might show that a child who is gifted has a low self-concept even though people around him say he is well adjusted. Or they might show that a child with retardation has an unrealistic view of her own abilities.

Measures of adaptive behavior can be obtained through such instruments as the Vineland Adaptive Behavior Scales and the American Association of Mental Deficiency Adaptive Behavior Scale. These scales are filled out through an interview of either someone knowledgeable about the child or a trained observer.

PROFILE

DEVELOPMENTAL

Diane: We can see how this assessment process works in the case of Diane, a 7-year-old. Diane was a slim child, somewhat small for her age. She was promoted to second grade mainly because of the hopes of her first-grade teacher; her actual performance was not good. In the second grade, Diane was having trouble with basic reading and arithmetic skills. She was an unhappy child who did not talk a lot and who did not have many friends in the classroom.

In some school systems, screening before kindergarten or at the beginning or end of first grade might have picked up Diane's problems. In this kind of screening, every child is examined quickly for major problems in vision, hearing, and learning ability. If a difficulty shows up, the child is referred for an intensive evaluation. In Diane's school system, academic performance takes the place of the screening process. In fact, most students find their way into special education through academic failure or through the perceptive observation of school personnel.

Diane's second-grade teacher recognized a problem and referred the child for diagnostic evaluation. Diane was given a series of tests and interviews to determine whether she did have a

▌Profile of Diane

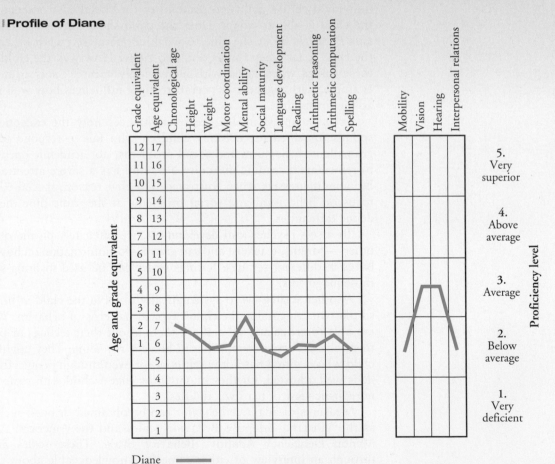

Diane ━━━

problem and to identify that problem. In the process, the diagnostic team eliminated a number of factors that might have caused Diane's difficulty. They looked for signs of physical disabilities, of serious emotional disturbance, of mental retardation, of environmental disadvantage. The goal of the assessment and referral was to identify the support Diane needed to maximize her potential.

In Diane's case, after the initial diagnosis and classification, a more thorough analysis of specific learning problems or difficulties was carried out. Earlier examinations had defined Diane's abilities and disabilities; now the educational team analyzed those abilities and disabilities to design a specialized program and teaching strategies for the child. Once the program goals were set and the individual program was implemented, a plan was set up to measure Diane's progress at subsequent points to see if the objectives had been met. This is done through the individualized education program (IEP).

The graph on the previous page provides us with a developmental portrait of Diane. While the profile seems unremarkable with few peaks and valleys it actually tells some important things about Diane to the educators struggling to find a reason for her poor reading. We know that her troubles are *not* due to low intelligence, since she seems average in mental ability. Both her vision and her hearing seem normal, so they cannot be the cause of her problems. Now we have eliminated some key potential causes, yet she is low on reading and related subjects.

What appears to be the cause is that Diane has a problem decoding written symbols and therefore is not reading well. Some specific exercises and practice are needed for Diane to cope with this learning disability. In each of the subsequent chapters, we provide a profile of one or two students to indicate what we have found out and what we need to do about our increased knowledge about individual children.

The Vineland measures adaptive behavior in four domains: communication (knows how to comprehend or receive a request), daily living skills (dresses self), socialization (takes turns in interactions), and motor skills (uses public transportation). Such measures—along with histories of past behavior—help complete the portrait of the child's behavior that is known only partially through his or her cognitive and academic performances (Sparrow & Cicchetti, 2002).

| Great care must be taken not to misinterpret behavior of a child from another culture.

An incorrect diagnosis can be made if a teacher misinterprets a child's behavior as disturbing or resistant because the child is from a different culture. Our expectations for students' behavior are shaped by the norms of the majority culture, and those expectations influence our evaluation of students' performance.

For all youngsters, special care needs to be taken to see that the procedures or tests used to assess them are fair and valid and to be sure that child and family cultural differences are considered in the design of an individualized education program.

Designing an Individualized Education Program (IEP)

One of the many innovations brought forth by the Education for All Handicapped Children Act is the requirement that every child with disabilities must have an individualized education program (IEP), a clearly documented and carefully monitored plan setting forth how to differentiate the curriculum and experiences of the exceptional child to meet the individual needs of that child. The instructional plan must include the following:

▶ The nature of the child's problem

▶ The program's long-term goals

▶ The program's short-term objectives

▶ The special education services the child will receive

▶ The criteria for gauging the effectiveness of those services

The implementation of the IEP in school systems across the nation has had both positive and negative outcomes (Gallagher & Desimone, 1995). On the positive side is evidence of better relations between teacher and family and improved understanding by the family of the special education program. There is also more information for parents about academic achievement and gains made by their child, as well as general agreement between school and family about the goals and program directions for the child.

On the negative side there is much evidence that the implementation of this idea has not gone smoothly in many places. The IEP is often seen as paperwork with no substantive meaning or use in the classroom (Mainzer, Deshler, Coleman, Kozleski, & Rodriguez-Walling, 2003). It places great demands on teachers' time, and is seen as one more meaningless requirement that must be fulfilled.

Although there are voices calling for the abandonment of the IEP, few wish to abandon the gains it has brought. How can we get rid of the nonessentials of the process and keep the things that are good? A continual problem for educators!

> Despite the additional time and effort required of teachers, implementing IEPs has increased family involvement in students' instructional programs.

Case Study: Frank's IEP

Frank, a 10-year-old fourth grader, could not concentrate on most tasks for more than two or three minutes at a time. Every ten minutes or so, he would turn around and bother the student behind him. His teacher had to stand over him and tap his desk every time he became disruptive. Writing was painstakingly difficult for Frank. It took him five minutes to write a five-word sentence. Most of the time he began sentences in the middle of the page. The letters were usually written very small, and some were written backward. His script *e* looked like an *l*, and he did not dot his *i*'s or cross his *t*'s. He often got frustrated and tore his paper up.

His teacher noted, however, that Frank was a "different boy" when he was working on his science lessons. He would sit quietly, focused on his experiment and documenting his results, waiting for his turn to present the information to the rest of the class. His teacher wanted an evaluation to determine why Frank performed so well in some areas and so poorly in others. She

The individualized education program describes the nature of the child's problem, the program's objectives and goals, the special education services the child will receive, and the criteria for gauging the effectiveness of those services.
© Robin Nelson/Photo Edit

believed that Frank had the ability to do well in all subjects and wanted information that might help her to motivate him or accommodate his learning style. In addition, she thought that he might benefit from special education services.

Frank's teacher felt he was having trouble in language arts and in maintaining attention. The teacher tried to introduce some special lessons and reward on-task performance. That helped a little, but Frank was referred for a comprehensive evaluation.

The Wechsler Intelligence Scale for Children revealed Frank to be of average intelligence but with a wide variation of performance on various subtests. Tests of spelling and visual motor tasks, however, showed Frank to be two grades below his age, as was his low written language production. His pattern of performance suggested a child with learning disabilities.

On the basis of that pattern, the special education teacher worked with the general education teacher to incorporate Frank's resource room work with the typical classroom activities. No time limits were set on his tasks. Some of the goals and objectives in Frank's IEP are listed in Table 2.2. After one year, Frank's progress toward the goals listed in his IEP will be evaluated and decisions about further steps made on the basis of that evaluation.

■ Government: A Support System of Educational Services

Most of the attention of special educators in the latter parts of the twentieth century was devoted to bringing a specially prepared teacher into direct contact with the child with special needs, so that the child could receive an

TABLE 2.2
Goals and Objectives of Frank's IEP

		EVALUATION SCHEDULE
ANNUAL GOAL	The student will increase his spelling scores from a grade level of approximately 2.5 to approximately 4.0.	Annual. Use a norm referenced test.
GENERAL OBJECTIVE	When the examiner pronounces words that begin with consonants, the student will demonstrate his ability to recognize initial consonant sounds auditorily by writing the correct initial consonant for twenty-one out of twenty-one different consonants.	Every three months. Use a criterion-referenced test.
IMMEDIATE SHORT-TERM OBJECTIVES	(*Note:* Objectives of this type are changed and updated frequently and typically are found in lesson plans.)	Weekly. Use a criterion-referenced test.
	When the examiner pronounces fifteen words with initial blends *sw, sk,* and *cr,* the student will demonstrate his ability to recognize the initial blend by writing the correct two letters with 100 percent accuracy.	
	When presented with three printed stimulus root words and requested to add a designated suffix (*ing* with doubled consonants; *ed* with doubled consonants; *ed* to words ending in silent *e*) to that root word, the student will correctly write the requested word with 100 percent accuracy.	Weekly. Use a criterion-referenced test.

Source: Adapted from Ronald R. Taylor, *Assessment of Exceptional Students* (pp. 510–519) (Boston: Allyn & Bacon, 1997). Reprinted with permission of Allyn & Bacon/Pearson Education.

appropriate educational experience. In the last decades, there has been increasing recognition that quality education requires, in addition to that well-prepared teacher, a series of support services (Mainzer, Deshler, Coleman, Kozleski, & Rodriguez-Walling, 2003).

In many ways such a support system resembles the well-organized system supporting the medical practitioner. Think about how limited your own physician would be without laboratories and x-ray technicians to help with diagnosis, active pharmaceutical enterprises producing new effective drugs, hospitals where special treatments can be applied, or the medical schools that do important research on new techniques and produce new generations of qualified physicians. So someone who says, "I have a really good doctor" actually means "I have a good health-care system."

TABLE 2.3
Needs of Special Education Programs Provided by Government and Other Institutions

PERSONNEL PREPARATION	The importance of programs designed to prepare specialists cannot be overestimated, and many institutions of higher education have cooperated in providing such programming.
TECHNICAL ASSISTANCE	Continued support for the on-the-job teacher has been achieved through such organizations as regional resource centers and the National Early Childhood Technical Assistance System, which provides consultation on individual cases and help with supporting local and state programs.
RESEARCH AND PROGRAM EVALUATION	There is a continual need for better techniques for diagnosing children with special needs and for assessing the effectiveness of the special programs now in existence. Major research centers, supported by federal and state funds, have appeared mainly in institutions of higher education to provide these key services.
COMMUNICATION	How does that special educator learn in a timely fashion about the latest ideas and procedures? With the growing use of the Internet, websites can help disseminate information. The difficulty with using the Internet is in evaluating the accuracy of the information. Selected Internet websites have been placed in the margins throughout this book so that readers can pursue further areas of interest. The information may be in the form of books and pamphlets but also may be video tapes or graphic design presentations, so that the teacher can grasp the new ideas more effectively.
DEMONSTRATION	Sometimes it is important for teachers and administrators to actually see new ideas and practices in action. It can be the best way to convince them to adopt a different approach or new instructional procedures. A series of demonstration centers in early childhood education for children with disabilities offer programs that illustrate for teachers and administrators the best of what can be done for the children now. For example, a demonstration could illustrate how to include children with disabilities in a typical preschool program.
DATA SYSTEMS	An often overlooked aid is a system of data collection that provides information about the needs for personnel by cataloguing the number of children and families needing services. Without such information, educational planners cannot allocate the necessary resources to meet the needs for special personnel or programs.
COMPREHENSIVE PLANNING	The need for long-range state planning has been well accepted. The issue is how to coordinate the various support elements so that educational resources are available at the right place, and at the right time, for local school systems

Source: From James J. Gallagher & Richard Clifford, The missing support infrastructure in early childhood, *Early Childhood Research and Practices,* 2(1) (2000): 1–24.

If we do not provide that hard-working general education or special education teacher with a similar collection of support services, then we are placing our specialist in the same situation the physician would be in if deprived of his or her supports. The quality support system consists of the components listed in Table 2.3.

EDUCATIONAL

EXCEPTIONAL CHILDREN

The nature of special education is to provide exceptional children with services not available to them in the typical education program. Special education programs are different from general education programs because they try to take into account the child's interindividual and intraindividual differences. It's important to realize that special education does *not* exist because regular education has failed. Classroom teachers and typical educational programs simply cannot respond fully to the special needs of exceptional children without a substantial change in the structure, program, and staffing of the typical classroom. Estimates of state, federal, and local expenditures for special education approach $50 billion dollars for 1999–2000, clearly indicating the extent of the financial commitment made by society on behalf of these children.

Instruction can be adapted to the interindividual and intraindividual differences found in exceptional children in several ways: We can adapt the learning environment to create an appropriate setting in which to learn, change the actual content of lessons or the specific knowledge being taught, adapt teaching strategies, and introduce technology that meets the special needs of exceptional students. Most chapters include a special Educational Adaptations section that is organized around the four areas listed in the table on the following page.

The school environment is where all of the many forces acting on exceptional children interact and influence each other. Laws regulate who receives services; courts interpret those laws and apply them to specific circumstances; and families support (or sometimes fail to support) the child's efforts and provide goals, values, and expectations that generally reflect the family's cultural background. The school is particularly important for exceptional children who may need very special kinds of help to become productive adults.

> Special education provides exceptional children with necessary services that are not available in the typical school program.

■ Adapting the Learning Environment

Often, a special learning environment is necessary to help exceptional children master particular content and skills. Making changes in the learning environment, however, has repercussions throughout the entire educational system. That may be one reason why environmental modifications are the subject of greater controversy than are changes in either content or skills.

When we decide to move youngsters from the general education classroom to a resource room for an hour a day, we generate a series of activities. First, we have to allocate space in the school for the **resource room.** Then the classroom teacher must modify instruction to accommodate the students who are out of the class for part of the day. And, of course, an array of special personnel must be brought into the system to identify eligible children and to deliver special services.

Educational Adaptations

ADAPTING THE LEARNING ENVIRONMENT

One can change the physical setting in which special services are delivered to make the instruction more likely to be effective.

ADAPTING THE CURRICULUM

It is often necessary to modify the curriculum content of the lessons to meet the needs of exceptional children who are performing markedly below or above the rest of the class. Special additional curricula are necessary for some students with exceptionalities. Some examples of these specialized approaches are Braille, sign language, and mobility education.

ADAPTING TEACHING STRATEGIES

Special attention is given to exceptional students to ensure that they have the necessary basic skills of reading and arithmetic and of processing information that are crucial to further learning.

USING ASSISTIVE AND INSTRUCTIONAL TECHNOLOGY

Special assistive-technology devices help students with exceptionalities to communicate and receive information; instructional-technology devices aid them in mastering necessary knowledge and skills.

The concept of **least restrictive environment** means that teachers attempt to educate a child in the environmental setting that maximizes the chances that the child with exceptionalities will respond well to the educational goals and objectives set for him or her. It should not be imagined, however, that the emphasis on inclusion has brought all exceptional children back into the general education classroom. About one in every five children with disabilities (usually the more severely impaired) are still educated in a separate classroom or resource room settings. The number of children in separate facilities (separate schools or institutions) has been reduced over the same time period from 7 percent to 4 percent.

Figure 2.1 reveals by age level the percentages of special needs children receiving help in an inclusive setting. At the elementary level about 56 percent of these children were provided services in the regular classroom in 2003. That number shrank appreciably in the middle school and secondary school programs, to less than 40 percent, becoming even smaller in the transition period between ages 18 through 21. Even so, there appear to be about 10 percent more children with
special needs being served in an inclusive setting today than was the case in 1988–1989. The legislation and court cases supporting inclusion have clearly had an effect (*Twenty-fourth Report to Congress,* 2003).

The Inclusion Movement

Inclusion is the most significant movement in special education in the past two decades. As an educational philosophy, it essentially says that exceptional

Supporters of the full-inclusion movement believe that all children, regardless of ability, should be educated in general education classrooms.

FIGURE 2.1

Students with Disabilities Served in Inclusive Setting 1999–2000

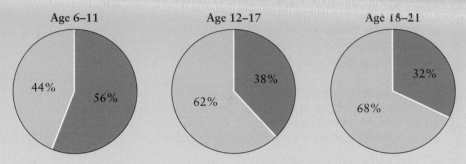

Age 6–11   Age 12–17   Age 18–21

44%   56%   38%   62%   32%   68%

◼ Students served in inclusive settings (more than 79% of the school week)

◻ Students served in other settings beyond the classroom (21% or more of the time)

Source: U.S. Department of Education (2003). *Twenty-fourth Annual Report to Congress.* Washington, DC: Office of Special Education Programs.

children should be *a part of, not apart from,* general education. The question that still bothers both special educators and general educators is how the philosophy of inclusion can be made operational in so many different schools in so many different communities. Additional questions include:

▶ Does inclusion mean that the exceptional child is always to be placed in the general education classroom?

▶ Does inclusion mean that the essential responsibility for the education of the exceptional child is in the hands of the general classroom teacher?

Instruction can be adapted to the differences found in exceptional children in several ways—by varying the learning environment, the content of lessons, and the skills being taught and by introducing technology that can meet special needs.
© Bob Daemmrich/
The Image Works

▶ Does inclusion mean that such children should receive special instruction only within the boundaries of the general classroom, or can they leave for special instruction for a period of time?

One of the keys for success is the collaboration between the general educator and the special educator, as illustrated in the Ecology of the Child on page 64.

Figure 2.2 shows the expected relationship between general education and special education with school-age children. The description in the far left column refers to students who need no accommodations or modifications in content or performance expectations. When there is a need for accommodations to the general curriculum, special education services enter the picture. Even if the content and performance expectations remain the same, the time allotted for learning may have to be adjusted, and the instruction may have to be modified.

As the distance of the child with disabilities becomes further from the norm, more modifications are expected, which may mean actual changes in the content fields or expectations and in the form of instruction. For the most seriously involved child, it may be necessary to set individualized curriculum goals and a separate functional curriculum designed to help the child to be independent in self-care and to learn vocational skills appropriate to his or her capabilities.

Inclusion in Context

Inclusion and the General Education Teacher Part of the inclusion argument revolves around what resources will be available to help general education classroom teachers. Will special education specialists be available in the classroom with the

FIGURE 2.2
Special Education and the General Curriculum

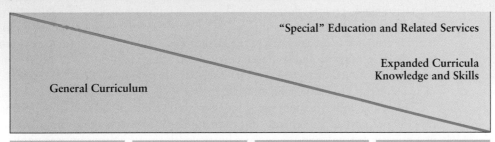

"Special" Education and Related Services

Expanded Curricula
Knowledge and Skills

General Curriculum

No Accommodations or Modifications	Accommodations	Modifications	Alternate
No changes to • Content • Performance expectations • Sequence and timelines • Instruction	No changes to • Content • Performance expectations Changes to • Sequence and timelines • Instruction	Changes some or all of • Content areas • Performance expectations • Sequence and timelines • Instruction	• Individualized curriculum goals • Separate functional curriculum

Source: From Victor Nolet & Margaret J. McLaughlin, *Accessing the General Curriculum: Including Students with Disabilities in Standards-Based Reform* (Thousand Oaks, CA: Corwin Press, 2000). Copyright © 2000 by Corwin Press, Inc. Reprinted with the permission of Corwin Press, Inc.

general education teacher for a significant amount of time to help with special instruction? Will paraprofessionals be present to provide necessary assistance to the children with special needs, particularly those with physical disabilities? Will general educators receive personnel preparation for their new roles concerning special needs children?

Those who support inclusion generally believe that supportive resources will be available for the general education teacher, whereas critics point to many situations where the support forces are not there. More important, such support will likely not be there for some time to come, judging by the attitude of school boards and state legislators regarding the resources they are willing to put into inclusion programs.

Nolet and McLaughlin (2000) present a useful distinction between the intended curriculum, the taught curriculum, and the learned curriculum.

► *The intended curriculum:* This is the official or adopted curriculum contained in state or district policy—the body of content that students are expected to learn as a part of their school experiences.

► *The taught curriculum:* This refers to putting the intended curriculum into operation. It means the minute-by-minute, day-to-day, and week-to-week events that actually occur in the classroom or relevant settings.

► *The learned curriculum:* This is what the students actually learn as a result of being in the classroom and interacting with the intended and the taught curricula.

A number of attempts have been made to bring together "access to the general education curriculum" and the "meeting of individual needs" in inclusive settings for children with disabilities. A junior-high science program in an inner-city neighborhood was designed to include students with disabilities by establishing teams of special education and general education teachers and constructing a variety of hands-on materials and tasks to aid in comprehension. Crucial to the programs was a training program for fifteen three-person teams of 100 hours to prepare them for team activities in the classrooms and to aid in bonding personnel to a common purpose and common curriculum. Fifteen students with a diagnosis of severe emotional disturbance (ED) or serious learning disabilities (LD) were included in the 114 students involved.

The results indicated that the students with disabilities had the same passing rate (69 percent) as the general education students (from a neighborhood school in a poverty setting), and the social adjustment during the program was good, with discipline referrals and attendance figures within acceptable limits (Cawley, Hayden, Cade, & Baker-Kroczynski, 2002).

A similar effort was reported in trying to determine if there were a blending of the National Council of Teachers of Mathematics (NCTM) standards with programs for students with emotional disturbance (ED) or learning disabilities (LD) at the middle school and secondary levels (Maccini & Gagnon, 2002). A total of 129 teachers were surveyed in Maryland districts, half of them special education teachers, half mathematics teachers. Surprisingly, 55 percent of the special education teachers said they had never heard of the NCTM standards, which have been around for over a decade.

The need for special planning and design seemed evident in the lack of suitable materials for students with LD and ED who require manipulatives, multiple representations, and varied examples as teachers progress through the

An alternative to full inclusion emphasizes providing a continuum of services based on each child's individual needs.

concrete-semiconcrete-abstract phases of instruction that are recommended by the NCTM standards.

Also, the general education teachers had little knowledge of teaching methods for EBD and LD students, which again suggests the need for additional training of both special education and general education teachers if such program blending is to be successful. How can the student who has been identified with a disability keep up with the general education classroom and the other students, since he or she was identified in the first place for inability to keep up? One of the strategies is to build flexibility into the instruction so that the products and environments can be usable by the largest possible number of students. This is called *universal design for learning* (UDL).

In universal design the assistive supports are built in, rather than added as an afterthought. These would include graceful ramps in new construction, instead of hastily constructed plywood entranceways when access to a building is a problem for some people with disabilities. One of the key elements of flexibility is *closed captioning,* standard on most TV sets, so that persons with hearing problems can see the text at the bottom of the screen; the same message is being delivered through two separate channels, visual and auditory.

Universal design also allows for flexibility in student expression. Instead of giving a paper-and-pencil answer, a student may use drawings or illustrations or respond through a computer. Street signs in two different languages would be another example of universal design flexibility.

A careful analysis of four secondary schools illustrates the new approach (Wallace, Anderson, Bartholomay, & Hupp, 2002). These four schools were in different states. As part of the Beacons of Excellence project, they were chosen from a roster of 114 schools nominated by a national advisory panel for their successful inclusion. The Beacons of Excellence project was funded by the Office of Special Education Programs in the U.S. Department of Education to increase the understanding of how schools can improve learning results for students with disabilities, within the context of efforts to achieve exemplary results for all children. After extensive observations of general education students and special education students, the authors reached the following conclusions.

▶ Merely including students with disabilities in the general education classroom is not enough to ensure their success.

▶ The school administration in each of the schools must support team teaching with special and general education teachers.

▶ A significant amount of time must be spent guiding students in their preparation for learning and teaching them directly, using a variety of strategies, including technology.

▶ Teachers must know a variety of instructional strategies in order to address the diverse learning needs of students, and they need to know how to work with each other to effectively implement the strategies (p. 357).

In short, success in inclusion is not an accident or attributable to good luck. It requires extensive planning, preparation, and teamwork.

Social Relationships in the Inclusive Classroom Social relationships seem to be the overriding concern for those supporting the inclusion movement, rather than mastery of certain academic and technical skills. This is the position of The Association for Persons with Severe Handicaps (TASH). The policy of full inclusion follows this path of reasoning: If we are to have, as a major goal, the *social integration* of persons with disabilities into adult society, then the school environment should foster the development of such skills, personal friendships, and relationships with children with disabilities. These skills are available to nondisabled persons in the natural course of their educational experiences (Snell, 1988).

Do friendships result from merely placing students in proximity to one another? Does the fact that some students are modeling appropriate behavior mean that the exceptional child will imitate such behavior? Probably not. Friendships generally grow between students who perceive similarities with each other. Students who are withdrawn gravitate toward others who are shy; an aggressive student often chooses another aggressive student to bond with (Dision, Andres, & Cosby, 1995). Reflect on your own youth. Did you always form friendships with peers with whom your parents wished you to be friends in the hope that they would be good role models for you? Or were your parents occasionally horrified to see whom you brought home, which friends stirred in you some bond of interest or some common feeling about the school or world around you?

One device that encourages closer social contact is the **circle of friends,** in which nondisabled children under the leadership of a teacher, counselor, or inclusion facilitator (Boathouse, 1993) take the responsibility for communicating with children with disabilities on a social level and spend time finding out about mutual likes and dislikes. To their surprise they may find little difference between themselves and the child with disabilities; that discovery is the beginning of wisdom and a degree of social acceptance.

Views on inclusion differ. TASH tends to support full inclusion. LDA emphasizes the importance of alternative instructional environments.

How Much Inclusion Is "Included"? The attitude of the Learning Disabilities Association of America (LDA) toward inclusion is quite different from that of TASH. LDA believes that the general education classroom is *not* the appropriate place for many students with learning disabilities—those who may need alternative instructional environments or teaching strategies that cannot or will not be provided within the context of the general education classroom. Neither group denies the legitimacy of the other's priorities. The issue is which should have precedence.

Evans (1996) points out that the inclusion philosophy requires the application of a variety of other strategies that can maintain a diverse group of students in the general education environment. These strategies include:

▶ consultant teacher models,

▶ collaborative consultation,

▶ collaborative teaching,

▶ cooperative professional development, and

▶ prereferral consultation.

In other words, it is not enough merely to decree that all exceptional children will be placed in the general education environment. If inclusion is to work, there must be a wide variety of support personnel to help the general education teacher provide a healthy educational environment for *all* students.

With a growing number of students with exceptionalities being "included" in general education classrooms, the roles and responsibilities of teachers have changed. General education teachers find themselves faced with exceptional students who have a range of needs and who require modifications. Special education teachers are now expected to collaborate with general education teachers in planning and implementing lessons for exceptional students in the general education classroom.

The results of a recent survey conducted by the Council for Exceptional Children indicate that while the expectations of what teachers will be doing have changed dramatically, little is being done to prepare and support teachers as they attempt to make these changes (Coleman, 2001). The report contains the following findings.

▶ General education teachers are working with greater numbers of children with exceptionalities, yet they have little to no time for collaborating with special educators for planning.

▶ Both general and special educators feel underprepared for their new roles, yet little is being done to provide additional preparation to address this gap.

▶ Teacher education programs have not kept pace in preparing graduates for their new roles, so the problem continues to grow.

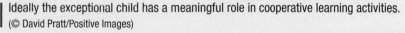

Ideally the exceptional child has a meaningful role in cooperative learning activities.
(© David Pratt/Positive Images)

▶ While the range and intensity of students' needs continue to increase, little is being done to provide additional support to teachers working to meet these needs (Coleman, 2001).

One of the most disturbing findings of the study was that although teachers see such difficulties clearly, administrators in a position to address these needs seem to feel that their teachers can meet the needs of students with exceptionalities in spite of these difficulties. Given the administrators' perception, it is hard to imagine that the situation will improve significantly in the near future.

Adapting the Curriculum

Assessing Progress

Accountability and Standardized Tests The word *accountability* throws a mild chill into every educator. The general public tells us that we are to be held responsible for the students that we release from the educational system. No longer will the general public take the educator's word about what progress is being made in education; it wants to be shown. The public wants proof that education and special education produce good results, and it does not react well when told how hard it is to produce that proof, however valid the reasons (Gallagher, 1998).

In the field of exceptional children, the goals of the IEPs might be quite different from one child to another, and so aggregating results into a total report on the special education program may be hard. For example, if Mary is trying to achieve social acceptance goals and Sam is working on spelling, it would be hard to assess Sam's progress with a social acceptance scale or Mary's progress with a spelling test or to add up all the scores of the special students on these measures as a way of judging progress.

Currently, most standard achievement tests don't accurately measure the knowledge and skills gains of the exceptional child.

As currently constructed, standard achievement tests do not adequately measure the attainments of many exceptional children. The child with mental retardation may be learning many practical sets of skills and knowledge that are not covered by the standard curriculum and standard tests, and the gifted child will surely have his or her abilities and attainments underestimated because of the lack of depth and conceptual complexity of most of these measures.

The increasing use of high-stakes testing has created special problems for children with exceptionalities because important decisions will be based on the results of such tests—decisions as to whether the student receives a diploma or passes from one grade to the next. Such decisions have been underlined by the federal No Child Left Behind Act of 2002 (PL 107-110), which places heavy demands on schools and school systems to meet state standards for achievement or suffer sanctions if they do not. The Council for Exceptional Children, the major professional association for children with special needs, wants policy that holds programs for exceptional children accountable as long as the measures used are appropriate.

a. All students with exceptional learning needs shall be included in all assessment and accountability systems and shall have available the opportunity to participate in general assessments....

b. Only assessment processes and instruments that have been developed and validated on student samples that included students who have exceptionalities and that validly demonstrate their performance shall be used.

(Council for Exceptional Children, 2003, sec. 4, pt. 3, p. 137.)

Some new approaches have appeared to supplement the standard achievement tests. They bear names like *performance assessment, authentic assessment,* and *real-life assessment.* Because performance is knowledge in use, **performance assessment** is a measure of the applications of knowledge. If a student is asked to write an essay on a particular topic, that essay could form the basis for a type of performance assessment. If a student is asked to conduct a research project or produce an oral presentation on a topic, that assignment could be a basis for performance assessment (Wiggins, 1992).

Authentic assessment involves the typical classroom performance of the student, rather than a contrived task. Quite typically, it might be an examination of a student portfolio providing evidence of student performance over time. In this way, we have an assessment in real time, using classroom work and assignments as the basis for evaluation.

These forms of evaluation still leave the task of determining just what performance is acceptable or outstanding. Often such judgments are rather crude three-point or four-point scales ranging from *excellent* to *unacceptable*. Added to that would be a substantive critique of writing style or scientific procedures revealed through the authentic assessment.

Cultural Differences and Assessment

As the student population becomes more diverse, the schools have a special responsibility in assessing students who come from various cultures. A student whose primary language is not English is liable to have his or her abilities or aptitudes underestimated by a standard assessment measure, unless some attention is paid to the individual's special circumstances (National Research Council, 2002). Special attention should be paid to the possible test biases caused by the assumption that the student has had a set of standard experiences in the mainstream culture. Such misdiagnoses have become so embarrassing for many educational administrators that they prefer to use the general education classroom as the base for special education services, rather than be accused of "segregating" students by race or ethnic origin into some separate setting in the school.

There has been such concern about the assessment of minority students that a panel was established by the National Academy of Sciences to answer key questions of assessment (Donovan & Cross, 2002).

1. *Is there a higher incidence of children with special needs or giftedness among some racial and ethnic groups?* Yes. Disproportionate numbers of minority students are in poverty. Major differences in measured aptitude between groups are documented at kindergarten entry.

2. *Does schooling contribute to these differences found in racial and ethnic groups?* Yes. Schools with higher concentrations of low-income minority students have fewer well-trained teachers and fewer resources.

3. *Does the current referral and assessment process reliably identify students with special needs and gifts, or is it biased by race and ethnicity?* The answer to this is not clear, although it does seem that minority status increases likelihood that the scores on assessment measures may be depressed.

4. *Is placement in special education a benefit or a risk? Is that outcome different by race or ethnic group?* There are insufficient data for answering the question, but there are substantial data that early identification and intervention are more effective than later identification and intervention.

The report clearly calls unwise the current policy of "wait to fail" before referring the student for help. Screening mechanisms exist for early identification of children at risk for reading and behavior problems and should be used.

This issue of ethnic and racial groups and their interaction with special education is dealt with in many of the subsequent chapters for individual categories of special needs children.

The Academic Standards Movement Meets the Inclusion Movement

Two of the major educational reforms facing school systems today seem to be on a collision course. They are the standards movement and the inclusion movement in general education for special education. The issue became so pressing that the National Academy of Sciences established a commission to study the matter (McDonnell, McLaughlin, & Morrison, 1997). The commission pointed out that the **standards movement** has made it clear that they expect all children to learn and achieve at high standards and that the term *all* includes children with disabilities. Such expansive statements raise some serious questions for exceptional children. Does that mean that Barry, with severe cognitive impairments plus cerebral palsy, is expected to meet the same high academic requirements in math, science, language arts, and social studies as all other students? What about Mary, who has autism?

Apart from the feasibility of applying such standards, there is the question of the desirability of such standards being applied to exceptional children. As the National Academy of Sciences report points out, many exceptional children take a secondary program that is vocationally oriented and directed to possible work practice and opportunities. "It is important that broader outcomes and school-to-work transition planning not be neglected in the move toward standards-based reform" (McDonnell et al., 1997, p. 149).

Is Carl, with a severe learning disability, going to have to give up his school-to-work assignment with the local bus company in order to take the challenging American history course so he can get his high school diploma? It is clear that a lot of work needs to be done to bring together, in an operational fashion, the desirable goals from both of these reform movements on inclusion and standards.

The increasing concern about standards has raised an important point about what action should be taken with students who don't meet the standards. Suppose, in the interests of higher standards, the schools establish a minimum standard of performance to be achieved before a student moves on to the next grade. Many exceptional children will not be able to meet that standard. What happens then? All too often, the answer is retention or holding the student back a grade in the hope that the student will, with the extra time, be able to master the basic skills or knowledge. Retention, however, has been long demonstrated to be one of the least useful of techniques. In general, students who are retained tend to drop out of school more and do not learn the necessary material that was the goal of the retention in the first place. Such results are also found in a research synthesis with children with learning disabilities (McLeskey, Lancaster, & Grizzle, 1995).

Adapting Technology

Special education has often led the way in the acceptance and use of technology in education. That achievement may well be due to the unique problems special educators face. Because they are educating children with special needs, they have been willing to try new devices that promise help, such as computers adapted to special needs, hearing aids, print magnifiers, and machines that trace eye movements as the student reads.

Assistive Technology

There are two quite different uses of technology for children with disabilities: assistive and instructional uses. **Assistive technology** consists of tools that enhance the functioning of people with special disabilities. For the person who is blind, it provides braille readers and typewriters; for the person who is deaf, hearing aids; for the person who cannot speak, communication boards for pointing to and composing messages. Assistive technology can be as sophisticated as a device that translates print into oral language or as simple as a headband and a pointer that allow students who have cerebral palsy to point to text or communication boards. Such devices have dramatically improved individual children's ability to receive and transmit information effectively and are most often used with children with moderate to severe disabilities that create major barriers to communication. Many of the subsequent chapters include examples of the uses of assistive technology.

New technologies in the classroom can both assist and instruct the student who is disabled.

www.abledata.com

Instructional Technology

Instructional technology involves the computer and related tools that support and expand the computer's usefulness. Instructional technology is developed primarily as a means to deliver content and instruction in an appropriate manner to exceptional children. The "Uses of Technology" table on page 62 provides a sample list of assistive- and instructional-technology devices.

Major attempts are being made to go beyond the traditional transmission of knowledge and to use technology as a means to aid exceptional children in thinking and problem solving. Hasselbring (1997) points out that a student may understand how the special characteristics of a camel may help the animal survive desert sandstorms yet fail to understand that this survival illustrates the phenomenon of *adaptation*. When asked about the concept of adaptation, the student may not

For resources, see this book: *Computer and Web Resources for People with Disabilities: A Guide to Exploring Today's Assistive Technology.* www.hunterhouse.com

Uses of Technology

ASSISTIVE TECHNOLOGY	INSTRUCTIONAL TECHNOLOGY
Tools for enhancing the routine functioning of people who have physical or sensory disabilities	Computers and related technology for the delivery and support of instruction
▶ Communication boards	▶ Computers and software programs
▶ Computer-screen readers	▶ Phone/fax
▶ Braille printers	▶ Internet
▶ Head pointers	▶ Data compression
▶ Kurtzweil reading devices for the visually impaired	▶ CD-ROM
	▶ Video discs

Source: Adapted from T. Hasselbring, *Florida's Future in Special Education: Applications of Technology.* Vision 2000 Conference, University of South Florida, Tampa. Reprinted with the permission of the author.

Rehabilitation Engineering and Assistive Technology Society of North America
www.resna.org

realize that his or her knowledge of camels is relevant or is a good illustration of the term.

There is good reason to believe that concept instruction is much more likely than fact-oriented instruction to produce transferable knowledge. That is why major efforts are being made to use technology not just to master specific information but as a tool to help in problem solving. It is especially important for teachers who work with children with exceptionalities to learn how to apply technology to their instruction. For the most part, teachers have been left on their own to learn as best they can, or they have been given short-term training introducing them to the technology but rarely allowing them sufficient time to explore the full potential of these new tools. Now, legislation (IDEA, 2004) mandates the mastery of technology on the part of special education teachers. Teachers must now consider the appropriateness of assistive technology as a tool for intervention (Lahm & Nichels, 1999). It can provide access to data and other programs. Even more important, computers allow children to learn at their own rate and provides immediate feedback and reinforcement. The child's learning becomes more active and self-directed. Now the rapid development of the Internet, the World Wide Web, and websites (Grabe & Grabe, 2000) threatens to leave children with special needs behind the rest of their classmates, unless special attention is paid to developing these children's skills in accessing and processing the information now available by computer.

The Alliance for Technology Access
www.ATAccess.org

The Government

A major social institution that has had a long-lasting effect on the education of exceptional children has been the government, both federal and state. The executive branches and the legislatures have the responsibility to create policies, draft laws, and find the necessary money for the special services and extra expenses involved in educating exceptional children.

Federal Actions for Students Who Are Gifted

The Javits Act, which provided resources for gifted students, pointed out the low incidence of cultural minorities identified as gifted.

Except for a brief period in the 1970s, there had been little movement at the federal legislative level to provide resources to aid in the education of children who are gifted. The Javits Act (Public Law 100-297), named after New York senator Jacob Javits, who showed early interest and support, provided a small sum of money to support research and demonstration programs that focused on the special needs of gifted students from economically disadvantaged circumstances, from different cultures, or with disabilities. The Javits programs have helped with the development of alternative identification methods designed to more adequately measure intellectual ability in minority populations (see Chapter 9 for a discussion of this movement).

A Summary of Special Education Legislation

One of the ways we express society's needs and intentions in a democracy is through legislation. At the turn of the century, individual states became involved in a limited way in subsidizing programs in public schools for children with sensory disabilities (blindness, deafness) and physical impairments. Some states helped organize and support classes for children who were mentally retarded or who had behavioral problems. After World War II, many states expanded their involvement, providing financial support for special classes and services in local schools for children with all types of disability. This expansion caused two problems that many believed could be solved only by federal legislation.

First, these new and larger programs created a personnel scarcity in the late 1940s and early 1950s. Professional special educators were in short supply, and the field of special education was not firmly established. Second, because not all states expanded their involvement in special education, organized parents' groups began asking why children with disabilities and their parents should be penalized through the accident of birth in a particular state or a particular region of a state.

Were not U.S. citizens (in this case, the parents of children with disabilities) entitled to equal treatment anywhere in the United States? Should parents, in addition to the burdens of having children with special needs, be forced to move their family to a community where special education resources were available, or to send their children to some institution far away from home and family because no local resources existed? The blatant unfairness of the situation called out for attention.

ECOLOGY OF THE CHILD

Teacher Collaboration

At its best, inclusion involves intense collaboration between the general education teacher, who knows the curriculum, and the special education teacher, who knows how to modify instruction so that students with exceptionalities can learn. When inclusion is working well, it goes somewhat like this:

Mrs. Brown was introducing the measurement of angles to her sixth-grade math class. She had created cards with various types of angles drawn on them—acute, obtuse, and right angles. Initially, she asked pairs of students to identify classroom objects that had angles and to select the card that showed the kind of angle they saw. Most of the students enjoyed this, moving about the room and listing the things they identified. During this phase of the lesson, Mrs. Brown and Mr. Fuller, the special education teacher, mingled with the students, asking them about the shapes of the angles they found: "Are they all the same?" "Which is the largest?" "Which looks the smallest?" "Can you find one angle that is middle-sized—that is, all the other angles are larger or smaller than that angle is? What is the middle-sized angle's shape?"

Next, the student pairs formed groups of four, and Mr. Fuller asked them to organize their angle cards by the size of the angle drawn, from the smallest to the largest angle. Then he held up a protractor and asked them what they thought this tool was for. Mrs. Brown handed out protractors, and Mr. Fuller showed the students how to use them to measure the angles on their cards.

As the students completed and recorded their measurements, both teachers circulated to offer help. Mr. Fuller gravitated toward Jason's group, knowing that Jason's learning disability might make it difficult for him to read and record the numbers accurately. He reminded Jason of a strategy they had practiced earlier, using graph paper to align Jason's numbers and keep his answers organized, and prompted Jason to get out his graph paper. The other students in the group saw the graph paper and asked Jason to record for the group because the graph paper made it look "cool."

Finally, Mrs. Brown led the class in a closing discussion where she asked the following questions:

"When you measured the middle-sized angle, how many degrees did it have? (Ninety degrees) Does anyone know the name for a ninety-degree angle? (A right angle) Does

---

Legislation has provided resources for children with special needs.

Federal legislation clearly was needed, both to bring qualified people into special education and to equalize educational opportunities across the country. But that legislation was not easy to obtain. It violated the strong tradition in the United States that education is a state and local responsibility. Still, organized parents' groups with the support of other interested citizens convinced Congress that they needed help.

Public Law 88–164

After much debate, in the late 1950s Congress began to pass limited measures directed toward research and personnel training in the fields of mental retardation and deafness. In 1963, PL 88-164 authorized funds for training professionals and for research and demonstration. The law represented a strong

anyone remember the names for angles that are smaller than ninety degrees? (Acute angles) What about angles that are larger than ninety degrees? (Obtuse angles)"

"Looking at how you arranged your angles, can you classify them by the type of angle they are?"

"When you found things in the room that had angles, which category did most of the angles fall into: acute, obtuse, or right? Why do you think this happened?"

And finally, Mrs. Brown gave the question for homework: "How can knowing about angles and their measurements help people in their work or in their lives?

The discussion led by Mrs. Brown was fast-paced and covered a wide variety of ideas. Mr. Fuller was fairly certain that Jason and some of the other exceptional students had been able to follow some of the discussion but that they had missed some essential points as well. Later that day, he went over the terms and discussion questions with his smaller group of students. He also had prepared a study guide on angles, with some additional measurement practice problems. Mr. Fuller and his students brainstormed ideas for the homework question, and he gave them time to think through their ideas in preparation for answering the question Mrs. Brown had given the class.

This type of collaboration takes time: time for planning, time for reflecting, and time for implementing. The benefit is that the exceptional students in Mrs. Brown's math class get access to the general curriculum *and* get additional support to help them succeed.

WHAT IS THE CONTEXT?

Both the special and the general education teacher play important roles in the education of a student with exceptionalities. While the general educator is an expert in the content and curriculum, the special educator knows how to modify learning experiences so that the exceptional student will more likely meet with success. Many middle schools and high schools are using approaches like the one at Jason's school, to ensure that students have access to teachers who are qualified in subject-area content and pedagogical methods.

PIVOTAL ISSUES FOR TEACHERS AND ADMINISTRATORS

- How can teachers find the planning time they need for making collaboration work well?
- How does Jason's school compare with schools that you have seen and worked with?
- What difficulties could prevent a model like this one from working well?

initiative by President John Kennedy, whose interest was heightened by his sister's mental retardation. Those first efforts were followed by many others, and from that small beginning emerged thirty years of legislation to ensure that all children with disabilities have access to an appropriate education.

Public Law 94–142

That flood of legislation served notice that the federal government accepted responsibility for providing support and resources for children with disabilities and for encouraging the states to carry out their basic responsibilities. Still, programs and resources were not consistent from state to state. To deal with that inconsistency and to help the states handle the costs of court-mandated

Bill Gates with a visually impaired student.
© Reuters/CORBIS

programs, Congress in 1975 passed PL 94-142, the Education for All Handicapped Children Act. The measure, which took effect in 1977, was designed

> to assure that all handicapped children have available to them a free appropriate public education which emphasizes special education and related services designed to meet their unique needs . . . to assure that the rights of handicapped children, and their parents or guardians, are protected, to assist states and localities to provide for the education of all handicapped children, and to assess and assure the effectiveness of efforts to educate handicapped children. (U.S. House of Representatives, 1975, p. 35)

Six key principles at the heart of PL 94-142 have shaped special as well as general education during the last three decades:

▶ *Zero reject.* All children with disabilities must be provided a free and appropriate public education. This means local school systems do not have the option to decide whether to provide needed services.

▶ *Nondiscriminatory evaluation.* Each student must receive a full individual examination before being placed in a special education program, with tests appropriate to the child's cultural and linguistic background. A re-evaluation is required every three years.

▶ *Individualized education program.* An IEP must be written for every student with a handicap who is receiving special education. The IEP must describe the child's current performance and goals for the school year, the particular special education services to be delivered, and the procedures by which outcomes are evaluated.

▶ *Least restrictive environment.* As much as possible, children who are handicapped must be educated with children who are not handicapped. The philosophy is to move as close to the normal setting (general education classroom) as feasible for each child.

▶ *Due process.* Due process is a set of legal procedures to ensure the fairness of educational decisions and the accountability of both professionals and parents in making those decisions. These procedures allow parents to call a hearing when they do not agree with the school's plans for their child, to obtain an individual evaluation from a qualified examiner outside the school system, or to take other actions to ensure that both family and child have channels through which to voice their interests and concerns.

▶ *Parental participation.* Parents are to be included in the development of the IEP, and they have the right to access their child's educational records.

To carry out the provisions of the law, the federal government authorized the spending of up to $3 billion by 1982, promising much larger sums of money to aid the states than had previously been provided. By 1990, the government was still spending about $1 billion a year. In return for that aid, states are required to show evidence that they are doing their best to help children with disabilities receive needed services. Specific provisions in the law placed substantial pressure on public school systems, demanding more in the way of assessment, parent contact, and evaluation than most school systems had been accustomed to providing.

Not surprisingly, many educators have protested the burden that these requirements place on them. But the law has become part of the educational landscape. In the last three decades, the federal government moved from little involvement in special education to becoming a major partner in local and state programs for students who have disabilities.

Public Law 99-457 and IDEA (Public Law 105–17)

The Education for All Handicapped Children Act was, in fact, misnamed. It wasn't for all children at all ages. As it became increasingly evident that early intervention was important, both for the exceptional child and for his or her family, pressure increased for the law to include younger children.

PL 99-457 (Education of the Handicapped Act Amendments), passed in 1986, provided that opportunity by allocating federal funds for the states to develop plans and programs for children and their families *from birth on.* PL 105-17 amendments of 1997 changed the title of the Education of the Handicapped Act to the "Individuals with Disabilities Education Act," or IDEA. The impact of IDEA will be discussed throughout the text.

IDEA 2004

IDEA 2004 represents the reauthorization of the basic legislation to account for flaws in earliers versions. Some of the major changes in IDEA 2004 involve the following:

▶ **Quality of personnel** Special education specialists must hold full state certification as a special education teacher and hold a license to teach.

They must demonstrate subject-matter competence in the academic programs they teach.

▶ **IEP standards (section 1400)** IEPs must reflect scientifically based instructional practices, cognitive behavioral interventions, and early intervention services, where appropriate. They must include plans for the use of assistive technology and short-term objectives for children with disabilities who take alternative assessments.

▶ **Transition services** Such services much be included in all IEPs for students at age 16 and for younger students if appropriate. Transition services must include instruction, community experiences, development of employment, and other postschool adult living objectives.

The intent of this reauthorization is to tighten the standards and ensure that a quality program is provided to children with special needs. The regulations that will determine how this law will be implemented were not written at the time of publication. In addition, how the federal government will handle news from local districts and states that they have been unable to obtain highly qualified personnel for all positions (as they will not, because of major shortages) will be important to the future of this legislation and to special education programs.

How Well Is IDEA Working?

Congress, in reviewing thirty years of experience with PL 94-142 (now IDEA), decided to embark on a series of initiatives to determine how the law is working and what can be learned from its various provisions.

▶ Children with disabilities will be included in statewide and districtwide assessments.

▶ Individualized education programs must indicate how the student will access the general education curriculum.

▶ More avenues are needed (e.g., distance learning) for preparing personnel to work with children with disabilities.

▶ A statement of transition needs for children with disabilities who are over the age of 14 will be included in the individualized education program.

▶ A series of longitudinal studies is authorized to follow children with disabilities for four to six years (*Twenty-fourth Annual Report to Congress, 2002*).

This is a first-rate example of how legislation can shape educational objectives and practices. Congress wants to have these children as closely aligned to the typical children as possible in their programs and assessments. Congress is underscoring the importance of transition from school to work and providing for research to track the progress of these students. The initiative also provides funds for personnel preparation, so that qualified instructors will work with the children.

Two other important pieces of legislation play a role in the life of children with disabilities. These are Section 504 of the Rehabilitation Act of 1973 (PL 93-112). The key provision of the act says it is illegal to deny participation in activities or programs solely because of a disability. Individuals with disabilities must have equal access to programs and services.

The second law was the Americans with Disabilities Act of 1992 (PL 101-336). This law extends to people with disabilities civil rights equal to those guaranteed without regard to race, color, national origin, gender, or religion through the Civil Rights Act of 1964.

These three pieces of legislation make clear that American society is determined to see that children with disabilities have equal access to educational resources and cannot be discriminated against solely on the basis of their disability.

■ The Role of the Courts

Courts have confirmed the right of children with special needs to a free, appropriate public education (FAPE).

Another of society's social institutions, the courts, has played a significant role in the lives of exceptional children and their families. It is the duty of the courts to rule on the interpretation of the laws and regulations generated by the executive and legislative branches. If the law says that every child is entitled to a "free and appropriate public education," how does that translate at the community level? Does that mean that a school cannot expel a child with disabilities? Many important court decisions have formed the foundation for special education.

The basic issue here is that children with special needs deserve a free and appropriate education, just as do all children in the United States. If that right is being abridged, or if other inequities are being created, citizens can appeal to the courts for justice and equity. During the last three decades, a series of legal cases solidified the position of exceptional children and their right to a free and appropriate education.

Although the courts have assumed the role of protector of the rights of exceptional children, their decisions have not always been that favorable. Despite the rules for compulsory attendance to school that were in place during the first third of the twentieth century, there were court decisions that allowed schools to expel students with various disabilities.

As late as 1958, the State Supreme Court of Illinois did not require a free public education for children who were mentally deficient and who "could not reap the benefits of education" (Yell, Rogers, & Rogers, 1998). Even in 1969, North Carolina made it a crime for parents to force attendance of the child with disabilities after he or she had been excluded from school.

A landmark case that began a series of court decisions in favor of exceptional children and their right to a free public education was the *Pennsylvania Association for Retarded Children* (PARC) v. *Commonwealth of Pennsylvania* lawsuit and decision. In this case, the court decided that children with mental retardation did have a right to free, appropriate public education (FAPE) and that when the state constitution said all children are entitled to a free education, the term *all* did, in fact, refer to *all* children.

The movement toward judicial action was, in part, a recognition of the success of minority groups in using the courts to establish their educational rights. In 1954 with the classic school desegregation case, *Brown* v. *Board of Education*, the courts began to reaffirm the rights of minority citizens in a wide variety of settings. If court decisions could protect the rights of one group of citizens, they should do the same for another group: those with disabilities. Soon, supporters of people with disabilities were working to translate abstract legal rights into tangible social action through the judicial system.

Class action suits have been influential in changing the status of children with disabilities in the United States. A *class action suit* provides that legal action taken as part of the suit applies not only to the individual who brings the particular case to court but to all members of the class to which that individual belongs. That means the rights of all people with disabilities can be reaffirmed by a case involving just one child.

The rulings in several court cases have reaffirmed the rights of those who are handicapped and have defined the limits of those rights.

Rights of Children with Disabilities

▶ A child with disabilities cannot be excluded from school without careful due process, and it is the responsibility of the schools to provide appropriate programs for children who are different (*Pennsylvania Association for Retarded Children* v. *Commonwealth of Pennsylvania*, 1972; *Goss* v. *Lopez*, 1974; *Hairston* v. *Drosick*, 1974).

▶ The presumed absence of funds is not an excuse for failing to provide educational services to exceptional children. If sufficient funds are not available, then all programs should be cut back (*Mills* v. *Board of Education*, 1972).

▶ Children with disabilities who are committed to state institutions must be provided a meaningful education in that setting or their incarceration is considered unlawful detention (*Wyatt* v. *Stickney*, 1972).

▶ Children should not be labeled "handicapped" or placed into special education without adequate diagnosis that takes into account different cultural and linguistic backgrounds (<u>*Larry P.*</u> v. *Riles*, 1979).

[handwritten in left margin: resulted in PL 94-142]

▶ Bilingual exceptional children need identification, evaluation, and educational procedures that reflect and respect their dual-language background (*Jose P.* v. *Ambach*, 1979).

▶ An individual with learning disabilities has a right to services whatever his or her age (*Frederick L.* v. *Thomas*, 1980).

▶ A child with disabilities is entitled to an appropriate, not an optimum, education (*Board of Education* v. *Rowley*, 1982). The *Rowley* decision was the first court decision that suggested there was a limit to the resources that exceptional children could expect.

▶ A subsequent case to the *Rowley* decision made it clear that such services, though not optimal, must be more than *de minimus*, must provide sufficient support so the child with disabilities can benefit educationally (*Polk* v. *Central Susquehanna Intermediate Unit 16*, 1988).

Inclusion and Funding Issues

Recently, the attention of the courts has turned to the issues of *inclusion* and *least restrictive environment* and what an appropriate program for exceptional children should be. The results are a mixture of rulings, some supporting a strong version of inclusion and some supporting a continuum of services (McCarthy, 1994):

▶ A child with a hearing disability was allowed to attend a school several miles from home instead of a neighborhood school because the centralized program at the special school better met the child's needs (*Barnett* v. *Fairfax County Board of Education*, 1991).

▶ A child with a serious attention deficit and acting-out behavior should be placed in a special school rather than in the general education classroom (*Clyde & Shela K.* v. *Puyallup School District*, 1994).

▶ A child with Down syndrome was placed in a general education program rather than in a special education class because of the presumed priority of inclusion in IDEA (*Greer* v. *Rome City School District*, 1991).

▶ A court ruled that it is the responsibility of the school district to demonstrate that the child's disabilities are so severe that he or she will receive little benefit from inclusion or will be so disruptive as to keep other classmates from learning (*Oberti* v. *Board of Education of the Borough of Clementon School District*, 1993).

Clearly, these rulings reflect the specifics of each individual case and the interpretation of local or district courts. It may take a Supreme Court decision to provide more general guidance on the issue. Nevertheless, when the courts speak, people listen because court decisions represent the law as we currently know it and must be obeyed.

A recent trend has focused the courts on the financial formulas used by educators to provide services for exceptional children and for all students. Three states, Alabama, Wyoming, and Ohio, have had major parts of their school financing system declared unconstitutional (Verstegen, 1998). The basic reason for these decisions resided in the unequal funding by the school systems within the state and the inadequacy of funding for special education, which caused it to be a drain on local general education funds.

It seems clear that some alternative method of state funding may have to be devised that can go further toward guaranteeing a free, appropriate education for all students that is equitable from one system to another in a state, regardless of the differences in wealth from one district to another.

The late nineties saw a much increased set of court cases around the provision of services for children with autism, with parents battling the schools for additional services for their children (Lord, 2001). The results of these court cases depended on local circumstances with both sides (parent or school) prevailing depending upon the facts of the case.

There remains a continual flow of court cases dealing with children with special needs (see Karnes & Marquardt, 2000; Grzywacz, 2001), but the key decisions appear to have been made in the 1980s and 1990s. The courts have decided that every child is entitled to a free and appropriate education and that education should demonstrate meaningful progress in the development of the child.

Current cases appear to deal with refinements of the IDEA regulations, establishment of the minimum required under the *Rowley* decision, various IEP requirements, and so forth (Grzywacz, 2001).

Just as laws have to be enforced and money has to be appropriated, so court decisions have to be executed. The court decisions created the expectation that something would be done, but they did not guarantee it. Closing down state institutions, reorganizing public schools, and providing special services to all children with disabilities were substantial and costly changes. They raised a serious problem for program administrators: Where would the money come from for implementation? Ultimately, school and local leaders turned to Washington, pressuring Congress to appropriate funds to help pay for the changes that the courts were demanding. Even with federal assistance, implementation has come slowly.

Much of the change that has been formalized in legislation and court decisions protects the rights of youngsters with disabilities. But laws and court rulings are subject to interpretation. Special educators have a unique responsibility to see that laws and rulings are implemented as they were intended: to guarantee that all children receive an appropriate education.

■ Transition: School to Community

For many years special education ended when the child with special needs left secondary school, either through graduation or through dropping out. There were few attempts to follow the children into the community in order to see if the work of special education teachers had paid off, or to establish linkages with various rehabilitation programs that could continue the special services those children had received in school.

One of the important elements of IDEA has been insistence on improved postschool outcomes. One reason for such insistence has been the evidence gathered as to what happened to students with disabilities after their secondary training.

Blackorby and Wagner (1996) reported that children with disabilities fell far behind their nondisabled peers in graduation rates and employment rates. Moreover, they did not seem to be receiving as much postsecondary continuing education.

What factors are associated with good postsecondary outcomes? During the last two years of high school, the successful students with disabilities received vocational education classes and paid work experience. They had functional reading and math learning and good social adjustment (Wehmeyer & Schwartz, 1997; Halpern, Yovanoff, Doren, & Benz, 1997). Also written interagency agreements structure postsecondary experiences for such students with disabilities, and a position in rehabilitation was established that was devoted to giving direct services to students in transition (Hasazi, Furney, & DeStefano, 1999).

Can our success rate be improved? One example is the Youth Transition Program operated collaboratively by the Oregon Department of Education, the Oregon Vocational Rehabilitation Division, and the University of Oregon, along with cooperating school districts (Benz, Lindstrom, & Yovanoff, 2000). This program worked with exceptional students in need of assistance during their last two years of high school and in the early transition years. The program included the following:

1. Transition planning on postschool goals
2. Instruction in academics, personal social adjustment, vocational content, and independent living
3. Paid job training while in the program
4. Follow-up services for two years after completion of the program

The results of this program were that 90 percent of YTP participants received high school completion documents and 82 percent were placed successfully in a competitive job or postsecondary training. The YTP program demonstrates yet again how careful planning and assignment of resources to a goal can pay off.

Another important addition to IDEA was the concern recognized by Congress that too many special education students were exiting school and entering adulthood without necessary survival competencies. Clearly, more attention must be paid to the transition period between school and the world of work if these students are to make a good adult adjustment.

Consequently, Congress now requires that a "statement of transition service needs" be added to the IEP, beginning at age 14, and that at age 16, the student's IEP must contain "a statement of needed **transition services**" including, when appropriate, "a statement of interagency responsibilities or needed linkages" (Turnbull & Turnbull, 2000, p. 200).

In this way, legislation reflects current professional thinking and practice on transition, deeming it important enough to put into the regulations of IDEA. It is quite evident that more attention will be paid to this transition period in the immediate future. Because of such emphasis, a section on transition appears at the end of each chapter, providing insight into specific transition issues related to the category of disability being discussed.

■ Conclusion

The impact of social institutions on all exceptional children has been recognized for many years. The schools provide the special instruction that is needed; the government has guaranteed a free and appropriate public education and provides the rules, standards, and special financing to help implement the special services; and the courts act to settle disputes between parents and schools as to what is just and equitable treatment for exceptional children.

Other social and educational reform movements, such as the academic standards movement or those relating to inclusion or sensitivity to cultural diversity, also have a tendency to shape the place for the delivery of special services, the content for the special services, and the special skills needed by these children. It seems clear that if we wish to improve these elements, one of the strategies is to work more closely with these social institutions, or social movements, that have been so impressive in their impact and influence on the children and on their families.

Summary

▶ The social institutions of school, government, and the courts all have important roles to play in the education of children with special needs.

▶ Instruction can be adapted to the individual needs of exceptional students in several ways: We can vary the learning environment, change the presentation of the curriculum, modify the skills taught, and adapt teaching strategies.

▶ Many exceptional children come from different cultural backgrounds and have distinctive values,

attitudes, and languages. It is the responsibility of special educators to take these differences into account in their special educational plans.

▶ There is a clear trend for more children with disabilities to be placed in the general education classroom than there was ten years ago.

▶ Technology can serve two separate purposes for children with disabilities. Assistive technology enhances routine functioning and communication. Instructional technology aids in the delivery and support of instruction.

▶ The assessment of exceptional children involves prereferral, screening, diagnosis, classification, placement, instructional planning, and program evaluation.

▶ An individualized education program (IEP) defines the nature of a child's academic situation, the program's long-term goals and short-term objectives, needed services, and criteria for evaluation. The IEP has received positive comments (it improves relations between teacher and parent) and negative comments (it places time demands on the teacher without helping the child).

▶ *Inclusion* refers to educational situations where children with disabilities are educated with same-age peers and one major goal is social integration.

▶ In addition to well-prepared teachers, there is needed a support system of educational services to provide continued assistance for those teachers.

▶ Legislation and court decisions have created a full range of educational opportunities for children with developmental disabilities.

▶ Courts now require school systems to have strong documentation before moving a child with disabilities from the general education classroom.

Future Challenges

1. *What is the future role of the courts in protecting the rights of exceptional children?*

During the last part of the twentieth century, the courts played a significant role in affirming the rights of exceptional children to a free and appropriate education. But who is to determine what is "appropriate"? Now that the courts have ruled in the *Rowley* case that it is sufficient for the schools to give reasonable help, there is need of clarification as to how much is enough. It is unlikely that the courts have the professional knowledge to make such decisions.

2. *Who will win the dispute—advocates of full inclusion, or advocates of a continuum of services?*

A major dispute exists between those who support a continuum of services to educate children with disabilities and those who insist that all children with disabilities belong in the general education classroom.

The impact of the exceptional child on the other children in the general classroom can be seen as both positive and negative. The fact that evidence for the benefits of either course of action is not currently available no doubt contributes to the intensity of the debate.

3. *How will the academic standards movement affect students with disabilities?*

At odds with each other are the academic standards movement and the inclusion movement. The academic standards movement expects all students to achieve at high levels in content subjects, which may not be feasible. Many secondary exceptional students may prefer vocational training to academics as they prepare for the workplace.

Key Terms

academic aptitude   *p. 40*

assessment   *p. 37*

assistive technology   *p. 61*

authentic assessment   *p. 59*

circle of friends   *p. 56*

context of the child   *p. 34*

continuum of services   *p. 36*

diagnostic achievement tests   *p. 42*

ecology of the child   *p. 34*

inclusion   *p. 36*

individualized education program (IEP)   *p. 45*

instructional technology   *p. 61*

interindividual differences   *p. 40*

least restrictive environment   *p. 51*

performance assessment   *p. 59*

resource room   *p. 50*

standard (norm-referenced) achievement tests   *p. 42*

standards movement   *p. 60*

transition services   *p. 72*

Resources

References of Special Interest

Grobe, M., & Grobe, C. (2001). *Integrating technology for meaningful learning* (3rd ed.). Boston: Houghton Mifflin. *An excellent manual for teachers interested in integrating technology with their teaching and their* students. *In particular, it provides good background in hardware and software and working with the Internet, and it offers useful suggestions on how to use technology to develop higher-order thinking skills.*

Grzywacz, P. (Ed.). (2001). *Students with disabilities and special education* (18th ed.). Birmingham, AL: Oakstone Legal and Business Publishing. *A valuable resource book that presents major legislation dealing with special education, synthesizes legal cases, and provides a detailed accounting of the federal regulations implementing IDEA. Legal cases dealing with placement, school liability, related services, and discrimination are included.*

Mainzer, R.W., Deshler, D., Coleman, M.R., Kozleski, E., & Rodriguez-Walling, M. (2003). *To ensure the learning of every child with a disability.* Love Publishing 35(5). *A report summarizing the Council for Exceptional Children's study of the conditions of teaching children with exceptionalities. It looks at issues related to paperwork, professional development role definition, caseloads and administrative support for teachers working with students with exceptionalities. Clear recommendations are given for strengthening the infrastructure to improve the conditions under which children with exceptionalities are educated.*

McDonnell, L., McLaughlin, M., & Morrison, P. (Eds.). (1997). *Educating one and all: Students with disabilities and standards-based reform.* Washington, DC: National Academy Press. *A report from the National Academy of Sciences on the attempts to combine the educational standards movement with the special needs of the student with a disability. How does one balance the "high standards for all" with the need for individual requirements for students with disabilities? The diversity of students with disabilities, the content standards, and the accountability and assessment issues are discussed in depth.*

National Research Council (2002). *Minority Students in Special and Gifted Education.* Washington, DC: National Academy Press. *A comprehensive report examining issues that lead to the disproportionately high representation of culturally/linguistically diverse students in special education and to their disproportionately low representation in gifted education. Complex factors are presented that create additional risk for children living in poverty. These risk factors are discussed in terms of their* impact on students' achievement and behavior in school settings. Recommendations for policy and practice are offered.

Salvia, J., & Ysseldyke, J. (2004). *Assessment* (9th ed.). Boston: Houghton Mifflin. *A comprehensive book that covers all aspects of assessment including both formal and informal measures and provides a basic discussion of measurement and its various problems. A special chapter is provided on how to adapt tests to accommodate children with disabilities. Special chapters are devoted to the assessment of perceptual-motor skills, socioemotional behavior and adaptive behavior.*

Remedial and Special Education [special journal issue on history]. (1998). 19(4), 196–238. *A series of articles that goes into interesting detail about the early years of special education and the identification and education of children with special needs. Most of the history begins in the nineteenth century and progresses to an increasing involvement of the educational system. Particularly interesting is a piece on the legal history of special education.*

Journals

Teaching Exceptional Children
  www.cec.sped.org/bk/abtec.htm/

Remedial and Special Education
  www.proedinc.com/journals.htm/

Journal of Special Education
  www.proedinc.com

Educational Leadership
  www.ascd.org/

Journal of Special Education Technology
  jset.univ.edu

Professional Organizations

Council for Exceptional Children
  www.cec.sped.org

Please visit the book's website at **http://education.college.hmco.com/students** for new and updated information on websites listed here and for the mailing addresses of the journals and organizations.

PART TWO

HIGH-INCIDENCE
EXCEPTIONALITIES

The seven chapters in Part 2 are devoted to children who each contribute more than 1 percent of the population of children in our schools. Chapters 3 through 9 focus on mental retardation, learning disabilities, communication disorders, emotional and behavior disorders, autism spectrum disorders, gifted students, and early childhood programs. The high numbers of children with these exceptionalities make it likely that schools will actively seek out the differentiated program suggestions that are central to these chapters.

3

EARLY INTERVENTION
PRIORITIES AND
PROGRAMS

FOCUS QUESTIONS

▶ Why is there an emphasis on early intervention for infants with disabilities?

▶ What is the meaning of the term *at-risk*?

▶ How do we identify children who are in need of early intervention?

▶ Who are some of the professionals involved in early intervention programs?

▶ Does early intervention improve the functioning of infants with disabilities?

▶ What is the role of the family in early intervention?

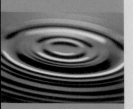

Nothing is more satisfying to parents than having a happy, cuddly, smiling, responsive baby. Not only do these babies make their parents happy, they also do well in life (Werner, 2004). However, not every baby is fortunate enough to have the disposition or the intact physiological system of the ideal baby parents hope for. Some babies will be developmentally delayed and not achieve the same goals that other babies of the same age do (such as sitting up, walking, and talking). Other babies may have such disabilities as deafness, blindness, or a range of physical or mental disorders that are genetically or environmentally induced. To respond to the range of developmental disorders and disabilities, the federal government has passed a series of laws that provide assistance to infants and toddlers as soon as their delays or disabilities are evaluated and diagnosed. Under the law known as the Individuals with Disabilities Education Act (IDEA), millions of children with disabilities receive special services provided for infants and toddlers and their families through an early intervention system (NICHCY, 2001). For school-age children and youth (ages 3 to 21), the school system is required to provide special education and related services (NICHCY, 2001).

To determine whether the child is eligible for services, he or she must receive a full individual evaluation. Early intervention services are provided for children from birth to age 2 for certain developmental delays—cognitive, physical (including hearing and vision), communication, social, emotional, or adaptive—or when a diagnosed condition is likely to result in a developmental delay (NICHCY, 2001). After the child has been evaluated, school districts may categorize those between 3 and 9 years of age as developmentally delayed. Those between 3 and 21 may also be identified by different disability categories, such as those described in Chapters 4 through 8 and 10 through 13. The major sources for information about early intervention are the child-family coordinators for each district, the principal or special education director of the school district, and the Parent Training and Information (PTI) center available in every state.

In this chapter, we examine the source and the effectiveness of early intervention, the nature and risk of disabilities, and methods of screening and evaluation, as well as strategies for effective intervention.

> Division for Early Childhood of the Council for Exceptional Children
> www.dec-sped.org

■ Overview of Early Intervention

Definitions and Goals

> Early intervention is designed to prevent deficits or to improve an existing disability.

Early childhood intervention consists of sustained and systematic efforts to assist young, developmentally vulnerable children with disabilities from birth to age 5 and their families (Shonkoff & Meisels, 2000). *Early intervention* is a term now used broadly to refer to a range of services provided to children, parents, and families during pregnancy, infancy, and/or early childhood (Dunst, 1996). Early intervention is designed to prevent deficits or to improve an existing disability by providing therapies (such as speech-language) or devices to help the child move (such as wheelchairs or braces for damaged limbs) and, most important in the new view of children with disabilities, by building strength through teaching and learning experiences. Early intervention cannot cure motor or sensory damage. However, it does work to prevent further loss and to improve functioning. For example, a child who is deaf may never hear sounds but can attain his or her cognitive and social potential through the use of sign language.

The time for early childhood intervention is usually divided into programs for infants to age 3 and programs for children 3 to 5 years of age and has become increasingly family directed (NICHCY, 1998; U.S. Department of Education, 1999). There is now an early intervention program in virtually every major community (Guralnick, 1998). Intervention programs may be federally, state, or privately funded. It is important to check with the local child find system to locate the range and types of services offered.

Origins of Early Intervention

Early intervention programs are a logical extension of early childhood programs, which have a long history in the United States, beginning in the late 1930s (Safford, Sargent, & Cook, 1994). Early childhood programs, known as nursery schools or preschools, were an outgrowth of psychologists' concerns for children's mental health (Cairns, 1983), which psychologists believed was fostered by positive child-rearing practices in the early years of life (Anastasiow & Nucci, 1994). Children with disabilities, however, were excluded from most of these programs. Many children with severe disabilities or mental retardation were sent to live in large state-run, hospital-like settings. These institutions provided custodial care and little training. Parents who could afford the alternative of a private residential school sent their children with disabilities there.

The prevailing opinion was that little could be done for a child with disabilities because intelligence and skills potential were fixed at birth. However, programs were developed for children who were deaf, hard of hearing, blind, or experiencing some loss of vision. Before 1900, children usually entered such programs at age 10; thereafter, they started as young as age 5. Not until the 1930s and 1940s were programs initiated for children with physical disabilities and cerebral palsy (Safford et al., 1994). But these programs were not widely available throughout the United States.

The belief that nothing could be done for children with disabilities was challenged by the children's parents, special educators, and members of allied therapeutic professions. This belief changed markedly as a result of Skeels and Skodak's work with orphanage children in the 1930s. These researchers found that children who were placed in foster homes or were adopted fared much better than a comparable group who remained in the orphanage (Skeels, 1966). The adopted group achieved normal intelligence, while many of the orphanage children were classified as mentally retarded. In addition, Kirk (1950) demonstrated that preschool experience could increase the rate of mental development and the social skills of children who were classified as mentally retarded (see also Bricker, 1993, for a more detailed history, and Farran, 2001).

Hunt's book *Intelligence and Experience* (1961) was extremely influential because it summarized research studies. It led directly to the development of **Head Start,** an educational program for children living in poverty. One of the assumptions was that children from families with higher economic status had higher IQ scores because of their more privileged environments. Once Head Start was established, families of children with disabilities pressed schools, communities, and Congress to establish programs for their children as well. They cited the principle that had led to the creation of Head Start: If children with disabilities were taught early in their lives, then their lives could be improved. As a result of pressure exerted by the families of children with disabilities, early intervention was born.

Legislative Support for Early Intervention

Early intervention led to the development of early childhood special education, or the special training of teachers to work with infants and toddlers (from birth to age 3) and children from 3 to 5 years of age. Before 1968, few training programs prepared special educators or other specialists such as psychologists to work with infants and young children. In addition, few training programs prepared educators to work with speech-language therapists, physical therapists, physicians, and the host of other specialists who could intervene to improve the life outcome of a child with disabilities.

Congress established the Bureau for the Education of the Handicapped in 1967 and in 1968 passed the Early Childhood Special Education Assistance Act (Gallagher, 2000). Early intervention programs were first started by a separate act or law, but they soon became one of the bureau's ongoing responsibilities and became known as the Handicapped Children Early Education Program (HCEEP), later referred to as the First Chance Network (De Weerd, 1981). This act set up programs in every state of the United States to serve as models of how to work with children with disabilities and improve their lives. The programs usually were categorically oriented: There would be one program for children with visual losses, one for children with hearing losses, one for those with cerebral palsy, and so on. The intent was to demonstrate to others in the state how to work with children with disabilities early in their lives to make them to the greatest extent possible like children of the same age who do not have disabilities. HCEEP later became a regular program in the bureau, and by 1980 a budget of more than $20 million had been allocated to support early intervention programs throughout the United States. The bureau's name was changed to the Office of Special Education and Rehabilitation Services in the 1980s.

In more recent years, as we saw in Chapter 2, Congress passed Public Law (PL) 94-142, which provides services to all handicapped children between ages 6 and 21 in regular or special schools. PL 99-457 expanded the mandate to include children younger than 5 years of age (including newborns). Both laws were extended to provide service to all persons with disabilities through the Individuals with Disabilities Education Act (IDEA) of 1990. PL 99-457 (Part H), enacted in 1986, was a major national step to ensure that infants and toddlers who were at risk for disabilities, were developmentally delayed, or possessed an identifiable disability received the total range of services that they and their families required (Gallagher, Harbin, Eckland, & Clifford, 1994).

However, amendments to IDEA in 1991 (PL 102-119) were designed to provide effective transitions between Part H and the preschool grant program.

> Early intervention led to the development of early childhood special education.

> Early intervention markedly improves the functioning of children with disabilities.

More than half of the states passed special legislation to provide collaborative transitions between programs. Still unresolved is the setting in which the children should be served: an inclusive setting with children without disabilities or a school designed for children with specific disabilities (Guralnick, 2000a)

In the current legislation, infants and toddlers with disabilities are located in **IDEA, Part C.** The new law encourages states to develop a system of services with multidisciplinary assessments and a plan that is family directed, and services are to be provided in a natural environment (NICHCY, 1998). In addition, the U.S. Department of Education (1999) funds 76 parent training programs and ten community resource centers to facilitate the training of children with disabilities and their parents (Zigler & Hall, 2002). The emphasis is on providing services to all members of the family and encouraging their participation in the child's development, whether in the home, at school, or in other settings (NEC-TAS, 2000; Cryer & Clifford, 2003). IDEA was reauthorized as PL 105-17 in 1997 and encourages inclusion not only in educational/development programs but also in neighborhood and community activities (Guralnick, 2001).

Current legislation encourages family involvement in the education plan and services that are promised in a natural environment.

■ Why Early Intervention?

From birth to the age of 3, the brain develops rapidly. Information from the environment is stored in pathways in the brain that are ready to receive it. During this period, the basic self develops in a transactional relationship with the caregivers in the environment and provides the foundation for autonomous emotional functioning (Schore, 1994). If information is not provided through experience, the pathways are unused. Enriched experiences build a better brain (Kolb, 1995). The purpose of therapies, training, and education of children with disabilities is to prevent further loss of function and to encourage their overall development. For example, children who are deaf who are provided with sign language by age 2 are more successful academically at a later age than those who do not receive intervention until age 6. Many children who have language disabilities and receive intervention by age 3 recover by age 5.6.

Because children are born able to learn and to respond positively to the effects of a supportive, stimulating environment, in this section we go into detail about why early intervention is important: to help children who are developmentally delayed achieve higher levels of intellectual and social function and to prevent secondary deficits in children with disabilities or sensory deficits (Reiss, 2003). Then we look at some of the research that supports the effectiveness of early intervention.

Avoiding Developmental Delays

Infants develop at varying rates. Some sit at 6 months of age, others at 4 months, and still others at 8 months (Lundy, 2003). Some walk early, and some walk late. These variations are the major reason for being cautious when deciding whether an infant is developmentally delayed. Delays must exist in more than one area to be considered a problem.

Delays in development are spotted by comparing an infant's development of physical, emotional, and intellectual skills with the development of other children of the same age.

Delays in development are identified by comparing an infant's development of physical, emotional, and intellectual skills with the development of other same-age children. The average ages of a task's accomplishment are put together in a **developmental scale.** If, for example, a child does not sit, stand, walk, or speak at the age when most children in his or her culture have acquired these skills, a disability or developmental delay is suspected.

It is well known that children with sensory deficits such as vision or hearing impairments, physical impairments, or genetic disorders linked to mental retardation do not achieve all their developmental skills as quickly as nondisabled children. In fact, without extra help in the form of therapies or educational stimulation, the child with disabilities may develop very slowly and, as an adult, reach a much lower level of functioning than the child with disabilities who has had the benefit of early childhood special education. Because some deficits are irreversible, not all children with disabilities can achieve what the average child achieves easily (Capute & Accardo, 1996; Guralnick, 1997). "When children receive appropriate stimulation, enrichment, an opportunity to learn, and reinforcement, the brain builds additional neurocircuits, which leads to a rich and functional brain" (*Today,* 2003).

Preventing Additional Deficits

Another major reason for early intervention is to avoid the development of secondary problems that can result from the lack of stimulation to the child because of a disability or sensory deficit. These secondary problems may include *self-stimulation* or *challenging behaviors* (such as hitting and biting).

> What seems most important in the long run is the quality of physical and emotional care provided by the family in early childhood.

Effective child-rearing practices can sometimes greatly improve a child's development and help overcome at-risk conditions present at birth. One of the best sources of knowledge is the Kauai Longitudinal Study, conducted from 1952 to 2000 (Werner & Smith, 1992; 2001). In that study, the developmental courses of individuals were followed from the time their expectant mothers made their pregnancies known (usually at 2 to 3 months) to when the children were 40 years of age (Werner & Smith, 2001). The Kauai study demonstrated that many children who are at risk for developmental delays from conditions such as lack of sufficient oxygen during birth (*anoxia,* usually occurring when the cord is around the baby's neck) or being born feet first (*breech birth,* highly associated with cerebral palsy) can achieve what the average child achieves, given a home that provides psychological warmth, low physical punishment, responsiveness, verbalness, and encouragement to develop. The phrase *encouragement to develop* can be defined as the knowledge the parent possesses about normal development and the parent's (or caregiver's) assistance to the child in achieving normal developmental milestones. Such child-rearing practices tend to help heal the negative effects of abnormal birthing processes (Kolvin, Miller, Scott, Gazonts, & Fleeting, 1990; Rutter, 2000; Werner, 2000). As Werner (2004) summarizes, large-scale longitudinal studies in the United States and across the world have demonstrated that early developmental competence, developed by consistent and supportive care, has a powerful effect on the child's adaptation and success throughout his or her life.

> Child-rearing practices can help offset the effects of disabilities.

Are Early Childhood Intervention Programs Effective?

Many authors have reviewed the effectiveness of early childhood intervention projects. We suggest *Handbook of Early Intervention* (Shonkoff & Meisels,

2000) and *The Effectiveness of Early Intervention* (Guralnick, 1997; Bailey, 1997) as good current sources of statistics and research results on early intervention. In general, mild retardation can be improved through early intervention programs so that these children can enter general education classrooms (McNulty, Soper, & Smith, 1984). Therapy for a broad spectrum of communication disorders can be very effective in eliminating those disorders or at least minimizing their impact on later speech and language (McLean & Cripe, 1997, p. 403). Deaf infants who are taught a manual communication system in the first years of life do much better as adults than those who are taught later in life (Goldin-Meadow, 1998; Marschark, Simple, Lillo-Martin, & Everhart, 1998); social and behavioral problems can be controlled (Upsur, 1990); and motor problems can be improved (Shonkoff & Hauser-Cram, 1988).

Many studies support early intervention's effectiveness. (Ramey & Ramey, 1998; Kavale & Forness, 2000; Espinosa, 2002); Guralnick and Bricker (1987) reviewed studies of children with Down syndrome and concluded that these children made more significant gains in intervention programs than they would have made had they not experienced early intervention. In an extensive review Farran (2001) notes that although the results of intervention for groups of children are positive they are modest (Gallagher, 1997, 2002). However, when one looks at the results of individual children, the results vary widely, suggesting the need for looking more closely at individual children in the total context of their environment (Gallagher, 1998). That is the intent of the requirements of individualized family services plans and IEPs. Important findings from Head Start early childhood programs show gains in cognitive, language, and socioemotional development (Emde, 2003; Administration on Children, Youth, & Families, 2001). Although these studies were done with children from low-income areas, the implications for children with disabilities seem appropriate (Langlois & Liben, 2003).

The importance of early intervention (besides lifesaving techniques) is to provide those protective factors of quality physical and emotional care that promote self-esteem and self-efficacy (Werner, 2000). These factors are the keys to a positive outcome for children in any intervention program, whether it be for the disabled or nondisabled (Rutter, 2000; Kolvin et al., 1990). Once these elements are in place, they appear to provide individuals with the lifelong skills they need to face and deal with various kinds of adversity (Vaillant & Milofsky, 1980; Werner & Smith, 1992, 2001; Werner, 2004; Lathor, Cicchetti, & Becker, 2000).

> Early intervention is important because it provides quality physical and emotional care that promotes self-esteem and self-efficacy.

> Intervention with children with disabilities needs to be individualized as much as possible and to focus on the ecology of the child—the broad range of issues affecting the child, the family, and the environment.

School Readiness

One purpose of early intervention is to help prepare young children for formal school when they enter kindergarten. The transition from preschool to kindergarten is important because a child's experiences during the early years of school typically set the pattern for later success or difficulty (Early, Pianta, & Cox, 1999; Love, Logue, Trudeau, & Thayer, 1992). This transition can be problematic as the expectations of kindergarten often differ widely from those of preschool. Kindergarten classes are much larger than preschool classes, there is more formal instruction and a greater emphasis on academic skills in kindergarten, and the physical demands for attending and sitting still increase significantly when young children enter school (Pianta & Cox, 2002). In addition to these concerns, children entering kindergarten also face larger school settings that have new environments like the lunch room, the library, and the playground. The challenges of moving into the school setting are often greater for children who are considered "at risk," and this group includes children with disabilities (Ramey & Ramey, 1998). Early intervention experiences are essential to assist the child and family in making a smooth transition into school. As with all preschoolers, we are also working to ensure that children with disabilities are ready to start school when they enter kindergarten.

■ What Puts Children at Risk?

An **at-risk infant** is one who, because of low birth weight, prematurity, or the presence of serious medical complications, has a heightened chance of displaying developmental delays or cognitive or motor deficits (Rossetti, 1986, p. 2). Researchers have identified three general categories of conditions that put children at risk: genetic disorders, events occurring during pregnancy and birth, and environmental risks (Garwood & Sheehan, 1989; Batshaw, 2002).

Genetic Disorders

More than one hundred genetic disorders are associated with lower developmental functioning and mental retardation (Kopp, 1983; March of Dimes, 2002). They include mental retardation, Tay-Sachs (an incurable disease leading to early death), and Turner syndrome (a condition that occurs only in women—a missing X chromosome, which leads to short height and possibly mental retardation). Although children with these disorders require immediate attention, they account for less than 1 percent of the school-age population with disabilities. Of sixteen infants born with a disability, in only one can the disability be traced to genetic causes (Batshaw, 2002). One reason why few children are born with genetic defects is that fetuses with genetic defects usually result in spontaneous abortions (Batshaw, 2002). Most disabilities are caused by events that occur during pregnancy and birth.

Events During Pregnancy and Birth

The second broad category of conditions that put infants at risk is events that occur in the womb during pregnancy or during the birth process. Prenatal care alerts mothers to the potential dangers of certain drugs as well as of infections and diseases (Schonberg & Tifft, 2002). For example, German measles and chicken pox can cause damage to the fetus but can be prevented by currently available vaccines (Graham & Morgan, 1997). The most common maternal illness that can lead to fetal malformation is diabetes. Control of diabetes can prevent the occurrence of many disabilities (Graham & Morgan, 1997; March of Dimes, 2000).

■ Environmental Risks

Environmental risks—factors in the life of the infant or child that interfere with development—are the major cause of disabilities of children by age 6. Some well-known environmental factors that interfere with development are child abuse, poverty, and parental substance abuse (March of Dimes, 2002, 2003). Parents who are unaware of the child-rearing strategies that facilitate development are particularly at risk in rearing low-birth-weight or premature babies, conditions that are known to be associated with disabilities. Other risks occur when family resources are too limited to provide adequate nutrition, medical care, and housing. These are briefly discussed in the following sections. (See Dunst & Trivette, 1997.)

Child Abuse or Neglect

Many of us may find it hard to understand the fact of child abuse, whether the child is with or without disabilities. How can an adult physically harm a baby or a young child, particularly one with disabilities? Yet most of us cannot imagine the stress that parents of children with disabilities endure. Imagine a child who screams constantly. For hours during the night, the parents try everything they can think of to calm him. They walk him, feed him, and bounce him, but nothing works. Throw into the equation a shaky marriage, pressures at work, and no prospect that tomorrow will be any better than today. If the child is perceived as the cause of all this, the formula for child abuse is in place. As many as three to ten million children are abused or neglected, of which 20 percent have diagnosable disorders (Sameroff & Feise, 2000). Research suggests that children with disabilities are abused more often than other children (Cosmos, 2001). Physical punishment is strongly associated with child abuse. Zigler, Finn-Stevenson, & Hall (2000) report that 60 percent of cases in which parents attempt to discipline their child physically lead to child abuse. Spanking can result in muscular, spinal, or skeletal damage.

> As many as 3 to 10 million children are abused or neglected, and 20 percent have disabilities.

Lower Socioeconomic Conditions (Poverty)

Women who live in poverty are likely to have insufficient medical care (including prenatal care), poor housing, and inadequate nutrition. A pregnant woman's poor nutrition rarely affects her fetus; a fetus acts like a parasite, drawing on the mother for what it needs (Batshaw & Perret, 1992). However, the poorly nourished mother may have an infant that is very small at birth (Rans-Bahrami, Short, & Batshaw, 2003).

In the absence of prenatal care, potential disorders that a physician could detect and treat are missed. For example, vitamin B_{12} or B (biotin) can cure one inborn defect in fetuses. If untreated, the child may be born with mental retardation and experience repeated episodes of vomiting (Batshaw & Perret, 1992, p. 165).

If the expectant mother is a teenager living in poverty, she is at great risk of having a premature or low-birth-weight infant, who itself is at great risk for a variety of disabilities. Teenage mothers who live in economically advantaged homes, have good prenatal care, and receive emotional support from their spouse or family are more likely to give birth to normal infants (Anastasiow, 1982; March of Dimes, 2003).

> Prenatal care allows a physician to detect and treat potential disorders.

Substance Abuse

Substance abuse by the mother or father can be linked to behavior problems and disabilities in children. A woman's use of alcohol during pregnancy may result in her infant's having **fetal alcohol syndrome** or alcohol-related disorders (Streissgath, 1997; March of Dimes, 2003). Fetal alcohol syndrome children have facial abnormalities, droopy eyelids, heart defects, small size, and usually some degree of mental retardation (Wunsch, Conlon, & Scheidt, 2002). Physical anomalies and growth deficiencies such as these persist in later childhood and adulthood. Alcohol-related disorders are more difficult to detect as causes, but the disability may appear as significant learning disorders (Streissgath, 1997).

Alcohol-related disorders can appear as significant learning disorders.

Expectant mothers who use heroin may give birth to premature or low-birth-weight infants. The infant may go through severe withdrawal symptoms and will be at risk for disabilities. Heroin and cocaine appear not to cause disabilities in utero but may cause premature births. The problems associated with the conditions at birth of low birth weight and prematurity may lead to physical or behavioral irregularities as the child matures (Hansen & Ulrey, 1993). In addition, children whose mothers use drugs tend to be more emotionally and developmentally delayed than the children of nonusers (Krauss, Thurman, Brodsky, Betancourt, Giannetta, & Hart, 2000). In their study of forty-nine children who were exposed to drugs prenatally, Cohen and Erwin (1994) found that half did not display any of the negative behaviors that one-quarter of the group did: anger, aggressiveness, and unoccupied behavior. It appears that there is wide behavioral variability among children prenatally exposed to drugs. Physicians and other health-care workers caution expectant mothers to avoid the use of drugs.

If the expectant mother smokes two packs or more of cigarettes a day, she risks giving birth to a premature or low-birth-weight infant. Major national campaigns have been mounted to discourage pregnant women from smoking and using substances that may harm their fetuses (March of Dimes, 2003).

■ Prevention Before Birth

The aim of prevention is to have a child without disabilities. Prevention involves two major activities: (1) genetic counseling, which includes an interview with the prospective parents to determine if the family has a history of disorder and, if so, what is the risk of their child having disabilities, and (2) prenatal care, which involves carefully monitoring the mother's health and fetal development to ensure that the infant is born healthy.

Prevention before birth involves genetic counseling and prenatal care.

Genetic Counseling

The first opportunity to detect potential disorders is **genetic counseling**. A counselor interviews the prospective parents about their families' histories of disabilities and analyzes samples of the clients' blood to determine if their gene pool contains defective genes that might be passed on to their children. Parents may choose to receive this counseling before the child is conceived. Some genetic disorders are most prevalent among certain racial groups, such as Tay-Sachs disease among Eastern European (Ashkenazic) Jews, Couley's anemia among Mediterranean Greeks and Italians, and sickle cell anemia among African Americans (Anastasiow, 1986). Individuals from populations at particular risk for these and other disorders may seek genetic counseling to determine the likelihood of their having a child with disabilities.

A genetic counselor can calculate the probability or odds of a couple's having a child with a disabling condition or genetic disorder (March of Dimes, 2003), but the counselor cannot confirm whether the child will be born with or without disabilities. If the parents have a high probability of having a child with disabilities, the expectant mother may choose to have a test that may detect if the child she is carrying has a disability.

Prenatal Care

In providing **prenatal care,** the physician checks the mother's health, monitors the progress of her pregnancy, and warns her about dangerous practices such as the use of alcohol, tobacco, and other drugs that can harm the fetus. Prenatal care can significantly reduce the number of premature or low-birth-weight babies. Even benign neglect—if, for example, the mother does not take iron or vitamin supplements or have other medical assistance during pregnancy—can have an adverse effect on the health of an infant. Prospective mothers are advised to take folic acid daily before they become pregnant to reduce the probability of neural tube deficits (March of Dimes, 2003). The physician can detect some deficiencies in the expectant mother's diet and prescribe the vitamins and minerals she and her baby need.

Teaching prospective parents good child-rearing practices can prevent disabilities from developing, even when the infant is at risk. For example, parents can learn that paint containing lead should not be used where a young child can get at it. Ingesting chips of lead paint can cause lead poisoning and mental retardation.

In the United States armed forces, prenatal care is provided uniformly to all pregnant women in the service and to wives of servicemen. It has been found that these women have the lowest instances of prematurity, low-birth-weight infants, and infant mortality in the United States. Interestingly, there are no racial differences in the infant death rates in this population. This finding is atypical of all other populations in the United States, where large racial differences exist (Pear, 1992).

An integral part of prenatal care is the tests that are available to screen the fetus for various disabilities. Some of the major prenatal tests are discussed next.

> Prenatal care can prevent some disabilities.

Triple Screen Test

Three kinds of blood screenings can be done during early pregnancy: the alpha-fetoprotein test and a test for two maternal hormones. Any of these can indicate increased risk and the need for further screening (March of Dimes, 2001). The **alpha-fetoprotein test** is a blood test that is offered to all pregnant women. Fetuses pass substances into the mother's blood, which can be examined to detect some disabilities. The blood sample is taken at sixteen weeks' gestation and can identify women who are at risk of having a fetus with a neural tube defect (a defect involving the spinal column or brain), Down syndrome, or some other birth defect (Batshaw & Rose, 1997; Blackman, 1983).

Because levels of fetal spinal fluid in the mother may vary, the results may or may not be accurate predictors of a disability, thus two other steps—sonography and amniocentesis—are taken to determine whether the disorder actually exists. Abnormal amounts of two hormones—that is, low levels of estrial and high levels of human chorionic gonadotropin—suggest an increased risk of Down syndrome (March of Dimes, 2001). Abnormal levels of other hormones are being investigated.

Sonography (Ultrasound)

Sonography, or ultrasound, is the use of sound waves to take a picture (like an x-ray) of the fetus. This picture allows specialists to determine the position of the fetus and possibly detect defects such as microcephaly (small head). It also detects the sex of the child and indicates whether there is more than one fetus (March of Dimes, 2003).

Amniocentesis

Amniocentesis is a relatively safe test in which a needle is inserted into the placenta (with the help of ultrasound to ensure that the needle does not damage the fetus) at 14 to 17 weeks' gestation (Batshaw & Rose, 1997; March of Dimes, 2003). The fluid can be analyzed to determine a number of (but not all) disabilities, such as Tay Sachs, Down syndrome, and spina bifida. If an incurable disability is detected, the prospective parents must choose between having the child and having an abortion, which is a personal family decision.

Ultrasound can help pediatricians determine the position of the baby as well as some birth defects.
(© Michael Pole/CORBIS)

Chorionic Villus Biopsy

A test usually not available or not recommended by many physicians is **chorionic villus biopsy.** In this procedure, some tissue is removed from the uterus of the pregnant woman during the first trimester (March of Dimes, 2000). When the tissue is examined under a microscope, some disabilities, such as Down syndrome, can be detected. The major drawback of this procedure is that it increases the risk of miscarriage, and it can also lead to internal bleeding and infection in the expectant mother (Batshaw & Rose, 1997). Batshaw and Perret (1992), however, suggest that if these risks could be reduced, chorionic villus biopsy would be very useful. It can be performed early in pregnancy, it is less expensive than amniocentesis, and it is less emotionally traumatic for the expectant mother, who may be afraid of having a needle inserted into the placenta.

A major issue is that not all disabilities are recognized at birth. For example, some children are not identified as having hearing impairments until they are two years of age. Autism may not be suspected until an infant exhibits communication delays.

Ann and Brian had a healthy three-year-old daughter and were expecting their second child. To their dismay, the prenatal tests revealed that they would have a boy with Down syndrome, a genetic disorder with possible physical problems and mental retardation. Their ethical orientation was one in which abortion was not an option. However, they were able to contact a local Parent to Parent program that put them in touch with other parents whose child had Down syndrome. From them Ann and Brian learned what typical physical and intellectual progress the child could be helped to make, and what kinds of early intervention could facilitate the child's development.

After their little boy was born, Ann and Brian were able to enroll him in an early intervention program. They also sought out in their community a variety of services to facilitate their child's progress, services that included, among others, physical therapy and the help of a speech-language pathologist. A range of such services can be found in most communities today.

However, Bailey (2002) indicates that only 2 percent of the eligible 11 to 12 percent of school-age children receive early intervention in the first three years of life, and fewer than 5 percent during the preschool years (p. 4).

■ Detecting Disabilities After Birth

If the infant is born with a defect that can be cured, treatment must begin early in life. For example, phenylketonuria (PKU) causes toxic accumulations of phenylalanine in the brain, which, if untreated, leads to multiple disabilities and mental retardation. Although infants have no obvious symptoms, PKU can be detected by a simple blood test, preferably when the infant is a week old. The treatment is to restrict the infant's diet to reduce the intake of phenylalanine. (Batshaw & Perret, 1992).

Screening at Birth

Can a physician or other professional tell whether an infant is disabled or at risk for a disabling condition within the first few minutes of the child's birth?

When a child is born, the physician administers the Apgar test to determine if the infant has any identifiable problems or abnormalities.

When a child is born, the physician administers the first screening test to determine whether the infant has any identifiable problems or abnormalities (Meisels, 1987). Screening tests are simple tests that are easy to administer and that separate infants without serious developmental problems from those who have a disability or are suspected of being at risk for a disabling condition (Anastasiow, Frankenburg, & Fandall, 1982). The first infant screening is done in the hospital at one minute and five minutes after birth. It is known as the **Apgar test,** after Virginia Apgar, who developed it in 1952.

In administering the Apgar test, the physician examines the infant's heart rate, respiratory effort, muscle tone, and general physical state, including skin color. A blue cast to the skin, for example, may indicate breathing or heart problems. Jaundice at birth is indicated by a yellow cast to the skin and eyes. A serious disorder, jaundice reflects the failure of the liver to process adequately because of its immaturity; as a result, bilirubin can accumulate. Many infants with jaundice recover in about a week. In more serious cases, the infant is placed under fluorescent lights for a day or two. This light treatment helps the infant process the bilirubin until the liver can function normally (Batshaw & Perret, 1992).

An infant with a below-average Apgar score at one minute or five minutes after birth is monitored by the physician to determine if a disability or medical problem exists and if medical intervention is needed. Lower-than-average Apgar scores are not necessarily predictive of disabilities, but they do serve to alert the physician that the infant may have special needs. Due to the fact that hearing impairments need to be detected as soon as possible for the child to make desired developmental progress, universal hearing assessment is recommended at birth. Twenty-six states offer it currently, and most states offer it for an additional fee.

Many states recommend a hearing assessment at birth.

Medical Intervention

Additional medical screening includes blood and urine tests to determine if the infant has known curable disorders that should be treated immediately to prevent the occurrence of a disability. Hypothyroidism, or the failure of the thyroid gland to function, can lead to *cretinism,* an irreversible condition of severe mental retardation. If thyroid supplement is given at birth and continued throughout life, however, the condition can be prevented and the child will develop regularly. The success in preventing mental retardation associated with a thyroid gland deficiency has done much to encourage research in the prevention of occurrences of developmental conditions identifiable at birth.

PKU (phenylketonuria) is an overproduction of an enzyme that can lead to mental retardation but that can be controlled by dietary restrictions. A screening test can be administered by taking a simple needle-prick blood sample in the early weeks after birth (March of Dimes, 2002). Other screening can be done for galactoseria, the inability to convert sugar in milk, which can lead to blindness, mental retardation, or death. Sickle cell anemia, which can be controlled through doses of penicillin at two months to five years of age, can be screened for at birth. Medical science is developing several other tests for inborn error in body chemistry as well (March of Dimes, 2002).

Early screening tests can determine whether an infant has any identifiable problems. If the infant is born with a defect that can be cured, treatment must begin early in life.
(© Bob Daemmrich/
The Image Works)

Developmental Screening

After the first screening tests, which are usually medical in orientation, other tests assess a broad range of infant capacities, including development in cognitive, social, emotional, physical, communicative, language, and self-help skills. Usually the tests are administered only if a problem is suspected.

Developmental screening is a brief assessment of a sampling of a child's developmental progress to determine whether the child is at risk for a delay, possesses an identifiable disability, is delayed in development, or is proceeding at the expected pace for his or her age (Meisels & Provence, 1989). The critical dimension of any screening test is its accuracy in not identifying children as being at risk who are normal (false positives) or labeling children as normal who are at risk (false negatives).

There has been a proliferation of infant screening devices in recent years, but many of them fail to achieve acceptable levels of confidence. Many practitioners rely on the Bayley scales of Infant Development–11 (Bayley, 1993) or on the Connecticut Infant and Toddler Assessment procedure (IDA) (Erikson, 2002), which provide more complete diagnostic assessments. Others administer some form of family assessment and gain critical information from the caregiver (Henderson & Meisels, 1994). There are a number of screening instruments for children 3 to 5 years of age. The Early Screening Inventory (Meisels, Marsden, Wiske, & Henderson, 1997) is among the most accurate.

■ Early Intervention Programs

The goal of early intervention programs is to help children with disabilities develop to their maximum potential. An outstanding example of intervention is research with Down syndrome, a disorder associated with mental retardation (Guralnick & Bricker, 1987). Untreated children with this disorder who were placed in institutions rarely learned more than fifteen or twenty words, whereas those who were reared in supportive homes and received early childhood special education developed language to the level of persons without disabilities and a high degree of competence in all other developmental areas. Although this genetic condition does not go away, the child with Down syndrome who is reared in an enriched environment in the home or a center will have an IQ score as many as 30 points higher than the score of a child who is untreated or raised in an institution (Guralnick & Bricker, 1987). Children who have mental retardation or reside in extremely restricted environments generally show a decline in IQ scores over time. Early intervention programs have been shown to prevent the decline (Guralnick, 2001).

In this section, we look at some intervention programs: where they take place and their strategies, how curricula are developed, and model programs. Some conditions can be prevented and others remediated, but many can be neither prevented nor remediated entirely. With most disabilities, however, improved conditions can be achieved through carefully planned and implemented intervention programs. The basis for planning intervention is the individualized family services plan.

> Children with Down syndrome reared in supportive homes and who receive early childhood special education have IQ scores much higher than untreated or institutionalized children with Down syndrome.

> Early intervention programs can prevent a decline in IQ scores among children with mental retardation who are in restrictive environments.

The Individualized Family Services Plan (IFSP)

Part H of PL 99-457 and Part C of IDEA require that an **individualized family services plan (IFSP)** be developed for each child from birth to 3 years of age who is diagnosed as disabled, developmentally delayed, or at risk for delay. When the child enters the public school early childhood special education services at 3 years of age, an IEP takes the place of the IFSP.

IDEA, Part C: Legal Requirements of the IFSP

IDEA, Part C requires that IFSPs be constructed to include the following:

► A statement of the infant's or toddler's present levels of physical development, cognitive development, communication development, social or emotional development, and adaptive development, based on objective criteria

► A statement of the family's resources, priorities, and concerns relating to enhancing the development of the family's infant or toddler with a disability

► A statement of the major outcomes expected to be achieved for the infant or toddler and the family and the criteria, procedures, and timelines used to determine the degree to which progress toward achieving the outcomes is being made and whether modifications or revisions of the outcomes or services are necessary

► A statement of specific early intervention services necessary to meet the unique needs of the infant or toddler and the family, including the frequency, intensity, and method of delivering services

The individualized family services plan acknowledges that a child with disabilities is a child in a family and that family members may need educational, financial, or emotional support to help the child achieve his or her potential.
(© Jerry Speier/Design Conceptions)

Because transition can be stressful, special transition efforts may be useful. An IFSP can address issues and goals related to the transition to an IEP for children 3 and older.

▶ A statement of the natural environments in which early intervention services shall appropriately be provided, including a justification of the extent, if any, to which the services will not be provided in a natural environment

▶ The projected dates for initiation of services and the anticipated duration of the services

▶ The identification of the service coordinator from the profession most immediately relevant to the infant's or toddler's or family's needs (or who is otherwise qualified to carry out all applicable responsibilities under Part C) who will be responsible for the implementation of the plan and coordination with other agencies and persons

▶ The steps to be taken to support the transition of the toddler with a disability to preschool or other appropriate services (Council for Exceptional Children, 1998)

The focus on the *family* is an important outgrowth of the findings of early childhood intervention programs: A child with disabilities is a child in a family, and family members may need educational, financial, or emotional support to be able to provide the best setting, support, security, and stimulation to

The family may need help in locating, obtaining, and implementing the services specified in the IFSP.

help the child with disabilities or developmental delays achieve his or her potential (Dunst & Trivette, 1997).

Consistent with an ecological position, the U.S. Department of Education encourages the training of parents in literacy skills and positive parent-child interaction skills, and also encourages parents to become involved in their children's development (NEC-TAS, 2000). One such program is Evenstart, which is funded under Title I, Part B, PL 103-382. As stated before, IDEA, Part C, is especially strong in its emphasis on family-centered delivery, providing services for all family members (U.S. Department of Education, 1999).

Parents can benefit from literacy skills training and learning positive parent-child interaction skills.

Inclusion in Context

The reauthorization of PL 105-17 is intended to promote inclusion in the broadest sense. Inclusion takes many forms and varies as to whether the child spends the total day or a portion of the day with typically developing students (Guralnick, 2001). Inclusion is primarily designed to promote social relationships among children with disabilities and those without disabilities (Guralnick, 1999). A major problem with many infants (0–3) with disabilities is that their needs are so intense and specialized that they cannot be in a group program but must receive individualized treatment in a one-on-one setting. In addition, some 0–3 child-care settings do not accept children with disabilities because of being unable to provide appropriate treatment.

To date in many states, fewer than half of the early childhood classes include children with disabilities. In addition, in those classes that enroll students with disabilities, few have teachers who have early childhood special education training or a collaborative special education teacher (Smith & Rapport, 1999). Thus, full inclusion for many children with disabilities may not provide the continuum of services (i.e., the multidisciplinary team) required in the law (Crockett, 2002). Further, children who have very special needs, such as those with deafness or autism or who are developmentally delayed, require one-to-one early intervention to enhance development. For example, the child with deafness will need early language intervention, whether it be sign, aural, or oral. These children may participate in play situations, but their communication may be nonverbal. Thus, inclusion may raise the level of social interaction for the child with disabilities, but not raise the level of his or her social competence (Guralnick, 2001).

Full inclusion for many children with disabilities may not provide the continuum of services (i.e., the multidisciplinary team) required in the law.

Early childhood teachers need to develop techniques to encourage peer-related social competence. Cavallaro and Haney (1999) and O'Brien (1997) have developed resources to assist child-care providers in serving infants and toddlers with special needs in inclusive settings. Another helpful technique is to include stories about children with disabilities, to make typically developing children aware of the strengths and needs of their peers with disabilities (Favazza, LaRoe, Phillipsen, & Kumar, 2000). While many studies demonstrate gains for children with disabilities in fully inclusive settings, Mills, Cole, Jenkins, and Dale (1998) demonstrate that it is the high-functioning children who can make these gains. Lower-functioning children appear to be more successful in special education classrooms and part-time inclusion.

It should be borne in mind that special education is designed to provide specific, individualized, intense remedial instruction (Zigmond & Baker,

1995). Instruction is the key ingredient, not placement (Crockett & Kauffman, 1998).

Yet children with disabilities do need a program that focuses on their total developmental needs. Most children with a disability are in other ways like children without disabilities and have similar needs (Buysse, Skinner, & Grant, 2001; Guralnick, 2001). Research from child-care studies suggests that the curriculum in high-quality programs is associated with cognitive and language gains as well as socialemotional development (Love et al., 2003). There are lower levels of aggression and fewer problem behaviors among children in high-quality programs. The curricula of these programs focus on children's self-determination, choice-making, and initiative-taking (Erwin & Brown, 2003), thereby encouraging the child to interact with the environment (people and objects) in appropriate ways. Maccoby and Lewis (2003) suggest that child care should have the following important features:

▶ Practice that builds attachment to the school and peers

▶ Initiative and planning activities on the part of the child

▶ Emphasis on intrinsic rather than extrinsic motivation

▶ A coherent focus on social development

The overall feature of an effective program is that the child receives pleasure from his or her own initiated activities, rather than from extrinsic motivation of rewards provided by the teacher (Maccoby & Lewis, 2003). The implication for special education is that while focusing on functional behavior and using drill and practice techniques may be necessary for some remedial academic skills, it is not the most efficacious method for the development of cognitive, social, and higher-level problem-solving skills.

Genes and environments cooperate in the development of the individual, and they do so best under conditions in which the child is the active initiator in supportive circumstances (Shonkoff & Phillips, 2000; Maccoby & Lewis, 2003). Child-directed play with social toys in groups of children with and without disabilities has been associated with more positive social activities (Kim et al., 2003). (See section on play and toys, below.)

Collaboration and the Multidisciplinary Team

The law also recognizes that families need more than friendly neighbors or relatives to help them. They may need a variety of services from specialists as well as a service coordinator to help them locate, obtain, and implement the services specified in the IFSP. Children who qualify for services under IDEA must have been identified, screened, and diagnosed by a **multidisciplinary team** as having a disability known to be associated with developmental delays or be at risk for the occurrence of developmental delays. The term *multidisciplinary* means that more than one professional needs to work with the child. The child may need physical therapy to improve functioning, speech-language therapy to assist control of the muscles involved in speech, and an educational program. Thus, a multidisciplinary team working in an early intervention program might include a member of each of those professions. Disciplines that are designated by law to be able to work with infants and children with disabilities are listed in Table 3.1.

The multidisciplinary team is a team of professionals who provide services to help a child with a disability.

TABLE 3.1
Multidisciplinary Team Members

SPECIALIST	FUNCTION
Audiologist	Determines if hearing losses are present
Ophthalmologist	Determines if vision losses are present
Early childhood special educator	Plans and administers program for remediation of deficits and coordinates special therapies
Physician	Determines if a biological or health deficit exists and plans treatment
Nurse	Provides a plan for adequate health care
Occupational therapist	Promotes individual development of self, self-help skills, play, and autonomy
Physical therapist	Enhances motor development and suggests prostheses and positioning strategies; provides needed therapies
Psychologist	Provides a comprehensive document of the child's strengths and weaknesses and helps the family deal with the stress of having a child with disabilities
Social worker	Assists the family in implementing appropriate child-rearing strategies and helps families locate services as needed
Speech and language pathologist	Provides necessary assessment plan for needed therapies and delivers services in appropriate cases

An ideal team includes a physician or health-care worker who examines the child and reviews his or her medical record for any signs of disorder. A special educator or developmental psychologist assesses the child's physical, emotional, cognitive, language, and social development. A special educator, social worker, or psychologist interviews the family members to determine their health history, child-rearing practices, and concerns for the child. The ideal team also includes other specialists as necessary. For example, a physical therapist assesses muscle tone and development, a language pathologist determines whether speech patterns are abnormal or delayed, an audiologist evaluates the hearing function, and in some cases a geneticist determines if the child has a genetic abnormality not detected previously.

When all the information on the child and the child's family has been gathered, the multidisciplinary team, including family members, discusses the case. The specialists might prescribe therapy or recommend an early intervention program. (Guralnick, 2000b). Their conclusion might be that the child should be reevaluated at a later age; if no disabilities or risk factors have been identified, perhaps the child should be discharged or monitored periodically. In cases in which the environment is the at-risk factor, the team may recommend parental counseling or identify sources of income assistance for the family.

The Americans with Disabilities Act (ADA) calls for public services (child-care programs) to make reasonable accommodations to prevent discrimination against children with disabilities. Child-care facilities may be required to

Child-care programs need to be sensitive to all cultures and languages.

do something different from their usual program or something additional to ensure full participation of all children in the program. These programs also need to be sensitive to the cultures and languages of families belonging to a nondominant group (Odom & McLean, 1996).

The IDA (Erikson, 1998; Hutchinson, 1997), which uses a multidisciplinary team to assess the child's health, development, and family situation, meets the requirements of IDEA. A typical case might be handled as follows.

Case Study: A Typical Family Situation

A pediatrician, a relative, or parents may raise concerns about a child's development. The family calls the state department of health, the state department of special education, or some other agency for help. The family is referred to a center where screening (a quick assessment of the child's current developmental status to determine whether the child needs further tests) is performed. (The child should not be labeled at any time, particularly after the screening.) Because the results suggest a potential problem, the IDA is administered by at least two persons from different professions. They conduct an interview with the family to collect a health history and a history of disabilities within the family. They request permission to examine the child's health records. They assess the child's motor, social, speech and language, and cognitive (intelligence) skills to determine whether the child can perform age-appropriate developmental tasks (such as stacking small colored blocks).

After collecting all the information from the family interview, the health history, and the developmental assessment, the team meets with the family to develop an IFSP and decide which of the following best describes the situation:

▶ The child is all right and needs no special assistance.

▶ The child appears to be somewhat delayed but not to such a degree that assistance is needed now; however, he or she should be brought back for another evaluation in three to six months.

▶ The child has a particular problem and should be in an intervention program.

▶ The family needs economic assistance, job training, or training in how to deal with the child and his or her disabilities.

The family may agree or disagree with the decision. If agreement is reached, a service coordinator is assigned to assist the family in finding the services they and their child need, such as an early intervention program for speech delays. This is the ideal situation and fulfillment of the hopes embodied in IDEA. If the family disagrees, they may remove their child from services. Most states do not have mandatory education for children from birth to age 3, whether they are with or without disabilities. So the parents can decide not to place their infant or preschooler in early intervention.

Settings and Strategies

An early intervention program can take place in a hospital, at home, or in an early childhood intervention center. The intervention strategies in each of these settings vary. Positive gains are made by children when the therapies, teaching, and/or curricula are designed to meet the diagnosed needs of the child. The crucial element is not the setting, but rather what happens in the setting, whether hospital, home, home/day care, or early childhood intervention classroom (Zigmond & Baker, 1995; Kavale & Forness, 2000). For example, infant massage has been shown to facilitate growth, reduce pain, increase alertness, and shorten the time of hospitalization for preemies as well as for infants born to drug-addicted mothers and mothers with AIDS (Field, 1998; Field, Hermundez-Reif, & Freeman, 2004).

In a Hospital

Assistance for a child with disabilities may begin in a hospital on the first day of his or her life. Assistance may also begin in the early weeks through medical intervention such as surgery (for example, to close the open spine in cases of spina bifida), the administration of drugs, or the use of diagnostic tests to determine if a disability exists.

Hospitals provide medical intervention to premature and low-birth-weight, medically fragile, and sick infants until they can be sent home. The treatment in the hospital is usually lifesaving in that the child was born before he or she was biologically ready to be in an environment other than the womb. Most babies at the time of discharge should be able to survive without continuous medical treatment in a hospital, although sometimes it is necessary to prepare the home in some way, such as for an oxygen-dependent child (one who needs a tube to obtain extra oxygen from a tank). It should be noted that infants having very low birth weight may survive, but many of them will have developmental problems throughout early childhood into middle-school age.

Als (1997) and her colleagues have developed a comprehensive intervention program in the hospital neonatal intensive-care unit for preterm infants. The program requires extensive training of the staff to implement the program and to attend to the infants' many needs. The philosophy of the program is to

Assessment of a child's strengths helps provide goals for a home or center program. (© Robin Sachs/Photo Edit)

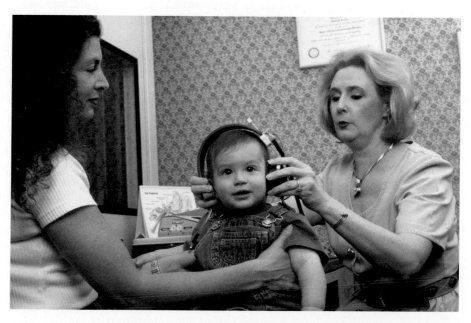

view the infant as a collaborator in the staff's efforts to help him or her survive and develop. The staff does that by engaging the infant in an ongoing relationship and determining through careful evaluation what supports the infant's needs. Observations include behavioral interpretations and consistency of caregiving through establishing a multidisciplinary team, including a therapist for each infant. The team works collaboratively to enhance the child's development. The results of one study showed a marked decrease in the number of days invasive techniques, such as tube feeding, were needed, as well as a decrease in the length of hospital stay and hospital costs.

A major movement is under way to establish intervention programs to follow the infant from the neonatal intensive-care nursery to the home. These programs aim to provide education to the parents, give them support, and help them find the services their infant requires (Affleck, Tennen, & Rowe, 1991; Beckwith, 1988; Infant Health and Development Project, 1990).

In a neonatal intensive-care unit, a multidisciplinary team should work collaboratively to enhance the child's development.

Natural Environments: Home and Family

IDEA (1997) encourages educating young children in natural environments— that is, settings that are normal for children of that age who do not have disabilities (Jung, 2003) (see Figure 3.1). The intent is to facilitate learning through naturally occurring experiences in daily activities (mealtimes, out-of-home shopping, and so on). The early childhood educator would provide parents with strategies to maximize their child's learning in their daily activities and routines and would identify learning opportunities in the home and community (Jung, 2003; Dunst, Herter, Shields, & Bennis, 2001). Promoting a child's competence through family routines and community activities also facilitates his or her movement into early intervention programs, particularly those in inclusive settings (Bruder & Dunst, 2000). If the child is in day care, child care, or an intervention program, the teacher would also facilitate learning through the imbedded material in the routine activities of the classroom (such as snack time, bathroom, entering and leaving) (Kaiser & Hancock, 2003).

Therapists, teachers, and other interventionists often provide services in the home for a number of reasons. A common belief among many educators is that education should take place in the setting in which the skills will be used; hence the home is the functional setting for very young children. Infants spend most of their time sleeping, and it is not practical to take them to an early intervention program that offers educational and therapeutic practice. In addition, mothers who are going through the process of accepting their child's disability may not be ready to take the child into public places. In some rural areas, early childhood special education centers are a long way from the home, and mothers would spend much valuable time traveling instead of interacting with and caring for the child. Furthermore, the mother's or caregiver's primary responsibility is to establish in-the-home routines that will facilitate the child's development. Attachments grow out of joint interactions with the child and are of fundamental importance to the infant's well-being.

Home programs emphasize helping the caregiver learn how to deal with the child in the child's setting.

A family's culture and community life and environment are major sources of children's learning opportunities (Dunst, 2001). Home programs tend to offer comprehensive services (therapies and education) and are very effective in assisting families with children at risk, the developmentally delayed, and those with disabilities (Shonkoff & Hauser-Cram, 1988; Clauss-Ehlers, 2003).

FIGURE 3.1
Natural Learning Environments

Locations
Car,
church,
mall, ranch,
grocery store,
beach, library,
relative's home,
recreational center,
department store,
playground, restaurant,
post office

Natural Learning Environments
Car rides, music concerts, parade,
swings, slide, sand (play), beach blanket,
beach toys, ocean, carnival, family gatherings,
swimming pool, stores, mail "pick up,"
friend's living room, neighborhood walks, sibling's
basketball game, riding in shopping cart, horse corral,
holiday displays, holiday dinner, chase games, wagon rides

Learning Opportunities
Listening to music, greeting people, splashing water, petting animals,
playing with rhythm sticks, touching rocks and grass, picking up sand,
eating with a spoon, drinking from a cup, being chased, rough housing,
crawling around, picking up shells, singing songs, hula dancing with mom,
watching fish (aquarium), playing with other children, carrying objects,
watching movies, "carrying" mail, watching mirror reflection, playing with balls,
parent/child games, vocal play, "singing," your turn/my turn play, sharing toys,
"pushing" a swing, going down a slide, give-and take child/child play

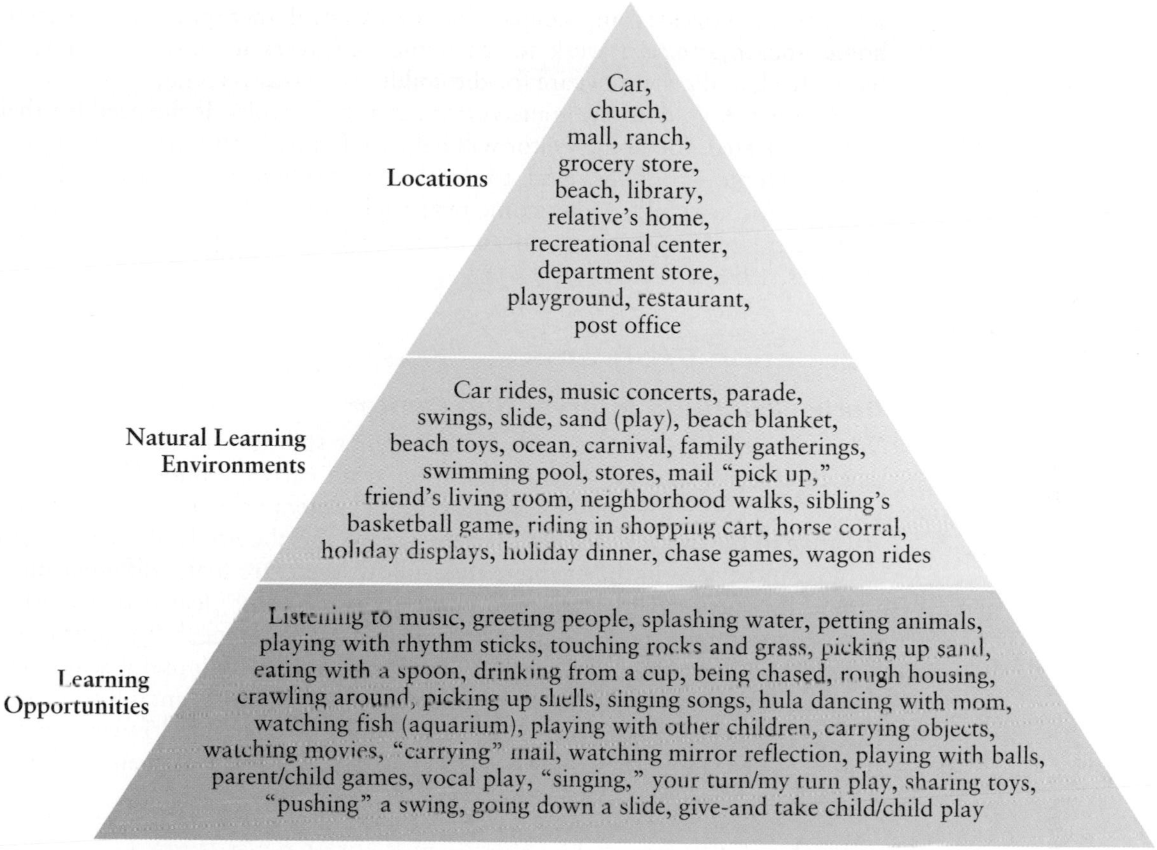

Note: These locations, natural learning environments. and learning opportunities are only a small sampling of the make-up of this child's community life.

Source: From C. Dunst, M. Bruder, C. Trivette, M. Raab, & M. McLean, Natural learning opportunities for infants, toddlers and preschoolers, *Young Exceptional Children,* 4(3) (2001): 22. Copyright © 2001. Reprinted with permission.

The data from research on home programs indicate positive gains for children as well as their parents. These strategies emphasize helping the caregiver learn how to deal with the child in the child's setting, thereby establishing a daily routine that is therapeutic. A National Association for Home-based Intervention has been formed to encourage service delivery in the natural environment (i.e., the home). This center is located at Utah State University.

The first person to visit the home may be a social worker who works with the caregivers in the home and helps them locate services to facilitate the child's development. Home visitors provide caregivers with information about the child's disability, child development in general, parenting practices, therapies, and a curriculum for the child (Affleck et al., 1991; Beckwith, 1988). In the process, the home visitor provides emotional support and contact with the

Part C of IDEA requires that services be provided in natural environments; for infants, that environment is the home.

family. The home visitor can also act as a service coordinator and help the parents apply for additional services for the child or the family. An example of additional services is an occupational or physical therapist who visits the home once or twice a week to teach the caregivers to position, carry, sit, bathe, feed, and generally care for the child.

Rarely, if ever, does the home visitor act as a therapist. If the need for therapy is indicated, the home visitor will help the family locate the necessary personnel. Home programs tend to teach the mother to be the teacher or therapist for her child. Many home programs have declined as a consequence of the increased employment out of the house of women with young children (Moores, 1996).

> Part C of IDEA requires that services be provided in natural environments; for infants, that environment is the home.

Education Programs

Early Childhood Intervention Center

When the child is 3 to 6 months old, a popular solution is to combine parent and child home education with education at an early childhood intervention center. The best early childhood intervention centers have a well-trained staff sensitive to the needs of the children they serve and the needs of their parents.

As can be seen in the chapters that follow, there are many different philosophically oriented early intervention programs. What is clear is that most effective programs are child centered, include developmentally appropriate practices, and are intensive in nature (Halpern, 2000). Two useful scales have been used to assess quality care: the Infant/Toddler Environmental Rating Scale (for 0–5) (Harms & Clifford, 1980) and the Early Childhood Environmental Rating Scale (Harms & Clifford, 1990). These scales assess appropriateness of

> Effective day-care and early childhood centers have low infant-teacher ratios and allow for child-initiated activities.
> (© Bob Daemmrich/The Image Works)

High-quality child care and early intervention classrooms aid cognitive and language development.

classroom practices, the quality of teacher-child interactions, and general classroom environment. High-quality child care and early intervention classrooms result in positive cognitive and language development (Burchinal et al., 2000; Love et al., 2003).

Early childhood centers provide families with a variety of personnel to assist them and their child. The infant program has the necessary therapists to work with the infant 30 to 45 minutes a day. A physical therapist works with children who have motor disabilities, and an occupational therapist might teach a child how to eat with a spoon or drink from a cup.

As infants move into the toddler stage, they usually need additional services. For example, it is expected that the children will begin to speak. Speech and language therapists are usually available to work with the child who has any identified problem. Because more infants and toddlers whose conditions require the use of technological equipment (oxygen tanks, respirators, and gastrostomy tubes) are entering public schools, specialists who know how to regulate the equipment are needed, as are personnel trained to catheterize the child who is paralyzed from the waist down.

Centers offer supplies and resources to the family, providing ample toys for the child to manipulate and explore. The natural (genetic) manner in which all human beings learn is through play (Lerner, 1986). It is particularly crucial for young children, who are innately curious, to look at objects, manipulate (for example, shake or rattle) them to see what they will do, and then play with them. Play is used in most early childhood programs (Buchanan & Cooney, 2000; Linder, 1993).

Evidence indicates that children who enter a well-planned, intensively structured program during the first five years of life and stay in that program for a longer period of time make the greatest gains and suffer the least loss (Guralnick, 1998).

Developmentally Appropriate Practice (DAP)

Developmentally Appropriate Practices
www.dec-sped.org

Concern over the education of young children led the National Association for the Education of Young Children (NAEYC) and the National Education Association (NEA) to publish guidelines called **developmentally appropriate practice (DAP)** (Bredekamp & Cupple, 1997). These guidelines encourage early childhood teachers to do the following:

1. Match early childhood practices to the ways children learn.
2. View the time of early childhood not as discrete age/grade levels.
3. Create classrooms that encourage exploration and facilitate learning and development.
4. Consider parent involvement as a critical and essential element in the curriculum.
5. Use ongoing evaluation for decision making and curriculum development. (Gullo, 1992, p. 11)

Using Technology with Children from Birth to Age 8
www.techandyoungchildren.org

Following that effort, special educators met and developed a handbook of recommended practices for early intervention programs (Odom & McLean, 1996; Sandal, McLean, & Smith, 2001). These suggested practices include assessment, curriculum transitions, and teacher training.

Although special educators tend to agree with the goals of DAP, their list of suggested practices tends to include more teacher-directed suggestions. For example, the activity-based intervention program (Bricker & Cripes, 1992), though consistent with the goals of DAP, looks for opportunities for the teaching of specific skills that the child has not mastered (Norvick, 1993). The major difference between the programs resides in how one engages the child. Child engagement is defined as the amount of time the child spends in developmentally and contextually appropriate behavior (Fox, Hanline, Vail, & Galant, 1994). Special educators recognize that children with disabilities do not always readily engage and have to be taught to do so.

Children with disabilities tend to be less active (passive) and less curious about the world around them (Field, 1989). They have fewer coping skills with which to respond to environmental demands (Zeitlin & Williamson, 1994). Thus, an interventionist may have to teach a child with disabilities how to play so the child can use play to learn (Anastasiow, 1996). Although the child with a disability may require more assistance than a child without a disability, great care must be taken to help the child with disabilities to develop independence, self-reliance, and critical skills for lifelong functioning (Wehmeyer, Agran, & Hughes, 1998).

Day-Care and Early Childhood Centers

Day-care and early childhood centers are usually established for children who do not have disabilities. They vary greatly in quality, organization, staff-child ratio, and program orientation (Katz, 2003). The most effective centers have a low infant-teacher ratio (2:1), well-trained personnel, observational methods, child-initiated activities, access to other professions, a skilled administrator, and low staff turnover. Child-initiated structured play is available in the effective centers (Linder, 1993).

In their longitudinal study, Schweinhart and Weikart (1998) found many positive personal and social effects among adults who as children had experienced a program oriented to intellectual, social, and physical development that encouraged them to make decisions, compared with adults who had attended a direct-instruction early childhood center.

These centers are required to accommodate infants and toddlers with disabilities. Many day-care and early childhood center teachers need additional training to accommodate and teach children with disabilities (Bruder, 1998). The School of Nursing at the University of Colorado has made an effort to meet those needs by developing materials that provide information about infants and toddlers with a wide spectrum of disabilities and suggestions on how to work with them (Krajicek, Steinke, Hertzdeng, Anastasiow, & Skandel, 2003). Video tapes and other materials are available from PRO-ED and Paul H. Brookes publishing companies.

Assessment and Curriculum

Most children go through comprehensive assessments before they are assigned by a committee on special education. These assessments are conducted with a variety of instruments and personnel such as those we described earlier in the chapter. Teachers and therapists evaluate a child's progress in motor development, fine motor development, speech and language, social and emotional

In school, teachers and therapists evaluate a child's progress in gross and fine motor development; speech and language; cognitive, social, and emotional development; and self-help skills.

development, and self-help skills. The special education teacher's role is to coordinate therapies, provide age-appropriate in-class experiences, and assist the student to capitalize on his or her abilities to attain, insofar as possible, the skills of a child of the same age without disabilities.

Play as Assessment Transdisciplinary play-based assessment (Linder, 1993a) and transdisciplinary play-based intervention (Linder, 1993b) provide techniques for assessing children in their natural settings (usually a preschool) during play and curriculum suggestions. Play has long been known to involve children's thinking, their motivation, and their socioemotional development. Linder's books help parents and the multidisciplinary team assess the child's functioning and, following assessment, provide curriculum suggestions for intervention if needed. Linder (1995) developed two training videos that demonstrate both assessment and intervention strategies through the medium of play. Forms are available to record the child's behavior.

Curriculum Options

The first curriculum issue is that most infants and toddlers with disabilities are subject to increased risks of health problems. Thus, they may need special equipment (such as wheelchairs, hearing aids, braces) and an individualized treatment program. In Chapters 4 through 8 and 10 through 13 we describe modifications for specific disabilities. An effective curriculum that takes these needs into account must be designed and begun early in the child's life, as soon as the disability is diagnosed. The following curricula are frequently used as a basis for designing an individual child's curriculum.

Helping Babies Learn: Developmental Profile and Activities for Infants and Toddlers (Furuno, O'Reilly, Hosaka, Inatsuka, & Falb, 1993) is a well-designed developmental scale with suggested activities in five areas: Home Routines,

With toddlers and children 3 to 5 years old, toys and play are the primary mode of teaching the names of objects, colors, concepts of volume and space, and of overcoming weaknesses in motor skills and physical ability.
(© Susie Fitzhugh)

ECOLOGY OF THE CHILD

SCHOOL **Welcome to Holland**

I am often asked to describe the experience of raising a child with a disability—to try to help people who have not shared that unique experience to understand it, to imagine how it would feel. It's like this...

When you're going to have a baby, it's like planning a fabulous vacation trip to Italy. You buy a bunch of guidebooks and make your wonderful plans. The Coliseum. The Michaelangelo *David*. The gondolas in Venice. You may even learn some handy phrases in Italian. It's all very exciting.

After months of eager anticipation, the day finally arrives. You pack your bags and off you go. Several hours later the plane lands. The stewardess comes in and says, "Welcome to Holland."

"Holland?" you say. "What do you mean Holland? I signed up for Italy. I'm supposed to be in Italy. All my life I've dreamed of going to Italy."

But there's been a change in the flight plan. They've landed in Holland and there you must stay.

The important thing is that they haven't taken you to a horrible, disgusting, filthy place, full of pestilence, famine and disease. It's just a different place.

So you must go out and buy new guidebooks. And you must learn a whole new language. And you will meet a whole new group of people you would never have met.

It's just a different place. It's slower-paced than Italy, less flashy than Italy. But after you've been there for a while and you catch your breath, you look around and you begin to notice that Holland has windmills, Holland has tulips. Holland even has Rembrandts.

But everyone you know is busy coming and going from Italy, and they're all bragging about what a wonderful time they had there. And for the rest of your life, you will say "Yes, that's where I was supposed to go. That's what I had planned."

Indoor Activities, Excursions, Social Development, and Health and Safety. These scales and activities are organized in three-month sections from birth to 3 years of age. The activities encompass a range of skills and describe situations in which the parent or teacher can observe and interact with the infant and facilitate his or her development.

The Hawaiian Early Learning Profile (HELP) (Furuno et al., 1989) has similar goals for 0- to 3-year-olds. The HELP contains nine scales and describes discrete tasks (such as drinking from a cup) and the average age at which most children accomplish the skill. By comparing an infant's or toddler's general profile across the nine areas, the teacher can pinpoint areas of delay and identify the areas that will constitute the curriculum.

Gathering systematic observations of children's activities and samples of their naturally occurring classroom work can be a method of assessing young children's growth and development. It is also an excellent way to communicate to parents their children's developmental status and academic achievements. The Work Sampling System (Meisels, Jablon, Marsden, Dichtelmiller, & Dorfman, 2001), designed for children age 3 through grade 6, is the most

And the pain of that will never, ever, ever go away, because the loss of that dream is a very significant loss.

But if you spend your life mourning the fact that you didn't get to Italy, you may never be free to enjoy the very special, the very lovely things about Holland.

Source: Emily Perl Kingsley, in T. W. Wesley & B. C. Dennis. Inclusive Child Care Training Series in Early Childhood Professionals, Chapel Hill, University of North Carolina Frank Porter Child Development Center, Partnership for Inclusion, 2000.

WHAT IS THE CONTEXT?

This passage describes the experiences of a mother whose child has been diagnosed at birth as having Down syndrome. The metaphor used, a trip to Holland captures the mixed emotions that parents struggle through as they work to come to peace with their child's disabilities. This is a very personal journey and every parent will find their own path through the difficulties they encounter. As professionals we must respect these difficulties and honor the parents' rights to handle them as they see fit.

PIVOTAL ISSUES FOR THE TEACHER

- How can we support parents as they struggle to understand and accept the special needs of their child with exceptionalities?

- How will our ability to provide genetic counseling and prenatal detection of disabilities impact the journey parents take as they deal with possible disabilities for their children?

- How might the parents' involvement in the interdisciplinary planning team for their child impact the parents' ability to cope with their child's disability?

---

widely used and extensively researched observational assessment (for example, see Meisels, Bickel, Nicholson, Xue, & Atkins-Burnett, 2001).

The Ounce Scale (Meisels, Dombro, Marsden, Weston, & Jewkes, 2003) is an adaptation of this approach from birth to age 3.6. The scale is organized around six areas of development: personal connections, feelings about self, relationships with other children, understanding and communicating, exploration and problem-solving, and movement and coordination. The scale relies on the observations and recordings of parents and child-care workers and provides explicit guidelines for the developmental expectations of typical infants and toddlers. The Ounce Scale assists caregivers and parents in learning more about their children and how they can interact with them in order to advance the children's development while also providing a model observational assessment.

The Carolina Curriculum (Johnson-Martin, Attermeier, & Hacker, 2004; Johnson-Martin, Jens, & Attermeier, 2004) is similar to the HELP in that it provides an assessment as well as a curriculum to assist the child in accomplishing skill development. It is now available in two volumes. The first is designed for children from birth to age 3, the second for children from ages 3 to 5.

These curricula are in essence large developmental scales, breaking down each area of development into small, discrete steps. The teacher presents each task and determines whether the child is able to accomplish it, such as identifying a cup and spoon and, later, naming objects presented in a series of pictures or actual toys. If the child is able to accomplish a task, the teacher moves on to the next task, until reaching a task the child is unable to accomplish. This process provides the teacher with information on where to begin instruction.

Young children with disabilities will tend to spend time observing rather than interacting. They engage in more solitary or isolated play, which is functional and on a low sensory level, rather than in higher-level dramatic or constructive play (Kim, Vaughn, Elbaum, Hughes, Sloan, & Sridhar, 2003). To encourage higher-level learning, the importance of toys and play activities cannot be overemphasized. There are many positive social outcomes from providing children with toys, allowing them to choose toys, and encouraging them to play with other children, with or without disabilities (Erwin & Brown, 2003).

Settings to encourage higher-level social play include dress-up clothes, a housekeeping corner, blocks, puppets, and group block play. While computers, books, and art materials all have their place in instruction, their use leads to more necessary functional skill development (Kim et al., 2003). For computers to be introduced most effectively, children should be trained in their use as part of daily activities in the classroom. Once children are comfortable and knowledgeable in using the computer, they may select programs that interest them and enhance their skill development. Many appropriate software programs are available. For an excellent guide to software companies and programs, see Judge (2001) or go to http://school.aol.com.

Houghton Mifflin Special
Education Resource Center
website
http://education.college.hmco.
com/students

■ Transition

The transition to formal schooling in kindergarten is recognized as a landmark event by millions of families across the country. This normal developmental milestone may be more difficult for children with disabilities and their families. A smooth transition depends on several factors coming together. The readiness of the child, as discussed earlier, is critical, but the readiness of the school to receive the child is just as important. School strategies that can facilitate this transition include sending letters home to parents, holding open-house visits, calling parents, and making home visits (Pianta & Cox, 2002). One difficulty is that families who need support during this transition (those who live in poverty, those who reside in urban and rural communities, and those who have children with disabilities) may in fact receive fewer services. Transition planning for children with disabilities who are receiving early intervention is essential. These children and their families should have a transition plan that is developed and implemented by a team (Pianta, Cox, Early, & Taylor, 1999). Transition planning for a smooth entry into school is key to ensuring that gains made by early intervention are not lost.

In addition, care for at-risk or developmentally delayed children, or children with disabilities does not end in infancy. Many of these children require continual monitoring and support. For example, as children with disabilities grow, bigger wheelchairs or braces may be required. Although many children experience a diminishment of or outgrow their earlier at-risk states—particularly children with mild retardation who have the benefit of an early intervention program—most children with sensory disabilities will need long-term assistance. The employment rate of adults with the most disabilities is very low, less than 30 percent.

Because a child with disabilities is likely to outlive his or her parents, this poses the real problem of who will care for the child later in life. Fortunately, many national associations have been established to serve as guardians for children with disabilities when the need arises. Parents bequeath their estates to these associations to cover the cost of caring for their child, and the associations assume the responsibility for placing the individual in a foster home, group home, or independent living situation, and they monitor his or her needs as necessary.

The long-term outcome for young children with disabilities is varied. Some achieve high school graduation, even further training after high school; some may go on to a community college or to universities. Others may live in group homes and be engaged in supportive employment.

Early intervention attempts to maximize the child's abilities so that at every transition point, the child moves easily into the new environment and gains increased competencies.

■ The Family-Centered Approach and Cultural Diversity

Increasingly it is being recognized that the family is fundamental to the development of any child, with or without disabilities (Osofsky & Thompson, 2000). The key is the ability of the mother and father to relate to the child and provide a responsive affect-caring environment. Most parents will provide the kind of environment their children need, and if the child is disabled, the parents will seek out professionals and learn desired methods of facilitating growth from them. However, parents from some cultures may not see the disability as a problem to be solved and therefore may not agree with the professional line of treatment. Others may see the child's need for intervention but not change their own behavior—for example, not perceiving the child as someone to play with or talk to (Garcia & Magnuson, 2000). The teacher should be aware of the following aspects of culture and cultural differences:

National Parent Information Network
www.npin.org

1. What is the child's primary language, and how is it used in the home?
2. What are the parents' expectations as to the use of language to communicate? How is language use valued in the home?
3. What are the preferred strategies of learning: verbal, nonverbal, observation, imitation?
4. To what degree is the family acculturated? Do they agree or disagree about cultural values and mores?
5. What goals does the family have for the child?

Teachers may find the Culturally and Linguistically Appropriate Services (CLAS) website helpful for locating culturally and linguistically appropriate instructional material (http://clas.uius.edu) (Corso, Santos, & Roof, 2002).

One of the strongest movements in special education recently has been the *family-focused* or *family-centered* practices. The current opinion is that the family needs to be placed at the center of any early intervention system, and their goals and opinions addressed and honored (Parette & Petch-Hogan, 2000). This does not mean professionals would give up their positions if they differed from those of the family. Rather, they would first gain the family's trust before attempting to modify their behavior by encouraging them to accept proven practices (Harry, Rueda, & Kalyonpurin, 1999). These differences may occur more frequently with families from cultures that are different from that of the professional. Team members dealing with these difference can find excellent resources—CD-ROM, books, articles, and Web pages—in Parette and Petch-Hogan (2000). The legislation IDEA calls for a family-oriented approach by requiring an individualized family services plan (IFSP), which spells out what services will be available for the family as well as for the child with disabilities (Barrere, 2000; Reiss, 2003; Turnbull & Turnbull, 1997).

Culture

Cultural relevance is one of the criteria established for the developmentally appropriate practices. These criteria are an important part of assessing the appropriateness of services for children and families from a variety of cultural backgrounds. Curricula need to be antibiased and culturally appropriate (Banks, Milagros, & Roof, 2003; Garcia & Magnuson, 2000).

Coping with Stress

All parents suffer from stress. Dryson (1991) found that parents of children with disabilities are under greater stress than are parents of children without disabilities. For the caregivers of children with disabilities, the key challenge is to develop the hope and conviction that they will need to cope with their stress as well as find the benefits they will need (therapeutic and educational services for the child, financial and emotional support for the caregiver) throughout the child's life. Several national programs are designed to teach parents how to cope cognitively, that is, to learn how to think positively about a problem and to enhance self-esteem (Turnbull & Turnbull, 1997).

Moving from early child care to kindergarten is a critical step for young children, and carefully formulated transition plans can facilitate their adjustment and success in school (Pianta & Kraft-Sayre, 2003). Successful transition requires communication among the preschool teacher, the parents, and the kindergarten teacher, preferably before the child enters the class. It should be a collaborative process in which past experiences are linked to future goals.

Affleck and associates (1991) suggest that the key to a mother's successful management of her child's disabilities appears to be the extent to which she perceives that she has control of the child's development, the degree of positive outcomes that she perceives, the finding of emotional support and needed services, and her acceptance of the child's disability without seeking to blame anyone for it. Mothers who cannot accept their child's disability are likely to seek a cause for it, and in most cases they attribute it to their own behavior (pp. 130–132).

National Parent Network in Disabilities catalog of toys
www.npnd.org

Parents Helping Parents Resource Center
www.php.com

Remember that the human body is genetically programmed to remain healthy and to ward off or overcome illness. Thus, children who are at risk have their body's systems helping them overcome their risk state. In addition, persons in the environment can greatly assist the child's biological system by providing support in the form of positive child-rearing practices (Werner & Smith, 1992). As Sandra Scarr (1982) writes,

> In this view, humans are made of the newer plastics—they bend with environmental pressure, resume their shapes when the pressures are relieved, and are unlikely to be misshapened by transient experiences. When bad environments are improved, people's adaptations improve. Humans are resilient and responsive to the advantages the environment provides. (pp. 852–853)

WWWW Equal Employment Opportunity Commission guide for people with disabilities seeking employment www.eeoc.gov/facts/adaguide.html

Similarly, Affleck and associates (1991) quote Taylor (1988) as follows:

> Despite serious setbacks . . . the majority of people facing such blows (e.g., personal tragedies) achieve a happy quality of life or level of happiness equivalent to or even exceeding their prior level of satisfaction. Not everyone readjusts, of course, but most do. (p. 142)

Summary

▶ Early intervention begins before pregnancy when the mother-to-be has a checkup to determine any vitamin or nutritional deficiency and takes recommended supplements, including folic acid. Following conception, the woman would avoid alcohol, tobacco, and drugs such as heroin, cocaine or marijuana.

▶ At birth, physicians will check for the infant's overall functioning and specifically for PKU, thyroid deficiency, hearing, and other potential disabilities. If the infant is a premature or low-birth-weight baby, intensive-care nurseries supply needed lifesaving care.

▶ Following the birth, if a developmental delay or disability is diagnosed, intervention programs are available to ameliorate or improve or prevent declines in functioning.

▶ Early intervention programs vary as to philosophical orientations; however, involving the parent directly in the program and recommended interventions with the multidisciplinary/collaborative teams is desired.

Future Challenges

1. What is the effect of advanced medical lifesaving techniques?

New lifesaving techniques are keeping extremely-low (under 1500 g), very-low-birth-weight (between 1,500 and 2,000 g), low-birth-weight (under 2,000 to 2,500 g), and premature infants from dying. However, large numbers of these children acquire disabilities as a result of being born too soon and too small. This will mean an increase in the number of infants to be served by early intervention.

2. What would be the impact of universal prenatal health care?

Primary prevention through prenatal care is not available to all expectant mothers, particularly those who live in poverty. Even when it is available, some individuals—adolescents, for example—do not take advantage of it. If prenatal care were provided universally, as it is in the United States armed forces, it would markedly reduce the number of premature and low-birth-weight children, who are at risk for disabilities, thereby saving millions of dollars despite the costs of prenatal care.

3. How can more children with disabilities be included in preschool and day care?
Inclusion of children with disabilities in Head Start, day care, or private preschools for the nondisabled has been a slow process.

4. How will caregivers continue to work and find appropriate care for their children?
Many women work outside the home because of preference or economic necessity. Forty-nine to 75 percent of mothers are employed outside the home. The primary caregiver of a child with disabilities, however, may not have the choice to continue working because of the difficulty of finding appropriate child care. Personnel of day-care centers usually are not trained to care for children with disabilities, and extended day care is not widely available.

5. Can staff of early intervention programs receive higher pay to reduce the turnover rate?
Consistency is an important feature of successful intervention programs. Yet the yearly turnover of some staff is 100 percent in Head Start, 81 percent in licensed day care, 75 percent in private early childhood programs, and 63 percent in public schools. The high turnover is usually attributed to low pay. High turnover in early childhood special education is usually attributed to the stress and strain of working with children with disabilities, particularly among those working with persons who have severe and profound disabilities.

Key Terms

alpha-fetoprotein test   *p. 88*

amniocentesis   *p. 89*

Apgar test   *p. 91*

at-risk infant   *p. 85*

chorionic villus biopsy   *p. 90*

developmental scale   *p. 83*

developmental screening   *p. 92*

developmentally appropriate practice (DAP)   *p. 103*

early childhood intervention   *p. 79*

environmental risks   *p. 86*

fetal alcohol syndrome   *p. 87*

genetic counseling   *p. 87*

Head Start   *p. 81*

IDEA, Part C   *p. 82*

individualized family services plan (IFSP)   *p. 93*

multidisciplinary team   *p. 96*

prenatal care   *p. 88*

sonography   *p. 89*

Resources

References of Special Interest

Fisher, D. & Ryndak, D. (Eds.). (2001). The Foundations of Inclusive Education. see www.tash.org/publications/foundations_for_inclusion or call 410-825-8275, ext. "0." *A compendium of articles originally published in JASH, which deal with the theory and practicalities of achieving inclusive education as well as strategies that have been shown to be effective. A series of three yearly publications devoted to issues of early intervention. A wide range of topics is covered by distinguished researchers and practitioners.*

Krajicek, M., Steinke, T., Hertzdeng, D., Anastasiow, N., & Skandel, S. (Eds.). (2003). *Handbook for the care of infants and toddlers with disabilities and chronic conditions and Instructor's guide for the Handbook for the care of infants and toddlers with disabilities and chronic conditions.* Austin, TX: PRO-ED. *These materials cover a wide range of disabilities, providing information about conditions as well as techniques (such as positioning) for treating them. They were prepared under the leadership of Marilyn Krajicek, Ed.D., R.N., at the University of Colorado School of Nursing.*

Frank Porter Child Development Institute. *Early Development.* Campus Box 8185, University of North Carolina, Chapel Hill, NC 27599-8185 www.fpg.unc.edu.

March of Dimes (1997–2003). Public Information Sheets. P.O. Box 1657, Wilkes-Barre, PA. 18703 *These information sheets cover a wide range of disabilities. They describe the nature of the disability, cause, if known, and treatments. They are very valuable for parent information sessions. A basic set is free of charge.*

Odom, S. L., & McLean, M. E. (1996). *Early intervention/Early childhood special education: Recommended practices.* PRO-ED, 8700 Shoal Creek Boulevard, Austin, TX 78757–6897. *This book contains a discussion and a comprehensive list of recommended practices, including assessment, development of IFSPs and IEPs, curriculum and intervention strategies, evaluation, transition, and personnel preparation. It is an essential source for all phases of program development and implementation.*

Siegel, L.M. (2001). The Complete IEP Guide. How to Advocate for Your Special Ed Child. NOLO. Call 510-549-

1976 or website www.nolo.com. *A wonderful resource for parents on the nature of the IEP, special education law, and the rights of parents to insure their child with a disability has the services recommended from the assessments. The guide also provides guidelines for resolving disputes through due process.*

Journals

Infants and Young Children

Journal of Early Intervention
Council for Exceptional Children
www.cec.sped.org/

Topics in Early Childhood Special Education
PRO-ED Journals
www.proedinc.com

Young Exceptional Children
www.dec-sped.org/publication.html

Professional Organizations

The Beach Center on Disability
www.beachcenter.org
Division for Early Childhood of the Council for Exceptional Children
www.dec-sped.org
March of Dimes Resource Center Birth Defects Foundation
www.modimes.org

National Center for Early Development and Learning (NCEDL)
www.ncedl.org

Parents Helping Parents Resource Center
www.php.com

Please visit the book's website at http://education.college.hmco.com/students for new and updated information on websites listed here and for the mailing addresses of the journals and organizations.

4

CHILDREN WITH SPECIFIC LEARNING DISABILITIES

FOCUS QUESTIONS

▶ How are specific learning disabilities defined by law?

▶ Is there one known primary cause of specific learning disabilities?

▶ How do we identify children with specific learning disabilities?

▶ How does inclusion work for children with specific learning disabilities?

▶ What technology is available to support academic learning?

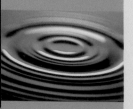

Perhaps no area of special education is generating so much multidisciplinary research and stimulating so much debate as learning disabilities. Researchers are intrigued by learning disabilities because children who possess them have near-average or higher IQ scores but do not succeed in areas that the IQ scores predict, particularly in learning how to read and write. Essentially, persons with learning disabilities belie one fundamental assumption about human beings: If you do not experience mental retardation, mental disturbances, visual or hearing impairments, or environmental deprivations, you should be able to do well in school.

The field of learning disabilities has had the problem of distinguishing between students with learning problems that arise from neurological defects or differences and students with learning problems resulting from a variety of social and physical problems (Fuchs, Fuchs, Mathes, Lipsey, & Roberts, 2002). This has led several investigators to suggest eliminating the category.

However, a consensus report of fifteen prominent researchers in the field concludes that there is strong evidence to support the category and that it should be labeled *Specific Learning Disabilities* (SLD) to distinguish it from a category of specific learning problems. The prominent features of SLD would involve disorders of learning and cognition that are intrinsic to the individual but are not primarily due to other conditions, such as mental retardation, behavioral disorders, lack of opportunity to learn, or primary sensory deficit (Bradley, Danielson, & Hallahan, 2002b, p. 792), and unexpected underachievement and intraindividual deficits (Scruggs & Mastropieri, 2002). This is not to suggest that there are no problems with identifying students with SLD, but the problems of assessment and identification should not lead to altering or eliminating the category (Scruggs & Mastropieri, 2002).

Why children with learning disabilities do not do well has fascinated and baffled researchers in the fields of reading, cognition, speech and hearing, neurology, learning, vision, audition, and special education in general. What is clear is that there is no one cause of the difficulties experienced by all persons who are said to have learning disabilities. There appear to be multiple causes, and not all children with learning disabilities have the same set of deficits. Most have trouble learning to read and write. Others have trouble with math. Some have trouble with all three.

SLD is a hidden disorder or deficit. You cannot see it as you can blindness or other physical disabilities. It is a disorder in an individual's ability to interpret what he or she sees or hears, or to link information from different parts of the brain. It can be a narrow or a multifaceted disorder and a lifelong condition (Neuwirth, 1996).

National Center for Learning Disabilities
www.ncld.org

Not all learning problems are learning disabilities.

■ A Historical Overview

Children who have average intelligence and no classifiable disability yet do not succeed in school have been a concern to teachers, parents, researchers, and the children themselves. Researchers began investigating the causes of the conditions now known as learning disabilities in the 1800s, and research continues today. Lack of effort by the student has been ruled out as a causative factor, but many questions remain.

Learning Disabilities
Association (LDA)
www.ldanatl.org

A number of intriguing hypotheses have been proposed to account for the disorder. Orton (1937) believed that the difficulty resides in the failure of the left hemisphere of the brain to take on the role of language as it typically does in human beings. He called students who had difficulty learning "minimally brain damaged." Kirk and Kirk (1971) and Myklebust (1965) perceived the problems as a specific language disorder and followed that line of reasoning in their research. Frostig, Lefever, and Whittesey (1964), Getman (1965), and others investigated perceptual and motor processes as possible factors. Fernald (1943) and Gillingham and Stillman (1960) believed that the disorder is primarily in the area of written language. These differences in opinion produced a fragmented body of research and no consensus among researchers as to the causes of the disorder or what to call it. At a meeting of concerned parents, Samuel Kirk (1963) proposed the term *learning disabilities* to describe the condition; the term was widely adopted and is still used.

Today most of the older hypotheses about learning disabilities involving brain damage have been abandoned or revised, but the causes of the disorder are still largely unknown (Lyon, 1994; Stanovich, 1986; Torgesen & Wong, 1986). Many researchers are working to determine the source of the disorder and to develop curricula and methods to remediate academic problems.

■ Definitions

Council for Learning
Disabilities
www.cldinternational.org

The specific learning disability label assists persons in identifying and classifying children who need special help. Their neurological patterns seem somewhat different from those of children of the same age without disabilities. Persons with learning disabilities have in common some type of failure in school or in the community. They are not able to do what others with the same level of intelligence are able to accomplish.

The *Federal Register* (1977) includes the regulations for identifying and defining students with learning disabilities under the Education for All Handicapped Children Act of 1975 (PL 94-142):

> "Specific learning disability" means a disorder in one or more of basic psychological processes involved in using language, spoken or written, which may manifest itself in an imperfect ability to listen, think, speak, read, write, spell, or to do mathematical calculations. The term includes such conditions as perceptual handicaps, brain injury, minimal brain dysfunction, dyslexia, and developmental aphasia. The term does not include children who have learning problems which are primarily the result of visual, hearing, or motor handicaps, of mental retardation, of emotional disturbance, or of environmental, cultural, or economic disadvantage. (*Federal Register*, 1977, p. 650; NICHCY, 2000)

The *Federal Register* definition has four criteria that teachers must consider when identifying students with learning disabilities:

Learning disabilities are indicated by a great discrepancy between intellectual ability and actual school achievement.

1. *Academic difficulties.* The child with learning disabilities has difficulty learning how to read, write, spell, organize thoughts, or do mathematical calculations, compared with other children of the same age.

Specific learning disabilities refers to a heterogeneous group of disorders manifested by significant difficulties in acquiring and using listening, speaking, reading, writing, reasoning, or mathematical abilities.
(© Will Hart/Photo Edit)

2. *Discrepancy between potential and achievement.* The child with learning disabilities experiences a serious discrepancy between intellectual ability and achievement in school; this is known as an **aptitude-achievement discrepancy.**

3. *Exclusion of other factors.* A person may not be classified as having learning disabilities if the learning problem is caused by visual or hearing impairments, mental retardation, motor disabilities, emotional disturbance, or environmental factors.

4. *Neuropsychological disorder.* Basic learning disabilities are the result of some type of neuropsychological disorder.

Using the discrepancy between IQ score and academic performance as a criterion has been highly criticized. However, Kavale (2002) and Scruggs and Mastropieri (2002) feel it is a very important indication of a potential learning disability and should be used along with other comprehensive identification processes. Students with SLD exhibit average or above-average intelligence across many domains, but have a specific deficit in a narrow range of performance (Bradley, Danielson, & Hallahan, 2002).

The National Joint Committee for Learning Disabilities (1991) proposed the following definition:

Special education programs for students with learning disabilities focus on strategies to help them learn the traditional curriculum.

Specific learning disabilities is a generic term that refers to a heterogeneous group of disorders that are manifested by significant difficulties in the acquisition and use of listening, speaking, reading, writing, reasoning, or mathematical abilities. These disorders are intrinsic to the individual and are presumed to be due to central nervous system dysfunction. Even though a learning disability may occur concomitantly with other handicapping conditions (e.g., sensory impairment, mental retardation, social and emotional disturbances, insufficient/inappropriate instruction, psychogenic factors), it is not the real result of those conditions or influences. (p. 16)

"Central nervous system dysfunction" is currently more commonly called *neuropsychological dysfunctioning* and/or *differences*. These terms mean that the definition assumes that the brain or perceptional systems or both are not damaged but work in a way that is different from the way they function in children without learning problems. However, there is general agreement that specific learning disabilities arise from neurological deficits in the brain (Bradley, Danielson, & Hallahan, 2002). The location of the area in the brain where the deficit occurs is currently the subject of intensive research (Council for Exceptional Children, 2003; Gorman, 2003).

Both definitions point to the need to present an alternative set of lessons to match the unusual neurological patterns of these children. Much of the special education designed for these children focuses on strategies to help them master lessons they cannot learn from the traditional curriculum.

It is important to bear in mind the following:

▶ All children with learning disabilities have learning problems.

▶ Not all children with academic problems have learning disabilities.

At this time, we can make the following general statements about learning disabilities:

▶ *Learning disabilities* is a general term that refers to a heterogeneous group of disorders that includes different subgroups.

▶ Learning disabilities are viewed as a problem not only of the school years but also of early childhood and adult life.

▶ A learning disability is intrinsic to the individual; the basis of the disorder is presumed to be a central nervous system dysfunction.

▶ Learning disabilities may occur with other disabilities as well as within different cultural and linguistic groups (Kavale, Forness, & Bender, 1988).

■ Prevalence

Incidence figures for children with learning disabilities vary. The U.S. Department of Education (1999) reports that slightly less than 5 percent of school-age children are receiving special education services, with 2.9 million served in the 1997–1998 school year. However, considering the special education population alone, the learning disabilities category contains the largest number of children: approximately 50 percent of all students with disabilities (*Twenty-fourth Annual Report to Congress*, 2002). According to that same report, most of these children are in regular schools; 48 percent spend most of their time in the regular classroom, and 48 percent spend 20 to 60 percent of their time in regular classrooms and 10 percent of their time in separate public facilities. Fuchs, Fuchs, Mathes, and Lipsey (2000) report an incidence of 7 percent.

Ninety-eight percent of the states exclude from the learning disability criteria children with mental retardation and low academic achievement due to environmental disadvantage. However, MacMillan and Speece (2000) report that the evidence reveals that between 52 percent and 70 percent of children identified by schools as learning disabled do not meet the standard established

Over 43 percent of students with learning disabilities are served in the regular classroom.

Because reading and arithmetic are similar in many ways (e.g., numbers and words stand for concepts), a child with language difficulty is likely to have difficulty in learning to calculate.
(© Monika Graff/The Image Works)

by state and federal criteria. Gottlieb, Alter, Gottlieb, and Wisner (1994) note that in the urban areas they studied many of the children classified as learning disabled previously would have been classified as educable retarded because of their lower IQ scores.

How children are served varies among states. For example, 81 percent of the children with specific learning disabilities are served in regular classrooms in Ohio, but only 23 percent in Delaware (U.S. Department of Education, 1999).

The problem with prevalence figures lies in the lack of a uniform definition of learning disabilities across the states and a failure to administer a complex multidisciplinary assessment that encompasses social, genetic, cultural, and educational factors. Because there is no single cause of school failure, some factors have to be ruled out (such as severe hearing impairments or cultural deprivation) before a child is considered as having learning disabilities (Interagency Committee, 1990, p. 140). Some schools tend to identify all students in academic trouble as having learning disabilities. A more realistic estimate with comprehensive identification measures would be 4 to 5 percent of the school population (Bradley, Danielson, & Hallahan, 2002b).

Keep in mind the concept of individual and intraindividual differences when thinking about children with learning disabilities. These children have some disabilities in common; for example, 75 to 80 percent of students with learning disabilities have reading or language deficits (Council for Exceptional Children [CEC], 1997; Cramer & Ellis, 1996). However, some students have other disabilities that are idiosyncratic characteristics of only a small subgroup of the population with learning disabilities. Although children in a subgroup may have characteristics in common, they will differ from one another on some dimension, some having several problems and some having only one. For example, Snowling and Perrin (1988) found that some children with learning disabilities have problems in reading, spelling, and writing, whereas others are excellent readers but poor spellers. Learning disabilities may be of a verbal or a nonverbal nature (Rourke, 1995; Morris, 2002).

■ Is There a Single Cause?

No one has discovered a single cause of learning disabilities. Rather, studies that focus on subgroups within the larger population of children with learning disabilities have identified some neurological differences and sensory deficits associated with their learning problems (Hynd, 1992; Lyon, 1995; Rourke, 1994). For example, although visual-perceptual-motor deficits do not appear to be a single cause of learning disabilities, they do appear to be a factor for a small sample within the group.

Research now clearly supports the rejection of a single cause or a single deficit. The field recognizes multiple problems and teaches each child, keeping his or her particular deficit clearly in mind. Instruction varies from child to child, depending on the problems he or she faces.

Learning disabilities result from a variety of causes.

■ Characteristics of Children with Learning Disabilities

Case Study: Manuel and Ray

Children with specific learning disabilities vary in their personal and social characteristics. Manuel, a fifth grader with a measured IQ score of 170, was an excellent reader but a very poor speller who loved to disrupt his class with distracting antics. Meetings with his parents revealed strong pressure from them for Manuel to improve his spelling with daily practice sessions at home. They were also skeptical of his measured IQ. Manuel had few friends; his classmates thought him weird.

Ray, a nonreader, was happy to volunteer for all art projects (in these, he excelled). Because of his poor academic performance, his classmates considered him retarded. Both students had specific learning disabilities. Manuel's parents never accepted his disability or his talents, and he stayed in the school through high school. Ray had an eighth-grade teacher who recognized his spatial abilities and helped him acquire reading skills. He later became a career military officer. Some children with learning disabilities have difficulty making friends (Vaugh, McIntosh, & Spencer-Rowe, 1991), and they do not seem to hear all that is said or respond quickly to questions (Curtis & Tallal, 1991). Some have trouble learning the rules of games, but once they learn them, they insist on strict adherence to them (Valletutti, 1987). Specific learning disabilities are frequently experienced throughout life and are apparent when the individual has difficulty in meeting the demands of work or living (Bradley, Danielson, & Hallahan, 2002a).

In the literature on learning disabilities, authors have used many negative terms to describe children with learning *disabilities*. These terms, however, are equally descriptive of children with learning *problems*. The main point to keep in mind is that children with learning disabilities have normal intelligence and have difficulty in one or more school subjects—difficulty that is *not* associated with a known disability such as cerebral palsy or mental retardation. It is hoped that the earlier we identify a child with learning disabilities and institute a successful educational program, the less likely are boredom, lack of motivation, and lack of interest to set in. But if a child continues to fail in elementary school, problem behaviors may be established by adolescence.

■ Classification of Learning Disabilities

Learning disabilities information, bulletin boards, and resources www.ldonline.org.

Researchers generally take one of the following perspectives on learning disabilities: developmental or academic achievement or a combination of these two approaches. Those who take a neuropsychological/developmental perspective seek an underlying cause for students' difficulties in academic subjects. The upper part of Figure 4.1 contains the hypothesized neuropsychological/developmental disorders: biological/genetic, perceptual-motor, visual, auditory, memory, and attentional disorders. A large number of researchers are pursuing the source or causes of these disorders (Kavale, Forness, & Bender, Vols. 1–3, 1988).

Researchers who take the academic perspective investigate the specific problems that students have with the content and processes (executive functions) they need to learn to master academic subjects. The middle part of Figure 4.1

FIGURE 4.1
Types of Learning Disabilities

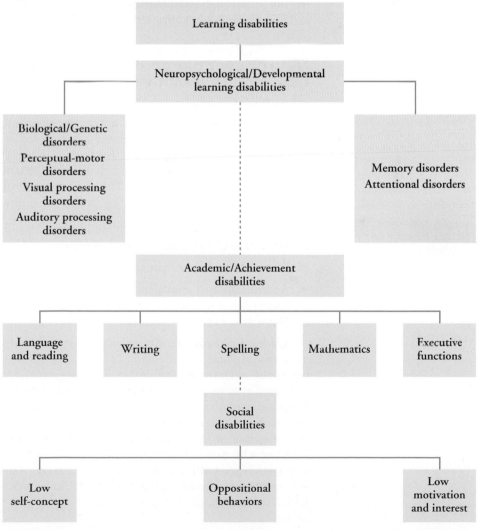

lists the academic areas that teachers are most concerned with: language and reading, writing, spelling, mathematics, and executive functions. A large group of researchers are focusing on how to solve these difficulties by developing teaching strategies and curriculum (see Lenz, Ellis, & Scanlon, 1996; Lyon, 1999; Sturomski, 1997; and Kavale & Forness, 2000).

The developmental-academic model implies that the child with learning disabilities comes to school with a set of developmental problems in processing information. **Developmental learning disabilities** (also called **neuropsychological learning disabilities**) include attention problems, memory problems, and disorders in thinking and using language. These problems are rarely detected before the child enters school because few serious demands are made of the preschool child in these areas. Efforts are currently being made to identify early risk factors, which may help school personnel to identify children with learning disabilities (Stanton-Chapman, Stanton, & Scott, 2001).

These developmental learning disabilities lead to **academic achievement learning disabilities** in listening, reading, spelling, writing, or arithmetic. Again, not everyone who has these academic problems has a learning disability, but a thorough examination can determine the presence of developmental learning disabilities (Lyon, 1994, 1999).

Neuropsychological/Developmental Learning Disabilities

Inherent in the term *learning disabilities* is the understanding that the disorder or disorders exist in the person, not in the environment. Hence, the first hypotheses proposed that these individuals suffered from brain damage, brain dysfunction, or brain differences resulting in disordered thinking skills, poor memory, poor attentive skills, and challenging behaviors (for example, lack of motivation, passive aggression). The neuropsychological/developmental model assumes that learning disabilities are due to the following:

> Learning disabilities occur within the child, not within the environment.

▶ Something wrong with or different in the child's brain or perceptual systems

▶ Some type of neurological dysfunction

▶ Disturbances in perceptual-motor functioning

▶ An imbalance of intelligence abilities and academic achievement from some type of damage to the brain (Kantrowitz & Underwood, 1999; Neuwirth, 1996; Rourke, 1994)

We have already mentioned that most children with learning disabilities have trouble learning to read. This may be the source of many of the disputes about learning disabilities. Learning to read depends on several perceptional systems: vision, hearing (matching one's auditory system to print), attention, previous experience, and so on. Thus, a researcher who pursues one of these topics may come to assume that one particular disability is the major source of learning disabilities. What is being discovered is that a researcher who makes this assumption is both right (accurately perceiving that some students with learning disabilities have vision processing problems) and wrong (overgeneralizing that all children with learning disabilities have vision problems).

In the following sections, we look at attempts by researchers to discover a cause (or causes) of learning disabilities.

Biological and Genetic Explanations

Researchers have reported biological, hereditary, and genetic explanations for some subtypes of learning disabilities. Pennington (1997) and Gorman (2003) demonstrated that some learning disabilities have a genetic base and are inherited. Greschwind (1985) proposed elevated hormone imbalances as a source of learning disabilities. Several researchers have demonstrated relationships between brain damage and some types of learning disabilities (DeFries and Alarcon, 1996; Rourke, 1994; Shaywitz, Pugh, Jenner, Fullbright, Fletcher, & Gore, 2002).

It has been known for a long time that persons with damage to the frontal lobe of the brain have problems in planning and using appropriate strategies in solving problems, but it is not correct to assume that persons who display these problems have frontal lobe damage. By analogy, if a baseball player who is nearsighted misses a ball hit to him, that does not mean everyone who misses a fly ball is nearsighted. A player may or may not be nearsighted, just as students with learning disabilities may or may not have brain damage. The student's disability may be a brain dysfunction or a way of operating different from that of most other children.

Perceptual-Motor Problems

Early childhood educators believe motor development is the key to sound overall development, particularly in regard to students without physical disabilities (Lerner, 2000). Whereas some children experience problems in coordination, balance, rhythm, and/or spatial awareness, it is an error to assume that these problems are the source of learning disabilities (as was hypothesized by the early learning disabilities researchers referred to above). Some children with learning disabilities *will* have motor problems. However, utilizing perceptual-motor integration practices (although many teachers believe in them) as a cure for learning disabilities has little research support (Kavale & Forness, 2000). Many remedial activities were suggested to increase perceptual-motor integration. Modern concern, however, tends to focus on techniques for remediating specific deficits—such as reading, spelling, or mathematical disorders—rather than on activities to increase proposed lacks in body integration. It is "unexpected underachievement" that is at the core of today's thinking about learning disabilities (Lyon, 1994, p. xv).

Visual Processing Deficits

Because reading depends partially on vision, many people assumed that visual deficits were the cause of learning disabilities. Children with visual deficits were observed to have difficulty moving their eyes from left to right to follow printed text, and they moved their eyes frequently back and forth across a line. These visual processing deficits were perceived to signal not a problem in seeing but instead a problem in how visual information was processed in the brain and how the children used their eyes to gain information. Visual processing deficits should not be ignored. Testing for them should be part of the diagnostic process so children with these deficits can be identified and receive appropriate remediation (Atkinson, 1993; Satz & Morris, 1981; Swanson, 1987).

Auditory Processing Deficits

Curtis and Tallal (1991) and Tallal, Miller, and Fitch (1993) suggested that auditory processing is slower in children with language delays. Language delays are common in children with learning disabilities. These children take longer to process auditory as well as visual information (Blakeslee, 1991). If the information takes longer to get into the short-term memory, it may not get into long-term memory. In addition, these children take longer to respond to questions or to solve problems. They differ from their peers in the rate at which they process sensory information (Curtis & Tallal, 1991). The impairments are perceived to be in the rate of processing as well as slower access to long-term memory for response. This point of view has not been accepted by all researchers, and some seriously question the results (Cucase & McFarland, 1998). These deficits have strong educational relevance, as we explain later in the chapter.

Central Auditory Processing Disorders in the way the brain receives auditory messages, interprets them, and retains them are key to central auditory processing. These disorders can be determined by a series of psycholinguistic tests, and several disability groups, including specific learning disabilities, have been found to have this problem.

Memory Disorders

A deficit in auditory processing affects storage in short-term memory (Curtis & Tallal, 1991). The slower auditory processing doesn't allow enough time for information to be entered into short-term memory. So, much of what is presented to the learner is lost, does not enter short-term memory, and therefore is not transferred to long-term memory (Tallal, Miller, & Fitch, 1993; Vellutino, 1987). The deficit related to learning disabilities appears to occur in semantic memory and affects encoding, cataloging, and recalling information that one has been taught (Interagency Committee, 1990; Mann & Liberman, 1984).

Nonverbal Specific Learning Disabilities Most of the work in this area has been conducted by Rourke (1995). By neurological assessments, he has identified a subpopulation of children whose academic problem range includes tasks of mathematical reasoning, reading comprehension, and complex concept formation (Torgesen, 2002). It is this pattern that distinguishes them from the more typical child with SLD who has problems in learning to read. These children have more difficulty with complex tasks than with ones requiring rote learning.

Attention Deficits and Hyperactivity

It has long been thought that most children with learning disabilities have attention deficits and are easily distracted, impulsive, hyperactive, or poor listeners (Morris, 2002). Some of the professionals who identify children as having learning disabilities prefer to regard the condition as an **attention-deficit hyperactivity disorder (ADHD)** (see Chapter 6). The basic assumption was that attention deficits and **hyperactivity** (impulsivity, acting before thinking, excessive moving about) were the source of the academic problems. Silver (1990) suggested that *learning disability* should be used to describe persons whose brains interfere with their learning, not persons unavailable for learning because of

Several disability groups, including specific learning disabilities, have been found to have central auditory processing deficits.
(© Richard Hutchings/CORBIS)

their increased activity and inattention. There is no conclusive evidence that children with learning disorders are fated to develop antisocial behavior. Rourke (1994) suggests most students with learning disorders appear to achieve adequate behavioral control.

Those who believe that ADHD causes learning problems might agree to use drugs to calm the individual. The most commonly used stimulants are ethylphenidate and mphetamines (Stein, Effron, Schiff, & Glazman, 2002). Although many professionals in the field of learning disabilities object to the use of these drugs, Forness and Kavale (1998) reported positive results in improving academic learning, and Hallahan and Kauffman (1995) found that the effect of these drugs in improving learning is conclusively documented. However, Kavale and Forness (2000) found little support for drug or diet effectiveness with groups of children with learning disabilities. Some believe, however, that the student's failure to learn at the same rate as his or her peers is the source of the behavioral problems.

Academic Achievement Learning Disabilities

Lerner (2000) and Lyon (1999) defined academic achievement learning disabilities to include deficits in school subjects such as listening, speaking, reading, writing, spelling, and mathematics. How to teach these subjects to

ECOLOGY OF THE CHILD

PEERS | **"A Student Helps Other Students with Dyslexia"**

Writer's block was more than a passing problem for Joan Corsiglia. The only way she could write a paper was to cut out each sentence of the laborious first draft, put the sentences on a table like pieces of a jigsaw puzzle and sort them under topics to form coherent paragraphs.

Only when she was a junior at Harvard did she learn why it took her ten times as long as other students to do reading and writing assignments. She had assumed that she was not trying hard enough.

She was diagnosed by tests at the Harvard health office as a dyslexic, one of average or better intelligence who has difficulty learning to read, write and organize language because of abnormal interactions in the brain. But her problems did not stop there. She found that there was no policy of remedial counseling or help, such as untimed exams, for dyslexic students.

"The deans and the tutors congratulated me on my strategies of coping, and the Bureau of Study Skills people told me that my skills were as good as any, but I was concerned that there was no help for students who had the same problems. Two percent of each entering class at Harvard have dyslexia."

The determined student organized a group of students with the same disorder to talk with faculty on what to expect from them and how to accommodate their needs. She turned to the Orton Dyslexia Society for speakers and films about the disorder, which affects some 15 percent of the nation's schoolchildren.

Then, during her senior year at Harvard and while she was preparing for medical school, Corsiglia was tutored by Jeanne Chall, professor of education at the Harvard Graduate School of Education, and one of her students, Martha Freeman.

Now a third-year medical student at Dartmouth, Corsiglia has helped to develop support policies there for dyslexics. More than 150 educators from 20 colleges met at Dartmouth in mid-April for a symposium that she organized on dyslexia and learning disabilities, and many more were turned away for lack of space.

Corsiglia's success at Harvard and Dartmouth in establishing support policies for dyslexics earned her an award from the New England Branch of the Orton Society at a dinner April 25 to raise $200,000 for dyslexia research. Dr. Drake D. Duane of the Mayo Clinic in Minnesota told her that any medical residency program will be lucky to have such a highly motivated person.

She calls herself lucky to have had so much help from her parents, Joseph and Sharon Corsiglia of Darien, Conn., and teachers who gave her confidence to overcome her learning handicaps.

"My father owns his own business, so his hours were flexible," says Corsiglia. "He and my mother took us to historic sites all over New England on three-day weekends so that we could learn history that way, as well as by reading. He had a horrible time in school, and so did my brothers, but they weren't diagnosed as dyslexic until after I was.

"My biggest thing was how do things work and why things are the way they are. I asked a lot of questions in school." Corsiglia says teachers told her that she was careless with her spelling, although she spent hours memorizing words, but they praised her for good ideas and extensive reports that gave her a chance to build models and do creative artwork to supplement her essays. Her mother checked her homework and sent her to the dictionary. "But my biggest problem was getting as far as the first draft of a paper," she says.

In the ninth grade, teacher Joan Burchenal sparked Corsiglia's interest in biology. She and her husband, Dr. Joseph Burchenal, an oncologist, helped Corsiglia build an incubator in her basement for experiments on the effects of chemotherapeutic drugs for leukemia on chick embryos.

Determination and fascination with learning won high marks for Corsiglia and helped get her into Harvard, but, by her junior year, her coping strategies began to break down. There wasn't enough time to do every assignment over and over again.

Carroll Williams, her biology adviser, was helpful in getting a diagnosis because he has a son with the same disorder. He had recognized the discrepancy between her laboratory work and written work, and encouraged her. She worked in his laboratory on her honors thesis on "Hormonal Control of Molting in the Tobacco Hornworm." "He helped me to get back my confidence," she says.

Another mentor was Martha Freeman, a graduate student of Jeanne Chall's at the Harvard School of Education.

Corsiglia talks of the tutoring given by Martha Freeman. "She set me to reading editorials in *The Boston Globe* and the *New York Times* and writing summaries." Corsiglia says, "Then I had to turn my summaries into paraphrases without going back to the originals." Medical papers and literate essays such as those of Dr. Lewis Thomas' "Lives of a Cell" captured her attention during long hours of tutoring.

Sports are an important outlet for Corsiglia. She runs from 3 to 5 miles a day and makes time for varsity cross-country track as well as skiing, basketball, soccer, tennis and golf.

With her record of advocacy for and interest in dyslexia, Corsiglia has been doing research on the anatomical differences between dyslexic and non-dyslexic brains. She has been working with Albert Galaburda, associate professor of neurology at the Harvard Medical School and director of the Orton Society's Dyslexia Neuroanatomical Laboratory at the Beth Israel Hospital. She plans to specialize in neurology and direct her efforts toward research and clinical practice.

"I want to work with patients as well as in the laboratory," she says. "I feel it is terribly important for young people with dyslexia to get help early so that they won't be discouraged from fulfilling their potential."

Source: Phyllis Coons, "A Student Helps Other Dyslexics," *Boston Globe,* June 14, 1987. Reprinted with the permission of The Boston Globe.

WHAT IS THE CONTEXT?

Joan Corsiglia's support system at Harvard included organized advocacy groups like the Orton Society as well as her family and professors. The supportive context promoted the development of alternative methods of learning and evaluation to accommodate her dyslexia. Joan's experience demonstrates the importance of finding an approach to education that is tailored to the particular needs of students with learning disabilities and that focuses on their strengths rather than their weaknesses.

PIVOTAL ISSUES FOR TEACHERS

- Discuss the various methods of learning and evaluation that Joan and her teachers used.

- Why were they effective for Joan?

- How can teachers learn to adapt their teaching to the needs of individual students with learning disabilities?

students with learning disabilities has been the subject of a long debate; there is a growing consensus about how to teach them (Kavale & Forness, 2000).

Language and Reading Disorders

Language disorders is a general term referring to difficulties in listening, speaking, phonological mastery, word recognition, reading, spelling, and writing (see Lyon, 1994, 1999; Okolo, Cavalier, Ferretti, & MacArthur, 2000, for a discussion of each area and its measurement). The most common difficulty identified for children with learning disabilities is mastery of phonological systems, which leads to deficits in reading, spelling, and writing (Cramer & Ellis, 1996; Tallal, Miller, & Fitch, 1993; Torgesen, 1999; Jenkins & O'Connor, 2002; Wise & Snyder, 2002).

About 80 percent of children with learning disabilities have difficulty in word and letter recognition or reading comprehension (Lerner, 2000). Becoming a skilled reader is so important in our culture that an unskilled reader is at a great disadvantage in school and the workplace. The following problems may prevent a child with learning disabilities from learning to read:

▶ Faulty auditory perception without hearing impairment

▶ Slow auditory or visual processing

▶ Inability to distinguish or separate the sounds of spoken words

▶ Lack of knowledge of the purpose of reading

▶ Failure to attend to critical aspects of the word, sentence, or paragraph

▶ Failure to understand that letters represent units of speech (Clark & Urhy, 1995; Curtis & Tallal, 1991; Liberman & Liberman, 1990)

Dyslexia

International Dyslexia Association www.interdys.org

Currently, dyslexia is accepted as a disorder within the learning disability population, and it has been widely studied (Clark & Uhry, 1995; Deshler, Ellis, & Lenz, 1996). The International Dyslexia Association defines **dyslexia** as follows:

> One of several distinct learning disabilities. It is a specific language-based disorder of constitutional origin characterized by difficulties in single word decoding, usually reflecting insufficient phonological processing. These difficulties in single word decoding are often unexpected in relation to age and other cognitivie and academic abilities; they are not the result of generalized developmental disability or sensory impairment. Dyslexia is manifested by variable difficulty with different forms of language, often including, in addition to problems with reading, a conspicuous problem with acquiring proficiency in writing and spelling. (Orton Dyslexia Research Committee, 1994)

The brains of children with dyslexia probably operate differently from those of children without dyslexia.

The major conclusion is that children with **dyslexia** have a variety of deficits resulting from brain dysfunction (that is, the brain is not damaged, but it operates differently from the brain of a child without dyslexia) (Rourke, 1991).

While persons with dyslexia have difficulties in language-based tasks (reading, spelling, writing, and phonological awareness), many have well-developed abilities in visual, spatial, motor, and nonverbal problem solving

(Dickman, 1996; Clark & Uhry, 1995). They do not have mental retardation (Gray & Kavanaugh, 1985).

Despite the enormous problems children with dyslexia face, the general consensus among researchers and teachers is that they can improve (Clark & Uhry, 1995; Deshler, Ellis, & Lenz, 1996). When the diagnosis of dyslexia is made in the first two grades, more than 80 percent of the children are brought up to grade level. However, if it is not made until fifth grade, only 10 to 15 percent are helped (Fletcher & Forman, 1994, p. 187).

It is important to remember that not all children with learning disabilities have dyslexia. The term *dyslexia* is overused in the popular press, which gives the inaccurate impression that everyone with reading or literacy problems is dyslexic.

> Eighty percent of dyslexic children diagnosed in first and second grades are brought up to grade level.

Writing Disorders

Dysgraphia is the inability to perform motor movement or extremely poor handwriting. It is associated with a neurological dysfunction. Agraphia is an acquired disorder in which the ability to write and make patterns is impaired. Writing involves three subprocesses: planning, sentence generation, and revision (Wong, 1999). Other writing problems include difficulty in composing a cohesive story, less complex sentences, fewer types of words, organizing a written composition, or outlining in a logical sequence (Zipprich, 1995).

Spelling Disorders

Many children with language and reading problems are poor spellers. However, that is not always the case; some excellent readers are poor spellers. This finding suggests that the skills involved in spelling and reading may not be connected (Moats, 1994). Moats suggests that prior research has shown spelling to be a complex process that is not simply mechanical. A sign that a child may be learning disabled and not have a learning problem is the ability to read well coupled with poor spelling ability. Spelling may be the most obvious performance deficit for children with a learning disability.

> A sign that a child may be learning disabled is an ability to read well but an inability to spell well.

Mathematics Disorders/Nonverbal Disorders

About one-third of all children identified as having specific learning disabilities have nonverbal disorders neurologically based in the right hemisphere of the brain; they have difficulty with tactile and visual-spatial problems (Morris, 2002). These students perform better when instruction is given verbally (Telzrow & Bonar, 2002). The technical term for mathematical disorders called *dyscalcula* refers to selective impairment in mathematical thinking or in calculation skills (Fleishner, 1994). Often mathematical learning disability occurs without deficits in reading or in other verbal skills.

Deficits in Executive Function or Cognitive Strategies

To be able to learn in the way that schools present as learning, children must master a set of skills known as **executive function, metacognition,** or **cognitive strategies;** these are the internal processes that children use to select, control, and monitor the strategies they use to solve problems or to learn (Torgesen, 1994). They include monitoring one's behavior, planning how to learn, and self-regulation (keeping oneself on task and not becoming distracted). These

PROFILES

DEVELOPMENTAL

Distinguishing students who have learning disabilities from those who have learning problems is not always easy. Individuals in both groups often present similar academic problems. Note that both students have wide intra-individual differences in academic subjects.

Massie: Massie, a fifth grader, had serious academic problems in all areas of the curriculum (see the "Developmental Profiles" graphs about Massie and Yuet). She had occasional outbursts of anger and rarely participated in group activities or outdoor play. The exception was her love of creative dance, in which she excelled.

Discussions with the principal and previous teachers revealed a history of academic failure and a very troubled home life. The parents believed her to have mental retardation in spite of excellent intelligence test scores. Further psychological testing indicated serious emotional problems. A health evaluation determined that she was grossly overweight and nearsighted. Her parents refused to come to school or to allow a home visit to discuss these problems. The psychologist and other evaluators considered Massie maladjusted but not learning disabled. Her learning problems stemmed from environmental issues, not neurological ones.

Developmental Profiles of Two Children

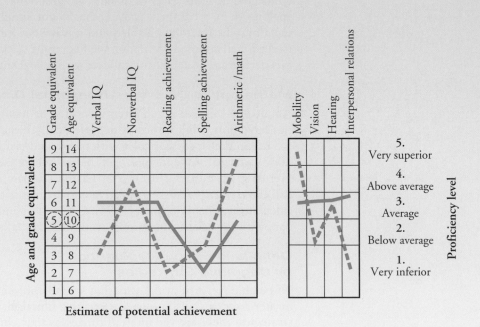

Yuet: Yuet, a fifth-grade student, could read only extremely frequently appearing words such as her name, street signs, and the names of comic strip characters. Yet she was a talented artist and an excellent oral problem solver, and she possessed excellent fine motor skills. Her nonverbal IQ score was well above average, whereas her verbal IQ score was near the range for mental retardation (see the graphs).

Yuet was completely unmotivated to do most classroom work and, if allowed, spent her time drawing masterful three-dimensional pictures to accompany the current social studies lessons. A meeting with her parents revealed that they were as puzzled about Yuet as the teacher was.

The psychologist's report noted superior fine motor skills and suggested that Yuet be taught reading with a nonaural method that took advantage of her visual capacity, using pictures, stories, and a whole-word approach. This nonaural approach was effective with Yuet, and after two years of specialized help in the resource room her reading greatly improved, as did her self-esteem and motivation.

Yuet has a learning disability. The wide difference between her nonverbal IQ and verbal IQ scores is often a sign of the disability. Her superior art work along with her poor reading are other signals of her disability. Yuet probably falls into the subgroup of children with learning disabilities who have damage to their left hemisphere.

strategies are gained from experience, being taught, or learning and are stored in long-term memory. For most adults, they seem automatic. They are the way a person thinks about how to learn. Some children with learning disabilities do not possess or do not use these strategies to solve problems and must be taught them (Denckla, 1994; Stone & Conca, 1993).

Social Problems

Children with SLD are more likely to be accepted poorly, rejected, or ignored by classmates than are their peers without SLD (Tur-Kaspa, 2002). Tur-Kaspa further notes that this relationship persists over time. It is suggested that some children with SLD have poor social skills in relating to others, lower self-esteem, lower self-concepts of their academic abilities, and a poor understanding of what it means to be SLD (Cosden, Brown, & Elliot, 2002). This occurs partly because children with learning disabilities are, by definition, intelligent but have difficulties in learning what the school expects them to learn. This failure, when often repeated, can lead to depression, lack of motivation, oppositional behaviors, and a poor self-concept. These side effects are often interpreted to be part of the syndrome of learning disabilities, but evidence suggests they are not (Rourke, 1994). Children with learning disabilities are likely to attribute their failure to their lack of ability, which lowers their feelings of self-esteem (Stone & Conca, 1993).

Some children with learning disabilities may have mild-to-severe disturbances in socioemotional development, particularly students with nonverbal learning disabilities. They may enjoy verbal interaction but have difficulty in entering into or initiating conversations (Morris, 2002), as well as difficulty in reading environmental and nonverbal social clues. Some children with learning disabilities appear to achieve adequate psychosocial adaptation. There is no uniform pattern of personality characteristics, psychological adaptation, social competence, self-concept, or other indicators of socioemotional functioning (Rourke, 1994).

Seventy percent of students with learning disabilities rate themselves low on academic self-perception but also rate themselves as being as smart as other students (Vaughn & Erlbaum, 1999). These self-perceptions appear to be accurate; that is, they are not doing as well academically and have normal intelligence. These students also rate themselves positively on global self-worth in spite of their academic difficulties.

Teachers can help children with learning disabilities recognize that their academic problems are not due to a lack of effort or intelligence and learn what it means to be learning disabled (Cosden, Brown, & Elliot, 2003). Early intervention and identification of learning disabilities can decrease social deficits.

Many students with learning disabilities have positive feelings of global self-worth.

■ Identification and Assessment

Identifying children with learning disabilities is not easy. First, learning disabilities must be distinguished from other conditions; then the difference between potential and achievement must be evaluated. How large a discrepancy is acceptable? Must a child have an identifiable developmental learning disability that has contributed to educational underachievement? Who makes the decision?

School systems, according to the provisions of PL 94-142 and PL 101-476, are required to assemble a multidisciplinary team of professionals to examine the child psychologically, mentally, socially, and educationally and, with the parents, come to a decision about whether the child is eligible for special education. The identification process that most school systems follow includes several steps.

Identifying Students with Learning Disabilities

1. A teacher or parent refers the child for evaluation.
2. A committee that includes the educational evaluator, the special education teacher, and the parent evaluates the referral to determine whether a multidisciplinary team should assess the child.
3. Once an assessment is approved, parental permission for the assessment is obtained.
4. A multidisciplinary team that includes psychologists, a speech-language pathologist, a neurologist, social workers, the classroom teacher, and the special education teacher conducts the evaluation.
5. Team members hold a conference and decide whether the child is eligible for special education.
6. If the child is eligible, an IEP is formulated, and the child is provided with the appropriate service.

To adequately assess the child with learning disabilities, specific deficits, dysfunctions, or difficulties, skilled personnel are needed to select the appropriate measure, whether it be in the neuropsychological domain or the academic achievement domain. Lyon's book (1994) is a valuable tool for selecting specific measures in all the subtypes of learning disabilities currently identified.

A new model for identifying children with specific learning disabilities is called Response to Instruction (RTI) (Gresham, 2002). The model is defined as a change in behavior in response to a specific teaching instruction. If a student fails to master the skills taught, he or she is considered a candidate. This model has received support and criticism from a large number of research workers (Marston, Muyskens, Lau, & Canter, 2003; Vaughn, Linen-Thompson, & Hickman, 2003; Vaughn & Fuchs, 2003; Scanlon, 2003; Scruggs & Mastropieri, 2003) who argue that RTI does not address all the problems associated with identification and only a comprehensive assessment may avoid overreferrals.

The reason for this RTI approach is that some students fail in school because of poor instruction, while others fail because of personal learning deficits. In order to tell one student from another, intensive positive instruction is applied. If the student still doesn't respond, the assumption is that a learning deficit is present in the student and that different approaches to learning are called for.

As we are noting throughout this book, all assessments and identification procedures with culturally diverse children should be conducted by personnel who are of the same linguistic group or are experienced in working within a particular culture and community. This will serve as a safeguard against differences being identified as disabilities.

Diagnosis

A **differential diagnosis** is used to pinpoint an atypical behavior, explain the behavior, and differentiate it from similar problems of other children with disabilities. A differential diagnosis allows teachers to determine the remedial program best suited to educating the child. Methods of identification and diagnosis are somewhat different for preschool children and school-age children. Preschoolers are identified through developmental discrepancies, or measured strengths and weaknesses in their developmental abilities. School-children are identified through discrepancies between aptitude and expected school achievement.

Educational diagnosis is different from identification of the type of a disability. As a teacher, you will need to know what the academic deficit is and then plan a strategy to remediate it. Achievement tests based on national norms are still the most commonly used and readily available in most school districts. A Curriculum-Based Measurement (Deno, 1985) is a technique in which the assessment is based on what has been taught specifically in the classroom (Fuchs, Fuchs, Hamlett, Phillips, & Bentz, 1994). A newer, comprehensive approach, the Work Sampling System (Meisels, Jablon, Marsden, Dichtelmiller, & Dorfman, 1994), offers guidelines about what to sample of children's classroom work and compares the sample to developmental age norms. These methods avoid the pitfalls of achievement tests that contain items and content that may not have been taught.

Early Intervention

Obviously, the earlier we identify children with learning disabilities, the sooner we can begin intervention programs to help them. More important, if we can identify youngsters who are at risk for learning disabilities, we may be able to prevent those disabilities (Fletcher & Forman, 1994; Wolery, 1992).

Badian (1983, 1988) found that two tests—the information subtest and the sentences subtest of the Wechsler Preschool and Primary Scale of Intelligence— predict with a fairly high degree of accuracy the long-term performance of students in reading. (The information subtest assesses factual knowledge; the sentences subtest assesses the ability to repeat increasingly complex sentences.) Moreover, certain characteristics—troubled birth history, family history of learning disabilities, late order of birth among siblings, delayed speech development, and lower socioeconomic status—differentiate poor readers from good readers (Badian, 1983, 1988).

The identification of learning disabilities in preschool children depends on our being able to observe behavior on age-appropriate tasks. These tasks often involve preacademic readiness skills (cutting with scissors, holding a crayon, sharing an experience with a classmate). Some children have trouble with fine and gross motor development. Others are slow to develop oral language and reasoning abilities. These delays in information processing can affect the child's learning, ability to communicate, and social and emotional adjustment. The most common disorders among preschoolers are delayed language development, poor perceptual-motor skills, and lack of attention.

A potential danger of early assessment of preschool children is that children who do not mature at the same rate as the norms of the assessment instrument may be mislabeled as learning disabled or as having a disability. Many preschoolers who lag in an area of development will catch up by first grade (Lerner, 2000).

Current research suggests that many students' reading difficulties stem from such factors as poor instruction, lack of reading readiness, or cultural differences. For these students, their reading deficits can be ameliorated by intensive reading instruction, particularly in phonological awareness and processing (Adams et al., 1998; Council for Exceptional Children, 1997; Cramer & Ellis, 1996; Lyon, 1995).

In diagnosing preschool children, examiners rely on the observations of parents and teachers, rating scales, informal clinical diagnoses, and norm-referenced and criterion-referenced tests.

Language Disabilities

The most common learning disabilities noted at the preschool level are language disabilities. Measures of phonological awareness such as the Comprehensive Tests of Phonological Processing are very useful (Wagner, Torgesen, & Rashutte, 1999; in Shapiro, Church, & Lewis, 2002). To diagnose a language disability, psychoeducational examiners follow a series of steps:

Diagnosing a Language Disability

1. Obtain a description of the language behavior as observed by the parent, the preschool teacher, or both.
2. Review the medical record to see whether the disability can be explained medically. Is the child deaf or hard of hearing?

Language disabilities are the most common learning disabilities among preschoolers.

3. Study the family situation to determine whether factors in the home contribute to the disability.
4. Using formal and informal tests, examine the child's abilities and disabilities in understanding language, relating things heard to past experiences, and talking.
5. Determine what the child can and cannot do in a specific area. For example, if the child functions well in most areas but does not talk, the next step is to find out if he or she understands language. If the child does not understand oral language, the next step is to find out if he or she can discriminate among words, among phonemes, or among common sounds in the environment.
6. Organize a remedial program that moves the child step by step into areas in which the child could not initially perform.

To identify potential language difficulties early, an assessment of the infant's or young child's *prelinguistic* behaviors must be made. These behaviors before words are spoken include eye contact, mutual gaze, prespeech vocalization, and gesture (Dromi, 1993).

Perceptual-Motor Disabilities

Children with **perceptual-motor disabilities** (also called **nonverbal disabilities**) have difficulty understanding and responding to the meaning of pictures or

(text continues on page 150)

The appropriate instruction is based on the child's individualized needs.
(© Michael Zide)

EDUCATIONAL

CHILDREN WITH LEARNING DISABILITIES

A large group of researchers in the field of learning disabilities have been focusing on the academic problems of children with learning disabilities. Their focus: to analyze what the children must learn and to identify the problems they have in mastering the material. Although this trend has many proponents, there are major differences in recommendations about how to adapt the educational process to help each child.

From an educational point of view, the best help for teachers working with children with learning disabilities is to provide those teachers with tools for identifying the academic and social problems that children with learning disabilities possess and a curriculum with strategies and materials that will help the children use their strengths to overcome their weaknesses (Lerner, 2000).

> Children with learning disabilities require an individualized teaching plan.

■ Adapting the Learning Environment

Where should students with learning disabilities be taught? The answer to this question is subject to lively debate about inclusion. (See Kauffman & Hallahan, 1995; Stainback & Stainback, 1992.) The consensus of fifteen researchers is that the field of special education has moved away from instruction specifically designed for students in need of special education, which was its original purpose. They suggest that there is a need to reaffirm special education's original intent: that it is instruction directed to the individual needs of the child in an environment based on the needs of the child (Bradley, Danielson, & Hallahan, 2002b, p. 794).

Inclusion in Context

> Depending on the teacher's support system, students with learning disabilities can learn as much in a general education class as they can in a special education class.

Several professional organizations argue for full inclusion of all students with disabilities in general education classrooms (see Chapter 11). However, the Division for Learning Disabilities, the National Joint Committee on Learning Disabilities, and the Learning Disability Association of America do not support full inclusion for all students with learning disabilities (Lackaye, 1997). They suggest that while many students with learning disabilities may profit from the general education classroom, others may need alternative instructional environments and teaching strategies that cannot be provided within the context of a general education classroom.

Issues of Achievement

One of the studies supportive of inclusion demonstrated that students with learning disabilities in general education classrooms achieved as much as students with learning disabilities in special classrooms (Affleck, Madge, Adams, & Lowenbrau, 1988). Other studies have not supported inclusion. Zigmond and Baker (1990) reported that students with major learning disabilities did not make progress in academic subjects in regular classrooms. In a further study, Zigmond et al. (1995)

concluded that the achievement outcomes of 40 percent of the students with learning disabilities did not reflect gains. In fact, the students fell further behind. In general, the setting in which special education students are educated has almost no influence. The important factor is what happens in that setting (Kavale & Forness, 2000).

One reason for the failure may be that teachers tend to teach the total class but the student with learning disabilities does not profit from group instruction (Fuchs, Fuchs, Hamlett, Phillips, & Korn, 1995). In general, students with learning disabilities believed the general classroom was better for social reasons but the resource room was better for learning (Kettman et al., 1998). Early childhood and elementary classrooms may be more successful in educating children with learning disabilities, but high school teachers are under greater pressure to cover course content (Schuman et al., 1995), and the culture of the school is content oriented (Tralli et al., 1996). Crockett and Kauffman (1998) and Keogh (1996) recommend tutorials, one-on-one teaching, and specialized instructional arrangements for students with learning disabilities. One model currently regarded as a solution is the collaborative model.

Collaboration and Inclusion

Collaborative team models composed of a general education teacher and a special educator bring together the former's knowledge of content and grade-level expectations with the latter's expertise in strategies and skills designed for the student with learning disabilities (Snell & Janney, 2000).

Successful inclusion requires patience, perseverance, and time. Teachers, both regular and special education, who work in collaborative arrangements need to

Successful collaboration requires good problem-solving and interpersonal skills and knowledge of the goals and vocabulary of all team members.

Listening to a story to be read assists the child with reading difficulties.
(© Elizabeth Crews)

Adaptations for Students with Learning Disabilities in Inclusive Classrooms

GENERAL ADAPTATIONS

APPROACHING THE STUDENTS

Respect students as individuals with differences.
Provide reinforcement and encouragement.
Establish personal relationships with students.
Help students find appropriate ways to deal with feelings.
Communicate with students, the special education teacher, and parents.
Establish expectations for students.

LEARNING ENVIRONMENT

Establish routines appropriate for students.
Adapt classroom management strategies that are effective with students.
Adjust physical arrangement of room for students.

INSTRUCTION

Make adaptations for students when developing long-range plans.
Make adaptations for students when developing daily plans.
Plan assignments and activities that allow students to be successful.
Allot time for teaching learning strategies as well as content.
Monitor the students' understanding of directions and assigned tasks.
Monitor the students' understanding of concepts presented in class.
Provide individual instruction.

MATERIALS

Adapt general classroom materials for students.
Use alternative materials for students.
Use computers to enhance learning as a tool for practicing skills.

GROUPING STUDENTS

Pair each student with a classmate.
Involve students in small-group activities.
Involve students in whole-class activities.

EVALUATION AND ASSESSMENT

Provide extra time for students.
Adapt pacing of instruction.
Keep records to monitor students' progress.
Provide students with ongoing feedback about performance.
Adapt evaluations for students.
Adapt scoring/grading criteria for students.

TEXTBOOK ADAPTATIONS

APPROACHING READING ASSIGNMENTS

Determine students' reading levels to identify students with potential problems with textbooks.
Read textbook aloud to students.
Create interest in reading assignments to motivate students.
Teach reading strategies to improve comprehension of text.
Provide students with questions to guide their reading.
Preview reading assignments with students to orient them to a topic and budget reading and study time.
Substitute or supplement textbook reading assignments with direct experiences.
Provide students with purposes for reading.
Reduce length of assignments.
Introduce key vocabulary before a reading assignment.

VARYING MEDIA AND VISUALS

Use film, videotapes, and recordings to supplement or substitute for textbook reading.
Use computer programs to supplement or substitute for textbook reading.
Use different colors to mark key words, definitions, and important facts throughout textbooks.
Teach students to use graphic aids.
Avoid use of textbooks.
Audiotape textbook content.
Use CD-ROM of textbook.
Use publishers' visual and interactive textbook materials.

ADAPTING TEACHING STRATEGIES

Teach study strategies to improve retention of text material.
Work with students individually or in small groups to master textbook material.
Provide assistance for answering text-based questions.
Structure postreading activities to increase retention of content.
Summarize and reduce textbook information to guide classroom discussions and independent reading.
Demonstrate and model effective reading strategies and comprehension techniques.
Determine level of difficulty of textbooks.
Explain textbook information thoroughly in classroom lectures and presentations.
Pair students to master textbook content.
Construct abridged version of textbook content or use publisher's abridged version.
Develop a study guide or study outline to direct learning from text.
Preview textbook with students to orient them to textbook organization and learning tools.
Place students in cooperative learning groups to master textbook content.
Use multilevel, multimaterial approach.
Teach comprehension-monitoring techniques to improve ongoing understanding of text.

Source: Adapted from J. S. Schumm & S. Vaughn, Getting ready for inclusion: Is the stage set?, *Learning Disabilities Research and Practice 10* (3) (1995): 169–179 (pp. 178, 179). Reprinted with the permission of Lawrence Erlbaum Associates, Inc.

develop clear-cut responsibilities to be effective. When a collaborative team is first established, the members should receive training in small-group interpersonal skills and problem solving and review each other's vocabulary and goals (Wood, 1998).

Supportive Inclusion

Tralli et al. (1996) have proposed a model of **supportive inclusion** for the secondary school. Students with mild learning disabilities are given intensive instruction in strategy learning in the resource room on a daily basis until they achieve mastery. Following mastery of learning strategies, students are then taught content enhancement routines the teacher uses in the classroom. When the students have mastered those skills, they are taught empowerment skills geared to enable them to perform their best, make friends, and interact in positive ways with teachers and peers (Tralli et al., 1996, p. 205).

The success of supportive inclusion depends on the ability of teachers to plan and work collaboratively to support the students with their newly acquired skills. Some individuals with learning disabilities have become very successful, such as President Woodrow Wilson and Governor (and later Vice President) Nelson Rockefeller. For others, although they may have graduated from high school, employment opportunities have been mixed. Recent results show marked gains for persons with learning disabilities, who are employed at nearly equivalent rates as members of the general population (Blackorby & Wagner, 1996). However, many hold jobs that are low paying, for instance, dishwashing, clerking, and working in the fast-food industry. Some need on-site job training or job coaches. IDEA requires that transition services be included in the IEP when the student is 14.

■ Adapting Curriculum

The curriculum for students with learning disabilities is the general school curriculum. The major challenge facing teachers is how to organize and present instruction to students with learning disabilities on the basis of diagnosis and evaluation of their strengths and weaknesses. The teachers' task is to familiarize themselves with the school's required curriculum and to organize it so students with learning disabilities master as much of it as possible. The box on the facing page contains many suggestions on how to adapt the curriculum for students in inclusive classrooms as well as techniques for individualized instruction. Many students with learning disabilities do not profit from large-group instruction (Zigmond, 1997). Rather, small-group instruction has been found to be an effective technique for teaching children with learning disabilities, including children from a variety of cultural and economic backgrounds (Erlbaum, Vaughn, Hughes, Moody, & Schumm, 2000).

> Curriculum for students with learning disabilities is the same as for all non–learning disabled students in the general education classroom.

For some students, one-on-one tutoring is the most appropriate instructional strategy, designed after the evaluation is complete and the IEP has been written. For others, the resource room can provide a person specially prepared to work with students with learning disabilities. In the resource room or general education classroom, augmented communication devices and computers can be useful, but most of them require the student to be able to read and follow directions. Strategy learning (see Pressley et al., 1990) may be required before instructional technology is introduced.

Supportive inclusion consists of mastering learning strategies, content enhancement routines, and empowerment skills to perform well socially.
(© Ellen Senisi/The Image Works)

Learning disabilities articles, e-texts, and resources www.ldresources.com

In junior and senior high schools, some students have not yet mastered the basic skills sufficiently to cope with content subjects. English, mathematics, science, social science, and history require reading, and most of that reading is beyond the ability of youngsters with learning disabilities. These students also continue to have difficulty with tasks that require specific types of information processing. Many of them need the developmental programs that are appropriate for their age. Most schools offer these programs in resource rooms and self-contained special education classrooms.

Another technique is to modify the textbook (Meese, 1997), which can be done by highlighting the basic information to be learned or by recording the textbook. Recordings for the Blind and Dyslexic, 20 Roszel Road, Princeton, NJ 08540 is a valuable source for tapes. However, listening of itself may not be as effective as teaching reading orally. Students will need previews of what they will hear, as well as guiding questions and summaries (Lackaye, 2001).

Adapting Teaching Strategies

The approaches presented here can be adapted to subject matter including mathematics, writing, spelling, and reading or dealing with dyslexia. These techniques can be used in the general classroom, resource room, or special class.

Applied Behavioral Analysis

Applied behavioral analysis (ABA) is frequently called *behaviorism* because it grew out of earlier work on the modification of challenging behaviors and emotional disturbances. Behaviorism is based on the work of Skinner (1953) and has been used widely to control or modify unacceptable behavior in school. The same techniques are used for teaching academic skills and subjects (Trieber & Lahey, 1983). In theory, ABA is concerned with the causes of disorder only insofar as they help teachers to formulate a treatment plan (Tindal & Marston, 1986). The learning programs are based on individual analyses of the child's functioning rather than on the child's assumed biological problems. Before the steps of ABA can be implemented, the task to be learned must be thoroughly analyzed (*task analysis*), and the child's skill and academic strengths and weaknesses must be thoroughly assessed (Trieber & Lahey, 1983).

Koorland (1986) suggested the following steps in ABA:

1. Pinpoint the child's behavior to be targeted for change.

2. Measure the behavior directly and repeatedly.

3. Institute a change in events antecedent and consequent to the behavior (what happens in the environment immediately before and after instruction).

4. Evaluate and record results.

5. Try again if goals are not attained. (Koorland, 1986)

6. If the child is successful, reward or reinforce the success.

7. If the child is successful, increase the demand with additional or more complex tasks.

8. Chart the results of the child's work.

9. Involve the child in identifying target behaviors.

Demonstrating, modeling, and feedback are recommended antecedent and consequent strategies in ABA. The instruction is always direct and focused on the specific fact or skill to be learned. At times, prompting or cueing is used to help the student focus on the task (Koorland, 1986). Direct instruction can be used with individual children or with small groups of children who have similar problems. It has proven to be an effective strategy for students with learning disabilities, particularly in small-group settings, and can be used in inclusive classrooms (Kavale & Forness, 2000). Direct instruction includes the following:

1. Explicit, step-by-step strategy

2. Development of mastery at each step in the process

3. Strategy or process corrections for student errors

4. Gradual fading from teacher-directed activity toward independent work

5. Use of adequate systematic practice with a range of examples

6. Cumulative review of learned concepts (Kavale & Forness, 2000, p. 314).

These techniques are useful with children of all ages and cultural backgrounds who have been identified and diagnosed as learning disabled. They may be delivered in general education/special education teacher consultation; in team

Applied behavioral analysis uses demonstration, modeling, and feedback to teach and reinforce desired behavior.

teaching; while utilizing teacher aides; or in limited pull-out services for individualized instruction.

Programs have been developed to teach students how to multiply and solve word problems (Cramer & Ellis, 1996). In summary, teaching strategy programs fall into two main categories: (1) teaching strategies that can be applied to all content areas and (2) those that apply to specific areas.

Cognitive Strategy Instruction

Teaching strategies are often modified for children with learning disabilities.

The cognitive strategy model (Pressley et al., 1995) is designed to remediate *executive functions, metacognitions,* or *organizational strategies.* The model, which focuses on the teacher's behavior as well as the student's, can be applied to all academic areas and to children with and without learning disabilities. The approach uses many behavioral principles and includes teaching children strategies for approaching learning problems. Psychologists refer to these strategies as *metacognition,* or the ability to think about one's own thinking and monitor its effectiveness. Pressley's overall plan is presented in the box on the following page.

Learning strategies are techniques, principles, or rules that help students learn how to solve problems, complete tasks, self-regulate, and use past learnings (Lackaye, 1997). A learning strategy program teaches the students strategies that can be used in a variety of content areas as well as with specific content; for example, mathematics or reading (Deshler, Ellis, & Lenz, 1996). If the child is not

Teaching Strategies for Increasing Students' Metacognitive Skills

- ▶ Teach a few strategies at a time, intensively and extensively, as part of the ongoing curriculum.
- ▶ Model and explain new strategies.
- ▶ Model again and re-explain strategies in ways that are sensitive to aspects of strategy use that are not well understood.
- ▶ Explain to students where and when to use strategies.
- ▶ Provide plenty of practice, using strategies for as many appropriate tasks as possible.
- ▶ Encourage students to monitor how they are doing when they are using strategies.
- ▶ Encourage continued use of and generalization of strategies.
- ▶ Increase students' motivation to use strategies by heightening students' awareness that they are acquiring valuable skills that are at the heart of competent functioning.
- ▶ Emphasize reflective processing rather than speedy processing; do all possible to eliminate high anxiety in students; encourage students to shield themselves from distraction so they can attend to academic tasks.

Source: From M. Pressley and Associates, *Cognitive Strategy Instruction That Really Improves Children's Academic Performance* (Cambridge, MA: Brookline Books, 1995), p. 18. Reprinted with permission.

successful in the task, the strategy may have to be repeated. It may also be advisable to reconsider and perhaps modify the behaviors of the teacher, change the setting of the learning, or change the nature of the reinforcement (to ensure that it is rewarding).

The cognitive strategy model approach can be applied to all subject areas from elementary to high school. It emphasizes self-monitoring by the teacher and the student. Facts, skills, and strategies may be taught in tutoring sessions, through peer teaching, or in small groups. The teacher may use prompts such as pictures of a word or of the idea of a story, object aids for counting or understanding fractions, or the actual object when introducing a word such as *ball*.

There are several other models for teaching strategies to help students learn new materials and integrate new information with what was previously taught (Sturomski, 1997). DEFENDS (a writing strategy) (Deshler, Ellis, & Lenz, 1996) reads as follows:

- ▶ Decide on audience, goals, and position.
- ▶ Estimate main ideas and details.
- ▶ Figure best order of main ideas and details.
- ▶ Express the position in the opening.
- ▶ Note each main idea and supporting points.
- ▶ Drive home the message in the last sentence.
- ▶ Search for errors and correct.

Other strategies include questioning and paraphrasing, reciprocal teaching, questioning to find the main idea, and story mapping (NICHCY, 1997). An approach that is supported by research evidence is the Strategies Intervention Model (SIM) (Deshler, Ellis, & Lenz, 1996). First, the teacher selects a strategy or strategies to be taught, then follows these steps:

Strategies Intervention Model

1. Pretest students and get them interested in learning the strategy.

2. Describe the strategy and give examples of ways it can be used.

3. Model the strategy; for example, talking aloud as one works on a real task.

4. Practice the strategy; have the student think aloud.

5. Provide feedback.

6. Provide generalization; show how the strategy can be applied to a different problem.

Guided practice and generalizing the strategies to new problems and different contexts assist the student with learning disabilities in mastering and using the strategy independently (Sturomski, 1997). Note that Swanson (1999) found that both the ABA model and the Strategies Intervention Model were effective in improving reading skills. However, when they were used in combination—that is, "top down and bottom up"—it produced a greater effect (Scruggs & Mastropieri, 2003).

Mnemonic Devices

A mnemonic device is a very effective teaching strategy (Kavale & Forness, 2000). It is a technique for putting difficult-to-remember facts into an accessible form; that is, a device or rhyme that helps people to remember words or concepts. One simple example is this mnemonic sentence that helps us remember the planets in order of distance from the sun: Mary's (Mercury) violet (Venus) eyes (Earth) make (Mars) John (Jupiter) sit (Saturn) up (Uranus) nights (Neptune) period (Pluto). More sophisticated examples can be found in Snowman and Biehler (2000).

Cooperative Learning

In cooperative learning, students of all levels of ability work together to solve a problem.

Cooperative learning is a teaching strategy that involves students of varying ability levels working together to solve a problem. The students may ask the teacher for help if necessary, but for the most part the group works on the problem without the teacher. When used appropriately, cooperative learning has positive results. Students with difficulties are assisted by others who have mastered the skills needed to solve the problem; those students in turn have their understanding of the problem reinforced by helping others in the group.

Another form of cooperative learning is **peer tutoring,** in which a capable student works with a student who needs help on a specific topic. The success of peer tutoring depends on balanced interaction between the tutor and the student, with the tutor teaching, rather than telling, the student what to do. Care should be taken with peer teaching. Many students with learning disabilities have difficulty understanding new concepts, to the frustration of themselves and their peers in these cooperative settings. This can lead to further social rejection of the student with a learning disability.

Mastery Learning

Mastery learning was developed in the educational reform movement of the 1960s. It is a combination of ideas of Bloom (1985), Gagne (1985), and others. The basic concept is to begin instruction at the student's current level of functioning and to break the instructional tasks into learnable units based on the individual student. In addition, continuous evaluation of the student's progress is conducted, and students proceed at their own learning rate. Guskey, Passaro, and Wheeler (1997) suggest that by applying mastery learning strategies in general education classrooms, teachers can effectively deal with the larger range of achievement levels inclusion presents to them.

> Mastery learning breaks instruction into learnable units at each individual's level.

Cognitive Instruction

Other approaches for teaching students with learning disabilities are based on cognitive (information-processing strategies) and cognitive-learning theory (a combination of ABA and cognitive principles). The distinction between ABA and cognitive approaches is becoming blurred because they use similar techniques. The major difference is that cognitive approaches rely more on theories of how children process information, along with direct and indirect teaching.

Wong (1986) emphasized that all cognitive approaches attempt to have the child with learning disabilities become aware of his or her own learning processes. Thus, in learning how to read, the child first focuses on the knowledge that words have meaning, that they are made of letters that stand for sounds, and that the sounds are part of the child's auditory system. Cognitive approaches combine knowledge of letter recognition, phonemes, syntax, word knowledge, and strategies for abstracting meaning from the printed page (metacognition) (Baker & Brown, 1984; Short & Ryan, 1984). Wong (1986) suggested that basic knowledge of four cognitive strategies aids reading:

▶ Awareness of the purpose of reading

▶ Knowledge of reading strategies

▶ Self-monitoring comprehension

▶ Spontaneous looking back while reading (Wong, 1986, p. 21)

Teaching cognitive strategies has been popular with both cognitive and behaviorally oriented curriculum planners. One major project (Kline, Deshler, & Schumaker, 1991) teaches educators how to teach the strategies and also presents a curriculum for teaching students with learning disabilities.

Learning how to learn has long been a goal of modern education because it provides students with the ability to be lifelong learners. Many students without disabilities acquire these strategies quickly; for students with learning disabilities, the teaching has to be more direct, explicit, repetitive, and in smaller steps (NICHCY, 1997). Students with learning disabilities usually need daily and sustained instruction and multiple opportunities for practice (Swanson, 2000).

Approaches to Content Instruction

Preschool Curriculum Preschool curriculum for those at risk for learning disabilities is not too different from the regular preschool curriculum. The major difference is the mode of presentation, which focuses directly, in a supportive manner, on the child's strengths as well as on deficits, allowing the child ample time to engage in the tasks. The tasks may need frequent repetition and review for the child with potential learning disabilities. Tasks include the following (see Lerner, 2000, for other ideas):

▶ *Gross motor:* walking forward, backward, and sideways; line walks

▶ *Fine motor:* cutting, pasting, buttoning, tracing, throwing, and assembling puzzles

▶ *Communication:* listening, talking, explaining, rhyming, and engaging others

▶ *Visual:* recognizing similarities and differences in pictures, objects, shapes, and letters

▶ *Auditory:* phonological awareness, word games, rhyming games

▶ *Cognitive:* learning relationships and differences; classifying objects by use, color, and shape

▶ *Social:* communication with peers and adults, sharing, turn taking, cooperative play

Recordings for Blind and Dyslexic in Princeton, NJ, offers recorded texts that can be supplemented with previews and summaries of the material.

Reading A child first learning to read matches his or her own auditory sound system to an abstract system of print. In English, the twenty-six letters of the alphabet are abstract symbols of a sound system consisting of consonants and vowels. The vowels (*a, e, i, o, u,* and sometimes *y*) combine with the consonants to make up forty-eight *phonemes,* the smallest units of sound meaning. Thus, reading is a recognition of phonemes, leading to phonemic awareness in spoken words as a sequence of sounds, phonemic blending to make a word (*b a t* to *bat*) and phonemic segmentation to separate sounds within a word (*bat* to *b-a-t*) (Newman, Copple, & Bredekamp, 2001).

To read, a child must have a rich store of auditorially perceived words that have meaning, such as knowing that a bat can be either a flying rodent or a stick used in baseball. The child must next break the abstract code. Although words contain letters, it is not knowing the alphabet in sequence that helps in reading, but understanding the relationship of the letters as phonemes and being able to decode (figure out the sound the letter stands for) and blend the letters into words (Liberman & Shankweiler, 1985; Torgesen & Wagner, 1998). Deficit in phonology appears to be the major problem causing children with learning disabilities to fail in reading (Lyon, 1996).

Ehri (1998) and Torgesen (1999) emphasize that understanding the alphabetic principle and the grapheme-phoneme correspondence are necessary and critical components of skilled reading. Skilled readers will process every word and letter in the text as they read. Thus, those children who do not understand the written and oral equivalents of letters will have difficulty in learning to read. These students will profit from phonetic training reading-strategy instruction (Wong, 1999).

Approaches to teaching reading to students with learning disabilities are based on one of three philosophies of how children learn to read: bottom-up, top-down, and interactive. The *bottom-up approach* attempts to teach children phonics, letter-sounds combinations, and isolated words, and then how to use those skills to decode text. The *top-down approach* uses the child's prior knowledge and experience to construct meaning from a text. Programs that use whole-language or literature-based methods are examples of the top-down philosophy, which emphasizes that meaning and understanding can be generated only from within the reader in the context of working with real literature. The *interactive approach* combines the top-down and bottom-up philosophies, which appears to be most effective. The student might be encouraged to use top-down strategies when the text is familiar and bottom-up strategies when the text is unfamiliar (Mercer, 1992, p. 501).

Many schools use basal readers in reading instruction. Basal readers are prepared by grade level and provide material for the development and practice of reading skills and reading comprehension. Stories are selected that will appeal to the child and introduce skills in a sequential fashion. There usually is a teacher's manual for each grade that contains suggestions on how to present the story. Basal readers generally take an interactive approach; however, some series introduce bottom-up activities earlier than others.

Most basal readers suggest a *directed teaching approach;* the teacher introduces new words contained in the story, motivates children to read by telling them what kind of story it is (fairy tale, mystery, and so on), and lets them know in advance what to look for in the story. Students read silently, sometimes reading the story aloud after reading it silently. The teacher questions them about the content of the story and plans follow-up activities.

For students with learning disabilities, any of these approaches may need to be used with one-to-one or small-group instruction so the teacher can identify a student's learning style and the particular difficulties the student is experiencing.

Research-supported critical factors in the teaching of reading and other academic subjects include the following:

▶ Control of task difficulty

▶ Instruction in small interactive groups of six students or less

▶ Direct-response questions: procedures that promote thinking aloud (Vaughn, Gersten, & Chard, 2000)

Many techniques have been used to teach children with dyslexia to read: tracing over letters, using the sense of touch, showing pictures along with the word, using toys along with the word, and using a general language enrichment program. Persons with dyslexia usually have deficits in the ability to process information into language or cognitive systems. Some teachers rely on tape recordings of books. After the tape has been played, the teacher asks the child a series of oral questions about its content. If the child has major problems with audition as well as dyslexia, however, this method may not work. Teachers need to try different approaches to determine which works best with the individual student.

The Internet-Expanded Writing Process

WRITING PROCESS PHASES	TYPICAL ACTIVITIES	INTERNET ACTIVITIES
Prewriting	▶ Brainstorming ▶ Outlining ▶ Clustering ▶ Collecting information	▶ Keyword searches ▶ Browsing ▶ Downloading information
Writing	▶ Series of drafts	
Revision	▶ Peer response ▶ Teacher response ▶ Editing ▶ Revision	▶ E-mail drafts to other kids for response ▶ E-mail drafts to experts for response ▶ Final draft reviewed for possible hypertext links to other WWW sites ▶ Additional searches made for possible links ▶ Story is pasted into a WWW creation program ▶ Hypertext links added
Publishing	▶ Final drafts ▶ Bound into a book ▶ Can be read by others in class ▶ Parents can read it	▶ Story file is transferred to a classroom WWW site on a networked computer ▶ URL address is established ▶ The story WWW page is registered with search page, Yahooligans!, for international access

Source: Adapted from S. Smith, R. Boone, & K. Higgins, Expanding the writing process to the Web, *Teaching Exceptional Children,* *30*(5) (1998): 25. Copyright © 1998 by The Council for Exceptional Children. Reprinted with permission.

Spelling and Writing Spelling is a more difficult skill to master than reading, because there are no clues, such as context, to help students spell (Lerner, 2000). In addition, the English language contains many exceptions (for example, *tough, through, thorough*) to orderly phonetic rules, and each exception must be taught separately. Word processors with spell checks are invaluable for students with spelling difficulties. Remember that the resource the child uses to achieve the correct spelling is not as important as the fact that the child was able to select an appropriate source and solve the problem (this is equally true in mathematics and other subjects).

Using the spell check on the computer is a legitimate way to circumvent problems with spelling.

If a motor writing problem is also present, the teacher may ask an occupational therapist for techniques to help the child hold and control the pencil as well as techniques to make writing legible.

The student who has difficulty in composing a story needs to be taught the strategies for composition: planning what is to be written, making an outline of the story's sequence, considering the parts of the story. Discussing the story with the teacher or the tutor before writing may aid the student in avoiding sparse, uninteresting one-paragraph compositions. See the box above, which is available on the World Wide Web (Smith, Boone & Higgins, 1998).

Mathematics Students receive higher results in mathematics when they understand its basic principles. For example, subtraction represents a difference, not just simply a take-away approach (ERIC/OSEP, 2002). Most children with math learning disabilities profit from working with basic counting, matching, and measuring activities with real objects. Tongue depressors, small discs, and water pitchers are useful objects. Repeated counting to obtain the correct numerical sequence is basic. Recognizing how many objects are present without having to count them is a good exercise. Most arithmetic manipulatives help students gain a firm foundation for later arithmetic operations. Once children have learned the basic signs of the four basic arithmetic operations, a simple calculator can be useful to assist them in accomplishing the calculations needed to solve mathematical concepts (Lerner, 2000).

Children with reading problems may need to have word problems read to them. This can be easily accomplished by a peer or in a cooperative learning group.

Adapting Technology

See the Houghton Mifflin Teacher Education website for an expanded list of assistive technology equipment.

> Houghton Mifflin Teacher Education website
> http://education.college.hmco.com/students

Although there are many software programs designed for students with disabilities, some students with learning disabilities have difficulty learning how to use the computer. Many are not trained. Tony is a case in point. Like many students with learning disabilities, he repeated one grade in high school and dropped out before graduating. He successfully completed a training program and secured a job as a skilled mechanic. His success brought difficulty because his employer upgraded him to a position that required the use of a computer. Rather than fail, Tony quit his job and took a lower-paying position that did not require sophisticated skills. Wong (1998) reports that many women on welfare have previously undiagnosed learning disabilities and are untrained and thus unable to meet the demands under many current work-welfare programs. As technology increasingly dominates the workplace, instruction designed to assist students with learning disabilities to acquire computer skills is essential.

> The quality of the software programs is related to positive results with students.

Given that students are trained to use the computer, a large number of software programs are available to enhance literacy skills (Okolo, Cavalier, Ferretti, & MacArthur, 2000) including phonological awareness, rapid word recognition, fluent word processing, and comprehension in text (Lesar, 1998). It is the quality of the software, not the computer, that is related positively to student gains.

Multimedia instruction is a computer-based environment that utilizes graphics, motion video text, and sound. These programs stress basic skills and mastery learning. Other software is available—and has been proliferating—for direct instruction, writing, reading comprehension, and study skills (Wissich & Gardner, 2000).

Dictionaries, thesauruses, encyclopedias, and programs with grammar checks and spell checks are available to assist students in reading, writing, and other academic areas (Skinner, Gillespie, & Balkam, 1997). Comprehensive database resource directories offer over 20,000 different instructional devices and software products (Castellani & Jeffs, 2001).

> Comprehensive database resource directories
> www.abledata.com
> www.closingthegap.com

(text continues from page 135)

numbers. In diagnosing perceptual-motor disabilities in a preschooler, psychoeducational examiners ask the usual questions about medical and home background, and through ratings, interviews, and formal tests they try to discover the contributing factors and areas in which the child experiences major difficulties. In the process, examiners try to answer several questions:

▶ Can the child interpret the environment and the significance of what he or she sees?

▶ Can the child match shapes and colors?

▶ Can the child recognize visual objects and pictures rapidly?

▶ Can the child assemble puzzles?

▶ Can the child express ideas in motor (nonverbal) terms through gestures and drawings?

Attention Disorders and Other Disabilities

Examiners use observation and formal and informal tests to diagnose attention disorders as well as other disorders. They are trying to answer these kinds of questions:

▶ Can the child sustain attention to auditory or visual stimuli?

▶ Is the child easily distracted?

▶ Does the child persevere in the face of difficulty or initial failure?

▶ Can the child discriminate between two pictures or objects (visual discrimination), between two words or sounds (auditory discrimination), or between two objects felt or touched (haptic discrimination)?

▶ Is the child oriented in space? Does he or she have right-left discrimination?

▶ Can the child remember immediately what was heard, seen, or felt?

▶ Can the child imitate the examiner orally or with gestures? Can the child mimic?

▶ Does the child have adequate visual-motor coordination? Is the child clumsy?

■ Transition

Transition to the workplace may require a job coach and job training.

National Adult Literacy and
Learning Disabilities Center
www.nifl.gov

Individuals with learning disabilities have their disabilities throughout their lives. The U.S. Vocational and Rehabilitation Department has developed programs on the national and local levels to assist persons with learning disabilities in making a successful transition from school to work.

One effort to assist persons with severe and profound disabilities is *supportive employment*. Supportive employment places the individual in an actual work setting and provides a supervisor to assist in mastery of the required tasks. As the person masters the tasks, coaching is diminished, and the supervisor gradually is removed but may remain available for counseling and emotional support. Supportive employment grants pay for this on-the-job preparation and for the supervisor's time. Although strategies vary, most of these programs have a common goal: to enable the person with learning disabilities to be independent and self-supporting. Bear in mind that persons with learning disabilities vary greatly in skill performance. Some function quite adequately; others need a great deal of help.

With students whose learning disabilities are severe, a variety of strategies are used: peer tutoring, functional skills development (at the work site), counseling about social skills (how to dress, how to talk to coworkers and supervisors), and counseling about good work habits (low absenteeism, punctuality).

Students with learning disabilities make up the majority of students with disabilities in American colleges. These students will need direct transitional strategies instruction when entering college, as mandated by Public Law 504. Students with learning disabilities will succeed best in colleges that offer special advisement, tutoring, and personal and academic counseling.

> Information about post–high school training for adults with disabilities
> www.nichcy.org/transitn.asp

■ Diversity

Students with learning disabilities make up the larger percentage of students in special education. Students with learning disabilities from diverse cultures may have parents who find it difficult to accept the disability. They might perceive the child's school failure as a lack of effort on the child's part. Teachers must become sensitive to the verbal and nonverbal styles of the parents if they are to succeed in communicating their concerns for the child. In addition, in diagnosing students from different cultural groups, caution must be exercised to ensure that a nonverbal communication style preferred by the parents and taught to the children is not mistaken for a disability (Banks, 1994).

Language may also present a problem, particularly when translators of a particular dialect (such as a Mexican, Puerto Rican, or South American variant of Spanish) are not available. Many Hispanic parents are dissatisfied with the services they and their children receive (Bailey, Skinner, Rodríguez, Gut, & Correa, 1999).

Successful progams design teaching, learning, and schooling in a social context and construct a culturally compatible approach with very successful results. These should serve as models for other cultures (Tharp & Gillmore, 1988; Comer, Haynes, & Joyner, 1999).

■ Family and Lifespan Issues

> Families need to be informed that the child's problems are not due to lack of effort.

The parents of a person with severe learning disabilities are constantly challenged to make adjustments. They must consider their own needs as well as the special needs of their child, needs that change as the child moves into adolescence and adulthood. Some people with learning disabilities may continue to live in their parents' home until early middle age (National Institute for Health, 2003), while others go on to independent living.

Parents play an integral part in any plan to assist their child with learning disabilities. At times, parents and other family members need help to become fully empowered to make decisions for themselves. O'Hara and Levy (1987) suggested the questions listed in Table 4.1 to help practitioners determine how parents can best assist the student to function independently.

TABLE 4.1
For the Practitioner: How Can You Best Assist Parents of Children with Learning Disabilities?

▶ How do parents describe their child? Do they use primarily positive or negative terms?

▶ What is their statement of the problem?

▶ What do parents expect from professionals? Remediation or cure?

▶ What do parents understand about the cause of the problem? Do they think it is their fault their child is learning disabled? The fault of one parent? Is it genetically linked? Are the parents blaming each other? Are they blaming professionals?

▶ What do parents understand about the child's ability to influence the problem?

▶ What diagnostic information have they heard previously?

▶ What is their understanding of learning disabilities?

▶ What is their perception of their own relationship to the ongoing nature of the problem? To what extent do they believe they can influence the course of the disability? How have they tried in the past to influence the situation?

▶ What has their experience been with other persons presenting problems similar to those of their child?

▶ What is the parents' assessment of how this problem affects their lives?

▶ How do they regard previous experiences associated with this problem? What was it like for them to take this child for diagnostic testing? Was their pediatrician supportive? What was diagnostic counseling like for them? How was the information presented? Were both parents present for the informing session? Were they able to support one another? What have their experiences been like with the school system thus far?

▶ What are their expectations for their own performances in relation to the problem?

▶ How do the parents feel about this situation? Are they angry or sad? Are they able to express any feelings at all?

Source: Adapted from D. O'Hara & J. Levy, Family intervention, in K. Kavale, S. Forness, & M. Bender (Eds.), *Handbook of Learning Disabilities* (Boston: College-Hill, 1987), p. 215. Reprinted by permission of the author.

Families must be intimately involved in every aspect of the life of the child with a disability, from diagnosis and intervention programs to transitional services, not only because of the law's requirements but because the family is key to the child's success. This is particularly true of families with children with learning disabilities. These children do not function as other children do, and they confuse the family. Too often the child is seen as lazy, not working hard enough, or resistant to instruction. From the earliest days of the child's life, children with learning disabilities tend to be less consistent, less flexible, unpredictable, and prone to temper outbursts (Breske, 1994).

The quality of the child-parent transactions, the extent to which the family provides diverse activities, influences the child's progress. Families of children with learning disabilities are at risk themselves if they lack social support and are undergoing stress due to having a child with disabilities. They may fall into the trap of teaching by being more "demanding" than "interacting" and using meaningless drills rather than *transacting* (taking turns in conversation, for example).

Harbin (1993) pointed out that families with children with disabilities have an ever-changing source of stress that affects the entire family. For children with learning disabilities, the struggle can be, and usually is, lifelong. Parents may feel guilty that they have genetically passed on the disability. However, families are unique and may display amazing strengths as well as needs. Many recognize that their children with learning disabilities need to be taught strategies (executive functions) for learning as well as information and facts. Families are key to convincing their children with learning disabilities that they are not "stupid" or "lazy," and families need to find ways to motivate their children to persist in the face of academic failure.

Teachers working closely with families can develop an individualized learning program appropriate for the child. Teachers can do much to help families use the appropriate teaching strategy for the particular child. At times, this may require a revision of the family's child-rearing techniques; at other times, it may require a reinforcement of the effective techniques the family has been using. Regardless, transaction occurs in four areas: (1) teacher-family, (2) teacher-child, (3) family-child, and (4) parent-teacher. Each influences the other as progress is made. The task, as Heinicke (1993) suggested, is to consolidate a helping working relationship in three areas: (1) encouraging communication, (2) providing mutual support, and (3) revising and evaluating child instruction and progress.

There is a particular distinction between families of children with learning disabilities and families of children with other disabilities. Learning disabilities are diagnosed later in life, and the child may exhibit emotional problems growing out of difficulties in learning that occur before his or her condition is known (O'Hara & Levy, 1987). The family's way of life may therefore have to be altered once the diagnosis is made, and the change can disrupt the functioning of the family and its flow of development. Whereas the family of a child with other kinds of disabilities usually has to make changes early in the child's life, the family of a child with learning disabilities has to make changes much later.

Summary

▶ Although the cause or causes of learning disabilities are largely unknown, the most commonly accepted cause is a dysfunction in processing information at the neurological level (not damage to the system).

▶ Accurate diagnosis of a student with a learning disability who has academic deficiency is key to planning appropriate instructional remediation.

▶ In most cases, a student with a learning disability will need, regardless of instructional setting, individual, tutorial, peer, or cooperative instruction to become academically successful.

▶ A student with a learning disability can be integrated best in general education class settings in the areas of his or her competence.

▶ All students with learning disabilities require a full range of support for their disability as well as instruction designed to utilize their strengths to resolve their academic deficits.

▶ Transitional programs are needed for persons with moderate-to-severe learning disabilities.

▶ Persons with learning disabilities face a lifelong problem, because the deficits are at the neurological processing level, and dysfunction will continue throughout the lifespan.

Future Challenges

1. How will learning disabilities be defined and will the causes be discovered?

The definition of *learning disabilities* is not uniform across the country. Some states may include children with mild mental retardation in this group, thereby inflating the prevalence figure.

2. Can early intervention be established?

Techniques have not been fully developed for the early identification of individuals with learning disabilities. At present, we do not know if the development of deficits associated with learning disabilities can be prevented early in life. For effective intervention, attention must be given to indications of potential problems during the earliest stages of the brain's plasticity.

3. What transition programs are needed?

There is a need for more programs throughout the United States to help individuals with learning disabilities make the transition from high school to work or college.

4. What is the range of inclusive options?

There is strong debate as to the appropriate instructional setting for students with learning disabilities. Some argue for full inclusion in the general education classroom. Others suggest partial inclusion with remedial instruction in the resource room. For some, individualized tutoring is deemed advisable. For others, the special class is still maintained in some settings. There is no consensus on where to most effectively educate students with learning disabilities.

5. How can shortages of personnel and funding be addressed?

Students with learning disabilities are a heterogenous group with a wide range of individual needs. For schools to provide the multiple range of services for individual students strains financial resources.

In addition, there are shortages in available trained personnel.

Key Terms

academic achievement learning disabilities *p. 122*

applied behavioral analysis (ABA) *p. 141*

aptitude-achievement discrepancy *p. 117*

attention-deficit hyperactivity disorder (ADHD) *p. 124*

cognitive strategies *p. 129*

collaborative team models *p. 137*

cooperative learning *p. 144*

developmental learning disabilities *p. 122*

differential diagnosis *p. 133*

dyslexia *p. 128*

executive function *p. 129*

hyperactivity *p. 124*

metacognition *p. 129*

neuropsychological learning disabilities *p. 122*

nonverbal disabilities *p. 135*

peer tutoring *p. 144*

perceptual-motor disabilities *p. 135*

specific learning disabilities *p. 117*

supportive inclusion *p. 139*

Resources

References of Special Interest

Adelman, H., & Taylor, L. (1993). *Learning problems and learning disabilities.* Pacific Grove, CA: Brooks/Cole. *The authors distinguish between students with learning problems and those with learning disabilities. This comprehensive text is a rich source of instructional techniques and intervention strategies.*

Bradley, R., Danielson, L., & Hallahan, D. (Eds.). (2002). *Identification of learning disabilities: Research to practice.* Mahwah, NJ: Lawrence Erlbaum Associates. *This text contains a series of nine research papers dealing with reform issues for LD identification and treatment and were sponsored by the U.S. Department of Education Office of Special Education Programs.*

Clark, D. B., & Uhry, J. (1995). *Dyslexia: Theory and practice of remedial instruction.* Parkton, MD: York Press. *The author presents a comprehensive view of dyslexia and the designing of educational strategies to assist dyslexic individuals.*

Deshler, D., Ellis, E., & Lenz, B. (1998). *Teaching adolescents with learning disabilities: Strategies and methods.* Denver, CO: Love Publishing. *A valuable text rich with suggestions and methods for working with adolescents with learning disabilities.*

Hallahan, D., Kaufman, J., & Lloyd, J. (1999). *Introduction to learning disabilities.* Boston: Allyn & Bacon. *An excellent text full of research findings, inclusive models, and teaching strategies.*

Journal of Learning Disabilities (Nov/Dec 2001). "Neurology and Genetics of Learning and Disorders," *34*(6), 489–584. *This issue is devoted to discussion, research, and viewpoints of our current understandings of learning disabilities. It is recommended for its discussion of current issues.*

Lerner, J. L. (2000). Learning disabilities: Theories, diagnosis and teaching strategies (8th ed.). Boston: Houghton Mifflin Company. *This text is a comprehensive introduction in the teaching of students with learning disabilities. Its balanced coverage of theory and practice has made it a standard in its field.*

Lyon, G. R. (Ed.). (1993). *Understanding learning disabilities.* Baltimore: Paul H. Brookes. *This book is an exploration of the theories and implications of practice for persons with learning disabilities.*

Pressley, M., & Associates. (1995). *Cognitive strategy instruction.* Cambridge, MA: Brookline Books. *This is an excellent source of strategies for teachers and students and of ways to design and conduct instruction for all children.*

Rourke, B. P. (Ed.). (1995). *Syndrome of non-verbal learning disabilities.* New York: Guilford Press. *The writings in this collection constitute a comprehensive overview of subtypes of learning disabilities whose assets and deficits have predictable academic outcomes.*

Siegel, L. M. (2004). *Nolo's IEP guide: Learning disabilities.* Berkeley, CA: Nolo. *The author, an attorney, provides a comprehensive and useful guide specifically designed to help parents of students with learning disabilities understand their child's rights, identify learning needs, prepare for meetings, develop IEPs, and resolve disputes.*

Special Issue of *Journal of Learning Disabilities—Neurology and the Genetics of Learning: Related Traits and Disorders.* November/December 2001, *34*(6). *This issue contains the latest information available on the role played by genetics in the development of learning disabilities. The articles focus upon dyslexia and reading and language abilities and presents compelling evidence for the linkage of various genetic characteristics and the problems of children in learning.*

E. Swanson, Harris, K., & Graham, S. (Eds.). (2003). *Handbook of learning disabilities,* New York: Guilford Press. *This volume is a collection of expert opinions on the various aspects of learning disabilities, including psychological neurological, sociocultural, and education issues. The critical analysis of the research, the synethesis of what is known, and the evaluation of what we still need to know make this volume a valuable asset regardless of your own approach to learning disabilities.*

Wong, B. Y. L. (1998). *The ABC's of learning disabilities.* San Diego, CA: Academic Press. *A concise summary of the research, teaching, methodologies, and issues in the field of learning disabilities. This book is an excellent combination of research findings and practical applications.*

Journals

Annals of Dyslexia
 www.interdys.org/serlet/bookstore?section-annalsofdyslexia

Journal of Learning Disabilities
 www.sagepub.co.uk

Professional Organizations

International Dyslexia Association (formerly Orton)
 www.interdys.org

Learning Disabilities Association (LDA)
 www.ldanatl.org

National Center for Learning Disabilities
 www.ncld.org

Please visit the book's website at **http://education.college.hmco.com/students** for new and updated information on websites listed here and for the mailing addresses of the journals and organizations.

5 CHILDREN WITH MENTAL RETARDATION AND DEVELOPMENTAL DISABILITIES

FOCUS QUESTIONS

▶ How do educators define mental retardation and developmental disabilities?

▶ How has inclusion influenced the education of children with mental retardation or developmental disabilities?

▶ How can teachers prepare students with mental retardation or developmental disabilities to function in the workplace?

▶ How has the standards movement influenced children with mental retardation or developmental disabilities?

▶ What assistive and instructional technology is available for supporting students with mental retardation or developmental disabilities?

▶ How do we help families cope with the presence of a child with mental retardation or developmental disabilities?

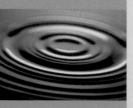

Awareness of the existence of children with mental retardation or developmental disabilities has been present for centuries, but the exact nature of the condition, its identification, and societal attitudes toward it have been constantly changing. Above all, we are trying to discover what can be done educationally for children and youth with the condition.

Maria and Diego Cortez have been worried about Ruiz, their eight-year-old son, who is slow in school. Now the school principal is talking about "developmental disabilities" and the need to provide Ruiz with special instruction. Though Maria had noticed that Ruiz was developing more slowly than his brothers and sisters, she had thought that would straighten out in time. How will Ruiz adapt to present-day complex society, and who will help him?

Organized attempts to help children who learn slowly began less than two hundred years ago, when Jean Itard, a French physician, tried to educate a young boy who had lived by himself in the woods—the so-called Wild Boy of Aveyron. Although Itard failed to achieve all his objectives, one of his students, Edward Seguin, later developed Itard's approaches and became an acknowledged leader of the movement to help children and adults with mental retardation.

Over the years, the care and education of children with mental retardation have moved gradually from large state institutions to the public schools and within the schools to the least restrictive environment.

One other person worth noting is Maria Montessori (1912), who worked with retarded children in the physiological tradition, using what is now called *sense training.* Her work was so successful that her teachings were applied to the teaching of young normal children. Today she is best known for her educational play materials and methods, even though her original work was with children who had mental retardation.

■ Definition

Definitions of what constitutes mental retardation and developmental disabilities (MR/DD) are not cast in concrete. As we learn more about a condition and its treatment, we modify the way we refer to it and to the individuals the condition affects.

Over the past decades, emphasis in the diagnosis of mental retardation and developmental disabilities has shifted from strictly a measurement of cognitive abilities (primarily IQ tests) to the mix of cognitive abilities and adaptive behaviors. This change has been due in part to realization of the role played by the environment (particularly poverty environments) in the development of mild mental retardation. We do not merely try to help a child adjust to his or her disability; we also try to intervene early in the life cycle to keep the condition from developing in more serious forms.

Defining Mental Retardation

The "AAMR Definition" box on page 158 highlights the current definition of mental retardation set forth by the American Association on Mental Retardation (AAMR). It refers to two separate domains where limitations must be found before we refer to a person as having mental retardation. The first is significantly subaverage intellectual functioning; the second domain reflects limitations in two or more of ten separate indicators of adaptive skills. Despite the problems that the AAMR definition poses, most educators and psychologists see the wisdom of using the dual criteria—*intellectual subnormality/developmental delay* and *deficits in adaptive behavior*—as important in identifying mild mental retardation.

Many people think that definitions of matters relating to children with mental retardation have existed over generations. It is important to realize that this is not true. In fact, since 1908 there have been ten different definitions of mental retardation. When new information based on research becomes available, the definition changes. The newest definition is presented in the box shown below, but it is not likely to become the final definition (AAMR, 2002).

What separates the current definition from those of the past is the recognition that mental retardation is a set of conditions that blend together intelligence and adaptive behavior. Since the quality of the environment in which the child develops is important, the condition can be modified and improved. This environment is not something that is fixed at birth by genetic factors, and this is encouraging for educators who now see avenues for improvement and change.

Mental retardation is not something that you *have,* like blue eyes or a heart defect. Nor is it something you *are,* like short or thin. It is neither a medical disorder nor a mental disorder. **Mental retardation** is a particular state of functioning that begins in childhood and is characterized by limitation in both intelligence and adaptive skills. Mental retardation reflects the "fit" between the capabilities of individuals and the structure and expectations of their environment.

The AAMR Definition of Mental Retardation

Mental retardation is a disability characterized by significant limitations both in intellectual functioning and in adaptive behavior as expressed in conceptual, social, and practical adaptive skills. The disability originates before age 18.

FIVE ASSUMPTIONS ESSENTIAL TO THE APPLICATION OF THE DEFINITION:

1. Limitations in present functioning must be considered within the context of community environments typical of the individual's age peers and culture.

2. Valid assessment considers cultural and linguistic diversity as well as differences in communication, sensory, motor, and behavioral factors.

3. Within an individual, limitations often coexist with strengths.

4. An important purpose of describing limitations is to develop a profile of needed supports.

5. With appropriate personalized supports over a sustained period, the life functioning of the person with mental retardation generally will improve.

Source: From American Association on Mental Retardation (2002). Reprinted with permission.

TABLE 5.1
Defining Developmental Disabilities

Developmental disability means a severe, chronic disability of a person five years of age or older that:
1. Is attributable to a mental or physical impairment or combination of mental and physical impairments
2. Is manifested before the person attains age twenty-two
3. Is likely to continue indefinitely
4. Results in substantial functional limitations in three or more of the following areas of major life activity: (a) self-care, (b) receptive and expressive language, (c) learning, (d) mobility, (e) self-direction, (f) capacity for independent living, and (g) economic self-sufficiency
5. Reflects the person's need for a combination and sequence of special, interdisciplinary or generic care, treatment, or other services that are lifelong or of extended duration and are individually planned and coordinated.

Source: From M. Beirne-Smith, M. Ittenbach, & J. Patton, *Mental retardation* (Upper Saddle River, NJ: Merrill, 1998), p. 83. Reprinted with the permission of Pearson Education, Inc.

The context of the child affects his or her ability to adapt positively.

The context of the child can determine his or her eventual ability to adapt, positively or negatively. The term **developmental disabilities** includes mental retardation plus other conditions of mental and physical impairment likely to need lifelong help from a variety of health, social, and educational agencies (see Table 5.1). And there is a trend toward referring to these children as developmentally disabled, in order to avoid the negative connotations of mental retardation.

Intelligence

The definition of mental retardation/developmental disabilities must include retardation in intellectual development and in adaptive behavior.

No definition, no matter how comprehensive, is worth much unless we can translate its abstractions into concrete action. Intellectual subnormality has traditionally been determined by performance on intelligence tests. Children with mental retardation are markedly slower than their agemates in using memory effectively, in associating and classifying information, in reasoning, and in making sound judgments—the types of performance measured on intelligence tests. One of the earliest of these tests was developed by Alfred Binet for the express purpose of finding children who were not capable of responding to the traditional education program in France at the turn of the twentieth century.

Later on, individual tests of intelligence developed by David Wechsler (1974) became popular and widely used. Part of the popularity of the Wechsler scales is that they provide for ten subtests (for example, similarities, information, and block design) and scale scores that allow psychologists to develop a profile of the skills of the individual tested and allow teachers to distinguish between verbal IQ scores and performance IQ scores. Other group tests of intelligence were designed to test large numbers of students in a shorter period of time. Though considerably less expensive than the individual tests, they are also less reliable and less valid and should be used only for screening.

Adaptive Skills

The current emphasis on the environment and the context of the child has resulted in an extended attempt to distinguish among various categories of adaptive behavior. Table 5.2 lists ten areas of adaptive skills that can be described and rated. To be considered to have mental retardation, a child or adult must be significantly deficient in at least two of these areas. This delineation of ten areas of adaptation is much more extensive than past efforts to define adaptive behavior and reflects the growing concern for adaptive skills as a key element in special education programs. Thus, it is possible to have a low IQ score and still possess usable adaptive skills, be self-sufficient in the community, be able to interact reasonably with other citizens, and maintain a part-time or full-time job. Under such circumstances, an individual would still be considered intellectually subnormal but would not be considered mentally retarded. The lowest score on an IQ test that a child with an intact, undamaged nervous system would achieve is not zero but about 60 or 70. Any score lower than that is generally an indication of some type of organic pathology.

The identification of ten areas of ability in assessing mental retardation shows the emphasis now put on adaptive behavior.

Levels of Mental Retardation

Historically, psychologists and educators distinguished among levels of intensity of mental retardation by assigning students to various categories (first *idiot*, *imbecile*, and *moron*; later *educable*, *trainable*, and *dependent*; then *mild*, *moderate*, *severe*, and *profound*). *Mild* indicated development at between one-half and three-fourths of the normal rate; *moderate*, development at about one-half of the normal rate; *severe*, development at slightly more than one-fourth of normal cognitive growth; and *profound*, less than one-fourth the normal rate. This chapter focuses on the mild and moderate levels of mental retardation. The severe and profound levels are covered in Chapter 13. Psychologists and educators assess how well these children are adapting to their environment in the ten categories of adaptability listed in Table 5.2, as well as their level of measurable intelligence.

The formal definition places the issue of mental retardation or developmental disabilities within the individual, but another way of viewing the individual is to define the level or intensity of support necessary to allow the child or individual to operate effectively. The intensity of support is measured as *intermittent*, *limited*, *extensive*, and *pervasive*.

Intensity of support—intermittent, limited, extensive, pervasive—emphasizes the level of support needed by a person who has mental retardation.

▶ *Intermittent* refers to support as needed but not necessarily present at all times.

▶ *Limited* refers to support provided on a regular basis for a short period of time.

▶ *Extensive* support indicates ongoing and regular involvement.

▶ The *pervasive* level of support describes constant high-intensity help provided across environments and involving more staff members than the other categories.

While these four terms line up well with the *mild*, *moderate*, *severe*, and *profound* AAMR categories, they emphasize what will be needed to provide necessary supports for the individual (Luckasson et al., 1992).

TABLE 5.2
Adaptive Skills and Mental Retardation

CATEGORY	SKILLS
COMMUNICATION	Skills involving the ability to comprehend and express information through symbolic behaviors (e.g., spoken word, written word/sign language) or nonsymbolic behaviors (e.g., facial expression)
SELF-CARE	Skills involved in toileting, eating, dressing, hygiene, and grooming
HOME LIVING	Skills related to functioning within a home, which include clothing care, housekeeping, food preparation, and home safety
SOCIAL	Skills related to social exchanges with other individuals, including initiating interaction and terminating interaction with others; responding to pertinent situation cues; recognizing feelings
COMMUNITY USE	Skills related to the appropriate use of community resources, including traveling in the community; shopping at stores and markets; purchasing or obtaining services (e.g., gas stations, doctor's and dentist's offices); using public transportation and public facilities
SELF DIRECTION	Skills related to making choices; following a schedule; initiating activities appropriate to the setting; completing necessary or required tasks
HEALTH AND SAFETY	Skills related to maintenance of one's health in terms of eating; illness, treatment, and prevention; basic first aid; sexuality; basic safety considerations (e.g., following rules and laws)
FUNCTIONAL ACADEMICS	Cognitive abilities and skills related to learning at school that also have direct application in one's life (e.g., writing, reading, using basic practical math concepts, awareness of the physical environment and one's health and sexuality)
LEISURE	The development of a variety of leisure and recreational interests (i.e., self-entertainment and interaction) that reflect personal preferences and choices
WORK	Skills related to holding a part- or full-time job or jobs in the community in terms of specific job skills, appropriate social behavior, and related work skills (e.g., completion of tasks, awareness of schedules, ability to take criticism and improve skills)

Source: Adapted from R. Luckasson, D. Coulder, E. Polloway, S. Russ, R. Schalock, M. Snell, D. Spitalnik, & I. Stark, *Mental retardation: Definition, classification, and systems of support* (Washington, DC: American Association on Mental Retardation, 1992), pp. 40–41. Reprinted with permission.

Coping with children with mental retardation has progressed over the last few decades from being concerned mainly with measuring cognitive abilities and classification, to being concerned about adaptive behavior and its various components, to now focusing on supports that are designed to help the individual with his or her cognitive and socioemotional adaptation.

Table 5.3 lists the supports (needed resources and strategies) that should be in place for children and youth (and adults) with mental retardation. These supports show our interest in devising ways to help individuals adapt in social and behavioral ways and our confidence that such supports can meaningfully help these children improve their adaptation.

As noted in Chapter 1, there has been a major reduction in the number of schoolchildren identified as having mental retardation. Such reduction in numbers seems to reflect the unwillingness or reluctance of educators to label students "mentally retarded," as well as greater refinement in diagnosing autism, learning disabilities, and so forth.

Accordingly, there have been some attempts to find a term more in keeping with our current understanding of the condition. One suggestion has been to refer to children with mild mental retardation (MMR) as those with *generalized learning disabilities* (MacMillan, Siperstein, & Gresham, 1996). Such a term would indicate an "across-the-board" developmental delay in academic and cognitive abilities and distinguishes it from children with specific learning disabilities, which would indicate a specific deficit in a particular area such as processing auditory input. Under such a category many youngsters now being called learning disabled could be included in the *generalized learning disabilities* label. And the *specific learning disability* term could be restricted to those youngsters that have a clear deficit in information processing.

TABLE 5.3
Examples of Support Areas for Individuals with Mental Retardation

Human development activities	Providing social and emotional developmental activities to foster trust, autonomy, and initiative
Teaching and education activities	Learning and using functional academics (reading signs, counting change, etc.)
Home living activities	Participating in leisure activities within the home
Community living activities	Shopping and purchasing goods
Employment activities	Interacting with coworkers
Health and safety activities	Avoiding health and safety hazards
Behavioral activities	Controlling anger and aggression
Social activities	Making and keeping friends
Protection and advocacy activities	Belonging to and participating in self-advocacy/ support organizations

Source: American Association of Mental Retardation, *Frequently asked questions about mental retardation,* retrieved from www.aamr.org/Policies/faq_mental_retardation.shtml, October 5, 2004. Reprinted with permission.

Changing the name of a well-established group (MMR) is no small matter. It would mean changing the name of journals, professional societies, and two generations of legislation, so the term "mild mental retardation" will likely be with us for some time to come.

■ Genetic and Environmental Factors

Genetic Factors

The question of how a tiny gene can influence the complex behavior of children and adults has puzzled scientists for many years. The breakthroughs of James Watson and Francis Crick helped to explain the functions of DNA and RNA, and it is now possible to provide a general answer to that question. According to McClearn (1993), "Genes influence the proteins that are critical to the functioning of the organ systems that determine behavior" (p. 39). Thus, genes can influence anatomical systems and their functions—the nervous system, sensory systems, musculature, and so on.

Do certain patterns of genes predetermine certain types of behavior? Are we unwitting automatons driven by mysterious bursts of chemicals? Not really. No particular gene or protein forces a person to drink a glass of whiskey, but some people have a genetic sensitivity to ethanol that may increase their tendency to become actively drinking alcoholics. The relationship between genes and behavior is complex, and environmental influences are almost always an important factor.

According to Plomin, DeFries, and McClearn (1980), human genetic abnormalities are common, involving as many as half of all human fertilizations. They don't show up in the general population because most genetic abnormalities result in early spontaneous abortion. About 1 in 200 fetuses with genetic abnormalities survive until birth, but many of these infants die soon after they are born. So although many deviations occur, most are never seen. More than 100 genetic disorders have been identified. Fortunately, most of them are relatively rare.

As we learn more from research like the Human Genome Project, we become more conscious of the continued interaction between environment and genetics. A recent study of 3,886 twins (Spinath, Harlaar, Ronald, & Plomin, 2004) chose to focus on the lowest 5 percent of the children in verbal and nonverbal abilities. They found twin concordance for mild mental impairment in 74 percent of the monozygotic (single egg) low-ability twins, while only 45 percent of same-sex dizygotic (two separate eggs) twins had shown mild mental impairment. (See Figure 5.1.) Such findings underline the importance of considering genetics along with environment in understanding developmental disabilities.

The Human Genome Project, an ambitious attempt to identify the genes on every chromosome, gives promise that in the near future, we will be able to identify many more genetic influences linked to the condition of mental retardation/developmental disabilities (Olesen, 1996). At present, of the approximately 4,434 genetic disorders known, mental retardation is present in over 400, or about 10 percent of them (Beirne-Smith, Ittenbach, & Patton, 2001). The mapping of the genes through the Human Genome Project will almost

The Human Genome Project may reveal much about mental retardation and may even help toward its prevention.

FIGURE 5.1
Twin Concordance Rates of Mild Mental Impairment

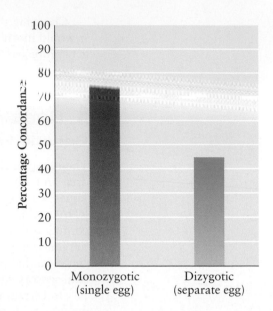

Source: From F. Spinath, N. Harlaar, A. Ronald, & R. Plomin, Substantial genetic influence on mild mental impairment in early childhood, *American Journal of Mental Retardation, 109,* (2004): 34–43. Reprinted with the permission of Allen Press.

certainly reveal more connections between mental retardation and a variety of genetic disorders and perhaps be a step toward preventing many of them.

Sometime in the near future we can expect to see gene therapy in utero or soon after birth as a means of correcting some birth defects. Gene therapy is a rapidly developing area with extraordinary potential. But we also know that much genetic vulnerability may be manifested only in the presence of an environmental trigger. In fact, cultural practices remain an extraordinarily powerful force in shaping development (Warren, 2002).

Forness and Kavale (1998) complain about the great attention being paid to various subgroups of mental retardation and excessive focus on distinguishing between various disorders. They point out that widely varying conditions such as traumatic brain injury (TBI), fetal alcohol syndrome (FAS), prenatal substance abuse (PSA), and fragile X syndrome (FXS) all have produced many children with similar educational problems such as low IQ scores, underachievement, inattention and impulsiveness, and conduct disorders. These conditions can all be treated with similar educational strategies despite the differences in causes. In other words, determining the cause of a condition is not necessarily helpful in regard to what the special educator can do about it.

Here we look at three of the most common genetic disorders: Down syndrome, phenylketonuria, and fragile X syndrome.

Down Syndrome

One of the most common and easily recognized genetic disorders is **Down syndrome.** Down syndrome occurs once in every 600–900 live births (Schachter & Demerath, 1996). Although clearly genetic, the condition is not hereditary, with the problem existing in the chromosome division. The vast majority of Down syndrome children are produced through *nondisjunction,* which is the failure of some chromosomes to divide properly, resulting in forty-seven chromosomes instead of the normal forty-six (Lejeune, Gautier, & Turpin, 1959) (Figure 5.1). The condition in most instances leads to mild or

National Down Syndrome Society
www.ndss.org

FIGURE 5.2
Chromosomal Pattern of a Girl with Down Syndrome, with an Extra Chromosome in Pair 21

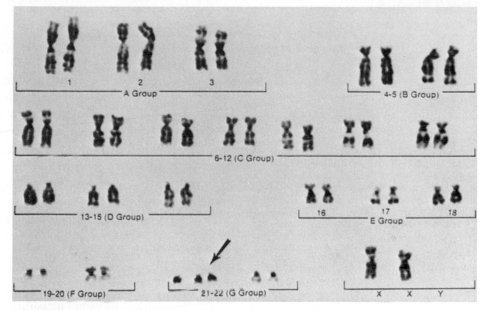

Source: From S. Pueschel, The child with Down syndrome, in M. Levine, W. Carey, A. Crocker, & R. Gross (Eds.), *Developmental-behavioral pediatrics* (Philadelphia: Saunders, 1983). Copyright 1983 by W. B. Saunders & Co. Reprinted by permission.

moderate mental retardation and a variety of hearing, skeletal, and heart problems. The presence of Down syndrome is related to maternal age; the incidence increases significantly in children born to mothers age 35 and older. According to current figures, more than 50 percent of children with Down syndrome are born to mothers older than 35. We do not know exactly why age is related to the condition. We do know, however, that the mother is not the exclusive source of the extra chromosome. The father contributes the extra chromosome in 20 to 25 percent of all cases (Abrams & Bennett, 1980). The age of the father does not seem as significant as the age of the mother. Down syndrome can also be caused by a chromosomal abnormality called *translocation.* The child may have forty-six chromosomes, but one pair breaks, and the broken part fuses to another chromosome.

Before the 1970s, the diagnosis of Down syndrome and a number of other pathological conditions was not made until the child was born or even later. **Amniocentesis,** a procedure for drawing a sample of amniotic fluid (the fluid that surrounds the fetus in the uterus) from the pregnant woman, has made earlier diagnosis possible. Fetal cells in the fluid are analyzed for chromosomal abnormality by **karyotyping,** a process in which a picture of chromosomal patterns is prepared (see Figure 5.2). Tests of prenatal maternal alpha-fetoprotein and ultrasonography can also reveal the presence of a fetus with Down syndrome. Such early diagnosis has posed a major dilemma for families and physicians (Pueschal, 1991). It allows parents to decide whether the pregnancy

ECOLOGY OF THE CHILD

FAMILY   ## Jon Will's Aptitudes

Jon Will, the oldest of my four children, turns 21 this week and on this birthday, as on every other workday, he will commute by subway to his job delivering mail and being useful in other ways at the National Institutes of Health. Jon is a taxpayer, which serves him right: he voted for Bill Clinton (although he was partial to Pat Buchanan in the primaries).

The fact that Jon is striding into a productive adulthood with a spring in his step and Baltimore's Orioles on his mind is a consummation that could not have been confidently predicted when he was born. Then a doctor told his parents that their first decision must be whether or not to take Jon home. Surely 21 years later fewer doctors suggest to parents of handicapped newborns that the parental instinct of instant love should be tentative or attenuated, or that their commitment to nurturing is merely a matter of choice, even a question of convenience.

Jon has Down syndrome, a chromosomal defect involving varying degrees of mental retardation and physical abnormalities. Jon lost, at the instant he was conceived, one of life's lotteries, but he also was lucky: his physical abnormalities do not impede his vitality and his retardation is not so severe that it interferes with life's essential joys—receiving love, returning it, and reading baseball box scores.

One must mind one's language when speaking of people like Jon. He does not "suffer from" Down syndrome. It is an affliction, but he is happy—as happy as the Orioles' stumbling start this season will permit. You may well say that being happy is easy now that ESPN exists. Jon would agree. But happiness is a species of talent, for which some people have superior aptitudes.

Jon's many aptitudes far exceed those few that were dogmatically ascribed to people like him not long ago. He was born when scientific and social understanding relevant to him was expanding dramatically. We know much more about genetically based problems than we did when, in the early 1950s, James Watson and Francis Crick published their discoveries concerning the structure of DNA, the hereditary

molecule, thereby beginning the cracking of the genetic code. Jon was born the year before *Roe* v. *Wade* and just as prenatal genetic tests were becoming routine. Because of advancing science and declining morals, there are fewer people like Jon than there should be. And just in Jon's generation much has been learned about unlocking the hitherto unimagined potential of the retarded. This begins with early intervention in the form of infant stimulation. Jon began going off to school when he was three months old.

Because Down syndrome is determined at conception and leaves its imprint in every cell of the person's body, it raises what philosophers call ontological questions. It seems mistaken to say that Jon is less than he would be without Down syndrome. When a child suffers a mentally limiting injury after birth we wonder sadly about what might have been. But a Down person's life never had any other trajectory. Jon was Jon from conception on. He has seen a brother two years younger surpass him in size, get a driver's license and leave for college, and although Jon would be forgiven for shaking his fist at the universe, he has been equable. I believe his serenity is grounded in his sense that he is a complete Jon and that is that.

Shadow of Loneliness

Some of life's pleasures, such as the delights of literature, are not accessible to Jon, but his most poignant problem is that he is just like everyone else, only a bit more so. A shadow of loneliness, an irreducible apartness from others, is inseparable from the fact of individual existence. This entails a sense of incompleteness—we *are* social creatures—that can be assuaged by marriage and other friendships, in the intimacy of which people speak their hearts and minds. Listen to the wisdom whispered by common locutions: We speak of "unburdening ourselves" when we talk with those to whom we talk most freely.

Now, try to imagine being prevented, by mental retardation and by physical impediments to clear

Exceptional children are children first with some special characteristics that require educational attention.
(© Lauren Shear/Photo Researchers, Inc.)

articulation, from putting down, through conversation, many burdens attendant on personhood. The shadow of loneliness must often be somewhat darker, the sense of apartness more acute, the sense of incompleteness more aching for people like Jon. Their ability to articulate is, even more than for everyone else, often not commensurate with their abilities to think and feel, to be curious and amused, and to yearn.

Because of Jon's problems of articulation, I marvel at his casual everyday courage in coping with a world that often is uncomprehending. He is intensely interested in major league baseball umpires, and is a friend of a few of them. I think he is fascinated by their ability to make themselves understood, by vigorous gestures, all the way to the back row of the bleachers. From his season-ticket seat behind the Orioles dugout, Jon relishes rhubarbs, but I have never seen him really angry. The closest he comes is exasperation leavened by resignation. It is an interesting commentary on the human condition that one aspect of Jon's abnormality—a facet of his disability—is the fact that he is gentleness straight through. But must we ascribe a sweet soul to a defective chromosome? Let us just say that Jon is an adornment to a world increasingly stained by anger acted out.

Like many handicapped people, Jon frequently depends on the kindness of strangers. He almost invariably receives it, partly because Americans are, by and large, nice, and because Jon is, too. He was born on his father's birthday, a gift that keeps on giving.

Source: George F. Will, Jon Will's aptitudes, from *The Leveling Wind* by George Will. Used by permission of Viking Penguin, a division of Penguin Putnam, Inc.

WHAT IS THE CONTEXT?

This article discusses Jon Will's capabilities, wants, and joys as he progresses from the inner circle of family to the outer circle of community. His father describes Jon's abilities and inabilities, joys and frustrations, but above all shows how Jon's life is simple but whole. Jon copes with a difficulty in articulating his thoughts by showing resolve and gentleness in adversity.

PIVOTAL ISSUES FOR TEACHERS

- What does the author value about Jon and his abilities?

- How is Jon's personality affected by Down syndrome?

- How has the way Jon's family raised him affected Jon's current abilities and attitudes?

- How does Jon's love of baseball give a sense of wholeness to his life?

- Now that Jon has reached adulthood, what does he contribute to the community, and in what other ways might he contribute?

should be terminated. The decision is not an easy one, generating questions about the right to life and genetic selection.

The effects of Down syndrome extend well beyond the child's early development. School age children with Down syndrome appear to have higher social and adaptive skills than would be expected given their slow intellectual development and less developed language and communication skills. Adults with Down syndrome seem particularly disposed to depression, dementia, and Alzheimer's disease (Loveland & Tunali-Kotoski, 1998). Systematic efforts to prevent or control these later risks have yet to be made (Epstein, 1988).

Part of the context of the child with Down syndrome is the distinctive physical appearance of the child, which may evoke negative responses from other children and adults. Recently, suggestions have been made for plastic surgery to remove some of the distinctive physical features.

Phenylketonuria

Normal growth and development in the embryo and fetus depend on the production of enzymes at the right time and place. When enzymes are not produced or fail to perform their normal functions, a number of unfavorable developmental conditions can result. These conditions are called *inborn errors of metabolism*. One of them is **phenylketonuria (PKU)**, a single-gene defect that can produce severe retardation. In PKU, the absence of a specific enzyme in the liver leads to a buildup of the amino acid *phenylalanine*.

PKU is an unusual genetic disorder in that it can be modified by environmental treatment, a special diet. The diet is very strict, however, and many families have difficulty holding to its requirements. PKU can be detected at birth, and every state has established a screening program to identify such children so they can be started on a nutritional regime early (Simonoff, Bolton, & Rutter, 1998).

The importance of staying on this strict diet can be judged by the following facts: The earlier treatment is begun, the less will be the loss in intelligence. Children with PKU who abandon the diet at school age suffer social and intellectual setbacks. Mothers with PKU can have a high proportion of children with birth defects unless they maintain this diet. As a child with PKU grows, he or she can eat only small quantities of high-protein food (such as meat and cheese) but can have fruits and vegetables (low protein). Peer pressure, however, can often pull the child off this restrictive diet.

Fragile X syndrome

The Fragile X syndrome is now considered the leading cause of inherited developmental disability. **Fragile X syndrome (FXS)** results from a mutation on the long arm of the X chromosome, and it affects about twice as many males as females—about once in four thousand. Extensive investigation has found that the condition causes a deficiency in protein production necessary for normal brain development. The diagnosis can be determined by DNA testing.

A study pursuing the characteristics of children with Fragile X syndrome (Bailey, Hatton, & Skinner, 1998) revealed that a sizable number (25 percent of these children) also showed the symptoms of autism (see Chapter 8). Therefore, some of the early symptomatology formerly linked to Fragile X syndrome may be attributable to the presence of autism as well. In children who

Prenatal tests can now determine if a fetus has any genetic abnormalities.

Kathy May noticed a problem with her son, Sam, within weeks of his birth. He was not easy to comfort and always seemed to keep his hands clasped. When he was 6 weeks old, she tried unsuccessfully to get Sam to look at her when she clapped her hands. At 15 months, Kathy's doctor expressed concern that Sam's language development was behind. She took Sam to an early-intervention service provider, who, suspecting he was autistic, recommended that he be tested at the local children's hospital. At 20 months, the diagnosis was confirmed: Sam had Fragile X syndrome (FXS).

Compared to most families of children with FXS, the Mays were fortunate. Sam was diagnosed with FXS earlier than most such children. According to a recent Frank Porter Graham Child Development Institute study, the average child with FXS is not diagnosed until nearly age 3, and many others not until much later. Had these children been identified earlier, they would have been immediately eligible for early intervention services under the Individuals with Disabilities Education Act.

Source: Frank Porter Graham Child Development Institute, Screening newborns for fragile X, *Early Developments, 8* (2004): 11–13. Reprinted with permission.

have Fragile X syndrome but no autism, there is very often mental retardation, but not social and communication problems to the same degree as in children with both Fragile X and autism. The receptive abilities of children with Fragile X are relatively superior to their other abilities (Bailey, Hatton, & Skinner, 1998).

When both conditions are present, the autistic behaviors of eye-gaze avoidance, perseverative behavior, poor imitation, and hypersensitivity to sensory stimuli (e.g., loud noises) are more easily noted. Also, there appears to be in increase in aggressive behavior (Hatton & Bailey, 2001). The box describing Sam explains the importance of early identification.

Teachers of children with fragile X have noted that the behavior problems, rather than the cognitive delay, cause the most difficulty (Hatton et al., 2000). The recommendations from these teachers strongly resemble those for children with autism:

▶ Have a consistent routine with structured activities.

▶ Have a structured environment.

▶ Use visual cues and modeling.

▶ Use picture schedules.

▶ Break tasks down into manageable steps.

The wide range of individual differences in this condition, however, does call for individual planning and treatment based upon a child's own profile and patterns of development.

Toxic Agents

The remarkable system whereby a pregnant mother transmits nutrients through the umbilical cord to her fetus is also the highway by which many damaging substances can pass to the developing child. Our increasing ability to monitor fetal development and the rapidly growing body of research from studies of animals have raised concerns about the effects on the unborn child of substances ingested by the mother. A teratogen (from the Greek, meaning "monster creating") is a substance that adversely affects fetal development. Drugs (including alcohol) and cigarette smoke are prime examples of teratogens. The heavy use of alcohol or other drugs creates a prenatal and postnatal environmental context that is unfavorable for the infant's and child's early development.

Fetal Alcohol Syndrome

For centuries we have been generally aware of the unfavorable effects that alcohol consumption by the mother has on her unborn child. But only in the past few decades have those general concerns been substantiated with specific statistics and detailed descriptions of the consequences of what is now referred to as **fetal alcohol syndrome (FAS)**. Most of these findings have stirred even more alarm and concern. About 7 out of 10,000 births result in FAS, with greater frequencies in African American and Native American families (Baumeister & Woodley-Zanthos, 1996).

Far too many women are unaware of the potential consequences of drinking while pregnant. The National Organization on Fetal Alcohol Syndrome (2004) presents three key facts:

▶ When a pregnant woman drinks, so does her baby.

▶ The baby's growth can be altered and slowed.

▶ The baby may suffer lifelong damage.

Physical impairments in addition to mental retardation can follow, and there are often behavioral consequences such as hyperactivity and attention problems. FAS is not something that is outgrown. Once present, it is likely that

According to the "least restrictive environment" principle, children should be moved from the mainstream of education only as far as necessary to meet their special needs.
(© Ellen Senisi/The Image Works)

special educational plans need to be made and help provided into adulthood. Even small amounts of alcohol can affect some children, so a mother need not be a binge drinker for FAS to occur.

Obviously, not every fetus is affected by maternal drinking; otherwise we would be awash with children with FAS. It is sufficiently prevalent, however, to be a major cause of concern. Milder effects of alcohol consumption during pregnancy, known as *fetal alcohol effects (FAE)*, include distractibility and hyperactivity, which may go unnoticed because they do not have FAS's catastrophic impact on the child.

One of the distressing aspects of FAS is that it directly affects the development of the brain, and its results last long into adulthood. FAS is currently considered one of the leading causes of moderate or severe organic mental retardation (Menke, McClead, & Hansen, 1991). It is also one condition that is preventable.

The Effects of Lead

Ingesting heavy metals, such as lead, cadmium, and mercury, can result in severe consequences, including mental retardation. Most attention is currently focused on lead, and much of the lead that enters the brain comes from the atmosphere. One of the most effective steps that has been taken, on a societal level, was the reduction of lead amounts permitted in gasoline. This reduction resulted in a lowering by one-third of the average lead levels in the blood of U.S. men, women, and children. The reduction in lead levels paralleled the declining use of leaded gasoline (Mahaffey, Annest, Roberts, & Murphy, 1982; Beirne-Smith, Ittenbach, & Patton, 1998).

Also, legislation has restricted the use of lead in paint and mandated that lead paint be removed from the walls and ceilings of older homes—a common source of lead poisoning in youngsters. Some children are born with high levels of lead in their blood (prenatal exposure to lead can be determined by examining the umbilical cord). On tests of intelligence, these children scored 8 percent below children who had lower levels of lead in their blood (Bellinger, Leviton, Waternaux, Needleman, & Rabinowitz, 1987). Children, who will place anything in their mouths, are known to ingest peeling paint chips with some regularity. Davis (1988) pointed out that good nutrition can prevent lead-related damage by reducing lead absorption in the body. The susceptibility of many children from low economic backgrounds to lead poisoning may, in part, reflect a combination of poor nutrition and the greater availability of lead in their environment, another contextual feature. Medications can be prescribed that can have the effect of flushing the system of lead, once it has been discovered (Pueschel, Scala, Weidenman, & Bernier, 1995).

The context of mental retardation includes the susceptibility of children from low socioeconomic backgrounds to lead exposure in their homes.

Infections

The brain begins to develop about three weeks after fertilization. Over the next several weeks, the central nervous system is highly susceptible to disease. If the mother contracts **rubella** (German measles) during this time, her child will likely be born with mental retardation and other serious birth defects. A rubella vaccine that is now available has drastically reduced the number of rubella children. Children and adults are also at risk of brain damage from viruses that produce high fevers, which, in turn, destroy brain cells. **Encephalitis** is one virus of this type. Fortunately it is rare, as are other viruses like it.

Environmental Factors

There has long been an enormous gap between what we know about the brain and its function and the set of behavioral symptoms by which we define mental retardation. With current advances in understanding the central nervous system, we are able to make some reasonable assumptions about the links between that system and behavior. Huttenlocher (1988) suggested that experience influences the development and maintenance of certain structures in the brain. The implications are exciting. If the development of the nervous system is not preset at fertilization by genetic factors, the nervous system can grow and change as the individual experiences new things. That means environment and human interactions can play a role in neurological and hence intellectual development. Such speculation on the influence of experience on brain development has been largely confirmed (Jensen, 1998).

Sameroff (1990) raised the issue of possible biosocial influences on the child, or the effect of the interaction of the environment with the biological state of the child. He pointed out that many children with birth complications actually grow up to show no evidence of their unhappy start, and he concluded that "social conditions were much better predictors of outcome for those children than either their early biological status, as measured by birth and pregnancy complications, or their psychological status, as measured by developmental scales" (p. 95).

When children who tested in the "low" or "mentally retarded" range as pre-schoolers are retested at ages 10 to 12, the correlation between the two measurements tends to be very high. Researchers have often interpreted this high correlation as an indication of the consistency with which the slow developmental rate of intellectual growth is maintained. When Sameroff tested the influences of external environment over time, he found similarly high or higher correlations between the preschool child's unfavorable environmental conditions and the preadolescent's environmental conditions. So the environmental conditions that the child experienced were as consistent as the measurements taken of the child's intellectual performance. Sameroff observed (1990):

> When predictions on how children will turn out are based on their early behavior, the predictions are generally wrong. When such predictions are based on their life circumstances, the predictions are generally right. In this domain, an understanding of the context may have greater developmental importance than an understanding of the child. (p. 97)

Sameroff (1990) identified a set of ten environmental risk factors (such as breadwinner employed in unskilled work, poor maternal health). Only in families with *multiple risk factors* did the child's competence seem to be in jeopardy. The multiple pressures of (1) the amount of stress from the environment, (2) the family's resources for coping with that stress, (3) the number of children who must share those resources, and (4) the parents' flexibility in understanding and dealing with their children play a role in fostering or hindering the child's intellectual and social competencies.

| Life circumstances, or the child's environment, are a strong predictor of how well a child will do in school and in society.

Characteristics of Children with Mental Retardation or Developmental Disabilities

Special programming for children with mild and moderate MR/DD is shaped in part by the characteristics that distinguish these children from their age-mates. There are marked differences in factors linked to level of intellectual development, such as the ability to process information, the ability to acquire and use language, and emotional development.

Ability to Process Information

The most obvious characteristic of children who have mild or moderate retardation is their limited cognitive ability, a limitation that inevitably shows up in their academic work. These children may lag by two to five grades, particularly in language-related subjects (reading, language arts). To help children who are not learning effectively, we must understand what is preventing them from learning. To do this, we must understand how they think—how they process information.

To help children learn, teachers need to know how children with mental retardation or developmental disabilities process information.

Many children who have mental retardation have problems in **central processing,** or the classification of a stimulus through the use of memory, reasoning, and evaluation. *Classification*—the organization of information—seems to be a special problem for children who have mental retardation. School-age children quickly learn to cluster (or group) events or things into useful classes: A chair, a table, and a sofa become "furniture"; an apple, a peach, and a pear become "fruit." Children who have mental retardation are less able to group things. They may have difficulty telling how a train and an automobile are alike.

Memory, another central-processing function, is also difficult for children who have mental retardation. Memory problems can stem from poor initial perception or poor judgment about applying what has been stored to a given situation. Most children use "rehearsal" as a memory aid, saying a string of words or a poem to themselves until they remember it. Children with retardation are less likely to rehearse information because their ability to use short-term memory appears limited.

Executive function—the decision-making element that controls reception, central processing, and expression—is a key factor in the poor performance of children who have mental retardation (Bebko & Luhaorp, 1998). It is not so much that these children cannot perceive a stimulus as it is that they cannot pay attention to the relevant aspects of a problem. It is not so much that they cannot reason as it is that they do not have the metathinking strategies to organize information to a point where reasoning can take place. And it is not so much that they do not have a repertoire of responses as it is that they too often choose an inappropriate response. Their teachers often say that they lack good judgment.

A common way to refer to the difficulty in processing information is to say there is a lack of good judgment.

For these children, learning problems are not limited to a specific cognitive function; instead, the whole information-processing system substantially breaks down. Most children whose IQ score is 50 or lower suffer from neurological damage that can make information processing very difficult.

Cognitive Processes

One of the questions posed by researchers in this area is "Do children with mental retardation follow the same developmental patterns, only slower, or do they have a unique pattern of development?" Weisz (1999) synthesized the results of many experiments and came to the conclusion that the evidence strongly supports a similar developmental sequence with children with mental retardation, only slower!

This raises another issue, that of *learned helplessness*, a feeling that nothing you can do can make a positive difference. If the child with mental retardation consistently fails on tasks, does he or she have a tendency to quit trying because of a feeling built up by consistent failure in academic tasks and situations? Think of your own abilities in some sports. If you are not able to kick the ball well in soccer and cannot run fast, isn't there a strong tendency to abandon that game in favor of something that provides some measure of success?

Several studies that matched children with mental retardation with nonidentified children of the same mental level indicated that following failure experiences, the children with MR showed a significant decline in the use of effective problem-solving strategies (Weisz, 1999). This issue of learned helplessness becomes a significant challenge in inclusion, since children with mental retardation can hardly fail to see that their own performance does not match those of the typical children in the classroom.

Ability to Acquire and Use Language

The ability to develop language is one of the great achievements of humans, and there always has been curiosity as to how, if at all, language development is changed or modified in children and adults with mental retardation. The close link between language and cognition has long been noted (Cromer, 1991) as well as its reciprocal interaction. Not only is language limited by cognition, cognition (especially thinking, planning, and reasoning) is limited by language (Fowler, 1998). In addition, there is the problem of limited input and an impoverished database during the language learning years that can add up to an impoverished linguistic system (Locke, 1994). Remember the great differences, in exposure to language, of young children from professional, working class, and welfare parents reported in Chapter 1 (Hart & Risley, 1995).

Recently, the study of language in persons with mental retardation has become more complex in two specific ways. First, an increasing attempt has been made to study the elements of language for such children separately so that *semantics* (meaning and comprehension) is separated from *pragmatics* (the use of language for communication) and *phonology* (speech expression), and also the study of language development of children with specific etiologies. Children with Down syndrome can be compared with children with Williams syndrome, for example (Tager-Flushberg & Sullivan, 1998).

The question as to whether language develops in the same fashion, only slower, with children with mental retardation or in a special fashion has been answered largely in favor of the first choice. It is largely just slower; for example, a child at age 5 would match in linguistic skills a child of 10 with mental retardation whose mental age was 5.

Yet there are intriguing variations on this generalization. Children with Down syndrome have retardation in language even lower than that of their general mental deficit (Yoder & Warren, 2004), while children with Williams syndrome seem to have advanced language beyond their general

Recent studies attempt to separate the ability to use language for communication and language for comprehension.

mental abilities. This puzzle guarantees that there will be much more research on these topics in the near future (Fowler, 1998).

Ability to Acquire Emotional and Social Skills

For many years, there has been a modest understanding of the link between emotional and social problems and the condition of mental retardation. But what that link signifies and what should be done about it remain issues of some dispute (Korinek & Polloway, 1993). We know that emotional and social difficulties can undermine vocational and community adjustment. We are also aware that emotional and behavior problems probably lower the level of social acceptance experienced by children with mental retardation in comparison with their peers in the classroom. It is entirely possible that this low level of social acceptance is related to the behavioral and social problems rather than to the condition of mental retardation.

As has been the case with language development, recent studies on social development have focused on the specific problems of children with special etiologies such as Down syndrome (Kasari & Bauminger, 1998). A range of studies reveal many problems in peer relationships for children with mental retardation. With the current stress on inclusion, it becomes particularly important to find ways to improve the social relationships of children with mental retardation, since that is one of the key purposes for inclusion in the first place.

Certain skills appear to be important for social acceptance. They include sharing, turn taking, smiling, attending, and following directions. A person with social competence uses such skills appropriately in social situations.

Korinek and Polloway (1993) have called for a major emphasis in the curriculum on the development of social skills and social competencies. This means a goal not only to improve social adaptability in order to increase academic efficiency but also to develop social skills for their own sake and because of their importance in adult adjustment. Indeed, students who do not have social skills are ill prepared to adapt to the inclusive classroom or school. One serious remaining problem involves the specific curriculum for teaching social skills. How can such a program fit into the general classroom activities and objectives? If most of the general students have already learned these skills without specific instruction, then how can the teacher take the time to engage in this training with students with mental retardation?

Social Adaptation

Since social adaptation has become critical for the child with mental retardation, both in the classroom and later, in vocational settings, it is important to determine what barriers stand in the way of social adaptation. A study on the interpretation of social cues was most revealing in this regard (Leffert, Siperstein, & Millikan, 2000). One hundred seventeen students in elementary grades, with and without mental retardation, were shown video tapes depicting various social conflicts (e.g., a child knocking a book off another child's desk accidentally or being rejected when wanting to join a group on the playground). The students watching the video tapes were then asked for their reactions.

The children with mental retardation much more often interpreted that the other child was being mean. They were focusing on the negative outcome of

---

Emotional and behavioral issues associated with mental retardation may lower social acceptance by peers in the inclusive classroom.

The current stress on inclusion makes it particularly important to find ways to improve the social relationships of children with mental retardation—one of the main goals of inclusion.

To be socially accepted, children need to know certain social skills, such as sharing, smiling, and following directions, and when to use them.

the event and ignoring social cues that would indicate that the event was an accident. They also more often referred to an adult authority to solve the social crisis, rather than suggesting social strategies for resolving the incident.

These results suggest a reason why children with mental retardation are not well received in peer groups and also point the way to some necessary curricular additions for them. They clearly need practice in identifying social cues so that they can better interpret social situations and also should have practice through role-playing or discussions about useful strategies for prosocial interaction. One of the helping roles that the special educator, working as a collaborator with the general education classroom teacher, can play is to provide such experiences in some group situations and help children with MMR to work out their own strategies for response.

Role-playing helps children identify social cues.

Two of the common characteristics ascribed to persons with mental retardation have been *credulity* (inability to see through untruthful assertions) and *gullibility* (the ease with which one can be duped); in other words, the inability to judge the truthfulness of even highly ridiculous statements (Greenspan, 1999). These cognitive shortcomings in evaluation and adjustment result in serious social consequences.

The ten adaptive skills noted in Table 5.2 are well recognized, but a wide variety of investigators have been trying to cluster adaptive skills around three or four categories that would comprise the core of adaptive behavior. Factor analysis, cluster analysis, and a wide variety of other methods have been used for this purpose (Schalock & Braddock, 1999). One investigator (Schalock, 1999) found three areas that appeal to many: practical skills, conceptual skills, and social skills.

Practical skills include self-help skills, motor functioning, and community living skills; *conceptual skills* include receptive and expressive language, reading and writing skills, and nonverbal communication; and *social skills* include forming and maintaining friendships, participation in group activities, self-direction, responsibility, and so forth. These three areas seem reasonably independent of one another, and an individual can be judged on each of these three dimensions.

■ Identification

The first step in adapting the standard educational program to meet the needs of children with mental retardation or developmental disabilities is to identify those children who need special help. How does a child find special education services? Although referrals can come from many different sources, most students with mental retardation or developmental disabilities come to the attention of special education services because they fail in school. The inability of the child to adapt academically or socially to the expected standards of his or her age group sets off alarm bells in the teacher and calls for action.

Until recently, the response to such alarm bells was a diagnostic examination by the school psychologist to determine if the child was eligible for some form of special education. Now, many school systems use a *prereferral team,* which includes the classroom teacher, the principal, someone from special education, and relevant other special personnel. The team tries to see if it can help the classroom teacher devise some adaptation of the general classroom program to cope with the student's problems without more intensive (and more expensive) intervention (Chalfant, 1989). If the student makes no apparent gain as a result of the recommendations of the prereferral team, the child may then be referred for more

American Speech-Language-Hearing Association
www.asha.org

National Association of School Psychologists
www.nasponline.org

detailed diagnostic examination by the psychologist and, if found eligible, placed in more intensive special education services with an IEP decided by the multidisciplinary IEP team working with the child's parents.

What is the purpose of a multidisciplinary team? Each team member brings important information to an individualized education program (IEP) meeting. Members share their information and work together to write the child's IEP. Each person's information adds to the team's understanding of the child and what services the child needs. Table 5.3 lists the team members and describes their contributions.

The diagnostic examination assesses the child's intellectual development and adaptive behavior, the two key elements in the AAMR definition of mental

(text continues on page 179)

TABLE 5.3
Who Is on the Multidisciplinary Team?

GENERAL EDUCATION TEACHER

At least one of the child's general education teachers must be on the IEP team if the child is (or may be) participating in an inclusive classroom. That teacher may talk about the curriculum in the general education classroom and the aids, services, or changes to the educational program that would help the child with behavior, if behavior is an issue.

PARENTS

Parents know their child very well and can talk about their child's strengths and needs as well as their ideas for enhancing the child's education. They can offer insight into how their child learns, what his or her interests are, and other aspects of the child—aspects that only a parent can know.

SPECIAL EDUCATION TEACHER OR RESOURCE ROOM TEACHER

The child's special education teacher contributes information and experience involved in modifying the general curriculum to help the child learn. For example, the supplementary aids and services that the child may need in order to be successful in the regular classroom and elsewhere; modifying testing so that the student can show what he or she has learned; and individualizing instruction to meet the student's unique needs.

SPEECH AND LANGUAGE PATHOLOGIST

The American Speech-Language-Hearing Association (ASHA) is the national professional, scientific, and accrediting association for more than 103,000 audiologists; speech-language pathologists; and speech, language, and hearing scientists. Audiologists specialize in preventing and assessing hearing disorders, as well as providing audiologic treatment, including hearing aids. Speech-language pathologists identify, assess, and treat speech and language problems, including swallowing disorders.

SCHOOL PSYCHOLOGIST

The school psychologist will often present and interpret the child's evaluation results. The psychologist is also involved in teacher consultation and in developing interventions for the child both during and following the evaluation process. More information on school psychologists is available from the National Association of School Psychologists.

THE STUDENT

The student may also be a member of the IEP team if he or she is age 14 or older. If transition services are going to be discussed at the meeting, the student must be invited to attend. More and more students are participating in and even leading their own IEP meetings. This allows them to have a strong voice in their own education and can teach them a great deal about self-advocacy and self-determination.

TRANSLATOR OR SIGN LANGUAGE SPECIALIST

This professional can play a crucial role for children and families that speak Spanish or other foreign languages; also for children who are deaf or hard of hearing.

OTHER PROFESSIONALS

Other professionals who work with the exceptional child can make a great contribution to the multidisciplinary team. These include physical and occupational therapists; the school principal; an individual representing the school system; and an individual with special knowledge or expertise about the child.

Source: From www.asha.org. Reprinted with the permission of the American Speech-Language-Hearing Association.

PROFILES

DEVELOPMENTAL

Look at the graphs showing the developmental profiles of Bob, a child with mild familial retardation, and Carol, a child with moderate organic retardation. Both children are 10 years old. The patterns revealed in the graphs are not unusual for children of their intellectual development, although individual differences from one child to another within each of these groups may be great.

Bob: Bob's physical profile (height, weight, motor coordination) does not differ markedly

from the profiles of others in his age group. But in academic areas such as reading, arithmetic, and spelling, Bob is performing three and four grades below his age group. Depending on his classmates and the levels at which they are performing, Bob would fall at the bottom of the regular class group or be placed in a special program in a resource room. Bob's mobility, vision, and hearing are average, but he is having problems with interpersonal relationships. Although he is a likable boy under non-threatening conditions, he is quick to take

**Profiles of
Two Children
with Mental
Retardation**

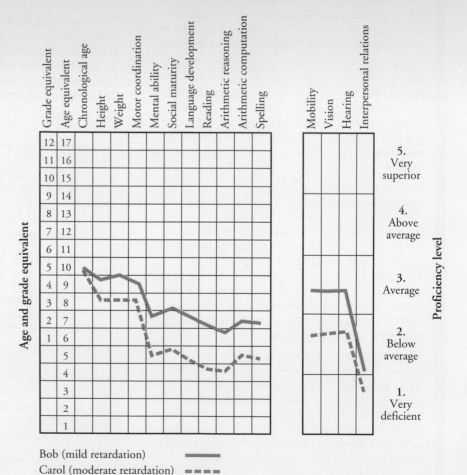

Bob (mild retardation) ———
Carol (moderate retardation) ------

offense and fight on the playground. In the classroom, he has a tendency to interrupt other children at their work and to wander aimlessly around the room when given an individual assignment. All these characteristics add up to a situation in which Bob has only a few friends, although he is tolerated by his classmates. With special help, he is able to maintain a marginal performance within the general education class.

Carol: Carol has moderate retardation and a much more serious adaptive problem. Her development is at the level of a 5-year-old (her IQ score is in the 50s). Like many other children with Down syndrome, she shows poor motor coordination and some minor vision and hearing problems that complicate her educational adaptation.

Carol's developmental profile shows that her academic performance is below first-grade level; indeed, at maturity, Carol's reading and arithmetic skills may not exceed a third-grade level. She can learn important skills or concepts in an educational setting, but the standard academic program is clearly inappropriate for her. To develop her capabilities to their maximum potential, Carol will need some special experiences with specially trained personnel.

(text continues from page 177)

retardation. The individual intelligence test remains the most common instrument used to determine intellectual subnormality. A student whose scores fall below those of 98 percent of his or her agemates is considered intellectually subnormal, unless cultural differences call the results into question.

Adaptive behavior is more difficult to assess because behavior can differ depending on the environment. Adaptive rating scales may indicate that a child is adapting well to the larger environment, but the child is acting out in the classroom. The Adaptive Behavior Scales of the American Association on Mental Retardation (AAMR) (Nihira, Leland, & Lambert, 1993a), and the Adaptive Behavior Inventory for Children (ABIC) measure adaptation to the community. Most children do well on these and similar scales because they are not asked to perform academically and constraints on their behavior are minimal. But a total measure of adaptation should measure how well students respond in the school environment, where they spend five or six hours a day, five days a week. The school edition of the AAMD Adaptive Behavior scale does focus on behavior in the school setting (Nihira, Leland, & Lambert, 1993a) and therefore may be the more appropriate measure to use.

Fuchs and Deno (1992) introduced an interesting alternative to the use of intelligence or aptitude tests to determine the student's performance level. Their curriculum-based measurement uses readings from various textbooks and asks students to read aloud from a hundred-word passage from the text. The number of words said correctly in one minute is the index of performance of the student. A variety of texts of differing levels of difficulty can fix the approximate reading level of the child. Such a simple method seems to correlate highly with standard measures of reading skills. It also provides the teacher with a clear sense of the student's developmental level of reading. If the teacher uses material of several grade levels to determine the proper reading level for the student, then the teacher should be able to adjust the difficulty level of the lessons that he or she provides to the student.

| Primary prevention of mental retardation occurs before birth, secondary prevention occurs in early childhood, and tertiary prevention occurs throughout the lifespan.

CHILDREN WITH MENTAL RETARDATION OR DEVELOPMENTAL DISABILITIES

Since the 1970s, thanks to major investments in research by the federal government, there have been significant advances in discoveries and attempts to find ways to aid in the development of the children with disabilities and in the support available to their families (see Chapter 2). The context in which children with mental retardation have been growing up also has changed. The context of modern life, with its increasing emphasis on advanced education and complex understandings, has not always been kind or favorable to children and adults with mental retardation. Opportunities for employment seem to be shrinking at the same time that acceptance of such individuals as a part of our society appears to be growing.

Several forces have come together to increase interest in early intervention in the young lives of children who might be at risk for mild or moderate mental retardation and for school failure. Discoveries in brain research indicated that the brain grows partly through the experiences that the young child has (Jensen, 1998). The number of women in the work force increased to the extent that over half the mothers with children under a year old work outside the home (Bureau of Labor Statistics, 1999), necessitating some form of child care. The low ratings that traditional child-care environments receive for their ability to stimulate cognitive and social development of children (Helburn, 1995) are a cause for concern. These factors have presented a picture of less than satisfactory environments for young children at risk during a crucial period of their development. This has led to proposals that a more vigorous role be played by education at earlier and earlier ages.

Can Special Education Make a Difference?

Researchers have made numerous efforts to assess in students with mental retardation the gains that accompany changes in their learning environment, curriculum, or skills mastery. Does the type of learning environment make a difference in the academic achievement, adaptive behavior, or cognitive development of children with mild and moderate retardation? Research findings suggest that changes in the learning environment alone do not make a striking difference. A large number of studies have tested the effectiveness of inclusive education for children with mental retardation, but the information derived from such studies is not often educationally significant. Few of the studies discuss the nature of the program the students received, and that surely is just as important as, if not more important than, "where" the student has been placed.

Although most of the intervention programs that have been assessed have focused on children with mild mental retardation, some assessments have attempted to test the impact of programs for children with moderate mental retardation as well. In one such program, eleven centers in Washington State were devoted to the education of children with Down syndrome and other developmental delays (Delwein, Fewell, & Pruess, 1985). The eleven centers emphasized enhancing five skill areas: gross motor, fine motor, cognitive, communicative, and social/self-help. The Developmental Sequence Performance Inventory (DSPI), a developmental checklist for children from birth to age 8, was used to test the effectiveness of the program. The children with Down syndrome exceeded developmental expectations in cognitive and communication areas and showed modest progress in the gross and fine motor areas. Only in the social/self-help areas were no substantive developmental gains noted.

It seems that teachers can accelerate developmental trends by giving specific instruction to children with moderate handicaps. This point is echoed by Castro (1987), who reviewed seventy-four intervention studies for all levels of disabling conditions and found evidence supporting the usefulness of special intervention programs for a wide variety of students.

Effectiveness of Intervention

As with other programs in special education, we are interested in knowing how much and in what way intervention is paying off for children with mental retardation or developmental disabilities. Bryant and Maxwell (1999) have reviewed the series of studies that attempted to chart gains from special programming for these children. They found support for an intensity and/or duration-of-treatment effect. In other words, the heavier the dose of educational treatment, the greater the children's gains. The same can be said for the length of time that the treatment is applied: the longer, the better. As a matter of fact, when special treatment stops, there is a tendency for the children to lose some or most of the gains that they have made.

We might attempt an analogy with diabetes, in that the patient must keep receiving treatment (insulin or other medication and/or adherence to diet) in order to get the desired results. It is not just a matter of giving a one-time dose of medicine and saying, "That takes care of that." What we have learned is that special education needs to be intensive and ongoing, for the children's initial gains to hold.

■ Adapting the Learning Environment

Inclusion in Context

How should the educational program be adapted to meet the needs of children with mental retardation? One intriguing aspect of the reform movement for inclusion is that it highlights principles of interpersonal interaction that are designed for life in the larger society. Proponents of inclusion wish the child with disabilities to be welcomed into a community of equals in the classroom, no one to speak disparagingly about others, everyone to be helpful to one another, and no one to be put down by others because of an inability to do certain things. But can such a philosophy of fairness and love be implemented in the school as we know it, particularly when the school has a number of competing academic goals that may make

Intervention programs result in moderate improvement in the development of adaptive behaviors.

Hands-on activities are important for children with mental retardation to master concepts.
(© Photo courtesy of the National Down Syndrome Society.)

achieving such interpersonal goals difficult? Implementation would be particularly difficult in the absence of support personnel to assist the classroom teacher, who otherwise would have to bear sole responsibility for inculcating such values.

The U.S. Congress left little doubt as to their preference for education in the general education classroom for all special needs children with the following language (from the Individuals with Disability Education Act amendments of 1997):

Teachers can build students' self-confidence by presenting lessons that are challenging but within the range of their ability to perform.
(© Bob Daemmrich/The Image Works)

To the maximum extent appropriate, handicapped children, including children in public or private institutions or other care facilities, are educated with children who are not handicapped, and that separate schooling, or other removal of handicapped children from regular educational environment occurs only when the nature or severity of the handicap is such that education in regular education classes *with the use of supplementary aids and services* cannot be achieved satisfactorily. [20 U.S.C. §1412(5)(B)]

Stainback and Stainback (1992, p. 13) describe the way inclusion should be. Teachers in inclusive classrooms should be able to call on reading specialists, compensatory education personnel, students in the classroom, school counselors, physical and speech therapists, other classroom teachers, math and science teachers, and a variety of other people to provide suggestions or participate in the classroom to make classes more flexible and relevant to the needs of all students.

Those who worry about a terrible traffic jam as these counselors, special teachers, and psychologists bump into one another trying to get to the classroom teacher need not be concerned just yet. The availability of these personnel is uncertain in many school districts, to say the least. It is not the ideals of inclusion that are being argued, but the ability to achieve or implement them. All three of the major areas of change—learning environments, curriculum content, and skills mastery—seem to require attention for students with mental retardation.

The Socialization Agenda of Inclusion One of the distinguishing features of inclusion is the emphasis on socialization of the child with disabilities within the inclusive setting. This is the primary objective of the schools, from the standpoint of inclusion advocates, and in their view is more important than academic achievement.

Children need to go to school in their own neighborhood, to attend classes with typical children their own age, and to be involved with kids in activities outside of school. Adults should not interfere but at the same time should understand that some children may need help in being introduced to others, in sharing their gifts with them and in making personal connects (Strully & Strully, 1997, p. 153).

Individualized Education Programs (IEPs)

One of the first efforts to develop long-range plans for child and family came forth from the IEPs, mandated in 1975 by the Education for All Handicapped Children Act (PL 94-142) to increase the collaboration between professionals and parents and to ensure some thoughtful consideration about how children would be served within the special education program.

One of the major changes in the educational planning for children with disabilities is that instead of focusing on their deficits and disabilities, we now wish to document the developmental and personal strengths of each such student in order to plan the most effective educational intervention for him or her. Students with limited verbal proficiency may be able to express themselves through dance or through other arts, or they may be relatively proficient in working with their hands, as in carpentry. IEPs now are stressing the strengths to be built upon as well as the developmental weaknesses that have been revealed.

The IEP has brought both positive and negative effects to the education of children with mental retardation or developmental disabilities.

The case study of Tanisha, a child with mild mental retardation, shows the annual goals and short term objectives on her IEP. The objectives are written in such a way that we can easily tell if they have been achieved. Tanisha's IEP provides goals and measurable objectives along three major dimensions: academic, social, and physical (see the box below). The academic goals are written to meet Tanisha where she is developmentally, so she can perform at some level in school. The social and physical goals are designed to improve Tanisha's behavior and enable her to interact with peers in recreational activities. Whenever these short-term objectives have been achieved, a new and more advanced set can be designed. It is important that the written IEP include the nature of the supplementary aids and services to be provided, who will provide the services, anticipated benefits for the child, and how data are to be collected to gauge achievement of objectives (Etscheidt & Bartlett, 1999).

A new concept in use for children with mental retardation is the development of social supports that are necessary to help the individual move toward independence and interdependence in the community. They may include, for older

Tanisha's IEP

Tanisha (CA = 7–3, IQ = 58)

AREA	ANNUAL GOALS	SAMPLE SHORT-TERM OBJECTIVES
Academic	1. Tanisha will count out any number of items between 1 and 20.	Given 5 items on the computer screen, Tanisha will press the correct number in 4 out of 5 trials.
	2. Tanisha will decode new words.	When presented with a new, one-syllable, printed word consisting of familiar letter sounds, Tanisha will say the word correctly in 4 out of 5 trials.
	3. Tanisha will print her full name.	When instructed to print her first name. Tanisha will print all the letters legibly in the correct order in 9 out of 10 trials.
Social	Tanisha will stay in her seat unless given permission to leave it.	During reading period, Tanisha will ask permission before leaving her seat without exception on 4 out of 5 days.
Physical	Tanisha will play kickball.	When instructed to kick, Tanisha will kick the ball in 7 out of 10 trials.

Source: Adapted from L. Hickson, L. Blackman, & E. Reis, *Mental retardation: Foundations of educational programming,* (Boston: Allyn & Bacon, 1995), p.153. Copyright © 1995 by Pearson Education. Adapted by permission.

children, everything from financial planning, to technology assistance, to carpooling, to mobility training.

General Education Classroom

Special educators have long been aware that merely moving an exceptional child from one educational setting to another does not of itself accomplish very much. The rationale for moving a child to another setting is that it will allow the teacher to accomplish goals that otherwise would not be possible.

The philosophy of *inclusion,* or bringing the exceptional child into the general education classroom, depends upon three specific questions:

▶ Can the presentation of the general education curriculum be modified to meet the special needs of the child with mild mental retardation (MMR)?

▶ Are the teachers able to assess the student's needs and modify the curriculum appropriately?

▶ Are teacher-training and inservice programs available to help teachers acquire the skills for teaching a diverse group of students (Crockett & Kauffman, 1998)?

The current stress on high standards for curriculum content and the emphasis on testing to ensure student mastery of that content have in many quarters raised doubts that the general education teacher can meet the three criteria listed above.

> Many students do not have the ability to keep pace with the curriculum the way it is structured within the general education classroom and thus may experience a different kind of segregation—the exclusion from the basic right to learn (Schumm et al., 1995, p. 335).

One of the main concerns of many special educators about the inclusion strategy that brings children with disabilities into the regular classroom is placing students back into the very environment in which they failed in the first place (Keogh, 1996). These students found their way into special education by being referred by the general education teacher as not being able to adapt to the general education classroom.

Those stressing the inclusion strategy point out that the classroom situation will be much different, with support personnel and a specific program (IEP) designed to meet the needs of individual students (Stainback & Stainback, 1996). So one of the keys is, "How much support is actually being given?" The answer may well be different from one school system—indeed, from one school—to the next.

Teacher Consultants or Facilitators

Just about everybody agrees that simply placing a child with special needs in a general education classroom, without making additional and necessary resources available to the classroom teacher, is a recipe for failure. A *support facilitator* can help broaden regular education curriculum by

▶ Encouraging and organizing support networks for the child with special needs

▶ Serving as a resource locator for the regular classroom teacher

▶ Playing the role of *team teacher.*

The child with mental retardation can participate in many activities that help facilitate peer acceptance.
© John Henley/CORBIS

Inclusion facilitators can play a larger role by helping all students, with or without disabilities, who are having difficulty in educational tasks or in gaining peer acceptance. It is crucial that facilitators provide support only when it is needed and not be overprotective. Finally, the inclusion facilitator is the teacher's resource and should not assume the role of a personal teacher for students needing support in the general education classroom (Schaffner & Buswell, 1996, p. 55).

The acceptance of any new child into a classroom group is rarely an easy process. When various characteristics make a child discernibly different from the other children, as a child's special needs would, the task requires special attention. Therefore, the inclusion of children like Bob or Carol needs careful planning.

How to Use the Resource Room

A resource room provides children with mild or moderate retardation an opportunity to work with special education teachers and focus on particular learning problems that are interfering with their performance in the regular classroom. These children leave the classroom for about an hour a day to take part in special lessons. The number of children in the resource room at any one time is usually much less than the number in the general education classroom, giving the resource room teacher an opportunity to work individually or in small groups with children who have retardation. In some schools, resource room programs combine other children with mild handicaps who are at a comparable developmental level with the children with mild retardation, allowing the teacher to plan for them in small groups. Although the resource room has come under increasing criticism, it still is a model used for delivering special educational services.

Special Classes

The greater the degree of disability, the more likely a child is to need a special learning environment to learn distinctively different material. In the special class, a trained teacher provides a distinctive curriculum for a small group of children, typically no more than fifteen. The curriculum may include exercises in personal grooming, safety, preprimary reading skills, or any subject not appropriate for the normally developing child in the regular classroom but highly appropriate for a child like Carol, whose cognitive development is half or less of what is normal for her age. The argument against the special class is that such a setting does not allow for social interaction with general education students.

■ Adapting Curriculum

What Are the Goals?

There has been much discussion about the most desirable curriculum for children with mental retardation. Should the content be different from that given to the average child? If so, where in the educational sequence should the branching take place? In secondary school? In middle school? Or should the curriculum be different from the beginning? The important questions to be answered in the development of curricula for students with mental retardation are, "What are our goals? What are our immediate objectives to reach that goal?"

For students like Carol, who have moderate retardation, reasonable goals are to:

▶ Learn to read at least to the "survival words" level (*stop, poison, restroom,* and so on)

▶ Do basic arithmetic and understand the various denominations of money

▶ Learn social skills, such as the ability to work cooperatively with others

▶ Have some leisure-time skills

▶ Communicate with persons such as storekeepers and community helpers

▶ Learn some work skills to be partially or fully self-supporting in adulthood, if possible

The more difficult curriculum decision involves children with mild mental retardation, who can be expected to reach a medium-to-high elementary school level of skills and knowledge. This decision is particularly difficult if the child is in an inclusive classroom. The curriculum will be the general education curriculum—which may or may not meet the needs of the child, except for the social contacts the student will be having in the class. Patton (1986) suggested that it is possible to infuse relevant career education topics into regularly assigned lessons. Though possible, such a process would require more knowledge and teamwork between special education and regular education than are often present.

At what point does the student with mild mental retardation branch off into a separate secondary school program that is designed to provide work skills rather than help the student reach the next level of education? Inclusion advocates do not expect students with mild or moderate retardation to take advanced high school physics or calculus. It is in the secondary program where attention is traditionally paid to community adjustment and work skills.

Oddly, the recent national emphasis on educational excellence may be a special problem for marginal children such as Bob. They may face academic difficulties when confronted with policies that do not tolerate academic mediocrity and insist on a minimal competence level in order to continue in middle school or secondary school programs.

Educational Reform and High-Stakes Testing

One of the distinctive characteristics of the educational reform movement is its commitment to high standards and accountability. "High standards" generally refers to high conceptual learning in traditional subjects such as language arts and mathematics. This is surely not good news for students with mental retardation or developmental disabilities who do not do well on high-level conceptual material and whose secondary program may even be focused on learning community living. Yet the reform movement increasingly insists on including children with disabilities in these districtwide assessments following those principles:

▶ All students should have access to challenging standards.

▶ Policymakers and educators should be held publicly accountable for every student's performance. (McDonnell, McLaughlin, & Morrison, 1997)

As yet, little is known about the performance of children with disabilities on accountability measures, because many of these students, particularly students with mental retardation or developmental disabilities, have been exempted from the exams by local school systems (Vanderwood, McGrew, & Ysseldyke, 1998). But there is increasing call for testing *all* students in a school system, so we have another issue emerging as to what to do with students who do not perform well on the tests.

Differentiated Instruction

The most common adaptation suggested to teachers for children with mental retardation is **differentiated instruction**, but what exactly does this term mean? It means that each teacher adjusts the level of difficulty of tasks to fit the level of development of the child with mental retardation. For example, if the rest of the class is doing complex multiplication or division problems, the child with mental retardation may be given addition and subtraction problems at his or her level of comprehension. Or in a cooperative learning situation, teams of four or five students might be working on a particular problem related to the early American colonists in our country. The child with mental retardation would be given a task such as finding pictures of colonial life to be used in a report, and other students would be challenged with a complex question such as why these settlers abandoned their homeland to come to the New World. Sometimes such differential lessons are referred to as *tiered assignments,* and they allow the child with mental retardation to participate meaningfully in the group activity.

In such situations it becomes important to have a special education teacher as consultant to help the general education teacher design tiered assignments.

Failure to differentiate lessons for the child with mental retardation runs the risk of discouraging the child, who faces failure once again in the academic setting (see the earlier discussion on learned helplessness).

In most programs for children with mild and moderate retardation—particularly for those who are grouped with other students of limited abilities or performance—differentiated instruction takes place in four major areas:

▶ *Readiness and academic skills.* With preschoolers and elementary school children, basic reading and arithmetic skills are stressed. Later, these skills are applied to practical work and community settings.

▶ *Communication and language development.* The student gets practice in using language to communicate needs and ideas. Specific efforts are directed toward improving memory skills and problem-solving skills at the level of the student's ability.

▶ *Socialization.* Specific instruction is provided in self-care and family living skills, beginning at the preschool level with sharing and manners, then gradually developing in secondary school into subjects like grooming, dancing, sex education, and avoiding drug abuse.

▶ *Prevocations and work-study skills.* The basis for vocational adjustment through good work habits (promptness, following through on instruction, working cooperatively on group projects) is established. At the secondary level, this curriculum can focus on career education and include part-time job placement and field trips to possible job sites.

We will examine each area separately. Because of current awareness of the value of early intervention, many of these skills are being included in the school curriculum at various levels.

Ronald: This child and his parents have been told that he will be part of a new program at school, called *inclusion,* that will bring Ronald into the regular fifth grade, even with his diagnosis of mild mental retardation. Previously he was in a resource room program; he spent an hour or more each day with a special education teacher who worked with him in areas of language and basic arithmetic. He was achieving at the second-grade level.

His parents felt gratified that Ronald would now be with all the other fifth graders, but worried, too. Would he get along with the other children? How could he keep up with the other students, when he was reading at only a second-grade level? The school principal told Ronald's parents that he would be seeing his special education teacher for some lessons, but within the general education classroom. The fifth-grade classroom teacher worried about the very same issues as the parents, knowing that having him in a seat in her class didn't mean that Ronald would find friends there, or that he would be happy with the high standards of instruction directed toward students now. One major task for this teacher is to make Ronald feel at home, feel like part of the class. A second is to ensure that he receives individualized instruction to meet his needs. Making inclusion work for Ronald will require professional teamwork on the part of the school (Wilson, 1999). That may be why many observers remain unconvinced about the utility of inclusion policies. It is not so much that inclusion may not work but that it may demand more attention and planning by school and classroom personnel then they are willing or able to provide (Crockett & Kauffman, 1998).

Martin (1995) expressed his fears about inclusion as: that they would offer less individualized instruction to children, that they would suffer from some of the same problems of organization, planning, and coordination that affect current programs. . . (p. 194).

Basic Academic Skills

To develop a curriculum for primary-grade children with mental retardation, we use **task analysis**—breaking down a complex task into simple subtasks that are within the child's abilities. Reading, for example, combines auditory perception (auditory discrimination and sound blending) and visual perception (matching letters and letter-word recognition) (Wolery & Brookfield-Norman, 1988). By helping the child master these basic skills, we are preparing the child to read.

In much the same way, we prepare the child to think about numbers in sets and to match numbers and objects by first teaching the child how to count. And we prepare the child to write by focusing on simple visual-motor activities (imitating a specific stroke, then tracing letters). The process offers dual benefits. First, the subtasks are the source from which academic skills will develop. Second, mastery of the subtasks gives the child with retardation an opportunity to succeed and gain self-confidence.

One of the discoveries that teachers make about children like Bob with mental retardation, is that one cannot assume that because he has acquired some skill or knowledge in one setting, it will automatically be generalized to other settings or situations. Such students need special help with their memory and attention.

Some of the cognitive strategies that have to be specifically taught are rehearsal strategies, such as shadowing or vocalized thinking or thinking aloud, and the use of verbatim notes with the student copying text, such as spelling words, in written form (Rosenthal-Malik & Bloom, 1998). One way to enhance the students' ability to organize information is by helping them ask a standard set of questions such as (1) What do I need to do? (b) What will happen if . . . ? (c) How am I doing? (d) Did that work achieve my goal? Though a teacher might not want to go to such trouble with other students, it is almost a necessity for children with mental retardation, to help them combat the natural limitations of memory or organization.

When we teach reading to Carol and other children with moderate retardation, we focus on functional reading (Snell, 1987). Although these individuals are unlikely to ever read for comprehension or recreation, they need to be able to:

▶ Identify key words in simple recipes

▶ Develop a protective vocabulary (*walk, don't walk, stop, men, women, in, out*)

▶ Recognize the skull and crossbones that denotes poisonous substances.

Language and Communication

There is a substantial effort in elementary schools to help children with moderate retardation use language as a tool for communication. Students may be asked to describe a simple object such as a table (it is round; it is hard; you put things on it; it is brown). And they may learn to communicate feelings of happiness, anger, and sadness by using language.

Language exercises for children with moderate retardation aim to foster the development of speech and the understanding and use of verbal concepts. Communication skills such as the ability to listen to stories, discuss pictures, and tell about recent experiences are stressed. Two important areas of study are the home and the community. Children learn about holidays, transportation, the months of the year and days of the week, and contributions to home life. Classes make use of dramatization, acting out a story or a song, playing make-believe, engaging in shadow play, and using gestures with songs, stories, and rhymes.

> The functional use of language is a critical goal for children with mental retardation.

For students with moderate retardation, there may be an expectation of mastery of reading and arithmetic to the second- or third-grade level. That means special attention should be paid to their learning key words that operate in our society to start or stop actions. Such "survival words" (and phrases) are listed in the box on page 192. Direct instruction in these words can help the child with moderate retardation exhibit proper behavior in the community even without extrinsic mastery of more complex reading skills.

Socialization

Social skills are a critical component of the primary school curriculum for children who have mental retardation, but instruction at this level should be informal. Children can learn to take turns, share, and work cooperatively as part of

> In peer-buddy systems, a classmate may help a classmate with disabilities negotiate the school day.
> (© Photo courtesy of the National Down Syndrome Society)

their daily activities. The lunch table is an excellent location for teaching social skills. Then, youngsters learn table manners as well as how to pass and share food, help others (pouring juice, for example), and wait their turn. The lunch table is also a good place to review the morning's activities and talk about what is planned for the afternoon or the next day. Although the teaching is informal, it is both effective and important to the child's social development.

Children with retardation have difficulty transferring or applying ideas from one setting to another. Thus, we teach needed social skills directly. We do not expect the children to automatically understand these skills and apply them from experience.

Part of the process of growing up is gradually mastering social skills to establish effective communication and relationships with others. We rarely think about these skills because they emerge through adult and peer modeling without our being conscious of them. If we are asked how we meet strangers, break unpleasant news, communicate with someone we haven't seen for a long time, or tell someone that he is intruding on our space and time, it is likely that we will have to think for a while before we can recall the coping strategies that we use without conscious effort. These skills are the lubrication that allows each of us to move smoothly through our daily contacts and tasks. Someone who is markedly deficient or awkward in such skills stands out in a crowd. Many children with mental retardation lack these social skills and need direct instruction in them if they are to establish a useful personal and community adjustment.

Bob, for example, usually got too close to the person he was speaking to. He made the other person uncomfortable but was not aware of this reaction. Through role-playing a number of social situations with Bob and others, the teacher was able to establish that each person has a personal space that is not to be invaded without permission (for example, to kiss an aunt good-bye). Such social rules may seem trivial, but their importance is magnified substantially when they are violated.

A Functional Reading Vocabulary

Go	Up	Dynamite	School
Slow down	Down	Explosives	School bus
Stop	Men	Fire	No trespassing
Off	Women	Fire escape	Private property
On	Exit	Poison	Men working
Cold	Entrance	Wet paint	Yield
Hot	Danger	Police	Railroad crossing
In	Be careful	Keep off	Boys
Out	Caution	Watch for children	Girls

Source: From C. Drew, M. Hardman, & D. Logan, *Mental retardation: A life cycle approach* (6th ed.) (Upper Saddle River, NJ: Prentice-Hall, 1996). Copyright © 1996. Reprinted with the permission of Prentice-Hall, Inc. Upper Saddle River, NJ.

It is important that the sense of privacy is established and understood when the child begins to cope with sexual relationships. Parents and other adults worry about the susceptibility of young people with mental retardation to sexual abuse or unwanted sexual contact merely because they lack the skills to fend off others in sexual encounters. The closer the student is brought to the inclusive classroom, the more likely he or she is to have a variety of contacts with members of the opposite sex. Therefore, some type of counseling and role-playing of relationships or situations with the opposite sex are often part of the curriculum for students with mild or moderate retardation.

The **social learning approach** (Bandura, 1989) aims to foster critical thinking and independent action by those with mild retardation. Lesson experiences focus on psychological needs (for self-respect, mastery), physical needs (for sensory stimulation), and physical maintenance and social aspects (for independence, mobility). For example, in the middle school, lesson experiences teaching the importance of economic security could include the following objectives: (1) choosing a job commensurate with skills and interests, (2) locating and acquiring a satisfactory job, (3) maintaining a job, and (4) effectively managing the financial resources earned from a job.

For students with mental retardation, gaining social acceptance in the inclusive classroom requires special planning by educators.

To meet a socialization goal of inclusion, those educators endorsing inclusion have devised a series of activities that enhance social contact and learning. In *peer-buddy systems,* a classmate may help a classmate with disabilities negotiate the school day; *peer support networks* help students become part of a caring community; and in *circles of friends,* an adult facilitator helps potential peer buddies sensitize peers to the friendship needs of students with disabilities (Villa & Thousand, 1995).

One of the strategies designed to enhance socialization is the creation of a MAP (for *making an action plan*). This may seem similar to an IEP, but is different in that it is constructed by those students and adults directly involved in the person's life instead of by a team of professionals constructing an IEP. The key question in the design of a MAP is, "What do the child and the family want?" Goals are established, along with the means to reach them.

A person identified as an *integration facilitator* may have the skills necessary to help relevant individuals create a MAP for Bob or Carol. Emphasis is placed on the individual strengths of the children and what actions need to be taken to allow them to achieve their dreams. The focus is not on academic learning but on the social skills that will serve the children in adult life (Pearpoint, Forest, & O'Brien, 1996). Supporters of these activities point out that students without disabilities have some important learning to do to realize the diversity of the general population and the importance of being a part of a caring community.

Prevocations and Work-Study Skills

As the child with mild retardation reaches middle school or junior high school, many special education programs focus on the development of work skills. Important knowledge and skills need to be mastered in five areas—consumer economics, occupational knowledge, health, community resources, and government and law. This approach is preferable to teaching generalizations or abstract principles that the child then has to apply to specific situations—a

When students with mental retardation reach middle school, their special education programs often begin to emphasize work skills.

skill in which children with retardation are not proficient. The problem for the teacher comes when other students in the classroom are learning different materials more appropriate for their age level. It takes a good deal of joint planning with the classroom teacher or the middle school teaching team to integrate functional competencies with the standard educational program. Some of the specific requirements have been noted as modifying teacher worksheets, specific instruction in assignment completion, in self-monitoring, setting performance goals and goal evaluation (Copeland, Hughes, Agran, Wehmeyer, & Fowley, 2002).

Vocational training focuses on dimensions beyond the job itself: banking and using money, grooming, caring for a car and obtaining insurance, interviewing for jobs, and using leisure time. Adjustment to the work world involves adapting to the demands of life as well as to a specific job.

Some programs try to build a set of vocational skills progressively over time, involving a variety of social agencies in the educational activities. Fundamental activities and skills are taught in a special class setting. Then specific areas of prevocational and vocational training, including on-the-job training, are covered in the adolescent years. Finally, with the help of vocational rehabilitation, attempts are made to provide a useful work experience in either a sheltered workshop facility or a competitive employment setting. This plan has the merit of establishing developmental tasks and long-range goals that those who have moderate retardation can approach step by step.

The recent movement toward including in general education classes children who have mild retardation has created a difficult conflict. As long as children with retardation are in general education classrooms, they are receiving the regular curriculum or some variation of it. But the secondary school curriculum of content subjects (English, history, science) may not be the most appropriate for them. These students could profit more from a program that emphasizes the practical and vocational skills needed for independent living.

Nevertheless, if the school is to be held accountable through testing standards, it is likely that students with mental retardation will endure the general curriculum anyway.

■ Adapting Teaching Strategies

Special education draws heavily on learning theory to help children achieve a level of constructive behavior. Many of the learning principles we use to help children with retardation associate ideas or remember events have been used intuitively in classrooms and families for years. One popular approach, Premack's principle (Premack, 1959), is to attach a wanted but low-probability behavior to a high-probability behavior, which then becomes a positive reinforcer. Practically, the teacher says, "If you clean up your workplace on time, you can do a puzzle or listen to records." (Premack's principle has been called "Grandma's law": "First you eat your vegetables, then you get dessert.")

Scaffolding and Reciprocal Teaching

The special learning problems that children with mental retardation have require special teaching strategies. Two of these strategies are scaffolding and reciprocal teaching. In scaffolding, the teacher models the expected behavior and then guides the student through the early stages of understanding. As the student's understanding increases, the teacher gradually withdraws aid (hence the name "scaffolding"). The goal is to have the student internalize the knowledge and operate independently.

In **reciprocal teaching,** small groups of students and teachers take turns leading a discussion on a particular topic. This exercise features four activities: questioning, clarifying, summarizing, and predicting. In this strategy (as in scaffolding), the teacher models how to carry out the activities successfully. The students then imitate the teaching style while the teacher plays the role of the student. In this way, students become active players in a role they find enjoyable.

Positive Behavior Supports (PBS)

One technique that is useful for educators is **positive behavior supports (PBS).** PBSs are used to reduce or eliminate obnoxious nonadaptive behaviors (Koegel, Koegel, & Dunlap, 1996). Combining *functional analysis* (to determine the possible triggers to the undesirable behavior) with *modification of the environment* around the child has been found to be effective.

With the PBS technique, environmental conditions are remediated, and positive behavior repertoires are built. *Applied behavior analysis* techniques, as part of PBS, use positive reinforcement to strengthen the desirable behavior and the mastery of social skills. *Environmental conditions* could involve lack of choice, inadequate teaching strategies, and lack of access to materials or activities. Building positive behavior repertoires can include self-management skills, social skills, and other constructive behaviors.

A synthesis of 10 years of research projects using PBA (Carr et al., 1999) revealed that PBS was widely applicable to persons with behavior problems and significantly reduced problem behaviors in one-half to two-thirds of the cases. This relatively new PBS approach deserves the attention of teacher trainers as well as teachers.

Fading and Self-Instruction

Earlier in this chapter, we presented the IEP goals and objectives for Tanisha. To achieve those objectives, though, it often would be necessary to adopt special instructional strategies to adjust to Tanisha's limited ability to generalize or to maintain desired behaviors even after they have appeared.

The "Case Study: Tanisha" box (see the following page) is a sequence of self-instruction training designed to aid Tanisha's ability to reach the objective that "Tanisha will ask permission before leaving her seat without exception on 4 out of 5 days." The trainer or aide first models the desired behavior by raising her hand and asking the teacher permission to go to the water fountain, then encourages Tanisha to do the same. Tanisha is taught to say aloud to herself, "Each time I want to leave my seat, I must raise my hand and ask my teacher for permission," then to whisper it to herself, then finally to use private, nonvocal speech to remind herself to ask permission. The process of going from speaking aloud to whispering to nonvocal speech is known as *fading.*

This long and involved sequence may strike some as a complicated series of events for the "simple" task of getting a student to raise her hand before leaving her seat, particularly since most students learn this behavior automatically. However, unless this systematic and sequential system is followed, children with mental retardation, like Tanisha, may not learn the social and academic skills necessary to their adaptation in the classroom and the community.

Intrinsic Motivation

It is generally accepted that children with mental retardation seem to be motivated more by **extrinsic motivation** (if you are good, I will buy you an ice cream cone) than by **intrinsic motivation** (if you do your homework, you will feel much better about yourself). This finding is translated into educational strategies through the use of various extrinsic rewards—such as positive social reinforcement by means of praise, gold stars, or tokens to be cashed in for toys—to motivate the student to greater effort. Some, however, maintain that an intrinsic motivational approach is helpful to children with special needs (Switzky & Schultz, 1988). They maintain that children with intrinsic motivation work harder and longer on tasks than do those with extrinsic motivation and that therefore it is important to help instill an attitude of intrinsic motivation in youngsters. The problem with extrinsic motivation, they point out, is that someone will not always be present and ready to give immediate and tangible rewards for proper behavior. Then what will extrinsically motivated youngsters do?

Some maintain that students who are intrinsically motivated work harder and longer on tasks than do students who are extrinsically motivated.

| Tanisha's Self-Instruction Training Sequence

CASE STUDY: Tanisha (CA = 7–3, IQ = 58)

Self-Instruction Training Sequence

Student: _Tanisha_   Date: _December 3, 1992_

Short-Term Objective: _During reading periods, Tanisha will ask permission before leaving her seat without exception on 4 out of 5 days._

Training Sequence

1. *Cognitive Modeling.* The trainer sits in a student seat in the classroom and raises her hand, saying aloud, "Each time I want to leave my seat, I must raise my hand and ask the teacher for permission." Then the trainer says to the teacher, "May I go the the water fountain?"

2. *Overt External Guidance.* The trainer instructs and verbally prompts Tanisha to raise her hand and ask the teacher for permission to go to the water fountain.

3. *Overt Self-Guidance.* Tanisha raises her hand, whispering to herself aloud, "Each time I want to leave my seat, I must raise my hand and ask my teacher for permission." Then Tanisha says to the teacher, "May I go to the water fountain?"

4. *Faded, Overt Self-Guidance.* Tanisha raises her hand, whispering to herself, "Each time I want to leave my seat, I must raise my hand and ask my teacher for permission." Then Tanisha says to the teacher, "May I go to the water fountain?"

5. *Covert Self-Instruction.* Tanisha raises her hand, and says to the teacher, "May I go to the water fountain?" This time, she uses private, nonvocal speech to remind herself that she must raise her hand and ask permission to leave her seat.

Source: Adapted from L. Hickson, L. Blackman, & E. Reis, *Mental retardation: Foundations for educational programming* (Boston: Allyn & Bacon, 1995), p. 153. Copyright © 1995 by Pearson Education. Adapted with permission.

Cooperative Learning

Interestingly, emphasis has switched from a focus on one-on-one instruction for the individual student with special needs, as represented in the policies for an IEP, to the importance of student participation in *cooperative learning* or *team-assisted individualization*. With the inclusion of many children with special needs in general education classrooms has come the need to develop strategies that will help the teacher integrate students with disabilities with the other students. Cooperative learning is one of these strategies. There are many versions of it (Johnson & Johnson, 1991; Kagan, 1989; Slavin, 1988), but all have some characteristics in common.

In **cooperative learning,** the teacher gives a task to a small group of students (typically four to six), who are expected to complete the task by working cooperatively with one another. The teacher may assign different responsibilities to different members of the group or ask each child to play a specific role (such as recorder, reporter, searcher, or praiser). Although group members are expected to work cooperatively, most advocates of cooperative learning insist that the students be evaluated individually. The child with disabilities may have the same overall objective as other students but be operating with a lower level of task expectations, a reduced workload, or partial participation. As long as the child feels a part of the enterprise, some good social interactions can occur.

Group instruction may actually be more advantageous than one-on-one instruction because of the economy of teacher effort, students learning how to interact with peers, and students learning from peers. Small-group instruction is the mode for the regular classroom if the students are to be mainstreamed (Collins, Gast, Ault, & Wolery, 1991).

Skills Mastery

One of the most important questions facing the teachers of children with mental retardation and developmental disabilities is how to motivate these children to learn. There are a lot of reasons for them not to be motivated in school. Bob, for example, comes from a home in which there is little interest in school learning. He is 10 years old and has had a few years' experience in school. But those years have not been full of positive experiences. Bob has known a lot of failure, and failure is a distinct turnoff for most children and adults.

People who believe they are likely to fail can develop a condition known as *learned helplessness*. They think, "I can't do anything about my situation, and I know things are going to turn out badly" (Dweck & Leggett, 1988). Students who experience this feeling tend to avoid situations in which they think they probably will fail. They avoid the very learning situations that they need to experience if they are going to improve their situation. Such individuals need a strong dose of *self-efficacy* (Bandura, 1989), the belief that they are competent at some tasks. But if failure is their constant diet, how can they develop feelings of competence? Finding an answer to that question is the basic challenge facing the educator who will work with Bob.

Carol, however, faces a different situation. Many special educators believe that their students' fundamental goal is not the mastery of knowledge or skills but the mastery of adaptive behaviors such as social skills, communication skills, and work skills. After all, they ask, who cares very much if Carol reaches third-grade or fourth grade mastery of academic skills? What is important is that Carol develop adaptive skills that will serve her well in adulthood and in the world of work. Thus, it is important for Carol to participate in cooperative learning exercises, not necessarily to learn what the other students learn, but to experience positive social interaction and learn how to work constructively with others.

A large part of the positive experience of school stems from success in learning how to learn and learning how to work constructively with others. Such skills, if they become habits, serve the individual well beyond the school years. So the mastery of social skills becomes a major objective of programs for exceptional children. It is unwise to assume that students with mental retardation absorb these skills any more readily than they do academic skills. It is much more likely that teachers need to design activities to help students achieve social skills and replace with prosocial skills disruptive behavior such as aggression, excessive talking, and out-of-seat behavior.

One goal of teachers is to help students develop a sense of competence. Self-confidence comes in part from being able to do well the work that is expected of you. The teacher can build students' self-confidence by presenting lessons that are challenging but within the range of their ability to perform.

Teachers also need a variety of skills that will help them nurture positive, prosocial skills and diminish negative patterns of behavior that a student may be showing.

■ Adapting Technology

The rapid development of technology linked to education provides a variety of opportunities for children with disabilities. These technological aids can be divided into two areas: assistive and instructional. *Assistive technology* exists to help the child with disabilities gain access to the information needed for learning. *Instructional technology* is used to help the student learn that information. The **universal design for learning** (UDL) is a way of presenting the information to be learned in the style most accommodating to the individual student's needs.

Assistive Technology

One of the support features of an individualized education program (IEP) can be assistive technology, equipment or product systems that can meet some of the special needs of individual children with developmental disabilities (Parette, 1998). The low-tech devices are relatively inexpensive, whereas the high-tech devices tend to be complex, expensive, and difficult to maintain. The high-tech devices often require extensive explanation from the IEP committee before a school system will invest in them, but may be required for meeting the educational needs of some children.

The purchase of a device without sufficient investment in time, proper supervision, and maintenance to make sure it is being used appropriately has resulted in many assistive technology devices ending up in closets and storage rooms, so special attention must be given to proper use of this equipment. See the Houghton Mifflin Teacher Education website for an expanded list of assistive technology equipment.

www Houghton Mifflin Teacher Education website http://education.college.hmco.com/students

The child with mental retardation needs guided practice with technology.
(© Paul Conklin/PhotoEdit)

Some of the uses of assistive technology (Blackhurst & Edyburn, 2000) include devices to aid mobility, communication, and instruction. These assistive devices are either low tech (such as communication boards or adapted books) or high tech (such as computerized visual amplification systems or augmentative communication devices that use digitized speech). The high-tech devices are sophisticated and expensive, and it pays to be aware of the low-tech devices that can be helpful for students with special needs (Parette, 1998).

Instructional Technology

Instructional technology in the classroom has many applications for students with mental retardation, as well as for other students. Serna and Patton (1989) indicated that the computer can be used for *drill and practice*—in reading and arithmetic particularly—*tutorials, simulations,* and *problem solving.* A disadvantage of using computers is that the teacher cannot merely point to the computer and say, "Bob, go and do your exercises." Students with mental retardation need consistent monitoring, and some need considerable instruction in the use of the computer and in the use of some of the simulation and problem-solving programs.

Parette (1991) pointed out that state-of-the-art *hypermedia*—an information storage and usage design that enables text, graphics, animation, and sound to be

Technology, when properly used, can help the child grasp unfamiliar ideas.

With organized training programs and support services, many young people with mental retardation or developmental disabilities can adjust well in community settings.
(© Mike Greenbar/The Image Works)

combined to suit individual needs—can be adapted for use with children with mental retardation. Such approaches may help students who otherwise would have problems linking ideas and thoughts.

This increasingly available technology can be a valuable adjunct to the well-prepared teacher particularly when the student becomes stuck in the mastery of a particular skill or set of information. It has the additional social value to students with retardation of signaling their ability to use sophisticated equipment, just as the other students do (Gardner & Bates, 1991).

What proportion of the child's social and cognitive development depends on biology and what proportion on the social environment remains a major issue. Horowitz and Haritos (1998) pointed out that few intervention programs with the goal of improving the social and cognitive experiences of young children born into poverty showed large increases in IQ scores. Most of those programs did show benefits in areas of school achievement, behavioral functioning, and personal adjustment. They concluded that the growing body of evidence points to biological factors strongly controlling the developmental outcomes but that environmental intervention can result in modest improvement.

■ Transition

School to Work

In the not-too-distant past, little or no information was available about the progress of students with mental retardation after they left school. Today, a growing number of studies indicate how these students are doing in adult life. The news is mixed.

A major study looking at 8,000 youths with disabilities, the National Longitudinal Transitional Study of Special Education Students (Blackorby & Wagner, 1996), was begun in 1987. Researchers used a careful sampling design to ensure that their sample was nationally representative and generalizable to the population as a whole as well as to students in eleven disabilities categories. Large samples of youngsters with disabilities from 300 public school districts and from 25 state-operated schools for children who are deaf or blind were surveyed and interviewed. In addition, a subsample of more than 800 parents of youth who had been out of secondary school between two and four years was interviewed.

What happened to youths identified as having mental retardation? Let's look first at performance in secondary school. Half of the students with mental retardation graduated from high school; the rest either dropped out or aged out of school. The reasons for dropping out of school appeared to be related to behavior rather than to academic performance. Twenty-eight percent of the students with disabilities who dropped out were identified as individuals having serious discipline problems.

What about social relationships? About 1 out of every 4 individuals with mental retardation was identified as a social isolate in school. But the percentage of students with mental retardation who regularly saw friends was no lower than the percentage among those who were visually impaired, speech impaired, or learning disabled. Children with mental retardation were less likely than other students with disabilities to be members of organized groups such as the Boy Scouts, religious youth groups, or sports teams. Only about 1

Ryan, a 22-year-old with mental retardation, was referred to an occupational therapist after unsuccessful community-based job placements. Several professionals recommended that he return to a sheltered day program for "work skills training."

While working with a new occupational therapist, Ryan said he'd like more jobs similar to the ones he had previously lost due to excessive absence or poor performance. Ryan was capable of doing the necessary tasks for those jobs but had seemed to lose interest in them very quickly.

He took a look at some new job ideas on video and was excited about the possibility of working as a housekeeper at a motel. It wasn't easy to find an employer who was willing to give him a try. But one motel owner agreed to give Ryan a job on a 30-day trial basis. It took only a short time for Ryan to become one of the most efficient and reliable housekeepers on the motel's staff. His employer was so impressed that she requested other people with disabilities seeking employment.

Ryan had many successes at this job. He was named Employee of the Month and given a cash bonus, and later was promoted to "second floor supervisor" and given a raise. Ryan eventually moved up to supervising a group of motel employees without disabilities.

Source: Adapted from Becky Blair, Ryan's story: From job placement challenge to employee of the month, *Teaching Exceptional Children* (March/April 2000): 47. Reprinted with permission.

out of every 3 of the students with mental retardation was identified as belonging to, or having some regular membership in, a group.

What about the arrest rate of youth with disabilities? Children with mental retardation ranked fourth in the eleven categories of youth with disabilities who were arrested while they were in secondary school, and they ranked fifth in the "out of school" arrest category. Roughly 1 out of every 10 of the school youth with mental retardation had an arrest record. A factor significant to the arrest record was gender: Males were arrested four times more often than females.

One of the major ethical issues in our society is whether a person with mental retardation should receive capital punishment for a crime he or she has committed. This is anything but a philosophical question. It has been estimated that anywhere from 12 to 20 percent of persons waiting to be executed in this country are mentally retarded (Beirne-Smith, Ittenbach, & Patton, 2001).

That number chiefly reflects the inability to raise a proper defense, and the low economic standing, of many mentally retarded persons under sentence. The Supreme Court (*Penry* v. *Lynaugh*, 1989) considered this issue through two questions:

▶ Should jurors be advised to consider mental retardation as a mitigating factor when considering the death penalty?

▶ Is it cruel and unusual punishment to execute persons who are mentally retarded?

In a five-to-four decision the Supreme Court stated that mental retardation should be considered a mitigating factor but that persons who are mentally retarded can legally be executed. Nevertheless, this issue bothers the conscience of many who wonder about the justice of executing a person who might have been unaware of what he or she was doing or about the consequences of the actions.

What about responsibilities at home? Out-of-school youth with mental retardation had roughly the same amount of household responsibilities as youth in other disability categories. Although the number of students with mental retardation who were performing in an unsatisfactory fashion was not encouraging, their adaptation seemed to be similar to that of students with other disabilities.

What about living independently? In the first or second year after secondary school, fewer students with mental retardation were living independently than were students with other disabilities. For example, 9 percent of the students with mental retardation, 22 percent of the students with learning disabilities, and 26 percent of the visually impaired students were living independently. These figures improve, however, three to five years after high school. Then, 24 percent of adults with mental retardation were living independently. There also were encouraging increases in employment rates and wages (Blackorby & Wagner, 1996).

Figure 5.3 indicates the percentage of youths with mental retardation who were competitively employed within three to five years after they left school. On the graph, the general population of students show a 70 percent rate of employment, and when all the figures for youths with disabilities are included, slightly more than half are competitively employed. In contrast, the number of

One young woman with Down syndrome achieved these goals: certification as a teacher's aide for an early intervention program, advisory board member on a magazine for parents of children with disabilities, and an Associate in Science degree.

**FIGURE 5.3
Youths Competitively
Employed 3–5 Years
Out of School**

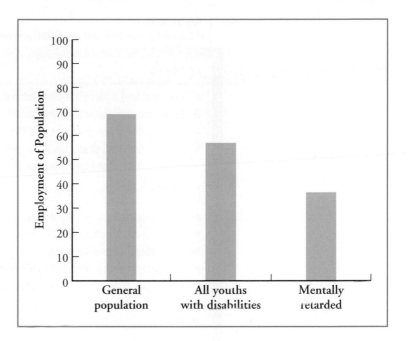

Source: From M. Wagner & J. Blackorby, Transition from high school to work or college: How special education students fare, in D. Terman, M. Lerner, C. Stevenson, & R. Behrman (Eds.), *The Future of Children, 6*(1) (1996): 4–24.

youths with mental retardation is between only 30 and 40 percent. Such a figure underscores the importance of vocational training and counseling in that transition period between school and work, so that these youths can make an effective adjustment to the world of work.

Table 5.5 provides a series of events for secondary students who have mental retardation. Basically, by getting a part-time job at age 16, enrolling in vocational classes at age 17, and setting vocational goals at age 18, the student is preparing for a transition to work and the community. It does not make much sense to continue to enroll this student with mental retardation in traditional secondary courses, many of them designed for college-preparatory programs.

Such results have convinced special educators that assistance to many students with mental retardation has to be continued beyond the school years, if the goals of becoming self-sustaining and independent are to be achieved. Accordingly, there has been more attention paid to the transition years between school and vocational work (and adulthood). While inclusion appears to be a viable goal for children with mental retardation through middle school, there needs to be a significant plan, a transition plan, which can be every bit as important as the IEP established earlier in the child's career. (See Table 5.4.)

Table 5.5, "Career and Economic Self-Sufficiency," shows the career plan for Garland, a student with moderate retardation who has only a 30-word sight vocabulary and basic math skills. This plan was worked out with Garland, his parents, his teacher, and his vocational rehabilitation counselor. The detailed steps in this plan are recognition that Garland will continue to need help in order to achieve vocational independence. The transition plan also includes goals related to community integration, transportation, and social relationships, without which the vocational training might be wasted.

TABLE 5.4
Planning for Secondary Students with Mental Retardation

AT AGE 16

► Find and hold a part-time job in school or in the community.
► Write transition knowledge into the IEP meetings.
► Invite adult service providers to IEP meetings.
► Discuss how long student will attend high school—for four years or until age 21.
► Attend information night meetings that offer information about future planning.

AT AGE 17

► Enroll in vocational education classes.
► Establish a graduation date.
► Write transition goals into IEP.
► Invite adult service providers to IEP meetings.
► Investigate guardianship procedures and determine what is in the best interest of the child.

AT AGE 18

► Apply for SSI and Medicaid card.
► Make application to PACT Inc. for residential or case management assistance.
► Apply to adult service provider. Take time to visit all providers to find the best match.
► Schedule a vocational evaluation to better assist in determining the child's interest and setting a vocational goal.
► Write transition goal in IEP. Discuss services needed for best transition from high school to adult services.
► Attend a job fair.

Source: From A. M. Goldberg, Transition timeline, retrieved July 15, 2004, from www.ndss.org. Reprinted with permission.

The lesson here is that we cannot release young people with retardation from school and expect them to adjust to a working environment without help and planning. With organized training programs and support services, many of these individuals can adjust well. The support resources that can be brought to bear fall into four categories:

▶ *Individuals:* skills, competencies, the ability to make choices, money information, spiritual values

▶ *Other people:* family, friends, coworkers, cohabitants, mentors

▶ *Technology:* assistive devices, job/living accommodations, behavioral technology

▶ *Services:* habilitation services that can be used when natural resources are not available

We should think of the total resources for helping young adults present in the community instead of merely the resources of the school system. Attention

Children with mental retardation can and do make good adaptations in adulthood.

TABLE 5.5
Career and Economic Self-Sufficiency

1. EMPLOYMENT GOAL	Garland will work full-time in the deli department of a local grocery store with supported employment.
Level of present performance	Garland has been employed by school enclaves at two sites and has taken a vocational food preparation course at school.
Steps needed to accomplish goal	(1) Assist Garland with applying for jobs at local groceries; (2) arrange for transportation by carpool; and (3) provide job training assistance and support as needed.
Date of completion	6/05
Person(s) responsible for implementation	VR counselor
2. VOCATIONAL EDUCATION/TRAINING GOAL	Garland will work part-time with supported employment prior to graduation.
Level of present performance	Garland has received vocational situational assessment at two grocery stores and has been assigned a Department of Rehabilitative Services (DRS) counselor.
Steps needed to accomplish goals	(1) Meet with DRS counselor and assist in job application is needed; (2) arrange Garland's school schedule to accommodate work schedule; (3) provide staff for job-site training; (4) provide transportation; and (5) share information and responsibilities with DRS counselor.

to the individual's adaptive skills at adolescence may yield the best chance for a meaningful adult adjustment. Helping adults with mental retardation find employment and social opportunities surely will be an important goal in the twenty-first century.

■ Family and Lifespan Issues

What happens to children with mental retardation when they finish their schooling? Do they find work? At what kinds of jobs? Where do they live? What kinds of support do they need in order to adapt to society?

Many jobs in the community can be filled by persons with mental retardation.
(© James Shaffer/PhotoEdit)

Family Support

ARC parents' group newsletter
www.thearc.org

One of the common feelings of parents whose children have developmental disabilities is loneliness. They feel different from their neighbors and often do not know how best to help such a child. An important resource, designed to help them cope can be an organized parents' group. The Arc of the United States (established in 1951 as the Association for Retarded Citizens) is a national organization with many chapters throughout the country. It is able to provide access to resources for parents and to advocate for them and for their children. Often another parent who has been through the same experience can be a valuable friend and confidante, and parents' organizations such as The Arc have well-developed support help. Visit The Arc's website for leads to a wide variety of useful information.

The Arc of the United States
www.thearc.org

One of the strategies that professionals use to help families cope with the extra stress that often accompanies living with children with disabilities is respite care. **Respite care** is the provision of child-care services so the parents are freed, for a few days, of their constant care responsibilities. Parents who may not have had a "day off" from child-care responsibilities for years greatly appreciate such assistance. Respite care is an effective way of reducing parental depression and stress and enabling parents to be more effective in their role (Botuck & Winsberg, 1991).

Respite care is one of the simplest and most effective aids to families.

There is little doubt that many of these parents are under an additional burden of stress, and one of the responsibilities of professionals who interact with family members is to recognize and support the family members with understanding and empathy. One of the ways to accomplish that goal is to reflect the feelings of the parent as a way of showing understanding and sympathy with what the parent is facing.

Family member: Everything seems to be a burden these days, doing the housework, taking care of the kids, paying the bills. I just don't know how much longer I can keep up the pace.

Professional: All your responsibilities really cause a drain on your time and energy.

Family member: Ever since Eliot was born, my family and friends have put a wall up between me and them. I guess they don't want to do the wrong thing, but what they don't realize is that the worst thing of all is doing nothing and staying away. I have no one to turn to and feel my "resentment gauge" going up by the day. It really hurts me and makes me angry when I've always tried to be there for them, and now when I need them most, they just seem to back away.

Professional: You're feeling very let down by family who you thought would always be there for you. (Turnbull & Turnbull, 1997, p. 66)

Another role for the professional is to help the family in establishing a sustainable daily routine (Gallimore, Bernheimer, & Weisner, 1998). Many parents react to their stressful situation by saying that they are merely going "one day at a time"—all the more reason to emphasize the importance of developing a daily routine that meets the needs of each family member in some optimal way.

As difficult as this life situation may be for the two-parent family, it becomes even more of a strain when only one parent is present or if the family unit is in poverty. One should not overlook the role of available resources or money to pay for child minding, laundry appliances, and cleaning services to relieve the parents of certain household tasks.

Too often in the past, when we said we were involved with the family, we really meant the mother. We now realize the importance of relating to the father as part of the family unit. This is especially true since there is evidence that the typical father tends to play less of a family role when there is a child with disabilities (Lillic, 1993). Some direct counseling and support for the father in his role may be important to achieve the sustainable daily routine that seems so necessary to keep the family on an even keel.

We used to assume that every family who has a child with disabilities was in a crisis situation. We have since discovered that many families adapt well to these special pressures (Bristol, Gallagher, & Shopler, 1988), while others require special attention. A popular program called Parent to Parent matches a trained "veteran parent" (someone who has experience as a parent with a child with disabilities) and a "referred parent" (one who is dealing with the issues for the first time). Although only twenty years old, there are 550 Parent to Parent programs serving nearly 30,000 parents (Turnbull & Turnbull, 1997). An example of just what such a program can mean comes from a referred parent:

> Parent to Parent has been my lifeline. When I first heard the diagnosis, I was devastated. Well-meaning doctors and nurses, as well as friends and family, simply did not understand. It was only when I finally connected with another parent through the Parent to Parent program that I could begin to hope for a future for us all. My veteran parent was gently there for me whenever I needed her. (Turnbull & Turnbull, 1997, p. 181)

Parent to Parent
www.netnet.net/mums

Transition to Community: Special Olympics

A goal of almost everyone, regardless of their educational philosophy, is to increase community contacts and interaction for students with mental retardation and developmental disabilities. Whether it is on-the-job vocational training, boarding a community bus to an athletic event, or field trips to various community sites, there is a manifest advantage in these students interacting in the community where they will live as adults.

One of the most successful of these ventures is a program called Special Olympics, which uses the format of the Olympic Games, but in which all the persons participating have developmental disabilities. The program was begun in 1968 by Eunice Kennedy Shriver, a sister of President John F. Kennedy. It has grown to an international event, with several thousand participants and many thousands of spectators. The purpose of the games is to allow children with disabilities to participate in races, swimming meets, field events, and team games and to feel what other athletes feel in competition, in winning and losing—an experience they rarely are able to achieve elsewhere. It has received substantial community support and is now touted as the largest athletic event now operating besides the traditional Olympics.

Interestingly, some negative voices are heard about the Special Olympic games—they are not designed to integrate the students into the mainstream but are special games only for children with disabilities, emphasizing that they are different from the general public. Of course, most of these youngsters could never compete for the basketball or track and field teams of their mainstream schools, so the idea of integration is not possible anyway. The sheer joy that these youngsters and their parents get from their Special Olympics experience is obvious to any observer.

Summary

▶ The current definition of mental retardation/developmental disabilities focuses on two major components: intelligence and adaptive behavior. An educational diagnosis of mental retardation depends on the characteristics of the child and on the demands of the social environment.

▶ Many factors contribute to the cause of mental retardation. They include genetic abnormalities, toxic agents, infections, and environmental factors.

▶ Early intervention programs are one means of preventing retardation caused by environmental factors, but they are not a cure-all for the effects of poverty and social disorganization in the home.

▶ Children with mental retardation have difficulty processing information. For many, the problem lies in limited memory, perception, and the way they organize information and make decisions.

Children with mental retardation have a general language deficit and specific problems using interpretative language.

▶ The elementary and secondary curricula for students with mental retardation stress academic skills, communication and language development, socialization, and prevocational and vocational skills. The emphasis, particularly for students with moderate retardation, is on functional learning.

▶ By reducing failure, increasing success, and modeling appropriate behaviors, teachers can improve the attitudes and behaviors of children with mild and moderate retardation.

▶ Social learning theory is generating teaching strategies to help youngsters with retardation to learn.

▶ Planning and vocational training are needed to ease the transition from school to work of those with mental retardation.

▶ Families with a child with mental retardation may need support and assistance to function at an expected level.

Future Challenges

1. Which issues of poverty contribute to slow development?

We still are not sure what factors in the culture of poverty are responsible for the slow development of children with mild retardation. Until we can determine the nature of the problem (lack of motivation, poor language, inattention and hyperactivity, lack of effective adult models), it is difficult to design effective methods for preventing it.

2. How can positive employment prospects be increased?

The future of students with mental retardation depends as much on the environment or context in which they live as on their education and training. The increasing complexity of modern society casts a shadow over the goal of independence for these students, although they may be able to get jobs in the service sector. Do individuals with mild or moderate retardation have a place in a shrinking job market, or will they be part of a "surplus" population?

3. How can more effective instruction be offered to students with mental retardation who are from a variety of cultures?

The changing demographics of the American population make it certain that more and more students from different cultures and ethnic backgrounds will be referred for special education services. Some will be mislabeled because of the difficulties of communication; others will find it difficult to adapt to classrooms where the demands are high and not in line with their own experience or even their family values. Special educators need to develop greater understanding and sensitivity to the diversity of families bringing children to the schools, in order to serve the students well.

4. How can inclusion and the best placement options be achieved?

By including individuals with mild mental retardation in the general education classroom at the secondary level, we limit them to a standard curriculum. Yet these students need special instruction in prevocational and survival skills. How do we balance the benefits of inclusion with these special vocational needs?

Key Terms

amniocentesis p. 165

applied behavior analyses p. 195

central processing p. 173

cooperative learning p. 197

developmental disabilities p. 159

differentiated instruction p. 188

Down syndrome p. 164

encephalitis p. 172

executive function p. 173

extrinsic motivation p. 196

fetal alcohol syndrome (FAS) p. 170

fragile X syndrome (FXS) p. 168

intrinsic motivation p. 196

karyotyping p. 165

mental retardation p. 158

phenylketonuria (PKU) p. 168

positive behavior supports (PBS) p. 195

positive reinforcement p. 195

reciprocal teaching p. 195

respite care p. 206

rubella p. 171

social learning approach p. 193

task analysis p. 190

teratogen p. 170

universal design for learning (UDL) p. 198

Resources

References of Special Interest

Beirne-Smith, M., Ittenbach, R., & Patton, J. (2001). *Mental Retardation* (6th ed.). Upper Saddle River, NJ: Merrill. *A comprehensive view of children with mental retardation from definition to assessment to characteristics. Much space is devoted to lifespan issues, including infancy and early childhood, educational programming in the school years, and the transitional years preparing for adulthood. Family consideration, individual rights, and legal issues are also addressed.*

Blacher, J., & Baker, B. (2002). *Families and mental retardation.* Washington, DC: American Association on Mental Retardation. *This book is a compilation of 32 articles about families and mental retardation that were originally* published in AAMD journals over 100 years. It reviews how professionals have changed their views concerning families over that period of time. The content covers family responsibilities, the reactions of families to mental retardation (they are not all negative, by any means), and family interventions and support.

Burack, J., Hodapp, R., & Zigler, E. (1998). *Handbook of mental retardation and development.* New York: Cambridge University Press. *An important book that synthesizes what we know about the development of children with mental retardation. Major chapters are devoted to cognitive and linguistic development, social and emotional development, and the effects of environment and family. There is little stress on education, but the global portrait of children with mental retardation provides a good basis for discussing these children's special needs.*

Davis, S. (Ed.). (2003). *A family handbook on future planning.* Silver Spring, MD: Arc of the United States. *A guide to help families develop a plan for their sons and daughters with cognitive, intellectual, or developmental disabilities. The plan deals with issues of personal finances and how to ensure the safety and well-being of the children after their parents' deaths.*

Hilton, A., & Ringlaben, R. (Eds.). (1998). *Best and Promising Practices in Developmental Disabilities.* Austin, TX: Pro-Ed. *A wide variety of chapters covering the best of what we know in current practices for children with disabilities. Issues related to definition, assessment, curriculum, specific instructional strategies, individual needs of children, systematic and data-based instruction and management, and family involvement are discussed.*

Schalock, R. (Ed.). (1999). *Adaptive Behavior and Its Measurements.* Washington, DC: American Association on Mental Retardation. *Adaptive behavior is a key element in the definition of mental retardation. This monograph from the AAMR explores its complexities, its relationship with intelligence, and the implications of the definition of mental retardation.*

Stainback, S., & Stainback, W. (1996). *Inclusion: A guide for educators.* Baltimore: Paul H. Brookes. *The authors defend the inclusive school movement by presenting suggestions about how school curricula should be modified to take into account the presence of children with special needs. They attempt to answer the questions of critics of the inclusive classroom approach by presenting practical suggestions for curriculum adaptations in the classroom for exceptional children.*

Turnbull, A., & Turnbull, H. R. (2000). *Families, professionals and exceptionality: Collaborating for empowerment.* 4th ed.). Upper Saddle River, NJ: Prentice Hall. *A rich text that focuses on the many roles played by the family members of a child with disabilities. It is designed to help professionals understand families, collaborate with families to help family empowerment, and aid family roles in the community and educational system improvement. Many practical quotes from family members bring the issues to life.*

Zigler, E., & Bennett-Gates, D. (Eds.). (1999). *Personality Development in Individuals with Mental Retardation.* New York: Cambridge University Press. *This book brings together a wide array of topics and specialists concerned about the personality development of children with mental retardation. The focus here is less on the cognitive limitations of these children than on their motivation, outer-directedness, and self-image. It is a valuable contribution.*

Journals

American Journal on Mental Retardation
aamr.allenpress.com

Education and Training in Mental Retardation and Developmental Disabilities
www.cec.sped.org

Mental Retardation
aamr.allenpress.com

Research in Developmental Disabilities
www.elsevier.com

Professional Organizations

American Association on Mental Retardation
www.aamr.org

Association for Retarded Citizens (The Arc)
www.thearc.org

National Down Syndrome Society
www.ndss.org

United Cerebral Palsy Association
www.ucpa.org

Please visit the book's website at **http://education.college.hmco.com/students** for new and updated information on websites listed here and for the mailing addresses of the journals and organizations.

Children with Emotional and Behavior Disorders

FOCUS QUESTIONS

▶ What are several potential causes of emotional and behavior disorders?

▶ What techniques do we use to teach children to manage and control their own behavior?

▶ How does functional assessment differ from other treatment programs?

▶ What is the impact of inclusion on students with emotional and behavior disorders?

▶ How successful are special education programs in helping students with emotional and behavior disorders make the transition from school to workplace?

▶ What are positive behavioral supports, and how can they be used with children with behavior disorders?

Few experiences are as disturbing to teachers as trying to teach children who are chronically unhappy or driven to aggressive, antisocial behavior. The teachers feel distressed, knowing there's a problem but feeling unable to do anything about it.

Children with behavior problems carry a burden that children with other disabilities do not. We don't blame children who have mental retardation or who have cerebral palsy for their deviant behavior. But many people assume that children with behavior disorders can control their actions and could stop their disturbing behavior if they wanted to. The sense that they are somehow responsible for their disability colors these children's interactions with those around them: their families, their agemates, their teachers.

■ History

We have always been aware of children with behavior or emotional problems. Yet for generations there has been amazing variation in what was believed to be the causes of such behavior, and a correspondingly wide array of treatments. Two centuries ago children with behavior problems were believed to be possessed by the devil or insane or mentally deficient. When attention was paid to them at all, they were shut away in large institutions with very little attention directed to their education. The professionals who dealt with them were largely clergy (if they were "possessed," it was up to the "holy men" to cure them) or physicians.

In general, our views of the causes and cures of mental disturbance have followed the broader trends of the times. That is, when we as a society became interested in genetics, heredity was considered an important cause of behavioral aberrations. When the society became interested in Sigmund Freud's style of psychoanalysis, we became interested in the inner life of the child with behavior problems.

In the late 1800s, children who were manifestly different from their agemates were being put into special ungraded classes, but with little attention paid to their individual or special needs. Itard and Seguin, both physicians, became important figures for treating children with behavior problems as well as children with mental retardation because there had been few other attempts to differentiate the two conditions.

After World War II, the responsibility for such children gradually shifted from the medical or mental health professionals to education. The schools assumed greater responsibility for their treatment, and the treatment became increasingly behavioral and educational. As we became aware of the power of ecological and social factors to influence children's development, treatment also included changing and improving their social and educational environment. Therefore, we discuss in this chapter the current view of causes, as well as the methods and current curricula based on humanistic, ecological, and behavioral principles (Kaufman, Brigham, & Mock, 2004).

As we look at these implications for children in today's schools, we will introduce you to a few actual students. Pete is a good example of a child with both academic and behavior problems that interfere with school. He has been a constant trial to his middle school teachers. He belongs to a gang known as the Griffins who, on occasion, terrorize other students in the school. They are

Because practically all children exhibit inappropriate behavior from time to time, criteria for identifying problem behavior depend largely on the frequency and intensity of specific behaviors.
(© David Young-Wolff/Photo Edit)

suspected of stealing from local stores and perhaps marketing drugs in the school. Pete does not appear to be depressed or anxious, but his acting-out behavior causes great stress for his teachers and his parents.

The definition of SED does have a serious shortcoming. A number of observers have pointed out that the federal definition places *all* responsibility for the problem on the child and none on the environment in which the child exists, thus making it the responsibility of the special education program to change the *child*—but not the *learning environment*, which can be considerably flawed (Maag & Howell, 1992; Nelson, Crabtree, Marchand-Martella, & Martella, 1998).

Cultures define appropriate behavior in varying ways. A behavior may be due not to underlying pathology but to a clash of cultural values of school and home.

■ Definition

It is not easy to define behavior and emotional problems in children. Most definitions assume that a child with a **behavior disorder,** or **serious emotional disturbance (E/BD),** reveals consistent "age-inappropriate behavior" leading to social conflict, personal unhappiness, and school failure.

A behavior disorder implies that the child is causing trouble for someone else. Serious emotional disturbance can be merely manifesting personal unhappiness. But almost all children reveal age-inappropriate behavior at one time or another. Moreover, a child's behavior is not the only variable that determines classification in this category. The person who perceives the child's behavior as "inappropriate" plays a key role in the decision. Clearly, some kinds of behavior, such as physical attacks, constant weeping or unhappiness, and extreme hyperactivity, are unacceptable in any setting. But the acceptability of a wide range of other behaviors depends on the attitude of the perceiver.

In our pluralistic society, behavior that is acceptable in some groups or subcultures is unacceptable in others. Our definition, therefore, must allow

www

One professional organization for children with behavior disorders is part of the Council for Exceptional Children. www.ccbd.net

A definition of acceptable behavior must allow for cultural differences.

for cultural differences. Can we say that a child's behavior is deviant if the behavior is the norm in the child's cultural group, even though we may find the particular behavior socially unacceptable?

The federal government's definition of children with serious emotional disabilities is important because it determines who receives federal funds to help with their exceptionality. In the Individuals with Disabilities Education Act (IDEA), PL 101-476, that definition is as follows:

> . . . a condition exhibiting one or more of the following characteristics over a long period of time and to a marked degree that adversely affects educational performance—
> A. An inability to learn that cannot be explained by intellectual, sensory, or health factors;
> B. An inability to build or maintain satisfactory interpersonal relationships with peers and teachers;
> C. Inappropriate types of behavior or feelings under normal circumstances;
> D. A general pervasive mood of unhappiness or depression; or
> E. A tendency to develop physical symptoms or fears associated with personal or school problems. [*Code of Federal Regulations*, Title 34, §300.7(b)(9)]

We noted earlier how this definition focuses on the child, but not on the child's environment. The learning environment may be exactly what is at issue for children who come to school from very different cultures with different lifestyles and values. Juan, a newly arrived Hispanic child, has trouble with the different ways he is supposed to react to authority. He is expected to look teachers in the eye when they are talking to him ("Look at me when I am speaking to you!"). But if he did that at home, he would be severely reprimanded because such eye contact would be considered defiance of parental authority. Juan's reaction to this very different environment may cause him to exhibit behavior within the range of the current definition of behavior disorder. That behavior would be due not to some underlying pathology but to the clash of cultural values of the school and of the home (Harry, 1992).

What treatment is prescribed for such a child? Should Juan be made to change his behavior patterns to fit the new environment, or should we try to reach an accommodation between the two? The issue of an individual child with maladaptive behavior may turn out to be an issue of clashing societies with a very different prescription for social remediation that extends far beyond the reach of special education.

The student caught between two cultures can still manifest behaviors that are certain to cause him trouble now and in the future in the school environment and in the community. In short, the problem may start out as a cultural clash, but it is transformed into a personal adjustment problem. Should the child receive some type of intervention to help in that situation? In this situation, it is appropriate to think of the entire family as the focus of attention. Increasingly, the family unit is involved in the attempts at behavior change in the child.

There is a disturbing gap between the number of children receiving special services in the schools and the number of children who have either se-

Context often plays a role in defining problem behavior.

rious emotional disturbance or behavior disorders (variously estimated between 5 and 15 percent). This category lacks the quantitative character of an index like IQ scores, and many of the judgments are subjective and left to local personnel. This is not to say, however, that there is not a core of children who can readily be identified as having an emotional or behavior disorder. A child who attacks another child with a weapon such as scissors, a knife, or a hammer leaves little doubt; neither does a child who weeps five or six times a day without apparent cause. As always, confusion about whether a child is eligible for special services exists at the margin of the category.

When a first-grade teacher sees a child who harms others and damages property, who breaks the rules, fights, lies, and yells, the teacher first wonders what to do about this child, then worries about what is to become of him. Will he continue to show these aggressive tendencies? Will they fade away as he gets older? Will he, in fact, be in trouble with society as an adult?

A sample of 297 male children who were first assessed at age 6, then evaluated at each grade level through seventh grade, and finally evaluated through interviews at ages 19 and 20 provides some answers to these questions (Schaeffer, Petras, Ialongo, Poduska, & Kellam, 2003).

These authors were able to sort these children into four groups: *chronic high aggressive* (the child was aggressive when starting school), *increasing aggressive* (including those who seemed to become aggressive while in school and increased their aggressiveness over the years), *moderate aggressive*, and *nonaggressive*. Figure 6.1 shows the comparison of the aggressive behavior in school with later adult consequences. The figure shows that almost three-quarters of the chronically high aggressive and the increasing aggressive

> A child's emotional or behavior disorders in school are strong indications of future difficulties in school and society.

FIGURE 6.1
Prediction of Adult Aggressive Behavior from Young Children

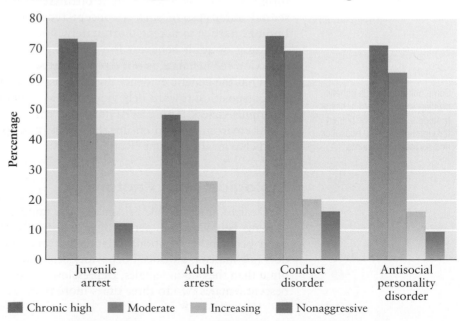

children had juvenile arrests, and half of them had adult arrests. Also, almost three-quarters of the chronically high aggressive and the increasing aggressive were identified as having conduct disorder or antisocial personality disorder.

Other studies have essentially shown the continuity between early aggressive behavior and adult aggressive behavior (Kauffman, 2002). In the study discussed, there also seems to be a linkage between aggressive behavior and attention-deficit hyperactive disorder (ADHD) that suggests a contributing or comorbid (joint) relationship. The fact that the increasing aggressive may suffer from concentration problems in school contributes to the portrait of a student having difficulty adjusting to the classroom. The authors called for an increasing and improved screening and tracking of behavior problems in elementary schools or before, so that preventive intervention can take place before the problems ripen into adult antisocial behavior.

Although not every child who is aggressive and violent in school will show such behavior in adulthood, it is hard to find an aggressive and violent adult who did not show that behavior in his or her youth (Simpson, Miles, Walker, Ormsbee, & Downing, 1991). It is in everyone's best interests that such students are identified early in their school career and positive steps taken to modify maladaptive behavior patterns.

■ Factors Related to Behavior Problems

Parents and professionals looking for the reasons why some children have behavior disorders and emotional problems should examine an array of potential influences, which include the individual's biological makeup and cognitive ability, along with family factors and the relationship to the larger society. Some ideas are harder to accept than others. One hypothesis is that future behavior is determined at birth (see the film *The Bad Seed*). The essential unfairness of such a concept repels us and makes genetic research findings harder to accept. Fortunately, we can now say that the final determination of adult behavior is a mix of genetics and environment; criminal behavior, for instance, is *not* fixed at birth.

What the genetic evidence does tell us, though, is that some children have a predisposition toward behaviors such as hyperactivity, attention problems, or impulsiveness. Those behaviors may call for some special educational or social environments to ensure that such predispositions do not flower into real behavioral problems (Rutter, 1997).

Biological Risk Factors

McClearn found credible evidence of the important role that heredity plays in shaping behavior and personality, specifically the sex-linked differences in many behavioral conditions. Infantile autism, hyperactivity, and conduct disorders (alcoholism, antisocial behavior) occur in males four to eight times more often than they do in females. Depression and social phobias appear in postpubescent females two to three times more than they do in males. Of course, we

Some children have a genetic predisposition toward behavior problems. This can be helped through both special education and social environments.

can tie these differences—at least in part—to the very different ways in which society treats males and females. But they also suggest that a sex-linked genetic factor may be at work.

The evidence of the genetic influence on behavior has been traced through the study of identical twins (identical heredity), adoptive children (Is the child more like the biological parents or the adoptive parents?), and statistical analyses of the prevalence of conditions in certain families or populations over generations (McClearn, 1993).

Interaction Between Genetics and Environment

Although it has now been widely accepted that there is an interaction between genetics and environment in the development of aggressive and hostile behavior in children, if we are to develop good remedial practices, we need to know *how* such an interaction works.

An ingenious study has taken us forward (Ge et al., 1996). The researchers studied forty-five teenage children who had been separated from their biological parents at birth. The biological parents were identified as having two or more pathological disorders, one pathological disorder, or no pathological disorders. The children were measured for their own level of hostile and aggressive behavior, and the adoptive parents were measured for their own pathological behavior and for the type of discipline that they applied (warmth versus harsh or inconsistent).

There was a strong relationship between the amount of pathology in the biological parents and the amount of aggressiveness shown by the children, confirming the genetic link between parental pathology and aggressive behavior in a child (Plomin & Petrill, 1997).

An unusual finding was a high correlation between the biological parent's pathology and the harsh discipline handed out by the adoptive parent. But why would there be any connection between the problems of the biological parents and the behavior of the adoptive parents, when these adults were unknown to one another?

An answer evolves when we compare the level of hostility that the child shows and harsh discipline revealed by the adoptive parents. The greater the aggressiveness in the children, the more harsh discipline was used by the adoptive parents. So we may conclude that this is another example of how a child's behavior (although originally influenced by the biological parent) now creates its own environment and directs the reaction of others (adoptive parents). In other words, the child's aggression brings forth a hostile reaction from the adoptive parents, thus continuing what has been referred to as a **coercive cycle** that has to be broken if we are to make progress with these hostile children.

Although there clearly is some genetic influence in conduct disorders, particularly those associated with hyperactivity, inattention, and poor peer relationships, there is no reason to believe that environmental experiences cannot counteract those influences. After all, if you can get a lion to sit on a chair and a bear to ride a bicycle (hardly gene-driven behavior), as happens in many circuses, you can control the behavior of a child with tendencies to hyperactivity.

What does seem clear is that there are two-way interactions between the various forces at work. That is, while aggression can change psychosocial factors, so can psychosocial factors change levels of aggression. Similar interactions occur with biological factors. Grisso (1996) provided a useful illustration of one potential sequence of events

> For example, Ritalin may reduce the aggression of an attention-deficit, hyperactive-disordered child, but the reduction in aggressive behavior may also produce a change in the family's response to the child. Whether that response is positive (e.g., interpersonally rewarding) or negative (e.g., the child is suddenly ignored) may influence the continued benefits of the biological intervention. (p. 6)

Such complex interactions have resulted in an increase in multidisciplinary research and treatment since these problems spill over into the domains of many disciplines.

Family Risk Factors

Children who are victims of abuse and violence often learn to inflict those behaviors on others.

One interesting indicator of a family risk factor is family violence, which includes child abuse. Violence against children is a behavior that the children themselves are likely to display when they are old enough to inflict violence on those weaker than they.

The intergenerational aspect of this disorder is distressing. A child with serious emotional disturbance rarely comes from a stable home with warm and loving parents. And the child who is abused is likely to be an abusive parent and to reproduce the entire negative pattern unless the school or community intervenes.

Ramsey and Walker (1988) compared two groups of boys drawn, as pairs, from the same fourth-grade classrooms. The thirty-nine boys in one group exhibited antisocial behaviors; the forty-one boys in the other group did not. Data that came from structured family interviews confirmed that the antisocial children lived in an unstructured, negative environment where discipline was harsh and inconsistent. Although these factors may not have "caused" the antisocial behavior, they certainly did not contribute in a positive way to the child's social development. These factors, once again, indicate the importance of involving the entire family when possible.

A generation ago, feelings were strong that parents were in large part responsible for their child's behavior problems. Today, many believe that the child's atypical behavior may cause parents to react in ways that are inappropriate and make the condition worse in a downward spiral of unfortunate sequential events.

School Risk Factors

The child risk factor most frequently associated with social and emotional disturbance is below-grade achievement in school. Do these children act out *because* they are academically slow and not able to keep up with their classmates? Is their acting out a reaction to their failure in school? The idea is an interesting one, but the evidence does not seem to support it. For one thing, studies that measure the abilities of children with conduct disorders consistently find that as a group, they score in the below-average range of intelligence (Kauffman, 2002). For another, the aggressive behavior that gets these youngsters into trouble in school is clearly observable *before* they enter school.

Jim, for example, was in trouble in school as early as kindergarten. His school records are peppered with teachers' statements: "He seems bright but doesn't want to apply himself." "He's unmotivated and an angry little boy." "This boy will not take the time necessary to learn the basics."

In the general education literature, *time on task* is a well-established predictor of school success (Berliner, 1990). In other words, the common-sense conclusion that the more time you spend on learning a topic the more likely you will be to master it turns out to have solid research backing. This principle is relevant to the school performance of children who are seriously emotionally disturbed because they spend less time engaged in academic activities in the classroom—and probably outside the classroom as well (Walker, Stieber, & O'Neill, 1990).

Children with serious emotional disturbance probably spend less time on task, so they may be less likely to master the subject matter.

Social Risk Factors

Violence in the Schools

There are few things more disturbing to teachers than a child who is disruptive to classroom procedures, openly defiant of authority, and threatening or using physical violence to get his way. (We say "his" because the majority of such students are male.)

Dramatic events such as school shootings and killings highlight what has come to be seen as a serious and continuing problem to the schools. Several major questions come to mind:

▶ How much violence exists, and is it getting better, or worse?

▶ Can we identify students who are prone to violence?

▶ What are the methods and procedures for lessening and controlling such violence?

The answer to the question "How much violence is occurring in the schools?" is that a great deal of violence occurs there.

▶ Over 100,000 students bring weapons to school each day, and more than 40 students are killed or wounded with these weapons annually.

▶ Large numbers of students fear victimization (bullying, sexual harassment) in school and on the way to and from school.

▶ More than 6,000 teachers are threatened annually, and over 200 are physically injured on school grounds.

▶ Schools are major sites for recruitment and related activities by organized gangs (Sprague & Walker, 2000).

Safe and Responsive Schools Project
www.indiana.edu/~safeschl/

The amount of youth violence has diminished somewhat from its peak in the early 1990s but remains a serious societal problem. The Surgeon General's report on Youth Violence (2001) contained the following figures.

In 1999, there were 104,000 arrests of people under age 18 for a serious violent crime—robbery, forcible rape, aggravated assault or homicide. Of these, 1,400 were for homicides committed by adolescents and, on occasion, even younger children. . . . For every youth arrested in any given year in the late 1990s, at least 10 were engaged in some form of violent behavior that would have seriously injured or killed another person, according to the several national research surveys in which youths report on their own behavior. (p. 1)

A subset of juveniles commits virtually all of the serious offenses, and members of the subset begin their violent behavior when quite young.

Can we identify children prone to violence? The answer is yes, and they can be identified quite early. Loeber and Farrington (1998) suggested that a small subset of juveniles commits virtually all of the serious offenses and that these students began their violent activities when quite young. Sprague and Walker (2000) suggest that 6 to 9 percent of children account for more than 50 percent of total discipline referrals and virtually all of the serious offenses. Furthermore, early discipline problems predict later adjustment problems quite accurately (Walker, Calvin, & Ramsey, 1995), so it is important to intervene as early as possible.

What can be done? First of all, we should consider what does *not* appear to work with the violent child. The "zero tolerance" approach adopted by many schools, which includes suspensions, expulsions, metal detectors, guards in the hallways, and so forth, does not seem to reduce violence. This "zero tolerance" amounts to counterhostility on the part of the school, rather than an attempt to deal with the individuals. Some suggest that such strategies may well be used to impress or reassure parents and other citizens that "action" is being taken on the problem.

Also, there appears to be sufficient evidence now that counseling does not appear to have an effect on antisocial or predelinquent youth (Elliott, Hamburg, & Williams, 1998; Gottfredson, 1998). Of course expulsions may solve the "problem" of the school administration, but not that of the community, since violent youths would be roaming the neighborhoods, free of monitoring or supervision.

One of the most popular approaches to coping with violence is a series of procedures known as *functional assessment*. These approaches have become so popular that they have been embedded in the 1997 IDEA Amendments with the expectation that children with behavior disorders would be expected to undergo functional assessment, which looks at patterns of behavior across different settings and circumstances. The goal is to identify the environmental triggers for the behavior so that these can be minimized and replaced with *positive behavior supports* (this is discussed later in the chapter).

Cultural and Ethnic Factors

Many observers have noted the increased prevalence of minority and immigrant children identified as children who are socially or emotionally disturbed (Leone, 1997). However, even though there might be a clear *correlation* between ethnic background and behavior, this does not mean there is *causation:* that is, that their condition was caused by their ethnic or racial membership.

Bronfenbrenner (1989) focused on the family as a child-rearing system, on society's support or lack of support for that system, and on the effects of that support or lack of support on children. He maintained that the alienation of children reflects a breakdown in the interconnected segments of a child's life—

family, peer group, school, neighborhood, and work world. The question is not "What is wrong with children with emotional or behavior disorders?" but "What is wrong with the child's social system?"

The conflict between the values of those in authority in society (and in the school) and the values of their subculture can create tension. For example, what does a child do who sees a friend cheating? Honesty—a valued societal ethic—demands that the child report the incident. But loyalty—a valued subcultural ethic—demands silence. Even more serious in its impact is the situation in which the subgroup devalues education or pressures the individual to use drugs or violence.

Lynam, Moffitt, and Stouthamer-Loeber (1993) suggested that school failure plays a more important role in the delinquency of African American boys from low-income families because the school can provide a source of social control that is lacking in the neighborhood. The boy who finds school so frustrating that he rejects it and what it represents is removing himself from its control and influence. Neighborhood delinquents and pressures are free to rush in and fill the social void (p. 195). So we have evidence that the school, the neighborhood, the social class, and the family as well as some individual characteristics of the child are all implicated in behavior problems.

One question that requires an answer is, "Are there differences in violent behavior according to ethnic background, and if so, are these differences due to the ethnic background or to other factors?" Marsh & Cornell (2001) conducted a survey on high-risk behavior (weapon possession, gang involvement, and fighting) of 7,848 seventh-, ninth-, and eleventh-grade students in a large population area in Virginia.

Differences in behavior were found between ethnic groups. African American students were significantly higher than the Caucasian population in reported weapon possession and fighting, the Asian American students were high in gang involvement, and the Hispanic population was high in weapon possession. The Caucasian populations ranked high in drug use and in being threatened by other students.

The African American students reported less support from both peers and adults in school as well as lower academic grades. In another study, student experience with violence in the community was the most important risk factor for carrying weapons at school (Kingery, Coggeshall, & Alford, 1998).

Marsh and Cornell sum up their findings as follows:

> Counselors and educators concerned with the prevention of school violence should address the concerns of students who are academically unsuccessful and feel unsupported by adults or peers at school. Students who feel endangered, threatened, or unsupported at school may be most likely to seek some sense of increased security by carrying a weapon or joining a gang. (p. 161)

Leone points out, as well, that we have been following a "the problem is within the child" philosophy without considering that the ecology surrounding the child may contribute some important factors to the condition, and this refers to the school ecology as well as the family ecology. The ways in which schools and classrooms are organized, the roles that students and teachers are expected to play, and the nature of the curriculum all shape the experiences of children.

Students who feel unsupported or threatened at school are more likely to seek security by carrying a weapon or joining a gang.

Children with conduct disorders learn that aggressive behavior is a way of getting what they want, particularly when parental punishment is sporadic and ineffective and provides another model of aggressiveness.
(© Carl Glassman/The Image Works)

Children with conduct disorders are a serious problem in a school setting. They are easily distracted, unable to persist at tasks, and often disrupt class. The problems of asocial and antisocial behavior, unless dealt with vigorously in childhood, can lead to antisocial behavior in adulthood, which in turn can create a new generation of antisocial children. And so the cycle continues.

Substance Abuse

One of the serious side problems of many children with behavior disorders is substance abuse. The public's attention is often directed to the use of exotic drugs, but the use and abuse of alcohol and tobacco are much more common. There is evidence (Elmquist, Morgan, & Bolds, 1992; Leone, Greenberg, Tricket, & Spero, 1989) that children with behavior problems have rates of substance abuse much higher than the rates of their peers in special education or in general education. Despite this information, there appears to be little systematic effort to include prevention programs in the school curriculum for these students.

Does the presence of behavior or emotional problems predispose an individual to use drugs? If you are anxious, depressed, or angry, are you more likely to take drugs? Common sense would answer "Yes," but research is not clear.

Substance abuse is a growing problem in U.S. schools. The prevalence of alcohol abuse and drug use is substantial, and it has been theorized that exceptional children may be overrepresented among those who use drugs and alcohol. Think about the characteristics of drug users: low self-esteem, depression, inability to handle social experiences, and stress. These are the same characteristics that mark children with behavior disorders. The primary handicap is a behavioral disturbance; the secondary handicap is a chemical dependency. Special educators, then, must know the signs of chemical dependency, what to do when they suspect drug abuse in their students, and how to work with drug treatment programs.

In addition to the general teen culture that can encourage substance abuse in some communities, children or teenagers with behavioral and emotional problems often are influenced by a series of additional factors that may predispose them to substance abuse. These factors would include prescribed medication, chronic medical problems, social isolation, depression, and a higher risk of being in a dysfunctional family (McCombs & Moore, 2002).

The link between substance abuse and behavior problems has been well established. One notable study is the longitudinal Pittsburgh Youth Study of inner-city boys. Substance use was classified in five categories: beer and wine, tobacco, hard liquor, marijuana, and other drugs. Tobacco was being used by 23 percent of the 13-year-olds, while beer and wine were already experienced by 32 percent of those boys. By the time the boys in this study reached 13 years of age, 9 percent of the boys had used marijuana.

These investigators (Loeber et al., 1998) found that the different levels of substance use correlated with the severity of delinquent acts. The factors that seemed to be most linked to substance abuse were low achievement, depressed mood, the presence of ADHD, and a lack of guilt on the part of the child for such substance use. Substance abuse cannot be said to cause emotional problems or problem behavior, but it is clearly part of the syndrome of behaviors linked to early problems and later delinquency.

Suicide

A strong feeling of hopelessness can be the predominant reason for teenagers to think about suicide or even to attempt it. For some time, suicide has been one of the major causes of adolescent death. Today it is the third leading cause of teenage deaths in the United States, with 272 deaths recorded along with about eight times more attempted suicide. The ratio of males to females in such attempts is about 4:1 (National Institute of Mental Health, 2001). A number of suicides are also linked to substance abuse.

The following are some currently cited signs of a potential suicide.

▶ Extreme changes in behavior

▶ Previous suicide attempts

▶ Suicide threats and statements

▶ Signs of depression

Special education or general education teachers who note such signs should make referrals to appropriate crisis teams or mental health facilities. Most communities now have such services available. In addition, there is a National Hopeline Network (1-800-SUICIDE) that is available 24 hours a day and seven days a week for emergency counseling. The teacher remains the first line of defense in these crisis situations and needs to be alert for any signs that students may provide.

Children who are anxious and withdrawn have problems with excessive internal control and often feel helpless and unable to be spontaneous.
(© Elizabeth Crews)

Anxiety-Withdrawal: Internalizers

Children who are anxious or withdrawn are likely to be more of a threat to themselves than to others around them. Because they usually are not disruptive, they generally do not cause classroom management problems. But they are a source of concern for teachers.

In contrast to children with conduct disorders, children who are anxious and withdrawn have problems with excessive internal control; in most settings they maintain firm control over their impulses, wishes, and desires. Children who are anxious and withdrawn may be rigid and unable to be spontaneous.

Where do fearful children come from? We know that many of them have parents with similar problems. In addition, most professionals agree that chronic anxiety in children comes from being in a stressful situation, not being able to get out of the situation, and not being able to do anything to improve it. This inability to change the situation adds to feelings of helplessness and reinforces low self-image.

For students, a crucial examination looming on the horizon can create chronic anxiety. For younger children, anxiety can stem from homes where they feel unwanted or are abused. Children are often too young to understand that their parents may be working out their own problems or that their parents' actions have little to do with them. All they understand is that no matter what they do, they are not getting praise or love from their parents.

> Children who are anxious or withdrawn are likely more a danger to themselves than they are to others.

> Children develop chronic anxiety when they are frequently exposed to stressful situations and are unable to control or remove themselves from those situations.

Attention-Deficit Hyperactivity Disorder (ADHD)

As we learn more about conditions that we wish to study, we establish different descriptions of those conditions. We tend to separate out conditions such as infantile autism for the purpose of understanding their specific causes and identifying the most effective treatment. For **attention-deficit hyperactivity disorder (ADHD),** the intent of establishing a new condition is to distinguish ADHD from other conditions that belong to the general category of developmental disorders or delay.

A child with ADHD, such as Dave, a compact and energetic 6-year-old, displays significant signs of inattention, distractibility, and disorganization but does not show the typical signs (such as delayed cognition) of a child with mental retardation. Such patterns of behavior show up typically in the preschool age. Dave's parents describe Dave like this: "He hits the floor running every day and has us all worn to a frazzle by midmorning." "He seems driven by some unseen force to be always on the go." "I never seem to be able to catch his attention to read him a story or get him to slow down to pay attention to what I want to tell him." It is not clear what the cause of such a condition is, but whether the cause is nutritional or neurological or an imbalance of neurotransmitter chemicals, the impact on the family and the teacher is predictable. Dave is hard to teach because he won't pay attention long enough for a person to communicate meaningfully with him.

To help students with ADHD, teachers might supplement verbal instructions with visual instructions.

One standard possible treatment for ADHD is medication, primarily to slow the child down so that someone can catch his or her attention long enough to teach needed information. Drugs such as Ritalin, Dexedrine, or Cylert are prescribed, often with the desired result of increasing the child's control of his or her own behavior (Pueschel, Scala, Weidenman, & Bernier, 1995). Dave's parents are reluctant to give such powerful medicine to a 6-year-old, but his uncontrollable behavior may cause them to eventually give in.

Whether or not Dave responds positively to such medical intervention, he needs special educational programming, because he will miss many important educational experiences while he engages in this whirl of physical activity that can be so wearing on his parents and teachers.

Where do children with ADHD fit into the complex categories of exceptional children? On the one hand, they appear to have specific learning problems associated with learning disabilities. On the other, they show the inappropriate impulsivity characteristic of children with emotional and behavioral disorders.

One thing is clear: Such children have a combination of factors requiring special services if they are going to have a good experience in the schools. Children with ADHD show an inability to sit still and pay attention in class and may engage in an array of disruptive behaviors, all troublesome to the teachers and to their peers.

Take Carl, for instance. Carl's record is filled with his primary-grade teachers' comments that he seems physically driven to the point where he has poor control of his own behavior. His excessive energy causes him to interact with other students in an often inappropriate way, and he rarely pays attention long enough to master the lessons his fourth-grade teacher presents. Since his reading is far below where it should be, Carl is currently being given medication as well as remedial treatment in the class.

PROFILES

DEVELOPMENTAL

The graph below about emotional and behavior disorders shows the profiles of two students, Jim and Molly. Both have behavior problems, and both are experiencing academic difficulties. The two children, however, manifest these problems in different ways.

Jim: Jim is an 11-year-old who seems sullen and angry most of the time. He rarely smiles and has a history of temper outbursts. When he is frustrated, he sometimes blows up and attacks the nearest person with such frenzy that

other children give him a wide berth and hesitate to interact with him.

Stories in the neighborhood recount Jim's cruelty to animals, how he has tortured and killed cats and dogs. His language borders on profanity, and he has been known to challenge his teachers by asking, "What are you going to do about it?" Jim is a threat not only to his peers but also to his teachers' sense of their own competence. His physical skills are advanced, even though his interpersonal skills are not, which tends to complicate the situation.

Profiles of Two Children with Emotional and Behavior Disorders

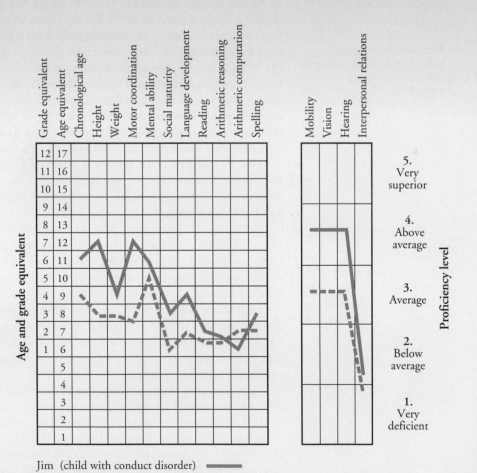

Jim (child with conduct disorder) ———
Molly (child with anxiety) — — —

As he grows older, he will become less manageable physically. Although we can tolerate the temper tantrums of a 5-year-old, the same outbursts from a 15-year-old are frightening.

School personnel are actively seeking alternative placement for Jim on the grounds that they are not capable, either physically or psychologically, of coping with his problems. Jim comes from a father-absent home; his mother is somewhat disorganized and seems to have given up trying to control her son. Attempts have been made to coordinate the program for Jim with mental health services for his mother in hopes of strengthening the family as a viable social unit. Although some progress has been made, the situation remains difficult. His social contacts are limited to a few other youngsters who have similar propensities for acting out when they become angry. Adults who are close to Jim are worried about his future. Jim's performance in school, as shown in the profile, is from two to five grades below his grade level, and his hostility and unwillingness to accept correction or help have caused his teachers much anxiety.

Molly: The second profile in the box is of Molly, a 9-year-old girl in the fourth grade who is having a difficult time at school. In contrast to Jim, who tends to externalize his problems, Molly seems to internalize hers. She is in tears and depressed much of the time. She is not able to make friends with the girls who have formed the major social group in the classroom, and she seems lonely and alone. Molly is so quiet that if it were not for the manifest unhappiness that shows in her face and physical demeanor, she would likely go completely unnoticed in school. She, like Jim, is seriously behind in her academic work. Jim is clearly externalizing his problems and, in the process, is causing problems for others. Molly is internalizing her problems and making herself miserable but is not directly confronting others.

Molly's middle-class parents are concerned about her and have taken many different steps to help her, including therapy from a psychiatrist in the community, but so far their efforts have met with little success. She is a source of great frustration to her parents, who cannot understand why she is not like her older sister, who seems to succeed effortlessly in both academic and social spheres. Molly is not the personal threat to teachers that Jim is because she does not challenge their ability to control the classroom. But she does challenge those teachers who want the children in their classes to be happy in school and who are upset by their inability to modify her sadness and low self-concept.

The Ecology of the Child segment about Amy shows another student struggling with ADHD and resisting the medication that in the end was a positive force in her life. One of the limiting factors in such cases is the need for proper medical monitoring of the drugs being given, since most schools do not have medical staff immediately available.

ADHD Drug Treatments

There have been numerous analyses for the efficacy of drug intervention with children who have emotional and behavior disorders. For example, for children with ADHD (Forness, Kavale, Sweeney, & Crenshaw, 1999), the clear drug of choice has been the stimulant medication named Ritalin. The central question is when the medication is most effective: when used alone, or when

ECOLOGY OF THE CHILD

SCHOOL   ## A Teenage Student Comes to Terms with Medication

My name is Amy. I am a 15-year-old girl from Erie, Pennsylvania, and I have attention deficit disorder (ADD). Part of my treatment is working with Jennifer Girts, a counselor at the Achievement Center near my home. One afternoon when I was really frustrated, she gave me an article on ADD and adolescents. Wow! I loved it! It really helped me understand a lot about myself. Now I feel moved to write my own article telling my story; about when I was diagnosed, the ways I felt about it then, and how I am coping now. Having dealt with ADD for nine years I know how other kids with ADD feel. I was there at one time too, and I hope my story will help.

Before we found out about ADD, my childhood was good. I have wonderful parents and a younger brother, Bran, who means the world to me. I was good and bad, just like another child. Then, in first grade we found out I have ADD. My life changed from then on.

Coming to Terms with ADD

When I first heard about ADD, I did not know what it was. I remember asking my parents about it. They explained it to me and I asked, "Will it ever go away?" The answer: "No." This made me really upset. They assured me that ADD could be treated, but that I needed to want the help.

My parents thought bringing me to a psychiatrist, who could give me medication, would help me. I thought I was going to lose my head trying all the different kinds of medications suggested. I ended up trying eight different kinds. Can you believe it? I took kinds that made me less hungry, some that made me depressed, and others that made me confused. Finally, my doctor found a combination that works. Now I am on Adderall and Clonidine.

Making a Choice

Finally we found the right medication, but then I never wanted to take it. I would hide it in my dog's chew toys or put it up my sleeve. Now I find myself wondering why I would want to do that since the medication really does help me. My mom assures me there was a time when I didn't care if it did or not. Here is the real reason: I wanted to be normal. After all, no other kid I knew took medication. But when I did not take my medication, I always had difficulty paying attention, and my grades dropped. I was a grouch—definitely not a nice person—all because I did not take my medication.

Finally, my counselor said to me, "Amy, it is your choice to take your medication or not. A lot of people take medication for all different kinds of reasons. You need to decide if you want to be in control of your

---

used in conjunction with psychosocial treatments such as parent training and cognitive behavior modification?

A major study initiated by the National Institute of Mental Health has given us considerable insight into this disorder and its treatment (MTA Cooperative Group, 1999). For the study, 579 children were randomly assigned to four types of treatment lasting fourteen months. The first treatment approach was medication management designed to impact impulsiveness and hyperactivity. The second approach was intensive behavioral treatment involving both school and parent. The third approach was a combination of the medication and behavioral intervention, and the fourth was standard community care.

moods and impulsivity. What kind of person do you want to be: someone in control or a grouch?" I finally realized that I need the medication to help myself. That's the way my father put it. He would say, "You need to help yourself before you can help others."

Listen, it's up to you. It's your choice; no one can force you to take your medicine. I know which person I would rather be. It was up to me to make the right choice—not my parents or my counselor. Other people can ask me to take medication, but I need to be smart enough to realize that I need it. I found out that it was the best thing for me. So my advice to others is: be smart and take your medication. It will help you—take my word for it.

Now my life is pretty good. I am in the eighth grade. I make good grades and have tons of friends. I still take my medication every morning and at night. And I still see my counselor every once in a while. She helps me sort out my feelings and ask myself the right questions. But, hey, I have ADD. And I am normal.

Don't get me wrong, I still have my ups and downs—everyone does. It's not because of ADD; it's because I am human. My life has changed over the years. I've come to understand what ADD can mean to me. ADD may never go away, but I have the power to control it. I will not let it control me again. I have made my choice. The right choice. You have to decide how you want to live: as Oscar the Grouch, or as a person in control with a wonderful life. What is your choice?

Amy is an eighth-grader at Walnut Creek School in Erie, Pennsylvania. Her favorite subject is English and favorite pastimes are hanging out with her friends, going to the mall, school dances, camping with her family, and helping other people. She wants to be a counselor for children with ADD. She enjoys talking with Jennifer Girts, her own counselor, and feels that it would benefit children with ADD to talk to a counselor who has had first-hand experience with the disorder.

Source: From Amy Wojtkielewicz, My choice for my life: Coming to terms with ADD, *Exceptional Parent Magazine* (November 2000): 113. Reprinted with permission.

WHAT IS THE CONTEXT?

Amy is an eighth-grade student who has struggled with her decision to take medication for ADD. She realizes that this is a decision that only she can make—no one else can do it for her. She concludes that she wants to feel less grouchy and better able to concentrate. She learns to see herself as a normal eighth grader.

PIVOTAL ISSUES FOR TEACHERS

- What can you do to support students with ADD/ADHD in your classroom?

- What support will you need from other professionals?

- How will you discuss ADD/ADHD with the student's family?

Although all four groups showed a decrease in symptoms over the course of the study, the combination of medication and behavioral treatments produced the strongest positive result of the four groups.

Educational Programming

In earlier times the programming for such children was left to mental health specialists. Now it is largely a task for educators because the close interaction between academic performance and socioemotional development has been recognized.

■ Identification and Placement

The decision to refer a child for special education services is an important one; it must be made carefully. It is often difficult to distinguish between children with behavior disorders and those who just have a series of transient adaptation problems: Each child shows unacceptable behavior, but one shows it longer and more intensely than the other.

Adolescents need to find their way out of learned helplessness through being taught alternative coping mechanisms and offered experiences designed to improve their feelings of self-esteem and self-worth. In these situations, as well as many others we have discussed, multidisciplinary teams of professionals seem called for.

One effort to thwart suicide attempts has been the formation of crisis teams at both the school and the district levels. Team members learn procedures to cope with suicidal individuals, and the team has access to resources that it can bring to bear quickly. A teacher who sees the danger signs has the immediate task of providing relief from the feelings of helplessness or hopelessness that the student may be expressing and of instilling in the student some feeling of being in control. Some positive change, no matter how small, must be made to prove to the student that the situation is not hopeless.

Long-range treatment may demand services from community and mental health agencies, and teachers should be aware of good referral sources. For schools, the best method of prevention is an educational program that enhances feelings of self-worth and self-control. Explicit instruction in positive coping skills can be one way of providing feelings of self-control.

Learned helplessness in children is the belief that nothing they do can stop bad things from happening. Learned helplessness results in severe deterioration in performance after failure, as though the children have said to themselves, "It's all happening again." These children often have such low self-concepts that failure in a school task or a social setting only confirms for them their worthlessness and helplessness in the face of an unfriendly environment (see Seligman & Peterson, 1986). These children's poor performance in the classroom may be much worse than they are capable of doing, simply because they are so pessimistic about themselves and their abilities. Low self-esteem seems to be at the heart of much of the underachievement of children who are anxious and withdrawn.

For example, Larry has become increasingly disruptive and irritable in class, far beyond what the teacher was used to from Larry, who had always been a reasonably friendly and happy boy. A further discussion with parents revealed that Bart, Larry's older brother, had gone off to college. Bart had been a true role model and friend to Larry, and they did many things together. Larry is having trouble adjusting to Bart's absence, but given some patience combined with firm application of the rules, this transient adaptation problem will likely fade away.

The placement of a disproportionate number of minority students in special education programs has raised questions about the process that many school systems use to identify students with behavior problems. Are these systems mistaking cultural differences for aberrant behavior? Are the personal biases of some decision makers playing a role in decision making? Or are some subgroups especially likely to show the symptoms of behavior problems? The

| Learned helplessness comes from low self-esteem and depression.

Articles on behavioral issues and behavioral support. www.ericec.org/faq/behavdis.html

It often is difficult to distinguish between children with behavior disorders and those who just have a series of transient adaptation problems.
(© David Young-Wolff/Photo Edit)

answers to these questions can be made only on an individual basis by a multidisciplinary team of professionals.

The Individualized Education Program (IEP), when used properly, is an effective guide for teachers who are trying to cope with children who show emotional or behavior problems. The IEP is shaped not only by the student's specific problem but also by available resources. The presence of professional consultants in the mental health area, or an active remedial program in the school, gives both the assessment team and the parents more options to consider.

Despite a liberal definition of children with behavior problems that includes the perceiver as well as the child, most diagnostic instruments now in use focus exclusively on the characteristics of the child and do not take into consideration the nature of the environment. Judgment about the role of the environment still is left to the discretion of the individual observer, clinician, or special educator.

Summing Up: Characteristics and Classification

Substantial advances have been made in our linking a variety of predictive factors for behavior disorder or serious emotional disturbance (B/ED) from early childhood to adult behavior. The most powerful predictive factor is physical aggression exhibited early in life (Frick et al., 2003; Broidy et al., 2003), but there also are other factors, including early language impairment (Brennan et al., 2003), gender — males being more at risk (Moffitt et al., 2001), and a variety of environmental risk factors such as family dysfunction, poverty, and abuse (Tolan et al., 2003).

Rutter (2003), in summarizing what has been learned, also presented what we have yet to learn, and these statements represent a challenge for the next generation of researchers and educators:

1. Most of the research falls well short of identifying the crucial mediators of the causal process or the effective elements of prevention or treatment.
2. We have only a very limited understanding of what is required to bring about beneficial change. It is evident that parental abuse and neglect provide significant risks for children, but it is not so obvious what would succeed in preventing abuse and neglect.
3. Even when we know which interventions are effective, we lack good means of ensuring that those who might benefit from the interventions participate.
4. Most research has focused on individual differences rather than on (a) differences in level, (b) why the crime rate now is much higher than in 1950, (c) why most forms of antisocial behavior are more common in males than in females, or (d) why the homicide rate in the United States is some dozen times the rate in Europe (p. 376).

■ Intervention Strategies

There are several dimensions through which attempts have been made to modify the educational program for children with emotional and behavior disorders. The original focus was, naturally, the child and his or her deviant characteristics. The accumulation of evidence that implicated factors in the social and physical ecology around the child has directed attention to those surrounding features for both diagnostic and treatment strategies.

Merely dealing with a child's aberrant behavior without attending to his or her adaptation to the school program was a poor strategy. The comorbidity (strong association) of academic failure and behavior problems has meant that the IEPs for such children should *also* recognize the academic adjustments needed for the child.

These changes in academic and social programming have also meant structural as well as instructional adaptations for the school. So inclusion and other modifications of the structure of educational programming have to be included, as would the development of multidisciplinary teams to contribute knowledge from the health, psychology, and education fields for these E/BD students.

■ Functional Behavior Assessment

One of the most popular intervention methods for coping with children with behavioral and emotional problems (B/ED) has been **functional behavioral**

assessment (FBA). The purpose of FBA is not to respond directly to the dysfunctional behavior of the child (such as throwing a book) but to understand the conditions surrounding the event and change them so as to prevent a repetition of the behavior.

Starting from the premise that even puzzling and self-destructive behavior has a rational purpose, functional assessment aims to discover that purpose. Much aberrant behavior is a reaction to fear or anger, but if we don't know precisely what the fear or anger refers to, we have difficulty knowing how to respond to the sometimes provoking behavior.

The five primary behavior outcomes of FBA have been noted as follows:

1. A clear description of the problem behavior
2. Identification of the events, times, and situations that predict when the problem behavior will or will not occur
3. Identification of the consequences that maintain the problem behavior
4. Development of summary statements or hypotheses describing the problem behavior, the specific situations in which it occurs, and the outcomes that maintain the behavior in those situations
5. Collection of direct observation data that support the summary statements (Fox & Gable, 2004).

In one instance the book throwing might represent embarrassment of a student who is performing badly in an oral presentation in front of his peers; for another child it might be a reaction to teasing; and so forth. Until the situation is analyzed, the particular dysfunctional behavior may be incomprehensible.

This does not mean, of course, that the teacher should ignore the book throwing, which is obviously against classroom rules, but it does mean that consistent disruptive behavior such as this requires some grasp of the motivations or patterns of behavior involved if we are going to contend successfully with the behavior itself.

When we conduct a functional assessment, we ask questions and then make a series of direct observations. The basic, two-part question is "Is this behavior aimed primarily at getting something (such as attention, material things, or support), or is the behavior aimed primarily at *avoiding* something (such as a difficult task, humiliation by peers, or being left out)?" Once we begin to see the primary motivation behind the behavior, we can look for patterns and triggers with follow-up questions like these:

What type of tasks tend to be associated with the difficult behavior?
Who is likely to be in close proximity when the difficult behavior emerges?
What seems to be the immediate results of the difficult behaviors?

Let's look again at Pete (introduced earlier in the chapter). In the functional assessment of Pete's behavior, his teachers have noted that he seems to act out more during language arts and social studies classes when students are asked to read silently and respond to questions at the end of a chapter. During these tasks Pete "roams around the room." His activities seem to start with a purpose (e.g., sharpen a pencil, throw away a paper, get a dictionary), but they usually degenerate into disruptions as he knocks books off another student's desk, tips a student's chair as he walks by, or makes a sarcastic remark to a classmate. Within minutes the quiet class environment is gone and a fight, either physical or verbal, is under way. Often the student involved in this is Jason. Pete's classmates have learned to stay clear of him and try to avoid all contact. It seems as if the more they try to avoid him, the more aggressive he becomes.

As we analyze Pete's behavior with a functional behavior assessment approach, we may conclude that Pete is both trying to "avoid something" (in this instance, a task he finds very difficult, reading and writing) and trying to "get something" (attention from his peers). We can note, too, that the major peer conflict often centers around Jason and that the immediate consequence for Pete is that he is removed from the class and must go to the in-school suspension room (the Tiger Pause room in his school, where a tiger is the mascot). With this functional assessment in hand, teachers will work to develop some positive behavioral supports to help Pete be more successful. We look at these later in the chapter.

Despite the enthusiasm displayed for functional behavior assessment (FBA), even extending to the incorporation of the approach in legislation (IDEA), cautionary voices have been raised about the approach (Sasso, Conroy, Stitcher, & Fox, 2001). Since the basis of FBA is to identify conditions motivating the child to engage in problem behavior, discover which events trigger and reinforce the behavior, and find alternative behaviors to substitute for the target behavior, it makes sense to ask whether those tasks can be efficiently carried out.

In the literature review conducted by Sasso, Conroy, Stitcher, and Fox (2001), the typical target behaviors were noncompliance, disruption, aggression, inappropriate vocalizations, talking out, making noise, and so forth. Investigators appear to have reached only modest agreement on the processes used in determining reasons for aberrant target behaviors, and little agreement as to what hypotheses could be formed on the basis of the assessment.

Despite the promising nature of the FBA approach itself, a great deal needs to be known about the technology of executing it. Sasso et al. (2001) concluded that "existing evidence suggests that we currently know very little about the use of functional assessment for students with or at risk for E/BD" (p. 288). Despite these reservations it is likely that FBA will continue to be used as a promising clinical approach, one that will be increasingly researched and improved.

In earlier chapters, we discussed the various ways that educators can modify the standard educational program to meet the special needs of exceptional children. They can change the *learning environment* in which the child is currently placed, they can change the *content* of the lessons provided to the child, and they can teach the child *skills* to process information and to work effectively with peers and adults. In addition, teachers must be given intervention strategies as well as training to accomplish these differential tasks. It is important to think of modifications in all these areas for children with behavior and emotional disorders.

Educators are using a wide variety of approaches to try to change behavior. Their objectives are to change behavior patterns, encourage constructive behaviors, and help children develop effective strategies for coping with their disorder.

Major strategies in this area have a base in what we have learned about operant conditioning and ecological strategies. Drug therapy may also be an option. Intervention strategies often are used in combination with one another.

Positive Reinforcement

One of the most commonly used strategies has been that of **positive reinforcement**. This is the application of a positive stimulus immediately following the response that we wish to strengthen. If the child is paying attention for a set period of time, the child will be rewarded with praise or with a tangible reward, such as a token to be later turned in for something the child wants. There have been objections to this approach saying that we shouldn't be rewarding students for doing what they are expected to do. But such rewards are only a temporary condition that can be reduced or faded when the response that we wish (e.g., attention to teacher) is well established.

One of the key elements of a positive reinforcement system is providing some type of external reward (extra time at recess, free time, a field trip) when the child exhibits the target behavior (Paul & Epanchin, 1986). Once the student starts behaving appropriately, the teacher can begin to use positive reinforcement. But a teacher can't reinforce behavior that isn't there. As one teacher commented, "I am more than ready to give positive reinforcement. When is *he* [the student] going to show some positive behavior that I can reinforce?"

Some object to the use of such reinforcement techniques because they treat the child like a slot machine (insert a quarter, get good behavior) and have little impact on the child's basic personality. This criticism is not fair. The educational objective is to create in the child a positive response that can be expanded and used for better overall social adjustment.

> To help children experience success, teachers can establish goals and organize tasks in small steps.

Positive Behavior Supports

With the recognition that the environment can have either a positive or a negative effect on an individual's behavior comes the responsibility to create educational environments that enhance positive behavior outcomes. Three levels of behavioral support seem to be necessary for good school operation (Lewis & Sugai, 1999). The first of these is *universal group behavior support,* for most students. This involves establishing schoolwide management strategies, setting rules and standards for expected student behavior in such venues as the cafeteria, the hallways, and the bus. Such an approach has been documented as sharply reducing office referrals for misbehavior (Taylor-Green et al., 1997).

The second level is *specialized group behavior support,* for students with at-risk problem behavior. A separate plan made by school staff with special attention to the 5 percent of the students who create 50 percent of the behavior problems. These students may not be influenced by the universal program, but a consistent strategy for the staff to apply to such students can pay dividends.

Finally, there is a need for *specialized individual behavior support,* for students with chronic problem behaviors. For these students a functional behavior assessment is often the starting point.

When we look at Pete's functional behavior assessment, we see that there are a few things we could do to modify the classroom environment and provide positive supports for his better behavior. We might, for example, establish a work carrel for Pete where distractions are minimized and he has all supplies (such as pencils, Franklin speller, paper, etc.) in one place. This might help with the initial "out of the seat" behavior—but we need to go further if we want to address the task avoidance. We already know that Pete avoids tasks with reading and writing because they are very difficult for him, so we look for ways to support his academic progress and thereby foster competence and success. Since Pete's listening comprehension is much stronger than his reading comprehension, one strategy we can use is allowing him to listen to a chapter on headphones as he follows along in the book. If we combine this with having him highlight main ideas and take a few notes on the material (study skills that we can teach him to use), we can begin to establish sound work habits.

We also need to address Pete's disruptive behavior with classmates, especially his continued difficulties with Jason. Much can be learned by talking with both boys. In this case, we discover that Pete and Jason used to be good friends in elementary school, but that in moving to middle school Jason has broadened his friendship circle and Pete does not seem to fit in with this new group. Part of Pete's volatility around Jason is a reaction to feeling left out. Pete is angry at being abandoned, and his behavior with Jason is a misplaced attempt at getting something: Jason's attention and friendship. At this point we can work with Pete to help him see how his aggressive behavior drives more people away from him. Part of the positive behavioral supports for Pete will include working with the school counselor on (1) recognizing the consequences of negative behavior and (2) developing specific behaviors that will help him make and keep friends.

Figure 6.2 gives some sample goals that would likely be in Pete's individualized education program. These goals address both academics and behavior. The specialized individual behavioral support plan is part of Pete's IEP and thus becomes part of our educational interventions to help Pete succeed in school.

These goals will be the basis for developing a complete IEP with objectives and measures for documenting success. They will also help the school personnel understand their roles in providing support for Pete's achievement. With a child like Pete the special education teacher, counselor, and classroom teacher will all have to work together to create an optimal learning environment.

(text continues on page 251)

FIGURE 6.2
Two IEP Goals for Pete: Academic and Behavioral

Academic Goal	Behavioral Goal
Pete will learn to use specific study skills (learned from his special education teacher and reinforced in his general education classes): • Books on tape • Highlighting main ideas • Note-taking from chapter material to assist him with academic success.	Pete will work with the guidance counselor to develop strategies for making and keeping friends.

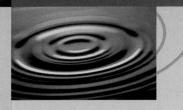

CHILDREN WITH EMOTIONAL AND BEHAVIOR DISORDERS

EDUCATIONAL

■ Adapting the Learning Environment

The learning environment for children with behavior disorders who passed through the prereferral stage and are determined eligible can include inclusion in the general education classroom, a resource room, a special class, and special residential schools where a total therapeutic environment is provided for children who do not seem able to cope with the general school program or vice versa.

Understanding Emotional and Behavior Disorders

There are two elements in any disruptive behavior in the classroom. The first element is the *immediate crisis,* which is often of interpersonal conflict; the second is the *underlying dynamics* that nudged the students to the immediate crisis.

> Paul is engaged in a verbal exchange with Mike in which he couldn't convince Mike to do things his way. Suddenly, Paul leaps on Mike, pounding him to the floor.

There is no question that the immediate crisis must be dealt with quickly and decisively. No matter the provocation, physical violence is unacceptable, and Paul must be taken aside and reminded that he has broken the rules of the classroom and the school and that sanctions will have to be applied.

Once the immediate crisis is over and relative peace has been restored, we need to pursue the underlying reasons for Paul's outburst. Unfortunately, such an outburst gives us few clues as to the cause except that Paul has fragile control over his impulsive behavior. Perhaps Paul is worried about a forthcoming test, was abused by his father before school today, or was humiliated at recess by a bigger boy. Unless we are able to tease out these dynamics, which are different for each individual incident, we will be hard pressed to help Paul avoid a similar episode in the future. The value of the multidisciplinary team is that different members may be able to fit together more pieces of the puzzle, and together they can plan for a longer-range strategy to help Paul in the future.

Inclusion in Context

The goal of special education has been to place children with behavior disorders in the least restrictive environment, which is the general education program, whenever possible. The reasons are to give these students a chance to:

▶ Interact with children who do not have disabilities

▶ Have constructive models of behavior

▶ Keep in step academically

One of the most serious barriers to the proper educational and mental health programming for students with behavior disorders is that the intensity of the treatment does not match the intensity of the disorder. Students did not acquire their dysfunctional patterns of behavior overnight. The dysfunctional patterns have been years in the making, and it is not realistic to believe that they can be eliminated and positive responses substituted for them as a result of an hour of remedial education two times a week. We often shortchange such children because of staff or financial limitations and then wonder why they don't show more immediate improvement.

On the basis of phone interviews with over 130 programs across the country and site visits to twenty-six programs, Knitzer, Steinberg, and Fleisch (1990) concluded that the resource room strategy has generally been nonproductive. They recommended that it be replaced with direct supportive services brought into the general classroom, together with substantial collaboration between mental health services and educators.

There has been an unfortunate tendency for general education teachers to refer children to special services or special education to get themselves out of an awkward situation. The prereferral strategies mentioned in previous chapters seem to be a preferred strategy, with a team of personnel in the school building meeting with the teacher to see what adjustments or adaptations might be made in the general education classroom before a referral is made to special education. Substantial questions have been raised about whether sufficient support services will be available to support the general educator. Kauffman (1994), for example, worried about whether there are sufficient general classroom resources to cope with the most violent or disturbed children in an inclusive classroom:

> Special education is intellectually bankrupt and morally derelict to the extent that it embraces a philosophy that insists on the same placement decision for all students. A second topic for discussion is how does this philosophy of inclusion and the practices derived from it fit with the nature of schools as they exist now, their changing priorities, and the processes of reform? At the same time that teachers are faced with increasingly difficult tasks, they are being asked to do more and to do better with less.
>
> Many of the students now identified for special education because of their emotional or behavioral disorders are kids with very serious problems who require intensive sustained services from many well-trained people who are continuously available. (p. 14)

The issue surrounding inclusion of children with behavior disorders essentially boils down to whether one has confidence that the schools will be able to provide the support personnel necessary to allow a particular child, the teacher, and other students to have a positive and constructive experience. Clearly, the consensus that emerges from the current literature is that necessary social skills instruction and behavior management support are not in place in many general education environments, and general educators are not prepared at this time to accept and teach students with challenging behaviors.

One of the major challenges for special educators is to report the necessary conditions under which children with serious behavior and emotional disorders can prosper in an inclusive setting. One such attempt was reported for fourteen

It is possible to create a positive social environment through instruction and prior preparation, so that children in general education classrooms can reach out to children with disabilities in an informed, empathic way.
(© Myrleen Ferguson Cate/Photo Edit)

students with emotional and behavior disorders in a suburban junior high school (Gibb, Allred, Ingram, Young, & Egan, 1999).

Each of the fourteen students had been in a school designated specifically for students with severe behavior disorders for an average of three and one-half years, having been sent there after failing to adjust to a general education setting. In addition to the general educators teaching the content subjects at the junior high, there were four special education teachers. Two of them were serving as support personnel to the general education classrooms, and the other two were "trackers" who followed the students with emotional and behavioral disorders to class, helped them with direct instruction or assistance within the classroom, and cued them about proper classroom behavior.

The overall results were viewed positively by administrators, general education teachers, special education teachers, and the students themselves—who managed to adapt well to the classroom setting. Although this is only one school, it demonstrates what can be done with a collaborative approach and support for the students. The role of *tracker* was seen as crucial to the success of the program. The authors noted that this approach was labor intensive and were concerned about whether the costs would be considered too great despite the success of this program.

Teacher Preparation for E/BD

If your school has made a commitment to inclusion, there remains the question of how the general education teachers are going to be supported and who is going to provide special education help. Policy makers differ as to whether the field of emotional and behavior disorders merits a specialist training program or can be folded into the usual special education program. In a survey on this topic, 28 of 47 states reported that they required a certificate in E/BD, whereas the remaining 19 states required merely special education training (Katsiyannis, Landrum, Bullock, & Vinton, 1997).

Likewise, only about half of the 101 universities, representing 32 states, providing special education training required specialist training in E/BD. Movement toward preparing E/BD specialists would need to offer strong evidence that such specialists would have demonstrably superior ability to cope with E/BD children, and such evidence has not been obtained.

Polsgrove (2003) mentions types of articles he would like to read in the literature, but which currently are not available.

▶ The effects of inclusion on academic and behavioral outcomes for children with emotional or behavior disorders: a longitudinal study

▶ A comparison of traditional programs for children with emotional or behavior disorders with schoolwide, positive behavior support/comprehensive services

In short, do we specialists in E/BD make a meaningful difference in our interventions? The special problems of the general education teacher faced with inclusion are captured in the "The Teacher and the Pressures of Inclusion" box.

The Teacher and the Pressures of Inclusion

Anne, a devoted elementary-school teacher in a local rural school district for 15 years, tells me that her job has become emotionally and physically overwhelming. After her school district moved to "full inclusion" several years ago, her fifth-grade classroom of 25 now includes 2 children diagnosed with autism, 3 with E/BD (emotional and behavioral disabilities), 8 with learning disabilities (LD), and about 5 others with mild cognitive disabilities. Anne is not certified in special education, but she gets some support from a special education teacher who works with the children with autism and a child with LD about 30 minutes each day. Although the reading levels of the children range from preprimer to grade level, she is required by the state to use standard textbooks for the fifth-grade level. She is finding it an increasingly difficult struggle to meet the needs of such a widely diverse class of students and is seriously considering resigning her position at the end of the year.

Source: From L. Polsgrove, Reflections on the past and future, *Behavioral Disorders 28* (2003): 221–226. Reprinted with permission.

The Support Teacher (E/BD Specialist)

The support teacher concept fits well into the inclusive classroom.

One innovative suggestion for supporting classroom teachers is the **support teacher,** a person who comes into the general classroom and provides the teacher with support for children with special needs. Obviously, a classroom teacher with twenty-five or thirty children cannot cope with all aspects of the classroom environment without help. Who can provide that help? The strategy rests on five assumptions and principles:

▶ Even a child who has serious behavior problems is not disturbed all the time. There are *only certain periods* when the pupil cannot function in the larger group setting. These periods may be at certain regular times or in the press of a crisis. But most of the time, the child can benefit from and fit into the class.

▶ Teachers need direct assistance. Consultation is one thing, but real help is something else. Psychologists and similar professionals might offer advice, but they do not know what it is like to try to administer a classroom that includes children who have behavior disorders.

▶ The direct-service support teacher should work full-time in the school to which he or she is assigned, should not be itinerant, and should be trained as a special teacher. The support teacher should be able to respond to the child who is in crisis but also be able to help all children with academic and emotional problems. Many of these youngsters need direct counseling help with issues such as self-concept, but just as many can achieve growth through therapeutic tutoring.

▶ Sometimes the support teacher can assist best by taking over the classroom while the regular teacher works through a phase of a problem with a child.

▶ Help should be based on the reality of how the child is able to cope with the classroom and not on categories, labels, or diagnostic criteria.

The support teacher generally uses techniques that are an extension of regular education procedures, emphasizing help and encouragement. In addition, the support teacher is able to provide important liaison services that are not within the capabilities of the heavily burdened classroom teacher. Children with behavior problems often need the help of pediatricians, psychologists, and paraprofessionals, and the support teacher can coordinate these sources of assistance as the service coordination noted above.

The role of the E/BD specialist is to help the general education teacher carry out the specific remedial strategies that are likely to improve the academic and social status of the student. The general education teacher does not have the time or setting to carry out such analytic reading techniques as *reciprocal teaching* (Palinscar & Brown, 1986), a one-on-one technique for teaching the student how to analyze a reading passage (i.e., asking questions about the text) and then reversing roles, having the student become the teacher and teach the skills to the specialist.

Other devices such as *transenvironmental planning* (Anderson-Inman, 1987), meaning the transfer of learning to different settings, can also be employed by the E/BD specialist. Once the student learns the value of highlighting and note-taking for a specific text, he or she is asked to transfer the skill from the special remedial setting to the general education setting. The two teachers', joint planning can solidify the technique for the student, who then can use it in other settings as well.

Collaboration: The Role of the Multidisciplinary Team

One realization that has emerged from experiences with children with behavior disorders or emotional disturbance (or both) is that various professional skills are required to make a difference in the life situation for such students. Multidisciplinary teams that may include educators, counselors, social service personnel, mental health personnel, paraprofessionals, and parents are increasingly popular (Simpson, Miles, Walker, Ormsbee, & Downing, 1991).

The multidisciplinary team is coordinated by a *case manager* (also known as a *service coordinator*). This person may come from any of these professions and is directly responsible for seeing that the treatment program is carried out. Among the case manager's functions are:

▶ Coordinating the various services going to child and family

▶ Providing follow-up to ensure that goals are being met

▶ Guiding the work of paraprofessionals and volunteers who work with the child

It is a substantial advantage to have one person who knows all aspects of the treatment program and who has responsibility to see that forward progress is being made (Johnson, 1989).

This may seem to be an enormous expenditure of staff for one student, but it has become increasingly clear that this type of approach is necessary to obtain positive results. Minor tinkering with one or another part of a student's environment is not likely to effect major changes in students prone to aggressiveness and violence.

The Wraparound Approach

Since behavior problems seem to include many different dimensions of self, family, culture, and community, it makes good sense to try a multidisciplinary approach using professionals from education, psychology, psychiatry, social work, and perhaps other related fields, combined into a treatment team. Such an approach involves a commitment to blend and create services for children, their teachers, and their families (Eber, Osuch, & Redditt, 1996).

This team approach to "wraparound" planning and treatment resembles IEP meetings and planning, except that these terms often originate in community agencies rather than the schools. In addition, the **wraparound approach** makes extensive use of agencies outside the school program, though they are expected to include school personnel in the planning (Eber, Nelson, & Miles, 1997).

With regard to Jim, such wraparound planning might include counseling for his mother, who has become depressed about her inability to handle his behavior; some psychological counseling for Jim to help him understand the reasons for his hostile outbursts; and some plans for the teacher to find some examples of success in schoolwork for Jim, so that he will get some satisfaction from being in school.

The wraparound approach has resulted in children's showing good improvement, but it will be successful only to the extent that the various professions and agencies involved can agree to work together and avoid status battles and competitive attitudes (VanDenBerg & Grealish, 1996).

The plan focuses on the strengths of the student as well as on attempts to mute any deficits in performance that the student may have. Although it is often used as a vehicle for maintaining the student in the general education classroom by bringing additional resources into that classroom, services might be delivered in a resource room or a self-contained special class if that is what represents the least restrictive environment for that student (Kerr & Nelson, 2002).

Adapting Teaching Strategies

Skills Mastery Techniques The difficulties of teaching students with emotional and behavior disorders does not lie in knowing what should be done, but in the ability of the teacher to carry out these principles in the face of resistance and misbehavior. Some of the established principles are (Wehby, Symons, & Canale, 1998)

▶ Provision of appropriate structure and predictable routines

▶ Positive teacher-student interaction with adequate praise and systematic response to problem behavior

▶ Frequent implementation of instructional sequences that promote high rates of academic engagement and high levels of student response

But when the teacher approaches Pete, a disruptive student, with a reading assignment and is confronted with "No, I won't do it!" the teacher is thrown back on her personal resources to cope with such outright defiance. It is not surprising that the evidence shows that teachers tend to avoid students like Pete and have fewer interactions with them than with other students. This is particularly true when the giving of assignments typically is followed by disruptive behavior. It is not clear that additional preservice training would help, but some form of mentoring of new teachers by teachers who have "been there" can be more effective.

Specialists working with children who have behavior disorders have focused much of their attention on behavior change, which can occur with or without the child's participation. That means reducing some unacceptable behavior or encouraging proactive, socially desirable behavior. Behavior change that occurs without the child's participation results from operant conditioning. Specialists apparently can also help children to actively change their behavior. They can help them (1) to see the signals in their environment that trigger their unacceptable behavior, (2) to inhibit the impulse to respond immediately, and (3) to develop a plan of action to meet different situations. In many respects, the goal of learning those three skills is as important to the education of students with behavior disorders as are the academic goals of reading and arithmetic. Until these children are able to exercise self-control and to develop other social skills, they are unlikely to learn traditional academic skills.

Teachers can use various strategies with students who have behavior disorders, but each strategy imposes costs or demands on the teachers, whether they are trying to communicate with students, support desirable behavior, or control problem behavior. For example, reminding a student about the rules of the classroom costs the teacher less in energy or effort than does conducting a group meeting on a problem behavior. High-cost teacher behavior, however, may be needed to bring some benefits to the situation. Teachers often find themselves having to decide whether to use these high-cost strategies, and all sorts of factors—professional and personal—can affect the final decision. A variety of strategies have been developed to cope with children who manifest these disorders.

Cognitive Strategy Approaches There is a family of strategies currently known as the *cognitive strategy approach*. Whether called *self-monitoring, self-instruction,*

Virtual resource center on behavior disorders teacher training modules
www.coe.missouri.edu/~vrcbd

or *self-control,* these methods rely on the cooperation of the child and encourage the development of effective cognition coping skills. With the development of the child's skills comes more self-confidence and a more positive self image as the child achieves greater control over his or her impulses.

Self-management for behavior change has received much favorable comment. One attraction of self-management techniques is that students who successfully apply them assume greater responsibility for their behavior, instead of being externally controlled or "forced" to change by various kinds of conditioning.

Suppose Pete has trouble staying in his seat. The first step is to teach him to recognize the behavior and then to record its frequency. Next, Pete negotiates a reward that is satisfying to him (perhaps some time to work on the computer) for staying in his seat for a specified period. Once he has shown the ability to control the behavior, he can be given the opportunity to control his own schedule and make decisions about the content or skills he would like to work on in the time slot.

There are several self-management techniques:

▶ *Self-monitoring* requires students to determine whether a target behavior has occurred and then record its occurrence. For example, if Pete feels an aggressive attack coming on, he can note it in a journal. This helps him become increasingly aware of the clues identifying a potential outburst.

▶ *Self-evaluation* asks the student to compare his or her behavior to some criteria and make a judgment about the quality of the behavior being exhibited, for example, "On a scale of 1 to 5, am I paying attention to the teacher?"

▶ *Self-reinforcement* means that the student rewards himself or herself with a token or a tally after meeting some performance standard, such as avoiding aggressive outbursts for a set period of time. For example, a timer set for ten minutes that goes off without an aggressive outburst earns for the student a token that he or she can cash in later for game-playing time or a specially designed activity.

▶ *Self-instruction* is a method by which students can, in essence, talk to themselves, encouraging themselves with verbal prompts to persist in solving an academic or social problem.

Those techniques are designed to increase students' awareness, competence, and commitment to eliminating negative behaviors and to encourage the acquisition of constructive ones. For Pete, this means the teacher works with him to improve self-awareness skills that will enable him to increase his own control over his hyperactivity or distractibility. One practical way of increasing the student's personal responsibility is to let the student participate in developing his or her own IEP.

A review of eleven studies regarding the effectiveness of self-management has determined that such techniques were successful in changing the behavior of students with behavior disorders (Hughes, Ruhl, & Misra, 1989). The majority of the behaviors that changed, however, involved fairly simple tasks, such as increasing on-task performance. Whether these techniques work as well with changes in more complex behaviors or last over an extended period of time remains to be determined.

The greatest advantage of this approach is that the child gains self-confidence by exerting control of his or her previously out-of-control behavior. There is an

Students using self-management assume greater responsibility for changing undesired behaviors.

important additional advantage. Many children with behavior disorders spend part of their time in the general education classroom as a result of the least restrictive environment and inclusive philosophies. Many general education classroom teachers do not wish to, or feel they cannot, engage in the complex monitoring and recording of individual student behaviors that some of the other behavior-shaping techniques require. Therefore, because students who use self-management monitor themselves, once the students learn what they are to do in a self-management program, they can proceed with only modest teacher supervision.

Students can use self-management in the inclusive classroom to monitor their own behavior, allowing only modest teacher supervision.

Student Contingency Contracts Behavior contracts can be a useful way to help teachers and students identify key areas for change. These contracts identify the specific behaviors being targeted, the impact of the behavior on self and others, the rewards for appropriate behavior, and the consequences of inappropriate behavior. If we think about Pete again, one of the most disruptive of his behaviors is starting fights with classmates—with Jason, in particular. In addition to working on his IEP goals, we might establish a behavior contract with him that focuses on his interactions with classmates, especially with Jason. The contract might look like the "Contract for Pete" in the box

---

Contract for Pete

Behavior and impact: I, Pete Walker, understand that when I start fights with Jason, I disrupt the class, I don't do my own work, I make my teacher get mad at me, and Jason and I sometimes get hurt.

Target for change: This week I will work on leaving Jason alone.

Reward for change: If I do not get into a fight with Jason this week, I can pick three classmates to play my favorite computer math game with me on Friday during independent worktime.

Consequence for no change: If I do fight with Jason this week, I will use my independent worktime to do a classroom chore. That way, I can give something back to my classmates.

Date: 9/15/05.

Student Signature:_____   Teacher Signature:_____

What is most important about behavior contracts is that they are directed by the student: The student identifies specific objectionable behavior, articulates the impact of this behavior, identifies its consequences, and describes rewards for not indulging in it. This ownership, for students, is critical to helping them take responsibility for their behavior and for the impact it has on those around them. It is also essential to remember that the more specific a contract is regarding the targeted behavior, the more likely it is that the student will be able to succeed in changing it. So in Pete's case, the wording "leaving Jason alone" is much better than a vague phrase like "trying to get along with Jason." The reward, too, critical: It should appear desirable to the student, but it should also foster positive growth. For Pete, the ability to invite other students to play a math game fosters

Social skills can be developed through modeling, role playing, performance feedback, generalization, and maintenance.
(© Ariel Skelley/CORBIS)

growth in both academic and social skills. Finally, the consequence for *not* fulfilling the contract must be logical and must be seen by the student as nondesirable. In this instance, Pete's behavior disrupts the class and takes away class time, so it is logical that his consequence should give something back to the class.

In some cases parents would be involved in the contracts, but this was not seen as possible for Pete because he receives very little support from home. Still, the most productive contracts are those that can be carried forward in the setting where the behavior is taking place—in this case, the classroom.

Developing Social Skills Many children with behavior disorders not only engage in nonadaptive behaviors that cause them trouble with their peers and teachers but also lack positive social skills. One specific goal of a special education program, therefore, is to enhance the use and practice of socially acceptable behaviors.

Molly's periodic weeping "turned off" her peers, and she had few positive skills to re-establish social contact with her classmates. One positive skill that can be introduced to Molly is how to approach another child with a request to play or talk.

Kerr and Nelson (1998) described a sequence of activities by which such skills might be developed:

1. *Modeling.* The skill can be introduced through live, audio, or video modeling. Peers can demonstrate such skills.

2. *Role-playing.* The skill can be played out in a pretend real-life situation. The role-play can be highly structured so that the person has a good chance of performing acceptably.

3. *Performance feedback.* Just as drama students are critiqued for their performance of a scene, so the teacher can discuss with the student the pluses

(always first) and the minuses of the performance. The student might be asked to do the scene again after the critique, and the performance is almost always improved.

4. *Generalization and maintenance.* The student must be able to use the skill in a variety of situations. Self-monitoring techniques can be helpful in keeping the skill foremost in the student's mind.

The supportive atmosphere that teachers and peers can establish in this process usually is extraordinarily helpful in its own right. This means that the teacher takes pains to set the situation up as a helping situation with perhaps more than one student as the focus of the social skills practice. Such extensive efforts require much time and attention on the part of the teacher and are best done with a teacher consultant in the classroom or in a small-group setting such as a resource room or special classroom.

Preventing Social Problems Specialists in behavior disorders strive not only to remediate behavior problems that have been observed but also to prevent their occurring in the first place. One of the most ambitious prevention projects has been carried out in four separate communities in the United States, with 198 first-grade intervention classrooms from 48 high-risk elementary schools along with 180 randomly selected comparison classrooms (Conduct Problems Prevention Research Group, 1999).

Two levels of child intervention were applied with the entire classroom in the 198 first grades. PATHS (Promoting Alternative Thinking Strategies), a 57-lesson curriculum in social competence, focusing on self control, awareness of one's own feelings, and peer relations, was utilized to improve social skills for the whole class.

Ten percent of these first-grade students who were identified by teacher and parent reports as "high-risk students" in kindergarten were given additional parent support classes, small-group social skills interventions, and academic tutoring, together with home visiting.

This "fast track" prevention program was designed to reduce the total level of aggressive, hyperactive, and disruptive behavior by having the full classroom become proficient in understanding their own feelings and by learning self-control skills. At the same time, additional effort was being made to help the 10 percent of students at particular risk, in the hope of reducing the likelihood that such students would have a negative impact on the total class behavior.

The detailed statistical analysis of the results indicated that the intervention classrooms showed less aggression than the comparison classrooms and also less hyperactive-disruptive behavior. No differences were found in prosocial behavior.

The authors also pointed out that the students with the teachers judged most effective in their application of the PATHS program showed greater improvement than students with teachers who were judged less effective. One lesson to be learned from this large project is that it is possible to combine an overall effort at teaching social skills in first-grade classrooms with special interventions for high-risk students to reduce those behaviors that can cause greater difficulty in later school years.

A similar preventive effort in Canada was carried out in Montreal schools: examining the effect of a parent training program combined with a social skills program given to 96 high-risk students identified in kindergarten as high-risk for aggression. A comparison group of "observation only" students and a third control group of students with "no treatment" were randomly chosen for the study. The particular advantage of this study was that these students, originally identified in their inner-city kindergartens, were followed until the age of 15 as to what the long-range effects of this program were (Tremblay, R., Pagani-Kurtz, L., Masse, L., Vitaro, F., & Pihl, R., 1995).

The students under the treatment program were able to remain in an "age appropriate" classroom to a greater extent than the students in the comparison groups and at yearly assessments from 10 to 15 years of age, reported significantly less delinquent behavior than the comparison groups. (A cautionary note—these differences in academic and teacher ratings in favor of the treated groups remained clear during the elementary school years but disappeared when the students reached ages 14 and 15, prompting the authors to recommend that some form of "booster program" be initiated at the secondary-school level.)

What we have learned from these and other studies is that students, even those from high-risk families and neighborhoods, can respond positively to parental and social skills training while these children are below age 8, often assumed to be the age at which serious aggressive behavior crystallizes (Eron, 1990).

The Needs of the Individual Student The emphasis in programs stressing positive reinforcement is that "work comes before play." This means that highly preferred activities (play) are contingent on less preferred activities (work). When successful, these programs have an additional advantage in that a sense of pride emerges

Activities such as participating in a community project or helping a charity give students an environment where they can observe and model positive behavior.
(© Robert Brenner/Photo Edit)

in the child for accomplishing valued tasks—if the teacher is skilled enough to present tasks of sufficient difficulty that the student has a true sense of accomplishment when they are completed.

Are our treatments or educational interventions effective? Which methods appear to be more effective than others? What are the odds that educational treatment of children with serious emotional and behavior disorders can be effective? A consensus of experts in this field (Walker, Zeller, Close, Webber, & Gresham, 1999) suggested that there was little, realistically, that educators could do about the risk factors that propelled youths to violence: (1) early involvement with drugs and alcohol; (2) easy access to weapons, especially handguns; (3) association with deviant, antisocial peer groups; and (4) pervasive exposure to violence in the media. They concluded:

> The most viable strategy for educators to consider in addressing the needs of at-risk antisocial youth is usually to develop protective factors (e.g., reading ability, academic skills, friendship-making skills, self-control strategies) that can buffer and offset the negative effects of their prior exposure to risk factors (p. 298).

One of the difficulties in answering such questions is that the treatment of children with behavior disorders is individual and based on the needs of a particular child, making comparisons among children difficult.

An innovative attempt to bring together the results of sixty-four single subject studies (reporting the results of one student at a time from a beginning baseline to performance after treatment) revealed moderate positive results for social skills training (Mathew, Kavale, Quinn, Forness, & Rutherford, 1998). Delinquent students seemed to respond better to social skills instruction than do children with emotional or behavior disorders or children with autism. The modest nature of the impact of social skills instruction suggests that further work needs to be done to improve such training and also reminds us how difficult it is to change patterns of human behavior once they have been established.

A summary of the research on social skills training to produce socially acceptable learned behaviors such as cooperation, assertion, responsibility, empathy, and self-control revealed a modest positive gain for that training (Gresham, 1998). There was even some suggestion that improvement in academic skills instruction might improve the behavior of many students as well as the social skills instruction itself. One of the biggest problems was that there was a failure of *generalization;* that is, the student might learn a skill in one setting (e.g., proper greeting) but be unable to generalize it to other settings, such as the playground. Gresham has proposed a contextual approach to teaching social skills that would take advantage of events that occur naturally in the school environment; most social skills instruction in home, school, and community settings can be characterized as informal. Thousands of behavioral incidents occur in these settings, creating numerous opportunities for successful learning experiences (p. 22).

A recent comprehensive review of social skills training and its effect on children with behavior and emotional disorders (Kavale, Mathur, & Mostert, 2004) found only limited positive results and concluded that social skills training is still an "experimental intervention and needs to be rebuilt as part of a comprehensive treatment for students with E/BD." This serves to remind us that it took years for many of these students to develop their dysfunctional behavior patterns, which cannot be eliminated without great effort and professional attention.

■ Adapting Technology

Computers: Aiding Content Mastery and Avoiding Negative Response

A computer can be an especially useful learning tool for a student with a behavior disorder because it provides an objective, neutral response to the child's sometimes provoking or challenging behavior. Children with a long history of social interaction problems may respond poorly to teacher feedback, particularly when criticism or correction is involved. The child who is adept at manipulating others can quickly change the focus of a discussion from his or her inadequate academic performance to the teacher's behavior. "Why are you always picking on me?" is a common theme. With a computer, however, the student must find a different approach.

Obviously, a computer isn't able to interact emotionally with the child. If the student has difficulty solving a problem, he or she must find out why and determine the right answer in order to proceed with the computer program. The student cannot resort to emotional manipulation or accuse the machine of being unfair.

Children who are hyperactive or who have an attention-deficit hyperactive disorder often have difficulty concentrating and can be helped by a computer. When working with a computer, they must pay some degree of attention to get results. The orderliness and sequence of the software programs can provide a systematic structure for students who have very little cognitive structure or self-discipline. Given the extensive possibilities for the use of computers with students who have behavior disorders, it is surprising that little research on their impact with such students has been published.

A number of technological aids have been made available that can provide some supportive help for those working with children with behavior or emotional difficulties. Some take the form of board games that enhance social skills development with topics such as social greetings, handling anger at school and work, appropriate and inappropriate touching, good sportsmanship, and so on. In another classroom behavior game, students move around the board and are exposed to ten strategies that are positive solutions for managing anger. They include taking responsibility for one's own actions, encouraging self-control, and dealing with the acting-out behavior of others.

See the Houghton Mifflin Teacher Education website for an expanded list of assistive technology equipment.

| Students with ADHD may benefit from working on a Computer.

| www.pcicatalog.com

| Houghton Mifflin Teacher Education website
http://education.college.hmco.com/students

Time-Out

The time-out is frequently used to control the misbehavior of children.

One of the techniques used most frequently to control the behavior of children with behavior disorders is the time-out—sending students who have violated classroom rules to a secluded place in the room or in a space nearby with instructions to come back when they feel they have regained control of themselves. Time-out takes the student away from possibly negative interactions with other students and gives him or her a chance to cool off.

Schools are important microsystems in treatment of children with behavior and emotional disorders.

One version of the time-out approach is the Think-Time strategy (Nelson, Crabtree, Marchand-Martella, & Martella, 1998). This approach requires the cooperation of another teacher who can provide the think-time area. The student engaging in disruptive behavior is sent to an area in another classroom previously designated in cooperation with another teacher. This enables the teacher to cut off a negative social exchange or a power struggle and provides the student with time to think about future performance. Once the student has calmed down, the cooperating teacher can get the student to review the inappropriate behavior, what the student was trying to do, and what he or she needs to do on returning to the classroom. Such an intervention cuts short what could be a serious situation and allows all parties time to cool off.

There is a version of time-out, however, that has received negative views from the professional community. *Seclusionary time-out* (placing an individual in an area that the person cannot leave until others decide that he or she can) is a highly intrusive behavior and should be used only as a last resort. As with any other technique, time-out should be used as a positive behavior-enhancement tool, not as punishment.

Many children with behavior disorders engage in nonadaptive behaviors that cause them trouble with their peers and teachers and also lack positive social skills.
(© Michael Newman/Photo Edit)

One teacher in Albuquerque, New Mexico, has used an innovative approach to students' needs for time-out. His classroom is a self-contained setting for bright students with extreme learning, behavioral, and/or emotional problems. (These are students who are often called "twice exceptional" because they are gifted and have disabilities. See Chapter 9 on gifted children.) In the course of studying weather, this fifth grade class did a special project on hurricanes and built a large papier-mâché model of a hurricane—complete with an "eye" large enough for one student to crawl into. The model stayed in a corner of the room for the entire year, and the eye of the hurricane became a calm spot where any child could go when feeling the need to "get out of the storm." In this classroom, time-out was seen as a positive self-regulatory strategy that students controlled and activated when they needed peace and quiet. The eye of the hurricane provided a positive outlet when any student began feeling overwhelmed, frustrated, or angry, and children who used this option instead of acting out were praised for their insight and responsibility.

Transition

One of the unsolved challenges involving the education of E/BD students is their poor record of school completion, together with limited success in the vocational arena following school. The Office of Special Education Programs reported (2003) that only about 40 percent of these students completed their secondary schooling. These findings suggest (1) entering a labor market with low and uncertain wages, (2) possible trouble with the law, and (3) the unlikelihood of seeking additional training on their own.

The findings are consistent with those of earlier studies (Valdez, Williamson, & Wagner, 1990; Rylance, 1997). Kortering, Braziel, and Tomkins (2002) interviewed individually 33 students, who were receiving services for behavior disorders, to find out their perceptions of the problems with completing school. Students' responses are listed in Table 6.1 and indicate that additional support is needed during the difficult transition period.

One of the major questions facing families is what happens to their children in secondary school and beyond. To what extent do they find jobs? To what extent are they personally independent?

Since the family unit has been often identified as one of the factors in the behavior disorders of their children, that family unit becomes an obvious target or goal for remediation. Unfortunately, few families that are dysfunctional are prime candidates for counseling, as they can be very defensive about what is going on within that family unit.

One strategy that seems to have some success is Parent Management Training (PMT), which uses the Patterson coercion model as its base and focuses treatment on four main targets; effective monitoring of children's behavior, prosocial fostering, well-focused discipline, and good social problem solving (Rutter, Giller, & Hagell, 1998). The treatment appears to achieve modest success when the parents follow through, but many families drop out, with resistance focusing on discipline practices at home (Patterson & Chamberlin, 1994). The treatment works best when the children involved are young and their families less disturbed.

TABLE 6.1
Responses from E/BD Students on Staying in School

ARE THERE ANY ADVANTAGES OR DISADVANTAGES TO STAYING IN SCHOOL?	
ADVANTAGES	Better education and jobs. Getting a better job and better pay. Diploma means a better job. Good education and a job. So I can get in the army and get a job. You will get a better job. Good Job.
DISADVANTAGES	Getting into trouble with peers. A lot of homework and not much free time. Can't get a job. Can't work. Working in class is too hard. Don't get a lot of time with friends.
WHAT CHANGES WOULD HELP AN INDIVIDUAL STUDENT FINISH SCHOOL, AND HOW?	
MORE SUPPORT	Help me pass. Help me with my homework. Help me get good grades. Give me more help. Help me control my anger.
WHAT CHANGES WOULD HELP MORE STUDENTS STAY IN SCHOOL?	
CURRICULUM	More detail in classes. Up-to-date books. Newer texts. Social studies books should be easier for kids in special education classes. Some of the books are too difficult. More fun things in class. Put tutors in [classes].

Source: From L. J. Kortering, P. M. Braziel, & J. R. Tomkins, The challenge of school completion among youths with behavioral disorders: Another side of the story, *Behavioral Disorders,* 27 (2002): 142–154. Reprinted with permission.

A relatively new way of viewing the professional and parent relationship is by seeing it as a *partnership of experts.* The parents are experts on their own children and on those children's feelings and behavior. They are really case managers, policy makers, and legislative advocates. The professionals are experts in such general fields as special education and mental health. Under these assumptions we can establish a relationship between the two parties with the best interests of the child in hand (Duchnowski, Dunlap, Berg, & Adiegbola, 1995).

A possible problem in establishing such collaboration or partnership could be any cultural diversity between families and professionals. In such instances

Behavioral Disorders magazine for August 1998 contains special articles on transition issues.

Students with behavior disorders have lower grade point averages than students in other disability categories.

the parents of children from nonmainstream cultures are more likely to be seen by the professionals as "needing training," rather than as full-fledged partners in the remedial efforts. A sense of "learned helplessness" felt by many such parents has to be combated by the professionals, so that the parents can maintain self-respect and the desire to be the professionals' partners (Harry, 1997).

There are many different approaches to children with emotional and behavior disorders. However, most experts feel that intensity of treatment is one key to success. Several experts (Kauffman, 2003; Nelson, 2003) have wondered whether the inclusive classroom will allow for the appropriate treatment to be given. Nelson (2003) has made the following recommendation:

> Advocate for the full continuum of services and placements for our students, and work to replace the concept of "full inclusion" with that of "supported inclusion" and insist that the support extend to the teachers and other caregivers in these inclusive environments as well as students with disabilities. Require that this support be in the form of valid technical assistance provided by the personnel who have the qualifications to deliver it (p. 215).

Summary

- Unlike children with other disabilities, children with emotional and behavior disorders are often blamed for their condition. This affects their interactions with the people around them.

- The definition of *emotional and behavior disorder* takes into account the intensity and duration of age-inappropriate behavior, the situation in which the behavior is exhibited, and the individual who considers the behavior a problem.

- Although fewer than 1 percent of schoolchildren are receiving special education services for emotional and behavior disorders, studies show that the number of children who actually need those services is at least 5 percent and may range as high as 15 percent.

- There is an increased prevalence of minority and immigrant children referred for special services for social and emotional disturbance. Such students often report less support from peers and adults as well as low school achievement. Favorable changes in the school environment for these children have positive results.

- Intervention for the child who is anxious and withdrawn should have as its primary objective instilling a sense of self-worth and self-control. Positive experiences play an important role in preventing suicide—a serious problem among students who are deeply depressed and withdrawn.

- Violence in the schools has been a continuing problem. Serious physical violence is caused by a small percentage of students, many of whom can be identified at an early age.

- Although traditional methods such as counseling and the "zero tolerance" approach do not appear to reduce violence, functional behavior assessment that seeks the personal cause of the violence does seem to have favorable results.

- We currently lack a graduated intensity of treatment programs and settings to cope with the various levels of behavior disorders.

- Inclusion appears to offer a viable setting for some students with behavior disorders, if the classroom teacher has received training in special instructional strategies, the other students have been alerted to the special needs of the student with behavior problems, and adequate support services are made available.

- Ecological strategies focus on the interactions between children and their environment and attempt to design therapeutic settings for the children. Social skills training has been only a modest success and should focus on the need for generalization from specific training to general classroom.

▶ Positive behavior supports are strategies by which the student can be encouraged to substitute prosocial behavior for negative ones.

▶ Drug therapy, in combination with educational intervention, is effective in the treatment of many children with hyperactivity, although the reaction to drugs is a highly individual matter that needs careful monitoring.

Future Challenges

1. What are the conditions for emotional health for culturally diverse students?

Despite findings that there is increased prevalence of social and emotional problems in minority and immigrant groups, the vast majority of such children are not so affected. A study of emotionally healthy children from these backgrounds and their families could help us understand and assist in the emergence of emotional health in these groups.

2. Can increasing uses of multidisciplinary teams provide the necessary increase in services?

One serious condition limiting the delivery of quality educational services to children with behavior problems is the need for highly trained personnel. Unless a way can be found to use paraprofessional personnel, as has been done in behavior shaping programs, it will not be possible to provide the help needed by the large number identified as having behavior problems.

3. How early should we begin?

The more research that is done, the stronger is the felt need to begin education and therapy as early in the child's life as possible—and that includes family counseling. For children with emotional and behavior disorders this would mean starting well before the school years. Ideally, some therapeutic treatment for children with E/BD and their families should begin by ages 2 or 3. This often means arranging for relationships with pediatricians and other professionals, who frequently are the first contact that the family has about these problems.

4. How can violence be prevented?

Longitudinal studies of children who are socially maladjusted and act out their aggressive feelings suggest strongly that they do not outgrow these tendencies. Unless something significant is done with these children or with the environment surrounding them (positive behavior supports), we can predict that aggressive children who hurt people will become aggressive adults who hurt people. The need for large-scale intervention within the school, family, and neighborhood is clear.

Key Terms

attention-deficit hyperactivity disorder (ADHD) *p. 225*

behavior disorder *p. 213*

coercive cycle *p. 217*

functional behavior assessment (FBA) *p. 232*

learned helplessness *p. 230*

positive behavior supports *p. 235*

positive reinforcement *p. 235*

serious emotional disturbance (E/BD) *p. 213*

support teacher *p. 240*

transient adaptation problems *p. 230*

wraparound approach *p. 242*

Resources

References of Special Interest

Bender, W., Clinton, G., & Bender, R. (Eds.). (1999). *Violence prevention and reduction in schools*. Austin, TX: Pro-Ed. *This text, written by a team of experts, contains practical, current information. Offering an overview of critical issues and potential solutions, it can be helpful to both educators and parents who want to be better informed.*

Committee for Children (2002). *Second step: A violence prevention curriculum*. Seattle, WA: Author. *This curriculum is a classroom-based social skills program for children ages 4 through 14. Designed to teach socioemotional skills, its goals are to reduce impulsive and aggressive behavior in children and to increase their levels of social competence. The program teaches, models, practices, and reinforces skills in empathy, impulse control, problem solving, and anger management and is packaged in a teacher-friendly format for use in the classroom. Over twelve evaluations of the Second Step Curriculum have been conducted; all have found overall decreases in aggression (both verbal and physical), along with a decrease in discipline referrals.*

Forum. (2003). *Behavioral Disorders, 28*, 197–228. *A special issue of this journal containing the retrospective thoughts of key figures in the field. Steven Forness, James Kauffman, C. Michael Nelson, and Lewis Polsgrove sum up what they have learned and what they believe to be the key issues of the present and the immediate future. Younger leaders in the field comment on these summaries with ideas of their own.*

Kerr, M., & Nelson, C. (2002). *Addressing behavior problems* (4th ed.). Upper Saddle River, NJ: Prentice Hall. *An organization of the best practices for educating students with behavior disorders in ways that are accessible and meaningful to practitioners. It reflects the results of new research and provides refinements for improved implementation and outcomes.*

Kerr, M., & Nelson, C. (2002). *Strategies for managing behavior problems in the classroom* (4th ed.). Upper Saddle River, NJ: Merrill. *This book is rich in the wide varieties of strategies and techniques for dealing with children with behavior problems. It includes principles for selecting interventions and for dealing with specific behavior problems, aggressive behaviors, and psychiatric problems. It also presents survival skills for the teacher.*

Lane, K., Gresham, F., & O'Shaughnessy, T. (Eds.). (2002). *Interventions for children with or at risk for emotional and behavioral disorders.* Boston: Allyn & Bacon. *A multiauthored text whose sections include coverage of prevention and identification, academic instruction, management of challenging behaviors, and the integration of services to children with E/BD. One section deals with internalizing disorders such as phobias, anxiety, depression, and so forth. Much of the book focuses on the specific problems teachers have in coping with these children, and there is a call for continued research on the linkage between academic difficulties and behavior problems.*

R. Rutherford, Jr., Quinn, M., & Mathur, S. (Eds). (2004). *Handbook of Research in Emotional and Behavorial Disorders.* New York: Guilford Press. *The editors have gathered together many of the most outstanding researchers and scholars in this field to present the most recent knowledge, research, and practices for educating students with emotional and behavior disorders. The content allows easy access to historical and conceptual foundations, assessment and evaluation, student characteristics and intervention, and treatment. It is an admirable source book for anyone interested in this field.*

Sugai, G., & Horner, R. (Eds.). (2000). Special Issue: Functional Behavioral Assessment. *Exceptionality, 8*(3), 145–230. *A special issue devoted entirely to a discussion of functional behavioral assessment. A series of experts discuss the conceptual and empirical foundations of this process, how functional behavioral assessment fits into recent legislative efforts, how to design plans for functional assessment, and the use of information technology to prepare personnel to use this new set of instructional strategies.*

Journals

Behavioral Disorders
www.ccbd.net

Exceptional Children
www.cec.sped.org

Journal of Applied Behavior Analysis
www.seab.enumed.rochester.edu/jaba/

Teaching Exceptional Children
www.cec.sped.org/bk/abtec.html

Professional Organizations

American Psychological Association
www.apa.org

Council for Children with Behavioral Disorders
www.ccbd.net

National Alliance for the Mentally Ill
www.nami.org

National Mental Health Association
www.nmha.org

Society for Research in Child Development
www.srcd.org

Please visit the book's website at **http://education.college.hmco.com/students** for new and updated information on websites listed here and for the mailing addresses of the journals and organizations.

Children with Communication Disorders in Speech and Language

FOCUS QUESTIONS

▶ What is the difference between a speech disorder and a language disorder?

▶ What are some language and listening strategies for a child with frequent otitis media?

▶ What are the advantages of early language intervention when a disorder is identified?

▶ How are non-English-speaking children assessed?

▶ What adaptations can be made to the environment, to teaching strategies, and to curriculum?

▶ What technology is available?

othing is more exciting to parents than their infant's amazing ability to begin to acquire speech and language in the first year of life. So it is not surprising that parents are often devastated if their infant fails to acquire verbal language and to speak in a manner that is understandable.

Communication through speech and language is a complicated but natural human process that grows out of the child's prelinguistic communication through cries, grunts, smiles, and gestures (Dromi, 1993). It involves cognition (thinking) and audition (hearing). It means receiving information and sending information back. It means learning how to control air for sound production and muscles of the mouth for articulation and speech in a fashion that another person of the same culture can understand.

Speech and language development occurs in most individuals who are not disabled. Thus, failure to learn to produce sounds (words) that have meaning in a given culture (language) is indicative of almost all major communication disabilities. When such a disability is suspected, it must be identified and appropriate remediation initiated as early in the child's life as possible so the child will be able to communicate with others and, at school age, learn to read and write.

■ Definitions

American Speech-Language-
Hearing Association (ASHA)
www.asha.org

Communication is the exchange of thoughts, information, and ideas. Most commonly, we think of verbal communication as occurring through speech or talking. Messages can be transmitted in other ways, however: through writing, sign language, telegraphy, and the electrical impulses of the telephone and the computer modem. Communication can be nonverbal, through gestures and facial expressions. Sign language uses an ordered form of gestures to convey meaning. Necessary for communication to take place are a sender, a message, and a receiver (Figure 7.1).

Speech is the systematic oral production of the words of a given language. Sounds become speech only if they produce words that have meaning. Speech has a rhythmic flow with stress and intonation and words with stressed and unstressed syllables. Figure 7.2 presents a simplified overview of the production of speech. A thought occurs in the brain; it is translated into symbols and sent to the larynx area for phonation and resonation, which takes place in the

FIGURE 7.1
The Communication Process

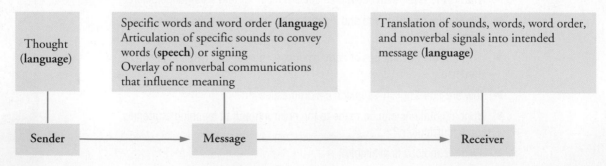

FIGURE 7.2
Processes Involved in the Production of Speech

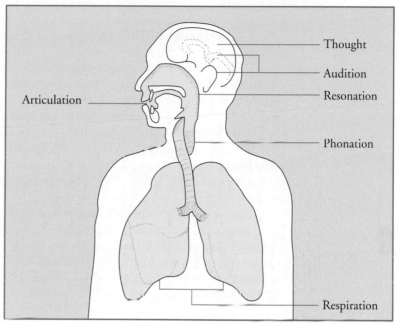

vocal tract; then air is sent to be modified by movements of the tongue and passage over the teeth and lips, which combine to form the sounds, words, and sentences of a particular language (articulation). The thought transformed into words is received by a listener through hearing, in a process called **audition.**

The following four processes are involved in the production of speech:

▶ **Respiration** (breathing) generates the energy that produces sound.

▶ **Phonation** is the production of sound by the vibration of the vocal cords.

▶ **Resonation** gives the voice a unique characteristic that identifies the speaker. It is the product of sound traveling through the speaker's head and neck.

▶ **Articulation** is the movement of the mouth and tongue that shapes sound into phonemes (the smallest unit of sound), which make speech.

Damage to any of these processes can result in a speech disorder but does not necessarily interfere with language learning or reading and writing. Hearing losses can also cause speech disorders (NICHCY, 2003). A child will fail to produce speech if he or she cannot hear it spoken or hear his or her own sound production. Fortunately, most children with hearing losses have some audition, and they can learn to speak when provided with amplification through hearing aids (children who are deaf or hard of hearing are the subject of Chapter 10).

Language is an organized system of symbols that humans use to express and receive meaning (Jusczyk, 1997). Language systems evolved over time and largely replaced the innate communication system of emotions by means of gestures and facial expressions, which convey meaning, though the range of meaning they convey is limited. When a given community selects a series of sounds to convey meaning, it creates speech. Spoken language has many advantages other than expression of emotions. It can convey meaning through speech and writing, and it can express the past and future as well as the present.

An infant is innately programmed to communicate through smiles, eye contact, sounds, and gestures (the prelinguistic system). Infants are very social beings and are motivated to relate to persons in their environment (Bloom, 2000). The language system uses these talents, and parents teach the child that people and objects have names and particular sounds to identify them. Because they are rational beings, children learn early in life that things have names (Bower, 1989) and are genetically prepared to learn a language (Stromswald, 1996). The language they learn is the one spoken in the home.

Causes of speech and language disorders are varied and multiple. They include genetic and congenital sources, mental retardation, physical impairments (Wang & Bacon, 1997); traumatic brain injury (NIDCD, 1998); extreme prematurity (Briscoe, Gatherole, & Morland, 1998); auditory loss and auditory processing disorders (Cucase & McFarland, 1998); and neurological dysfunctions (NICHCY, 2000).

■ Differences Between Speech Disorders and Language Disorders

| *Communication may be oral (speech), gestural, or written.*

A **communication disorder** is a disorder in speech, hearing, and/or language. It is important to distinguish between disorders in speech and disorders in language because they have different origins and require different interventions. A **speech disorder** is a disorder affecting articulation, voice, or fluency. A **language disorder** is the impairment or deviant development of comprehension or use (or both) of a spoken, written, or other verbal symbol system. Cromer's 1978 definition is still a standard. Cromer defined a language disorder as a disorder that exists without other disabilities, such as deafness, mental retardation, motor disabilities, or personality disorders. Language problems can coexist with all those deficits, however, and need to be treated.

The definitions of communication disorders in speech and language presented in Table 7.1 (pp. 262–263) are those of the professional organization of specialists in speech and hearing, the American Speech-Language-Hearing Association (ASHA).

■ The Elements of Verbal Language

| *Infants begin to identify the sounds of language at about six months.*

Verbal language is language expressed in words, through speech and in writing. To be considered a verbal language, spoken or written words must have several elements in common so that members of the culture in which the words are used are able to understand what the speaker or writer wants to communicate.

Speech therapists encourage production and understandable articulation.
(© Christina Kennedy/Photo Edit)

There must be agreement about semantics (what the words mean) and **phonology** (how to pronounce the words). Many researchers believe all human infants have language mechanisms that enable them to figure out the rules (syntax) and sounds (phonology) of their language (Pinker, 1991). As Knight (2003) stated, "The evidence that language is a biologically determined, specie-specific genetically transmitted capacity is simply overwhelming" (p. 4). The mechanisms that enable an infant to identify the sounds of his or her language begin to operate when the infant is about 6 months of age. The mechanisms that enable the infant to figure out the rules of the language (morphology, syntax, and pragmatics) begin to operate shortly before the child's second year of life (Bloom, 1991, 2000; Jusczyk, 1997). These mechanisms may be similar to cognitive mechanisms; however, they can exist when a child has mental retardation and faulty cognitive mechanisms but is linguistically sophisticated, as children with Wallace syndrome are (Bellugi, 1988; Pinker, 1991).

In summary, the production of meaningful spoken and written language depends on a multitude of working parts of the biological system. It also requires the child to learn rules of pronunciation, grammar, and usage. Children without disabilities generally master spoken language quickly and display an amazing competence by the third year of life. Because our culture highly values proficiency in spoken language and expects everyone to master it, a great deal of research has been conducted to identify discrete disorders of language, specialists are trained to remediate them, and curriculum is devised to improve them. Spoken language is considered the hallmark of human functioning, and when it does not come naturally, a great deal of attention is paid to correcting it.

TABLE 7.1
ASHA Definitions of Communication Disorders
and Variations

I. COMMUNICATION DISORDERS

A *communication disorder* is an impairment in the ability to receive, send, process, and comprehend concepts of verbal, nonverbal, and graphic symbol systems. A communication disorder may be evident in the processes of hearing, language, and/or speech. A communication disorder may range in severity from mild to profound. It may be developmental or acquired. Individuals may demonstrate one or any combination of communication disorders. A communication disorder may result in a primary disability or it may be secondary to other disabilities.

A. A *speech disorder* is an impairment of the articulation of speech sounds, fluency, and/or voice.

   1. An *articulation disorder* is the atypical production of speech sounds characterized by substitutions, omissions, additions or distortions that may interfere with intelligibility.
   2. A *fluency disorder* is an interruption in the flow of speaking characterized by atypical rate, rhythm, and repetitions in sounds, syllables, words, and phrases. This may be accompanied by excessive tension, struggle behavior, and secondary mannerisms.
   3. A *voice disorder* is characterized by the abnormal production and/or absences of vocal quality, pitch, loudness, resonance, and/or duration, which is inappropriate for an individual's age and/or sex.

B. A *language disorder* is impaired comprehension and/or use of spoken, written, and/or other symbol systems. The disorder may involve (1) the form of language (phonology, morphology, syntax), (2) the content of language (semantics), and/or (3) the function of language in communication (pragmatics) in any combination.

   1. Form of Language
      a. *Phonology* is the sound system of a language and the rules that govern the sound combinations.
      b. *Morphology* is the system that governs the structure of words and the construction of word forms.
      c. *Syntax* is the system governing the order and combination of words to form sentences, and the relationships among the elements within a sentence.
   2. Content of Language
      a. *Semantics* is the system that governs the meanings of words and sentences.
   3. Function of Language
      a. *Pragmatics* is the system that combines the above language components in functional and socially appropriate communication.

C. A *hearing disorder* is the result of impaired auditory sensitivity of the physiological auditory system. A hearing disorder may limit the development, comprehension, production, and/or maintenance of speech and/or language. Hearing disorders are classified according to difficulties in detection, recognition, discrimination, comprehension, and perception of auditory information. Individuals with hearing impairment may be described as deaf or hard of hearing.

   1. *Deaf* is defined as a hearing disorder that limits an individual's aural/oral communication performance to the extent that the primary sensory input for communication may be other than the auditory channel.
   2. *Hard of hearing* is defined as a hearing disorder, whether fluctuating or permanent, which adversely affects an individual's ability to communicate. The hard-of-hearing individual relies on the auditory channel as the primary sensory input for communication.

D. *Central auditory processing disorders* (CAPDs) are deficits in the information processing of audible signals not attributed to impaired peripheral hearing sensitivity or intellectual impairment. This information processing involves perceptual, cognitive, and linguistic functions that, with appropriate interactions, result in effective receptive communication of auditorily presented stimuli. Specifically, CAPD refers to limitations in the ongoing transmission analysis, organization, transformation, elaboration, storage, retrieval, and use of information contained in audible signals. CAPD may involve the listener's

(continued)

TABLE 7.1
(continued)

active and passive (e.g., conscious and unconscious, mediated and unmediated, controlled and automatic) ability to do the following:

► attend, discriminate, and identify acoustic signals;
► transform and continuously transmit information through both the peripheral and central nervous systems;
► filter, sort, and combine information at appropriate perceptual and conceptual levels;
► store and retrieve information efficiently; restore, organize, and use retrieved information;
► segment and decode acoustic stimuli using phonological, semantic, syntactic, and pragmatic knowledge; and
► attach meaning to a stream of acoustic signals through use of linguistic and nonlinguistic contexts.

II. COMMUNICATION VARIATIONS

A. *Communication difference/dialect* is a variation of a symbol system used by a group of individuals that reflects and is determined by shared regional, social, or cultural/ethnic factors. A regional, social, or cultural/ethnic variation of a symbol system should not be considered a disorder of speech or language.

B. *Augmentative/alternative communication* systems attempt to compensate and facilitate, temporarily or permanently, for the impairment and disability patterns of individuals with severe expressive and/or language comprehension disorders. Augmentative/alternative communication may be required for individuals demonstrating impairments in gestural, spoken, and/or written modalities.

Source: American Speech-Language-Hearing Association Ad Hoc Committee on Service Delivery in the Schools, Definitions: Communication disorders and variations, *ASHA, 35* (Suppl. 10) (1993): 40–41. Reprinted with permission.

Augmentative communication devices such as hearing aids assist individuals with hearing impairments.

■ Prevalence of Communication Disorders

Because of the many systems and processes in which communication problems can originate, it is difficult to get an accurate picture of how many communication disorders are speech deficits and how many are language deficits. Speech and language impairment affected over 1 million children in 1997–1998, composing 21 percent of the total number of children with disabilities (U.S. Department of Education, 1999). Not all children with language disorders are in special education classes. In fact, 89 percent of children with speech and language impairments are served in regular classes; only 7 percent are in resource rooms and 4 percent in separate classes. Children with speech and language disorders are more likely than children with other disabilities to be served in the regular classroom.

Prevalence figures also tend to be distorted because mental retardation, cerebral palsy, and many other disabilities affect communication. Although a communication disorder may be secondary to another disability, it still requires treatment and therapy as part of a total special education program (Table 7.2).

Some patterns in communication disorders have been found. Tallal, Curtis, and Kaplan (1988) demonstrated that speech-language problems tend to run in families. They occur in about 33 percent of the children whose mothers

TABLE 7.2
Disabilities That Communication Disorders May Accompany

DISABILITY	CHARACTERISTIC OF COMMUNICATION DISORDER
MENTAL RETARDATION	Delayed language is a universal characteristic; disorders may be present in all aspects of language production and reception.
CEREBRAL PALSY	Poor muscle control and impaired breathing of the child with cerebral palsy result in communication difficulties ranging from language delays and voice disorders to the inability to speak.
LEARNING DISABILITIES	Major problems in learning to read, write, spell, and do arithmetic. The most likely hypothesis is that an unknown brain dysfunction interferes with auditory and visual perception and thus with all language reception and production.
SEVERE AND PROFOUND MULTIPLE DISABILITIES	Inability to speak; possibly able to learn a limited number of receptive words. Those without mental retardation may have no difficulties or may experience delays in language development; the child with severe physical disabilities may need a head pointer to type or some other form of augmented communication device to communicate by pointing to pictures, letters, or words.
AUTISM; CHILDHOOD MENTAL DISTURBANCE	Spoken language may not be present, but some can learn to communicate by using augmented and alternative communication devices. Autistic children with mental retardation and other severe mental disturbances may have disordered language in terms of syntax and semantics.

have such problems and 18 percent of the children whose fathers have such problems. Knowing that a member of the family has a specific language problem alerts parents to the risk of their children having a similar problem.

■ Language Development

It is far beyond the scope of this chapter to list all aspects of language development. As you read this overview, keep in mind that a child is a hypothesis maker and an active creator of theories about his or her world and language (Bower, 1989). When children hear speech, they try to figure out the rules of speech. They do so without explicit instruction, because they are motivated to learn language on their own, and they monitor their own learning (Pinker, 1991; Shantz & Ebeling, 1991). The basic motivation to learn a language is assumed to be social; that is, the desire to communicate with individuals (at first, the caregiver) in the environment (Bloom, 2000; Snow, 1999). Chomsky (1988) states it well: "Language learning is not really something the child does, it is something that happens to the child placed in an appropriate environment" (p. 62).

In this chapter, we discuss spoken language (speech). Gestural languages are covered more fully in Chapter 10.

Characteristics

In most, if not all, societies, children who are not disabled learn to speak the language of their culture very early in life. The sequence in mastering a language is similar across cultures. Language is social in origin, and it arises in the context of a close interaction with basic caregivers (usually the child's parents). Linguists generally agree that the infant learns language during interactions with his or her basic caregivers.

The caregiver's sensitive responsiveness to the child and to the child's requests greatly facilitates the child's acquisition of language. The interaction of caregiver and child in games such as "peekaboo" and "I'm going to get you" is enjoyable play for the child and encourages the child to fulfill his or her genetic push to learn language. Children learn language when interacting with caregivers in a setting (usually the home) in which they are provided with psychological warmth and encouragement. At first, the child's contribution may be smiles, gestures, and babbling, and the caregiver's role is to take turns and provide words. The rate of prelingual vocalization is positively related to the development of expressive vocabulary (McCathren, Yoder, & Warren, 1999).

Most caregivers use what psycholinguists call *motherese* to talk to their children. Motherese is a form of language in which the adult uses a high-pitched voice, which infants seem to respond to, speaks in simple sentences, repeats words and sentences, uses the present tense, and asks a lot of simple questions about what is going on in the context. Examples of these questions are "Where's Daddy?" "See the doggie?" "Where did the doggie go?" "More milk?" and "More cookies?" Motherese is spoken slowly and pronounced carefully. The clear pronunciation may help babies learn sound categories, and the questions may help babies identify objects by name. The use of motherese seems to be widespread; it has been found in fourteen different languages.

Thus, nature (genes) and parents combine to enable the child to master the language of his or her home.

The Sequence of Language Development

Language is acquired by engaging in a world of persons, objects, and events, and the child engages with the persons in his or her environment (Bloom & Tinker, 2001). By 2 to 3 months of age, infants begin to coo, make eye contact with their caregivers, and emit a socially communicative smile. By 2 months of age, they can detect the rhythm of the language of their home (Garnett, 1996).

Around 5 to 6 months of age, infants babble and parents begin to match the sounds the infants produce to words in the home language. When the infant

---

Most adults simplify their language (spoken or gestural) when communicating with a young child.

Parents in many cultures use motherese to communicate with infants and toddlers.

The caregiver's sensitive responsiveness to the child and to his or her requests greatly facilitates the child's acquisition of language.
© Jonathan A. Meyers

produces sounds such as "ba ba, da da, na na, ma ma," the mother will tend to select "ma ma" and reinforce it. Thus, the infant "learns" to say "ma ma." At 6 months of age, babies change from being "universal linguists" who can learn any language of the world into specialists in their own language (Bloom, 1991, 2000). By 7 months, infants appear to recognize major features of their home language (phonology, syntax, and phrases) and lose the ability to distinguish sounds not found in their own language (Leonard, 1998).

At this point, the infant learns (cognitively) a major fact about the world: People and objects have names (Bower, 1989; Brown, 1958). The child appears to be able to abstract meaning from the environment and figure out the words associated with objects at home by looking where the caregiver is looking while saying a word—for example, the name of an object like *ball*. At this point in the infant's development, usually by the age of 9 months, the child's speech or oral sounds take on meaning, and they become language by the time the child is 12 months of age, when the first words appear.

When the first word appears, the child may string together a series of nonsense syllables with the word. The child seems to understand that one word isn't enough, but combining words is beyond his or her ability at this age.

Learning language involves a combination of genetic and environmental inputs.

The child's first sentences are one-word sentences that convey the total meaning of what the child is trying to communicate. Thus, the word *ball* may mean "See the ball," "I want the ball," "Throw me the ball," or "Where is the ball?" For parents, deciphering meaning is a guessing game. They have to be in the same context as the child to determine what the child is communicating. Words have meaning only in a particular context.

Around 18 months, most children are speaking in two-word sentences, usually a verb and a noun, such as "See doggie," or "Daddy go." The verb in the two-word sentence conveys much of the meaning (Bloom, 1991). By 3 years of age, most children are speaking in multiple-word sentences and using generally correct syntax, although some common errors are present, such as overgeneralizations ("I runned" instead of "I ran") and errors in making plurals (*sheeps* for *sheep* and *deers* for *deer*). By 6 years of age, the child is a good communicator with a knowledge of several thousand words. He or she is using speech and language in various logical forms and has mastered most of the phonology of the community's language. Learning the rules of how to pronounce all the sounds of the home language extends through infancy and childhood into adulthood (Gleason, 1993). Remember that children go through these language acquisition stages at roughly the same ages but with some degree of individual variation.

It is important to understand language development, because it is in the early stages of language development that disorders appear. Some elements of language, such as correct pronunciation and articulation, will improve with age. Problems with other elements indicate the need for early therapy if they are to be remediated.

■ Classification of Communication Disorders

There are four categories of communication disorders; articulation-phonology, fluency and speech timing, voice, and language.

Communication disorders usually fall into four broad categories: (1) disorders of articulation-phonology, (2) disorders of fluency and speech timing, (3) disorders of voice, and (4) disorders of language. The first three classifications are traditionally considered speech disorders.

We want to emphasize that these classifications are not mutually exclusive. Individuals with one kind of disorder are by no means protected from having another. The relationship between articulation-phonology disorders and language disorders is well established, and researchers are exploring other connections among these areas.

Disorders of Articulation-Phonology

Articulation-phonology disorders are misproductions of speech sounds. They are the most common communication disorder among children in public schools. Although historically these disorders were considered speech disorders, they can be considered language disorders as well. We discuss them here as a distinct category of disorder and later as a subcategory of language disorders.

In recent years, the terminology used to describe articulation-phonology disorders has become more precise (ASHA, 1993). Today, the term *articulation errors* indicates misproductions associated with speech motor activity, such as saying "pop" for "top." The term *phonological errors* indicates misproductions of speech sounds associated with the dysfunctional use of the sound system of the language (Paul, 1996a). There is a strong relationship between phonological errors and reading problems, which will be discussed more fully later in this chapter.

ECOLOGY OF THE CHILD

COMMUNITY **Have you ever wondered what it would be like not to be able to communicate? It's very frustrating. It's very lonely. It hurts.**

Think about it. You feel, you think, you know and understand the words yet you cannot speak them. You hear everyone around you in an interesting conversation, but you cannot join in.

You cannot express any of the feelings or emotions that are just as deep inside of you as anyone else. You are furiously angry and you have to hold it in; or you are extremely happy and you can't show it. Your heart is so full of love you could just burst, but you can't share it. I know what it is like because for years I could not communicate or express myself. I am a 19-year-old girl. I have cerebral palsy and cannot talk. I do not have coordination in my hands to write or use sign language. Even a typewriter was out of the question when I was younger. I know what it is like to be fed potatoes all my life. After all, potatoes are a good basic food for everyday, easy to fix in many different ways. I hate potatoes! But then, who knew that but me?

I know what it is like to be dressed in reds and blues when my favorite colors are mint greens, lemon yellows and pinks. I mean really, can you imagine?

Mama found me one night curled up in a ball in my bed crying, doubled over in pain. I couldn't explain to her where or how I hurt. So, after checking me over the best she could, she thought I had a bad stomachache due to constipation. Naturally, a quick cure for that was an enema. It didn't help my earache at all!

Finally, help came! I was introduced to Blissymbols.

My life changed! Blissymbols were originally developed for a universal language but they have been a miracle for me and others like me. Blissymbols are a combination of the written word and a symbolized picture that anyone can learn, which are displayed in a way that can be easily used. There was a tray strapped to my wheelchair. It was covered with a sheet of paper which was divided into little blocks of words to form sentences. At last, I could communicate!

Naturally, one board could not hold all the words needed. I had to learn to make up my own, combining two or more words to mean another. As in "story sleep" for dream or "bad night horse" for nightmare.

My teachers started me on ten words a day to see if I could learn them. I learned as fast as they could give me new words. I was ready to communicate! I could even stutter! That's what my uncle calls it when it takes three or four tries to point to one word.

Once I mastered Blissymbols I left the symbols behind and changed to words and sentences. I got my first computer. It was an Autocom.™ I programmed my Bliss board into it and much more. It also had a printer. Finally, I could write!

The number and kinds of misproductions and their effect on intelligibility are among the criteria for judging the disorder on a continuum ranging from mild to severe. Articulation-phonology disorders may range from a mild frontal lisp, a fleeting hesitation in words, to mispronunciations of speech sounds so severe that the speaker is unintelligible to listeners in his or her own community. Persons with severe and profound disabilities may never develop speech and must rely on learning how to use their prelinguistic system for communication (Dromi, 1993). Tallal, Galaburda, Llinas, and Von Euler

I didn't stop there. I went on to a more advanced system. I had fun learning about computers by using my Express III.™ I was doing the programming all by myself and even did some of the "funny" spelling.

The first thing I learned about computers was to think of them as "hotel." My "Hotel Express III™" had 99 floors or levels. Each floor had 128 rooms or spaces for programming. In each room I could put one person as in a letter or a number, or a whole family as in a sentence; or I could just throw a wild party with several paragraphs. So you see my "Hotel Express III™" had almost unlimited accommodations.

Did I stop there? Surprise, I got a new device. It is called a Touch Talker™ with Mindspeak software. This one has the same basic features as my Express III,™ but I can connect it to an Apple computer to either store the memory on a disk or just use the screen to make my paragraphs all in one instead of having to say bits and pieces at a time. Everything in it is coded like my Express III,™ but it is much easier to get the words or sentences out because everything is coded by pictures instead of numbers and it is a lot easier to remember pictures. The Express III™ had number levels and it was harder to remember where I put everything, so as you can see, the Touch Talker™ makes it a lot easier for me to communicate with you or anyone else.

Communicating for me has opened a lot of doors. It even let me act in a play. I have been a guest speaker at a Kiwanis Club meeting. It has done a lot more, too. There's help out there, just don't give up.

Source: From American-Speech-Language-Hearing Association, *I Can Even Stutter Now!* Copyright © ASHA. Reprinted with permission.

Note: Let's Talk ..., a publication for people with special communication needs, is published by the Consumer Affairs Division of ASHA, 10801 Rockville Pike, Rockville, MD 20852, (800) 638-TALK.

WHAT IS THE CONTEXT?

It is difficult to be part of any community if you can't communicate. Sara can now make a difference by expressing her ideas and feelings to others. Prior to using Blissymbols, she had no way to communicate many important messages to her family, friends, and teachers. Basic needs were difficult to communicate, and her knowledge and ideas were nearly impossible to get across. Since Sara started using Blissymbols and other assistive technology, she can communicate her basic needs as well as more complex thoughts and desires. What activities can Sara participate in now that she couldn't previously? Does this allow her to be a part of the community—to join in and make a difference? How?

PIVOTAL ISSUES FOR TEACHERS

- Students like Sara need assistive technology to be able to speak about what they already know but don't have the ability to communicate.

- Assistive technology makes it possible for students like Sara to learn and grow.

- Notice that Sara has excellent writing skills as she tells her story in this article. That is one of her strengths.

- Identify the strengths of children in your classroom who have communication disorders.

- Are there students in your class who would benefit from assistive technology to help them communicate.

- What professionals can you ask about advances in technology that might help your students?

(1993) proposed that some children are unable to process auditorially the rapidity of speech. This failure to be able to process and integrate speech begins with phonological difficulties and eventually leads to defects in language development and difficulty in learning to read.

The Nature of Articulation-Phonology Disorders

Imprecise phoneme production or articulation errors are described as substitutions, distortions, omissions, and, infrequently, the addition of extra sounds

(McReynolds, 1986). When the intended phoneme is replaced by another phoneme, the error is one of *substitution*. Common examples are *w* for *r* (*wight* for *right*), *t* for *k* (*toat* for *coat*), and *w* for *l* (*wove* for *love*). The influence of multiple substitutions on intelligibility becomes apparent when *like* becomes *wite*. In other instances, a misproduction makes a phoneme sound different, but the difference is not enough to change the production into a different phoneme. These productions are known as *distortions* (for example, *brlu* for *blue*). When a disorder involves *omissions*, certain sounds are omitted entirely (*pay* for *play*, *ka* for *cat* or *cap*).

Misarticulations are not always consistent. In some phoneme sequences, sounds are articulated correctly; in others, they are not. Often the position of a sound (at the beginning, middle, or end of a word) or the position of a word influences the production.

Disabilities Associated with Articulation-Phonology Disorders

Obvious handicaps associated with disordered articulation are cleft palate, hearing loss, cerebral palsy, and other disorders of the central nervous system.

Cleft palate is a structural deficiency caused by the failure of the bone and soft tissue of the roof of the mouth to fuse during prenatal development. It is often associated with cleft lip. Historically, these clefts have been of special interest to speech-language pathologists. Hypernasality (excessively nasal-sounding speech), which is a disorder of resonance, is the most familiar speech characteristic of children with clefts. Children with palatal clefts also make particular kinds of articulation errors related to impaired palatal function.

Sometimes an articulation-phonology disorder is associated with another speech disorder (for example, stuttering) or is part of a basic language disorder. Although researchers have examined many different causal factors, they have not reached a consensus.

Disorders of Fluency and Speech Timing

Stuttering occurs most frequently in young children between the ages of 2 and 6 (NIDCD, 1997).

Fluency is the flow of speech. The most common fluency disorder is stuttering, which is characterized by repetitions and prolongations of sound, syllables, or words; tension; and extraneous movement. **Stuttering** is a complex behavioral disorder with a variety of assumed causes. Some researchers believe that there is a genetic component to stuttering (Yairi, Ambrose, & Cox, 1996). Many children who stutter have spontaneous recovery by school age (Bloodstein, 1995). What is clear is that early intervention (begun by the age of 3) is very effective in reducing stuttering (Onslow, Costa, Andrews, Harrison, & Packman, 1996; Hancock et al., 1998).

Disorders of Voice

Voice is the production of sound in the larynx and the selective transmission and modification of that sound through resonance and loudness. When we talk about voice, we usually think of three characteristics: quality, pitch, and loudness. We evaluate these characteristics in terms of the speaker's age, sex, and culture (Moores, 1996). A **voice disorder** is an inappropriate variation in voice quality, pitch, or loudness.

Disorders of voice quality, generally called **dysphonia,** can be related to phonation, resonation, or both. Breathiness, hoarseness, or harshness are disorders of phonation. Problems with resonation include hypernasality (excessively nasal-sounding speech) and hyponasality (speech that sounds as if the speaker has a bad cold). Often phonation and resonation disorders are present in the same person, but they can be separate disorders.

Pitch indicates whether the speaker is male or female, young or old. Pitch breaks, a common problem, occur in adolescents and affect boys particularly. High-pitched and variably pitched voices are common among children with severe hearing impairments or cerebral palsy (Boone & McFarlane, 1988).

Disorders of Language

As we explained earlier, culturally determined rules of correct usage govern the elements of language. Each element—phonology, morphology, syntax, pragmatics, and semantics—is a potential source of language disorder. For example, some children are able to express age-appropriate ideas in correct sentence structures but are not able to use accepted rules of morphology; they might have difficulty with pluralization (*foot-feet*), with verb tenses (*run-ran, walk-walked*), or with the use of prefixes (*pre-, anti-*).

Language involves both *reception* (taking in information) and *expression* (giving out verbal information). In some manner, language is processed internally during both reception and expression, but language production and language comprehension do not always proceed at the same pace. Some children will speak but do not seem to understand the meaning of the sentence (Miller & Paul, 1995). Processing errors interfere with all types of learning, including language learning.

The stages and sequences of normal language acquisition give clues to language disorders. But it is often difficult to determine a specific cause for a specific language disorder in a specific child. Speech problems, developmental disorders, or other disabilities may all influence the child's ability to use language.

In summary, any deviation from linguistic competence involving the following is considered a disorder (revised and adapted from Dore, 1986, p. 4):

▶ Producing understandable sounds (articulation and pronunciation)

▶ Creating well-formed sentences and understanding grammatical structures (syntax and morphology)

▶ Creating sentences with meaningful content (semantics)

▶ Constructing logical sentences with appropriate knowledge (for example, saying "I see a bird," when the child sees a bird, not an airplane)

▶ Speaking appropriately in context (pragmatics)

■ Developmental Delay in Communication

Some children are slow talkers and with an enriched environment are able to achieve average scores by kindergarten age (Leonard, 1998). Other children, however, are slow to develop and possess a disability. The following categories describe different groups of slow developers.

Michele: The graph below shows the developmental profile of Michele, a 10-year-old girl who has a moderate articulation-phonology disorder (she mispronounces specific sounds). Careful evaluation indicates that Michele also has a language deficit. (Often a speech disorder signals an underlying language impairment.) Academically, she is performing below grade level on skills that require language mediation. Michele demonstrates a range of intraindividual differences. Her sound substitutions and omissions are not so severe that she cannot be understood, but oral productions call attention to her speech and set her apart from her peers.

Michele's speech is characterized by consistent sound substitutions (w/r as in *wabbit* for *rabbit;* t/k as in *tome* for *come*). She also sometimes omits sounds at the ends of words, including the sounds that represent verb tense and noun number (for example, the final /s/ in *looks* and *cats*). Careful listening to her conversational language reveals that she omits articles and that her sentence structure is not as elaborate as that of most 10-year-olds.

Profile of a Child with a Mild Speech and Language Disorder

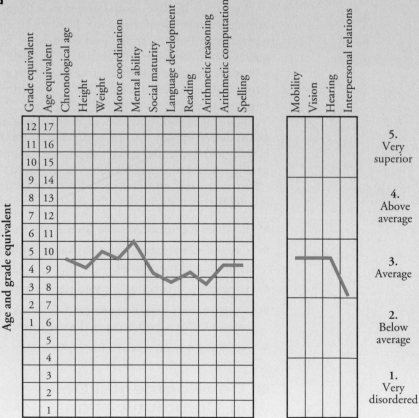

Michele is in a regular classroom but seems reluctant to participate in class. It has not been determined whether this reluctance stems from her sensitivity to others' reactions, an inability to formulate speech and complex language to express her ideas, or both.

In contrast to Michele, many children with mild speech disorders seem to develop normally in other areas and do not differ markedly from other children in educational performance or social skills. Young children often make developmental articulation errors that continue into kindergarten or first grade and then disappear as the child matures and acquires reading skills. Children whose misarticulations persist until about age 8 are less likely to correct inaccurate sound productions themselves. The teacher can do much to help Michele feel comfortable in spite of her disorder. The suggestions listed on pages 286–287 to help children who stutter would also help Michele develop a more positive self-esteem.

When misarticulations continue until age 8, the child probably needs the help of a speech-language pathologist.

Children with *slow expressive language development* (SELD) have fewer than the average 50 words in their vocabulary by 24 months of age. However, they usually move into the normal range of language expression by school age (Paul, 1995). SELD is a risk factor, not a disorder.

Children from lower socioeconomic conditions tend to have significantly lower vocabulary scores (Hart & Risley, 1995). Adults in lower-class environments tend to use and encourage language less than middle-class adults do.

At-risk preschoolers whose parents share books with them and read with them have more success with emergent literacy skills than children who do not have these experiences. Hearing and seeing the words in print appears to facilitate literacy (Capelline, Flanagan, & Colton, 2003). There is a plethora of material available to encourage language acquisition and literacy. The Linder set *Read, Play & Learn* (1999), designed for preschool and kindergarten, includes a series of booklets containing stories. The booklets encourage the use of language as well as learning the function of communication (expressing emotions, understanding different cultures, and so on).

As research indicates that families who reside in lower economic conditions do not read or use enriched language with their children to the same extent as middle-class parents (Hart & Risley, 1999), preschool and kindergarten teachers need to ensure that these children have the experiences needed for success in school (see also Tabor & Dickenson, 2001).

Some children who have slower acquisition rates are thought to have difficulty in auditory processing sounds in the normal pace of speech (Curtis & Tallal, 1991). This difficulty manifests itself in the child's failure to distinguish among phonemes such as "ba" and "da." The slower auditory processing does not allow enough time for the sound to enter short-term memory and then be stored in long-term memory. Thus, accurate recognition and production of phonemes do not occur, which leads to reading problems (Tallal et al., 1996). However, not all children who have delays in communication are found to have auditory processing problems (Bishop, Bishop, Bright, James,

Delaney, & Tallal, 1999). For some children, the source of the difficulty is unknown (Bishop, Carlyon, Deeks, & Bishop, 1999). While central auditory processing disorders occur in children, they are not implicated in all communication disorders (Cacace & McFarland, 1998). Some researchers believe that many children with specific language impairments have deficits in verbal working memory as well as a language deficit (Montgomery, 2002).

Families with a history of language impairments tend to have children with language impairments (Campbell et al., 2003). There appears to be a genetic component that manifests itself in 50 percent of the children in such families (Dionne, Dale, Boivin, & Plomin, 2003). These children tend to have significantly lower language scores in comparison to their matched-age peers in which both genetic material and shared environment influence the lower acquisition rates (Flax, Realpe-Bonilla, Hirsch, Brzustowicz, Bartlett, & Tailal, 2003).

Children with *specific language impairment* (SLI) have a limited language ability for which there are no known sensory, motor, emotional, psychosocial, or general cognitive deficits (Leonard, 1998). These children have a slow rate of language development that persists over time. They need to be carefully evaluated so they are not confused with risk groups such as children with SELD, who require enrichment rather than therapy. Children with SLI are at least one standard deviation below norms on language-production measures (Nelson, Camarata, Welsh, Butskovsky, & Camarata, 1996). These children require therapy, and as many as 50 percent of them will have trouble learning how to read (Leonard, 1998; Catts, Fey, Zhang, & Tomblin, 2002).

■ Identification and Assessment

Preschool Children and Early Intervention

Although much of language development begins before a child says his or her first word, most tests for language delays or disorders are not administered until the child is 2 years of age (Leonard, 1993). Leonard stated that the criterion for administering diagnostic tests is the failure of the child to master fifty words by age 2. Mastery of fewer than fifty words may indicate that the child has a communication disorder or a hearing impairment. In addition, preschoolers with delayed phonological development are likely to have other delayed language skills (Dale, Price, Bishop, & Plomin, 2003).

Early intervention is crucial, as it has been found that if the language impairment is still present by age 5.6, the child is at high risk for educational difficulties throughout childhood and adolescence. Early intervention has been successful in remediating speech and language delays for many children (Leonard, 1998).

Attention recently has been given to the nonverbal communication system (the prelinguistic system) that is a precursor to speech. Prior to the emergence of words, infants point to objects, respond to the caregiver's pointing, look at what the caregiver is looking at, and interact in basic play activities (Dromi, 1993). Infants also use gestures to make requests and to respond. If these prelinguistic competencies fail to develop at the expected time, a communication deficit may exist.

Irregularities in an infant's production of sound, sucking, swallowing, or breathing may portend a problem in the infant's development of spoken language.

Irregularities in the early nonverbal sound system (such as a strange infant cry) or in the sucking, swallowing, or breathing systems may predict a problem in spoken language development (Oller, 1985; Schiefelbusch, Sullivan, & Ganz, 1980). These difficulties will interfere with speech production. Deficient sucking or choking on fluids is an indicator of potential disorder, as is the child's swallowing excessive air or failing to chew by 18 months of age (Schiefelbusch et al., 1980). A pediatric neurologist should be consulted to determine if a disorder exists. A physician or surgeon may need to determine if abnormalities are present in the mouth, throat, or breathing apparatus.

The Multidisciplinary Team

A multidisciplinary team composed of speech-language pathologists, physical therapists, physicians, audiologists, occupational therapists, special education teachers, parents, psychologists, and social workers may be formed to plan early intervention services. Because speech disorders so commonly accompany other disabilities, the speech-language pathologist has a role in many different therapies. That role may be major or minor in the delivery of service, but it is always major in assessment, diagnosis, and planning a program for the remediation or improvement of a communication disorder.

The speech-language pathologist primarily should be responsible for the identification, diagnosis (as part of a multidisciplinary team), and design of the treatment plan and curriculum for children with language and speech deficits. The speech-language pathologist sits down with the teacher and suggests or designs lessons to include in the IEP or IFSP. The speech-language pathologist may formulate plans to encourage the spontaneous flow of language and assist non-English-speaking children in learning the English language. He or she may suggest activities for all children to encourage phonological discrimination and acquisition through rhymes and jingles that contain words with consonant and vowel combinations that are troubling the student. For example, the jingle "Polly put the popcorn in a big iron pot until it went pop, pop, pop" introduces the child to the sounds of *p* with vowels in initial and end positions. The IFSP may include plans for the therapist or teacher to send home simple activities such as this for the parent to model for the child.

The IFSP may include activities for the parent to model with the child.

The teacher's primary role may be to encourage talk, expand talk, and model correct forms and usage. Rarely should children with speech and language disorders be placed in a special class. These children will be part of the regular preschool classes (inclusion) and perhaps have extra instruction outside class several times a week in a resource room.

Rarely should children with speech and language disorders be placed in a special class.

School-Age Children

Many school systems use four procedures to identify children who have communication disorders (Neidecker, 1987):

1. Screening children who are suspected of having communication disorders and who may need additional testing or a full evaluation
2. Evaluating those identified during screening and from referrals with appropriate audiological, speech, and language assessment tools

3. Diagnosing the type and severity of communication disorder according to the criteria of the evaluation data
4. Making appropriate placement decisions for children who need speech or language intervention and developing an IEP or IFSP for them

Screening

Most school systems have formal screening programs for vision, hearing, and communication disorders. Often parents or teachers request that a child be screened. Speech-language pathologists may conduct screening in selected grades at the beginning of each year to identify children suspected of having disorders of articulation, fluency, voice, or language. Screening is sometimes a yes-no process: Yes, this child needs further evaluation; no, this child does not need further evaluation *at this time*. If there is any doubt, an assessment is conducted. The purpose of rapid screening is detection, not diagnosis; it must be well planned, fast, and accurate.

Federal regulations do not require a parent's permission before group screening; however, some school districts and some states require that parents be notified. Children who are identified through screening are then evaluated more thoroughly.

Evaluation and Diagnosis

Evaluating children who are suspected of having communication disorders and diagnosing those disorders usually involve the following steps:

1. *Obtaining parental permission.* Federal law requires that parents or legally designated caregivers give permission before a child is formally tested for communication disorders.
2. *Taking a case history.* During the evaluation process, the speech-language pathologist often obtains information about other people's opinions of the child's communication abilities and disabilities. This history may include background information about the child's development, a health history, family information, a social history, school achievement records, and data from earlier evaluations.
3. *Assessing the disorder.* The clinician assesses the type and severity of the disorder with formal audiological, speech, and language tests and informal procedures (language sampling, analysis of conversation). The speech-language pathologist also evaluates the structure and function of the speech mechanism.
4. *Assessing other areas.* Assessing intellectual development may be particularly important for children with language deficits. Psychologists usually are responsible for intelligence testing. Often psychological tests are administered to evaluate cognitive skills and identify differences between verbal and nonverbal abilities. Educational assessment and its consistency with other assessment data are important. Physical therapists, occupational therapists, and other health professionals may also contribute important assessment information.

5. *Making a diagnosis.* Diagnosis has been called the art and science of distinguishing one disorder from another according to the signs and symptoms that characterize each disorder. The speech-language pathologist makes a written report about the kind of disorder(s) observed and describes the symptoms of the disorder(s) on which the diagnosis is based.

Collaboration: Developing the IEP

The speech-language pathologist may lead the school team in developing an IEP for the child with a communication disorder. Parental permission is required for the plan to be implemented. Intervention for the communication disorder outlined in the IEP is based on assessment data, the diagnosis, and other characteristics of the child (intellectual function, learning deficits).

Linguistic Diversity

Children learn to speak the language that is spoken in their homes and neighborhoods. They tend to use language to express their needs and thoughts in the same way as their parents or caregivers do. In some homes, parents use language in ways that are different from the language some teachers expect students to use. For example, teachers may demand explicitness in language (Anastasiow, Hanes, & Hanes, 1982). Whereas the two sentences "He took it" and "Arthur took my truck" convey the same meaning, the listener has to be in the immediate environment to understand the

Children from communities that speak a language other than American English need assessments by speech-language pathologists who are skilled in the child's primary language.
(© Michael Newman/Photo Edit)

former, less explicit communication. Children who have not been exposed to explicit communication in the home may have difficulty when they encounter a teacher who expects it. Teachers must be aware that differences in language usage such as this are not treated as disorders. Such differences can be addressed by teaching rather than by therapy. Comparing the child's communication skills with the skills of peers from the same cultural background avoids labeling the child as language impaired rather than language different (Roseberry-McKibbin, 1997).

Assessment of Non-English-Speaking Children

Children from homes in which English is not the primary language are likely to encounter difficulty in using English in school. Language differences can and should be identified early, and language skills (how to relate to and speak to the teacher) should be taught to avoid failure by the child due to cultural differences in talking with adults. Children from cultures and communities that speak a language other than American English need assessments by speech-language pathologists who are skilled in the child's primary language (Salend & Selinas, 2003).

Ines is a three-year-old born into a New Mexico family living in economic poverty. She speaks primarily English, but her range of English vocabulary and language proficiency is lower on developmental tests than would be expected for her age norms. In part, these lower scores reflect a New Mexican dialect that some of the local families use, which varies from classic Spanish and includes some English called "Spanglish." It is to be hoped that the school personnel will be knowledgeable about this dialect when they assess Ines's functioning.

Ines is fortunate in some respects, as many children her age in New Mexico have not learned English and will not do so until they attend school. Ines's success will depend on the skills of her teacher and the speech therapist, and on the cooperation and support provided by her family.

> Assessments of bilingual children should include a specialist who is bicultural and bilingual.

Children who are bilingual vary in their English competence. Any assessment of these children should involve a specialist who is bicultural and speaks the language of their home and who can answer three basic questions (Metz, 1991): Who speaks what language? When is that language spoken? For what purpose is that language spoken?

Bilingual children, whether they understand both English and Spanish (or Hebrew, Chinese, French, or a Native American or other language), are usually more proficient in one language than in the other. For children with disabilities, intervention should occur first in the language in which the child is more proficient (Gutierrez-Clellen, 1999). For a discussion of family-centered approaches, see Chapter 3.

> Any interventions should occur in the language in which the child is more proficient.

Great care must be taken that children from different cultures who speak a different language receive an accurate assessment by a person well versed in the children's language and cultural mores. For example, Spanish-speaking children who speak a Puerto Rican dialect make a number of phonological errors that are consistent with their dialect. If the dialect of these children is not taken into account, lower scores will be obtained (Goldstein & Iglesias, 2001). Naglai (1991) reported that a child was referred for a hearing test and failed not because of hearing loss but because of the child's "inability to follow simple instructions in English" (p. 15). Situations such as that must be avoided.

Another issue is that the child may not understand the so-called native language. For example, Metz (1991), a person of Mexican-American Spanish background, reported that when she assessed a child from Puerto Rico, the child could not understand her dialect of Spanish because it lacked the intonation patterns of Puerto Rican Spanish. Spanish speakers use many variations of Spanish. The assessor and the child being assessed must be from the same Spanish-speaking subgroup. When a native speaker of the child's language is not available to conduct the assessment, a mediator who speaks the child's language can be hired as a neutral person to assist the evaluator and the family. During the evaluation, the mediator can relieve the family's stress by keeping the family informed about what is taking place (Metz, 1991). Language differences between Black English and Spanish-influenced, Native American, and Asian dialects and standard American speech can be found in Paul (1996b).

■ Transition

For a young child in a preschool program and in therapy, transition may be a daily occurrence (Bruder & Chandler, 1996). Care must be taken that communication from the two sources is consistent and involves parents. Because articulation and stuttering respond well to early intervention, when the child moves from preschool to regular school, he or she may no longer need therapy. If therapy does need to be continued into grade school, records detailing the therapeutic approach and diagnosis as well as the child's progress must follow the child to the new setting.

■ Family and Lifespan Issues

What lies ahead for the child who has a communication disorder? The answer to this question depends on the nature and severity of the disorder. Children who have primary articulation disorders (that is, a speech or language disorder not associated with other disabilities) seem to have few special problems as adults. In contrast, follow-up studies of children with severe disorders show that those with language deficits, in spite of early intervention, continue to have problems in academics, interpersonal relationships, and work. Intelligence seems to be an important variable in determining the outcome among children who have language disorders from brain damage or mental retardation.

Families are concerned by any and all irregularities in their child's spoken language. They need information about their child's condition, and they need to be taught appropriate techniques to use at home. Teaching parents to recast the child's pronunciation, articulation, or incomplete sentences is critical. Parents will tend to correct communications that are understandable but not correct in form. The techniques for teachers that we suggest in the Educational Adaptations section under "Intervention for Fluency Disorders" need to be taught to parents. Language learning proceeds best in a setting in which language is used naturally (Fey, Windsor, & Warren, 1995).

Research is giving us evidence that speech and language intervention programs decrease the severity of communication disorders. In 1987, forty-three

(text continues on page 291)

CHILDREN WITH COMMUNICATION DISORDERS IN SPEECH AND LANGUAGE

■ Adapting the Learning Environment

The organization of programs for speech and language disorders in the schools varies with the size of the district and other local factors. Most children with communication disorders are in regular classrooms. Special language classes and other alternatives are available in some school systems, and school services may be offered in various combinations of delivery models.

In the school year 2002–2003, most states (over 90 percent) predominantly used the regular classroom with resource room backup as the educational setting for children with speech and language disorders. Three states predominantly used the resource room as the place of service with the regular classroom as backup. Separate classes are infrequently used as the educational setting (U.S. Department of Education, 2003).

Inclusion in Context

> Children with primary speech disorders respond well to inclusion when they receive help for their communication needs.

Inclusion is an important option for the child with communication disorders. Children with primary speech disorders typically respond to the regular education program if they receive additional help for their special communication needs.

Speech-language pathologists increasingly are working directly with children in the general education classroom, supporting the academic program. They may alert students to pay attention to verbal or written instructions, encourage them to ask pertinent questions and to participate in discussions, and assist them in responding in a culture- and classroom-appropriate fashion (pragmatics).

Otitis media, a middle-ear infection almost universal in children of school age, can lead to hearing and language impairments. Preschool teachers can assist youngsters with frequent otitis media in critical language learning by utilizing the techniques listed in the "Listening and Language Strategies" box on the following page. These techniques are useful for the child identified as hearing impaired as well as for children in general.

Coordination of the Multidisciplinary Team

Consultative Service Consultative service provides a school system with a speech-language pathologist who serves as a consultant to regular classroom teachers, special class teachers, aides, curriculum specialists, administrators, and parents in organizing a speech and language development program. Specialized materials and procedures, inservice education, demonstrations, and other activities help educators, administrators, and parents improve the communication skills of

Listening and Language Strategies for a Child with Frequent Otitis Media

MAKE SPEECH LOUDER OR CLEARER.

▶ Get down on the child's eye level to talk whenever possible. Get close (no more than 3 feet away) and face the child to provide clear visual and auditory information.

▶ Gain the child's attention before speaking to make sure that the child is listening. Remind the child to listen when necessary.

▶ Speak clearly and repeat important words but use a natural speaking intonation or pattern.

▶ When possible, use visual support to help the child understand what he or she is hearing. For a young child, point to objects, pictures, or people and gesture when talking. For an older child, give written as well as verbal instructions.

▶ When there is a speaker in the classroom, seat the child close to the speaker but where the child also can see other children (e.g., at the side of the room).

MINIMIZE BACKGROUND NOISE.

▶ Turn off record players, radios, recorders, and television playing in the background, which can interfere with children hearing ongoing conversation.

▶ Repair noisy appliances (e.g., air conditioners, heaters, fans, vacuum cleaners) that make it hard to hear speech clearly.

▶ Reduce distractions by using movable barriers (e.g., bookshelves, flannel boards) to create small areas in a classroom where small-group and one-to-one interactions can take place.

▶ Hang washable draperies over windows to absorb sound, and close doors and windows, if there is noise that makes it hard to hear.

PROMOTE LANGUAGE LEARNING.

▶ Show an interest in what the child is talking about and in things that interest the child, and follow the child's topic.

▶ Play interactive games with children to encourage turn taking (e.g., peekaboo).

▶ Model desired language by describing ongoing activities.

▶ Respond immediately and consistently to a child's communication attempts.

▶ Pause to give the child time to talk.

▶ Check with the child to see if directions and new information are understood.

▶ Give positive feedback for language attempts.

▶ Elaborate on what the child says by adding words to the child's utterances.

▶ For older preschoolers, encourage discussions that explain things, predict what will happen next, describe feelings, and refer to children's own experiences.

INCREASE CHILDREN'S ATTENTION TO LANGUAGE.

▶ Sing simple songs with repeated words and phrases (e.g., "The Wheels on the Bus").

▶ Play word and listening games (e.g., I Spy) in which children listen to familiar patterns and fill in words.

▶ For older preschool children, play rhyming games (e.g., cat, fat, bat).

▶ Read frequently with children, labeling and describing pictures and referring to children's own experiences.

Source: From J. E. Roberts & I. Wallace, *Otitis media in young children: Medical, developmental, and educational considerations* (Baltimore: Paul H. Brookes, 1997), p. 155. Reprinted with permission.

children in natural settings—the classroom and the home (Salend & Salinas, 2002). The educational audiologist is becoming more involved in assisting teachers in working with children with communication disorders (English 1995). (See Chapter 10 on children who are deaf or hard of hearing.)

Itinerant Service In the past, the most common delivery system was the itinerant service provider, that is, a therapist who went from room to room or took children out of the classroom. In some areas, a speech-language pathologist still travels from school to school to give direct service to children in regular and special classrooms.

Intensive-Cycle Scheduling Another method of service delivery is the *intensive cycle,* sometimes called the *block system,* in which children are scheduled for therapy four or five times a week for a concentrated period, usually for four to six weeks. This type of scheduling is sometimes used in combination with the itinerant service provider, particularly where more than one speech-language pathologist is on the staff (Neidecker, 1987).

■ Adapting Teaching Strategies

Speech and Language Therapy

The speech-language pathologist brings to each therapy session a considerable knowledge base and set of skills to recognize and remediate each child's specific problem (such as errors in articulation, syntax, and voice). The choice of therapy depends on the assessment of the child's need. The most common therapeutic procedure for most young children with deficits is play (sometimes called role-playing). Play, as we mentioned earlier, is the way all children learn speech and language. In the therapy sessions, therapists model the way children who are not disabled learn language. For example, the therapist introduces an age-appropriate toy, talks about it, and encourages the child to examine and manipulate the toy and discover its aspects and the word for it. The therapist asks questions about the toy ("What will it do?" "Can you push it?" "What color is it?" "Can you make it go?") and encourages the child to respond. If the child responds in one word, the therapist expands the child's response and models the correct pronunciation and language form (Fey, Catts, & Larrivee, 1995; Ogura, 1991). Attempts are made to encourage the child to initiate the conversation and the adult responds and amplifies (Leonard, 1998).

Rarely is it advisable to break a word into syllables or to stop the child's communication to correct the pronunciation. If the therapist can understand the meaning the child intends to convey, expansion and modeling are called for. If the therapist cannot understand the child, the adult may query the child about what he or she wished to communicate. If the word did not communicate (for example, if the child had said "cookie" instead of "juice"), the therapist would correct the response. Because a portion of the treatment and intervention program may be delivered by parents or the teacher, the speech-language therapist may be responsible for training the parent or teacher and modeling correct behavior for them. For example, if the child says "Wa doo," the parent may say, "I don't understand; tell me again." The child repeats "Wa doo," looking at the refrigerator. The

If the child's language is not perfectly pronounced, the therapist (or teacher or parent) does not correct the form but recasts it into a correct form in the reply.

Most children with communication disorders are in general education classrooms. Speech-language pathologists give direct service to these children individually in resource rooms and in regular and special classrooms.
(© Bob Daemmrich/Stock Boston)

parent then says, "Oh, you want some juice," and gives it to the child (Camarata, 1995, p. 70). Camarata also calls it *recasting* when the parent models correct pronunciation without correction. For example, a child says "a wion," and the parent says, "yes, a lion." At no time does the parent or teacher interrupt the child and tell him or her, "Say lion." These responses by the adult that build on what the child is communicating are also referred to as *following directives*. They have been shown to be positively associated with language development (McCathren, Yoder, & Warren, 1995).

A program that involves repeated concentration on words to be taught also includes observation of the object that a word stands for—such as an actual nearby dog or one seen during a visit to a pet shop (Lederer, 2002). The word is presented in syntactically correct sentences that encourage the child to respond but do not require a response. Targeted words are developmentally appropriate and include sounds that the child has produced.

Parents also need to be taught that their child with a speech or language disorder needs everything a child without a communication disorder needs and perhaps something more in the form of aids or extra time.

The speech-language pathologist and the teacher must work as a collaborative team to ensure that a child's disorder is treated appropriately. Weekly conferences or planned in-class "talking" activities can be very beneficial.

The Speech-Language Pathologist Speech-language pathologists have specific terminology for some of the major disorders. (See the list below where some of these terms are listed and defined.) The terminology is necessary information for teachers. During the preparation of the IEP or the IFSP, speech-language pathologists use these terms to refer to common speech-language disorders, and teachers need to work closely with the speech-language pathologist to decide how to approach the child's disorder. Often the speech-language pathologist works individually with the child outside the classroom as well.

Speech-language pathologists use many techniques to promote the carryover of newly acquired communication skills into the classroom and everyday conversation. These techniques include children's notebooks prepared by therapists that are kept in the classroom for the teacher's regular review, weekly conferences with teachers regarding specific objectives, the use of devices and props as reminders, and carefully planned in-class "talking" activities. A major task of the communication specialist is to help the classroom teacher use these tools effectively, because the teacher's help is vital to success.

Many children outgrow articulation problems when they are between 5 and 6 years of age. The teacher needs to be aware of what therapies the child has received in kindergarten and work with the speech-language pathologist to determine which therapies to continue. The multidisciplinary team should determine what therapies (if any) to include in the IEP or IFSP.

General education teachers need to cooperate in scheduling out-of-class time for students' speech therapy.

The success of intervention depends on the teacher's cooperation in scheduling time out of class for therapy and sending children to "speech lessons" regularly. Some speech and language changes (the production of particular sounds, language targets, fluency patterns) are best learned in individualized structured therapy sessions; however, the teacher's creativity in adapting classroom opportunities to foster ways of talking will help the student to generalize new skills. The classroom is often the most appropriate setting for incidental and interactive functional teaching (Fey, Windsor, & Warren, 1995).

The speech-language pathologist and the classroom teacher often work side by side in the general education classroom.

Teachers often participate in innovative alternatives to traditional speech-language lessons. It is common practice for the speech-language pathologist and classroom teacher to work side by side each day in a classroom, focusing on the language components of reading, language arts, and socialization (Cole, 1995).

Terms That Speech-Language Pathologists Use to Describe Disorders

Term	Disorder
Apraxia	Impairment in the ability to plan the movement for speech
Aphasia	Impairment in the ability to communicate due to brain damage
Dysarthria	Articulation or voice disorder due to impaired motor control problems of throat, tongue, or lips
Anarthria	Loss of the ability to speak
Dysphonia	A disorder of voice quality
Stuttering	A disorder of fluency: repetitions, prolongations, and hesitations of sounds and syllables

Teachers recognize that there are differences between speech-language programs at the elementary and secondary levels. Often young children have therapy in their classroom, and older students have individual therapy. Because fewer standardized materials are available for students at the secondary level, the speech-language pathologist may have to design and develop or adapt materials for older students with speech and language disorders. Computer programs are very useful in helping high school students master a wide variety of language skills (Schery & O'Connor, 1995).

Secondary school students can use computers to work on language skills.

Additional Roles of the Speech-Language Pathologist From the variety of settings and options for delivery of services to children with speech and language disorders, it's obvious that a speech-language pathologist must be able to serve in more than one capacity. An itinerant speech-language pathologist must be prepared to deal with a broad range of disorders—primary articulation, fluency, voice, and language disorders—as well as the problems found among children with cleft palate, mental retardation, cerebral palsy, learning disabilities, and emotional disturbance, children who are learning impaired, or students who are deaf (Hanks & Velaski, 2003).

Speech-language pathologists often work with parents of children with other disabilities. Researchers have found that parents may not talk to a child with disabilities as much as they would talk to a child without disabilities, or they may overwhelm their child with talk. They appear to be more anxious about their child's progress, especially the progress of a low-birth-weight premature child who is less responsive to the parent and generally less fun to interact with than a child without disabilities. Mothers of children with hearing-language impairments may need help in being flexible and encouragement in communicating with their child. Some parents consistently change the topic of talk away from the child's focus or fail to respond to the child's talk and extend the child's topics (Snow, 1999). These parents may need help in how to facilitate their child's language learning (Hart & Risley, 1999).

Parents may need assistance in learning to speak frequently enough with their child.

Speech language pathologists assist children who have communication disorders in many ways:

▶ They provide individual therapy.

▶ They consult with the child's teacher about effective ways to assist the child in the classroom.

▶ At times they may work with the entire class.

▶ They work closely with the family.

▶ They work with vocational teachers and counselors to establish goals for work.

▶ They work with individual children in the classroom, cuing them when to ask questions and encouraging them to participate in discussion and interact verbally.

Interactive Approaches

It was once quite popular to use operant conditioning to train a child to repeat words spoken to him or her. (*Operant conditioning* is a technique of behavior modification that works by controlling the stimulus that follows a response.) If the child repeated the word correctly, he or she was rewarded for doing so. Some interventionists achieved success in having the child master a list of words, but they were disappointed when the child did not use the words in his or her own free speech. Bloom (1991) noted that these modeling procedures fail, at in part be cause children without disabilities imitate far less than was previously believed.

Teachers and therapists focus on the social use of language (pragmatics) and stress functional communication in natural language environments (Kaiser & Gray, 1993). This popular form of treatment is the *interactive approach*. The interventionist—the parent, special education teacher, or speech-language pathologist—tries to capitalize on the natural inclination of the child to talk about what he or she is doing, plans to do, or wants to do. To encourage correct word use and language use, interventionists provide remediation sessions while the child is eating, playing, or visiting community settings such as a fast-food restaurant (Warren & Kaiser, 1988).

This natural approach is frequently referred to as *functionalism*, which means using speech and language in a functional way to acquire and satisfy one's needs. Other terms for this technique are *incidental teaching* and **social language learning.** The intent of these techniques is to increase the child's amount of talk (Bloom, 1991). The more the child talks, the more the child will gradually gain accuracy and increase his or her vocabulary.

Intervention for Fluency Disorders

Intervention programs based on learning theory and principles of behavior have had a tremendous impact on all speech and language therapy, particularly for stuttering. Although parent counseling and training to change environmental stress continue to be important therapeutic tools for young children, direct speech intervention programs for children as young as age 2 have been developed and are working (Fey, Windsor, & Warren, 1995).

Many successful therapies recognize the importance of motivation, attitudes toward speech and self, and environmental interactions. In one successful approach developed many years ago by pioneers in speech-language disorders at the University, of Iowa, stutterers are taught to control stuttering, to reduce extraneous behaviors, and to stutter "normally." They are taught to face the problem rather than try to cover up their dysfluencies. The approach makes use of outside speaking activities (shopping, asking for directions, making telephone calls).

Classroom teachers can be particularly helpful to the child who stutters by working with the speech-language pathologist to plan opportunities for the child to participate in speaking activities that are appropriate for practicing newly acquired fluency skills at increasing levels of complexity. The following lists of suggestions can help teachers (Blance, Stedal, & Smith, 1994; Williams, 1999).

Teachers can help students who stutter by creating silence in interactions, reducing the rate of speech, and modeling vocabulary and grammar.

■ Suggestions to Improve Students' Self-Esteem

▶ Disregard moments of nonfluency.

▶ Show acceptance of what the child has expressed rather than how it was said.

▶ Treat a child who stutters like any other member of the class.

Evaluating children who are suspected of having communication disorders involves assessing the disorder with formal speech and language tests and with informal procedures such as language sampling and analysis of conversation.
(© Mary Kate Denny/ Photo Edit)

▶ Acknowledge nonfluency without labeling the child.

▶ Help the child feel in control of his or her speech.

▶ Accept nonfluency.

Focused Stimulation

Focused stimulations are procedures held in a naturalistic environment in which the therapist recasts a child's sentences to highlight desired language, particularly grammar. The naturalistic environment provides an opportunity for play and the stimulation of language, as in this example (Fey, Cleave, & Long, 1997):

> **Child:** I can play, too?
> **Adult:** Oh, you played it, too.
> **Child:** Him like that.
> **Adult:** Does he like that?

Phonological Training

Phonological awareness, the best predictor of reading achievement, is the ability to recognize that words can be divided into smaller units, such as syllables and phonemes (Leonard, 1998; Rivers, Lombardino, & Thompson, 1996). Children who have difficulty recognizing and mastering phonemes will have difficulty learning how to read.

Phonological awareness skills include rhyming; comparing sounds of words (*mat-cat*); isolating beginning, medial, and ending sounds; blending sounds (*c-a-t*); segmenting (what are the sounds in *cat*?); deleting sounds (*cat-at*); and substituting sounds (*cat-cap*) (adapted from Wanzek, Bursuck, & Dickson, 2003).

Augmented and Alternative Communication

At times, children with severe motor problems cannot produce intelligible speech. A common instructional strategy is called **augmented and alternative communication. American Sign Language (ASL)**, a system of gestures that contain meaning, is one example of this strategy. Another gesture system that is sometimes used is Signed English. Sign language is taught to some visually or motor-impaired children (Bower, 1989).

Other aids include communication boards of varying complexity, with letters or pictures to which the child can point to spell out a word or select a picture of the word (Beukelman & Mirenda, 1992; DiCarlo, Banajee, & Buras-Stricklin, 2000). The use of these aids has been shown to assist the child in acquiring language—many times without speech, but not always (McLean & Cripe, 1997).

Communication boards allow a child to point to letters or pictures to communicate.

■ Adapting Curriculum

Intervention Priorities

School systems must provide appropriate services to all students, and they can make decisions about types of services and where to offer them. A number of professionals are concerned about the priorities in providing speech and language services within the educational program. Neidecker (1987) suggested the following continuum of services based on a model developed by ASHA:

▶ *Communication disorders.* Children with moderate-to-severe articulation, fluency, voice, or language disorders require intensive intervention. These disorders often interfere with academic achievement and social adjustment, and a variety of professionals may be needed to plan a treatment program.

▶ *Communication deviations.* Children with communication deviations have less severe handicapping disorders, but their communication can cause adaptation difficulties in school. Children with developmental lags and mild mental retardation often are in this group.

▶ *Communication development.* All children may need some effort by speech language pathologists to prevent the progression of mild speech problems and to improve their primary linguistic skills and enrich their language.

The use of a dialect is not a sign of a speech disorder but is part of the linguistic diversity of society.

Dialects

Variations in word usage, pronunciation (phonology), word order (syntax), and meaning (semantics) influence the child's use of language (pragmatics). A **dialect** is a variety of language differing in pronunciation, vocabulary, or syntax from the literary form of the language. A dialect is used and understood by a group within a larger community. Dialects reflect regional, social, occupational, and other differences: "He done sold his car." "We be there tomorrow." "She be sick to her stomach."

Saying "warsh" for "wash" is a regional dialect, not a speech disorder.

Saying "warsh" for "wash" is not a sign of a speech defect but a regional dialect. If a child says "dog" for "cow," then a disorder may be suspected (though it may be that the child has not learned the new term).

A dialect is very much a part of a child's self-concept, and teachers must react to it carefully. They need to model standard literary usage and encourage children to use it when reading aloud and writing, but they should allow children to use dialect in their informal speech if communication is clear.

A major problem for teachers is that the existence of a dialect may mask a delay or disorder that will become increasingly difficult to diagnose the longer it remains undetected. A major failing of language assessment tools is that they are based on the average child's use of language, which is not necessarily the way language is used, taught, and encouraged in all families and communities. Therapists and teachers need to learn what a specific community considers accurate pronunciation and usage, and they need to teach children to respond to questions fully. Through "show and tell" and by dictating creative stories, with teachers encouraging expansion and explicitness, children can be encouraged to speak in sentences, to use standard American English, to be explicit, and not to overuse pronouns (as persons in noninclusive settings tend to do).

Adapting Technology

Because speech-language professionals use computers as therapeutic tools, it is essential for speech-language pathologists to be computer literate. ASHA and the national group Computer Users in Speech and Hearing (CUSH) both provide information about technological advances.

Instructional Technology

Computer programs are designed for a variety of specific purposes, for example, phonological evaluation and teaching children sentence structure. Another important use is word processing, which frees children from the burden of organizing bits and pieces of written language on the spatial confines of a page. There are several benefits of word-processing systems for children with disorders of written language (and for others as well):

▶ There is no penalty for revising.

▶ It is easy for students to experiment with writing.

▶ Interest in writing is maintained.

▶ Editing is simple: Spelling, punctuation, and grammar can be checked and corrected.

▶ Writing and editing are less time consuming.

▶ Frustration is minimized.

▶ It is easy to produce perfect copy.

Computers provide highly structured, totally consistent stimulus materials and response acceptance. They give students independence in routine activities, and they help maintain interest in practice and drill, areas that traditionally have bored both students and clinicians. They are also designed to provide specific communication skill training (Schery & O'Connor, 1995).

Word-prompt programs provide a list of words based on the letter being typed. For example, if the user types *b*, all the words beginning with *b* appear on the screen (Wood, Rankin, & Beukelman, 1997). More sophisticated programs provide words from a vocabulary list, others from dictionaries and some by context.

Speech-language pathologists must be computer literate in order to use therapeutic tools such as word-processing programs. These can provide an easy and less frustrating way for students to write and revise.

Computers can give secondary school students independence in routine drill and practice exercises.

Software for language-related difficulties: Co-Writing, Predict It, and Write Out Loud www.donjohnston.com

For children with severe motor problems who cannot produce intelligible speech, a common instructional strategy is augmented and alternative communication by means of communication boards.
(© Susie Fitzhugh)

Following are some examples.

www.pcicatalog.com

▶ *Play and Say Speech Cards* A language training system and symbolic language pictures designed to help children communicate and learn correct speech patterns through games and activities.

www.dynavoxsys.com

▶ *Day Write* A direct-selection communicator designed for those who can type and spell.

▶ *Link Plus* A direct-selection alternative and augmentative communication device that speaks by producing synthesized speech as the user types.

▶ *Look Hear* An auditory training activity for those with speech difficulties. The program includes three cassettes that feature sounds of people, home, school, transportation, and animals, as well as thirty-five color photographs of corresponding scenes and objects.

Houghton Mifflin Teacher Education website http://education.college.hmco.com/students

See the Houghton Mifflin Teacher Education website for an expanded list of assistive technology equipment.

(text continues from page 279)

studies were analyzed with special techniques to assess the overall effectiveness of language intervention with individuals who have language-learning disabilities. The composite results indicated that the average child with language disorders moved from the 50th to the 85th percentile as a result of language intervention (Shriberg & Kwiatowski, 1988).

The prospect for stutterers to learn good communication skills is very good. Controlled studies of children who stutter have demonstrated that they can achieve outcomes within normal limits (Hancock et al., 1998). Therapy with stutterers should begin by 2–3 years of age, at the first appearance of stuttering (Leonard, 1998). Since the 1980s, serious research has focused on the problems of maintaining fluent speech and preventing relapse. Evaluation of these studies and others indicated that scientifically based therapy is clearly effective (McLean & Cripe, 1997). Early intervention for stuttering has become so widespread that some authors refer to it as prevention in which the family plays the critical role (Culatta & Goldberg, 1995).

Important changes have come about in helping students with language disorders make transitions from high school to college and the workplace. Many colleges and universities have support services and special programs for these students. Special clinics and help sessions are staffed by speech-language pathologists, learning disabilities specialists, and psychologists, and individualized techniques for note taking, class participation, and writing are available to help students who have written-language deficits.

Summary

▶ Communication can be verbal, nonverbal, or a combination of both.

▶ *Language* is the system of symbols used to express and receive meaning. It can be verbal or nonverbal.

▶ Processes needed to produce speech are respiration, phonation, resonation, articulation, audition, and symbolization/organization.

▶ *Speech* is the systematic oral production of the words of a given language.

▶ Communication disorders include speech disorders of articulation, fluency and voice, and language disorders. Hearing loss can also cause speech disorders. Communication disorders can be secondary to other disabilities.

▶ A child who has a speech disorder is conspicuous, usually unintelligible.

▶ A child who has a language disorder shows skills in the primary language that are markedly below the skills expected for the child's chronological age.

▶ An understanding of normal patterns of language acquisition is an important part of identifying children with language disorders and developing remediation programs for them.

▶ Common models for the delivery of language and speech services are consultative services, itinerant services, intensive-cycle scheduling, and resource rooms—all of which fit well within the concept of inclusion—as well as training parents and teachers to deliver services.

▶ The role of the speech-language pathologist has expanded in the schools. This professional is a member of the multidisciplinary team that develops and monitors the child's IEP or IFSP.

Future Challenges

1. **With children in inclusive classrooms, how can students also receive needed individual therapy?**
Children with major speech disorders need one-on-one therapy. However, recent emphasis on inclusion raises questions on how individual

therapy can take place in the classroom without disrupting the classroom program. The problem of incorporating full inclusion with individual therapy is still unresolved.

2. How can early intervention materials be made more available to parents and physicians?

Most speech disorders are not identifiable until a child reaches 2 years of age, when verbal language ability usually appears. Unfortunately, parents frequently do not recognize early signs of potential speech disorders in the prelinguistic stage as signs of a potential problem. How to make this information more available to both pediatricians and parents remains an issue.

3. How can schools find personnel who speak a variety of languages?

The large number of immigrants from many different non-English-speaking cultures has introduced major challenges for U.S. schools. Because the number of languages sometimes can be as many as eight different ones, some schools find it difficult to cope with the demands of this diversity. How schools can locate personnel who speak these languages and how the schools can afford to hire them are unresolved issues.

Key Terms

American Sign Language (ASL)   *p. 288*

articulation   *p. 259*

audition   *p. 259*

augmented and alternative communication   *p. 288*

cleft palate   *p. 270*

communication   *p. 258*

communication disorder   *p. 260*

dialect   *p. 288*

dysphonia   *p. 271*

fluency   *p. 270*

language disorder   *p. 260*

phonation   *p. 259*

phonology   *p. 261*

resonation   *p. 259*

respiration   *p. 259*

social language learning   *p. 286*

speech   *p. 258*

speech disorder   *p. 260*

stuttering   *p. 270*

voice disorder   *p. 270*

Resources

References of Special Interest

L. Bloom, & Tinker, E. (2001). The intentionality model and language acquisition. *Monographs of the Society for Research in Child Development* 66(4): 1–91. *An excellent presentation of language acquisition as well as a critique of current theories and the presentation of an integrated theory.*

Fey, M., Windsor, J., & Warren, S. (Eds.). (1995). *Language intervention: Preschool through elementary years.* Baltimore: Paul H. Brookes. *In this collection, authorities in the field offer teachers many practical suggestions based on sound research.*

Hammil, D. (2004). What we know about correlates of reading. *Exceptional Children* 70(4): 453–468. *An overview of research on successful techniques of teaching reading.*

Kaiser, A., & Gray, D. (Eds.). (1993). *Enhancing children's communication.* Baltimore: Paul H. Brookes. *The articles in this collection offer a rich array of intervention techniques, such as parent-implemented language intervention, for dealing with language disorders.*

Lahey, M., & Bloom, L. (1988). *Language disorders and language development.* Columbus, OH: Merrill. *The first edition was a classic in the field, and this edition (with the title reversed) is equally valuable. The authors provide a clear and succinct description of speech and language disorders and how to deal with them in the classroom and in special therapy situations. Highly recommended.*

Paul, R. (1995). *Language disorders from infancy through adolescence: Assessment and intervention.* St. Louis, MO: Mosby. *A comprehensive presentation of assessment strategies for a wide array of speech-language disorders as well as suggestions for intervention.*

Watkins, R., & Rice, M. (Eds.). (1994). *Specific language impairments in children.* Baltimore: Paul H. Brookes. *This research-oriented collection sheds light on the genetic basis of language disorders and suggests intervention strategies.*

Journals

American Journal of Speech-Language Pathology
http://professional.asha.org/resources/journal/AJSPL-index.cfou

Journal of Speech-Language, Pathology, and Audiology
www.caslpa.ca/english/resources/jslpa.asp

Journal of Speech, Language, and Hearing Research
professional.asha.org/resources/journals/JSLHR-index.cfm

Topics in Language Disorders
http://www.lww/com/products/

Professional Organizations

The American Speech-Language-Hearing Association
(ASHA) www.asha.org/
National Stuttering Project
members.aol.com/nsphome/index.html

Please visit the book's website at
http://education.college.hmco.com/students for new
and updated information on websites listed here
and for the mailing addresses of the journals and
organizations.

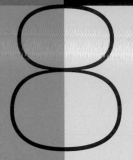

8

CHILDREN WITH AUTISM SPECTRUM DISORDERS

FOCUS QUESTIONS

▶ What are autism spectrum disorders?

▶ What is Asperger's syndrome?

▶ What is functional behavior assessment?

▶ What is a theory of mind?

▶ How do children with autism experience the world?

▶ What are some of the educational programs for children with autism?

▶ How can their social skills be improved?

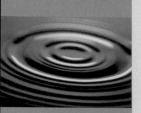

Mike Dolan was a poster boy of a child. With his blond curly hair and clear blue eyes he was, as neighbors and relatives said, a beautiful two-year-old. But Mike's parents were worried about him. Something was clearly wrong with their child. He wasn't talking as two-year-olds do. He had a series of physical motions with his hands that he kept repeating. And above all, he didn't interact socially with his parents or others the way he should.

He didn't look directly at people when they talked to him, and he appeared not to pay attention to many of the things his parents said to him. He seemed preoccupied with his toy trucks and would play with them incessantly. When he wanted something such as a glass of milk, he would go to the refrigerator, grab a bottle, and hand it to his mother rather than ask.

Finally, Mrs. Dolan decided to take him to the family pediatrician. Dr. Phinney examined Mike and found nothing physically wrong with his development, with the exception of some motor incoordination. However, having seen a child with similar behavior two months before, the doctor suggested that the Dolans bring Mike to a university clinic that had the multidisciplinary staff to diagnose the condition.

Mike was evaluated by physicians, psychologists, and speech pathologists at the university clinic. Then they met with the Dolans and explained that in their judgment, Mike had a condition known as autism. The lack of communication, his inability to interact socially, his obsession with particular toys, and his strange motor movements all pointed in that direction. Yet it was fortunate that the Dolans had come to them so soon. Early treatment was essential, and it would be important to begin a treatment regime right away.

The Dolans had many questions. What was this condition? What had caused the autism? Could other children that they might have contract the condition as well? Could it be cured, and what would be the treatment? Mrs. Dolan wanted to know if the schools could handle a child with this condition—or would Mike need to go to a special school?

Those are all good questions, ones that any parent might ask in a similar situation. There has been increasing awareness of this strange condition called autism with its patterns of symptoms, such as Mike had, that can be recognized by age two or even earlier. The number of children identified as having autism has been steadily growing over the past decade, but most authorities believe that this means more general recognition of a condition that formerly would have been called something else—perhaps mental retardation or severe emotional disturbance (Volkmar, 1998). As we attempt to answer some of the Dolans' questions, it is important to keep in mind that a great deal still is not known about autism and ways to treat it.

Autism Society of America
www.autism-society.org

■ Definition

What Are Autism Spectrum Disorders?

Mike belongs to that group of children classified as having *autism spectrum disorders*. The term refers to a variety of disorders affecting the children's social development and ability to communicate and having characteristic behavioral manifestations such as repetitive motor movements. Included in this group are pervasive developmental disorders not otherwise specified (PDDNOS), Asperger's syndrome (observable in high-functioning children with autism-like symptoms), and childhood disintegrative disorders, which cause children to regress in their development (for example, a child who once had speech no longer communicating) (Lord, 2001).

The disorders in these categories are neurological disorders that lead to deficits in the child's ability to communicate, understand language, play, develop social skills, and relate to others (IDEA, 1997). The Individuals with Disabilities Education Act Amendment of 1997 defines autism as

| Autism significantly affects verbal and nonverbal communication and social skills.

> a developmental disability significantly affecting verbal and non-verbal communication and social interaction, usually evident before age 3, that adversely affects a child's educational performance. Other characteristics often associated with autism are engagement in repetitive activities and stereotyped movement, resistance to environmental change or change in daily routines, and unusual sensory experiences.

■ History

The discovery of the condition of autism has been relatively recent. We have known about mental retardation for more than a century, but autism was first brought to our attention by Leo Kanner (1943), a psychiatrist at Johns Hopkins University. He described a group of children who did not relate to others, had delays in speech development, engaged in repetitive behavior, were upset by changes in routines, and so forth.

Later on, in England, Michael Rutter (1996) reported a study that compared children diagnosed as autistic with children who displayed other emotional disorders. He found three characteristics that almost always were present in the children with autism but only occasionally in children with emotional disorders:

1. Failure to develop social relationships
2. Language retardation with impaired comprehension
3. Ritualistic or compulsive behaviors

Whereas there has been general agreement on the nature of the syndrome of autism, the same cannot be said for understanding the causes of autism. During a period in the 1960s and 1970s, there was a widespread belief that the cause of autism was a cold and unfeeling mother. The child's social and communication problems were attributed to this breakdown in relationships. It was a doubly unfortunate theory because not only was it insulting to the mothers; it was dead wrong.

Now there is widespread acceptance of the idea that the child with autism has a neurophysiological condition with known brain differences in amygdala, hippocampus, and cerebellum. So what were these "experts" seeing when they said the mother was at fault? They probably were seeing the end product of maternal frustration with a child who was not responsive to any of the mother's overtures and who was very distant from all social contact.

■ Prevalence

The prevalence of autism spectrum disorders has been steadily rising in the spotlight of attention focused on them. Fombonne (2000) has reviewed the data in 10 countries and he estimated a prevalence of 4.8/10,000, or about 1 in every 2,000 children. Other estimates suggest it may be as high as 1 in every 1000. It may now exceed the number of children with Down syndrome and children with fragile X syndrome. Over 50,000 children in the United States under the age of 5 are affected. There is a diverse set of views on the true prevalence.

The early identification of these children is made possible with a few simple tasks provided to pediatricians, who are often the first professionals to come into contact with the family. Children with autism have difficulty with pretend play (such as pretending to drink from a teacup), or imitating adult behavior (rapping on the table), or pointing to objects upon request (point to the dog). The failure to respond well in these instances is often the cue for entering into a more comprehensive examination of child and family.

One of the screening devices that appears to be helpful with very young children is known as CHAT (Checklist for Autism in Toddlers). The originators of this checklist, Baron-Cohen and others (1996), claim that the absence of three key items at 18 months of age carries an over 80 percent risk of autism. These three items are *protodeclarative pointing* (the infant points at an object in order to direct another person to look at the object), *gaze monitoring* (the infant turns to look in the same direction in which an adult is looking), and *pretend play* (play involving object substitution: a stick becomes a gun or an airplane).

■ Causes and Characteristics

Because autism spectrum disorders tend to run in families, a genetic defect is suspected. Autism is more common among boys, with about four times as many boys as girls identified. Some children with autism may appear to be developing normally until around 2 years of age. Others may be seen as different from early infancy.

During the 1970s and 1980s, it became popular in the social sciences to emphasize environmental effects on children and adults. Now, with the growing capabilities for genetic research, it seems clear that many conditions that resulted in children with special needs are linked to an intertwining of genetics and environment. Conditions such as fragile X syndrome, mental retardation, attention-deficit hyperactivity disorder, and dyslexia (all learning disabilities), as well as autism, all seem to have genetic components (McGuffin, Riley, & Plomin, 2003).

Evidence is accumulating for a strong genetic linkage for autism. There is a striking concordance of autism among monozygotic twins (those with identical genetic makeup) over dizygotic twins (those with similar but not identical genetic makeup). This result, obtained in a number of studies across several countries, strengthens the belief that genetics plays a major role in this condition (Bailey, Phillips, & Rutter, 1996).

The advances in our genetic knowledge through the Human Genome Project and other research have even identified two of the chromosomes (7 and 15) as the sites for the disorder in many children with autism. In addition, linkages between autism and conditions such as fragile X and untreated phenylketonuria have been established (Smalley, 1997). Environmental factors can have a secondary influence on the intensity of the problem—but no credible linkage has been found to reactions to vaccines, as has been proposed in the popular media (Taylor et al., 2002).

Some of childhood's remarkable achievements in development are often taken for granted because the great majority of children demonstrate them at the appropriate age. As Shonkoff and Phillips (2000) pointed out in their comprehensive review of early child development:

> The second and third years of life appear to be pivotal for the child's emerging capacities and inclination to be cooperative and considerate toward others. Toddlers are developing the cognitive skills to understand parental standards and apply them to their own behavior and achieving capacities for self-regulation that enable them increasingly to comply with internalized standards of conduct. (p. 241)

But what happens when the child does not automatically develop such behaviors and is unable to understand the feelings of others and consequently express empathy for others in distress? That is what happens to children with *autism,* a puzzling disorder, which makes its appearance early and profoundly impacts the child's development.

Early identification of children with autism is one of the key elements of treatment. The key developmental areas of language development and social skills are critical at ages 18 months to 3 years, and these skills, in addition to imitation of motor behaviors and using eye gaze to communicate, need to be fostered at that time. If we wait for the child's autism to be discovered in kindergarten, we have lost valuable time that will be very difficult to recover.

Fortunately, a number of studies have shown that diagnosticians have the ability to correctly identify children with autism at age 2 or earlier (Stone et al., 1999; Lord, 1995; Baron-Cohen et al., 1996). This affords an early opportunity to begin therapy in language functioning and improvements in peer relationships. It is important for parents to be aware of the existence of such diagnostic services in their communities, so that this early identification and treatment be carried out.

These disorders are very troubling to parents, who tend to seek a cure or a miracle to transform their once developing child back to age-appropriate developmental functioning (Cohen, 1998). As Cohen notes, there is almost a sense of desperation among parents trying an array of approaches that may work for some children, but rarely for many, and never for all.

The combination of parental stress and the uncertainties of the causes of autism spectrum disorders has led to many attempts to find a cause, efforts that fall outside standard scientific investigations. One such attempt has been described in a *Wall Street Journal* editorial, "The Politics of Autism" (December 29, 2003) about the preservative thimerosal, used in preparing a variety of vaccines routinely given to young children.

The association in time between the taking of the vaccine with the appearance of symptoms of autism has led some to believe there is a causative rela-

The Politics of Autism

For any parent, there are few more traumatic diagnoses than that a child suffers from autism. But the increasing political attention to that affliction is having the unintended and dangerous consequence of limiting vaccines for all children.

This is a story of politics and lawyers trumping science and medicine. It concerns thimerosal, a preservative that was used in vaccines for 60 years and has never been credibly linked to any health problems. Nonetheless, a small but vocal group of parents have taken to claiming that thimerosal causes autism, a brain disorder that impairs normal social interaction. The result has been an ugly legal and political spat that has spilled into Congress and is frightening some parents from vaccinating their children against such deadly diseases as tetanus and whooping cough.

Like night follows day, the dispute has also brought in the trial lawyers. Vaccine makers are supposed to be protected from lawsuits by 1986 legislation, but the lawyers are exploiting loopholes to file billion-dollar suits that threaten to punish the few companies that still make vaccines.

Congress tried to fix this by including a liability provision in homeland security legislation a year ago. But three Northeast Republican Senators—Olympia Snowe, Susan Collins and Lincoln Chafee—demanded it be taken out until Congress could have a full airing of the thimerosal-autism issue. The Senators haven't yet honored their side of that deal.

Perhaps that's because if they did their position would be exposed as scientifically untenable. The claim is that thimerosal, an organic mercury compound, can cause neurodevelopmental disorders. But study after study has shown that there is simply no such link.

A 2002 University of Rochester study compared the blood mercury levels of infants who'd received vaccines with and without thimerosal. All had levels well below the supercautious EPA safety standard. This was followed last March by a study published in Pediatrics magazine, in which researchers compared the physical manifestations of autism and mercury poisoning. They found that the symptoms weren't the same, nor were the brain tissues similar.

Perhaps the best evidence comes from Denmark, one of those European nations that likes to monitor most everything about its citizens. Researchers recently examined the health records of all children born in Denmark from 1971 to 2000 for autism diagnoses. Though Denmark eliminated thimerosal from its vaccines in 1992, the researchers found that the incidence of autism continued to increase. A second research team reviewed the records of nearly 500,000 Danes vaccinated for pertussis. They also found that the risk of autism and related disorders didn't differ between those vaccinated with thimerosal and those without.

None of this is to deny that the incidence of autism may be rising, though there is a dispute about why. The definition of the disease has broadened in recent years, encompassing even mild learning disabilities, and doctors have become better at diagnosing it. Some statistics show that as autism diagnoses rise, those for mental retardation fall—suggesting children were previously misdiagnosed. Parents are also more keen to have a proper diagnosis, because many schools now offer more extensive educational services for autism than they do for other disorders.

The good news is that research is beginning to reveal autism's causes and signs, in particular evidence of a genetic link. Studies have found that if one identical twin has autism the other has a very high chance of having severe social impairment. Scientists are already focusing on a handful of genes that may play a role.

In an important study this year, researchers found that a small head circumference at birth, followed by a sudden growth spurt of the head before the end of the first year, is a reliable early warning sign. (Brain growth that early can't be triggered by vaccines.)

Autism is a terrible disease and it's understandable that some parents would want to look for scapegoats. One lobby group, Safe Minds, has been especially active in blaming vaccines and has found a powerful ally in Indiana Republican Dan Burton, who runs the House Wellness and Human Rights Subcommittee. His family has had its own painful experience with autism.

But their understandable passion shouldn't be allowed to trump undeniable evidence and damage childhood immunizations that are essential to public health. Vaccine makers stopped using thimerosal a few years ago, but the autism lawsuits threaten those companies with enough damage that their ability to supply vaccines is in jeopardy.

Senate Majority Leader Bill Frist has a proposal to offer liability protection against thimerosal claims and modernize the federal Vaccine Injury Compensation Program—which pays out to the rare family whose child is truly harmed by a vaccine. Congress could both redeem itself and improve public health by making this bill a priority when it reconvenes in January.

tionship between the two. As "The Politics of Autism" points out, numerous scientific inquiries have failed to implicate thimerosal, but publicity surrounding this posited cause has caused some parents to refuse to have their children vaccinated, thus leaving them open to other dangerous diseases. The need for scientific closure on the causes of autism is very apparent.

Special Characteristics of Children with Autism

Many persons have wondered what might be the fundamental mechanisms at the heart of the problems observable in children with autism, such as Mike Dolan. What is behind the inability to socialize or to communicate effectively with others?

Theory of Mind

One of the indicators of a fundamental developmental disability in autistic children has been lack of a **theory of mind,** the ability of human beings to understand the thinking and feelings of other people. A theory of mind is necessary for understanding, predicting, and shaping the behavior of others. In typical children, 4-year-olds have a developing theory of mind (Twachtman-Cullen, 2000).

One example of a test of *theory of mind* is known as the Sally and Anne Test (see Fig. 8.1). In this, the child watches while a doll named Sally leaves a marble in a round box and leaves the scene. While she is away the other doll, named Anne, moves the marble to the square box sitting beside the round box. On Sally's return, participants are asked to predict where she will look for her ball. To answer correctly, one must be able to understand what Sally's mental state would be—namely, that since she put the ball in the round box, she would expect to find it there. Most children as young as 4 can correctly respond as to where Sally will look. But children with autism have a great deal of difficulty with this test, and this suggests that they are not able to get inside Sally's thinking processes. A variety of tasks that depend upon understanding the feelings or thinking processes of others have been presented to children with autism, who do extremely poorly on them. An analysis of a series of studies on this topic (Yirmiya, Erel, Shaked, & Solomonica-Levy, 1998) revealed that children with autism have a major fundamental deficit in the development of theory of mind, compared with children of typical development and even seem less able to do these tasks than children with mental retardation who also have deficits in "theory of mind" ability.

Hypersensitivity to Sensory Stimuli

One of the characteristics shared by many persons with autism is a hypersensitivity to noises in the environment. It almost seems as if they have lost the ability to modulate sounds, as these sounds come through with terrifying impact. The following statement from Temple Grandin (1988) as an adult with autism, is typical.

FIGURE 8.1
How Autistic People Experience the World

Austistic people have extreme difficulty perceiving, or even inferring, other people's thoughts, feelings and intentions. In fact, autism is sometimes described as "mindblindness." Yet the condition is more than a disability. Autistic people excel at certain tasks.

THE IMPAIRMENTS PERCEIVING MENTAL STATES

1 Sally puts her marble in the basket, replaces the lid and leaves the room.

2 While Sally is gone, her friend Anne takes the marble out of the basket, moves it into the covered box and replaces both of the lids.

3 When Sally comes back into the room, the two containers look just the way she left them. Where do you think she will look for her marble?

A **normal 4-year-old** easily discerns that Sally will expect to find the marble in the basket where she left it.

Looking at the same scene, **autistic children** tend to predict that she'll look in the box, since that's where it is. They can't see things from Sally's perspective.

Normal child   **Autistic child**

Source: From Geoffrey Cowley, Understanding autism, *Newsweek,* July 23, 2000. Copyright © 2000 by Newsweek, Inc. Reprinted by permission.

Loud, sudden noises still startle me. My reaction to them is more intense than other people's. I still hate balloons, because I never know when one will pop and make me jump. Sustained high-pitched motor noises, such as hair dryers and bathroom vent fans, still bother me, lower frequency motor noises do not. (p. 3)

Sometimes this sensitivity to stimuli extends to the tactile, so that some children with autism are sensitive to touch and will shy away from relatives hugging them or from being touched by others. Such behavior can easily be misinterpreted and compound the social difficulties such children face.

Asperger's Syndrome

Named for Viennese physician Hans Asperger in 1944, this condition has in recent years received renewed attention, due to increased interest in the general condition of autism. One of the distinguishing characteristics of students with Asperger's syndrome is a developmental imbalance. On the one hand, they can be of average or superior intelligence; on the other, they are unfailingly years behind in social development.

In addition, they may have a preoccupation with certain subjects almost to the exclusion of other subjects (for instance, the solar system or insects) and can become experts in a narrow field that includes things but not people. They may also show stereotyped behavior such as "hand flapping" and various nonfunctional rituals (such as insisting that the objects on a shelf always be in the same place and order) (Attwood, 1998).

In the box about David, a ten-year-old student with Asperger's syndrome reveals high intelligence as well as some hidden emotions. David is one of those students called "twice exceptional," in that he would qualify as both intellectually gifted and autistic (Asperger's). Such students require an individualized education program that focuses on social development, establishing social contacts, and learning about others' feelings (theory of mind). Some can perform well in academic areas, yet they still have serious social and behavioral problems that require special attention.

David—A Boy with Asperger's

RAGE

Rage is Anger's brother.
Anger is a hurricane
And Rage is a tornado
They are powerful and strong.
Rage is an eruption of red hot lava
Running down a volcano.
Anger is pitch black
Like the bottom of the ocean.
Rage throws spears of lightning and
Pushes fire through your veins.
Rage is an earthquake shattering buildings.
Rage is a powerful force
That causes total destruction.

—David, age 10

Source: From D. Fraser, From the playful to the profound: What metaphors tell us about gifted children, *Roeper Review, 25,* no. 4 (2003): 183. Reprinted with permission.

PROFILES

DEVELOPMENTAL

The graph below indicates the development of two boys, one with autism (Sam) and one with Asperger's syndrome (Larry). Since there is great variation in the development of children with autism, many different developmental patterns can be seen.

Sam: Sam is ten years old and of somewhat low height and weight. His main problems are seen in school-related performance, in which his reading and arithmetic are at a first-grade level and on a par with his measured intelligence. Also, his interpersonal relations are at the bottom because of the special problems he has in relating socially. Since Sam is in the fifth grade (inclusion), he needs an enormous amount of support and help, in both the academic and the social realms. The regular classroom teacher is ready to recommend him for another placement because she cannot get his attention in order to

Developmental Profiles of Children with Autism Spectrum Disorders

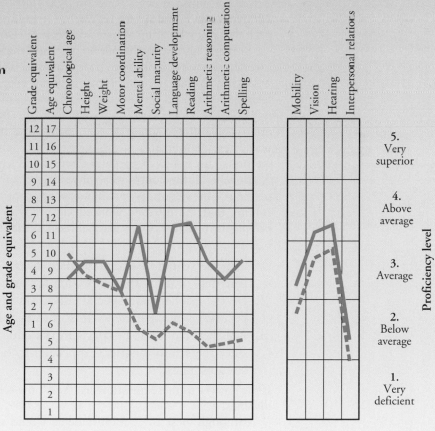

Larry (Asperger's Syndrome) ———
Sam (Autism) - - - -

do any meaningful teaching, even when she has the time to devote to him.

Larry: Larry, a child diagnosed with Asperger's syndrome, has a different type of profile than Sam's. In the area of academic performance, Larry appears to be above average in most of his academic work, and he is in the superior range of measured intelligence. His problems concentrate in the social area. His social maturity is that of a 7 year old, and the teacher is forever reminding him that "we don't tolerate this silly kind of behavior." Like Sam's interpersonal relationships, Larry's are at the bottom. He does not seem to be aware of what to do to have friends or keep them (Schopler, Mesibov, & Kunce, 1998). His IEP goals would focus on the development of social skills and social awareness, something his parents would dearly like to see improve.

The Courts

The importance of the courts in the development of programs for children with special needs has been noted in previous chapters. In no other category have the courts played such a significant role than with children with autism. A total of nineteen cases were brought into federal court between 1998 and 2002 as a result of disputes between parents and school districts on the appropriate way of educating autistic children (Nelson & Huefner, 2003).

In many instances, the parents insisted that the school district employ the Lovaas method of discrete trial training (DTT), while the school system wished to provide an alternative training program. The parents' intensity of feeling is not hard to understand because Lovaas has claimed that children under his program reached "normality" in many instances. Few other programs make this claim. The school districts, however, aware of the high expense and requirements of the Lovaas approach, often seek alternatives to this method. This results in parental distress and legal disputes.

In general, the courts were unwilling to substitute their judgment for that of the school system as to what was appropriate for an individual child, assuming that the districts worked closely with the parents and followed the provisions of IDEA. One case established the legal standard for sound education policy in these disputes (*J. P.* v. *West Clark Community Schools, 2002*):

1. Can the school district articulate its rationale or explain the "specific benefits" of using that approach for the given child?
2. Do the teachers and special educators involved have the necessary experience and expertise to do so successfully?
3. Are there "qualified experts in the educational community who consider the school district's approach to be at least adequate under the circumstances"?

If the answer to these questions is "Yes," the school system will prevail in such disputes.

Although these three requirements would seem to be reasonable propositions, many school systems may have difficulty in meeting them, especially in poor or rural districts. Until there exists a much larger cadre of specially trained teachers or other support personnel capable of meeting the needs of children with autism, it is likely that these disputes will continue.

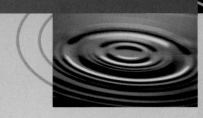

CHILDREN WITH AUTISM SPECTRUM DISORDERS

EDUCATIONAL

▌ Adapting Curriculum

The emphasis on early diagnosis also means that educational programming for the child with autism should begin early as well, sometimes as early as at 2 years of age. During the preschool years the goals are to help the child master basic skills that provide the foundation for future learning. The child must be able to communicate to others, so one major building block is to help him or her attain a *functional communication system*. Second, the child must be able to interact socially with adults and peers, so *basic social skills* (paying attention when others speak, not pushing people out of the way, and so forth) should be learned and practiced.

Functional behavioral analysis (p. 311) may be needed to cope with particular behavioral problems on an individual basis. Once these basic communication and social skills have been learned during the preschool period, the child with autism should be ready to participate meaningfully in the educational system, if there is proper staffing and support for the classroom teacher.

Educational Programs for Early Childhood

A wide variety of treatment programs have been suggested for these young children, based on the proposition that many social and linguistic skills that typical children learn easily by observation and experience, children with autism must learn through direct instruction.

Since language and communication are key problems for children with autism, methods for stimulating communication have received a great deal of attention. For children who are essentially without language or noncommunicative, we must start with very basic steps, often using *applied behavior analysis* methods to form the basis of communication. This means linking isolated words with objects such as a ball, a car, or a block, and rewarding the child for correct identification and speech. This can be the beginning of social and educational interaction for the child.

Later on, many therapists follow a developmental approach. One of the common features of that approach is being "child directed" (Lord, 2001). The child's environment is arranged to provide opportunities for communication, the child initiates the interaction or teaching episode ("I want a cookie!"), and then the teacher or communicative partner, perhaps a parent, follows the child's lead by being responsive to the child's communicative intentions and by imitating or expanding on the child's behavior.

In some cases where the child is unable to respond even at this basic level, an approach known as the augmentative and alternative communication (AAC) and assistive technology may be used. This includes supporting existing speech. Extensive use may be made of pictures displayed on communication boards so that the child, by pointing to the pictures, can communicate his wishes. AAC provides ways to communicate needs and can avoid the development of nonadaptive child behavior such as head banging, biting, throwing objects, and so on, when the child is frustrated in

Autistic children are often withdrawn and unresponsive, but teachers and parents can reach them through a structured early educational program focusing on applied behavioral analysis and reinforcement in both school and home settings.
(© Elizabeth Crews)

his or her attempts to communicate through standard ways. Some of the well-known organized approaches to young children with autism are noted briefly here.

UCLA Young Autism Project (Lovaas, Director) This program uses the principles of *applied behavior analysis* or operant conditioning to directly provide positive rewards when the child behaves correctly. In this way, the child learns to pay attention to adults, to imitate, and to use language for social purposes ("I want some juice"). This one-on-one interaction, with trained students or parents, is often an intensive and painstaking process, and Lovaas insists that 40 hours a week be spent on working directly with the child to ensure that he or she can be ready for first grade with typical children. The approach requires teaching many discrete skills, which are then chained into functional routines (Olley, 1999). The Lovaas program reports significant gains when these methods are closely followed (Lovaas & Buch, 1997).

Cohen (1998) estimated that the process may take several years. It is a very expensive program, and few families can afford the cost of $20,000 to $60,000 per year. Fortunately many states have been able to provide free intervention services for young children with autism so that parents don't have to bear the full burden of this expense. One major problem is that the early childhood teacher must be trained in the Lovaas method, must understand the principles of prompting, fading, and reinforcing desired behaviors, and must be able to administer or supervise the program in a one-on-one situation (Lovaas, 1993).

Other professionals in the field of autism have expressed considerable negative feelings about this approach, as a result of their belief that Lovaas suggested a "cure" could be had for this condition. Lovaas claims that he has been misunderstood and that he never claimed a "cure" for autism—only that a number of young children under his method had reached "normal functioning" by the time they started school.

The *applied behavior analysis* approach that has been a central part of the Lovaas method has been utilized by many others in the field who have adopted it and established treatment programs of their own. Lovaas cautions that unless there is careful monitoring by established and trained professionals (he calls it "clinic supervision") of those who are applying the treatment process, it cannot truly be called the Lovaas method.

TEACCH—University of North Carolina (Mesibov, Director) TEACCH is a statewide program (North Carolina) and has six regional centers. Intensive work is done with parents to help them become teachers for their own child with autism. Extensive use of pictures and other visual symbols are used to help communicate with the child (e.g., "Time to go to the bathroom"). The communication curriculum is based on behavioral principles but applied in more naturalistic settings (home and child-care) (Schopler, Mesibov, & Hearsey, 1995).

A study by Ozonoff and Cathcart (1998) taught parents of young children with autism to use TEACCH instructional methods in the home. In contrast to a "no treatment" control group, the children whose parents used TEACCH methods within the home showed greater improvement in a variety of skills over a four-month interval. The children in both groups were simultaneously receiving day treatment from a variety of settings. Early research by Harris (1995) suggested that most parents require ongoing consultation and support if they are to sustain their role as teachers within the home.

LEAP—University of Colorado (Strain, Director) This program, at its base, attempts to improve the social behavior of children with autism. The curriculum emphasizes independent play and social interaction in naturally occurring routines. Social skills are taught as discrete skills such as "play initiation." Applying the program in an integrative setting with typical children allows for practice in social skills. LEAP has used peer-mediation skills, intervention, training typical peers in ways to enhance social interaction with children with autism. There have been numerous studies demonstrating the effective acquisition of social skills by preschool children with autism (Strain, Kohler, & Goldstein, 1996).

Pivotal Response Model—University of California at Santa Barbara (Koegel and Koegel, Directors) This program often starts with discrete trial behavior analysis similar to the UCLA model, but then moves on to a goal of social and educational proficiency in natural settings. The goal is to achieve change in pivotal areas that have broad generalizations. The emphasis is placed on self-management, motivation, self-initiation, and other abilities that can be transferred from one situation to another. Koegel and Koegel (1995) have developed specific curricula to obtain their reported positive results.

Walden Early Childhood Program—Emory University (McGee, Director) The key to the treatment of children with autism in this program is *incidental teaching* using the spontaneous behavior of the child to teach specific skills such as functional verbal

www.lovaas.com

www.teacch.com

www.education.ucsb.edu/
autism/NIMH.2003.in

language, social responsiveness to adults, participation with typical peers, and methods of self-care (such as toilet training).

There is currently a dearth of scientific evidence to support the claims of these programs, although each program claims substantial success for their methods. Of course, a lack of evidence does not imply that they are not successful, merely that we currently lack the research data to confirm the claims.

Common Threads Among Treatment Programs

Despite the many unique features of the major attempts at treatment of children with autism, Dawson and Osterling (1997) identified five common elements of each:

1. *Common curriculum content.* This includes the ability to selectively attend to stimuli in the environment, stimulating imitative ability, stressing receptive and expressive language, appropriate toy play, and social interaction skills.

2. *Highly supportive and structured teaching environment.* This includes various attempts to encourage generalization from these structural settings to the natural environments of classroom and playground.

3. *Predictability and routine.* All programs contain set routines each day. These increase the security of the child with autism who can be very upset by changes in daily routines.

4. *Functional approach to problem behaviors.* Focus is placed on seeking the causes of problem behavior such as task escape or social inattention, rather than the specific problem behavior itself.

5. *Transition between preschool and kindergarten.* Teaching skills that are essential for functioning in integrated settings.

In addition, most programs put major emphasis on *family involvement,* although the nature of the involvement may vary from one program to another (Gresham, Beebe-Frankenberger, & MacMillan, 1999).

Cure, Recovery, or Improvement?

There is some controversy in the field regarding the terms *cure* and *recovery.* Experts such as Lovaas (1987) have maintained that if children with autism are identified early enough in the preschool-age range and given intensive treatment (40 hours a week), many of them can be indistinguishable from typical children by kindergarten or first grade. In a particular study carried out by Lovaas and his associates (1987), they found that almost half of the sample of children (9 out of 19) in the study who had received intensive treatment were admitted to first grade and were judged not distinguishable from the other students.

Other experts in the field say that while it is true that substantial advances can be made in social development, in communication, and in the reduction of problem behaviors, the child essentially will always have autism and will carry the essence of the syndrome of autism into adulthood.

Thus, while it seems true that children with autism can, with good education, learn to become socialized to a degree, the characteristics of autism (such as social reticence) will always be present. Regardless of the outcome of this controversy, all

Early intervention can greatly improve a child's social development and communication.

A Teenager with Asperger's Syndrome Reporting Her Struggles

IRONING OUT THE WRINKLES

Life was once a tangled mess.
Like missing pieces, in a game of chess.
Like only half a pattern for a dress.
Like saying no, but meaning yes.
Like wanting more, and getting less.
But I'm slowly straightening it out.

Life was once a tangled line.
Like saying yours, and meaning mine.
Like feeling sick, but saying fine.
Like ordering milk, and getting wine.
Like seeing a tree, and saying vine.
But I'm slowly straightening it out.

Life is now a lot more clear.
The tangles are unraveling.
And hope is near.
Sure there are bumps ahead.
But no more do I look on with dread.
After fourteen years the tangles have straightened.

—Vanessa Regal

Source: "Ironing Out the Wrinkles" by Vanessa Regal from Tony Attwood, *Asperger's Syndrome: A guide for parents and professionals* (London: Athenaeum Press, 1998), p. 153. Reprinted with the permission of the author.

of the major figures in the field agree that with early identification and treatment, substantial gains can be made by these children in the areas of special deficits. So the importance of early identification and early treatment becomes critical. The poem "Ironing Out the Wrinkles" is a good illustration of personal progress!

Inclusion in Context: School-Age Children with Autism

Children with autism at school age will undoubtedly have an individualized education program (IEP) planned for them. A multidisciplinary team will be necessary to provide a comprehensive set of plans and experiences for the child. Whether the child is successful or not will depend upon the makeup of the team. Surely there must be someone on the team who knows something about autism and its special issues. We would not think of planning for a child who is deaf without engaging a specialist in the education of children with hearing disabilities. Yet too often we engage in a program for these children with autism with only minimal expertise present.

It is important for the teacher to know that when things get difficult and she calls for help, someone will answer and come running. Few things can be more depressing to the teacher than believing herself totally alone in her attempts to help the children with autism and feeling she has been given a burden that is not shared.

IEP Elements for Sam

AREA	GOALS	SHORT-TERM OBJECTIVES
Academic	1. Sam will improve reading skills to third-grade level. 2. Sam will master fundamentals of addition and subtraction.	1. Sam will complete a book relevant to classmate topics but directed to his limited reading skills. 2. Sam will be given tiered assignments to match his developmental level in arithmetic. He will reach 90% correct level in addition and subtraction problems with two numerals.
Social	1. Sam will improve his social skills. 2. Sam will reduce by one-half his episodes of challenging behavior (fighting).	1. Sam will be placed in cooperative learning groups that have been primed to include him in activity. 2. Functional behavior assessment will be carried out by specialist to determine appropriate replacement behaviors for Sam.
Behavioral	1. Sam will reduce by 50 percent the repetitive movements with his hands (hand flapping).	1. Tasks will be chosen that will require Sam to use his hands in a constructive manner. 2. The teacher will reduce sensory overload and provide calming periods for Sam.

The academic lessons that the child with autism receives can be planned in advance by a team of teachers and aides so that they fit the child's own developmental level. The assignments can be short and not complex, so that the child can see progress and success in these appropriate tasks.

One would expect that each IEP would have some special plans for improving the social skills of the child and would also pay some attention to his or her language development, together with specific plans to cope with disturbing behavior patterns, if they are present.

The box above shows some elements of an individualized education program that might be planned for Sam. Such planning necessitates the presence of specialized assistance, consultation, aides, and others for the general education teacher if it is to work, since few such teachers have the skills or background knowledge or time to carry out that program unaided. Since Sam is behind in fundamental reading and mathematical skills, some specific attention is paid to special *tiered assignments* (assignments adjusted to the developmental level of the child).

Sam's social skills are in substantial need of improvement. Placing him in a small group stressing cooperative learning is one approach to give him experience working with others toward a common goal. The question as to what Sam's fighting is achieving for him (perhaps security, revenge, attention, or status) can be addressed through a *functional behavioral analysis*. We may be able to discover Sam's motivation and prepare some substitute or alternative behaviors to replace the fighting yet obtain the same psychological result for him.

One detriment to Sam's social adjustment has been his "hand flapping" that seems to emerge when he is under stress. His classmates view this repetitive

Strong one-on-one attention seems needed to help children with autism interact socially.
(© Ellen Senisi/The Image Works)

motor movement with his hands as "weird," and that doesn't improve his social standing. It seems appropriate to work on all of these problems simultaneously, and that also requires more personnel than just one classroom teacher in this situation.

One would expect very clear educational objectives, systematically taught with his levels of structure and repetition. The classroom teacher should have aides present to help, and should also have easy consultation available if needed.

Adapting Teaching Strategies

Structure and Routine

Since the child with autism often has difficulty confronting unorganized environments and becomes anxious in an unpredictable classroom, one adaptive strategy has been an approach called Structured Teaching (Mesibov, 1999). Presenting the child with autism an individual daily schedule that describes what is going to happen at each time in the school day becomes a useful support and reduces stress for the child. Creating a consistent physical environment around the child (everything is in the same place from one day to another) can be another source of security.

> A daily schedule and a consistent environment are critical for a child with autism to feel secure.

Since many of these children with autism need structure and order so that they can proceed academically, the teacher is encouraged to provide their assignments in a clear and predictable fashion, as follows (Hogan, 2000):

Child: What am I expected to do?
Teacher: Read pages 34 through 38 in your book *Airplanes of World War II.*

Child: How much am I expected to do?

Teacher: Write two paragraphs about the information you read in the book. Each paragraph should have five sentences.

Child: How will I know when I am finished?

Teacher: When you have finished writing, put your paper in the "Finished Assignments" bin on Mrs. Bates's desk.

Child: What will I do next?

Teacher: Check in your notebook for what is next on your daily schedule.

For a student who is not well organized, these precise instructions provide the structure he needs in order to make progress on his assignments.

If we accept, as we should, the proposition that children with autism rarely learn important concepts in the social or cognitive realms through incidental learning, then we must provide direct teaching experience. While the typical child may quickly observe that "getting in line" or "taking one's turn" is important to getting along in class and with one's peers, such ideas must be directly taught to the child with autism. Part of the problems that the child with autism has socially occur precisely because these observations of others and incidental learning are absent to a large degree. The advantage for the general education teacher is that the child with autism, once taught these rules and allowed to practice their use, can perform acceptably and thus show substantial improvement, over time, in classroom behavior.

Although the child with high-functioning autism can have general good proficiency in language, there is a tendency toward literal interpretation, which causes the child to not understand neither jokes that depend on a play on words, nor metaphors, nor common idioms such as these (Attwood, 1998, p. 77):

> Has the cat got your tongue?
> Keep your eye on the ball.
> You're pulling my leg.
> Pull yourself together.

This literal-mindedness lends an appearance of naiveté that can interfere with socialization.

Improving Social Skills

Since one of the prime areas concerning the education of children with autism is the lack of social sensitivity and social skills that most typical children display, there have been many attempts to counteract that lack. Of course, children with autism are not totally devoid of social skills. McGee and her colleagues (McGee, Feldman, & Morrier, 1997) found that young children with autism engage to some degree in play, social participation, and social interaction, only much less than the typical child of the same age. The special needs of children with autism spectrum disorders often require a change in the teaching approach to the student. Neihart (2000) suggests frequent use of diagrams, visualization, and pictograms in the lessons provided to children with Asperger's syndrome or high-functioning children with autism, since they think best in concrete and literal pictures.

The use of social stories is often employed by the teacher; this involves the child writing a very short story that describes a specific social situation with which the child struggles. These social stories are designed to teach the cues and

Using visual aids and pictures helps the child with autism to grasp concepts more easily.

behaviors for specific social situations. Here is an example (Neihart, 2000, p. 227):

> Sometimes my friend Toni tells me to "chill." This means I am getting loud and bossy. Toni doesn't want to sit with me when I am loud and bossy. I will lower my voice when Toni tells me to "chill." When Toni tells me to "chill," I can imagine putting my voice on ice.

The use of "free play" with young children is designed to allow them to explore various activities and areas of the classroom, and to gain much incidental learning as a result. Children with autism, however, must be guided into such activities, or their tendency toward withdrawal and self-stimulation will continue.

One attempt to intervene on their behalf was described in a study in which photographs of various play areas are identified, and the children with autism are asked to pick the areas they intend to play in (Morrison, Sainato, Benchaaban, & Endo, 2002). Their choice of photographs of play areas are placed on a bulletin board and they are encouraged to follow their choices.

Children with autism can follow such a schedule with encouragement, and the result is that autistic children can engage in more effective and interactive play behavior with other children. The lesson here is that the teachers have to be active in designing activities that increase autistic children's play and social behavior.

A wide variety of approaches have been tried to enhance the social abilities, and a recent attempt to summarize the results of many studies of these various approaches has been completed (McConnell, 2000). McConnell divided these approaches that are designed to improve social skills into five major categories and then assessed what the research had to say about each it applied to children with autism.

Ecological Variations This refers to changes in the physical environment for that child or modifications in activity, schedule, or structure designed to enhance social interaction. "Ecological variations can, under some conditions, produce weak to moderate effects on the social interaction of young children with autism."

Collateral Skills Interventions Collateral skills interventions are attempts to improve play skills, academic responses, or sociodramatic play. Do such improvements result in increased social interaction? "Collateral skills interventions may increase social interaction by bringing children with autism into contact with typically developing peers, and by activating social interaction processes by giving children with autism greater competencies and rewarding social contacts."

Child-Specific Interventions These interventions may include general instructional interventions to improve social problem solving (social stories), using direct social skills training, and various generalization promotion techniques (particularly self-monitoring). "Child-specific interventions, in isolation, would seem to have limited potential since these interventions tend to focus more on social initiations, rather than other elements of sustained and high-quality social interaction."

Peer-Mediated Intervention Procedures These are approaches in which the teacher helps peers to learn how to interact with the child with autism. By changing the related social behaviors of peers, they change the social interactions for young children with autism. "Peer-mediated interventions have demonstrated powerful and robust treatment effects across a number of studies. Such approaches must

Peer interaction is one important element in the special education of children with autism.
(© Robin Nelson/Photo Edit)

demonstrate lasting effects on the social behavior of children with autism to justify the efforts made."

Comprehensive Interventions These contain two or more components of the other intervention styles reported above. These include some form of social skills training for all children, some delivery of teacher prompts, reinforcement in free play, and the promotion of reciprocal interactions between children with autism and their peers. "Interventions directed to both young children with autism and their typically developing peers can produce pronounced effects on social interactions in intervention settings with some generalization to other settings."

Kennedy & Shukla (1995) have reported that children with autism can benefit from purposeful social interaction skills intervention. They believe that social interactions can be taught and learned, that "social interaction in typical settings can be successfully accomplished and substantial positive outcomes accrue." McConnell (2000) concluded that promoting social interaction development should be a routine component of any comprehensive treatment program for children with autism.

One of the favorite educational strategies designed to cope with some of the behavior manifestations of autism is **functional behavior assessment.** This means that instead of concentrating on the specific behavior of the child, the teacher or therapist or parent tries to assess the meaning of that behavior to the child.

If Mike attacks other people, in addition to dealing directly with the behavior, the educational team tries to understand how the attacks benefit Mike. Is he using this as a means for gaining attention, for communicating some need that he is unable to express verbally? We can then try to help him use alternative means for attaining his goals.

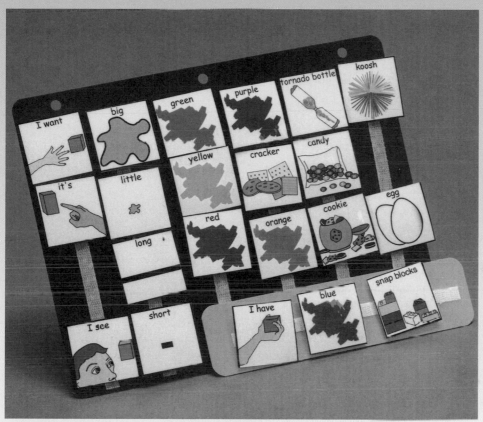

Example of Picture Exchange Communication System (PECS).
(© Pyramid Educational Products, Inc.)

This does not mean, of course, that you allow Mike to continue to hit people while you figure out the true meaning of his behavior, but if these attacks have become a constant problem, it means trying to deduce the motivation behind it and substituting some more acceptable way for him to achieve his goals of obtaining parental or teacher attention: perhaps a small bell to ring when he wants his parents' attention or a physical sign like raising his arm. This search for the child's intentions has proven to be more effective in modifying the child's actions than merely direct punishment for unacceptable behavior.

Adapting Technology

The importance of communication to the child with autism is universally agreed upon. When the child does not develop speech and receptive language in the usual fashion, a wide variety of devices (called augmentative and alternative communication [AAC]) are tried to augment or increase the child's communication skills (Miranda & Erickson, 2000). This may include the Picture Exchange Communication System (PECS) or on occasion teaching the child some elements of

www Houghton Mifflin Teacher Education website http://education.college.hmco.com.students

Children with autism may learn eye-hand coordination using a computer mouse. A touch screen helps a child understand sending commands to the computer by using touch.

American Sign Language. See the Houghton Mifflin Teacher Education website for an expanded list of assistive technology equipment.

Sometimes a communication board is used, such as the one shown in the box, so that basic communication is established between child and adult. Here the child can communicate basic needs and feelings and the adult can respond in kind. There is an increasing use of photographs to aid in this type of communication.

Now available are other aids, known as Voice-Output Communication Aids (VOCA), to store recorded messages that the child can trigger. These can range from a series of twenty messages, each 20 seconds long, to complex messages that can be changed according to the situation so that the student can participate ("Hi, how are you today?").

Also, a computer can be combined with synthetic speech to allow the child to enter the initial letter of a word to produce an onscreen list of common words that begin with the selected letter. Those who cannot read can use a mouse or arrow key to select words that are recited out loud by the speech synthesizer.

The improvement of communication devices also seems to have a favorable effect on controlling or reducing challenging behavior. Some challenging behavior seems to be caused by the inability to communicate needs and wishes. Augmentative communication aids that set up pictorial or written schedules help the individual to follow predictable sequences (Wood, Lasker, Siegel-Causey, Beukelman, & Ball, 1998) which, in turn, helps reduce this challenging behavior. Although evaluative research measuring the impact of these methods and devices appears to be largely missing, we will likely see an increase in the use of these methods and technology to aid children with autism in communicating.

| Sample Communication Board

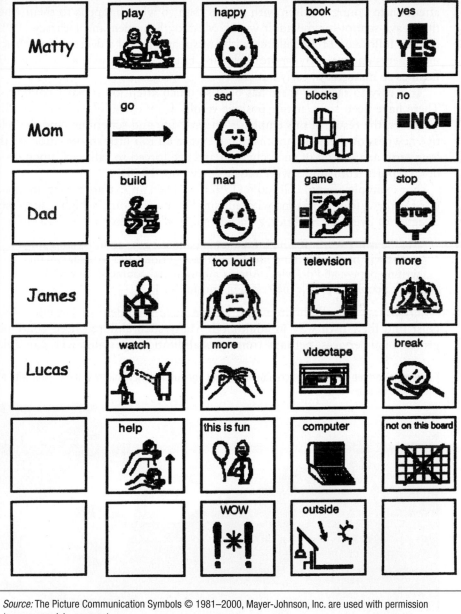

Source: The Picture Communication Symbols © 1981–2000, Mayer-Johnson, Inc. are used with permission (www.mayer-johnson.com).

■ Transition

What happens to children with autism spectrum disorders when they become young adults? The National Academy of Sciences report (Lord, 2001) calls for more longitudinal research, but the truth is that the field has paid much more attention to young children with autism than to what happens to them when they leave school for the adult world. Mesibov Schopler, and Hearsey (1999) did one follow-up of 59 children with autism and found a decrease in physical movements and repetitive motor behavior, but a continuation of the social difficulties so manifest in early autism.

It is easy to see why there has been so much attention to early childhood. There have been some major positive results from early intervention studies. However, the result of this emphasis on early life and schooling, and the relative newness of this field, means that we have all too little information on the long-term adaptation of such children and are forced to fall back upon anecdotal reports from adults with autism (Attwood, 1998).

For example, Temple Grandin (1992) has been an extraordinary ambassador for the cause of persons with autism. She has become a highly successful designer of livestock facilities, an academic, and an author.

> My life is my work. If a high-functioning autistic gets an interesting job, he or she will have a fulfilling life. I spend most Friday and Saturday nights writing papers and drawing. Almost all my social contacts are with livestock people or people interested in autism. (p. 123)

Of course not all children with autism have the talent of Grandin. They must find their own way in adulthood. Many such children need continued professional services, perhaps from a rehabilitation specialist who can guide

| Advocate Temple Grandin has created important agricultural technology while coping with autism. (© Rosalie Winard)

Successful vocational placements for teenagers with autism stress strengths and downplay social problems. (© Robin Nelson/Photo Edit)

young adults with autism spectrum disorders to appropriate community services and even help them find employment. There is a possible elevated rate of depression in adults with autism that needs medical and psychiatric attention.

The general recommendation for vocational placements stresses the strengths of the child with autism and plays down the social problems. The requirement in IDEA for beginning planning for adult adjustment in the IEPs of teenagers with disabilities seems very appropriate here. And we would expect to find them working with computers or going into engineering or a similar occupation that downplays social interaction and emphasizes focused work on inanimate objects.

One way to improve our limited knowledge is for centers for treatment of children with autism to maintain their contacts with these children as they go through adolescence and early adulthood, so that we can find out more about the challenges they face in early adulthood and how they have adapted to them.

Family and Lifespan

To provide an appropriate education for their child, parents of children with autism need specialized skills. Prime among these are the mastery of specific teaching strategies enabling them to help their child acquire new behaviors. Parents need, too, an understanding of the nature of autism and how it influences their child's learning patterns and behavior. They need to know special-education laws and regulations and how to negotiate on behalf of their child. In addition, some parents need help in coping with the emotional stress that can follow from having a child with a significant developmental disorder.

Among specific concerns expressed by mothers are worry about their child's welfare in the years ahead, the child's ability to function independently, and the community's acceptance of their child (Koegel et al., 1992). Mothers of children with autism also report more stress in their lives than do mothers of children with other disabilities (see, for example, Rodriguez, Morgan, & Geffken, 1990).

Mothers usually carry a much greater burden of care for these children than fathers do. The difference is not due solely to the father's employment outside of the home. Bristol, Gallagher, and Schopler (1988) reported that mothers who worked in jobs outside the home still felt a greater child-care burden than did their employed husbands. The siblings of children with autism can have their lives seriously disrupted, and they should be considered part of a comprehensive treatment program (Konidaris, 1997). Since siblings are often enrolled in the same school, a sensitive teacher can help a child respond to questions about his sibling's autism (Lord, 2001). Konidaris also found that expressive positive support from one's partner was an important predictor of the quality of parenting in the home.

One of the promising attempts to modify the behavior of young children with autism focuses on the relationship between the parents and the child.

Mahoney and Perales (2003) report a yearlong intervention with 20 young children with autism spectrum disorders (80 percent under the age of 3, the rest under 6).

The intervention approach is **relationship focused (RF)** that encourages parents to use responsible interaction strategies (for example, take turns) during routine interaction with their children. Parents of children with autism were seen in one-hour sessions for an average of 30 sessions. The parents were taught a variety of techniques for "responsive interaction" with their child, and they reported using these strategies with that child at home for about two hours a day.

Using a variety of measures, the authors reported significant improvements in social-emotional functioning that included decreases in detachment and underactivity, and increases in social competence, including empathy and cooperation. The authors concluded that enhanced maternal responsiveness encourages children to use the behaviors necessary for attaining higher levels of social-emotional and developmental functioning.

Gains in social behaviors and communication were reported in those children whose mothers showed substantial improvement in becoming more responsive, and few children gained when the mother did not improve.

Koegel, Koegel, and Carter (1999) reported on the importance of the child's mastering pivotal response behaviors such as attachment, empathy, cooperation, and self-regulation. These pivotal response behaviors then form the base for more advanced developmental behaviors for the child. It is extremely important that the parents be encouraged, or they may give up attempts to communicate with the child following initial frustrations and failure.

We can sum up the family issues for the child with autism as follows:

1. Parents can learn how to teach adaptive skills and manage the behavior of their child with autism.
2. For some families, having a child with autism creates measurable stress, and support services should be available for the parents.
3. Parents' use of effective teaching methods for their child with autism can have a measurable impact on the reduction of family stress.

Currently, we do not have extensive information as to what happens to the greater number of children with autism when their time in school is finished and they must find a way into the larger world. We do have some individual memoirs by persons with autism (Grandin, 1995), which remind us that even though the basic condition remains, these adults have made effective adaptation and are gainfully employed. One of the next steps surely is how we can help youths with autism to make the shift from school to work.

Many parents of children with autism have found to their dismay that although there is legislation establishing their child's right to a free and appropriate education (FAPE), this does not mean that these laws and regulations will be implemented at the local level. The huge expense (often $20,000 to $60,000 per child) of the intensive treatment programs have led local schools to plan for something less than the intensive treatment that many Lovaas followers and others insist upon. Indeed, the National Academy of Sciences report *Educating*

Children with Autism recommends no fewer than 25 hours of treatment a week for young autistic children (Lord, 2001).

The result of these intensive-treatment recommendations has been that many court hearings have been brought by parents trying to force the schools to provide necessary services, while the schools often respond that they are doing as much as they can (see the Rowley case in Chapter 2). This is still an unsettled policy issue, and court cases have been decided on an individual basis—sometimes in favor of the family, sometimes in favor of the schools (Mandlawitz, 1999).

These children with autism spectrum disorders have presented a puzzle to parents, to the schools, and to the professionals with whom they come into contact. In light of the substantial progress made in the last part of the twentieth century, we look forward in the twenty-first to needed breakthroughs.

Should There Be New Policies?

Do we need new educational policies for children with autism? A number of parents and advocates for children with autism wish to develop new legislation to ensure that these children will receive the maximum of educational benefits. There are others, however, who have pointed out that the Individuals with Disabilities Education Act (IDEA) really covers the essential needs of such children. To see how this works, we can go back to the six fundamental legal rights embedded in the original Education for All Handicapped Children Act (PL 94-142).

1. *Zero Reject.* All children with disabilities must be provided a free and appropriate public education.
   For children with autism, this means that no such child, regardless of degree of impairment or manifestation of difficult behavior, can be denied educational services.
2. *Nondiscriminatory Evaluation.* Each student must receive a full individual examination before being placed in a special educational program with tests appropriate to the child's cultural and linguistic background.
   For children with autism this means an appropriate evaluation to be carried out by personnel with the experience in the use of the appropriate tests and protocols for such children.
3. *An Individualized Education Program (IEP).* An IEP must be written for every student with a disability who is receiving special education.
   For children with autism, this is an important provision because it requires the schools to develop a program that fits the needs of this particular child and not to just routinely place the child in a special education program that already exists for other children with special needs.
4. *Least Restrictive Environment.* As much as possible, children with disabilities must be educated with children without disabilities. The edu-

ECOLOGY OF THE CHILD

FAMILY

My name is Viki Gayhardt. Autism/PDD is a hidden disability and, without a doubt, our children are some of the most physically beautiful children on earth. I think it's because of this reason that their needs are often misunderstood, underestimated, or just completely overlooked. This mistake is especially true for the less involved, more verbal children. I have two children: six year old Justine and two and a half year old Vinny. Both my children have been diagnosed with PDDNOS, but today I'm going to tell Jussy's story.

Justine was my first child after seven years of marriage. I was working full-time and quit my job to stay home with her. She received 150% of my attention, at least. I was very concerned when her peers started to skyrocket past her in various areas of development. Her idiosyncratic behaviors were plentiful. The list goes on and on. Justine was very active. She rocked. She lined up toys—miles and miles of toys all around the house. She liked to put hairy things in her mouth. She'd bite the hair off those little troll dolls. She always had something swirling around on her tongue. Above all, she would recite lines from movies with such character and animation that people would say, "That kid's got to be on Broadway," and urge me to get her an agent. "She's got to be a model, she's got to be in the movies."

The best advice the developmental pediatrician gave me on the day Justine was diagnosed was to contact the local support group leader, who is also a mother of a child with autism/PDD. I found other parents to be our greatest resource—their help was invaluable, and it still is to this day. Not only to me, but to our local Special Education (SPED) Director. One day he confessed to me that he really didn't know what he was dealing with concerning autism/PDD. He wanted to learn more. It was our local support group leader whom he called to get further direction and guidance. I think I have a really good relationship with the school and I feel we've built that relationship on a mutual desire: to learn more about autism/PDD. We've been learning together.

Regretfully, but truthfully, I'll admit that community inclusion has been a painful experience for me.

cational philosophy is to move the child with special needs as close to the normal setting as feasible.

For the child with autism this means that there is an expectation that this child should be interacting on a regular basis with children without autism if at all possible. The school must make a special statement as to why a child will not be placed in the regular classroom, when another placement is recommended.

5. *Due Process.* Due process is a set of legal procedures to ensure the fairness of educational decisions and the accountability of both professionals and parents in making those decisions.

For the child with autism this means that the parents can call a hearing when they do not agree with the school's plan for the child. They can

We've tried story hours, soccer, T-ball, church events, school events, old home events, and it's always a constant, painful reminder that autism will always challenge my family and separate us. I recently learned that there is a clinical term for this kind of mourning: it's called chronic sorrow. A good example of chronic sorrow would be a scene that took place at my daughter's sixth birthday party. We had it at a McDonald's PlayPlace, and we invited 20 kids from Justine's kindergarten. One of the children was a little boy who has autism/PDD, who was a bit more involved than Justine. On one side of the Play-Place was that little boy with his Mom. She was really struggling to keep him focused and prevent him from falling apart in this total sensory overload situation. On the other side of the PlayPlace were the parents of the typical kids, I call them "tippies." The tippies were laughing, drinking their coffee, and eating their burgers. They were totally oblivious to what a luxury their circumstances would be for the Mom on the other side. It was an opportunity for me to step back and watch and be objective for a change, but the only thing I could really see was that mother's pain. I could read it on her face. "God, get me through this next hour. I want to get out of here, I want to get out of here." She and I discussed this

afterwards, and we talked about how hard it is—it doesn't matter how long you do it, or how often you practice. That separateness is always going to be there. It's chronic sorrow.

Source: From Viki Gayhardt, *At home with autism: Three families' stories.* Reprinted with permission. This is a partial transcription from an oral presentation given by the author on the subject of community inclusion and autism.

WHAT IS THE CONTEXT?

Justine's mother is very involved with Justine and noticed early in her development that she displayed behaviors different from those of her peers. Becoming involved with other parents of children with autism has been a great support for Justine's mother. The awareness of her child not fitting in is a sorrow that stays with this mother.

PIVOTAL ISSUES FOR TEACHERS

- As a teacher, what can you do to include children with autism in classroom activities?

- How can you encourage consistency and routine in your classroom?

- In what ways will you need additional assistance to support students with autism in your classroom?

obtain an individual evaluation from a qualified examiner outside the school system or take other action to ensure that both family and child have channels through which to voice their interests and concerns.

6. *Parental Participation.* Parents are to be included in the development of the IEP and have a right to access their child's educational records. *For the child with autism this means that parents can obtain the test results and educational evaluation of their child and can participate as equals in the development of the IEP.*

This important legislation, IDEA, is essentially neutral with regard to particular children with special needs. It fits children with mental retardation, or cerebral palsy, or autism equally. The legislation can be used to deal with the special needs of each of these groups of special children.

Summary

▶ Autism is a pervasive developmental disorder affecting communication and social development and causing at times a variety of unusual behaviors and unusual reactions to sensory stimulation.

▶ This condition of autism can be recognized in a child as early as at 2 years of age. Beginning intensive treatment immediately is strongly recommended.

▶ Although the majority of children with autism seem to be developmentally delayed, there is a subgroup, children with Asperger's syndrome, who can be highly intelligent and academically able, but who have the same social problems as children with autism.

▶ The prevalence of children with this condition appears to be steadily rising. It now is estimated at 1 in 1000, or even more. The reason for the increase is not clear. It may be because we are now identifying as autistic children who previously would have been labeled differently (mentally retarded, for example). Or there may be a genuine increase in autism, for reasons not yet known. The gender ratio remains constant: Four times as many autistic boys are found as girls.

▶ Focus on social skills development includes changes in environment, the teaching of collateral skills, direct social skills training, or peer-mediated intervention.

▶ Improvements in communication are often carried out in natural environments, both home and school, using the child's natural interests in play to develop and expand communication.

▶ For children without the use of language, augmentative and alternative methods of communication are employed, such as pictures that are organized especially for communication.

▶ Many programs of treatment exist, often in competition with one another. All report clinical successes in terms of improving social and academic skills, but we still need careful research to document these treatments and their long-term effects.

▶ Despite the variety of approaches, all major treatment programs include common elements such as similar curriculum content, structured teaching environments, predictable routines, functional approaches to problem behavior, and the teaching of transition skills to prepare children for kindergarten.

▶ The major problem of implementation in the schools centers around both the high costs of such treatment and the lack of trained personnel to administer it.

Future Challenges

1. Will there be enough trained personnel?

The education of children with autism requires very special preparation. Few teachers, in either general or special education, have mastered the methods of applied behavior analysis or the other instructional strategies designed to enhance the social development and communication skills of children with autism. How will these needs for trained personnel be met?

2. Will new medical treatments become available?

To date, medical or pharmaceutical treatments have had uncertain effects on children with autism. With our increasing sophistication and understanding of brain function and the genetic code, can there be some future help for families affected by autism?

3. Who will pay for expensive educational treatments?

Some states have established emergency funds to aid the ability of local schools to supplement the education costs for these children. Medicaid has been used in other states to defray the education costs. No easy way out seems currently available.

4. Will there be enough funding to research new methods for developing social skills and communication?

We should anticipate the further validation and dissemination of the various methods used to improve the functioning of children with autism in behavior management, social skills, and communication, given sufficient research and development funds that would be obtained mainly from the federal governmental level.

Key Terms

Asperger's syndrome   *p. 296*
collateral skills interventions   *p. 314*
ecological variations   *p. 314*

Resources

References of Special Interest

Attwood, T. (1998). *Asperger's syndrome: A guide for parents and professionals.* Philadelphia: Jessica Kingsley Publishers, Ltd. *One special variation in the autism spectrum disorders is Asperger's syndrome. Although they have many standard characteristics of autistic children, such as inability to socialize, clumsy and ill-coordinated movements, and intense absorption in certain subjects, children with Asperger's syndrome often show high intellectual ability. This book is a fine introduction to a fascinating variation on the autistic condition sometimes referred to as high-functioning autism.*

Cohen, D., & Volkmar, F. (Eds.). (1997). *Handbook of autism and pervasive developmental disorders.* New York: Cambridge University Press. *This is a state-of-the-art account of what is known about autism, produced by a multidisciplinary set of experts. Individual chapters cover the psychological dimensions, neuropharmacology, educational approaches, and the evidence for a genetic component. A chapter on adult outcomes provides perspective on what lies ahead for children who have autism.*

Cohen, S. (1998). *Targeting autism.* Berkeley: University of California Press. *This distillation of thirty years of clinical experience informs parents, educators, and students about the condition of autism and particularly addresses the various controversies currently abroad in the professional fields that deal with children with autism. It contains many specific examples and useful quotes from parents about their autistic children.*

Lord, C. (Ed.). (2001). *Educating children with autism.* Washington, DC: National Academy of Science. *A multidisciplinary committee assembled by the National Academy of Sciences reports on the effectiveness of various attempts at providing educational programming for children with autism. A series of recommendations confront remaining problems and issues and point the way toward better resources and results.*

Mesibov, G., Shea, G., & Schopler, E. (2004). *The TEACCH approach to autism spectrum disorders.* New York: Springer. *A compilation of decades of work on children with autism at the Division TEACCH (Treatment and Education of Autistic and related Communication handicapped Children) center at the University of North Carolina at Chapel Hill. It highlights an individualized approach to each child and provides a description of structured teaching, surrounding the child with an organized physical environment, developing work schedules and work systems, developing clear and explicit expectations, and stressing the visual channel for instruction.*

Wetherby, A., & Prizant, B. (Eds.). (2000). *Autism spectrum disorders: A transactional development perspective* (vol. 9). Baltimore: Paul H. Brookes. *This volume is part of a communication and language intervention series designed to provide foundations for the use of intervention to enhance development of communication skills. The book has two main sections, each with a variety of chapters written by different experts. Part 1 deals with the theoretical and research foundations on the development context of autism. Part 2 deals with assessment and intervention issues.*

Journals

Journal of Autism and Developmental Disorders
    www.teacch.com/publications/journadd.htm

Journal of Applied Behavior Analysis
    www.envmed.rochester.edu/wwwrap/behavior/jaba/jabahme.htm

Journal of Child Psychology and Psychiatry
    uk.cambridge.org/journals/cpp/cppifc.htm

Topics in Early Childhood Special Education
    www.decs.act.gov.au

Professional Organizations

Autism Network International
    www.ani.ac

Autism Research Institute (ARI)
    www.autism.com/ari

Autism Society of America
    www.autism-society.org

Indiana Resource Center for Autism (IRCA) Institute for the Study of Developmental Disabilities
    www.iidc.indiana.edu/irca

On-line Asperger's Syndrome Information and Support (OASIS)
    www.udel.edu/bkirby/asperger

The National Information Center for Children and Youth with Disabilities (NICHCY)
    www.nichcy.org

Please visit the book's website at
http://education.college.hmco.com/students for new and updated information on websites listed here and for the mailing addresses of the journals and organizations.

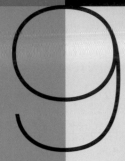

CHILDREN WHO ARE GIFTED AND TALENTED

FOCUS QUESTIONS

▶ How do public schools define children who are gifted and talented?

▶ What are some characteristics of children who are gifted and talented?

▶ How can we modify curriculum to accommodate a student's special gifts and talents?

▶ What are some special problems of gender for students who are gifted?

▶ How has the educational reform movement affected programs for students who are gifted?

▶ How can gifted and talented students from diverse cultures be better identified and served?

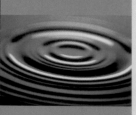

Two major values, *equity* and *excellence,* have driven American education for many years. We wish to ensure, first, that every child, whatever his or her background, disability, or ethnic origin, gets a fair and equal opportunity for quality educational services (equity). We even accept the concept of *vertical equity,* "the unequal treatment of unequals in order to make them more equal." Programs such as Head Start and legislation such as No Child Left Behind reflect that value. Next, we want to make sure that all students, including those with extraordinary talent in the arts, sciences, business, and other fields, have full opportunity to develop their gifts (excellence). And we do this because we recognize that their excelling in these fields means that society as a whole will flourish.

Since there are only scarce resources to be divided among our needs and goals, these two values, *equity* and *excellence,* sometimes bump into one another. In the first part of the twenty-first century, the scales seem to tip strongly in the direction of equity. So at the present time there are far fewer public resources available for gifted children than for children who need special help to be able to survive academically and socially in this culture.

Students who are gifted are different in many key ways from the other groups of exceptional children discussed in this text. Children with exceptionalities such as learning disabilities, mental retardation, or autism find themselves in trouble academically and have difficulty in catching up to the average students. It is the role of the special educator to help these students develop to the limits of their capabilities. The gifted students, in contrast, have already achieved more than average students and may be operating at two or three grade levels above their own. Yet students with a surplus of ability or talent can pose a problem for the classroom teacher. We should concern ourselves with such students because of evidence that they will fill many leadership positions and roles in our future society. They will make many of the new scientific discoveries, shape our future artistic productions. It is in the best interest of society as a whole to see to it that these gifted and talented students perform to the best of their potential—and we have evidence that this is not happening now.

In this chapter, we discuss the special characteristics that set these students apart from nonidentified students. We explore how the schools attempt to adapt programs to meet the special needs of students who are gifted, in what ways educational reform movements have been affecting their education, and what is currently being done to find "hidden giftedness" in our schools to help those students reach a higher level of proficiency.

One of the strong motivating forces supporting special educational opportunities for students who are gifted has been negative reports about how U.S. students perform in comparison with students of other countries. Our best students, in an academic sense, do not compare favorably with the best students from other countries. We have come to assume that Americans are in first place in everything. However, a series of international comparisons indicates that that assumption is far from accurate. Ross (1993) reports in a study on national excellence the following:

> Americans assume that our best students can compete with the best students anywhere. This is not true. International assessments focused attention on the relatively poor standing of all students. These tests also show

National Association for Gifted Children
www.nagc.org

The Association for the Gifted, a division of the Council for Exceptional Children
www.cec.sped.org

that our top-performing are undistinguished at best and poor at worst when compared with top students in other countries. (p. 8)

Another wake-up call to American educators came with the publication of the results of the Third International Mathematics and Science Study (TIMSS, 1998). This study, which involved about 15,000 schools around the world in tests of their mastery of mathematics and science at the fourth-, eighth-, and twelfth-grade levels, revealed disturbing results for American students.

American middle school students are below average in math and science compared with students in other countries.

At the fourth grade, American students appeared to be performing above average for the fourteen countries that participated in the TIMSS study. That result changed, however, at the middle-school level, with American students falling below average in both subjects. The twelfth-grade results were even more devastating, with the American students at or near the bottom of the over twenty countries with which they were compared.

Clearly, there needs to be concern about the performance of all our students in these critical curricular areas. The students who will be expected to go on to higher education and graduate education would be of particular concern, if they have not mastered the basics of mathematics and science in their elementary and secondary years.

■ Definitions

Children from all cultural groups, economic levels, and areas of human endeavor show outstanding talents.

The term *gifted* traditionally has been used to refer to people with intellectual gifts, and we use it here in the same way. Each culture defines *giftedness* in its own image, in terms of the abilities that culture values. Ancient Greeks honored the philosopher and the orator, and Romans valued the engineer and the soldier. From a society's definition of giftedness, we learn something about the values and lifestyles of the culture. We also learn that the exceptional person often is defined by both individual ability and societal needs.

In the United States, early definitions of giftedness were tied to performance on the Stanford-Binet Intelligence Test, which Lewis Terman developed during and after World War I. Children who scored above an agreed-upon point—such as 130 or 140—were called gifted. They represented from 1 to 3 percent of their age-group population (Terman & Oden, 1947).

Essentially, a high score on the Stanford-Binet or on other intelligence tests meant that children were intellectually developing more rapidly than their age-mates. What was unique was not so much *what* they were doing as *when,* developmentally, they were doing it. A child playing chess is not a phenomenon, but a child playing chess seriously at age 5 is. Many children write poetry, but not at age 6, when most are just learning to read. Early rapid development is one of the clear indicators of high intellectual ability, and that is what intelligence tests measure.

It was long thought that intelligence was distributed in society in conformity with the normal curve, with many students likely to have about average IQ scores of 100 and fewer expected to score extremely high. This "normal curve" distribution of scores was one of the reasons for assuming that intelligence was a biological property, since other characteristics such as height and weight showed similar normal curve distributions.

But now we have evidence that intelligence scores do *not* form a normal distribution, certainly not at the extreme ends (Robinson, Zigler, & Gallagher, 2000; Silverman, 1997). Few children's IQ scores fall below 70 without some pathological cause, and there seem to be many more youngsters at the top end of the distribution (scoring over 140) than would be expected on the basis of a normal curve distribution (Silverman, 1997).

When we combine this discovery with investigations that suggest that entire populations of countries are performing better on tests of ability than a generation before (Flynn, 1999), we must confront the notion that IQ scores are not fixed for an individual or a society but can be improved with education and experience. We are not limited in the number of highly intelligent students we can produce, but have as a prospect a gradually increasing supply of highly intelligent people—if we are wise enough to create the conditions for their development.

Over the past few decades, periodic efforts have been made to broaden the definition of giftedness to include more than abilities directly related to schoolwork. Table 9.1 presents a federal definition of children who are gifted. Within the definition in Table 9.1 are many phrases that reveal our current thinking about gifted students. The phrase "show the potential for performing" means we accept the idea that children can be gifted without showing excellent performance. "Compared with others of their age, experience, or environment" means we accept the important role of environment and context in producing gifted students. The phrase "require services . . . not ordinarily provided" means we expect that school systems will and should modify their services and programs to take into account the different levels of development of these students. "Outstanding talents are present in children . . . from all cultural groups, across all economic strata" means teachers should be encouraged to seek special talent from all cultural groups.

Other definitions of giftedness try to include the way an individual defines and then tackles a problem—the ability to *problem-find* and *problem-solve* (Gardner, 1985; Getzels, 1978; Siegler, 1986; Sternberg, 1991). In the real world, problems do not come in neat packages ready for solving. Usually, they

Teachers need to be aware of special talents present in children from all cultures and economic backgrounds.

TABLE 9.1
Federal Definition of Students Who Are Gifted

Children and youth with outstanding talent perform, or show the potential for performing, at remarkably high levels of accomplishment when compared with others of their age, experience, or environment.

These children and youth exhibit high-performance capability in intellectual, creative, and/or artistic areas, possess an unusual leadership capacity, or excel in specific academic fields. They require services or activities not ordinarily provided by the schools.

Outstanding talents are present in children and youth from all cultural groups, across all economic strata, and in all areas of human endeavor.

Source: P. Ross (Ed.). (1993). *National Excellence.* Washington, DC: U.S. Department of Education.

are hard to define and organize—they are what Simon (1979) called *ill structured.* The ability to take an ill-structured problem and organize it so the issue is clear is one indicator of giftedness.

Despite the addition of creativity, problem-finding and problem-solving skills, and different types of intelligence to our definition of giftedness, emphasis is still placed on intelligence tests as one means of identifying children who are gifted. Why? Because these tests have been effective in predicting performance in school-related activities for many students.

■ Components of Intellectual Competence

What are the components of intellectual competence? What does a student who is gifted need to be productive, and what must the schools offer to such a student? As noted in Chapter 1, Perkins (1995) believes that competence reflects three major factors:

▶ The power of a person's neurological computer

▶ The tactical repertoire or cognitive strategies that a person can bring to bear

▶ Context-specific content and know-how

Students who are gifted appear to have advantages across the full range of information processing. They tend to grasp new ideas faster, they see more associations between ideas, and they have a rich storehouse of concepts and systems of

A Poem Written by a Gifted Seven-Year-Old

INDECISION

She wears a colourful summery skirt
A thick dark purple coat.
Her house has a very dark blue roof
And a light yellow base
Her shutters are half closed half open

She likes to play with Crazy and Adventurous
But every time she goes to see them
She walks out the front door,
Then thinks she should have
Gone through the back door.

She really would like to eat hot food
But she prefers cold food.
She loves to cook
But normally eats out.

She would do things in the weekend
Except it takes till Monday to decide what.

(Katrina, age 7)

Source: D. Fraser, From the playful to the profound: What metaphors tell us about gifted children, *Roeper Review* 25 (4) (2003): 180–184. Reprinted with permission.

ideas to apply to individual problems. They also have a superior ability to use cognitive strategies, which increases their ability to cope with difficult assignments. In most instances, their ability to reason—that is, to use existing information to generate new information—is at a level two to three years or more beyond that of their agemates. Note the previous poem as an illustration of advanced thinking.

It is the responsibility of the schools to help students develop both learning strategies and content mastery. The notion that the student who is gifted will automatically learn these strategies or knowledge, however, is an idea that dies hard. The tactics or strategies that these students employ as they try to cope with difficult problems must be explicitly taught because they will rarely be spontaneously discovered. This collection of strategies is often referred to as the *executive function*.

The student will not naturally stumble on the process of multiplication (which, after all, is a strategy for processing information), principles of logical analysis, problem finding, and a number of other devices that are useful tools to the serious thinker. All these strategies must be taught. Occasionally, a student who is gifted will intuitively solve a problem in an innovative fashion, but unless the student explicitly recognizes the method, he or she will not likely have full use of the strategy (Glaser & Rabinowitz, 1986). Schools should deliberately attempt to teach the use of thinking strategies in many different content areas and tasks, because the conceptual transfer of a thinking strategy from one content field to another is not as easy as many people think.

> Schools need to teach thinking strategies in a variety of content areas and tasks.

■ One Gift or Many?

Should giftedness be regarded as one overriding mental ability or as a series of special abilities? Howard Gardner is one of the latest of a group of psychologists to view giftedness as a series of special abilities (1998). He has proposed a list of nine distinct and separate abilities that need specific educational attention (Table 9.2).

Everyone knows persons who are particularly good at one or two of the abilities listed in Table 9.2 but who are not superior in them all. Think of a student who is a math wiz but is not expert in linguistic or interpersonal intelligence. Some students seem to be particularly gifted in spatial intelligence but have only above-average ability in other areas. Whereas all these abilities seem to be positively correlated with one another, and students who have outstanding talents in one area are usually good in the other areas as well, we can find concrete examples of specialists in outstanding performance. Consequently, the educational issue becomes not only how to plan one *overall* program for students who have talents in many of these areas but also what should be done with students who have specialized talents in a single area such as mathematics, visual perception, or interpersonal relationships.

> There seem to be several types of intelligence. A student may be gifted in one area, such as linguistic intelligence, but not be gifted in other ways.

Students who are gifted provide a fine example of the need to view exceptional children *in context*. Although abundant evidence suggests that we are born with differing neurological systems that are differentially responsive to outside experience, factors within the family and the society also help determine the full extent of the development of the child who is gifted. (See the discussion in Chapter 1 on heredity versus environment.)

TABLE 9.2
Gardner's Multiple Intelligences

CATEGORY	CORE OPERATIONS
LINGUISTIC	
Mastery, sensitivity, desire to explore, and love of words, spoken and written language(s)	Comprehension and expression of written and oral language, syntax, semantics, pragmatics Example: William Shakespeare, Toni Morrison
LOGICAL-MATHEMATICAL	
Confront, logically analyze, assess and empirically investigate objects, abstractions, and problems, discern relations and underlying principles, carry out mathematical operations, handle long chains of reasoning	Computation, deductive reasoning, inductive reasoning Example: Paul Erdos, Isaac Newton
MUSICAL	
Skill in producing, composing, performing, listening, discerning, and sensitivity to the components of music and sound	Pitch, melody, rhythm, texture, timbre, musical themes, harmony Example: Charlie Parker, Wolfgang Amadeus Mozart
SPATIAL	
Accurately perceive, recognize, manipulate, modify and transform shape, form, and pattern	Design, color, form, perspective, balance, contrast, match Example: Leonardo da Vinci, Frank Lloyd Wright
BODILY-KINESTHETIC	
Orchestrate and control body motions and handle objects, skillfully, to perform tasks or fashion products	Control and coordination, stamina, balance, locating self or objects in space Example: Martha Graham, Tiger Woods
INTERPERSONAL	
Be sensitive to, accurately assess, and understand others' actions, motivations, moods, feelings, and other mental states and act productively on the basis of that knowledge	Ability to inspire, instruct, or lead others and respond to their actions, emotions, motivations, opinions, and situations Example: Virginia Woolf, the Dalai Lama
INTRAPERSONAL	
Be sensitive to, accurately assess, understand and regulate oneself and act productively on the basis of one's actions, motivations, moods, feelings, and other mental states	Knowledge and understanding of one's strengths and weaknesses, styles, emotions, motivations, self-orientation Example: Mohandas K. Gandhi, Oprah Winfrey
NATURALIST	
Expertise in recognition and classification of natural objects: e.g., flora and fauna, or artifacts; e.g., cars, coins, or stamps	Noting the differences that are key to discriminating among several categories or species of objects in the natural world Example: Charles Darwin, Jane Goodall
EXISTENTIAL*	
Capturing and pondering the fundamental questions of existence; an interest and concern with "ultimate" issues	Capacity to raise big questions about one's place in the cosmos Example: Søren Kierkegaard, Martin Luther King, Jr.

*Unconfirmed ninth intelligence

Source: Adapted from H. Ramos-Ford & H. Gardner, Giftedness from a multiple intelligence perspective, in N. Colangelo & G. Davis (Eds.), *Handbook of Gifted Education* (Boston: Allyn & Bacon, 1997). Copyright © 1997 by Pearson Education. Adapted with permission.

Of course being labeled as talented or being identified as gifted through high test scores does not guarantee an academic road of productivity or accomplishments following school. So what is the recipe for productivity on the part of a gifted student? Schneider (2000) reviewed an extensive literature on this topic and concluded as follows:

> Exceptional performance is usually based on an extremely rich knowledge base, acquired through a very long lasting process of motivated learning. (p. 173)

In other words, high ability is not the predictor of student productivity, but only the base on which the student must build. *Extended practice, dedication,* and *high motivation* to succeed are the characteristics necessary to complete the portrait of a productive person. Since they are easily recognized components of the successful athlete or musician, this should be of no surprise to educators. This is also where the school and educators can play a significant role in exciting the student about learning, providing resources and access to advanced knowledge that keep a student's high motivation alive.

Some decades ago there was an attempt to separate "High IQ" students from "High Creative" students, attributing different characteristics to each group (Getzels and Jackson, 1962). What now seems most likely is that these students all had high cognitive ability, but that the creative student possessed more of the characteristics noted above—dedication, practice, and high motivation (see Table 9.3). The other high-aptitude students, less highly motivated, continued in the routine high achievement vein without noticeable accomplishments other than high grades.

There is growing recognition that creativity is not so much a personal characteristic as it is a process that involves both thinking and personality. Treffinger, Young, Shelby, and Sheperdson (2002) present four different dimensions of the creative process shown in Table 9.3.

TABLE 9.3
The Dimensions of Creativity

DIMENSIONS	BEHAVIORS NEEDED
Generating Ideas	Producing multiple ideas to meet a task Cognitive characteristics like fluency, flexibility and originality, elaboration
Digging Deeper Into Ideas	Desire to understand complexity Analyzing, synthesizing, resolving ambiguities, bringing order from disorder
Courage to Explore Ideas	Curiosity, playfulness, risk taking, sense of humor, tolerance of ambiguity, openness to experience, self-confidence
Listening to One's Inner Voice	Understanding of who you are, where you want to go, commitment to do whatever it takes to get there Persistence, self-direction, concentration, work ethic

Source: From D. Treffinger, G. Young, E. Selby, & C. Sheperdson, *Assessing creativity: A guide for educators.* (Storrs, CT: National Research Center on the Gifted and Talented, 2002). Reprinted with permission.

"Generating Ideas" requires cognitive flexibility, while "Digging Deeper into Ideas" requires more synthesis and reasoning power. Personality becomes more of a player in the "Courage to Explore Ideas," requiring risk taking and openness to experience. The final stage, "Listening to One's Inner Voice," deals with clearly envisioning what you wish to accomplish and determining to overcome obstacles—again, personality characteristics.

One reason why there is such disagreement among observers as to the essence of creativity is that different persons focus on different properties. Therefore, some stress generation of ideas; others, the courage to explore ideas. What is clear, though, is that educators can help individuals develop these characteristics and reward them when they are acquired. It is also clear that no one is creative all the time or has all four of these components perpetually in play.

Students with high native ability still need support and help from the family, schools, and society to make the most of their outstanding abilities. The failure of these outside forces to provide support may result in such a reduction of usable talent that the student may no longer be referred to as "gifted" (Frasier, 1997) and no longer be eligible for special services.

■ Factors That Contribute to Giftedness and Talent

Are children born gifted and talented? Do outstanding abilities emerge no matter what opportunities or education a person has? What role does heredity play in giftedness? How important is the context of the child who is gifted?

Heredity and Environment

More than one hundred years ago, Francis Galton, in a study of outstanding Englishmen, concluded that extraordinary ability ran in families and was genetic in origin. (Galton overlooked the environmental advantage of being born into an upper-class family.) Ever since, there has been a strong belief in the powerful role that heredity plays in producing mental ability. Certainly, studies of twins and the close relationship of the abilities of adoptive children to the abilities of their natural parents demand that we recognize a hereditary element (Plomin, 1997).

One of the strongest arguments for hereditary influences on giftedness lies in the small—but still impressive—number of prodigies, children who develop extraordinarily fast. A young man named Michael Kearney has the following documented achievements. He first spoke at 4 months and began reading single words at 8 months. He has been listed in the Guinness Book of World Records for these distinctions (Schneider, 2000):

1. The youngest person in history to receive a high school diploma (at 6 years, 5 months)
2. The youngest person in history to enter college (at 6 years, 7 months)
3. The youngest person in history to have graduated from college (at 10 years, 4 months)
4. The youngest person in history to receive a master's degree in biochemistry (at age 14)

Such accomplishments cannot be explained by favorable environments alone, even though parental interest and support could have contributed. Other prodigies have shown similar, if not so dramatic, development (Morelock & Feldman, 1997).

Although researchers make a strong case for the importance of heredity in giftedness, environment, or the context of the child, is important as well. Extraordinary talent may be shaped by heredity, but it is nurtured and developed by the environment. We've discussed the role that society plays in defining gifts and talents and rewarding them. A more powerful influence, because it is closer, is the family.

> Students who are gifted appear to have both favorable hereditary and favorable environmental factors in their early development.

Benjamin Bloom (1985) attempted to uncover the factors that are linked to extraordinary ability. Bloom conducted a retrospective study of the early lives of world-class swimmers, pianists, mathematicians, and other gifted persons. In interviews with the subjects, their parents, and their former teachers, he found that several general characteristics seem important whatever the talent area:

- Willingness to do great amounts of work (practice, time, effort) to achieve a high level or standard
- Competitiveness with peers in the area of talent and determination to do the best at all costs
- Ability to rapidly learn new techniques, ideas, or processes in the area of talent

> Family encouragement is critical to the emergent talent of the gifted child.

Bloom suggested that the group's high motivation was stimulated in a powerful way by the early recognition of talent by parents and friends, who went out of their way to obtain special instruction and to encourage and nurture the talent. The enthusiasm and support of the family seemed to be a critical element in the emergence of these gifted persons into world-class performers.

■ Studies of Students Who Are Gifted

What sets students who are gifted apart from their agemates? How do those characteristics affect the way teachers plan their education? To answer these questions, we look for general patterns among youngsters who are gifted and for deviations from those patterns (the variance of characteristics within the group). Our objective is to identify and study, over time, groups of students who are gifted to see what form their development takes.

After his revision and the publication of the Binet-Simon Tests of Intelligence in 1916, Lewis Terman, a professor of psychology at Stanford University, turned his attention to children who are gifted. In 1920, he began a study of 1,528 such children, which was to continue for more than sixty years as he and his colleagues followed them into maturity and old age.

Terman conducted his search for children who were gifted in California's public schools. He used teacher nominations and group intelligence tests to screen subjects. Terman based the final selection of children on their performance on the Stanford-Binet Intelligence Scale. Most had IQ scores of 140 or higher; the average IQ score for the group was 151. The results, on average, were favorable in practically every developmental and socio-emotional dimension. The group did well not only in school and career but also in areas such as mental health, marriage, and character.

The final volume in the Terman series captures this population in their sixties and seventies (Holahan & Sears, 1995). The group continued to be superior in health, psychological well-being, and survival rates. Their feelings of lifetime satisfaction were positive, and they continued to achieve through these later years and to participate in intellectual and social events. The overall portrait was one of a privileged group of children who contributed substantially to their society as adults.

The findings of another longitudinal study are helping us determine whether gifted children fulfill their early promise. The Speyer School, a special elementary school in New York, was established through the work of Leta Hollingworth (1942), a pioneer in the education of gifted children. White and Renzulli (1987) conducted a forty-year follow-up of graduates of the school. Twenty-eight students were found; twenty of them returned questionnaires, and eight were interviewed in depth. Like the subjects in the Terman study, the majority of the men had entered professions, while the women tended to combine career and family. Their memories of the school were vivid. And "they all believed that their experience at Speyer School was instrumental in providing them with peer interaction for the first time, exposing them to competition, causing them to learn and like school for the first time, giving them a strong desire to excel" (p. 90).

Although no one in the group had made an earth-shaking discovery or contribution, most seemed to be contributing substantially to the quality of society in what they were doing. (Remember that individuals can be extraordinarily successful in their own field, such as business, science, the arts, or religion, and still be virtually unknown to the general public. Can you name three of the country's outstanding biochemists? Can you name one?)

Terman unbalanced his sample of gifted individuals through his identification process of young children. By using his own IQ test, the Stanford-Binet, as the tool for selecting gifted students for his sample, he eliminated many potentially bright youngsters from low-economic or immigrant status from the sample. As a consequence, what we are looking at in these lifespan results are largely what happens to gifted students from already well-established professional or managerial families.

One of the recurring questions regarding longitudinal studies such as the one that Terman and his associates did is, "Are the results due to the students or to the culture and times (the context) in which the study took place?" A more recent study provides some information on this issue (Subotnik, Kassan, Summers, & Wasser, 1993). In the 1940s, a special elementary school was established at Hunter College in New York City. The school was highly selective of the students it enrolled. Each year, fifty students with IQ scores ranging from 122 to 196 were enrolled (the average Binet IQ score was 157).

In educational attainment, the results were similar to those reported by the Terman group. Over 80 percent held a master's degree, and 68 percent of the men and 40 percent of the women held a doctorate in medicine, law, or some other area. They were in good health, mentally and physically, and were earning an income as impressive as their educational attainments would suggest.

One major difference between the Terman and the Hunter Elementary samples was in the careers of the women. The vast majority of the women in the Hunter Elementary sample were employed and were satisfied with their careers. Fewer than 10 percent were homemakers exclusively. The interviews made it clear that the women's movement (context again!) had had a decided effect on their becoming more oriented to work outside the home.

Subotnik and the other authors of the study were somewhat disappointed by the lack of drive for success or for extraordinary achievement that they found in the Hunter Elementary group. Most members of the group seemed content to do their professional job and enjoy their social life and the opportunities their vocational success provided. The well-rounded students had become well-rounded, complacent adults. One of them remarked,

> This is a terrible thing to say, but I think I'm where I want to be—terrible because I've always thought that there should have been more challenges. I'm very admired and respected where I work. . . . I don't want to be a senior vice president. . . . I want to have time to spend with my family, to garden, to play tennis, and see my friends. I'm very happy with my life. (p. 78)

On average, children who are gifted grow up to become well-adjusted adults, successful in their chosen careers.

There is little difference in emotional adjustment when comparing groups of gifted students to students of average ability.
(© Elizabeth Crews)

Is some degree of unhappiness or dissatisfaction necessary to create the obsessive concern with a particular goal and the single-minded drive and motivation to achieve that goal that lead to great attainments? On the other hand, the vast majority of these students became productive and useful citizens, and we might well ask if we should expect more of them than that.

■ The Challenges Associated with Giftedness

Heather [handwritten note in margin]

Despite their demonstrated ability to make friends and generally to adapt well, people who are gifted may shoulder some problems or challenges that stem from their exceptionality. Increased attention has been paid to the personality of gifted students.

A volume produced by members of the National Association for Gifted Children presented a summary of what was known about the social and emotional status of gifted students (Neihart, Reis, Robinson, & Moon, 2002). There have been substantial differences of opinion with regard to the linkage of giftedness to such issues as depression, delinquency, perfectionism, suicide, and response to stress. This disagreement appears to indicate that there is a wide variation of social-emotional adjustment in gifted students and that different investigators are looking at different parts of this wide distribution.

Giftedness does not provide an inoculation against emotional problems. The question is whether it provides a buffer against them because of gifted students' cognitive abilities to problem-solve and to examine their own feelings. Silverman (2002) discusses the special problem of *asynchronization of development* of gifted students: namely, that—for example—cognitively some may be 14 years old, physically and socially they may be only 8, and that this causes problems both for those students and for adults around them who are not aware of this atypical development.

Robinson (2002) points out that two implicit theories of intelligence are held by both adults and the students themselves. One has been entitled *entity theory,* meaning that intelligence is seen as a fixed trait and there is little we can do to change it. The second theory, an *incremental theory,* is that although people differ in native ability, intelligence is malleable and can be cultivated and increased through effort. Holding to either of these theories can result in differing emotional reactions to stress. Dweck (2000) points out that gifted students holding to the *entity theory* build the expectation that they will remain "smart" and should be able to handle new situations and stay at the top of the class with minimal effort. Faced with adults who remark on how bright they are, their concept of "born smart" is solidified. When such students are challenged by bright peers or difficult curricula, they often want to retreat from the uncomfortable situation, to seek low-risk tasks that can reconfirm their high abilities. Those individuals holding to the *incremental theory* seem to be in a better position to accept challenge and the need for effort and hard work to achieve success. That theory appears to be the one that comes closer to the facts as we know them.

Another characteristic that seems to be a part of some gifted students' emotional and social life is that of *perfectionism*. These are the combinations of thoughts and behaviors associated with high standards or high expectations for one's own performance. Superior performance depends upon setting high standards for oneself and would seem an essential part of the high productivity expected of such students. But now the question is whether perfectionism shades over into neurotic performance, since from their earliest years gifted children tend to be successful in almost everything they try—because they are being underchallenged. If perfectionism becomes neurosis, students can become "failure avoidant." Perfectionistic students can have a depressive reaction if they receive a 95 on a paper instead of the usual 100. In such instances it is important for teachers and others to point out to the student that great accomplishments usually are accompanied by failure in some part of the process.

Neihart (2002) points out that delinquency seems generally to be linked to a low-average intelligence, although it is clear that some gifted youth have committed serious violent acts. Delinquent youth are not a homogeneous group, and anyone attempting to understand the developmental trajectories of antisocial behavior in children and adolescents has to understand the various risks and protective factors involved in accelerating or reducing such behavior.

In the case of social and emotional development of gifted students it becomes all the more important to focus on individuals and to realize that group characteristics do not necessarily predict individual adjustment or response. That is all the more reason for developing individual plans and for understanding individual emotional adjustment.

Several reviews of the literature have been completed on this topic in recent years to determine the relative merit of these two opposing views (Neihart, 1999; Garland & Zigler, 1999; Gust-Brey & Cross, 1999) as to whether gifted students have more social and emotional difficulties than their less gifted peers.

Gust-Brey and Cross (1999) pointed out that an increasing incidence of suicide among adolescents in general would seem to mean that the incidence would likely be increasing in the gifted populations as well. There is some indication that youngsters who are extremely creative artistically have more vulnerability to mental illness than do their other academically gifted classmates. It goes without saying that teachers and counselors should be alert to signs of depression or anxiety in students, gifted or nongifted, and see that these young people receive appropriate attention.

The impact of gender on how gifted students decide to manage their giftedness has been an areas of interest to several scholars (Coleman & Cross, 2001; Reis, 2003; Roeper, 2003; Kerr & Cohn, 2001). Sociocultural standards regarding appropriate roles for boys and girls are very clear and may conflict with the emergence of giftedness in some instances. Let's look at how this might work for both gifted girls and gifted boys.

For gifted girls the message to be "feminine," meaning to be passive, modest, dependent, nurturing, and unselfish, can conflict with their expectations of such factors as independence, risk taking, full development of their potential, assertiveness, and a certain degree of competitiveness. These conflicting messages can mean that some gifted girls elect to camouflage their abilities in order to fit in better with society's expectations (Reis, 2003). While societal messages have changed somewhat since the women's movement of the 1960s (Roeper, 2003), these dilemmas remain critical for many gifted girls. (Further discussion of these issues is presented in this chapter in the section on special populations.)

PROFILES

We would like you to meet two children, Cranshaw and Zelda. Both are 10 years old and in the fifth grade. Cranshaw probably meets the criteria for intellectual, creative, and leadership giftedness; Zelda, the intellectual criteria. Their developmental profiles are shown in the accompanying graphs.

Cranshaw: Cranshaw is a big, athletic, happy-go-lucky youngster who impresses the casual observer as the "all-American boy." He seems to be a natural leader and to be enthusiastic over a wide range of interests. These interests have not yet solidified. One week he can be fascinated with astronomy, the next week with football formations, and the following week with the study of Africa.

His past history in school has suggested that teachers have two very distinct reactions to Cranshaw. One is that he is a joy to have in the classroom. He is a cooperative and responsible boy who can not only perform his own tasks well, but be a good influence in helping the other youngsters to perform effectively. On the other hand, Cranshaw's mere presence in the class also stimulates in teachers some hints of personal inferiority and frustration, since he always seems to be exceeding the bounds of the teachers' knowledge and abilities. The teachers secretly wonder how much they are really teaching Cranshaw and how much he is learning on his own.

Cranshaw's family is a well-knit, reasonably happy one. His father is a businessman,

Profiles of Two Gifted Students

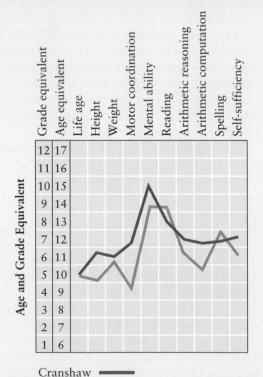

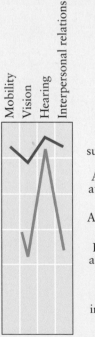

Source: From J. Gallagher and S. Gallagher, *Teaching the Gifted Child,* 4th ed. (p.12). Copyright © 1994 by Allyn and Bacon. Reprinted by permission.

Cranshaw ━━━
Zelda ━━━

his mother is an elementary school teacher, and the family is moderately active in the community. Their attitude toward Cranshaw is that he is a fine boy, and they hope that he does well. They anticipate his going on to higher education but, in effect, say that it is pretty much up to him what he is going to do when the time comes. They do not seem to be future-oriented and are perfectly happy to have him as the enthusiastic and well-adjusted youngster that he appears to be today.

Zelda: Zelda shares similar high scores on intelligence tests to those manifested by Cranshaw. Zelda is a chubby girl who wears rather thick glasses that give her a "bookish" appearance. Her clothes, while reasonably neat and clean, are not stylish and give the impression that neither her parents nor Zelda have given a great deal of thought to how they look on this particular child. Socially, she has one or two reasonably close girl friends, but she is not a member of the wider social circle of girls in her classroom and, indeed, seems to reject it.

Teachers respond to Zelda with two generally different feelings. They are pleased with the enthusiasm with which Zelda attacks her schoolwork and the good grades that she gets. At the same time, they are vaguely annoyed or irritated with Zelda's undisguised feeling of superiority toward youngsters who are not as bright as she is; they tend to repel Zelda when she tries to act like an assistant teacher, or to gain favors that are more often reserved for the teachers.

Zelda and her family seem to get along very well with each other. The main source of conflict is that the family has values which Zelda has accepted wholeheartedly but that are getting her into difficulty with her classmates. Her parents are college professors, her father in history and her mother in English literature. They seem to value achievement and intellectual performance almost to the exclusion of all other things.

Their social evenings are made up of intellectual discussions of politics, religion, or the current burning issue on the campus. These discussions are definitely adult-oriented, and Zelda is intelligent enough to be able to enter occasionally into such conversations. This type of behavior is rewarded much more by the parents than is the behavior that would seem more appropriate to her age level (Gallagher & Gallagher, 1994, pp. 11–12, reprinted by permission).

Cranshaw's adjustment is as good as his academic achievement; Zelda has social difficulties. She is not accepted by her agemates and doesn't understand why. The pattern of development is different for each of these students because of differing environmental factors.

The teachers of gifted students face several basic challenges: holding the interest of youngsters whose abilities are several years beyond their grade level, encouraging them to work in areas that may not interest them, and helping them deal with the social problems that may be linked to being gifted.

If messages for gifted students involve attitudes toward independence, risk taking, and competitiveness, you may wonder how these concepts can be problematic for gifted boys. Gifted boys face another type of dilemma. Those who are highly sensitive, aesthetically aware, insightful, emotive, and intuitive run a high risk of appearing "unmanly," and one needs only to contemplate the labels developed for boys who appear "unmanly" to understand this difficulty in the life of a gifted boy (Kerr & Cohn, 2001). When we look at the impact of gender on achievement patterns in school, it is impossible to ignore the fact that approximately three times as many boys are identified as underachievers as girls (McCoach & Siegle, 2003). (This will be examined in more detail in a later section on underachievers.)

Gifted children as a group have been described as being more androgynous (Coleman & Cross, 2001). This means that gifted girls tend to take on more traits that are identified as male (independence, assertiveness, risk taking, and so on) and that gifted boys tend to show more "feminine" traits (such as sensitivity, aesthetic awareness, and emotiveness). It is a complex issue: Some gifted students find that the gender expectations of society conflict with the direction of their gifts and talents, so they face difficult choices about managing their identities as gifted individuals.

One common adjustment problem of many students who are gifted is dealing with the boredom that comes from sitting through classes in which something they already know is being taught. Imagine yourself faced with learning the multiplication tables over and over, and you might begin to understand their dislike of a nondifferentiated educational program. In spite of their boredom, gifted students may avoid identifying themselves as being gifted, by using a coping style that denies interest in excellence and even by making fun of other gifted students (Coleman, 1985). It is interesting that at special schools for advanced students, the social norm is that it is OK to be interested in intellectual and academic goals (Kolloff, 1997). Under this social environment, students who are gifted find it comfortable to reveal their true selves and interests.

> The social pressures gifted students feel to conform to the dominant peer norm are very strong.

When we look at the profiles of Cranshaw and Zelda, we are reminded that individuals, within any category of exceptional children, are first and foremost *individuals*. Each has his or her own pattern of strengths and areas of need. Indeed, within any category of exceptional children, the intraindividual differences of a single child can seem more important than the interindividual differences across the group. Nevertheless, we need to remember that what both Zelda and Cranshaw have in common is an advanced cognitive ability that will require teachers to provide a more challenging curriculum in these two students' areas of strengths.

■ Identification

Before we can provide children who are gifted with special services to match their special needs, we have to find them. Identification is not an easy task! In every generation, many such children pass through school unidentified, their talents uncultivated (Johnson, 2004).

We generally expect that teachers can spot these children and do something for them. But studies have shown that teachers do not always recognize children who are gifted, even those with academic talent (Parke, 1989). The identification of these students requires an understanding of the requirements of the program for which they are chosen. If we want to choose a group of students for an advanced mathematics class, our approach would be different than if we are looking for students with high aptitude for a creative-writing program. Specific program needs and requirements shape the identification process.

Any program for identifying children who are gifted in a school system should include both subjective and objective methods of evaluation. Classroom behavior, for example, can point out children's ability to organize and use materials and reveal their potential for processing information, sometimes better than can a test. Products, such as superior essays and term projects, that can be kept in a student portfolio can serve as an indication of special gifts.

In the visual and performing arts, talent usually is determined by the consensus of expert judges, often in an audition setting. Experts in the arts are not enthusiastic about tests of artistic ability or musical aptitude. They trust their own judgment more, although their judgment is susceptible to bias. Sometimes, it is possible to judge the quality of a series of products or a portfolio of drawings or compositions that students produce over a period of time (Clark & Zimmerman, 1998).

Most schools have test scores available from group intelligence tests or group achievement tests. Such data can serve as a starting point for selecting candidates for a special program, but they do have limitations:

▶ Group intelligence tests are not as reliable as individual tests.

▶ Group tests seldom differentiate abilities at the upper limits because they have been designed largely for the average student.

▶ Group tests rarely measure creative thinking or cognitive areas beyond academic aptitude.

▶ Some children do not function well in a timed testing situation.

Despite those limitations, group intelligence tests are a practical means of screening large numbers of students, although the scores of students from culturally diverse families are likely to be underestimated because tests tend to be

The visual and performing arts use expert judgment to identify talented students.

Any program for identifying children who are gifted in a school system should include both subjective and objective methods of evaluation. Classroom behavior, for example, can point out children's ability to organize and use materials and can reveal their potential for processing information.
(© Will and Demi McIntyre/CORBIS)

culturally biased. It is financially prohibitive, however, to give all children individual examinations.

Achievement tests are even less discriminating. They detect only the children who are achieving well academically. Emotional disturbance, family problems, peer-group values, poor study habits, a non-English-speaking background, and many other factors can affect a child's ability to perform academically.

Another approach used to identify students who are gifted is to start with a particular program and find youngsters with the special abilities that meet program requirements. Stanley (1989) used this method to initiate a talent search for mathematically and verbally precocious youngsters—the Study of Mathematically Precocious Youth, now referred to as the Center for Talented Youth at Johns Hopkins University.

The Scholastic Aptitude Test and other aptitude tests are used to screen students who are extraordinarily capable in mathematics. Other characteristics—motivation and academic efficiency—determine the type of special attention suitable for those who score at the highest level on these tests. Most special education programs for students who are gifted now use a combination of aptitude tests, teacher ratings, nominations, portfolios, and scholastic records to help identify eligible students. A committee of teachers and other specialists often will try to match the child's talents with the special services that are available.

Identifying children who are gifted should be the first step to a differentiated program. It also can be used to determine eligibility for state financial aid that may provide a subsidy for local programs or to satisfy state or federal guidelines.

■ Special Groups of Children Who Are Gifted

The category of children who are gifted and talented contains many subgroups. How well individuals in these groups are adapting depends to a major degree on how their families raise them, how their schools utilize their special gifts, and how society sees them.

Girls Who Are Gifted

The limited number of girls being identified as gifted seems to be the result of societal preconceptions that girls do not have special abilities.

It seems strange in one respect to identify girls who are gifted as a "special" group, because girls make up more than 50 percent of the student population. But sufficient evidence shows that members of this group differ meaningfully on a number of indices from their male counterparts. The differences appear to rest in their perceptions of the world around them, often formed by the attitudes of those close to them.

As we discussed earlier, gender differences in self-perception appear to limit girls' intellectual performance, so it is extremely important for teachers to be aware of such differences and try to do something about them. These differences appear to be related to societal expectations. Although there is reason to believe (Roeper, 2003) that attitudes toward girls and women are changing, the forces at work to limit achievement of girls appear still powerful.

Math achievement is one area where gender differences remain. One study (Cramer & Oshima, 1992) places the key at about sixth through ninth grade, finding that girls who are gifted began at that level (but not before) to attribute math success to greater ability on the part of males. The males believed that their talent came from their greater effort. Such a belief in male superiority in math can have a smothering effect on girls' efforts to achieve in mathematics. Another study showed a relationship between the mathematics self-concept of high-ability girls and their parents' belief in the ability of their daughters (Dickens & Cornell, 1993). Girls with a high mathematics self-concept had parents who had a similarly high perception of their daughters' ability and high expectations for their performance. This finding seems to indicate the importance of high parental expectations in dampening the societal bias against girls doing well in mathematics.

But there remains much to be done before some form of gender equity is obtained. Consider positions now held in Congress, the media, university leadership, symphony orchestras, corporations, and so forth. The relative scarcity of female role models is another stumbling block, although that problem is easing now as more women become visible in desirable occupations (Reis, 2003). Van Tassel-Baska (1998) has suggested that the use of successful women as adult role models and mentors can help girls set goals and consider career decisions. She also advises the use of career development counseling and internships so gifted girls will have some direct experience with various career areas. Bright girls should also be helped to begin to confront the balancing act between career and family, which may affect their future.

Adolescence seems to be a particularly difficult period for gifted girls. It is the time when their self-esteem seems to be weakest and their concerns about social acceptance at their peak (Kerr, 1997). One suggestion is that gifted girls be encouraged to take risks: engaging in physical activities that are challenging, taking the most challenging courses available, and being encouraged to speak out and defend their points of view (Rimm, 2003). Teachers have not often encouraged these as feminine traits.

In recognition of the potential intimidation by males in the classroom at the adolescent age level, some attempts have been made to develop single-sex classes or schools, and these seem to offer real advantages in freeing up the girls' self expression and confidence (Hollinger, 1993).

Children of Extraordinary Ability

It is generally accepted today that superior intellectual ability often predicts high academic performance and personal adjustment. But doubts linger about the youngster of extraordinary ability—the 1 in 100,000 at the level of an Einstein. What happens to the student who is seven or eight years ahead of his or her age group in development?

Is there a relationship between extraordinary intelligence and later development? As IQ scores increase, do we see an increase in later accomplishments? Feldman (1984) compared two groups of adults among Terman's subjects. As children, one group obtained IQ scores of more than 180; the other, randomly selected from the average range of scores, had IQ scores in the area of 150. There was some evidence that men in the "very high IQ" group had accomplished more than men in the "high IQ" group. For example, one was an internationally known psychologist, another a highly honored landscape architect. Still, many of the men in the lower group were successful,

Career development counseling and internships give gifted girls direct experience with career options.

Adolescence can be a difficult time for girls who are gifted.

Genius includes more than intelligence. It includes personality and motivation, too.

if not eminent. Feldman also found a difference between the women in the two groups. Those with IQ scores around 180 tended to have full-time careers; those in the lower group tended to be homemakers. Despite the difference he found between the groups, Feldman concluded that genius is not solely a function of intelligence but rather reflects a combination of intelligence, personality, motivation, and environmental variables.

CASE STUDY: IMAGINATION, LOGIC, AND THE EXCEPTIONALLY GIFTED

Among my case studies of exceptionally gifted children is Peter Martin, a child whose IQ measured above 200 when he was tested with the Stanford-Binet L-M at the age of four. When Peter was five years old, I discussed Peter with his school guidance counselor. Peter loved learning facts about the world. One of his favorite books was the *World Book Encyclopedia*. He was interested in such things as how computers work and the intricacies of deciphering symbolic codes. But he wasn't much into imaginative play—a pastime typically enjoyed by children his age. The counselor was concerned about Peter's problem because she had read some research reporting how using imagination can help children cope with stressful situations. She thought that by helping him to develop his imaginative side a bit more, she would be assisting him in terms of coping skills and would be helping him to feel "more like a whole person and not just be the analytical, figure-out little person that's so tied into the real world."

A short time later, Peter revealed that an "analytical, figure-out mind" and an extraordinary imagination were not necessarily mutually exclusive phenomena. Around Christmas time, he discovered Stephen Hawking's book *A Brief History of Time*, which speculated on the origins of the universe. Fascinated with the book, he read it constantly, even to a point of falling asleep with it at night. About the same time, he happened to see the Sesame Street Christmas Special in which Big Bird was obsessively worrying about how Santa Claus would get down all those chimneys. Peter applied the knowledge he had gained from Hawking's book and came up with a solution. . . .

Hawking had theorized that if someone were able to enter a black hole, the person would become longer and thinner as he or she went deeper and deeper into the hole and further and further away from its boundary, the "event horizon" where light gets sucked in on one side but escapes on the other. In addition, time would slow down. "Peter," his mother reported, "reasoned that if Santa could direct and control the force of singularity (the force generated within the center of a black hole), he could make himself thin enough to get down chimneys. In addition, time would slow down and that he could get to all the houses in the world without any problem!" (Morelock, 1997, a1–a2)

The great developmental distance between these youngsters and their age peers necessitates individual programs for them, not unlike the IEPs proposed for children with disabilities. Such programs and services would consider acceleration, moving the student through the system more rapidly, and some form of tutoring or mentoring by adults with special knowledge in the student's area of special interest (Silverman, 1998).

Extraordinarily precocious students represent one of our greatest and rarest natural resources. We must learn more about them to understand the origin of their giftedness and ways to help them adapt to an often difficult social environment. As noted earlier, there are many more of these students than would be predicted by the normal curve of intelligence (Silverman, 1997).

Underachievers Who Are Gifted

One of the many myths surrounding children who are gifted is the cannonball theory. The idea, simply put, is that such children can no more be stopped from achieving their potential than a cannonball, once fired, can be diverted from its path. Like most simplistic ideas about human beings, this one, too, is wrong. There is a subgroup of children referred to as **gifted underachievers,** students whose academic performance consistently falls far short of expectations (e.g., a consistent C average).

A substantial proportion of children never achieve the level of performance that their scores on intelligence and aptitude tests predict for them. In the Terman longitudinal study, the researchers identified a group of 150 men who had not achieved to the level of their apparent ability and compared them with 150 men who had done well (Terman & Oden, 1947). In their self-ratings and in ratings by their wives and parents, four major characteristics separated the underachieving men from the achieving men: greater feelings of inferiority, less self-confidence, less perseverance, and less of a sense of life goals. More striking was an examination of teacher ratings made on the men twenty years earlier, while they were in school. Even at that time, their teachers believed that the underachievers lacked self-confidence, foresight, and the desire to excel.

A recent study looked at the predictors of underachievement for gifted students (McCoach & Siegle, 2003). Five factors were examined: academic self-perception, attitudes toward school, attitudes toward teachers, motivation/self-regulation, and goal valuation. The last two factors predicted underachievement the most. Interestingly, the academic self-perceptions of underachieving gifted students were high; they knew that they *could* do the work; and their attitudes toward school and teachers were mixed. Given that motivation/self-regulation and goal valuation were the critical factors predicting underachievement, the authors recommended that "teachers and counselors who work with gifted underachievers should assess whether these students value the goals of school and whether they are motivated to attain those goals" (McCoach & Siegle, 2003). The authors further pointed out that if these students value neither the specific task they are given (here, practicing algebraic formulas) nor the outcome of completing the task (an A in math), their motivation is likely to be very low.

One of the questions to be asked, then, is what is the nature of the gifted underachiever? If a student does not perform well on expected academic tasks, is he therefore an underachiever? Not necessarily: Neumeister and Herbert (2003) make a distinction between underachievement and selective achievement by discussing Sam, who doesn't do well in school because he is resistant to conformity and is seeking to find his own distinctive way in life. Selective achievement means that Sam will learn, all right, but in his own way, which is likely to be untraditional. Listen to Sam:

> Maybe I am not slacking off in what's really important. . . . A lot of people take the view that Academics have got to be the most important. But, if you take a more worldly view, I don't think they are. When, for instance,

there are people dying of starvation, how important is it that I get a little grade?

Some students have a tendency to rebel against authority and learn perfectly well if they are given tasks and allowed to use their own style of learning to solve them, and if the teacher is flexible enough to not get caught up in a student's campaign against authority.

Most teachers are able to describe at length the characteristics of underachievers. But what they really want to know is what to do about them. Whitmore reported on a special program at the primary-grade level. A group of twenty-seven underachievers who were gifted was placed in a special class where the children were encouraged to express their feelings and concerns. The teacher met monthly with each child and his or her parents. After a year, twelve of the students had gained from $1\frac{1}{2}$ to 3 years in reading scores; only three failed to reach grade level in reading or arithmetic. Social behavior and work habits also improved. Whitmore pointed out that many of the children had shown signs of emotional disturbance, but the creation of a warm, accepting environment apparently had overcome the outward symptoms of those problems.

A different approach to underachievement, one using the Renzulli Enrichment Triad model, seems to have some promise (Baum, Renzulli, & Hebért, 1995). For that model, seventeen underachievers in grades 3–9 were selected by their teachers as students who would qualify for the gifted and talented program but who were judged to be underachievers. The basis for the underachievement was judged in different children to be social and emotional problems, poor self-regulation, or negative response to the standard curriculum.

The teachers engaged each of the seventeen students in an enrichment activity, the goal of which was to provide an opportunity for the student to actually investigate real problems through suitable means of inquiry and to bring his or

A warm, accepting, supportive environment can significantly improve the academic and social performance of underachievers.

Gifted students who are seen as underachievers may benefit from enrichment activities based on investigating real problems.

Gifted and talented students can be challenged by participating in Outward Bound activities, such as these high schoolers on a nature hike with their teacher.
(© Davis Barber/Photo Edit)

her findings to bear on realistic audiences. The authors reported that positive gains in attitude, interviews, achievement tests, and other areas have shown that carefully designed programs over an extended period of time can make a positive difference in the academic and social performance of underachievers. Yet very few school systems offer these programs. Why? Because underachievers who are gifted do not often come to the attention of special educators. They don't fail in school, yet they can't perform at the level that would place them in programs for students who are gifted (see also Supplee, 1990).

It is indeed difficult to change the maladapted patterns of students who for eight to ten years have been developing precisely the wrong approach to academic stress or challenge. This task requires great intensity of effort on the part of both the student and those trying to help that student change. The best-known educational intervention strategies have established either part-time or full-time special classrooms for gifted underachievers. In these classrooms, as reported by Reis and McCoach (2000), "educators strive to create a favorable environment for student achievement by altering the traditional classroom organization. A smaller student-teacher ratio exists, teachers create less conventional types of teaching and learning activities, teachers give students some choice and freedom in exercising control over their atmosphere, and students are encouraged to utilize different learning strategies" (p. 164).

> Students who are high-achieving often prefer to be grouped together in honors classes.

Cultural Diversity and Children Who Are Gifted

Van Tassel-Baska (2004) has summarized the need for special curriculum units for low-income gifted students who are shown to be different from more advantaged gifted students in their lesser interest in reading and abstract ideas, greater interest in social acceptance, and lesser interest in long-term academic performance. Although low-income status and minority status often overlap and are consequently confused, the above characteristics appear to be present regardless of race.

Van Tassel-Baska proposes curricula that place emphasis on openness to experience and allow for creativity and fluency in thinking, opportunity to express ideas in the arts rather than verbally, preference for hands-on applications, and preference for oral expression. The problem-based learning approach contains many of these characteristics and has been shown to be effective with low-income gifted populations.

One example is the problem-based unit on the Black Death (Gallagher & Bray, 2002), which allows low-income sixth-grade students to take the role of council members in a medieval Italian town who have heard that this plague is coming. Their task is to determine how to protect their fellow citizens and what actions they need to take. The students are encouraged to explore the Internet for information, involve themselves in small-group study, and express their ideas on the actions to be taken. Using this whole-class method, a number of potentially gifted students were identified and then given special lessons in self-assessment, thinking about career goals, and believing in themselves and their abilities (Gallagher, Cook, & Shoffner, 2003).

These approaches provide teachers with an authentic lens for viewing their students, thus increasing each teacher's ability to recognize the potential of culturally-linguistically diverse and economically disadvantaged students.

Coleman and Gallagher (1992) analyzed the special changes that the fifty states made in their standard identification procedures to try to discover in nontraditional families and cultural groups children who were gifted. These strategies included

▶ Developing student profiles and case study examples of nontraditional gifted students

▶ Using multiple identification criteria with the clause "no single criterion should prevent identification"

▶ Using portfolios of student work samples to document giftedness

Such measures seemed necessary because cultural diversity often masks outstanding talent (CEC/TAG, 2001).

Structured teacher observations have proved useful in recognizing gifted students from culturally-linguistically diverse and/or economically disadvantaged families. This approach is not without risks, as teachers who have little knowledge of how giftedness can show itself in children with limited school readiness may fall into stereotypical patterns of who is gifted and who is not (Coleman, 2003).

Project U-Stars (Using Science Talents and Abilities to Recognize Students) capitalizes on the teachers' knowledge of their students to help identify young children with outstanding potential (Coleman, 2003). The U-Stars approach relies on three key elements:

1. Teachers who know what to look for (how to recognize potential)
2. Teachers who know how to structure their classrooms so that children will be engaged
3. Teachers who know how to provide a psychologically safe environment where students can show their best abilities

The structured observation approach used by U-Stars includes an observational note-taking system that gives teachers specific behaviors to look for. In this case the areas for observation include children who learn easily, show advanced skills, display curiosity and creativity, have strong interests, show advanced reasoning and problem solving, display spatial abilities, are motivated, show social perceptiveness, and have leadership strengths. Table 9.4 gives a few specific behaviors for each of these areas of observation. The observations are further structured by asking the teacher to complete them during specific lessons that focus on hands-on science problem solving and experimentation. The basic belief underlying this approach and similar ones is that we must go beyond the use of IQ scores and standardized measures of achievement if we hope to identify "hidden giftedness." Other programs that focus on using observational data to help teachers recognize students with outstanding potential have used problem-based learning experiences as the observational platform.

Another of the alternative ways of identifying gifted minority is to ask those who know them best, their peers. By asking which students learn quickly or which ones their peers would ask for help at school, you can gather a number of names that will serve as leads in your talent search. This information might then be followed up with more comprehensive identification. No such identification should be sought, of course, until there is a clear idea as to the nature of the special services that would be presented to those students.

TABLE 9.4
Sample of Structured Observations from U-Stars Early Recognition of Potential (Harrison & Coleman, 2004)

LEARNS EASILY
Has lots of information Completes assignments ahead of others
SHOWS ADVANCED SKILLS
Can tell or reproduce stories or events with detail Understands advanced number concepts
DISPLAYS CURIOSITY AND CREATIVITY
Questions, explores, experiments Puts unrelated ideas and materials together in new and different ways
HAS STRONG INTERESTS
Is able to lose self in something of interest Is recognized as "expert" by classmates
SHOWS ADVANCED REASONING AND PROBLEM SOLVING
Keen observer; spots details others miss Offers many different ways to solve problems
DISPLAYS SPATIAL ABILITIES
Figures out why and how things work Shows unusual talent in various art forms Invents games
IS MOTIVATED
Is a self-starter; requires little direction Is independent; likes to do things on own
SHOWS SOCIAL PERCEPTIVENESS
Is able to see another's point of view Displays strong sense of justice
DISPLAYS LEADERSHIP
Accepts and carries out responsibilities Can influence others

Source: From A. Harrison & M. R. Coleman, Do you teach some who . . . ? An observational reporting procedure to identify gifted behaviors in children (Chapel Hill: UNC-CH, FPG Child Development Institute, Project U-Stars Plus, 2004). Reprinted with permission.

Once gifted students from a variety of cultures are identified, by whatever method, we must develop an educational plan for their special needs and circumstances. One objective is to encourage a child's understanding of and respect for his or her own cultural background. Biographies and the works of noted writers or leaders from the particular cultural group are often the basis of special programs. Because there are so many groups with such diverse backgrounds, these programs are usually unique (Baldwin, 1987; Bernal, 1979).

Ford and Harris (1999) are concerned about retaining black children in programs for gifted students. Placing a child in a program does not guarantee that he or she will be happy to be there or will want to stay. This underscores a general rule about exceptional children: merely placing the exceptional child in a different setting is not sufficient for his or her success; special steps need to be taken to ensure that the child's adaptation is appropriate.

Ford mentions irrelevant curriculum; incompatible social, racial, and cultural backgrounds with the majority of the students; and even a lack of support from those parents who find themselves torn between the culture of the school and the culture of the home.

For instance, Jason and his parents were excited about his being nominated for the gifted program, but Jason eventually seemed reluctant to go to the special program and even resistant to what the program was presenting to him. His parents sought the reason for this change and found out that Jason was disturbed about being the only black child in the program and that he was also getting considerable static from other black boys for being black but "acting white." For the sake of these bright students, we have to be aware of the sociocultural environment as well as of the curriculum.

Some special counseling may help individual students come to terms with the differing values, attitudes, and norms of the dominant culture and their parent culture. Special multicultural counseling strategies are needed, together with use of mentors and role models. The ordinary school counseling program by itself does not seem adequate for this special task. Gifted students from culturally diverse families may need special career counseling so they are aware of the range of opportunities that are available to them (Perrone, 1997).

Children with Disabilities Who Are Gifted

Resources and facts relating to gifted students with disabilities www.eric.org/

A student's not being able to see or hear or walk does not mean he or she is not intellectually gifted (Hua & Coleman, 2002). It only means that the child stands a good chance of having special talents overlooked. In her seminal book, Whitmore (1980) described a child who not only went unrecognized as gifted but was actually thought to have mental retardation:

> Kim. At seven years of age, this child with cerebral palsy had no speech and extremely limited motor control. In a public school for severely handicapped students, she was taught only self-help skills. Her parents, who were teachers, observed her use of her eyes to communicate and believed there was unstimulated intellect trapped in her severely handicapped body. Upon parent request, she was mainstreamed in her wheelchair into an open-space elementary school. After two months of stimulation and the provision of a mechanical communicator, Kim began to develop rapidly. She learned the Morse code in less than two days and began communicating continuously to the teacher and peers through her communicator. Within four months, she was reading on grade level (second), and subsequent testing indicated she possessed superior mental abilities—an exceptional capacity to learn. (p. 109)

It is not hard to imagine what Kim's world would have been like if she had not been given the opportunity to learn and communicate.

A gifted student might also have a disability.
(© Michael Newman/Photo Edit)

One of the areas of disabilities to which researchers have given particular attention is the child who is both gifted and learning disabled. Some students can be gifted and also have neurologically based attention problems or visual perceptual problems that can cause reading or spelling errors.

Coleman (2002) studied the coping strategies used by students with learning disabilities who were gifted, as opposed to nonidentified students with learning disabilities. She found that the students who were gifted had many more constructive coping strategies—that they developed problem-solving plans—whereas the nonidentified student with learning disabilities often displayed *learned helplessness* ("there's nothing I can do"), *escape/avoidance* ("go out and play instead of do homework"), or *distancing* ("just shrug it off"). Coleman recommended that all students with learning disabilities be directly instructed in coping strategies as a way of helping them survive the educational environment.

Another area where there can be a mix of giftedness and another exceptionality is that of autism. Although the majority of children identified as autistic have average or below-average ability, there is a subset of children sometimes referred to as children with Asperger's syndrome, where the child can be highly intelligent (Attwood, 1998); see Chapter 8, on autism. This high intelligence takes on a special flavor with such children, who can be encyclopedic in their knowledge but very poor in their social relationships. Their *theory of mind* function (the ability to perceive the intentions and thoughts of others) remains a serious problem for them. They will need special help in the social adaptation, regardless of their academic proficiency.

(text continues on page 370)

EDUCATIONAL

Children Who Are Gifted and Talented

Consider the following three general educational objectives for programs or services for students who are gifted and talented:

▶ Mastering important conceptual systems that are at the level of their abilities in various content fields

▶ Developing skills and strategies that enable them to become more independent and creative

▶ Developing pleasure in and excitement about learning that will carry them through the routine that is an inevitable part of the learning process

The ecology of the school has been impacted by increased demands for accountability to ensure that schools are doing their best. One of the unintended consequences of the strong emphasis on accountability in the No Child Left Behind Act (PL 107-110) has been its effect on gifted students. In order to study this effect, over one thousand elementary teachers were surveyed nationwide, and twenty-one focus group discussions were held with teachers and students in three states: California, Virginia, and Texas (Moon, Brighton, & Callahan, 2003).

The results confirmed the suspicions of the investigators that the emphasis on helping students who were in academic trouble and might fail statewide tests resulted in less attention paid in differentiating the programs for gifted students. There was a consequent increase in boredom and disquiet among the gifted students. Some typical comments from the focus groups were as follows:

> [Teacher] Throughout the whole year it's constant tracking and assessing and collaborating with your teams to focus on the ones that are not working at grade level. Just once a year is when you hear about gifted nominations. . . . Our whole emphasis is on our low-achieving students. (p. 54)

> [Teacher] The gifted student doesn't have to do all of the drilling, working on the objectives day after day, but they have to follow the timeline, follow the same curriculum as the other kids. So they're losing out because I don't think they're being challenged.

> [Student] It's just stuff we already know. It's just a long review of what we've done all year. We've reviewed it a lot already before the [state test]. It is kind of a waste of time.

> [Student] With Shakespeare or the *Odyssey,* which we're reading now, our study is interrupted to do [state test] exercises. . . . It gets in the way of the time we have to be in class.

It seems that our heavy emphasis on *equity* has gotten in the way of our second goal of *excellence.* How to balance these two desirable goals is a constant challenge for the schools.

Although general education classroom teachers, in collaboration with other teachers and specialists, can help children who are gifted meet some of these goals, special programs are essential to consistently achieve. We can modify the school program for any group of exceptional children in three areas: learning environment, content, and cognitive strategies. A special type of change in learning environment involves moving the student more rapidly through school—educational acceleration. In this section, we explore these topics, focusing on children who are intellectually gifted.

A school program for students who are gifted involves modifications to the learning environment, to curriculum content, and to cognitive strategies.

Adapting the Learning Environment

Teachers can change the learning environment in many ways, but most of those ways are designed to bring children who are gifted together for instruction for a period of time. The aim is threefold:

▶ To provide students who are gifted with an opportunity to interact with one another and to learn with and be stimulated by their intellectual peers

▶ To reduce the spread of abilities and performance within the group on instructionally relevant dimensions (past achievement, for example) to make it easier for the teacher to provide instructionally relevant materials

▶ To place students who are gifted with an instructor who has expertise in working with such students or in a relevant content field

Because changes in the learning environment affect the entire school system, they have received more attention at the school district level than have changes in skills and content, which remain primarily classroom issues. Still, the three elements are closely related: Changes in the learning environment for students who are gifted are often necessary to meet the instructional goals of special skills and differential content mastery.

A number of strategies are being used to modify the placement of gifted students so as to meet their special needs. The strategies are of two main types.

Flexible pacing There are a variety of educational adjustments that allow students to move more rapidly through the standard curriculum after they have shown mastery over the standard lessons. Accelerating a student to the next grade would be one approach, or students may be allowed to "test out" for courses where they can show consistent mastery of the material. Students who manifest clearly advanced development can be considered for early entrance to the next level, whether it be kindergarten or college.

Grouping This strategy brings gifted students together for learning so that they can go at an advanced pace and be stimulated by others of like ability. This can be done through a special class, a part-time special class, or *cluster grouping*, which brings six to ten gifted students together to form a subgroup within the larger classroom. Sometimes students are allowed to volunteer for a *magnet school*, which can draw students who excel and are interested in specific subject areas.

The great current interest in the strategy of *inclusion* for children with disabilities has also influenced the education for the students who are gifted. Educators have renewed efforts to find strategies for effectively teaching students who are gifted within the framework of the general classroom (Maker, 1993; Parke, 1989). Devices such as cluster grouping and the use of a *teacher-consultant* have been revisited in an effort to avoid the physical separation of students who are gifted from their peers, particularly at the elementary level. Despite efforts at inclusion, many school systems rely on pull-out programs and resource rooms conducted by specially qualified teachers to modify the regular program in important ways to meet the educational needs of students with special gifts and talents.

The magnet school is a recent addition to the options available to bright students and is a type of performance grouping. Magnet schools often specialize in subject matter such as mathematics or in an activity such as art, and they encourage interested and qualified students to attend. Students who are gifted are interested in magnet schools that allow them to study at advanced levels and with other highly motivated students.

A study conducted in an elementary magnet school used interview techniques designed to reveal the students' perceptions about the magnet-school environment, with its clustering of gifted students in elementary classrooms. Getting the students to give their perceptions of the situation was done in addition to seeking objective descriptions of the situation. Questions were asked that allowed the

Changes in the learning environment for gifted students are necessary to meet the instructional goals of special skills and differential content development.
(© Elizabeth Crews)

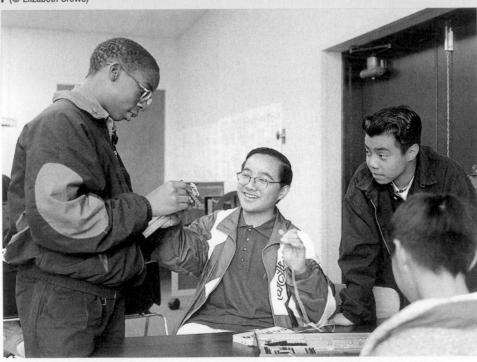

students to express their own feelings, such as "When you think of your experience of being a student in [the magnet school], what stands out in your mind?" (Cross, Stewart, & Coleman, 2003).

Fifteen gifted students at various grade levels were extensively interviewed. These students revealed that they felt more at home socially and academically in this school than they had in previous academic settings, and they discussed their ambitions to go to "Harvard or Yale." (Such students usually know little about either Harvard or Yale, but these universities are symbolic of the excellence to which they aspire.)

This approach to studies, one that taps the students' attitudes and perceptions, is becoming more popular as we realize that student performance on achievement tests is not as important as the students' own perceptions about their abilities and goals in life.

Among other recent developments are the designs for *charter schools* that are freed from some of the standard rules for public schools so that they can try innovative approaches to education. Gifted students can often find a more comfortable setting in these schools with their emphasis on individual performance and accomplishments. And there is another type of educational setting for gifted students that is about as far away as one can get from general education inclusion: the *residential schools*, established in ten states, that bring together highly talented students for their last two or three years of secondary school. Instead of floating through their last two years of high school, as many gifted students do, students in these residential schools are given a rigorous introduction to higher-level thinking and study.

Coleman (2003) conducted an ethnographic study of a number of these students, living in the dormitory with them for several months and gaining their confidence. Interested in finding out what life was like in this special school, he conducted interviews and tape-recorded conversations with them.

His first discovery was that students were genuinely shocked to learn that the "Greenhouse Institute" expected them to do homework and lots of it. The shock was that this type of homework takes time, is ever-present, and is never quite finished. Their local high schools had called for little or no studying. Most students claimed that they did not have homework or did not have to study at their home schools.

In a focus group of seniors in this residential school, Coleman found that the challenging nature of homework that required thinking rekindled their interest in learning for its own sake. Often the students also discovered that they did not know how to study or needed to learn study skills all over again. The students complete the equivalent of a high school honors diploma, and recent graduates have called the program more rigorous than courses at the colleges they attended next.

Another aspect of the school was that the students found themselves surrounded by other students as bright as they were—another shock! Coleman reported on four girls who took differing approaches to handling the new environment. Some maintained a social life, while others studied late into the night. Some maintained a physical exercise routine through it all.

All these students have learned how to live in a fast-paced high-energy environment among others who are like them in being serious about learning. They will not need much adjustment to college life, and the amount of content that they have mastered is far beyond what the gifted student in the general education high school will attain.

Flexible pacing versus grouping: These different approaches to educating gifted students represent different value orientations to education. Which is better? "Better for what?" is the response that will lead to appropriate answers.

At the secondary school level, various **special courses** often address the increasing diversity of achievement and aptitude found in that student body. Honors courses or Advanced Placement courses for which students may earn college credit are common and popular. Over ten states have advanced residential schools for high-performing students. The North Carolina School of Science and Mathematics, the Illinois Math and Science Academy, and other schools focus on math and science (Kolloff, 1997).

Regardless of the attractiveness of the context of learning, unless there are clear modifications in content and process (for example, in thinking strategies), not much is likely to be accomplished by merely grouping youngsters of high ability together (Kulik & Kulik, 1997).

Student Acceleration

We can also adapt the educational program by abandoning the traditional practice of going from grade to grade and by varying the length of the educational program. Because more and more knowledge and skills must be learned at the highest levels of the professions, students who are talented and gifted, who are seeking advanced degrees or professional training in fields such as medicine, can find themselves still in school at age 30 and beyond. While skilled workers are earning a living and starting a family, students who are gifted are often dependent on others for a good part of their young adult life. The process of **student acceleration**—passing students through the educational system as quickly as possible—is a clear educational objective for some children. Stanley (1989) described six ways of accelerating students:

▶ *Early school admission.* The intellectually and socially mature child is allowed to enter kindergarten at a younger-than-normal age.

▶ *Skipping grades.* The child can be accelerated by completely eliminating one semester or grade in school. The primary drawback here is the potential for temporary adjustment problems for the student.

▶ *Telescoping grades.* The child covers the standard material but in less time. For example, a three-year middle school program is taught over two years to an advanced group.

▶ *Advanced Placement.* The student takes courses for college credit while still in high school, shortening the college program.

▶ *Dual enrollment in high school and college.* The student is enrolled in college while finishing high school.

▶ *Early college admission.* An extraordinarily advanced student may enter college at 13, 14, or 15 years of age.

Stanley (1989) found that acceleration, particularly through dual enrollment in high school and college and early admission to college, is most effective for many students who excel in mathematics. In a field like mathematics, in which the curriculum content can be organized in sequential fashion, it is possible for bright students to move quickly through the material. Stanley developed a program for accelerating students in mathematics courses and for awarding college credit to children from 12 to 14 years of age. He described one student:

> Sean, who is $12\frac{1}{2}$ years of age, completed four and one-half years of precalculus mathematics in six 2-hour Saturday mornings compared with the 810 forty-five or fifty-minute periods usually required for Algebra I through III, plane geometry, trigonometry, and analytic geometry. . . . [D]uring the second semester of the eighth grade he was given released time to take the introduction to computer science course at Johns Hopkins and made a final grade of A. . . . While still 13 years old, Sean skipped the ninth and tenth grades. He became an eleventh-grader at a large suburban public high school and took calculus with twelfth graders, won a letter on the wrestling team, was a science and math whiz on the school's television academic quiz team, tutored a brilliant seventh grader through two and one-half years of algebra and a year of plane geometry in eight months, played a good game of golf, and took some college courses on the side (set theory, economics, and political science). (p. 175)

All this work allowed Sean to enter Johns Hopkins University as a sophomore with 34 credits at the age of 14. And Sean was just one example. Stanley reported that a number of youngsters with extraordinary talent in mathematics had academic programs that were shortened by accelerating either the student or the content.

From early admission to school to early admission to college, research studies invariably report that children who have been accelerated, as a group, have

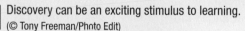
Discovery can be an exciting stimulus to learning.
(© Tony Freeman/Photo Edit)

adjusted as well as or better than children of similar ability who have not been accelerated. Despite these findings, some parents and teachers continue to have strong negative feelings about the practice, and some educational administrators do not want to deal with these special cases. The major objection to the strategy is the fear that acceleration can displace individual children who are gifted from their social and emotional peers, affecting their subsequent social adjustment (Southern, 1991). The result of these misgivings is that many students who are gifted spend the greater part of their first three decades of life in the educational system, often locked in a relatively unproductive role, to the detriment of themselves and society.

As more longitudinal studies are completed, it becomes possible to learn what actually happened to students who were accelerated, instead of what people hoped or feared would happen. Lubinski, Webb, Morelock, and Benbow (2001) conducted a ten-year follow-up on 320 profoundly gifted students who scored high enough on the Scholastic Aptitude Test to qualify as the top one in 10,000 students. Of these 320 students 95 percent had taken advantage of various forms of acceleration (grade skipping, college courses while in high schools, exams for college credit, early entrance to college, and so forth).

The perceptions of these students were highly favorable regarding their acceleration. They saw the procedures as an advantage in their academic progress and maintaining their interest in learning. They found little or no effect of such acceleration on their social life or peer relationships. By their early twenties, 23 had already attained a PhD, 9 had a law degree, and 7 were doctors of medicine. Another 150 or so of this sample continued to work toward advanced degrees. These results are even more positive than those of similar studies and clearly suggest that the fears of educators and parents that such acceleration would harm the students socially are largely unfounded.

There is little evidence to show that highly gifted students who are radically accelerated (more than two to three years) suffer unfavorable social or emotional effects (Gross & Van Vliet, 2003). These students do not burn out; they do not lose interest in their area of talent; and they do not suffer from large gaps in their academic or social knowledge. Rather, radical acceleration appears to offer extraordinary benefits for highly gifted children for both their intellectual development and their social and emotional health.

Although most acceleration for gifted students has been done on a student-by-student basis, there have been an increasing number of institutional attempts to bring groups of students together for acceleration. The residential schools noted above are one example. Another model is the Early Entrance Program at California State University at Los Angeles (Maddox, 2003). This program accepts about one hundred high-performing students under 16 for a college entrance program. The key elements in the students accepted are a strong desire to attempt a challenging program, cooperative parents, and a history of high achievement.

The accelerated students (under age sixteen) must be on the campus four days a week and have a schedule such as the one noted in Table 9.5, which resembles the usual program for an entering first-year student. In addition to the time saved (about two years), the students have the advantage of being in a group whose members encourage, mentor, and support one another.

TABLE 9.5
Sample of an Early Entrance Program Freshman Schedule of Curriculum

FALL	WINTER	SPRING
ENGL 101 Frosh Composition (A1)	ENGL 102 Composition 11 (A1)	ENGL 250 Literature (C1)
MATH 102 College Algebra (A4)	HIST 202B U.S. History 11 (A1^)	POLS 150 American Govt. (A1*)
HIST 202 A U.S. History 1 (A1)	Any Natural Science (C1–3)	Any Natural Science (C1–3)
Intro to Higher Ed. (IHE) (A5)	Any Elective*	Any Elective*
Frosh Study Hall		
*Math 101 for nonscience majors *AI is American Institutions	*science-based majors take: MATH 103 Trigonometry	*science-based majors take: MATH 206 Calculus I

Source: From Richard S. Maddox, Early Start: The early entrance program at California State University, Los Angeles, *Gifted Educator Communicator 34* (3 & 4) (2003): 42–49. Reprinted with permission.

A comprehensive report on the impact of educational acceleration brings together the views of a variety of scholars and research data to examine why schools do not use acceleration more often as one tool in the education of gifted students (Colangelo, Assouline, & Gross, 2004). The report considers why schools hold back America's bright students:

► Schools' lack of familiarity with the research on acceleration

► A belief that children must be kept with their age peers

► A belief that acceleration "hurries" children out of childhood

► A concern that acceleration could hurt students socially

► Political concerns about "equality" for all

► The concern that other students will be offended

None of these concerns is supported by research. Instead the report, *A Nation Deceived,* finds highly favorable results for these acceleration approaches.

Adapting Curriculum

Effective Education Programs

An important question to raise in the education of gifted students—and in all education—is "Are the practices we are using beneficial, or do they just represent established practice, which through repetition becomes the established way of doing things?"

Effective education programs support the cognitive and affective needs of all gifted students.

While a number of practices such as problem solving, problem finding, and use of microcomputers can be used effectively with all students, acceleration and high-level curriculum seem to be especially relevant to gifted students (Shore & Delcourt, 1996).

Curriculum Compacting

One strategy to help gifted students avoid the chronic boredom of having to "learn" things they already know is **curriculum compacting.** The basic principle of compacting is that if students already know something and have the basic skills to apply the knowledge, they should be allowed to move on to other areas of learning (Reis, Burns, & Renzulli, 1992). The critical point of compacting is that students are allowed to show their knowledge when *they* are ready, so they don't have to wait until the whole class is prepared for the assessment.

Showing their knowledge can involve a simple checkpoint or an exit slip, or it can involve a major test and a portfolio of work samples. The level of documentation needed to allow a student to move on depends on the amount of content being compacted. As a rule, the greater the amount of content being compacted, the more extensive the documentation needed. For example, if second-grade students will be released from a lesson on regrouping when adding two-digit numbers, a checkpoint with a sample of problems to work correctly is likely to be sufficient. If, however, a high school student is to be released (with credit) from French 1, a full set of documentation, including tests, work samples, and conversational interviews, is likely to be needed.

The most appropriate curriculum areas for compacting are those that focus on mastery of basic knowledge and skills. These might include vocabulary, basic application skills (such as grammar, arithmetic, and spelling), factual knowledge in a given subject, and basic comprehension in reading. These areas can be readily assessed to document mastery. Once students have shown mastery of the basics, they can be released from further direct instruction, guided practice (classwork), and independent practice (homework) on this set of knowledge and skills. Essentially, curriculum compacting allows students to "buy time" for other, more appropriate, learning experiences. How can this time be used?

Gallagher and Gallagher (1994) described how teachers can use *acceleration, enrichment, sophistication,* and *novelty* to individualize the curriculum of the student who is gifted. (See the "Curriculum Modifications" box.)

Educators can use content acceleration, enrichment, sophistication, and novelty to individualize a student's curriculum.

Content Acceleration and Enrichment

The purpose of **content acceleration** is to move students through the traditional curriculum at a fast rate. The process allows students to master increasingly complex sets of ideas. For example, by learning calculus in ninth grade, students have the foundation to begin physics and chemistry, subjects that require the skills of calculus. The curriculum modifications box shows how content can be accelerated in mathematics and other subject areas.

Content enrichment gives students the opportunity for a greater appreciation of the topic under study by expanding the material for study (exploring additional examples, using specific illustrations). Having students read the diaries of Civil War soldiers on both sides, for example, enriches their perspective on the war.

Curriculum Modifications for Students Who Are Gifted

MODIFICATION	MATH	SCIENCE	LANGUAGE ARTS	SOCIAL STUDIES
Acceleration	Algebra in fifth grade	Early chemistry and physics	Learning grammatical structure early	Early introduction to world history
Enrichment	Changing bases in number systems	Experimentation and data collecting	Short-story and poetry writing	Reading biographies of persons for historical insight
Sophistication	Mastering the laws of arithmetic	Learning the laws of physics	Mastering the structural properties of plays, sonnets, etc.	Learning and applying the principles of economics
Novelty	Probability and statistics	Science and its impact on society	Rewriting Shakespeare's plays to give them happy endings	Creating future societies and telling how they are governed

Source: From J. Gallagher and S. Gallagher (1994). *Teaching the Gifted Child* (4th ed.). Copyright © 1994 by Allyn and Bacon. Adapted by permission.

This form of differentiated content for students who are gifted is often used in the general education classroom because it requires no change in content, just additional assignments.

Content Sophistication

Content sophistication challenges students who are gifted to use higher levels of thinking to understand ideas that average students of the same age would find difficult or impossible to comprehend. The objective is to encourage children who are gifted to understand important abstractions, scientific laws, or general principles that can be applied in many circumstances. One example is *values,* an area rarely explored in general educational programs. The diversity in our society often causes us to overlook important common principles that we share with one another.

One example of content sophistication would be to introduce the abstract concept of *change* (see the box on page 364). The focus of the study is not on changes in culture, nor on changes due to the discovery of DNA, nor on change due to graduation from the football team, but on the process of change itself. The notion that there are properties of change that remain constant regardless of the particular focus of change is a substantial insight for a gifted student, and the idea that change is pervasive, affecting all aspects of our lives, is also a sophisticated insight. An instructional unit on change could generate a variety of independent study projects, each with a different content focus, from literature to popular music to the aging process.

Content Novelty

Content novelty is the introduction of material that normally would not appear in the general curriculum because of time constraints or the abstract nature of the content. Students who are gifted are often able to see relationships across content fields. Because of this ability, a teacher could describe one or two examples and have the students think of others.

Generalizations and Outcomes About change

GENERALIZATIONS	OUTCOMES
1. Change is pervasive.	Understand that change permeates our lives and our universe.
2. Change is linked to time.	Illustrate the variability of change on the basis of time.
3. Change may be perceived as systematic or random.	Categorize types of change, given several examples. Demonstrate the change process at work in a piece of literature.
4. Change may represent growth and development or regression and decay.	Interpret change in selected works as progressive or regressive.
5. Change may occur according to natural order or be imposed by individuals or groups.	Analyze social and individual change in a given piece of literature.

Source: From J. Van Tassel-Baska, *Guide to teaching language arts curriculum for high-ability learners,* (Williamsburg, VA: College of William and Mary, Center for Gifted Education, 1999). Reprinted with permission.

The distinction between *content enrichment* and *content novelty* is that enrichment is linked to the standard curriculum and takes off from that curriculum, whereas novelty can be totally apart from the standard curriculum.

Adapting Teaching Strategies

One of our goals in educating gifted students—and all students—is to capitalize on skills they already have: that is, the ability to generate new information from existing information. If I tell you that "Mary is taller than Joyce and Joyce is taller than Betty," you most likely will generate the new information that "Mary is taller than Betty." You have generated new information from old knowledge.

The ability to generate new information from old is extremely valuable. The cognitive processes for doing so can be simple exercises like the examples above, or they can lead to a new solution for global warming, the discovery of genes linked to cancer, or an improved transportation system. All students need to increase their ability to generate new information from old, but particularly gifted students, who have the capability for dealing with problems of greater complexity than do their agemates.

Focusing instructionally on the enhancement of thinking skills and dimensions such as creativity, problem solving, problem finding, and so on addresses higher-level thinking skills. Few students, no matter how bright, will be likely to discover, on their own, calculus, the scientific method, or the creation of depth perspective in art. These must be taught, and we expect students to produce findings and results that will demonstrate that they have learned the skills required for the generation of new knowledge or information.

Students need to be taught higher-level thinking skills such as creativity, problem solving, and problem finding.

Problem-Based Learning

There are specific strategies to help students learn search techniques so that they themselves can gather information that will allow them to solve a problem. The essence of **problem-based learning** (PBL) is as follows:

1. *The students are presented with an ill-structured problem.* (For example, a student has suddenly become ill with a number of odd symptoms. The cause of this condition is not evident.)

2. *The students are made stakeholders in the problem.* (They are to play the role of medical detectives tracking down the diagnosis for the condition and must use a variety of search techniques, such as surfing the Internet, to arrive at an answer.)

3. *The instructor plays the role of metacognitive coach, not information-giver.* (The teacher may point out possible sources of information or ways of accessing various sources, perhaps even suggesting that students interview community medical personnel, but will not provide the answer.)

Using a combination of small-group and individual work, the students try to arrive at the answer. (In the above problem, they finally decided that the cause was the West Nile virus. They recommended control of mosquitoes but not closing the school, since the disorder is not contagious.)

Teachers receive special training for the role of coach in the PBL model. These PBL methods have been used to teach economics, social studies, language arts, science, and even medical school subjects. The observations from diverse PBL programs are remarkably similar: The students are energized by the nature of the problems presented, play an active and enthusiastic role in seeking new knowledge to solve each problem, and report excitement and increased interest as a byproduct of the PBL approach (Barrows, 1988; Doig & Werner, 2000; Gallagher & Stepien, 1996; Maxwell, Bellisimo, & Mergandoller (2001).

The way to develop problem-solving skills in individuals who are gifted and those who are not is *not* to drill them on unconnected facts but to help them build a knowledge structure of interrelated information. And the key to this is

> practice, thousands of hours of practice. . . . There may be some as yet undiscovered basic abilities that underlie the attainment of truly exceptional performance . . . but for the most part, practice is by far the best predictor of performance. (Chase & Chi, 1981, p. 12)

To help students with problem solving, do not drill on unconnected facts. Instead, help students build a knowledge structure of interrelated information.

Creativity

Creativity is "a mental process by which an individual creates new ideas or products, or recombines existing ideas and products in a fashion that is novel to him or her" (Gallagher, 1985, pp. 268, 303). More attention has probably been paid to creativity than to any other single objective in the education of children who are gifted and talented. We expect that superior intellectual development or talent gives students the ability to generate novel and better solutions to problems.

An important part of problem-based learning is for the students to feel they are specialists as they search for information.

Creativity and Giftedness What is the link between high intelligence and creativity? These terms have become separated in the past because intelligence tests measure

Superior intellectual talent enables students to generate new and better solutions to problems.

Students use brainstorming to extend their intellectual fluency by discussing a particular problem and suggesting as many answers as possible for the problem. During brainstorming, criticism and evaluation are delayed until all ideas have been presented.
(© Susie Fitzhugh)

reasoning ability and past knowledge, whereas creativity represents the process by which students and adults produce unique products of value to themselves and to society. Not everyone who scores high on intelligence tests will be creative, though many will. What characteristics encourage or drive some students to be manifestly creative, and what can we, as educators, do to enhance them?

Many investigators and observers have studied the characteristics linked to creativity. Simonton (1999) has generated a list of creativity facilitators that gives us some clues as to how creativity comes about.

CHARACTERISTICS LINKED TO CREATIVITY

▶ A wide range of interests, providing a base for unique associations

▶ Openness to novel experiences, which stimulates creativity

▶ Ability to think of unrelated ideas at the same time

▶ Cognitive and behavioral flexibility, allowing investigation along unconventional paths

▶ Introverted personality, permitting solitary contemplation

▶ Being an independent, autonomous, and nonconventional thinker

It is increasingly clear that many general education classrooms with their standard curricula, worksheets, and restrictive management are destined to impede the development of independent thinking without meaning to do so. It is also clear that if one of your instructional goals is student independent thought, you will need to plan carefully to bring about this desired result.

Notice that evaluation becomes an important part of the process after the **divergent thinking**—that is, producing many different answers to a question— takes place. Once the ideas are produced, the group can choose those that seem

Creativity can be seen as an interaction among persons, products, and environment. Creativity can be stimulated by small-group activities.

most likely to solve the problem. Brainstorming, then, requires divergent thinking; judgment is more evaluative.

Divergent thinking requires fluency, flexibility, and originality.

Creativity has always been a fascinating topic. How did Mozart, Shakespeare, Newton, the Curies—and the thousands of other creative persons who made a difference in their culture with their discoveries and products—get to be creative?

In the last part of the twentieth century, there was a belief that there were two quite different types of students, the "high IQ score students" and the "high creativity" students. Studies were conducted to show how they were different (Getzels & Jackson, 1962). We now have a different view. Csikszentmihalyi said, "creativity can be defined as an idea or product that is original, valued, and implemented" (Csikszentmihalyi & Wolfe, 2000). Figure 9.1 shows a simplified model of complex interactions in which cognitive abilities, key personality traits, and favorable environments combine to generate the ideas or products noted in the definition. Note that the school is only one of many factors in the environment, but does the school facilitate creative activities of students, or hinder them? Csikszentmihalyi (1996) reports a study of exceptionally creative writers, musicians, Nobel Prize scientists, and others. These persons almost never mentioned their elementary or secondary schools as having helped develop their expertise and interest that led to their accomplishments. Almost all of them mentioned some influential teachers, but the classroom activities were remembered as boring and repressive.

If we look at the desired personality characteristics in Figure 9.1, we can ask ourselves if we, in our schools, emphasize risk taking or devote ourselves to

FIGURE 9.1
Components of Creativity

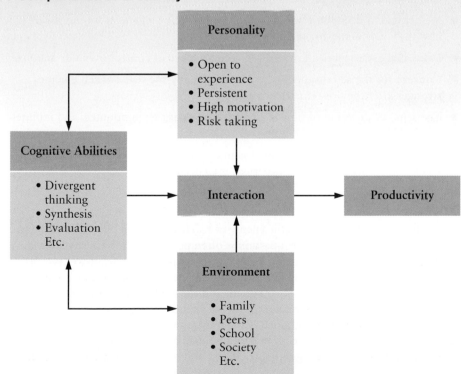

students' openness to experiences beyond the standard lessons. Some programs have been specifically designed to stimulate creativity in the schools, such as the Future Problem Solving program (Torrance, 1969), where students are asked to think about alternative futures, or Odyssey of the Mind, where teams of students design answers to the complex problems presented. Students may work intermittently on such projects for weeks. But these programs are exceptions rather than the rule. As our discussion of the influence of No Child Left Behind legislation makes clear, programs of this type are even less likely to be implemented today unless specific plans are generated to stimulate cognitive processes. And it is cognitive processes such as divergent thinking, originality, evaluation, and so forth, on topics of importance to the students that bring forth personality characteristics such as high motivation and persistence in creating a quality product.

Csikszentmihalyi (1990) describes a recognizable phenomenon he calls *flow*, which is a state in which "people are so involved in an activity that nothing else seems to matter; the experience itself is so enjoyable that people will do it even at great cost; for the sheer sake of doing it" (p. 4). Many creative artists and scientists report such experiences. It becomes a matter of importance as to whether we can individually create the conditions for such experiences for ourselves or for our students. Csikszentmihalyi reports some components of the flow experience:

▶ The experience usually occurs when we confront tasks we have a chance of completing.

▶ We must be able to concentrate on what we are doing.

▶ Concentration is possible because the task undertaken has clear goals.

▶ The task undertaken provides immediate feedback.

▶ We act with a deep but effortless involvement that removes from our awareness the worries and frustrations of everyday life.

▶ Enjoyable experiences allow us to exercise a sense of control over our actions.

▶ Concern for the self disappears, yet paradoxically the sense of self emerges stronger after the flow experience is over.

| Limited time often prevents teachers from presenting a sophisticated curriculum to students.

▶ The sense of duration of time is altered; hours pass by in minutes, and minutes can stretch out to seem like hours.

We need to reflect as to whether the design of our educational environment and curricula will easily allow these experiences to occur.

Time

The failure to recognize *time* as the enemy of teachers and teaching is at the heart of many teachers' disputes. The question is often posed, "Cannot the average student learn what is being taught to students who are gifted?" The answer is "Yes," if you disregard the time factor. For example, middle school students who are gifted can be taught about the solar system and the various theories about its origin in an enrichment lesson because they have already mastered the required curriculum in less than the time allotted. Could average students also master these theories? Of course, if they are given enough time. But they have not yet mastered the required lessons of the regular curriculum, and they also have greater difficulty with the concepts of distance, of orbits, and of centrifugal force—difficulty that will extend further the time they need to master the theories.

Time is a fixed constant. Between 180 and 200 days are available in a school year, so there is not an unlimited period in which students can master needed knowledge and skills. Youngsters who learn faster than others will be able to master more knowledge and practice more of the necessary skills than will other students in the same amount of time. Such differences are a fact of life that we, as educators, must adjust to, instead of pretending that they don't exist.

■ Adapting Technology

The rapid development of educational technology has made mountains of knowledge easily accessible to every student who has access to a computer. This development is a boon for gifted students. An entire encyclopedia is available on a single small disk—it's like having a library inside their home. The challenge for the teacher is to ensure that students learn the best ways to use the computer as a learning tool.

One of the half-truths about education has been that teachers cannot teach concepts and ideas any more complicated than they themselves understand, that they cannot instruct students in, say, Newton's laws or postimpressionism art if they themselves don't know about those topics. That perception is pessimistic and generally incorrect. If teachers know how to access major references or sources of information, they can open the door to more knowledge for their students, who can then explore for themselves. (Students who are gifted can—and often do—surpass their teachers in understanding selective fields.) Of course, teachers have access to these new sources of information as well and, by using the same technology, can become continuous learners themselves. See the Houghton Mifflin Teacher Education website for an expanded list of assistive technology equipment.

One of the advantages of increasingly accessible technology is that more challenging assignments can be legitimately given to gifted students. For example, some California schools have a senior high school project (the Quest senior project) that lasts the entire senior year, is designed by the student, and makes extensive use of outside resources to develop a credible project (Mrazik & Lind, 2003). Such projects can be used for legitimate accountability for gifted students, rather than routine statewide tests.

The role of the local teacher will change from one of *direct instruction* to that of *instructional coach* of individual students. Teachers also need to help students evaluate information they obtain from such sources as the Internet. The largely unscreened communications on the Internet allow many outrageously incorrect statements to be widely broadcast. A new challenge is teaching students the difference between legitimate information and spurious information.

> Teachers can help gifted students explore new areas of knowledge by teaching them to distinguish between legitimate information on the Internet and less credible information.

Of particular advantage to many gifted students in rural areas is *distance learning*—interactive television—to bring complex ideas to the bright students in remote areas. The North Carolina School of Science and Mathematics, a special statewide school for highly talented students, engaged its highly educated faculty to construct a precalculus course and beam it to all areas of the state (Wilson, Little, Coleman, & Gallagher, 1997). There will be much more use of distance learning in the near future, to the great advantage of gifted students.

> Houghton Mifflin Teacher Education website
> http://education.college.hmco.com/students

■ Transition

The typical student goes through many transitions: adjusting to the changes from kindergarten to first grade, elementary to middle school, middle school to secondary school, and perhaps to university or advanced technical training. These transitions can be even more difficult for students who have been accelerated. Some counseling is advisable where needed.

The gifted student may well add to that sequence the transition to graduate or professional training. The multiple talents of many gifted students cause difficult decisions between competing careers (in each of which they could be successful), and it is important that they receive the kind of career information that will enable them to make a good personal choice.

One of the authors of this book once knew a gifted student who was intent on following a career in music. His college adviser, aware of the young man's stratospheric scores in mathematics, pressured him to seek a career in physics or engineering where he could make a "tangible contribution" to society.

The student considered this advice and made his decision. He transferred to another university and continued his career in music! Not all students have such self-confidence in their own choices, however, so it is important that they receive an even-handed presentation of information and counseling.

■ Family and Lifespan Issues

Homeschooling

One of the educational phenomena of recent years has been a movement toward **homeschooling,** involving over one million children. They have been receiving their education at home (Ray, 1997). Although homeschooling originated with parents anxious to maintain a religious element in their child's education, it has become a vehicle for many parents of gifted and talented students. Many of these parents have despaired of the public schools' ability to meet the needs of their exceptional children.

Such education has now become feasible through the Internet. No longer is the school the gatekeeper or exclusive dispenser of knowledge. The access that the Internet provides opens wide the door to knowledge of all sorts. The student can focus on a particular project without having to stop at intervals to change classes, nor do children being homeschooled have to limit themselves to grade-level books or texts or curricula. The concern that such homeschooled children would be deprived of social opportunities has been proven largely untrue, for parents make plans for their child to join clubs, recreational sports, and other activities (Kearney, 1998).

There have been few serious efforts to evaluate the overall impact of homeschooling on students, but there have been enough favorable reports from parents to get the attention of other parents seeking an educational alternative for a gifted child. It has also caught the attention of educational administrators who are aware of losing some of their better students to this alternative and who therefore seek ways to entice these children back into the public school programs.

Prolonged Schooling and Financial Considerations

The economic and vocational futures for most individuals with gifts and talents are bright. The vocational opportunities awaiting them are diverse, including the fields of medicine, law, business, politics, and science. Only in the arts, where a limited number of opportunities exist to earn a comfortable income, do people who are gifted encounter major social and economic barriers to their ambitions.

It is virtually certain that when most students who are gifted finish secondary school, they will go on to more school. They often have from eight to ten *more* years of training before they can expect to begin earning a living. This is especially true if they choose careers in medicine, law, or the sciences. The delay in becoming an independent wage earner creates personal and social problems that researchers are just beginning to study. Prolonged schooling means that individuals who are gifted must receive continued financial support. The most common forms of financial support are assistance from family and subsidies from private or public sources. If financial aid takes the form of bank or government loans, then a man or woman who is gifted can begin his or her career with a substantial debt. This period of extended schooling also tends to cause gifted individuals to postpone marriage and raising a family.

The psychological problems that result from remaining dependent on others for financial support for as much as thirty years remain unexplored. We need to consider these issues before we burden students who are gifted with more schooling requirements intended to meet the demands of this rapidly changing world.

National Network of Families
with Gifted Children (NNFGC)
www.nnfgc.org

Summary

▶ Children who are gifted may show outstanding abilities in a variety of areas, including intellect, academic aptitude, creative thinking, leadership, and the visual and performing arts. They also can show talent in superior self-knowledge and interpersonal relationships.

▶ Intellectual giftedness appears to be created by a strong combination of heredity and environment, with a close and continuing interaction.

▶ Longitudinal studies indicate that most children who are identified as gifted are healthy and well adjusted and achieve well into adulthood. There are some exceptions (called underachievers).

▶ International comparisons of U.S. students with students from other countries in mathematics and science revealed that even top-level U.S. students lag behind top-level students of other countries.

▶ Ability grouping, combined with a differentiated program, has been demonstrated to be an effective strategy that results in improved performance by students who are gifted.

▶ Cognitive strategies—problem finding, problem solving, and creativity—are the focus of many special programs for students who are gifted.

▶ Creativity depends on the individual's capacity for divergent thinking, a willingness to be different, strong motivation, and a favorable context.

▶ Acceleration, the more rapid movement of gifted students through their long educational span, appears to have positive results for them.

▶ Society's traditional expectations of gender roles may provide special obstacles for gifted children, limiting their willingness to explore the full range of their talents

▶ Some gifted students may be labeled as underachievers due to personal characteristics (such as feelings of inferiority, low self-confidence, expectations of failure) while others may underachieve because of their resistance to traditional educational programs and practices.

▶ Many students possess giftedness that is "hidden" by differing cultural perspectives, linguistic backgrounds, and life experiences. A variety of tests, observations, and performance indicators seem necessary to discover these gifted students.

▶ Children with physical and sensory disabilities can be intellectually gifted, but often their abilities are undiscovered because less has been expected of them.

▶ The abilities of all gifted students can be enhanced by comprehensive and rigorous programming to meet their special needs.

Future Challenges

1. Will gifted students receive an appropriate education?

The conflicting education priorities between equity and excellence seem to be tilted in favor of equity. It will take deliberate planning and commitment to national excellence to provide our gifted students with a challenging education.

2. Are there programs for young children who are gifted?

The early years are increasingly seen as fundamental to a developing intellect. Prekindergarten programs are blossoming across the country and will need to provide for gifted prekindergarten students who already can read and do basic arithmetic. This is an early challenge for educators to develop a differentiated curriculum.

3. How can we ensure that gifted and talented students from culturally-linguistically diverse and/or economically disadvantaged families are recognized and served appropriately?

We continue to face the challenge of underrepresentation of some groups of children in our programs for gifted and talented students. Given the rapidly changing demographics across the country, this disproportionate representation will likely increase unless we take proactive steps to address it. We need to look to models that help teachers recognize and nurture potential, using structured observations of students engaged in meaningful and dynamic work.

4. What are best practices for identifying gifted students?

The identification of a student as gifted is a high-stakes decision. Access to educational opportunities hinges on this decision, and making the right decision may in fact be critical to the student's well-being. What can we do to (1) ensure that students who need services provided through gifted education are not overlooked and (2) make sure that we do not identify as gifted students who do not need those services? We need to use multiple types of information and multiple sources of input in the identification process; we need to match the information directly with the kinds of services that will be provided.

Key Terms

content acceleration   *p. 362*

content enrichment   *p. 362*

content novelty   *p. 363*

content sophistication   *p. 363*

creativity   *p. 365*

curriculum compacting   *p. 362*

divergent thinking   *p. 366*

gifted underachievers   *p. 347*

homeschooling   *p. 370*

problem-based learning (PBL)   *p. 365*

special courses   *p. 358*

student acceleration   *p. 358*

Resources

References of Special Interest

Colangelo, N. (Ed.). (2004). *Templeton national report on acceleration: A nation deceived.* Iowa City, IA: Bolen &

Blank International Center for Gifted Education. This report is a comprehensive compilation of the effects of educational acceleration on gifted students. Eleven specialists have written chapters reviewing research and practice.

Colangelo, N., & Davis, G. (Eds.). (2003). *Handbook of gifted education* (3rd ed.). Boston: Allyn & Bacon. *Over forty well-known authors in the field of gifted education have contributed chapters to this volume, which includes sections on instructional models, creativity and thinking skills, and psychological and counseling services.*

Coleman, L., & Cross, T. (2001). *Being gifted in school: An introduction to development, guidance, and teaching.* Waco, TX: Prufrock Press. *An introductory text stressing the concept that giftedness is the application of abilities. The book provides a variety of teaching and program models offering stimulation for such students. There is an interesting section on identification and an extensive section on teaching.*

Gallagher, J., & Gallagher, S. (1994). *Teaching the gifted child* (4th ed.). Boston: Allyn & Bacon. *A widely read general textbook on the education of gifted students. Topics such as differentiated curriculum, thinking processes, and administrative adjustments are discussed, along with several case studies.*

Heller, K., Monks, F., Sternberg, R., & Subotnik, R. (Eds.). (2000). *International handbook of giftedness and talent* (2nd ed.). New York: Elsevier. *A comprehensive international review of present knowledge of students with giftedness and talent. In addition to good summaries of what is happening in the United States, there are chapters dealing with giftedness in Germany, Israel, Australia, Canada, Russia, Taiwan, Latin American countries, and other countries that have not been covered by textbooks in the United States. There are fifteen chapters on gifted education and programming.*

Kerr, B.A., & Cohn, S.J. (2001). *Smart boys: Talent, manhood, and the search for meaning.* Scottsdale, AZ: Great Potential. *The role of society's expectations for boys and how these expectations interact with the development of gifts and talent are examined in this comprehensive treatment. The authors introduce us to the world of gifted boys and the often poignant struggles they face growing up. This book will be useful to counselors, parents, and teachers, and to gifted boys and young men themselves.*

Neihart, M., Reis, S., Robinson, N., & Moon, S. (Eds.). (2002). *The social and emotional development of gifted children.* Waco, TX: Prufrock Press. *A comprehensive review in 24 chapters of what we know about the special social and emotional problems of gifted students. The book covers topics such as perfectionism, depression, delinquency, and so on. It includes a section on promising practices and interventions and recommendations for future action.*

Reis, S. (1998). *Work left undone: Choices and compromises of talented females.* Mansfield Center, CT: Creative Learning Press. *An impressive work on the special and unique world of the gifted female in American society. Reis reviews two decades of research on the topic and also includes numerous case studies and vignettes to underline her points. She makes some major recommendations for gifted females, addressing parents, teachers, and administrators. This volume is also a source of curricular materials and resources for coping with the social and cultural factors affecting gifted females.*

Ross, P. (Ed.). (1993). *National excellence.* Washington, DC: U.S. Department of Education. *This report on the status of the education of students in the United States who are gifted and talented points out that studies have indicated American students fall behind students from other countries in areas such as mathematics and science and that the provisions for such students in the United States are fragmentary and not well supported. Recommendations for improving the situation are included.*

Van Tassel-Baska, J. (1998). *Excellence in educating gifted and talented learners* (3rd ed.). Denver: Love Publishing Company. *This general textbook focuses on curriculum differentiation and provides a number of good suggestions for teachers and administrators.*

Van Tassel-Baska, J. (Ed.). (2004). *Curriculum of gifted and talented students.* Thousand Oaks, CA: Corwin Press. *Differentiated curriculum has been widely recommended as the way to modify the traditional educational program for gifted students—but where is that differentiated curriculum to come from? This volume brings together a variety of experts to show how the standard curricula in math, science, and other content fields can be modified to better meet the needs of gifted students.*

Journals

Educational Leadership
www.ascd.org

Gifted Child Quarterly
www.nagc.org

Journal for the Education of the Gifted
www.prufrock.com/

Journal for Secondary Gifted Education
www.prufrock.com/

Parenting for High Potential
www.nagc.org

Roeper Review
www.roeperreview.org

Professional Organizations

National Association for Gifted Children
www.nagc.org
The Association for the Gifted
www.cec.org

Please visit the book's website at
http://education.college.hmco.com/students for new and
updated information on websites listed here and for the
mailing addresses of the journals and organizations.

LOW-INCIDENCE EXCEPTIONALITIES

The four chapters in Part 3 describe the educational conditions for exceptional children who comprise less than .5 percent of the students in our schools. In many instances, some special planning and individualized programming are required for children who are deaf or hard of hearing, children with visual impairments, children with multiple and severe disabilities, and children with physical disabilities and health impairments. In Chapters 10 through 13, we highlight how these exceptionalities affect students and schools and discuss how the most current research suggests that students should be educated.

CHILDREN WHO ARE DEAF OR HARD OF HEARING

FOCUS QUESTIONS

▶ How do we identify children with hearing losses?

▶ How do hearing losses affect a child's language development, and what can be done to maximize communication potential?

▶ Why is it critical to teach a gestural language to a person who is deaf and to his or her family?

▶ What are the trends in school placement for students who have hearing losses?

▶ What is the Deaf community, and how can it help a student who is deaf or hard of hearing?

▶ What is the effectiveness of cochlear implants?

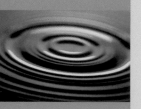

Children who are deaf or hard of hearing have a much greater chance of achieving a communication system (gesture-manual, speech, or both) and academic success than at any time in the past. There is now much broader acceptance of persons who are deaf or hard of hearing in society. In the past two decades, an actress who is deaf won a Tony award for her performance in a Broadway play, and another actress received an Oscar for her performance in the motion picture based on that play, as well as an Emmy for the leading role in a television series about a lawyer who is deaf. Miss America of 1995 is deaf. There is a player who is deaf on a major league baseball team, and one who plays professional football. During the 2000 Olympics, Terrence Parkin, a swimmer who is deaf, won a silver medal. Moreover, there are now doctors, lawyers, directors of government agencies, and other professionals who are deaf. The president of Gallaudet University is deaf. There are many students who are deaf or hard of hearing in regular schools and more adults who are deaf or hard of hearing in the workplace.

Children who are not hard of hearing are more likely to play, interact, and make friends with children who are hard of hearing in regular schools and in their communities. There are now more than 3,000 interpreters in the public schools to translate from speech to gestural language and vice versa (U.S. Department of Education, 1997).

National Deaf Education Center (formerly known as the National Information Center on Deafness) www.clerccenter.gallaudet.edu/infotogo

These advances have been greatly assisted by government mandates. Commissions established by Congress in 1986 and 1988 led to the establishment of the National Information Center on Deafness and the Helen Keller National Center for Technical Assistance and to rules and regulations requiring statewide telephone relaying systems. In addition, all television sets with screens 13 inches or larger sold in the United States now must be equipped to receive captioned broadcasts. The Individuals with Disabilities Education Act (IDEA; PL 101-476), the Americans with Disabilities Act (PL 101-336), the Rehabilitation Act (PL 102-569), and other laws and regulations have increased public awareness of the talents and educational needs of persons who are deaf and hard of hearing. Identification during infancy and early childhood has led to progress for parents and their children through early intervention and educational and communication training.

There is a strong movement to consider persons who are deaf or hard of hearing as a sociocultural language minority rather than as individuals who are disabled (Parasnis, 1997).

In spite of the gains, there is a lack of agreement in the field on several major issues, three of which are critical: what to teach, where to teach it, how to teach it. Our speech-language-oriented society has not readily accepted a sign language system. Thus, some educators of persons who are deaf and hard of hearing strongly advocate oral-speech language. Others advocate sign language or some combination of both. There is a strong movement to consider persons who are deaf or hard of hearing as a sociocultural language minority rather than as individuals who are disabled (Parasnis, 1997; Easterbrooks, 1999).

While reading this chapter, keep in mind that the essential deficit is a partial or total lack of auditory reception and that language can be communicated orally (speech) or by means of signs (manual-movement, visual). Hearing loss is a communication and sociolinguistic experience that begins in the family (Bodner-Johnson & Sass-Lehrer, 2003).

■ Definitions

Hearing losses are defined in terms of the degree of loss, the age at which the loss occurs, and the type of loss.

IDEA defines deafness as a hearing impairment, so "severe that the child is impaired in processing linguistic information through hearing, with or without amplification, that adversely affects the child" (NICHCY, 2002, p. 23). Being hard of hearing is defined as "an impairment in hearing, whether permanent or fluctuating, not adversely affecting a child's educational performance" but is not included under the definition of deafness (p. 2).

Degree of Hearing Loss

Children experience hearing loss before they acquire speech when their hearing loss is genetic or congenital caused by an event during pregnancy; this phenomenon is called **prelinguistic deafness.** Loss after the child has acquired some speech and language is called **postlinguistic deafness.**

The term *hearing loss* has different meanings for different authors. For some, it describes a slight-to-moderate hearing loss (Moores, 1989, p. 1). For others, it describes any hearing loss, mild or severe (Paul & Quigley, 1994). We use the terms *deaf* to refer to a profound or complete inability to hear and *hard of hearing* to refer to all other categories of loss.

The severity of hearing losses is determined by the individual's reception of sound as measured in *decibels (dB).* A loss between 15 and 20 dB is considered slight; increasing degrees of loss range from mild to severe and profound hearing loss or, to use a more common term, deafness (Moores, 2000). Table 10.1 presents the range of degrees of hearing impairments and their descriptive classification, etiology, and potential needs.

Individuals classified as hard of hearing may be able to hear and understand speech, or they can be assisted to do so with hearing aids. Only a small percentage (less than 1 percent) of persons who are deaf are unable to hear speech under any conditions.

The Structure of the Ear and Types of Hearing Loss

The ear is a complicated structure (Figure 10.1), and it functions in a complex way. The middle ear is composed of the tympanic membrane, or eardrum, and the three ear bones: the malleus, the incus, and the stapes. The stapes lies next to the oval window, the gateway to the inner ear (Green, 1999). The inner ear contains the cochlea and the vestibular apparatus, collectively called the labyrinth (Steinberg & Knightly, 1997).

Although defects are possible in structure and function, they can be classified into four categories: conductive losses, sensorineural losses, mixed losses, and central losses.

A *conductive hearing loss* occurs when something blocks the sound passing through the outer or inner ear (March of Dimes, 2000). The blockage can be caused by wax, infections (otitis media), or any type of malformation of the

TABLE 10.1
Degrees of Hearing Impairment

LEVEL OF HEARING LOSS	DESCRIPTION	ETIOLOGY	SOUNDS HEARD	DEGREE OF DISABILITY	POSSIBLE NEEDS
15–25 dB	Slight hearing loss	Serous otitis perforation, monmeric membrane sensorineural loss, tympanosclerosis	Hears vowel sounds clearly; may miss unvoiced consonant sounds	Mild auditory dysfunction in language learning	Hearing aid, lip reading, auditory training, speech therapy, preferential seating
25–40 dB	Mild hearing loss	Serous otitis perforation, tympanosclerosis, monmeric membrane sensorineural loss	Hears only some louder-voiced speech sounds	Auditory learning dysfunction, mild language retardation, mild speech problems, inattention	Hearing aid, lip reading, auditory training, speech therapy
40–65 dB	Moderate hearing loss	Chronic otitis, middle ear anomaly, sensorineural loss	Misses most speech sounds at normal conversational level	Speech problems language retardation, dysfunction, inattention	All of the above plus therapies
65–95 dB	Severe hearing loss	Sensorineural or mixed loss from a sensorineural loss plus middle ear disease	Hears no speech sounds of normal conversation	Severe speech problems, language retardation, learning dysfunction, inattention	All of the above plus sign interpreter
More than 95 dB	Profound hearing loss	Sensorineural or mixed loss	Hears no speech or other sounds	Severe speech problems, language retardation, learning dysfunction, inattention	All of the above

Source: Adapted from Nancy J. Roizen, Hearing loss, in A. J., Capute, & P. J. Accardo, *Developmental disabilities in infancy and childhood,* Vol. 2, *The spectrum of developmental disabilities* (Baltimore: Paul H. Brookes, 1996), p. 481. Adapted with permission.

ear canal. This type of loss is usually temporary and can be corrected by surgery or medication (NIDCD, 1999; Herter, Knightly, & Steinberg, 2002).

Sensorineural hearing losses are caused by defects in the inner ear (cochlea) or the auditory nerve, particularly in the delicate sensory hairs of the inner ear or in the nerves that supply them. Those nerves transmit impulses to the brain (Newton & Stokes, 1999).

Mixed hearing losses result from problems in the outer ear as well as in the middle or inner ear (NICD, 1999). Persons with this type of loss may hear distorted sounds as well as have difficulty with sound level. *Central hearing losses* result from changes in the reception of hearing areas in the brain or damage to the pathways of the brain (NICD, 1999). Central hearing losses are not frequently encountered.

FIGURE 10.1
Structure of the Ear

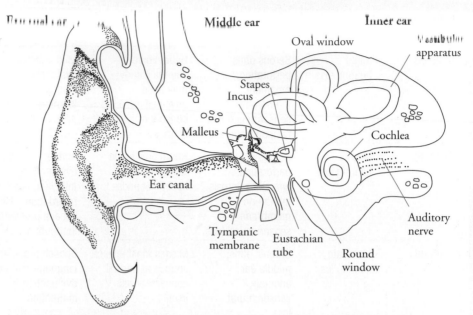

Source: From M. L. Batshaw (Ed.), *Children with disabilities* (3rd ed.) (Baltimore: Paul H. Brookes, 1992), p. 323. Used with the permission of the author.

■ Prevalence of Hearing Loss

About 23 million persons in the United States, or 8 percent of the general population, have some degree of hearing loss. Of these, about 1 percent are deaf (NICD, 2003). During the school year 2000–2001, 70,767 students were listed as deaf or hard of hearing (IDEA, 2002). They accounted for 1.3 percent of students with disabilities (NICHCY, 2003). Of these students, 31 percent were served in regular classes, 20 percent in resource rooms, 31 percent in separate classes, and 19 percent in separate or residential schools (U.S. Department of Education, 1997). Because of the impact of the Education for All Handicapped Children Act (PL 94-142) and IDEA, the education of most children who are hard of hearing and that of many who are deaf has moved from residential and day schools to local schools.

■ Causes of Hearing Loss

Over half the causes of permanent deafness or of being hard of hearing are prenatal in origin (Newton & Stokes, 1999). These causes are estimated to be one-third genetic, one-third environmental or acquired, and one-third unknown (Herter, Knightly, & Steinberg, 2002). Some authorities divide the causes into one-half genetic and one-half environmental (NICD, 2000). There are 70 documented genetic syndromes as well as many other single genetic causes of deafness and partial deafness. Environmental causes include exposure to bacteria, viruses, toxins, and trauma, as well as infection during the course of pregnancy or in the birth process (Herter, Knightly, & Steinberg, 2002). There are a number of illnesses, infections, or accidents that can lead to hearing losses after birth.

Genetic Causes

The genetic causes are disorders inherited from one or both of the parents. More than two hundred different types of genetic deafness have been identified and can be inherited from either a hearing parent or a nonhearing parent (NICD, 1989).

Children with other genetic defects may have associated hearing disorders. For example, children with Down syndrome (a genetic disorder associated with mental retardation) have narrow ear canals and are prone to middle ear infections, which may cause hearing losses. Individuals with cleft palates (an opening in the lip and aboral ridge) also may have repeated middle ear infections, which can result in conductive hearing losses (Roizen, 1997; Herter, Knightly, & Steinberg, 2002).

Congenital conditions such as Rh (hyperbilirubinemia) can develop incompatibility when a mother who is Rh-negative carries a fetus that is Rh-positive. The mother's immune system begins to destroy the fetus's red blood cells when they enter the mother's circulatory system. As a result, the fetus may become anemic and die in utero. If the child survives, he or she is likely to have a high-frequency hearing loss. The drug RhoGAM is available to block the formation of antibodies in the mother's system. Usually, the first pregnancy is not affected, but all subsequent ones are if the condition is not identified and treated (Ward & McCune, 2002).

Boothroyd (1988) reminds us that not all hearing losses due to genetic defects appear at birth. Babies born with perfectly normal hearing may lose it in months or years as a result of heredity (Herter, Knightly, & Steinberg, 2002). Teachers who suspect that a child may be exhibiting signs of a loss should be aware that loss can occur in a child who previously exhibited a normal range of hearing.

Some genetically based hearing losses occur during childhood and adolescence.

Environmental Causes

Some infections that the mother has during pregnancy can cause deafness in her child.

The environmental effects that begin before birth are associated with illness or infections the mother may have had during pregnancy. For example, uncontrolled diabetes in the mother may cause a hearing loss in her child. More specifically, a group of infections that affect the mother but cause severe hearing losses in the fetus have been labeled *TORCHS* (Newton & Stokes, 1999). The *TO* stands for toxoplasmosis, a parasitic disease common in Europe that may be contracted by handling contaminated cat feces or eating infected lamb that has not been cooked sufficiently (Batshaw & Perret, 1992). The *R* stands for rubella (German measles), which, if contracted by the mother, can cause not only serious hearing losses in the child, but also blindness and retardation as well. With the advent of the rubella vaccine, very few cases are occurring (Steinberg & Knightly, 1997). This vaccination must be renewed periodically.

The *C* stands for cytomegalovirus (CMV), an infection in the mother's uterus, which is a major environmental cause of deafness in the United States. CMV can go undiagnosed, or it can be misdiagnosed (sometimes as the flu). A particularly harmful virus, it can pass through the placenta and affect the fetus. It can also be passed through the mother's milk in nursing (Strauss, 1999). Specialists believe that some children with hearing losses caused by rubella may actually have been exposed to CMV (Gothelf, 1991). CMV is so strongly associated with low-birth-weight and premature infants that it has been considered as a possible cause of prematurity as well as of the resulting hearing loss. While the incidence of rubella has decreased 1 percent, CMV has increased from 1 percent to 2 percent (Holden-Pitt & Diaz, 1998). The *HS* stands for herpes simplex virus, which, if untreated, can lead to the death of 60 percent of infected infants. Those who survive may have serious neurological problems and potential hearing loss. Some believe that CMV is a form of herpes virus (Pappas, 1985).

Noise pollution, particularly loud and persistent noises, can cause hearing loss. It is suspected that the noise produced by isolettes for premature babies is related to hearing loss, but this has not been proven (Batshaw & Perret, 1988).

Infections after birth, such as *meningitis* (an inflammation of the membranes covering the brain and spinal cord), can damage the auditory nerve. Because the antibiotics given to treat the infection may also cause damage to the auditory nerve, the dosage for the infant must be measured carefully (Batshaw & Perret, 1992). All infants should be inoculated against meningitis.

The identification during infancy and in early childhood of children who are deaf or hard of hearing means these children have the opportunity for early access to instruction and assistive technology. This increases their potential for communication development and academic success.

(© Elizabeth Crews)

Otitis media is a universal infection among preschoolers.

Otitis media, a universal infection of the middle ear, may cause a hearing loss if it is persistent or recurrent and untreated. It is generally associated with mild-to-moderate hearing losses.

Asphyxia (lack of oxygen) during the birth process may bring about a hearing loss (NIDCD, 2000).

Premature and low-birth-weight infants, particularly very low-birth-weight infants weighing under 2 pounds and those born weighing less than 4 pounds are at greater risk of hearing loss. Because of increasingly successful lifesaving techniques now being used in neonate nurseries, we are seeing an increase in the number of infants with hearing losses (Newton & Stokes, 1999; Rais-Bahrami, Short, & Batshaw, 2002).

Hearing losses can be detected at birth. *Otoacoustic emissions* are low-intensity sounds produced by the middle ear. They can be measured by placing a microphone in the infant's ear canal. If a defect is suspected, it can be verified by the *auditory brain stem response test,* which is described later in this chapter. Because 20 to 30 percent of hearing deficits occur during early childhood, screenings should be conducted at regular intervals. If a hearing loss is identified at birth and fully diagnosed as a hearing deficit by 3 months of age, the infant can be fitted with a hearing aid. Early diagnosis also alerts the parents that the child is deaf and may need a manual language in order to avoid developmental delays (NIDCD, 1999; Herrer, Knightly, & Steinberg, 2002).

■ Characteristics of Children with Hearing Loss

Cognitive Development

Most children who are deaf or hard of hearing possess normal intelligence.

The most important thing to remember about children who are deaf or hard of hearing is that most of them possess normal intelligence. They are not deficient

When reading is taught visually or by a gestural method, deaf children are better able to learn how to read, write, and use language logic forms and to succeed in school.
(© David Young-Wolf/Photo Edit)

or deviant in their cognitive abilities; they are simply children who cannot hear as well as children with normal hearing. However, as these children develop, they have different background experiences, communication histories, and knowledge, and they should not be viewed simply as children who cannot hear. They will need specialized instruction to reach the same cognitive and developmental milestones as children who can hear (Marschark, Lang, & Albertini, 2002). Furthermore, hearing loss is often accompanied by other disabilities that require more complicated interventions. Hearing loss is a silent disability. It is not accompanied by pain, fear, or physical problems. It is only when verbal demands are made on the child that it becomes apparent (Lillo-Martin, 1997).

One of the major problems in the past in determining the intellectual level of children with hearing losses was that the intelligence tests used to measure their abilities were not appropriate for children with hearing losses. Orally (speech) administered intelligence tests greatly underestimate the abilities of a child whose primary language is gestural (Paul & Quigley, 1994). To assess children who are deaf or hard of hearing in written English is like testing a monolingual English-speaking child with Chinese characters (Marschark & Harris, 1996, p. 127). When nonverbal tests are used with a sign system familiar to the child, these children perform well within the normal range (Bellugi & Studdert-Kennedy, 1984).

A child who has not heard the sounds of the language will not be able to decode print if taught in the usual method of matching sounds to print. If reading is taught visually or by a gestural method (such as American Sign Language [ASL] or finger spelling, which are discussed later in the chapter), however, children who are deaf or hard of hearing are able to learn how to read, write, and use language logic forms (for example, past tense, questions, and logical propositions such as if-then or either-or) and will be successful in school. Depending on the degree of hearing present, the child may learn how to use both the gestural system and the oral system of language.

Why most children with hearing losses do not develop literacy skills commensurate with their intelligence is suspected to be a consequence of the hearing impairment not having been identified early. Children who are identified as being deaf and taught a sign language before the age of 2½ perform much better on all tasks than those identified after reaching 2½ years of age (Mauk & White, 1995). This fact is the basis for the position advocating universal auditory screening of infants while in the hospital. Screening is now mandatory at birth in thirty-five states (Marschark, Lam, & Albertini, 2002). In general, early intervention for children who are deaf or hard of hearing, regardless of the method used, has long-term positive results (Carney & Moeller, 1998). Hard-of-hearing children who are fitted with hearing aids before 3 years of age do better than those who receive them after age 3 (Calderon & Greenberg, 1997). What is clear is that children who are deaf or hard of hearing, who have parents who are deaf or hard of hearing, and who are taught a sign language (usually ASL) early usually do far better in school than other such children (Marschark, 2000).

Let us look at some information from linguistics about how all children acquire language and the implications for effective teaching of children who are deaf or hard of hearing.

Hearing screening is recommended at birth, before the infant leaves the hospital.

Language Development

Children who are born deaf or hard of hearing are no different from children born hearing (Lillo-Martin, 1997). During the first year of life, which is called the prelinguistic period (meaning without speech), they will exhibit the same behaviors, such as crying, making comfort sounds, and babbling to parents. In babbling, the child produces his or her first sounds that resemble words (*baba, dada*), and the parents reinforce these sounds and transform them into words. What many parents do not realize is that these behaviors are innately programmed and will appear whether the infant can hear or not. "The evidence that language is a biologically determined, species specific, genetically transmitted capacity is simply overwhelming" (Knight, 2003, p. 306). Infants who can hear typically produce their first word around 12 months of age. For the infant who is deaf, babbling does not develop into words. However, Petitto and Marentette (1991) found that children with severe hearing losses gesture at about the same developmental age as that at which hearing children babble. They concluded that infants are innately predisposed to learn language and do so by stimulating the environment by babbling; if they cannot hear, they use babbling-like hand gestures that are sign equivalents of speech sounds. These signs are not words, but they are similar to the babbling sounds. Parents who are deaf recognize these signs and begin teaching a gestural/manual/visual system, usually ASL. Each language, spoken or gestural, proceeds in similar fashion. If the parents do not help the child form gestures into language, the child may develop his or her own sign system, called *home sign*.

The point is that the innate language mechanism is so strong that children who hear will develop a spoken language and children who are deaf will develop a gestural one. Each will develop the language of his or her home. For the child who can hear, it will be English, French, Spanish—whatever language is spoken in the home. For the child who is deaf, it will be the sign system taught in the home or one developed by the child (Goldin-Meadow, 1998).

Thus, for all children, language begins before birth and proceeds during the first year of life well in advance of the production of the first word at around 12 months of age. The gestures of infants with hearing losses are precursors to learning language in the form of manual signs. Parents must recognize and reinforce these gestures in much the same way that they would reinforce oral sounds. The major problem is that 90 percent of children who are deaf or hard of hearing are born into homes with hearing parents who do not recognize the child's deafness or his or her attempts at a manual language.

These babbling-like gestures are seen in children of parents with severe hearing losses, who tend to reinforce them. Thus, the presence of both babbling and gestures tends to support the position of those who believe there is a strong, innate push to learn how to communicate in one's home, using the same mode of communication as the adults in the home (Goldin-Meadow, 1998). Not all educators of the deaf and hard of hearing prefer teaching a visual system. They introduce auditory-verbal or auditory-oral approaches as soon as identification is made (Stone, 1997; Goldberg, 1997). Both of these methods are discussed below.

Deafness may seriously hamper verbal language development.

The language learning patterns of children who are deaf or hard of hearing and of children who can hear are the same. As noted, most children produce their first word by 12 months of age. By 18 to 22 months of age, they master the logic forms of the language used in their home (Bloom, 1991), and they begin on their own to figure out the rules of language from the spoken examples provided by their environment (Pinker, 1991; Shantz & Eberling, 1991). This ability to independently generate the rules of grammar (particularly syntax or word order) tends to disappear after 6 years of age. If the child masters these rules of grammar by the age of 6, he or she can build on them through instruction. If the child has not acquired them by then, it is extremely difficult or almost impossible to teach them to the child.

Depending on the hearing loss, some children may not be able to distinguish phonemes in a crowded room, a critical skill in learning to read. Children with severe prelinguistic hearing losses who are not provided with amplification and early childhood special education are seriously deprived of the experience they need to use their innate mechanisms to figure out the grammar (syntax) and use (pragmatics) of their language. Not surprisingly, grammar and syntax are two aspects of language that children with prelinguistic hearing losses have difficulty mastering (Paul & Quigley, 1994).

For those who can hear no sounds, the introduction of sign language during the first year of life does much to encourage normal gestural language, which has most of the features of American English.

Our basic argument is that all children have a genetic push to acquire language (Chomsky, 1988). They can do so in rich language environments and in poor ones. If they cannot hear, they can develop an equally adequate system of sign language (Goldin-Meadow, 1998). If a speech or a sign language is not provided for children to master, however, each child develops a system that is unique, which is not considered normal (Paul & Quigley, 1994).

All children have a genetic push to acquire language. For those with severe and profound hearing losses, the introduction of sign language during the first year of life does much to encourage normal gestural language, which has most of the features of American English.
(© Ellen Senisi/The Image Works)

The NICD (1989) stated the following:

Deaf children have unique communication needs; unable to hear the continuous repeated flow of language interchange around them, children with severe hearing impairments are not exposed to the enormous amounts of language stimulation experienced by hearing children during the early years. For children with severe hearing losses, early, consistent, and conscious use of visible communication modes (such as sign language, finger spelling, and cued speech) and/or amplification and aural/oral training can help reduce this language delay. Without such assistance *from infancy,* problems in the use of English typically persist throughout the child's school years. With such assistance, the language learning task is easier but by no means easy. (p. 21; emphasis added)

These results point to the importance of *every* parent or teacher of a student who is deaf learning a signed or an oral/aural language, particularly in infancy and the preschool years, when the child's central nervous system is ready to learn language. The language of the child's culture, whether it be expressed in signed or oral form, must be provided with strong parental involvement if the child is to learn to communicate (Solnit, Taylor, & Bednarczyk, 1992). The teacher's and parents' abilities to sign not only will aid the child in developing a communication system but also will enhance the child's social skills, peer interaction, and play (Luetke-Stahlman, 1994; Spencer, Erting, & Marschark, 2000).

People who are deaf develop a sense of community and an awareness of their needs as a group, which have been translated into political and social action to protect their individual and group rights.
(© Bob Rashid)

Social and Personal Adjustment

A hearing loss often brings with it communication problems, and communication problems can contribute to social and behavioral difficulties:

> Personality inventories have consistently shown that deaf children have more adjustment problems than hearing children. When deaf children without overt or serious problems have been studied, they have been found to exhibit characteristics of rigidity, egocentricity, absence of inner controls, impulsivity, and suggestibility. (Meadow, 1980, p. 97)

Consider the boy with prelinguistic hearing loss who wants a turn on the playground swings. He cannot simply say, "I want my turn" or "It's my turn now." What does he do? He may push another youngster out of the way. Obviously, this kind of behavior is going to cause the child difficulties with interpersonal relationships. And when it is repeated many times, it can create serious social adaptation problems.

Several factors should improve the social adjustment of children who are deaf or hard of hearing.

▶ Early identification and intervention is very effective in markedly improving the child's overall functioning, thus giving him or her increased feelings of self-esteem (Marschark, Lyons, & Albertini, 2002).

▶ Increased parent training teaches families the most effective ways to interact with their child and facilitate his or her development, thereby reducing family stress and increasing the child's acceptance.

▶ The availability of sophisticated technological aids such as the Internet and the World Wide Web provides access to information and social contacts.

▶ The increasing number of sign-language interpreters in public schools gives these children an outlet for making friends and engaging in a larger variety of activities.

Promoting Alternative Thinking Strategies (PATHS) is designed to improve social competence and to reduce behavioral problems of children who are deaf. It teaches self-esteem and interpersonal competencies. It aims at assisting students to achieve self-control. The curriculum focuses on problem-solving techniques to resolve social problems and overcome frustrations. PATHS is useful from late preschool to sixth grade (Calderon & Greenberg, 2000).

It is not surprising that many children with severe hearing losses prefer to be with children like themselves, with whom they can feel socially accepted and comfortable (Antia, 1982; Guralnick, 2001). The desire to cluster extends into adulthood, and in many large cities there is a culture of people with severe hearing losses, a group of individuals who socialize with one another and intermarry—the Deaf community. This tendency to band together is not unusual. Most adults and children feel most comfortable with people like themselves. This does not mean that people who are deaf do not want to be or cannot be integrated into society. Nor does it mean that all people who are deaf are alike.

Being able to communicate and to insert the communicative response is an interactive process that enables a person with hearing loss to participate fully in his or her environment. Hearing is not the issue; communication is (Bodner-Johnson &

Lack of verbal language makes it difficult for children who are deaf to make friends with children who speak and do not sign.

Sass-Lehrer, 2003). Recall that 90 percent of the parents of children who are deaf or hard of hearing are not able to communicate fully with them through speech. Therefore, these parents will have to master a communication system that is appropriate for their child.

Expressing frustration over inadequate communication in their homes, five young adult deaf students mentioned family members with limited signing skills; attending gatherings with numerous untrained relatives; and watching television with family members who would summarize the program but not give the details (Bodner-Johnson & Sass-Lehrer, 2003). These students' main complaint was that communication issues prevented them from participating fully in family life. It is rare for all the hearing members of a family to learn a sign language.

A Note of Caution

Students who are hard of hearing, like most other populations of students with disabilities, are a very heterogeneous population (Wachs, 2000). There may be a wide fluctuation in what individuals can hear from day to day. Some students will have a loss in only one ear and will move their heads in the direction from which the sound is coming. These students may appear to the teacher as being "too squirmy in their seats" (Easterbrooks, 1999). Those who have high fluctuations may appear to be inattentive and ask the teacher to repeat oral instructions, particularly in large group settings. Students with fluctuations may have difficulty in discriminating among phonemes on one day but not on another. Teachers must learn the range of fluctuations and skills of individual children and be cognizant of these individual differences in hearing patterns, so as not to confuse them with behavioral problems.

Interpreters

Interpreters can greatly assist the successful inclusion of students who are deaf into the regular classroom. Interpreters have not necessarily been trained as teachers, so they need to be in close communication with the classroom teacher to be able to understand the teacher's goals and preferred way in achieving them. In some schools the interpreter is a regular member of the multidisciplinary team (Moores, 2000). In some classrooms, the interpreter may work individually with one or more children; in most cases, however, the interpreter's role is to sign oral instruction. In any event, good communication acquired through frequent meetings with the classroom teacher and discussing the individual child's needs and progress is recommended.

> Interpreters in the general education classroom sign oral instruction as a way to support children who are deaf.

Teachers should be aware, also, that while interpreters are accepted by general education students in inclusive classes, they are not welcome in informal situations, such as the playground or cafeteria. Further, if the interpreter is assigned to the class rather than to the student, the student may have only limited communication with his or her peers (Stinson & Foster, 2000).

The Deaf Community

> The cohesive Deaf community helps its members overcome a sense of isolation from mainstream society.

The Deaf community exists as a separate cultural group within our society and has exhibited considerable cohesiveness for more than a century (Moores, 2000). It is a very diverse group, composed of cultural, religious, social, and ethnic group membership. However, its members share similar values and traditions, and they have a common language, ASL. As we have noted, parents

Computer-generated programs provide meaningful practice for people who are deaf in learning a sign language.
(© NR Rowan/The Image Works)

World Council on Hearing Health
www.tdi-online.org

Telecommunication for the Deaf, Inc. (TDI)
www.tdi.online.org

who are deaf teach ASL to their children who are deaf. Many adults who are deaf learned ASL from their peers in residential schools in which they were able to establish close, long-lasting friendships (Stinson & Foster, 2000).

The Deaf community has state and local networks, holds world games for the deaf and a Deaf Miss America Pageant (Moores, 1996), and publishes a newspaper as well as other material. The community is strongly bonded, and most adults who are deaf in the United States move toward membership and involvement in it. The Deaf community has the status of a minority group within the mainstream culture. Its members are bilingual, using ASL for communication with others and American English for reading and writing. They provide one another with a sense of belonging and pride, and they help one another overcome their isolation from mainstream society.

■ The School's Role in Identification

Children with severe hearing losses are usually identified through screening at birth and/or public health screening or pediatric examinations before they enter school. Children with mild or moderate hearing losses often go undiagnosed until academic performance indicates a problem. Even then, an accurate diagnosis is not automatic. Many of the symptoms of a hearing loss are also indicative of other disorders. A child who stares blankly at the teacher may not be able to hear or may not understand what is being said.

PROFILES

DEVELOPMENTAL

The graph below shows the developmental profiles of three children: Kiesha, Juan, and Raymon. All three children are 10 years old. Their profiles are similar in shape, but their intraindividual differences increase with the severity of hearing loss and age at the onset of deafness. Kiesha is hard of hearing, Juan has a postlingual hearing loss, and Raymon has a prelingual hearing loss.

Kiesha: The upper profile in the graph is Kiesha's. She has a moderate hearing loss of 45 dB. Like Juan and Raymon, Kiesha is of average height, weight, and motor coordination. She also shows average mental ability and social maturity for her age. Her speech development is slightly delayed. She has some difficulty in articulation and needs speech remediation. This speech problem has affected Kiesha's reading skills, but her achievement in arithmetic and spelling is at grade level.

When Kiesha was first fitted with a hearing aid, her special education program included instruction in its use. Now an

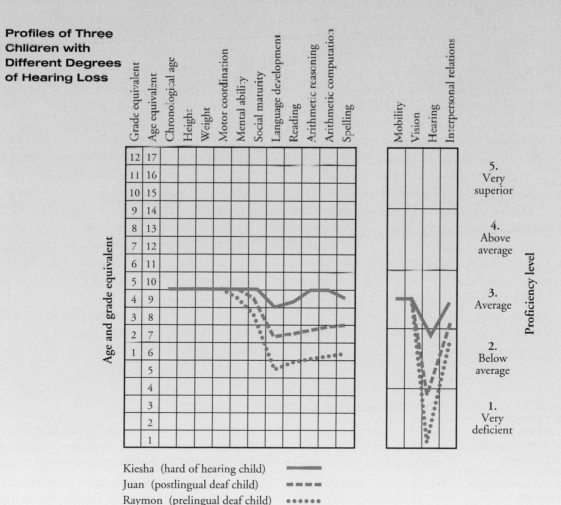

Profiles of Three Children with Different Degrees of Hearing Loss

Kiesha (hard of hearing child) ────
Juan (postlingual deaf child) ─ ─ ─
Raymon (prelingual deaf child) ••••••

itinerant speech-language pathologist gives her speech remediation, auditory training, and speech-reading lessons once a week.

Even though Kiesha's development and educational achievement are close to those of her peers, she does need some special attention from the classroom teacher. Her hearing aid makes her feel different from her friends, which could become more of a problem when she is an adolescent. Kiesha's hearing fluctuates somewhat when the weather changes or when she has a cold. Teachers who are not aware of this fluctuation may think that she is deliberately ignoring them when in fact she simply cannot hear them.

Juan: The middle profile in the graph shows the developmental pattern of Juan, who has a severe hearing loss. He was born with normal hearing but suffered a severe hearing loss in both ears at age 4. He is classified as having postlingual severe hearing loss. Although Juan is approximately normal in physical ability, intelligence, and social maturity, his speech and language have not developed normally. On audiometric testing, he showed a hearing loss of 75 dB even after he was fitted with hearing aids. Fortunately, Juan learned to talk normally before his loss of hearing and developed considerable language ability. That means he can learn through the auditory channel with the help of hearing aids. Still, his reading and other academic achievement scores are at a second-grade level. His hearing loss has interfered considerably with his educational progress, but with hearing aids, speech habilitation, and other special education services, he is moving ahead.

Juan relies a good deal on his speech-reading skills. For that reason, and to use his hearing aids to best advantage, he sits at the front of the classroom, facing the teacher. He needs extra help in developing social skills and making friends.

Raymon: The bottom profile in the graph is of a child with a profound hearing loss. Raymon was born with a severe hearing impairment. He has never heard a spoken word. Hearing aids might make him aware of environmental sounds but cannot help him develop speech and English. Because of the severity of Raymon's hearing loss—it tested at more than 95 dB—he is in a self-contained special class. He would need intensive tutorial services if he were integrated into the regular classroom.

Raymon's speech is difficult to understand. His English language development has not followed the pattern of hearing children. In reading and other academic subjects, he is about four grades behind his agemates.

Raymon's communication with his family and peers is limited; so are his sources of information and his social experiences. He often reacts to social situations in ways that are characteristic of a much younger child. If he were placed in the regular classroom, he would need help in making friends.

These are just two examples from the very heterogeneous population of children who are deaf or hard of hearing. Kiesha's learning profile is more uniform whereas there are wide intraindividual differences in Juan and Raymon's achievement.

A general education teacher can help identify a child with a possible hearing loss by observing his or her articulation, need for a higher volume of sounds, requests that information be repeated, and inattentiveness or unresponsiveness.

The General Education Teacher

How does the classroom teacher identify a child with a possible hearing loss so the child can be referred for comprehensive examination? Stephens, Blackhurst, and Magliocca (1982, pp. 43–44) suggested that teachers watch for several things:

▶ *Does the child appear to have physical problems associated with the ears?* The student may complain of earaches, discomfort in the ear, or strange

ECOLOGY OF THE CHILD

COMMUNITY **Brittany's Success**

My name is Brittany Sinclair and I am a 14-year-old student who is deaf. For as long as I can remember, I have worked with my mother to help develop my lip-reading skills. As I grew up, I was able to participate fully in the hearing world. My skills in lip-reading were already strong at a very early age, and so by the time I was six, doctors refused to believe that I was deaf.

My mother and Dr. Geraldine Detosta, who was the head of the child study team at a local hospital, arranged for a brainstem audio test. . . . It . . . produced evidence that erased all doubt—I have severe profound neurosensory deafness.

One of the major obstacles my family and I had to overcome was the ongoing dispute between whether I should attend the mainstream versus the deaf school, as well as signing versus oral communication. While I can sign, I have always been able to speak and read lips. It was difficult when I was very small to sit by as doctors told me that I should be mute and my lack of hearing would cause me to be delayed in my academic development. So each day, I go to school with my hearing aids, FM (a device that works with hearing aids which relays the voice of the teacher who is using a microphone), and my book-bag. Mainstreamed in the Walter T. Bergen public school in Bloomingdale, New Jersey, I attend honors classes and participate as if I were a hearing adolescent. I was invited to attend the summer gifted project at Boys Town, in Omaha, Nebraska, in the summer of 1995. This fall, I will start high school.

Learning from the Best

My Mom and Dad have always encouraged me. They are my biological grandparents who adopted me at birth. They have always made me feel that I can do whatever I want to, without letting my deafness stand in my way. . . .

I love music and I play several instruments. The eight instruments that I play are the flute, piccolo, trumpet, piano, organ, drums, guitar, and clarinet. I come from a family with a gift for music, as my mother is also talented. With my hearing aids in and from the vibrations of the instrument, I can tell that I am playing the right notes. I play with the Butler High School Band and I was appointed to the State Regional Band. . . .

Last year, I achieved the Excellence in Art award for my school. I also gained recognition at the state "Mini-Model Congress" for excellence in bill writing. I authored and debated a bill to have captioning put in movie theaters so that people who have hearing impairments could enjoy the latest movies without using an interpreter. I feel strongly that closed captioning should be available in all theaters.

Motivation

I am fueled by my desire to help students with disabilities feel safe and secure in the hearing world.

---

ringing or buzzing noises. Teachers should note these complaints and also be alert for signs of discharge from the ears or excessively heavy waxy buildup in the ear canal. Frequent colds and sore throats are occasional indicators of infections that could impair hearing.

▶ *Does the child articulate sounds poorly and particularly omit consonant sounds?* Students who articulate poorly may have a hearing problem that is preventing them from getting feedback about their vocal productions.

The great financial burden of the many devices needed for the hard of hearing led me to request the Lions Club to obtain flashing fire alarms for the hard of hearing at little or no cost to them, thus hopefully saving lives. 2,000 people die in fires each year because they did not hear the alarm. This is devastating. Being deaf makes you feel vulnerable. No one wants to feel unsafe. When you feel safe, it gives you hope and makes you feel that you are not at a disadvantage. It makes you feel that you are as important as anyone else.

I am very social and love to be the center of attention. At the moment, I am between boyfriends, but that is not a problem because I have good friends to spend time with. . . .

Making my friends laugh is one of my favorite things. Because of my deafness, my voice sounds a little different and people who don't know me will ask me what country I am from. I sometimes say France, but I will say any country that pops into my head. I answer this way because whenever I explain that I am deaf, I notice a change in the way strangers act toward me; they are astonished and want to know how I can talk. I have a good sense of humor about everything. I don't mind that I sound like "The Nanny" from television! . . .

Speaking Up

In the future, I hope to graduate law school. Since I enjoy problem solving, like the idea of protecting people, and need to have action in my life, I will probably become either a lawyer or an FBI agent. My music and acting are something that I can keep as a secondary pursuit.

I have learned from my parents that I can do anything I set out to do. I would say to other parents of kids with disabilities, do not hold them back! If your children are discriminated against, stand up for them, since they cannot do it themselves. My parents also taught me that if there is anything that you have to do that is difficult, deal with it head on and don't dodge it. Then it doesn't seem so hard after all.

Source: From Brittany Sinclair, Talking back, *Exceptional Parent*, (July 1998) 45. Reprinted with permision.

WHAT IS THE CONTEXT?

Brittany is an active part of her community. She plays in the high school band, contributes to the Lions Club, and participates in sports and many other school activities. Through her own motivation and the support of family, friends, and community, Brittany successfully carries out her interests and participates fully in the community.

PIVOTAL ISSUES FOR TEACHERS

- What factors contribute to how well Brittany has adjusted socially and personally?
- What kind of educational adaptations might Brittany need to accommodate for her deafness?
- What types of communication methods does Brittany use?
- What types of assistive devices or instructional technology might be useful to her?

Omission of consonant sounds from speech is often indicative of a high-frequency hearing loss.

▶ *When listening to radio, television, or records, does the student turn the volume up so high that others complain?* Because it is much in vogue among young people today to turn up the amplification of rock music almost "to the threshold of pain," this determination will sometimes be difficult to make. Teachers can get clues, however, by observing students listening to audio media that are not producing music, such as instructional records and sound-filmstrips.

▶ *Does the student cock the head or turn toward the speaker in an apparent effort to hear better?* Sometimes such movements are obvious and may even be accompanied by a "cupping" of the ear with the hand in an effort to direct the sound into the ear. In other cases, actions are much more subtle. Teachers often overlook such signs, interpreting them as symbols of increased inquisitiveness and interest.

▶ *Does the student frequently request that what has just been said be repeated?* Although some students pick up the habit of saying "Huh?" as a form of defense mechanism when they are unable to produce what they perceive as an acceptable response, such verbalizations may also indicate a hearing loss. When a particular student frequently requests repeated instructions, teachers should further investigate the possibility of hearing loss.

▶ *Is the student unresponsive or inattentive when spoken to in a normal voice?* Some students who do not follow directions or do not pay attention in class are frequently labeled as "troublemakers," which results in negative or punitive treatment. Often, however, these inappropriate school behaviors are actually caused by the student's inability to hear. They can also be caused if the sounds that are heard appear to be "garbled."

▶ *Is the student reluctant to participate in oral activities?* Although reluctance to participate orally may be symptomatic of problems such as shyness, insecurity with respect to knowledge of subject matter, or fear of failure, it also may be due to hearing loss. The child might not be able to hear the verbal interactions that occur in such activities.

The Audiologist

An audiologist is critical in assessing the degree, type, and extent of hearing loss.

With the passage of the Education for All Handicapped Children Act, the presence of the audiologist on the multidisciplinary team had an impact on the services that audiologists provide in the school setting (English, 1995). Audiologists continue to provide traditional clinical services: evaluating hearing level, recommending and fitting devices, and offering counsel on hearing conservation and room acoustics. In addition, they are involved in instruction in speech and in reading (listening skills as well as checking and monitoring all types of amplification devices), and they assist teachers in recognizing and resolving psychological issues of the child who is hard of hearing or deaf (English, 1995). In essence, audiology has developed a subspecialty: educational audiology.

■ Transition

Postsecondary Programs

In the mid-1960s, surveys of the vocational status of adults with severe hearing losses revealed some disturbing facts. The unemployment rate among the population was four times greater than that of hearing adults, and the level of employment was primarily fixed at unskilled or semiskilled positions (for example, see Moores, 2000). At about the same time, an effort to locate all persons with hearing losses who had enrolled in or graduated from regular colleges and universities was under way. It yielded just 653 persons, only 133 of them graduates, who had prelinguistic hearing losses (Quigley, Jenne, & Phillips, 1968). Clearly, one factor affecting the kinds of jobs that adults with severe hearing losses were finding was their limited educational opportunities.

Since the 1970s, the situation has changed. There are an increasing number of vocational programs for young adults with severe hearing losses. In 1967, the National Technical Institute for the Deaf was established in Rochester, New York. The institute, supported by the federal government, was founded to provide technical and vocational training for adolescents and adults with severe hearing losses.

New job opportunities come with educational opportunities. One academic alternative for students with severe hearing losses is Gallaudet University in Washington, D.C., the only college in the world devoted to the liberal arts education of students with severe hearing losses. The school is supported by the federal government. It is an accredited four-year liberal arts college and now includes a graduate school for deaf, hard-of-hearing, and hearing students. Gallaudet also operates the Kendall Demonstration Elementary School and the Model Secondary School for the Deaf.

Many state universities now have students with moderate-to-severe hearing losses on their campuses. They provide interpreting and note-taking services for these students. The impact of new educational opportunities is yet to be determined, but much depends on the quality of early education.

Many universities provide students who have hearing losses with interpreters and other support services.

■ Family and Lifespan Issues

The most important inclusion required by law in educational programs for the deaf and hard of hearing is the family. Family-oriented approaches have resulted in children who are deaf or hard of hearing attaining better communication skills. Moreover, when stress is reduced within a family, better interaction usually occurs among its members (Spencer, Ertling, & Marschark, 2000). IDEA stresses that the family is central to intervention programs (IDEA, 2000).

Focusing on the family system requires recognition of its strengths and respect for its values, beliefs, choices, and aspirations. It helps the family to recognize the critical role that sign language plays in the development of children who are deaf or severely hard of hearing. The child's development is facilitated when family members adopt interactive strategies, encouraging the child to request, respond, and take the initiative. All these interactive patterns are important factors in effective learning (Jamieson, 1994). They also stimulate the child to use language.

The teacher is faced with a dual problem—how to recognize the strengths of the family and how to improve (when necessary) the transaction patterns if parents are not aware of how they should be used to maximize the development of a child who is deaf or hard of hearing.

When the parents of a child who is deaf are also deaf, they are likely to prefer having the child learn a sign or manual language, usually ASL, first. Children in this situation are fortunate because they learn a language early and probably develop more quickly than children who are deaf and born to hearing parents, who may not recognize their child's condition for some time.

Most parents who can hear have little or no experience with deafness and may not know how to proceed with a child who is deaf. Feelings of guilt and

National Association of the Deaf
www.nad.org

(text continues on page 415)

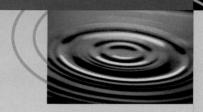

CHILDREN WHO ARE DEAF OR HARD OF HEARING

▮ Adapting the Learning Environment

Early intervention for children who are deaf or hard of hearing begins in the home as soon as the child is identified and is continued in early intervention centers. It has been shown to be very effective in assisting children who are deaf or hard of hearing to achieve optimal development and later academic success (Marschark, Lang, & Albertini, 2002).

Parent Involvement and Early Intervention

Infants learn about communication from the facial expressions, lip and head movements, gestures, touch, and vocal vibrations of those around them. That is why it is so important for the parents of children who are deaf or hard of hearing to establish effective communication as early as possible.

> Involving parents in early intervention programs for the deaf or hard of hearing assists both child and parent.

During infancy and early childhood, the innate language mechanism propels infants to learn a language. For the hearing child, it is the language of the home. For the child who is deaf and has parents who are deaf, it is a manual/sign/visual system. The critical factor is for the child to make at least 50 words (speech or manual) before 18 months to 2 years of age, when the innate grammar acquisition mechanism begins to function.

It is clear that children who are hard of hearing and those who are deaf with parents who can hear must receive early intervention if they are to accomplish these learnings during the critical language learning period. If the child has residual hearing, hearing aids or other technological devices are needed to allow the child to hear the language of the home and master it. Some professionals advocate both prostheses, such as hearing aids, and sign language. However, proponents of the oral-only orientation do not encourage sign learning for those with some residual hearing, which most children who are deaf or hard of hearing do possess (Green, 1999).

Many of the early education programs for preschoolers with severe hearing losses focus on the parents. Some provide counseling to help family members accept and adjust to the diagnosis of the severe hearing losses and to understand the condition. Others train parents to take an active role in teaching their children, carrying out in the home developmental tasks that are part of the overall program. The extent of the parents' involvement is a function of their readiness to participate and the willingness of educators to include them. Most parents of children who are deaf are not deaf themselves and have little or no experience with persons who are deaf. Many of them will not recognize that their child is deaf until he or she is 2 years of age or older. What most intervention programs for infants and toddlers who are deaf have come to stress is teaching the parents effective strategies for teaching their children. Current early intervention programs emphasize having the parents play a major role in teaching a communication system to their child, preferably in a natural

> Many parents won't recognize that their child is deaf until the child is 2 years old.

Good emotional and behavioral adjustment is one of the greatest challenges for children who are deaf, who may experience social difficulties.
(© Robin Sachs/Photo Edit)

environment (IDEA, 2000; Spencer, Ertling, & Marschark, 2000). Some of these strategies are listed here.

STRATEGIES FOR PARENTS OF DEAF INFANTS

▶ Develop a perception that is accepting of deafness.

▶ Learn a sign language, preferably ASL.

▶ Use gentle facial touch to gain the infant's attention.

▶ Use facial expressions to help the infant understand the sign.

▶ If the infant looks away, allow him or her to do so before trying to continue communication.

▶ Use short utterances.

▶ When referring to things, make signs and gestures near the object.

▶ Exaggerate, repeat, and prolong signs to make sure that they are seen and recognized.

▶ Use signs at a slower rate than you would for spoken language to an adult.

▶ Sign near the object to be identified or move the object into the infant's gaze. (Adapted from Jamieson, 1995; Koester, Karkowski & Traci, 1998; Lytle & Rovins, 1997; Marschark et al., 2002; Masataka, 1996; Waxman, Spencer, & Poisson, 1996).

▶ Learn an oral or an aural approach.

▶ Provide amplification of residual hearing.

▶ Utilize techniques (see those listed above) when presenting verbal stimuli.

Parent training and programs for very young children with severe hearing losses are often provided in the home by appropriate therapists and special education teachers. These programs are also available in nursery schools, day-care centers, and some public schools. Their primary objectives are as follows:

OBJECTIVES OF PARENT TRAINING PROGRAMS

► To train parents

► To develop communication skills

► To give children with severe hearing losses opportunities to share, play, and take turns with other children

► To help children with hearing losses use their residual hearing (through auditory training or with hearing aids)

► To develop readiness in basic English, reading, and arithmetic

Intensive preschool training is a fundamental step in preparing children with severe hearing losses for school. One important part of that preparation for children and their parents is learning to use sign language.

Inclusion in Context

Preschool Issues involving preschool inclusion of children who are deaf revolve around adequate and appropriate communication with the child, so that his or her language development will parallel that of a child who can hear. Antia and Levine (2001) indicate that the major reason why professionals who work with preschool-age children who are deaf recommend programs for the deaf is that these programs are likely to employ teachers and aides who are competent users of sign language. In addition, these programs usually have access to adults who are deaf, are competent signers, and can serve as models as well as interact with the child. In such segregated classrooms there is a large quantity of interaction containing quality language and communication complexities, which are not found in settings with less fluent signers.

Elementary School The increasing popularity of inclusion, or integrating children with disabilities into the general education classroom has triggered controversy among teachers of children with severe hearing losses. Academic programs that mainstream children with severe hearing losses must provide trained supplementary personnel, such as interpreters, speech-language pathologists, and audiologists, who are accessible to parents as well as to children. The child's major responsibilities during the elementary years are to develop reading, writing, arithmetic, science, and social studies skills.

With the growing impact of inclusion, the importance of using interpreters in the classroom cannot be overemphasized.

The trend in reading instruction for the child who is deaf is to use a whole language approach, which includes guided reading, language experience approaches, sustained reading, shared reading, and writing in journals. It includes both the bottom-up technique (word identification, phonemes, and syllables) and the top-down technique (comprehension and knowing what the word means) (LaSasso & Mobley, 1996). Finger spelling taught in conjunction with American Sign Language (ASL) assists the student in bridging the gap from ASL to written English, an important step in learning to read and write English (Schimmel, Edwards, & Prickett, 1999).

Knowledge of the alphabetic principle, which is essential for understanding the relationship among phonemes (vowels and consonants) and intonation, pause, and rhythm, is critical if the student is to learn the grapheme (print) of letters and words (Paul, 1996). This is not an easy process for the child who is deaf or hard of hearing, and specialists need to provide intervention to enable the child to acquire these skills. Decisions about the type of school placement and curriculum should be based on the needs of the individual child at his or her particular stage of development and the development of individual education programs.

In addition, there is a movement to teach reading by the whole word method. First, students learn to read words that stand for persons or things with which they are familiar; for example, *ball*. Then, after students have acquired a basic reading vocabulary, the teacher introduces phonics as a part of a continuing emphasis on teaching whole words (Hammil, 2004). For children who are deaf or hard of hearing, a picture of the object or person may accompany the presentation of the word. The child who can hear may have already made the association between the word and the object or person, but one cannot assume that the child who is deaf or hard of hearing has done so.

Children who are deaf or hard of hearing placed in inclusive classrooms tend to learn more in academic areas that are given greater emphasis in regular schools than they have traditionally been able to absorb in residential or special classes. These results are obtained when there is an interpreter or other support personnel present. It is not class placement that has been interpreted as accounting for gains, but the level of instruction (Moores, 2000).

Secondary School High school students with serious hearing losses often are several grade levels behind their agemates in achievement. When they are mainstreamed, these students need sign language interpreters in the classroom as well as supplementary resource assistance. Moores, Kluwin, and Mertens (1985; Moores, 2000) reported a tendency to mainstream children with severe hearing losses more in mathematics than in English, history, or science. Interviews with teachers and administrators revealed a consensus that there are fewer problems in mathematics achievement than in other academic areas.

A number of large metropolitan and suburban school districts offer a wide range of special services by centralizing programs (Moores, Kluwin, & Mertens, 1985). Schools within a district or several districts working together can combine their resources to provide special services to accommodate students with severe hearing losses within a large, comprehensive high school. This setting allows a range of environmental options, from self-contained classes for students with severe hearing losses to mainstreaming in all academic courses.

Residential School Many mainstream classrooms are not offering equality of education to children who are deaf or hard of hearing. Some have the student take the core curriculum in one room and receive special instruction in another. A dual-track education makes social relationships more difficult (Marschark et al., 2002). In addition, although interpretation is provided, if students have to look at a visual representation while a lecture is being conducted, their attention is divided between the visual and the interpreter, and they miss part of the lesson. Marschark et al. also present the following facts: Some parents choose residential placement so that full attention will be given to the individual needs of the student from the very heterogeneous population of the deaf and hard of hearing. Currently, the population in residential schools has dropped to about 10,000, with only 2,500 full-time students. These students tend to have more severe hearing losses, come from lower-income and lower-SES (socioeconomic status) families, and have poorer spoken language skills. Also, a greater number have parents who are deaf or hard of hearing (Marschark et al., 2002, p. 154).

The advantages that the parents perceive are as follows: The teachers are better prepared to deal with children with hearing impairments; the child is in a population of students who are similarly challenged, so he or she can relate to and establish friendships with classmates, develop a positive self-image, and achieve emotional security (Marschark et al., 2002). The parents decide what setting is best for their child.

The Multidisciplinary Team

A child with a significant hearing loss faces a variety of problems, which may require a team of professionals to produce a comprehensive program of education and therapy. A clinical audiologist must carefully assess the hearing loss and its physical and functional dimensions. A speech therapist helps the child reach his or her potential in speech reading and production. A special education teacher trained to work with children with severe hearing losses develops an individualized education program (IEP) and a sequence of lessons to help general education teachers understand the needs of the child.

> The multidisciplinary team includes an audiologist, speech therapist, and special education teacher.

The education of children with severe hearing losses is changing. Instruction must adapt to the students' needs, and their needs appear to include some form of manual interpretation. For this reason, it's important to have interpreters in the classroom and teachers trained not only in special education but in subject areas as well.

Family

One critical segment of the multidisciplinary team is not professional at all—the family. Less than 35 percent of the families of children who are deaf or severely hard of hearing use signs in the home (Trybus, 1985). In more than 90 percent of these families, parents and siblings do not have hearing losses. In addition, family members are providing important reinforcement and training throughout the critical preschool years. For individuals in the Deaf community, hearing aids, cochlear implants, and oral approaches emphasize the negative aspects of deafness. They believe that parents of children who are deaf should communicate with them through a sign system, thereby demonstrating acceptance of them (Lane, Hoffmeister, & Bahan, 1996). It should be clear, however, that not all educators of the deaf and hard of hearing prefer visual-signing systems, and some utilize verbal-oral approaches.

> Parents are critical members of the multidisciplinary team.

■ Adapting Curriculum

Three factors are related to the academic achievement of children with hearing losses: the degree of hearing loss, the presence of language, and experiences in the environment with people and things. If the child who is deaf is taught signing in infancy, or if he or she has some auditory perception and amplification is provided before the age of 2, and his or her environment is rich in terms of experiential language and activities, the child need not fail in school.

National trends in the reading achievement of children with hearing losses are exciting. Moores (2000) reports that each year, children who are deaf continue to make gains in reading scores, compared to the scores in previous years of those who are deaf. However, most children who are deaf do not read at the average national norm. New technology should help these students attain their age-appropriate academic levels.

Moores (2000) attributed some of these gains to the movement toward teaching, reading, and writing in a more functional (practical) and semantic (knowledge/meaning) manner. Many also affirmed that inclusion has increased students' academic achievement.

About 65 percent of the graduates of Gallaudet College are going on to graduate school and doing as well as their classmates who do not have hearing impairments (Moores, 2000). However, this is not to say that the academic achievement problem has disappeared. Several factors should be mentioned for persons with hearing losses at all age levels:

> Peer play and interaction can be limited, because peers who can hear usually cannot communicate with a sign language.

> Not all family members can use gestural communication. Although 70 percent of students with hearing losses use some form of signing, only 35 percent of their families use it at home (Paul & Quigley, 1994).

> The experiences of young children with hearing losses are limited. They cannot go into the environment without supervision because they cannot hear approaching cars or other dangers and the general populace cannot communicate with them.

Components of Successful Programs

In addition to fostering the teacher's individual efforts, programs should concentrate on the following components, which research has found to be desirable:

> *Reading training.* Over and above conventional reading instruction, a special program should train students with severe hearing losses in adjusting reading strategies for various purposes. After reading is mastered, emphasis should be placed on reading to learn (Kelly, 1995; Moores, 1996).

> *Cognitive strategies.* The teaching of cognitive strategies should be an important part of the curriculum (Moores, 1996). Students use these strategies to select, control, and monitor how they learn and solve problems. According to Moores, they are frequently neglected in programs for students who are deaf or hard of hearing.

> *Special programs.* Students with severe hearing losses who have high potential should be identified and should receive accelerated training.

> *Tutoring.* Even if a one-to-one situation cannot be maintained, with careful planning a low student-teacher ratio in programs for persons with severe hearing losses can lead to significant one-to-one and small-group instruction.

Most children who are deaf do not read at the average national norm.

Students who are deaf and also gifted should receive accelerated instruction.

► *Cooperative parent programs.* The alterable curriculum of the home can be manipulated to foster school achievement.

Encouraging Academic Achievement at Home

Early communication skills are usually taught in a one-to-one affective manner by parents of regular children in the home. This approach is now strongly recommended as the most appropriate means of teaching communication skills to the child who is deaf or hard of hearing (Lederberg & Everhart, 1998).

The idea behind the use of the alterable home curriculum is not to place the total responsibility for teaching on parents but to encourage academic achievement. The results have been excellent. Basic guidelines for parents include the following:

► Become actively involved in teaching a communication system.

► Keep television viewing to moderate levels (twelve hours per week or less).

► Monitor homework to see that it is completed.

► Encourage leisure reading.

► Discuss school with the child.

► Express interest in the child's progress.

► Learn a sign or gestural communication system if the child has a severe hearing loss.

Many programs at homes or with therapists and early intervention programs focus on teaching words and phonemes (the smallest units of sound with meaning) rather than on the broad set of literary skills. Children with hearing losses must be taught the following concepts (after Paul & Quigley, 1994, pp. 181–186):

► *Word meanings:* multiple meanings of the same word, such as *mole,* an animal, and *mole*, a spy whose task it is to collect classified information within an organization

► *Syntax:* variety of word order, such as in questions, declarative statements, and possessives

► *Figurative language:* similes ("he has a head like a rock"), metaphors ("she is a vixen"), and onomatopoeia ("the whir of the engine")

► *Idioms:* for example, "he pulled himself up by his bootstraps"

► *Inferences:* for example, "the cold wind blew snow around the house," from which it can be inferred that it is winter

Adapting Teaching Strategies

Learning Strategies

Currently, some educators hold that regardless of whether the language program is oral, aural-oral, or sign language, the technical title of this approach is *social constructivism* (Meyer, Akamatsu, & Stewart, 2002). The premise is that the learner is the one who constructs meaning, and he or she does so in transaction with the teacher. Teachers take the role of encouraging learning and base their instruction on the student's current level of functioning, utilizing his or her strengths, past experiences, and interests (Meyer et al., 2002). This model is appealing to educators of the deaf and hard of hearing, given the heterogeneity of this population in terms of skills, modes of communication, background experience, and interests (Meyer et al., 2002).

The teaching of reading through the language experience approach serves as an example of the process (Clerc, 2003). With young children, the student dictates a story to an adult, who writes it in English on a chart. The subject is chosen by the student, usually on the basis of his or her personal experiences or interests. Assisted by the teacher, the student then reads the story to the class in whatever form of communication he or she uses. The teacher may ask how the student feels about the story and whether it has communicated what he or she wished to say. Older students can dictate their story or write it, if they have developed the skills. Then it can be typed and shared with the class. Small groups of students can focus on a topic from social studies or science, participate in an activity related to it, and then dictate or write an essay about it. The typed version can be used as a text for reading instruction or expansion of ideas about the topic. Through this process, students engage in dialogue inquiry.

Communication Skills

The dispute over how to teach language to a child with hearing losses began in Europe, with Samuel Heinicke in Germany stressing oralism (speech) and Abbé de l'Eprée in France stressing manualism (gestures). A conference held in Milan in 1880 stressed oralism and claimed that sign language impeded language development (Paul & Quigley, 1994).

In the United States, the sign language approach was taken up by Thomas Hopkins Gallaudet, who founded the first school for the hard of hearing in Hartford, Connecticut, in 1817. The school was moved to Washington, D.C., in 1884. The oral approach was advocated by Alexander Graham Bell, inventor of the telephone and the audiometer. Interestingly, both men had mothers with severe hearing losses, and each was firmly convinced of the correctness of his position.

Not until the 1970s did Bob Holcomb (Gannon, 1981), a college graduate with a severe hearing loss, advocate the use of both systems and coin the term *total communication method* to describe this dual approach. In total communication, some type of sign language is used simultaneously with speech. However, according to Goldberg (1997) and Stone (1997), many educators of persons who are deaf or hard of hearing do not use a sign language as an instructional technique. The simple fact is that our culture prefers that people learn to speak with correct pronunciation, correct word order, and interpretable meaning appropriate to the setting in which speech is spoken. Given this strong societal bias, educators of students who have hearing losses stress oral language, and many of these children succeed very well (Lynas, 2000). Many specialists in educating persons with hearing losses argue that it is more important to teach a communication system that the child can master, regardless of whether it is gestural or oral.

The combination of sign language and oral systems in a total communication approach is now being more widely recommended for those with hearing losses, regardless of whether the loss is moderate or severe (Moores, 2000).

As mentioned earlier, there is a movement to consider ASL as the primary language for persons who are deaf and English as a second language. The position is that persons who are deaf constitute a language minority group and should be entitled to bilingual education (Lane, Hoffmeister, & Bahan, 1996; Parasnis, 1997). Given the importance of cultural diversity in the U.S. population, teachers and specialists may be confronted with students whose first sign language may be influenced by Spanish, Chinese, or some other spoken language. This population may sign (or speak if there is residual hearing) in a language that is not English; by learning ASL and English, they become trilingual. Technology may be the key for assisting members of other language groups who are deaf (Gallaudet Research Institute, 1997).

Many individuals in the Deaf community believe in communicating with a signing language, such as ASL, rather than using hearing aids or the oral approach to communicating.

Communication Methods

Oral methods of communication for persons who are deaf or hard of hearing use whatever hearing and speech abilities a person has. Oral methods include the auditory-verbal method and the auditory-oral method. Manual methods include the various types of sign language systems (ASL, for example) and finger spelling. The effectiveness of all these methods depends on the severity of the hearing loss and the availability of early intervention.

Auditory-Oral Method The auditory-oral method uses residual hearing through amplified sound, speech reading, and speech to develop communication skills. Auditory-oral programs do not use or encourage the use of sign languages or finger spelling, believing that manual communication impedes the child's adjustment to the hearing world (Stone, 1997).

American Sign Language is the only signing system of communication that is a distinct language with its own grammar and syntax.
(© Bill Aron/Photo Edit)

The effectiveness of any communication method depends on the severity of a person's hearing loss and how early the loss is diagnosed and intervention is begun.

One important skill in the auditory-oral method is **speech reading**, the visual interpretation of spoken communication (also known as *lip reading*). It is one means by which people with severe hearing losses receive communication from those who can hear. Because few hearing people go to the trouble to learn a complex system of manual communication, individuals with severe hearing losses who want to keep in meaningful contact with the hearing world must learn to speech-read.

Speech reading is possible because many sounds in the English language bring a particular expression to the speaker's face. For example, the *n* sound looks very different from the *k* sound. A major problem, however, is sounds that are homophones—they are articulated in similar ways and look the same on the speaker's lips and face (for example, *cite, height, night*). The fact that half of the words in the English language have homophones is one reason why speech reading is so difficult.

The approach that is used to teach youngsters speech reading depends on the child's age. When the child is young, the teacher or parent talks in whole sentences. At first the child may not pick up any clues, but as the teacher or parent repeats the same expression over and over in the same relationship to something that the child is experiencing—an object, an action, a feeling—the child begins to get an idea of what is being said. At a later stage, these vague whole impressions are converted into lessons that emphasize details and into exercises that help the child discriminate among different words and sounds. Eventually, the special education teacher uses speech reading to present lessons in school.

Auditory-Verbal Method The auditory-verbal method (or aural method) makes extensive use of sound amplification to develop listening and speech skills. It involves auditory training—teaching the child to listen to sounds and to discriminate among different sounds. Although the method is used widely with school-age youngsters who have mild or moderate hearing losses, it has been most effective with preschoolers, particularly children with a severe loss. Parents play an important part in the early training process, and one of the goals of hearing specialists is to instruct parents and include them in the training (Goldberg, 1997).

The auditory-verbal method is also called the acoustic method, the acoupedic method, and the **unisensory method,** which has also been called the **auditory global method.** The approach makes maximum use of residual hearing and is used with amplification as early as possible.

ASL is the language of the Deaf community.

HandSpeak
www.handspeak.com

Signing Language There are several sign language systems of communication: **American Sign Language (ASL)**, Pidgin Sign English (PSE), and Signing Exact English (SEE II). Of these, ASL is the only distinct language (Bellugi & Studdert-Kennedy, 1984). The others are manual codes based on English.

Like all languages, ASL has its own grammar and syntax. It is very different from the "home" language, be it American English, an Asian language, or Spanish as it is spoken in different parts of North and South America. The language of the Deaf community, ASL, is not easily learned by adults who learned another language first.

Because there are very few teachers who are deaf in intervention, school, and college programs, teachers who can hear face the challenge of teaching ASL to students who are deaf.

Each sign has three elements: the position of the hands, the configuration of the hands, and the movement of the hands to different positions (Moores, 1996).

Moores reports that Gallaudet University requires faculty members to attain proficiency in ASL within six years. He feels it may be unreasonable to expect parents who hear to learn ASL in a short period of time.

Differences in grammar and syntax between ASL and English have created a controversy over the use of ASL with students with severe hearing losses. Many educators believe that ASL inhibits the acquisition of English. Others, principally researchers, believe that ASL is (or should be) the first language of children with severe hearing losses and they should learn it *before* they learn English (Drasgow, 1998).

PSE and SEE II are manually coded systems that preserve the syntactic patterns of English. Of the two, PSE comes closer to ASL. It uses the same signs and occasionally omits English function words and inflections. SEE II maintains strict English structural patterns. One morpheme equals one sign. (For example, the word *cats* would be signed with two morphemes: *cat* plus *s*.) And SEE II treats each part of a compound word (such as *babysit*) separately (*baby, sit*).

Finger Spelling Finger spelling is writing in the air. The manual letters of the alphabet are presented in the box on page 409 that shows the alphabet. Instead of writing with a pencil, the child writes with his or her fingers, spelling out each letter of the word. Finger spelling evolves into a complete hand pattern like a sign, rather than individual letters (Ertling, Theman-Preziuso, & Benedict, 2000). The practice was very common in the USSR in the 1970s and 1980s among preschool children who were hard of hearing; finger spelling was used in conjunction with speech (Gallagher, 1974; Moores, 1996). In the United States, finger spelling with speech is commonly known as the Rochester method (NICD, 1989). In Russia, finger spelling is a common way to begin teaching speech to preschoolers who are deaf or hard of hearing. In the United States, it is used to establish the letter-phoneme correspondence to reading.

Approaches to Teaching Communication

Total Communication Method The **total communication method,** also known as the **simultaneous method** or **combined method,** combines finger spelling, signs (one of the several signed English systems), speech reading, speech, and auditory amplification. The Conference of Executives of American Schools for the Deaf (1976) defined *total communication* as a "philosophy requiring the incorporation of appropriate aural, manual, and oral modes of communication in order to insure effective communication with and among hearing impaired persons" (p. 358).

Combining the oral and aural (auditory) methods, total communication is the most common method of classroom communication; the auditory-oral method is the next most common. The two procedures together were used by more than 90 percent of the schools surveyed. Manual communication by itself was not reported as a major mode of instruction in any school (Paul & Quigley, 1994).

Diversity: Bilingual-Bicultural

Bilingual-Bicultural Approach This approach advocates that persons who are deaf are bicultural, in that they belong to the deaf culture as well as to the broader culture of the society in which they live. They are also bilingual, in that they possess the ability to use a sign language system (usually American Sign Language) to communicate, as well as the spoken or written language of their culture. In the United States, the language of the majority is English, and members of minority groups that speak a different first language would be considered trilingual if they mastered two verbal/written languages and ASL (Baker & Baker, 1997; Easterbrooks, 1999; Moores, 2000).

Some specialists in teaching people with hearing losses advocate postponing the introduction of speech. They believe that children should be taught a sign language first and be introduced to oral language later, as if it were a second language (the first being the sign language). Children with hearing losses who were taught in this manner would be considered bilingual. Children who are deaf would use ASL as their first language and the written or oral form of English as their second language. It should be noted that studies of persons who are bilingual indicate that they may develop full proficiency in only one of the two languages they speak. Therefore, an individual who is able to code-switch from ASL to the written or oral form of English with considerable linguistic skill may still be more proficient in the first language, in this case ASL.

> Mexican-American children who are deaf are one of the fastest-growing minorities in the U.S. school-age population.

Academic Teacher Strategies

Strategies under the control of the teacher are knowledge of subject matter and skill in communicating with children with severe hearing losses. The following general instructional strategies also enhance the teaching and learning process:

▶ *Reinforcement.* The teacher should provide appropriate reinforcement and positive feedback.

▶ *Mastery learning.* The addition of teaching and feedback procedures to conventional instruction enhances learning.

▶ *Graded homework.* Meaningful homework that is assigned, graded, and responded to will increase learning.

▶ *Time on task.* There is a positive correlation between the time spent on a subject and the amount learned. This may seem a rather simplistic statement, but many teachers—particularly teachers of students with severe hearing losses in academic content areas—spend surprisingly little time on task.

▶ *Class morale.* Teachers should strive to maintain cohesiveness, satisfaction, and goal direction in the classroom.

▶ *Support.* Someone who can sign (the teacher or an interpreter) needs to be in the classroom.

> An interpreter or a teacher who can sign needs to be in the general education classroom to support any students who are deaf or hard of hearing.

■ Testing Hearing Loss

Audiometry

Play Audiometry Play audiometry tests are conducted in a pleasant environment with toys that move and make sounds. The toys are used to elicit responses, such as eye blinks and changes in respiration or heartbeat (slower heartbeats indicate attention).

The child is brought into a room with his or her caregiver. An examiner distracts the child with an attractive toy. Sounds are piped into the room. A

I The Alphabet of Finger Spelling

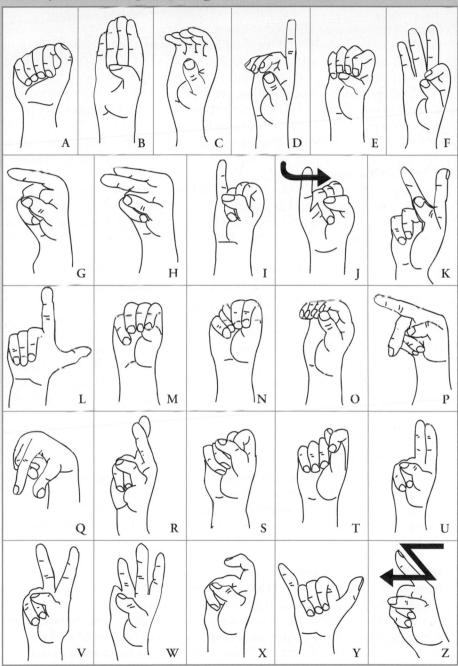

change in sound indicates that a curtain will be raised to reveal a more attractive toy. The child is not told that this will happen. Children without hearing losses hear the change of sound and turn to look at the hidden toy before the curtain is lifted to reveal it. If the child does not turn when the sound is changed, hearing losses are suspected (Herter, Knightly, & Steinberg, 2002).

Other play behavioral assessments are based on principles of conditioning children to respond to sound by rewarding them when they indicate that they hear it. The reward is usually allowing them to play with the toy. Paul and Quigley (1994) reported that play-conditioning audiometry is both reliable and an acceptable technique for assessing hearing in young children (p. 37). However, it is not suitable for infants (ASHA, 1991).

A sound is introduced into the child's ear and received by electrodes attached to his or her scalp. The sound is then transmitted to a computer that prints out the sound pattern received. The audiologist can determine the nature of the sound received (Green, 1999; Silberman, Bruce, & Nelson, 2004).

| Auditory brainstem response is the preferred method for testing an infant's hearing.

Auditory Brainstem Response (Otoacoustic Emissions) A click sound is played into the ear. In the ear of a typical child, an echo is generated. If there is no echo, further investigation into the child's hearing is advised (Green, 2000). Auditory brainstem response (ABR) is currently the preferred method of evaluating whether or not an infant can hear. It is based on the fact that as sounds move through the ear canal to the middle ear, they will stimulate thousands of hair cells, causing them to vibrate and emit a sound (Green, 2000). By using a small microphone, it is possible to receive and record this sound in the external ear (Mauk & White, 1995). If no sound is received, further evaluation is indicated.

Bone-Conductor Test With infants and preschool children younger than 3 years of age, it is common to use both a pure-tone test and a bone-conductor test, which measure the movement of sound through the hearing system to the brain. The reception of sound in the brain (auditory brainstem recognition) is recorded on a graph that charts the brain's response in vibrations (Linden, Kankkunen, & Tjellstrom, 1985). The vibrations are received by electrodes placed on the child's ear. By comparing the test taker's responses to the responses of a population of hearing persons, the audiologist can ascertain hearing abilities or losses (Linden et al., 1985).

Visual Reinforcement Audiometry This test can be used with children between 6 months and 2.5 years of age (Herter, Knightly, & Steinberg, 2002). The child is seated on the parent's lap, and at a 90-degree angle to one side is a darkened glass box with a toy inside. When a sound is played, a light goes on in the box, illuminating the toy. After the child is conditioned to associate the sound with the toy, the test is begun. If the child fails to turn to see the toy when a series of sounds are emitted, a hearing deficit is suspected.

Pure-Tone Audiometry Pure-tone audiometry, which is the most common means of determining hearing loss, can be used in children about 3 years of age and older. The audiometer—an instrument for testing hearing acuity—presents pure tones (not speech) to the individual, who receives the tones in a headset. The audiometer presents a range of sounds and measures the fre-

The artist we are going to take look at today utilizes geography, location, history and identity as integral aspects of her work. Judy Smith is a muralist working in Los Angeles, who has spent the past 30+ years incorporating politics, realities and histories into her artworks.

During late 1960s, Los Angeles became a major center for muralists. Smith was one of leaders of Citywide Mural Project that produced more than 250 murals. The project defined itself as "being about people standing up and

An instructor using a speech-to-print system is able to instruct the class by typing the content which students receive on their desktop receivers.

(© Photo courtesy of the National Technical Institute for the Deaf at the Rochester Institute of Technology.)

quency (vibrations) and intensity (pitch) that the individual is able to hear through the earphones. The individual being tested responds to the sounds by raising his or her hand (or speaking into a microphone) if he or she can hear the tone. These responses are recorded on a graph called an audiogram. From an examination of the results, an audiologist can determine the degree and range of hearing loss. More elaborate audiometers can present and measure speech reception and discrimination (Paul & Quigley, 1994).

Behavioral Observation Audiometry Audiologists use behavioral observation audiometry to test hearing in children younger than 3 years of age. The child is placed in an environment with attractive toys, and an outside observer notes the child's reactions as sounds are introduced into the room. Head turning, eye blinking, smiles, movements toward the sound source, and lack of response to presented sounds are recorded. Variations include distraction testing, visual reinforcement audiometry, and performance testing (see Green, 1999, pp. 24–25). All of these tests observe the child's response to sound events in the environment.

Adapting Technology

Assistive Technology

Assistive technology is any equipment or product that assists the learner with a disability. Federal law requires that assistive technology be considered for every student with a disability (U.S. Department of Education, 1997).

Alerting Devices/Systems Various alerting devices and alarm systems developed for the deaf and hard of hearing include a baby-cry alarm consisting of a wrist-worn vibrator activated by a sound-sensitive transmitter in the baby's room. Others are clocks and fire alarms with flashing lights (Di Pietro, Williams, & Kaplan, 1991).

Hearing Aids One of the most important developments in this century for those with hearing loss is the electronic hearing aid. Paul and Quigley (1994) explained how a hearing aid works:

> Three basic units are common to all amplification systems—the microphone, the amplifier, and the receiver. The microphone converts acoustic sound waves into a weaker but similar electrical energy. The amplifier driven by a power supply (usually a battery) increases the amplitude of the electrical signal. (pp. 45–47)

Thus, the receiver in the ear receives an electrical signal, which is transformed into speech.

Hearing aids have several different designs:

▶ In the ear (ITE)

▶ Behind the ear (BTE)

▶ Canal (fits into the ear canal) (IEC)

▶ Body aids, attached to the body and connected to the ear by a wire (NICD, 1999; Green, 1999)

An audiologist or an otolaryngologist (physician who specializes in the ear) will determine the best hearing aid to meet the needs of an individual.

The development of the transistor transformed hearing aids from heavy, cumbersome units to easily portable devices. And directional microphones have cut down on background noise, amplifying only the sounds coming from directly in front of the listener (Northern & Downs, 1978).

The following devices also facilitate hearing:

▶ Bone anchored hearing aids.

▶ Augmentative communication devices (symbolic black-and-white outline drawings, pictorial symbols, pointers) (MacDonald & Gillette, 1986).

▶ Assistive listening devices (ALDs), which increase the volume of the voice received and reduce other sounds in the environment. They are wired or wireless and are small enough to be portable for use in vocational or recreational settings (Beukelman & Mirenda, 1992).

▶ A hardware device with a direct line to the earphone set and to the microphone.

▶ An induction loop device, which is an audio loop system that surrounds a seating area connected to a microphone and amplifies the sound received by the hearing aid. The loop may be small enough to be worn around the neck or as large as a room.

▶ Frequency modulated (FM) systems, in which the teacher wears a microphone that sends a direct signal into the child's hearing aid.

The Federal Communications Commission (FCC) requires that all television screens 13 inches or larger have decoding chips, to enable deaf people to view programs with captions.

▶ Infrared devices, which transmit sound via invisible light waves. They can be directly connected to a hearing aid, to the ear without a hearing aid, or to a neck loop.

▶ A vibrotactic aid that transmits sound through vibrators worn on the skin.

The teacher should receive information from the multidisciplinary team about each child who wears a hearing aid as to its operation and how to be sure the child is receiving sound. The audiologist is skilled in this area and will be an invaluable resource for the teacher. The audiologist will periodically check to be sure the aid is in good working order (English, 1995). Because some children will lip-read in addition to wearing their aid, the teacher should make every effort to look at these children when speaking.

Cochlear Implants Cochlear implants involve a surgical procedure in which electrodes are inserted into the cochlea. A microphone worn behind the ear receives environmental sounds and sends them through the auditory system (Steinberg & Knightly, 1997; Edwards & Tyskiewicz, 1999). Cochlear implants bypass the damaged part of the ear and stimulate the hearing nerve. They do not restore hearing, but they do provide a sound system that can assist the user in understanding incoming auditory stimuli (Marschark, Lang, & Albertini, 2002). They appear to be effective over a longer period of use if worn consistently. Recent research indicates that children who receive implants, particularly during the preschool years, develop language at nearly normal rates and in sequences similar to those of children who are not deaf or hard of hearing (Serry & Blaney, 1999; Deafness Research Foundation, 2000).

Cochlear Implant Association
www.cici.org

While hearing aids simply amplify sounds, cochlear implants with 22 to 24 wires send sounds of different frequencies to the brain, thereby providing a direct connection between speech and sounds in the environment. However, these implants cost between $40,000 and $50,000 initially, with a follow-up expense of approximately $20,000 per year (Marschark, Lang, & Albertini, 2002). The Deaf community has not fully accepted cochlear implants, as many feel that they convey a negative impression of deafness.

Speech Viewer III Speech Viewer III provides a variety of visual displays, such as a balloon getting larger in proportion to the loudness of the speaker's voice. The program is designed to improve voicing, pitch, timing, and sustained production (Mahshie, 1998). Another program, the CyberSign project, provides students with line illustrations of a number of signs (Nakamura, 1997). The ERIC Clearinghouse on Disabilities and Gifted Education is an excellent source in this rapidly evolving field.

Speech-to-Print Systems

Speech-to-print systems reproduce the classroom dialogue on a computer screen. A captionist who is in the room types the dialogue as it occurs. This has a dual advantage, in that the student can read it as it is taking place and review it later in either a printout or a computer file (Stinson & Foster, 2000).

TTY A major advance in technology for children and adults with serious hearing losses is the teletypewriter-printer device (**TTY** or **TT**), which was developed in

1964 by an orthodonist and a physicist who were deaf. This machine enables persons with severe hearing losses to communicate by using a typewriter that transforms typed messages into electrical signals, then retranslates them into print at the other end of a telephone connector. To make a TTY call, the individual places an ordinary telephone receiver on a coupler modem or interface between the typewriter and the telephone. The acoustic coupler transforms the electrical signals into two sounds at different frequencies that are then transmitted over the telephone and converted back into printed letters on the receiving end (Compton & Brandt, n.d.). More sophisticated units that can work with a computer are available, and research is under way to determine how the TTY can be used to improve social language skills (Rittenhouse, 1985). Telephone relay services are in every state. Their locations and telephone numbers are listed in the NICD bulletin *What are TTY's, TT's, and TDD's?* (1999).

A series of similar systems, known as telecommunication devices for the deaf (**TDDs**), have been generated over the past two decades. Currently, more than fifty thousand stations send, receive, and print messages on TDD systems. Although costs for the machines and the messages are high, the systems provide a very effective way for people with severe hearing losses to communicate across long distances (NICD, 1994).

A telecommunication relay service (TRS) allows people who are deaf or hard of hearing to communicate through a communication assistant (CA) with those who use a standard telephone (NICD, 1999). A CA relays the input to the telephone user and types that person's response back to the text telephone user. CAs are well trained and all calls are confidential. NICD has available a list of telephone numbers for each state. One may call (800) 241-1055 (TTY) for the needed number.

See the Houghton Mifflin Teacher Education website for an expanded list of assistive technology equipment.

WWW Houghton Mifflin Teacher Education website http://education.college.hmco.com/students

Instructional Technology

Software programs to assist instruction are being developed at a rapid rate. High-speed computers make it possible to combine print, videos, sounds, and signs to help the student who is deaf or hard of hearing understand instruction. Multimedia programs are available that contain video dictionaries of sign language (usually ASL). When the user encounters an unfamiliar word, he or she moves the mouse and clicks the appropriate key, and a video appears with a person signing the word (Andrews & Jodron, 1998).

The usefulness of computers for children with hearing losses is comparable to their usefulness for those who have learning disabilities (see Chapter 4). Applied computer technology has advanced to such an extent that special word-processing systems can be used to translate written English into graphic finger spelling signed on the computer screen. The computer enables the student with severe hearing losses to practice both signed and written English.

Clymer and McKee (1997) report that 70 percent of the schools serving students who are deaf or hard of hearing have access to the Internet and the World Wide Web. Therefore, these students can have access to Web pages related to deafness, ASL, and deaf culture.

The majority of schools serving students who are deaf or hard of hearing have Internet access to Web pages related to deaf culture, sign language, and other deafness-related topics.

(text continues from page 396)

helplessness are common. In many instances, they initially misperceive the condition, believing it to be an inability to speak rather than an inability to hear. They tend to resort to spanking more often (the child cannot hear other commands) and exhibit a great deal of frustration. In turn, they also tend to be overprotective of the child, and the child tends to be more dependent.

Hearing mothers tend to be more controlling of a child who is deaf or hard of hearing. This behavior tends to work against the development of a healthy mother-child relationship and deprives the child of important trial-and-error learning (Marschark, Lang, & Albertini, 2002, p. 81).

Summary

▶ Children's hearing losses fall into several categories: mild hearing loss, some residual hearing (the children are hard of hearing), and severe hearing losses—these children are usually prelinguistically impaired (deaf). With sound amplification, the child who is hard of hearing can understand speech; the child with severe hearing losses (deaf) usually cannot and usually depends on a sign system.

▶ Prelinguistic deafness is the loss of hearing before speech and language develop; postlinguistic deafness is the loss of hearing after speech and language develop. Children who have prelinguistic severe hearing losses face the most serious learning problems.

▶ The causes of hearing losses are equally divided between genetics and the environment. Environmental causes include complications during pregnancy and birth; childhood diseases; infections; and injuries. Studies show that most children with serious hearing losses are cognitively normal. Their poor reading performance stems from their difficulty in reading and writing in English.

▶ The social adjustment of youngsters with severe hearing losses can be impeded by a lack of communication with those around them. Most early intervention programs for youngsters with severe hearing losses make the parents a critical part of the process. Most elementary and secondary programs bring children who have severe hearing losses into the public school, either in general education classrooms or in special classrooms.

▶ Methods of teaching communication skills to students with severe hearing losses include the auditory-oral method, the auditory method, and manual methods. Approaches to teaching communication include the total communication method and the bilingual approach. The total communication method, currently the most popular approach, combines oral and manual communication.

▶ Technology is having an impact on children with mild to severe hearing loss. The electronic hearing aid is used extensively, and computers give students the extra individual attention they need. Advances in telecommunications are allowing people with severe hearing losses to communicate across long distances. Cochlear implants offer individuals the promise of increased hearing. And captioned films and television programs are making visual channels more accessible.

Employment Issues

1. Employment prospects

With respect to unemployment, occupational level, wage earnings, and opportunities for advancement, in all groups persons with severe hearing losses fare worse than the general U.S. population.

2. Job performance

The favorable reports of most supervisors regarding the job performance of their employees who have severe hearing losses indicate that employed young adults who have severe hearing losses perform well in their jobs. Supervisors also seem willing to have subordinates who have severe hearing losses and to advance them if they receive further training.

3. Postsecondary training

A majority of current and former students who have severe hearing losses and their parents perceive a need for postsecondary training and indicate that they would support such programs if the opportunity were available. See PEP NET Postsecondary Programs Network (http://www.pepnet.org/)

Future Challenges

1. Will there be adequate early intervention?

Students will do better when their hearing problems are identified early. They will need to learn reading and how to access information like their hearing peers. An early start will be of great benefit.

2. How can educators stimulate language development?

The growing popularity of the total communication method reflects the importance of language to the academic performance of a child with a severe hearing loss. Can we alter teaching of the structural and conceptual aspects of language in sequence so that youngsters can move from preschool to elementary to secondary programs that build on and reinforce earlier learning?

3. Will teacher-training programs reflect innovative research findings?

Most teacher-training programs reflect traditional philosophies and methodologies, not the innovative educational approaches suggested by research findings. All too often, the preparation of teachers and the operation of research programs are mutually exclusive functions. Until teacher-training programs begin to integrate preparation and research through faculty appointments and university emphases, the students who graduate from traditional programs may continue to use methods that are not working.

4. Will students' reading and English language abilities improve?

Many adolescents who have severe hearing losses graduate from high school today with little control over the English language. Although the education of those with severe hearing losses has changed markedly over the course of this century, more improvements are needed. With new findings in language and cognitive research and new materials, we may see some changes in the achievement of youngsters with severe hearing losses. Of course, this means that new findings and materials must be assimilated directly into teacher-

training programs if we want them to be implemented as soon as possible.

Key Terms

American Sign Language (ASL) *p. 407*

auditory global method *p. 406*

combined method *p. 407*

finger spelling *p. 407*

mixed hearing loss *p. 379*

postlinguistic deafness *p. 378*

prelinguistic deafness *p. 378*

simultaneous method *p. 407*

speech reading *p. 406*

TDD *p. 413*

total communication method *p. 407*

TTY *p. 413*

unisensory method *p. 406*

Resources

References of Special Interest

American Speech-Hearing-Language Association. (1991). *ASHA, Supplement H, 33(3). This guide to position statements on children with hearing impairments or speech and language disorders is a must for all speech-language and hearing pathologists as a professional guide to practice.*

Batshaw, M. L. (Ed.) (2002). *Children with disabilities: A medical primer. Baltimore: Paul H. Brookes. A comprehensive guide to all disabilities, with a focus on medical causes and treatments, this book includes both genetic and environmentally induced dysfunctions. It is amply illustrated with photographs and diagrams of aids for children with disabilities.*

Bodner-Johnson, B., and Sass-Lehrer M. (2003). *The young deaf or hard of hearing child. Baltimore: Paul H. Brookes. A rich resource for a family approach to early education when a child is deaf or hard of hearing.*

Dolnic, E. (1993). Deafness as culture. *The Atlantic Monthly, 272, 37–53. In an accessible article, the writer explains the meaning and importance of the deaf culture in American society.*

English, K. (1995). *Educational audiology across the lifespan. Baltimore: Paul H. Brookes. The author describes the role of audiologists in the education of persons with hearing disabilities. The text includes suggestions for practice as well as ways in which an audiologist can contribute to collaborative teams.*

Moores, D. (2000). *Educating the deaf: Psychology, principles, and practices (5th ed.). Boston: Houghton Mif-*

flin. *This comprehensive textbook on children with severe hearing losses provides a rich historical background and up-to-date reports on current research, educational trends, and preschool and postsecondary programs.*

Stokes, J. (Ed.). (1999). *Hearing impaired infants: Support in the first eighteen months.* London: Whurr Publisher: Distributed by Paul H. Brookes, Baltimore. *An excellent source for the development of deaf and hard-of-hearing infants.*

Journals

American Annals of the Deaf
  Gallaudet University

Journal of Speech, Language and Hearing Research
  American Speech-Language-Hearing Association
  www.professional.asha.org

The Volta Review
  Alexander Graham Bell Society

Professional Organizations

Alexander Graham Bell Association for the Deaf
  www.agbell.org

Gallaudet University
  www.gallaudet.edu

National Association of the Deaf Captioned Film/Video Program
  www.nad.org
  www.cfv.org

National Deaf Education Center
Formerly known as the National Information Center on Deafness (NICD)
  www.clerccenter.gallaudet.edu/infotogo

Please visit the book's website at **http://education.college.hmco.com/students** for new and updated information on websites listed here and for the mailing addresses of the journals and organizations.

Some Special Services

Numerous social service agencies extend their programs to clients with severe hearing losses. In addition, various agencies and organizations—related either to hearing losses or to disability in general—provide specific services to people with severe hearing losses.

Captioned Films for the Deaf

Captioned Films for the Deaf lends theatrical and educational films captioned for viewers with severe hearing losses. It is funded by the Captioning and Adaptations Branch of the U.S. Department of Education. Its aim is to promote the education and welfare of people with severe hearing losses through the use of media. The Captioning and Adaptations Branch also provides funds for closed-captioned television programs, including the live-captioned ABC television news (NICD, 1989).

The Clerc Center–National Deaf Education Center, Gallaudet University, Washington, DC.

A wide range of materials for teachers, parents, and children. A unique feature, "Tips for Your Reading to Your Deaf Child," is available in 20 different languages. The bookmarks are free and available in lots of 100 per customer.

Deafness Research Foundation:

The National Campaign for Hearing Health 1050 1754, Washington, D.C. Provides grants for research and technique for dection, prevention, intervention, and research. http://www.def.org and www.hearing health.net.

Gallaudet University Press (http://gupress.edu)

A source of up-to-date material for teachers and parents, as well as colorful children's books to be read to infants and older children with hearing impairments. The illustrated books introducing the first signs are recommended.

National Information Center on Deafness

NICD is located at Gallaudet University, 800 Florida Avenue, NE, Washington, DC 20002-3695. It is a centralized source for information about hearing loss and deafness. NICD has a wealth of information available in a variety of written and visual forms and at nominal cost. Gallaudet also provides information on postsecondary education programs (http://www.pepnet.org/). This network is continually updated and should be consulted for current program availability.

Registry of Interpreters for the Deaf, Inc

A professional organization, the Registry of Interpreters for the Deaf (RID) maintains a national listing of persons skilled in the use of ASL and other sign systems. The organization also provides information on interpreting and evaluation and certification of interpreters for people with severe hearing losses (NICD, 1989).

Signaling Devices

Signaling devices that add a flashing or vibrating signal to the existing auditory signal are popular with users who are hard of hearing. Among devices that use flashing lights are door "bells," telephone-ring signalers, baby-cry signals (which alert the parent that the baby is crying), and smoke alarms. Alarm clocks may feature either a flashing light or a vibrating signal.

State Departments of Vocational Rehabilitation

Each state has specific provisions for the type and extent of vocational evaluation, financial assistance for education and training, and job placement help (NICD, 1989).

Telecommunications for the Deaf, Inc. (TDI)

Telecommunications for the Deaf (TDI) publishes an international telephone directory of individuals and organizations that own and maintain telecommunication devices for the deaf (TDDs) for personal or business use (NICD, 2000).

CHILDREN WITH VISUAL IMPAIRMENTS

FOCUS QUESTIONS

▶ What effects do limited visual experiences have on the development of children with visual impairments?

▶ Why is learned helplessness a problem for many children who are visually impaired?

▶ How do we adapt the instructional program for youngsters with visual impairments?

▶ How does the philosophy of inclusion affect the education of these special students?

▶ What effects has technology had on the communication skills and mobility of children and youth with visual impairments?

▶ How has the Universal Design for Learning influenced education for the visually impaired?

▶ What is needed to implement the expanded core curriculum?

Many children have correctable visual problems and are not our concern in this chapter. For one child in a thousand, visual impairments are so severe that they cannot be corrected. In this chapter, we discuss the special needs of children who are visually impaired and the educational adaptations that are—or should be—made for them.

Definitions

Visual impairment is a general term for a visual loss that affects learning in a school environment. Legally, a definition of children with visual impairments divides these children into two large groups on the basis of their ability to use the visual sense for learning after maximum correction. A child who is **legally blind** is one who can see at 20 feet an object that a person with normal sight can see at 200 feet. Legal blindness (less than 20/200 vision) still can mean that a child can be responsive to light and darkness and may have some visual imagery.

Children with **low vision** have a visual acuity of 20/70 to 20/200 in the better eye. They have difficulty accomplishing visual tasks, but they can learn through the visual sense by the use of various special technologies and teaching techniques. Children with low vision used to be referred to as "partially sighted," but the term is rarely used today.

The major educational distinction is that children who are blind use their tactile or auditory senses as their primary learning channels, whereas children with low vision can, with aid, still use the visual sense as their major avenue of learning.

Prevalence of Visual Impairments

Children with visual impairments qualify as having a low-incidence disability and make up a very small percentage of the school population. There are only about 4 of these children for every 10,000 students (U.S. Department of Education estimate, 2003), so it would be very difficult to cluster them for instructional purposes unless they were in a very large community or enrolled in a state school for the blind. Today there is a strong effort to provide them with an education within local schools. Another complication, described by a teacher of the visually impaired (TVI), is that many children with visual impairments also have other conditions, such as cerebral palsy, mental retardation, autism, and so on, which challenges the education planning for such students.

The Human Eye

Vision or visual interpretation is a function of the brain, experience, and the adequacy of the sense organ that receives stimuli from the outside world: the eye. Faulty visual interpretation can result from a defect in the brain, inadequate experience, or a defective eye. The process of visual interpretation is as follows: Light enters the eye, focuses on the retina, and is transmitted along the optic nerve to the brain, where visual information is interpreted. Two people

WWW
Association for Education and Rehabilitation of the Blind and Visually Impaired
www.aerbvi.org

Vision is a function of the sensation and perception of light.

with well-functioning sense organs can interpret a visual experience differently, depending on their training and experience.

Educators of children with visual impairments are concerned primarily with adapting instruction to the impairment. To accomplish this, they need to understand how healthy eyes operate and what some of the conditions are that can cause problems.

The human eye is a complex system of interrelated parts (Figure 11.1). Any part can be defective or become nonfunctional as a result of hereditary anomaly, disease, accident, or other causes. The eye has been called a camera for the brain. Like a camera, the eye has a diaphragm, the **iris.** The iris is the colored muscular partition that expands and contracts to regulate the amount of light admitted through the central opening, or **pupil.** Behind the iris is the **lens,** an elastic biconvex body that focuses onto the retina the light reflected from objects in the line of vision. The **retina** is the light-sensitive innermost layer of tissue at the back of the eyeball. It contains neural receptors that translate the physical energy of light into the neural energy that results in the experience of seeing.

As Figure 11.1 shows, other protective and structural elements in the eye can affect vision. The **cornea** is the transparent anterior (front) portion of the

FIGURE 11.1
The Human Eye

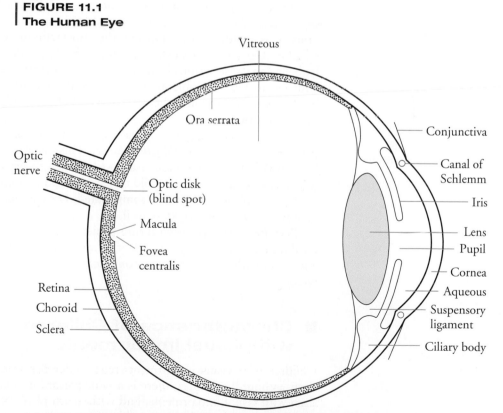

Source: From Anatomy of the eye, *Vision problems in the U.S.* (Schaumburg, IL: Author, 1994). Reprinted with permission of Prevent Blindness America.

tough outer coat of the eyeball. The **ciliary muscles** change the shape of the lens so the eye can focus on objects at varying distances. In the normal mature eye, no muscular effort is necessary to see clearly objects 20 feet or more away. When the eye looks at an object closer than 20 feet, the ciliary muscles increase the convex curvature of the lens so that the closer object is still focused on the retina. This change in the shape of the lens is called **accommodation**.

Extrinsic muscles control the movement of the eyeball in the socket. The change made by these muscles is known as **convergence** and refers to the movement of two eyes toward each other when focusing on an object at near range.

■ Causes of Visual Impairments

A wide variety of conditions can cause serious visual impairments in children from birth to age 5. The potential causes of visual impairment in children range from hereditary conditions to infectious diseases, to cancer, to injuries, to various environmental conditions. The actual cause of the disorder is not of primary interest to the teacher, who must deal with the functional consequences of the disorders—those functional consequences would seem to be similar from one condition to another. So whether the cause was an infection or a hereditary condition, a similar problem of limited vision is faced by the teacher.

The widely scattered prevalence of these conditions makes it difficult to assign percentages to particular causes, but some of them are reasonably well known as major causes. One of the most common infectious diseases is rubella (German measles), contracted by the mother during pregnancy. Rubella can cause serious birth defects, mental retardation, and hearing loss in addition to visual problems, but improved control measures and education have combined to reduce the percentage of children blinded by this and other infectious diseases.

Another major cause of visual impairment is **retinopathy of prematurity** (formerly called *retrolental fibroplasia*). This disorder was widely believed to be caused by the overadministration of oxygen to premature infants in an attempt to save the life of the child threatened by other conditions. However, the condition appears to be more complicated. For example, it seems to be associated with low birth weight as well.

Because there have been future projections of more children with multiple disabilities, there is a likelihood of more children with visual problems to be educated, with their condition complicated by a variety of other problems as well.

■ Characteristics of Children with Visual Impairments

Children with visual impairments tend to develop at a slower pace than children without disabilities; there is a wide variation in the development of children with visual impairments; and with a rich physical environment and with encouragement to take reasonable risks, parents can increase the adaptive skills of their children. (See Table 11.1.)

For additional information on blindness and multiple disabilities, see Chapter 13.

A Visit to the Beach for a Child Who Is Blind

Imagine that a girl who is blind goes to the beach for the first time with someone who takes pleasure in introducing her to the joys of summer. Her companion, who may be sighted or blind, has described where they are going so that she has some preparation for what awaits her as she first sets foot on the beach. She anticipates eating a picnic lunch on the beach, and she has helped to buy the food and pack it in the ice chest. The two beachgoers have loaded the chest into the car and carried it from the car to the beach. Together, they have paused to pick up some sand and feel it sift through their fingers before they venture to the shore. Her friend has pointed out how the sand becomes damper the closer they get to the water. She may have picked up some more sand on her own to examine the change in texture. She has helped spread the blanket on the sand, noticing how the wind makes it difficult to spread it flat. When she has listened to an explanation of why it is important to protect her skin from the sun, she is prepared to rub the parts she can reach with sunscreen and to ask for help with the parts she cannot reach. Her attention to the sounds, smells, and tactile sensations at the beach is appreciated and forms an important part of the friends' conversation. With assistance, she has stashed her shoes in a bag on a particular corner of the blanket; her friend hopes she will remember where to retrieve them when it is time to put them on and go home.

The day has been rich in information and less scary than it might have been. Her friend has answered questions and shown her, in small, understandable, and pleasant steps, what is enjoyable and interesting at the beach. She may not comprehend how huge the ocean looks or how beautiful the sky is that day, but she has had a better chance of relaxing in the sun, enjoying a swim, and feeling like one of the magicians who produced the lovely picnic at the beach.

Source: F. Liefert, Introduction to visual impairment, in S. Goodman & S. Wittenstein (Eds.), *Collaborative assessment* (pp.1–22) (New York: American Foundation for the Blind, 2003). Reprinted with the permission of the American Foundation for the Blind.

One of the difficulties in determining the characteristics of children with visual impairment was their low prevalence in the population, which made it difficult to assemble a large number of such children in one place. Accordingly, the Office of Special Education Programs in the U.S. Department of Education funded a large longitudinal study of young children (birth to 5 years) in seven sites around the country. This enabled the investigators to assemble data on a population of 202 youngsters receiving services from these sites and to draw some conclusions about their visual acuity, behavior, temperament, and environment, in an effort to see any differences between these children and typical children of similar age. This longitudinal study was named Project PRISM and administered 2,446 standardized tests to the 202 children during the course of the project (Ferrell, Shaw, & Deitz, 1998).

Some of the major findings from this effort were as follows.

▶ Sixty percent of these children had additional disabilities, and two-thirds of these disabilities were considered severe.

▶ The leading diagnoses for these children were cortical visual impairment (21 percent), retinopathy of prematurity (19 percent), and optic nerve hypoplasia (17 percent).

▶ The majority of developmental milestones for these children were delayed, in comparison with those of typical children. Children with additional impairments achieved these milestones later than children without such impairments.

▶ Measures of social maturity and cognitive development showed delay.

▶ Measures of parental stress found more high scores among the parents of these children with visual impairments.

These findings tended to underscore the importance of providing services to the child and family as early as possible and also emphasize the importance of special attention to those children with more than one disability.

Cognitive Development

In the 1940s and 1950s, educators generally believed that the intelligence of children with visual impairments was not seriously affected by their condition, except for their ability to use certain visual concepts (colors and three-dimensional space, for example). The thinking then was that intelligence unfolds on a genetically determined schedule and is affected by only the most severe environmental trauma. Samuel Hayes (1941) modified the Stanford-Binet for children with visual impairments. His examination of more than two thousand youngsters revealed overall average IQ scores.

Today, we hold a different view of cognition. We recognize that what we measure as intelligence in school-age children has been notably affected by their cumulative experiences in the early years of development. Lack of vision, then, is both a primary impairment and a condition that can hamper cognitive development because it limits the integrating experiences and the understanding of those experiences that the visual sense brings naturally to sighted children. These limitations are especially notable if the children do not receive early intervention in the preschool years. At present, the verbal section of the Wechsler scale would seem to provide the best measurement of intelligence for children with visual impairment.

> Visual impairment can hamper cognitive development.

Language Development

Sighted children acquire language by listening, reading, and watching movements and facial expressions. They express themselves first through babbling and later by imitating their parents and siblings. Children with visual impairments acquire language in much the same way, but their language concepts are not helped by reading or visual input. A sighted child develops the concept of a ball by seeing different balls; a child with blindness develops the same concept through tactile manipulation of different balls. Both are able to understand the word *ball*, and both are able to identify a ball.

A series of investigations into the language development of children with visual impairments yielded the following conclusions. Visual impairment does not interfere with everyday language usage or communication abilities. The language of children with visual impairments seems like that of their sighted peers. However, the children with visual impairments had less understanding of words as vehicles of, or as standing for, concrete experiences, and they were slower than sighted children to form hypotheses about word meaning. Children with severe visual impairment appeared to be restricted to word meanings from their own personal experience, whereas vision allowed children to broaden and generalize the meanings of words.

Warren (1994), in a review of the literature on the language of those with visual impairments, arrived at these conclusions:

> Visual impairment limits children's conceptual understanding and generalizations in language and vocabulary.

> It is clear from the literature that the vocabulary of children with visual impairments is heavily grounded in their own perceptual experience and is

not simply a parroting of sighted vocabulary. . . . This underscores the importance of the parents' role in ensuring not only that the child's perceptual experience is adequately rich, but also that it is embedded in a context of shared communication. (p. 326)

Sensory Compensation and Perception

Vision is a continuous source of information. We depend on vision to orient ourselves, to identify people and objects, and to regulate our motor and social behavior. People without sight have to rely on other senses for information and for all the other tasks that vision performs. How this is accomplished has been the focus of much speculation and research.

The false doctrine of **sensory compensation** holds that if one sense, such as vision, is deficient, other senses are automatically strengthened, in part because of their greater use. Although this may be true in certain cases, research does not show that the hearing or touch sensitivity of children with visual impairments is superior to that of sighted children. For example, Gottesman (1971) tested children ages 2 to 8 who were blind and who were sighted on their ability to identify by touch such things as a key, a comb, a pair of scissors, and geometric forms (triangle, cross). He found no difference between the groups.

Personal and Social Adjustment

No personal or social problems *inevitably* follow from being visually impaired. However, the restricted mobility and consequent limited experiences of children who are visually impaired appear to cause, in some children, a state of passivity and dependency.

Students with visual impairments may tend to spend more time in sedentary activities than their sighted peers.

The increasing interest in the social adjustment of students with visual impairments resulted in a study of the lifestyles of blind, low-vision, and sighted adolescents (Sacks, Wolffe, & Tierney, 1998). Using a device called a time diary, in which the students identified their primary and secondary activities in 1-hour blocks of time over a 24-hour period, the investigators found that students with visual impairments spent more time on the telephone, engaged in more sedentary activities, spent more time alone, and were bound to their homes by their inability to travel independently.

The students with visual impairments who were chosen for this study had no other impairments and were close to grade level in performance. One could anticipate that children with multiple impairments would fare even worse in the social domain than did these students.

There is a need for programs that prepare students with visual impairments for adult life.

What this study seems to indicate is a need for continued implementation of programs designed to prepare students with visual impairments for adult life. That would mean curricula that focus on career development and social skill competencies. Of course, the study also underscores the importance of mobility training as a key component to social contact for these students.

The teacher of the visually impaired must deal with many realistic issues; for example, spatial perception and communication. It is understandable that the teacher might overlook an issue that turns out to be one of the most

Self-esteem and self-acceptance in children with visual impairments are nurtured by positive interactions with sighted people.
(© Michael Newman/Photo Edit)

important—how the child feels about his or her situation. Recently, there has been an attempt to focus on the child's feelings and to make them a significant part of the instructional program. The child who is deeply depressed and feeling helpless is not a good candidate for braille, print reading, or anything else (Tuttle & Tuttle, 1996). For example, a child who is trying to deny the reality of blindness may resist special learning devices like viewers or magnifying glasses since these symbolize the disability.

Successful Coping

Several principles have formed the basis of a strategy to help the child go beyond these feelings of despair and create a climate of self-expression and self-esteem.

Successful coping includes the following:

▶ What a person can do is emphasized.

▶ The areas of life in which the person can participate are seen as worthwhile.

▶ The person plays an active role in molding his or her life constructively.

▶ Accomplishments are appreciated in terms of their benefits to the person and others and not depreciated because they fall short of some irrelevant standard.

▶ Pain that is suffered or difficulties that exist are felt to be manageable.

▶ The person is overcoming difficulties or ameliorating them through the application of medical procedures, the use of prostheses and other aids, the learning of new skills, and environmental accommodations (social, legal, economic, and so on).

> The person is living on satisfactory terms with his or her limitations. (Tuttle & Tuttle, 1996, p. 169)

Many people who have not had experience with persons with disabilities react to them by lowering their expectations. But those students don't want this kind of favor. "Don't treat me like I'm helpless. Don't do me any special favors. Let me do it on my own" is their response to well-meaning people who attempt to "help" them.

Great interest has been shown in the self-esteem of students with visual disabilities. However, self-esteem appears to be the by-product of good performance on tasks deemed socially valuable (for example, effective mobility around class and school). Good academic and social behavior will result in good self-esteem, rather than the other way around.

What happens to children with visual impairments over time? Does the lack of experience with the world around them cause developmental problems in motor and social domains? These questions have been difficult to answer because the relative infrequency of such children made it hard to bring together sufficient children to conduct a convincing study.

A national study of children with visual impairments was combined with agency data from a southern state to create a sample of 186 children (ages 1–7) who had developmental curves that could answer these questions (Hatton, Bailey, Burchinal, & Ferrell, 1997). The majority of these children had visual impairments that stemmed from retinopathy of prematurity,

Many sighted people who have not worked with children who are visually impaired tend to have low expectations of those children's abilities.

One Person's Reflections on the Consequences of Using a Unique Standard

I don't know when it began, this pervasive expectation that others would naturally give me a break because I am blind—probably as a very young child. I do remember in the first grade the teacher asked for volunteers to help me during recesses "so [I] wouldn't get hurt." I didn't need the help, but I have to admit I enjoyed the extra attention.

In fourth and fifth grades, the teachers let me complete only even-numbered problems in arithmetic homework while my classmates had to do them all. They told me that they were making this exception because I was blind and it took me longer to do my work. I had a teacher in seventh grade who required six book reports during the year for an A, but then turned to me and announced that four would be good enough for an A. Who was I to argue with such good fortune?

Through high school, I guess I began to work the system to my advantage. I learned that if I looked uncomfortable, I wouldn't be called on in class; if I turned in partial work, I would often get full credit; if I happened to be late turning in assignments, it was OK because I was blind. Before long, I expected everyone to give me a break because of my blindness.

My first summer job after my junior year in high school really jolted me to reality. I was hired by a used car dealer to wash, wax, and vacuum six cars a day. At the end of the first week I questioned my paycheck—I thought they shortchanged me. My boss didn't pull any punches. "You serviced four cars a day this week, so I paid you for four cars a day. If and when you get up to speed and you finish six cars, I'll pay you what we agreed upon." I didn't argue—I knew he was right. I got myself organized, hustled a bit more, and put in some extra time that next week. I was proud to get my first paycheck on Friday; I know I had earned it fair and square.

Source: From D. Tuttle, & N. Tuttle, Psychosocial needs of children and youths, in M. C. Holbrook & A. J. Koenig (Eds.), *Foundations of education* (2nd ed.), Vol. 1, *History and theory of teaching children and youths with visual impairments* (p. 167) (New York: AFB Press, 2000). Reprinted with the permission of the American Foundation for the Blind.

PROFILES

DEVELOPMENTAL

People with normal sight wonder from time to time what it would be like to be blind. It's obvious that adapting to sensory loss has implications that are profoundly personal and social as well as educational. A comprehensive special education program must involve all areas of development and adjustment. We introduce developmental profiles here of two visually impaired children to highlight some of the problems children with visual handicaps have in adapting to their disability. The graph below shows the patterns of development of

Renaldo and Susan. Renaldo has a severe visual disability; Susan has been blind since birth. Both are educated in public schools where special provisions, personnel, and equipment are available.

Renaldo: Renaldo is a tall, slim 11-year-old who has a severe visual impairment for which maximum correction has been obtained with the aid of thick glasses. He can read print material and, in the early grades, was able to make a reasonable academic adjustment. As

Profiles of Two Children with Different Degrees of Visual Impairment

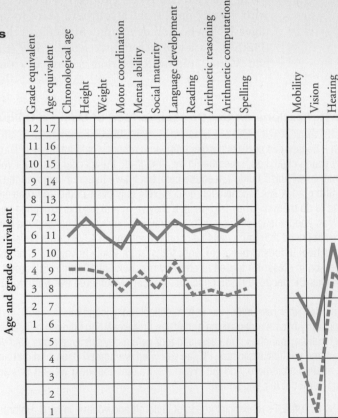
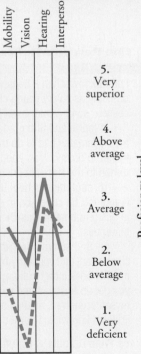

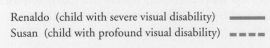

Renaldo (child with severe visual disability) ——————

Susan (child with profound visual disability) ━ ━ ━ ━

the profile in the graph shows, Renaldo scored slightly above average in intelligence as measured by an adaptation of the Stanford-Binet and is currently doing average work as measured by achievement tests administered with no time limits. Yet this profile, though favorable, tends to mask the academic problems Renaldo is likely to encounter. He will be required to use higher thought processes as he progresses through the educational system, and he is already beginning to experience the shift from concrete arithmetic to the more difficult (for him) abstractions of algebra and spatial concepts of geometry.

Renaldo spends most of his time in school with a regular sixth-grade class but leaves the program for about an hour a day to work with a specially trained resource teacher. Only three or four other students are in the resource room with Renaldo, so the teacher can give him a good deal of tutoring in the academic areas in which he needs help.

Of more concern is how Renaldo feels about himself. His visual handicap is serious enough that he is sometimes unsure whether he belongs to the sighted community or to the blind community. He feels deeply about his awkwardness and inability to perform in athletics—an important dimension in the life of an 11-year-old—but he does not discuss this with his schoolmates.

Renaldo also has some interpersonal problems. He reacts with a sharp tongue and a quick temper to any slights or negative comments, real or imagined, about his impairment. Consequently, many of his peers ignore or avoid him except when class participation requires interaction. Above all, Renaldo is beginning to wonder about his future: What is he going to do with his life when he grows up? How can he be independent? How will he establish friendships with girls? This is a topic of great importance to his older brother, Brian, who is in high school and whose life seems to

revolve around girls. Brian's behavior is a source of amusement to Renaldo now, but in a few years he will have to face social relationship problems more seriously.

Susan: Susan's profile is also shown in the graph on the previous page. She is an average-looking 9-year-old. Like many children who are blind, she has limited light perception that helps her move around. She has mastered a braille system that uses contractions, letter combinations, and shortened forms of words to save time and space in reading. In some respects, Susan is making a better adjustment than Renaldo, despite her blindness. She has a warm, understanding mother who has given her strong emotional support and a professional father who provides a comfortable income for the family. Her mother has tried to be a companion for Susan and has read to her extensively from the time Susan was 3 or 4 years of age. She has helped Susan through some difficult times, particularly when Susan was having trouble developing independent living skills. Susan's father is more distant; he doesn't seem to know how to approach her.

Susan shows some signs of mild neurological damage, which tends to make her physically awkward, but this condition is not serious enough to classify her as multiply disabled. As the developmental profile shows, Susan's performance on tests of mental ability and her development in speech and language are average, testimony perhaps to the intensive work with her mother in the early years. But in arithmetic and spelling, her performance is somewhat below average.

Susan has been affected in an important way by the educational trend of placing exceptional children in the least restrictive environment in their own school system. Susan lives in an urban area with a large population where a number of children are visually impaired. The school system buses these children from around the district to a school that provides a special

program for them, Susan is well accepted by her classmates and has one or two close friends who are sighted. She has not yet had to face problems in relationships with boys.

In the next three or four years, her mother and father will have to decide whether they want her to attend a residential school that provides advanced curriculum and educational facilities for youngsters with visual impairments. But for now, they are happy that she is at home and able to get special help within the local school system.

optic nerve hypoplasia, cortical visual impairment, and albinism. Forty percent of the sample also had a co-occurring condition of mental retardation or developmental disabilities.

The results clearly indicated delays in motor and social domains, with less delay in communications. The development of those with severe impairment or blindness (worse than 20/200) was clearly different from those with the most vision (20/70 to 20/200). The children with the additional condition of mental retardation and developmental disabilities were significantly slower than those who did not have that additional condition.

■ Early Intervention

A child's experiences during the period from birth to age 5 are critical to subsequent development. It is especially important that the systematic education of visually impaired children begin as early as possible. Sighted children absorb a tremendous amount of information and experience from their environment in the ordinary course of events. Parents and teachers must specially design parallel experiences for children who are visually impaired (see Chapter 3 for more information).

The characteristics we observe in a 10-year-old who has visual impairment are often a blend of the primary problem (loss of vision) and a number of secondary problems that have developed because the child has missed certain sequential experiences. For example, many youngsters with a visual disability are passive. Passivity is not a natural or inevitable by-product of low vision; it is present because the child does not have a well-established motivation to move.

For the sighted child, the environment is filled with visual stimulation: toys, bottles, people, color, and shapes. The child has a natural impulse to move toward these elements. The child with a severe visual disability isn't aware of these elements unless someone points them out. For an infant who is blind, the feeding bottle appears magically. The child is not motivated to go after it; in fact, the child does not even realize that he or she can do something—be active—to get the bottle.

An easily understood concept for the sighted child is **object permanence**. By the age of 6 or 7 months, sighted children realize that even when objects

When adapting instruction to the educational needs of children who are visually impaired, teachers should emphasize concreteness, unifying experiences, and learning by doing.
(© Steve Goldberg)

TABLE 11.1
Infants and Toddlers with Visual Impairments:
Suggestions for Early Interventionists

Establish reliable alliances (Turnbull & Turnbull, 2002) with families and other service providers based upon family and child strengths, respect for diversity and culture, and collaboration.

Collaborate with families and other professionals to complete the Individualized Family Services Plan (IFSP) process.

Serve as an effective member of the early intervention team, help families and other team members understand medical information, and be familiar with service coordination responsibilities.

Approach early intervention from a support, rather than a provision of services, perspective.

Make home visits that promote functional outcomes for both the child and the family.

Source: Hatton, D., McWilliam, R., & Winton, P. (2002). Infants and toddlers with visual impairments: Suggestions for early interventionists (Report EDO-EC-02-14). Washington, DC: Office of Educational Research and Improvement (OERI), U.S. Department of Education. (ERIC Clearinghouse on Disabilities and Gifted Education Digest E636).

It is important to let children take control of a task once they demonstrate an ability to do so.

disappear from their visual field (mother left the room; the ball rolled under the couch), they still exist. This knowledge makes the world more orderly and predictable. And it makes sense to go after objects even if they are not in the line of sight. Object constancy is a more difficult concept for children with visual disabilities to understand. They need deliberate instruction and an organized environment before they can understand the concept and begin to act on it.

Table 11.1 provides a series of suggestions for early interventionists to use.

Although it's important to help visually impaired youngsters learn tasks, it's also important to let them take over when they are able. Ferrell (1986) described a technique called **fading**, or gradually cutting back help as a child becomes competent at a task. She showed how the process works with the task of eating:

1. Begin by placing your hand completely around the child's hand as the child grasps the spoon. Move the child through the scooping and eating motions.
2. As the child gains control, continue the scooping and eating motions with your hand on the child's wrist.
3. Gradually move your hand from the wrist to the arm, and then to the elbow.
4. Eventually, just touch the arm to remind the child what he or she is supposed to do.

By teaching young children with visual disabilities to do things for themselves, we give these children some of the important experiences that sighted children get naturally.

It is important for parents and teachers to give the child with visual disabilities the opportunity to indicate what he or she wants and not to anticipate the child's needs. "By doing so, they eliminate the child's choice and control of the situation and they foster his dependence. Independence training begins in infancy, not at age 2, 6, or when college is imminent" (Ferrell, 1986, p. 130).

Children with visual impairments may exhibit delays in their play skills.

The importance of starting education early for children with visual impairments was pointed to in a study of thirteen children with visual impairments who were 40 months of age (Hughes, Dote-Kwan, & Dolendo, 1998). The study looked at the play behavior of these children in a special play setting. The results agreed with earlier studies in that the children with visual impairments were significantly delayed in their play skills, particularly symbolic play. Because the children were functioning at expected developmental levels in other domains, such as receptive language, the study underlined the importance of helping these children to develop and facilitate their play behavior. This is particularly important considering the heavy emphasis on play in most inclusive preschool settings.

The Individuals with Disabilities Education Act (IDEA), which mandates services for infants and toddlers with disabilities (see Chapter 2), provides for earlier identification and earlier professional services for children with vision problems. Such early intervention programs should reduce the number of secondary problems shown by children who did not have the advantages of earlier services. The work cited in Chapter 3 on early intervention provides additional evidence on the usefulness of early attention.

■ Identification and Assessment

Most children with severe and profound visual disabilities are identified by parents and physicians long before they enter school. The most common exceptions are children with multiple disabilities. It is possible for another condition—for example, cerebral palsy or mental retardation—to mask a visual impairment. The key to identification is a comprehensive examination. Many of these components do not require formal testing, just the observations of those around the child. For example, the family can be very helpful in determining whether a child has mastered functional living skills. And a classroom teacher is a good source of information about a child's social and emotional development.

Most states require preschool vision screening, which identifies children with moderate vision problems. Throughout this textbook, we discuss the importance of early experiences in cognitive development. Obviously, early identification allows us to broaden those experiences for the child with a visual disability through maximum correction and preschool programs.

The term *assessment* describes a process that must occur before a student with a suspected disability receives special educational services. Four specific steps are taken in assessments: screening, eligibility, instructional planning, and progress evaluation (Lewis & Russo, 1998).

Routine vision screenings are administered to many students before they enter school. While severe visual impairments are readily apparent without formal screening, some milder problems might escape notice. Screening merely identifies students with possible developmental problems. A medical diagnosis of blindness is often sufficient to demonstrate the need for special educational services, but sometimes a functional visual evaluation may be necessary to determine the degree of usable vision. These results can do much to shape the approach taken by special education teachers.

Mild, correctable visual impairments often go undiagnosed until a child enters elementary school. School systems use different methods to detect visual impairments in children. Some refer children with suspected problems directly to an ophthalmologist or an optometrist. Others routinely screen youngsters to determine whether they have vision difficulties, and they refer those who do not pass that screening for more comprehensive assessment.

The standard school screening instrument is the Snellen chart, which has rows of letters in gradually smaller sizes that children read at a distance of 20 feet. A variation that is useful for screening young children and people who do not know letter names consists of capital *E*s pointing in different directions. The individual is asked to indicate the direction in which the arms of the *E* are pointing. Scores are based on how accurately the subject identifies the letters (or directions of the *E*s) using one eye at a time. A reading of 20/20 is normal.

The National Society for the Prevention of Blindness is the oldest voluntary health agency involved in preventing blindness. For preschoolers and

FIGURE 11.2
Near-Acuity Cards from Lighthouse International

Source: From M. Wilkinson, Clinical low vision services, in A. Corn & A. Koening (Eds.), *Foundations of low vision: Clinical and functional perspectives.* (New York: Lighthouse International). Copyright © The Lighthouse International. Reprinted with permission.

school-age children, it has developed a number of screening tests that use the Snellen chart or modifications of it. For infants, evaluation is based on observation of how the eyes are used. For 3- to 5-year-olds, both observation and the Snellen *E* chart are used. The consensus is that early diagnosis and treatment can prevent visual impairments in some children.

Figure 11.2 provides examples of some near-acuity cards provided by Lighthouse International. These lists would seem to have considerable advantage over the typical Snellen chart for low-vision children. It becomes important to know what the students can read at near point, and the gradations of print here can give some understanding of the student's limits in responding to print.

More extensive tests use elaborate equipment (such as the Keystone Telebinocular and the Bausch & Lomb Orthorater) to measure vision at far and near points and to test muscle balance, fusion, usable vision, and other characteristics. The Titmus Vision Tester (manufactured by Titmus, P.O. Box 191, Petersburg, VA 23804) is the most widely used test of visual acuity and is used to screen vision in preschool children, school-age children, and adults. Most people who have taken a driver's license test have been screened for vision problems by the Titmus.

TABLE 11.2
National Agenda Goal Statement for Children with Visual Impairments

1. Students and their families will be referred to an appropriate education program within 30 days of identification of a suspected visual impairment.

2. Policies and procedures will be implemented to ensure the right of all parents to full participation and equal partnership in the education process.

3. Universities, with a minimum of one full-time faculty member in the area of visual impairment, will prepare a sufficient number of educators of students with visual impairments to meet personnel needs throughout the country.

4. Service providers will determine caseloads based on the needs of students and will require ongoing professional development for all teachers and orientation and mobility instructors.

5. Local education programs will ensure that all students have access to a full array of placement options.

6. Assessment of students will be conducted, in collaboration with parents, by personnel having expertise in the education of students with visual impairments.

7. Access to developmental and educational services will include an assurance that instructional materials are available to students in the appropriate media and at the same time as their sighted peers.

8. Educational and developmental goals, including instruction, will reflect the assessed needs of each student in all areas of academic and disability-specific core curricula.

Source· A. L. Corn, P. Hatlen, K. M. Huebner, F. Ryan, & M. Siller (Eds.), *National Agenda for the Education of Children and Youth with Visual Disabilities Including Those with Multiple Disabilities.* © 1996. Reprinted with permission from the American Foundation for the Blind.

Just as the pediatrician is the first line for identifying children with disabilities in preschool years, so the teacher is the prime source of identification of mild disabilities in school-age youngsters.

■ A National Agenda

Table 11.2 provides a roster of national agenda items for children with visual impairments. The items include students' and parents' rights, appropriate and timely service, and appropriate case loads and personnel preparation programs. This list presents the professional expectations of what should be happening if good educational practice for children with visual impairments is to be observed. For those programs that are not meeting these needs, it is a wake-up call that they are falling short of appropriate norms for good practice. The list itself can be a checklist for parents and others who want to make sure good practice is being adhered to.

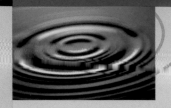

CHILDREN WITH VISUAL IMPAIRMENTS

Formal efforts in the United States to educate children with visual handicaps began in Boston in 1829 with the establishment of the residential school now called the Perkins School for the Blind. Not until 1900 was the first public school class for children who were blind organized in Chicago. Some thirteen years later, another class for children with severe visual impairments was established.

Prior to the twentieth century, no distinctions were made between children with low vision and children who were functionally blind. During the last few decades, a rapid growth in public school programs for children with visual impairment has been stimulated by the Education for all Handicapped Children Act (PL 94-142). Currently, there are thirty-five teacher preparation programs and fourteen orientation and mobility (O&M) programs based in universities preparing professionals to work with children with visual impairment (Goodrich & Sowell, 1996).

The history of the education of children with multiple handicaps that included visual disabilities is that they often were refused education in schools for the blind and were placed in settings that focused on their other disabilities while often ignoring the visual problems. As Hatlen (1998) pointed out, it is no longer possible for educators of the visually impaired students to ignore multiply impaired children.

> Today, these previously underserved students constitute the majority of students who have visual impairments. Reported increases in the percentage of students who have visual impairments with other disabilities are dramatic. Since the mid-1980s estimates regarding the prevalence of these children have risen from 50% to as high as 75% of the total number of children with visual impairment. (p. xv)

Adaptations in both materials and equipment are needed to fully utilize the visually handicapped person's senses of hearing, touch, smell, vision, and even taste. Lowenfeld (1973) proposed three general principles that are still important for adapting instruction to the educational needs of children who are visually impaired:

1. *Concrete experiences.* Children with severe and profound visual disabilities learn primarily through hearing and touch. To understand the surrounding world, these children must work with concrete objects they can feel and manipulate. Through tactile observation of real objects in natural settings (or models of dangerous objects), students with visual handicaps come to understand shape, size, weight, hardness, texture, pliability, and temperature.

2. *Unifying experiences.* Visual experience tends to unify knowledge. A child who goes into a grocery store sees not only shelves and objects but also the relationships of shelves and objects in space. Children with visual impairments

Children with visual impairments need teachers to give them concrete experiences and to explain the relationships among those experiences.

cannot understand these relationships unless teachers allow them the *experience* of the grocery store. The teacher must bring the "whole" into perspective, not only by giving students concrete experiences—in a post office, on a farm—but also by explaining relationships.

Left on their own, children with severe and profound visual disabilities live a relatively restricted life. To expand their horizons, to enable them to develop imagery, and to orient them to a wider environment, it is necessary to develop experiences by systematic stimulation: Lead children through space to help them understand large areas; expose them to different sizes, shapes, textures, and relationships to help them generalize the common qualities of different objects and understand the differences. Their verbalization of similarities and differences stimulates mental development.

3. *Learning by doing.* To learn about the environment, these children have to be motivated to explore that environment. A blind infant does not reach out for an object unless that object attracts the child through other senses (touch, smell, hearing). Stimulate the child to reach and to make contact by introducing motivating toys or games (rattles, objects with interesting textures).

Children with visual impairments have the ability to listen, relate, and remember, skills that must be developed to the fullest. These children have to learn to use time efficiently because the process of acquiring information or performing a task can be cumbersome and time consuming. For the teacher, that means organizing material, giving specific directions, providing firsthand experiences, and using sound principles of learning.

To design an instructional plan one must first find out what the student's current level of achievement is, what his or her potential is, and other information about learning style and responsiveness to various forms of instruction. A comprehensive assessment would contain information about the child's skills (see Turnbull, Turnbull, Shank, & Leal, 1995):

▶ Concept development and academic skills

▶ Communication skills

▶ Social and emotional skills

▶ Sensory motor skills

▶ Daily living skills

▶ Orientation and mobility skills

▶ Career and vocational skills

In addition to a variety of formal tests (for example, the Test of Visual-Motor Perceptual Skills, which provides information on how the student's brain processes visual imagery) designed to capture the above skill areas, assessment is made from observations and criterion reference tests. For example, if you want to know if the student can borrow in subtraction, you give him or her some additional problems and watch what the student does (Lewis & Russo, 1998; Silberman & Brown, 1998).

All this information is drawn together with input from the parents into an IEP meeting, in which the basic goals and objectives of the program for the student are determined, together with the strategies that will be used to reach those goals.

Finally, there is the question of whether the student is progressing toward these goals in a satisfactory manner. If a student is not progressing satisfactorily, readjustments in the IEP and the instructional program are called for.

If a student is not progressing toward the IEP goals, the IEP can be revised.

Adapting the Learning Environment

The goal of moving students with visual impairments into the general education classroom or as close as possible (least restrictive environment) is proceeding, as the bar graph below indicates. Almost half of the students with visual impairments are found in the general education classroom, and another 20 percent are in a resource room program, which means they spend the majority of their time in the general education classroom. Only 11 percent of these children can now be found in a residential school, and they probably have a variety of disabilities requiring very specialized education and care.

As is true of children with other kinds of exceptionality, the various learning environments provided for children with visual impairments represent a continuum of services. The goal of full inclusion is modified by the particular needs of the individual child and, sometimes, by the availability of services. The specialist in vision will examine the lighting, ensure class traffic patterns, and prevent clutter as much as possible.

Percentage of Students with Visual Impairment in Educational Environments, 1997–1998

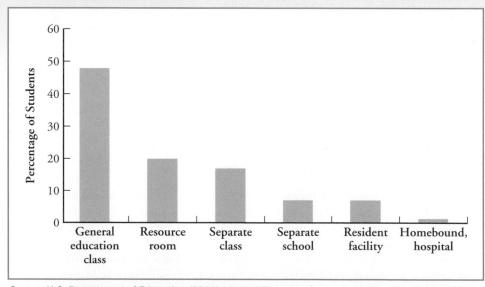

Source: U.S. Department of Education (2000). *Annual Report to Congress on the Implementation of the Individuals with Disability Education Act.* Washington, DC: U.S. Department of Education.

Inclusion in Context

Inclusion has a major impact on young children with visual impairments, raising the question of how thoroughly such children should be integrated into typical preschool settings. There are serious arguments within the profession about the merits of integration compared with the merits of specially trained personnel and special equipment that can be found in a residential or day school for the visually impaired.

Erwin (1993) laid out a series of guidelines for the effective inclusion of young children with visual impairment. Not surprisingly, merely placing the child within a typical preschool setting, without careful planning and without support personnel, will not produce good results. An important aspect of the integrative approach that Erwin describes is a partnership and teamwork between the classroom teacher and the visual consultant teacher; otherwise, the visually impaired child may be socially isolated in integrated settings, particularly when the only focus in such a setting is academic (Kekelis & Sacks, 1988).

Placement in a typical preschool requires careful planning and support personnel.

Collaborating with the Education Team: The Itinerant Teacher The move toward inclusion has made the role of the itinerant teacher very important for children with visual impairment. This teacher travels from school to school providing special materials, consultation with school personnel, and individualized instruction. An unsolved problem is how to provide within the framework of the ordinary school the specialized training that children with visual impairments need. It is clear from the educational environments bar graph on the previous page that the vast majority of children with visual impairments are being educated in general education classrooms.

The itinerant teacher ensures that instructional materials can be used easily by children with visual impairments.

Children with visual impairments can be very active when they are under supervision.
(© Mitch Wojnarowicz/The Image Works)

The successful inclusion of the exceptional child does not happen by chance or accident. It requires a well-thought-out plan and capable people applying themselves to the task; otherwise, the possibility for social isolation of the child is great. An additional complicating factor is cultural differences between the child with visual difficulties and the school. For example, a child who is blind and from a Hispanic background has numerous challenges to overcome as well as, possibly, a language barrier and a set of family values differing from the values taught at school.

Wherever the child with visual impairments is placed, ideally one professional—often the classroom teacher or the teacher with special skills in instructing students with visual impairments—should take the role of **case coordinator.** This individual brings together all the information that relates to the child (the comprehensive assessment, for example) and leads a team of professionals who, with the parents, develop an IEP for the student. The creation of a working team made up of persons of different backgrounds and skills is of paramount importance if an IEP is to be written and executed.

Itinerant teachers are especially important for general education teachers, most of whom have had limited experience in meeting the special needs of children who are visually impaired. Itinerant or resource room teachers can help classroom teachers understand the problems these children face.

For example, the classroom teacher of a boy with a severe visual impairment was upset because he wanted to sit near the closed-circuit television monitor and because he tended to hold books close to his eyes. The teacher was afraid he would damage his vision. The expert advice of a resource room teacher dispelled that misconception. Another classroom teacher believed that a very bright light should always be available for children with visual disabilities. In fact, dim light does not harm the eyes and may be more comfortable for students with cataracts, albinism, and certain other conditions.

Children with Other Exceptionalities As we noted earlier in the chapter, many children with visual impairment may have other disabilities such as mental retardation, learning disabilities, neurological disabilities, behavioral disorders, or deaf-blindness (Silberman, 2000). It has been estimated that the prevalence of children with visual impairment who have dual or multiple disabilities may be over 50 percent (Hatlen, 1998). The more involved cases of such multiple disabilities, including children with deaf-blindness, are covered in detail in Chapter 12, on children with multiple and severe disabilities.

For those children with milder versions of visual impairments, there needs to be some type of *collaborative team* formed that can plan to meet the needs of a particular child. In addition to the teacher of children with visual impairment, that team may include psychologists, speech and language therapists, audiologists, and other specialists.

Silberman (2000) considers the *transdisciplinary* model the most desirable. In this model, therapists and other specialists provide direct services to students in classrooms or other natural environments as part of the daily routine, instead of in some isolated therapy room. The Individual Education Program (IEP) needs to reflect the goals of all of the professionals working with the child.

Multicultural Issues As in the case of children with additional exceptionalities, the presence of children from different ethnic or racial backgrounds adds an element of complexity to the planning and programming for children with visual impairments. This is particularly an issue whenever English is not the primary language of the child or family (Milian, 2000), as is the case with many Hispanic families. Again a collaborative team of professionals seems called for, although in this case it might include a translator familiar with the first language of the student. Consultations between the English as a Second Language teachers and the teachers of students with visual impairments can yield positive results. An ESL teacher can learn how to modify the curriculum to take visual problems into account, while the teacher of children who have visual impairment can learn about the sequence of acquiring a second language.

A substantial percentage of children with visual impairments come from African American homes (perhaps 10–15 percent), so cultural factors such as family views on education, on child-rearing practices, or on the origins of disability have to be factored into the plans for the student. Adding to the challenge of planning is a shortage of minority teachers in special education, but a determined effort to recruit more teachers from these ethnic or racial backgrounds is under way (Milian & Ferrell, 1998). The same type of adaptations are obviously called for in regard to Asian American families and families of yet other cultural backgrounds.

Individualized Education Program

The IEP for children with visual disabilities should include a variety of goals—some focusing on the effective use of the learning environment, some on instructional content, and some on skills that the student will need to perform effectively in the inclusion classroom. It will likely take a team of professionals to implement the goals.

As Sacks and Silberman (1998) pointed out, one of the consequences of the diversity of children with visual and other disabilities is that the teacher becomes a team member rather than teaching in isolation.

> They are working as members of a team that includes professionals in specializations such as visual impairment, severe disabilities, deafblindness, early childhood, learning disabilities, general education and occupational and physical therapies and also includes the families of these children and youth. (p. xix)

Some sample IEP goals for such a child are shown in the box on page 442 Note that Jerry has both academic and social goals in his IEP, reflecting the comprehensive goals of the program. The general education classroom teacher may need some help from an itinerant teacher to carry out these objectives successfully.

Special Schools

Before the 1980s emphasis on the least restrictive environment and the inclusive classroom began, the education of children with visual impairments was often conducted in large residential state schools. With the rapidly growing trend for

Sample IEP Goals and Objectives

LONG-TERM GOALS	SHORT-TERM OBJECTIVES
Jerry will use special devices and materials in order to perform at grade level in reading and mathematics.	1. Jerry will demonstrate effective use of various tools of magnification. 2. Jerry will demonstrate effective keyboarding skills that allow him to do word processing. 3. Jerry will score within one grade level of the class norm in academic achievement tests.
Jerry will establish effective social relationships with some of the nondisabled members of the class.	1. Jerry will join and participate in one of the clubs or organizations in the school that stress social interactions. 2. Jerry will receive a number of votes by other students to work on class projects with them. 3. In class parties, Jerry will join in the activities and interact with other class members.

such students to be educated in the local schools, the question of what happens to the residential school and its often elaborate facilities arose.

Erin (1993) pointed out that the children attending residential schools may have additional disabilities and that the schools have been redesigned to provide an effective environment for such children. Also, these schools provide outreach services, offering information, assessment, and technical assistance to students who are visually impaired and to their teachers in the public schools. Erin proposed a future in which such schools could play three distinct roles:

▶ *Resource centers for students with visual impairments.* These facilities would function as state or regional sites to distribute materials and provide technical assistance and outreach services to neighborhood schools. They would also participate in professional preparation activities.

▶ *Life skills centers for students with severe disabilities.* These centers would specialize in assisting students with severe and multiple disabilities, with an emphasis on those with visual impairments.

▶ *Magnet schools for students with visual impairments.* These schools would provide direct instruction for the academic learner with a visual impairment. Short-term placements that would be arranged by contract with individual school districts and that would address functional needs would be common.

In short, residential schools would address diverse needs while playing a role in the future education of children with visual impairments.

Another reason for placing a child with visual impairment in a special school is to receive a curriculum that cannot be provided in the general education classroom. The Texas School for the Blind and Visually Impaired, for example, is implementing a career education model that begins in the elementary school and

Orientation to possible careers is often part of the curriculum for children with visual impairments.

continues through secondary school and beyond. At the elementary school level, the emphasis is on career awareness. Students may interview persons about their jobs and what they do to function in those jobs. At the middle school level, the emphasis is on career investigation. Students take a course in Introduction to Work and assess their own abilities, aptitudes, and interests. At the secondary school level, students focus on career preparation and career specialization, and the academic subjects are tailored to those objectives.

Obviously, such a curriculum would not be appropriate for students without disabilities in the public school, but it is beneficial for students with visual disabilities. For children with visual disabilities who attend public schools during the school year, the Texas School for the Blind and Visually Impaired also provides summer programs with an emphasis on career education.

Program Evaluation

Despite vigorous arguments about which setting is best for children with visual impairments, little evidence is available to support the various points of view. Does the child with visual disabilities profit from being in an inclusion classroom?

Some agree with Harrell and Curry (1987):

> There is no evidence that the provision of educational services to visually impaired students in regular classrooms and integrated settings is of greater benefit to the pupil than are more intensive segregated programs that offer carefully planned opportunities for successful interactions with nonhandicapped peers. (p. 372)

Falvey (1988), however, pointed out that if a great deal of money is spent on residential school programs, little is left for strengthening the delivery of services in local schools. Also, although residential schools allow children with visual disabilities to form friendships, these friendships inevitably are limited to others with visual disabilities. But the low incidence of children with visual disabilities means that many local schools will have few such children, so necessary, intensive special education in areas such as personal hygiene, grooming, eating, and cooperative living—to say nothing of mobility training—may be difficult to obtain in general education classrooms.

■ Adapting Curriculum

Two major challenges related to the curriculum for children with visual impairment face special educators. Table 11.3 lists the existing core curriculum and the expanded core curriculum. In the existing core curriculum there have to be major adaptations to the standard lessons in English, social studies, science, and so forth to allow children with visual impairments to absorb the concepts.

In addition, there is need of an expanded core curriculum exclusively for children with visual impairments that deals with the use of assistive technology, orientation and mobility, independent living skills, and so on. This will call for specially trained teachers who have learned how to present the expanded core curriculum to these students.

TABLE 11.3
Curricula for Children with Visual Impairments

EXISTING CORE CURRICULUM		EXPANDED CORE CURRICULUM	
English language arts	Other languages to the extent possible	Compensatory academic skills, including communication modes	Orientation and mobility
Mathematics	Science	Social interaction skills	Independent living skills
Health	Physical education	Recreation and leisure skills	Career education
Social studies	History	Use of assistive technology	Visual efficiency skills
Economics	Business education		
Fine arts	Vocational education		

Source: From P. Hatlen, The core curriculum for blind and visually impaired students, including those with additional disabilities, in A. J. Koenig & M. Cay Holbrook (Eds.), *Foundations of education* (2nd ed.), Vol. 2, *Instructional strategies for teaching children and youths with visual impairments* (p. 781) (New York: AFB Press, 2000).

Existing Core Curriculum

How are we to educate children who have visual impairments, when so much of the standard education is based upon the ability to see? That is the question addressed by the National Agenda developed by specialists in this field (Hatlen, 1996). Table 11.3 shows the components of both a core curriculum and an expanded core curriculum for children with visual impairments. The Core Curriculum makes clear that there are expectations that these children will and should master the standard curriculum of such subjects as language arts, mathematics, social studies, science.

In order to achieve those curricular goals, children with visual impairment need to master a wide variety of skills that will enable them to access the information in the standard curriculum. Many of the skills learned naturally by the typical student (such as how to get to school or how to work cooperatively with others) have to be deliberately and directly taught to the student with visual impairment. That is the nature of the Expanded Core Curriculum that will be elaborated upon later in this chapter.

Literacy An important thing to realize in the increasing trend toward including children with visual problems in the general education classroom is that they cannot just be placed there and forgotten. Special adaptations of the environment and the instruction are called for, as are specially trained personnel to help the student.

For example, a common practice in typical elementary classrooms is *round robin reading*, or having each student read to the class in turn. Such a practice can be discouraging for children with visual problems because it highlights their reading problems and their need to use magnification tools.

Koenig and Rex (1996) suggest targeted practice in reading fluency so that a student with visual impairment becomes comfortable with the use of the optical tools and also comfortable reading in front of others. Other devices, such as *echo reading* (teacher and student reading together) and *choral reading* (small groups of readers read aloud at the same time), can bring more confidence to the child with visual problems.

Choral reading brings confidence to the child with visual problems.

The writing skills of students with visual impairments can be helped by the use of bold-lined paper, felt-tipped pens, and mounted magnifiers. While manuscript and cursive writing are always desirable and need to be practiced, keyboarding skills are equally important. Computers can be equipped with screen enlargement programs and synthetic speech output to allow students to use all aspects of the writing process: prewriting, drafting, revising, editing, and publishing.

Computers with an enlargement screen or synthetic speech allow students with visual impairments to work on writing skills.

Mathematics For children who are blind, direct teaching of mathematical concepts is essential and should not be left to incidental learning. Since mathematics involves the manipulation of symbols as well as words, the teacher has to have a well-organized set of lessons so that the fundamental understandings of arithmetic and the most abstract algebra and geometry are grasped. (See Table 11.4.)

Special attention must be paid to the use of measurement tools and to the concepts underlying the addition, subtraction, multiplication, and division of fractions, difficult for many students with visual impairments. Creating examples of these operations can test the ingenuity of the teacher but is essential if the student is to master these abstract ideas (Kapperman, Heinze, & Sticken, 2000).

Blind children in kindergarten through third grade can master fractions by working with three-dimensional circles of wood and placing them in a form board nest that can include fractional parts to make up a full circle. Once they have placed a whole circle, the children can learn to assemble blocks representing a third of a circle and put them together in the nest to form the whole. This kind of tactile experience helps children who are blind not only master the idea of fractional parts but discriminate among the relative sizes of various fractional parts (for example, halves versus quarters) along with their sighted peers.

In the middle grades (fourth through eighth or ninth grade), students who are visually impaired work with supplementary materials to help themselves absorb the information that sighted children learn.

A standard tool for learning mathematics is the abacus, used in many Asian countries to instruct all children. The Cranmer Abacus, a special version of the device, is a substantial help to persons who are visually impaired. The beads in the Cranmer Abacus do not move as rapidly as the beads in the usual abacus and thus can be read more easily by touch. Also, the rods are spaced farther apart for more convenient finger access to the beads. This is another example of the adaptation of devices to meet the special needs of children with visual impairments.

TABLE 11.4
Mathematics Example

Suppose a math teacher uses the Universal Design for Learning approach to convey the critical features of a right triangle. With software that supports graphics and hyperlinks, he prepares a document that shows

1. Multiple examples of right triangles in different orientations and sizes with the right angle and three points highlighted

2. An animation of the right triangle morphing into an isosceles triangle or into a rectangle, with voice and onscreen text to highlight the differences

3. Links to reviews on the characteristics of triangles and of right angles

4. Links to examples of right triangles in various real-world contexts

5. Links to pages that students can go to on their own for review or enrichment on the subject

The teacher could then project the document onto a large screen in front of the class. Thus, he would present the concept not simply by explaining it verbally or by assigning a textbook chapter or workbook page, but by using many modalities and with options for extra support or extra enrichment.

Source: From C. Hitchcock, A. Meyer, D. Rose, & R. Jackson, Providing new access to the general curriculum or learning, *Teaching Exceptional Children, 32* (2002): 13. Reprinted with permission.

Expanded Core Curriculum

A student with visual impairment may have a diverse curriculum that includes science, algebra, choir, mobility, and even cheerleading as an extracurricular activity.

In addition to adjustments to the core curriculum, Hatlen (2000) points out, there needs to be an expanded core curriculum that includes those skills needed by the child with visual impairments. One of these is *orientation and mobility,* which enables a child to master spatial concepts and physical environments. There are trained specialists (certified orientation and mobility specialists, or COMS) who help children who are blind learn to orient themselves in space, and to travel safely around their home or their community. The goal is to make children with visual impairments as independent as possible.

Independent living skills also need to be specifically taught. These would include dining skills, bathing, toileting, and so on (Koenig & Holbrook, 2000). These need to be taught in natural environments at home and in school, and they are needed to combat *learned helplessness,* the children's feeling that they cannot do anything worthwhile or useful.

Other aspects of the expanded core curriculum are learning about *recreation and leisure skills* and *career education*—which can begin with identifying jobs, community workers, and skills such as cleaning up, restacking books, using audiotapes, and more (Wolffe, 2000). Students also can learn to use *assistive technology* to communicate, with the help of some additional switches or expanded computer keyboards, for instance. Finally, the teacher of the visually impaired can help the students increase their *visual efficiency* in the school day by enhancing localization, fixating, scanning, or tracking.

One of the assistive technology devices is a *closed circuit television* (CCTV) that will present enlarged print material from a monitor. The background and the font size can be adjusted to the individual student.

Universal Curriculum The idea of creating a flexible environment that serves a broad range of consumers originated with universal design in architecture. Retrofitting buildings with added-on ramps and automatic doors to accommodate people with disabilities is costly, marginally effective, and often esthetically disastrous.

The Universal Design for Learning (UDL) framework helps us to see that inflexible curricular materials and methods are barriers to diverse learners, just as inflexible buildings with stairs as the only entry option are barriers to people with physical disabilities. Universally designed curricula include a range of options for accessing, using, and engaging with learning materials—recognizing that no single option will work for all students (Hitchcock, Meyer, Rose, & Jackson, 2002).

The increasing emphasis on inclusion as a policy for all of special education has led policy makers to try to ensure that children with visual impairments receive the special services that they need. The IDEA Amendments of 1997 (PL 105-17) provide that Individual Education Program (IEP) teams are required to make provision for instruction in braille and the use of braille for children who are blind or visually impaired, unless the IEP team determines that instruction in braille or the use of braille is not appropriate. This puts the burden of responsibility for *not* having braille available for such students directly upon the IEP and the school (OSERS Policy Guidance for Educating Blind and Visually Impaired Students, August 14, 2000).

A similar addition to the "related services" part of the law adds "orientation and mobility services" to the list of supportive services identified, so there is no doubt that such services should be made available to students in need of them.

An example of how a team composed of a specialist in visual impairment and a general education teacher can work is exemplified in their discussion and planning about Doug, a 9-year-old who is blind (Topor, Holbrook, & Koenig, 2000).

"Now about Doug's slow reading . . . ," began Ms. Valencia. "I've finished my assessment of his reading skills, and Doug knows the braille code well. However, his speed while reading is only 50 words a minute. It isn't unusual for a braille reader to reach this rate and level off, but a reading speed this slow interferes both with comprehension and reading pleasure—not to mention completing assignments on time. We certainly don't want Doug to remain at that rate! Doug tells me that he doesn't like to read and never reads outside of class. I wonder if one approach to help him pick up his reading speed may be simply to promote outside reading."

Ms. Krause commented, "I've seen it work with other reluctant readers. Sometimes children just haven't found the right books to interest them."

"Well, I have some sources of braille books for children," said Ms. Valencia, "and if we look through my catalogs, maybe you can identify some that may be just right for Doug."

"Good idea," said Ms. Krause. "Maybe I can find books that match some selections in our class library. Then when Doug reads one of them, I can find another child who really enjoyed that book to discuss it with him. You know, a really enthusiastic reader. . . ."

Social Interaction Skills One of the most significant dimensions of the educational programs for children with visual impairment should be the social needs of the children. Such needs are shortchanged in inclusive settings if the general education teacher knows little about the special needs of visually impaired children. Merely placing children with special needs in a classroom with other children does not guarantee good social interaction. And the same is certainly true for visually impaired children (Sacks, 1992). Some organized efforts to improve social skills are required, because visually impaired children are rejected by classmates more often than are other children (Jones & Chiba, 1985).

Training packages have been designed to help visually impaired children with their posture, facial expressions, assertiveness, and speech (Kekelis, 1992). In one instance, attempts were made to bolster the social skills of these children by means of teacher instruction and peer prompting. The training consisted of modeling, using prompts, discussing the need for social behaviors, and role playing. The peer-mediated training turned out to produce more improvement than did

For some children who are visually impaired, the least restrictive environment is an inclusive classroom; other children need some form of special resource room program.
(© Steve Goldberg)

the teacher instruction, and the social behavior that the children learned was maintained over time.

Sacks and Kekelis (1992) pointed out that recess and lunchtime offer opportunities for students to practice social skills and interactions.

The teacher may ask himself or herself a number of questions:

▶ Does the visually impaired student play with and talk to peers as much as his or her classmates?

▶ Do students talk with their visually impaired classmates in the classroom, play with them on the playground, and invite them to after-school and weekend activities?

▶ Does the visually impaired child show affection and display preferences for classmates?

▶ Do I observe interactions during recess and, when necessary, intervene so that the visually impaired child is not isolated on the playground? (Kekelis & Sacks, 1988).

A negative answer to any of these questions calls for constructive action by the special teacher working with the general education classroom teacher. One cannot count on a favorable social adaptation without some help and assistance from the teachers involved.

Although the field of educating children with visual impairment was one of the first to include students in the general education classroom, opinions differ about the usefulness of the inclusive approach as it is now being conducted. For example, educators disagree about whether the child with visual impairment is harmed by being labeled as a student with special problems. Instead, the treatment program, for many professionals, includes the student's acceptance of his or her visual impairment as part of his or her identity (Harrell & Curry, 1987). Also, placing all services in a noncategorical program with children with other disabilities may result in children with visual disabilities not receiving the special services (such as braille and mobility) that they need in order to perform well in

Teaching Assertive Behavior

THE SITUATION	ASSERTIVE STATEMENT
You want to ask for time or distance.	"I need to think about that one for a while."
You need to get a commitment from someone.	"When can you give a firm answer?"
You want to make sure the receiver is getting your message.	"I want to make clear the point that_____.
You want to make sure you are getting the message.	"I'm confused; tell me again."
You want to share a positive feeling.	"I really like the way you _____."
You are feeling upset.	"I get embarrassed when _____."

the educational setting. Hatlen and Curry (1987, p. 7) asked, "Can 'generalists' in special education teach blind children to prepare lunch—let alone fulfill the children's basic instructional needs?"

The necessity for ongoing teamwork between professionals is clear. Teamwork is a prerequisite for a successful educational plan for the student with visual impairment. One problem that such students need to overcome is the tendency to lapse into passivity because they lack the skill to assert themselves in a socially acceptable way. The sample assertive statements listed in the "Teaching Assertive Behavior" box on page 449 can help students develop effective relationships with others. A clumsy statement can complicate social relationships considerably.

The increasing popularity of *inclusion* as an educational philosophy raises questions about how to ensure appropriate social interaction for the child with visual impairments. There are few existing studies on social interactions for children with visual impairments across the range of elementary and secondary programs.

An investigation of the social interactions of nine children with visual impairments, who were enrolled in six different preschool programs (Crocker & Orr, 1996), was performed and then matched with social interactions of nine sighted children of same age and gender. The investigators found that the children with visual impairments were capable of social interactions, but they also found that the children with visual impairments rarely initiated social contacts and that those they did initiate were often with the teacher.

These results make clear that social development should not be taken for granted when merely placing the child with special needs in the general education classroom. The teacher and the special educator need to plan and organize class activities so that appropriate social interactions take place (Workman, 1986).

Recreation and Leisure Skills Recreation and leisure skills are important, as they offer opportunities for relaxation and social interaction. The teacher might wish to assess the student's ability to manage leisure time, playing independently or with friends, and skills related to physical games and sports, arts and crafts, and music and dance (McGregor & Farrenkopf, 2000).

Many people find amazing the range of sports and leisure activities that students with visual impairments can participate in, given special instruction and aids. Such activities include bowling, bicycling, skiing, swimming, ice skating, and wrestling. In addition, card games and board games such as Scrabble and various arts and crafts are well within their capabilities when the materials are modified to fit the child with visual impairment. It must be stressed, though, that special instruction is needed before the student with visual impairment will feel comfortable and seek out such activities.

One way to think about this issue is to think of a recreation or leisure activity that you enjoy. Analyze the activity on the following basis.

▶ What modification would need to be made for a blind person or someone with low vision to participate in the activity?

▶ Would someone with a visual impairment need to take more time, in order to participate in the activity?

▶ Are there other benefits of this activity (social interactions, physical fitness) (McGregor & Farrenkopf, 2000)?

Orientation and Mobility

One of the greatest limitations imposed by blindness is the problem of becoming oriented to one's environment and to one's need for mobility in that environment. The situations that force dependence and can cause the greatest personality and social problems for individuals who have visual impairments usually involve mobility. For improving mobility, adults use tools such as long canes, guide dogs, and sighted guides. But children also must learn to move about their environment independently and safely, so orientation and mobility have become part of the curriculum in all programs for children with visual impairments.

Simply defined, **orientation and mobility (O&M) training** involves an understanding of one's location in a given environment (orientation) coupled with the ability to physically move through that environment safely and independently (mobility) (Cioffi, 1995). It is not uncommon for young people to have one of these skills in greater amount than the other, so attention has to be focused on one of them. The goal of any mobility program is to bring the individual to his or her highest desired level of safe, independent travel. Students with visual disabilities become independent when they can move about in the environment to meet their own needs. These skills are central to a strong curriculum that stresses independence.

The adult adjustment of persons with visual impairments relies heavily on the person being mobile. A key element of special education for such children has been O&M services. Much of the O&M training involves teaching visual skills that can be used. One of these visual skills is *scanning*, which is the use of head and eye movements to search for and localize a target. Horizontal scanning can pick up vertical targets such as poles that hold street signs, and vertical scanning helps locate the street sign itself.

Another visual skill is *tracing*, visually following single or multiple stationary lines to help maintain a line of direction. Hedgelines, overhead fluorescent lights, and contrasting baseboards can serve as tracing cues. Also important for effective mobility is *tracking*, visually following a moving target, whether a car or a pedestrian (Smith & Geruschat, 1996).

Although much of this training is a matter of supervised practice, there are some optical devices that can help. Using a telescopic device to read street signs or magnification at near point for maps, timetables, and price tags can enhance mobility efficiency.

As in other skills, the earlier such training is instituted the better, with preschool ages being none too early to begin (Smith & O'Donnell, 1991). The role of the O&M specialist has many dimensions to it. He or she can contribute as a member of the educational team, provide developmentally appropriate goals for the educational plan, develop and implement educational activities for working with the child and family, analyze the child's travel environments for safety factors and possible modifications, and train other educational service providers in O&M principles (Anthony, Fazzi, Lampert, & Pogrund, 1992).

Orientation and Mobility Specialists Because learning mobility with a degree of personal independence is one of the most desirable educational goals, special teachers provide O&M instruction to teach the child to use sensory information to establish and maintain his or her position in the environment and move safely,

The goal of an O&M program is to develop a child's mobility skills to the safest, most independent level possible.

The general education teacher can help by identifying landmarks and clues in the classroom, for example, attaching braille markers to important areas in the room.

efficiently, and gracefully (Hill, 1992). The skill areas that are covered in such instruction include the following:

▶ Ability to identify and make use of landmarks and clues

▶ Knowledge and use of compass directions

▶ Knowledge and use of indoor and city number systems

▶ Ability to align the body to objects and with sounds for the purpose of maintaining a straight line of travel

▶ Use of systematic search patterns to explore novel objects and environments

▶ Recovery skills

▶ Knowledge of where, when, and how to solicit aid (Hill, 1992, pp. 25–26)

The ability of many children and adults with visual impairment to avoid obstacles has been noted. Research a half century ago (Cotzin & Dallenbach, 1950) determined that it is the sense of hearing that helps them sense an obstacle in front of them. It is *not* that persons with disabilities have a special sense, but merely that they use their remaining senses with greater efficiency than do sighted persons.

| O&M practitioners believe the cane has many advantages.

Despite a variety of experiments with more sophisticated devices to aid in travel, the long white cane, so long recognized as a symbol of the individual with visual impairments, continues to be the instrument of choice, even to its use with preschoolers (Pogrund, Fazzi, & Lampert, 1992). There seems to be a consensus among active O&M practitioners that the cane has numerous advantages over alternatives, even though there is little firm research evidence to support that position (Leong, 1996). It certainly extends the mobility of young children during a period when exploration and orientation to objects in the environment are very important.

Personal mobility and independence have particular importance for adolescents who are ready to break away from family restraints and protection. The ability to control oneself and one's environment is essential to becoming independent and gaining the respect of peers. The schools are using physical education programs to sharpen the orientation and mobility skills of visually impaired youngsters. Barraga and Erin (1992) suggested that "for children who are blind or who have low vision, movement may be the most accurate replacement for vision in clarifying information about the world." (p. 45).

Removing Barriers In most cases, we increase the mobility of individuals who are visually impaired by teaching them ways to get around or to use available tools. But there is another way to ease the restrictions on those who are blind. Society has a responsibility to remove obstacles wherever possible. That responsibility became law in 1991 with the passage of the Americans with Disabilities Act, which directs businesses and public officials to remove barriers for persons with disabilities (see Chapter 2). Removing barriers includes attaching braille symbols to elevators, widening aisles for wheelchair access, and making public telephones accessible.

Independent Living Skills

Independence at School The itinerant or resource teacher in the public school must often instruct students and classroom teachers on some of the special skills that the child with visual disabilities should master. Some of these skills are important keys to the child's effectively mastering the learning environment (Torres & Corn, 1990):

▶ *Fire drills.* The child with visual disabilities needs to be instructed to take hold of the nearest moving child or adult and quickly follow the others. No particular child should be assigned to the task of aiding the child because he or she might be absent or away when needed.

▶ *Field trips.* Giving prior notice to the place where these children will be visiting is important. The person in charge (such as the museum director) might be able to make adaptations that will aid the child with vision problems.

▶ *Auditorium.* The child should be allowed to sit close to the stage to get the maximum amount of information from the experience.

▶ *Lunchroom.* Some type of orientation is needed so the child with visual disabilities learns where the essential things are. The cafeteria staff can be alerted to help the student with food choice, and peers can help with finding a seat.

Some daily living skills are noted in the "Life Skills Training" box below. Thinking of a plate as the face of a clock facilitates finding food on a plate. Other useful adaptations of daily activities are the different ways of folding one-, five-, and ten-dollar bills and special arrangements of clothes in a closet. Such simple steps can make the daily life of the child with visual impairments easier. The things that sighted children learn as a matter of easy experience have to be planned for

▌ Life Skills Training for Children with Visual Impairments

How do people with visual impairments pay for things when they can't see their money?

Coins are easy to recognize by feeling them. Dimes are small and slim with ridges around the edges; pennies are small with smooth edges; nickels are bigger and thick; quarters have ridges and are bigger but thinner than nickels.

People who are visually impaired use this trick to recognize dollar bills: In their wallet, one-dollar bills are left unfolded; five-dollar bills are folded in half the short way; and ten-dollar bills are folded in half the long way.

How do children who are visually impaired find their toys and clothes?

Children with visual impairments have to be very neat. They have to put their things in the same place every day in order to find them.

To pick out what to wear in the morning, children who are visually impaired can feel the texture of their clothes. They know jeans feel different from wool pants. Or they may remember in what order their clothes are hung in the closet.

To decide what top matches what bottom, aluminum clothing tags can be sewn in each piece of clothing. On the tags, braille markings indicate the color. Children with visual impairments must learn what colors go together.

How do children with visual impairments find the food on their plate?

To find the food on their plate, imagine the plate is a clock. They are told at what time the food is placed.

On this plate, the hamburger is at 12 o'clock, the salad is at 3 o'clock and the french fries are at 8 o'clock.

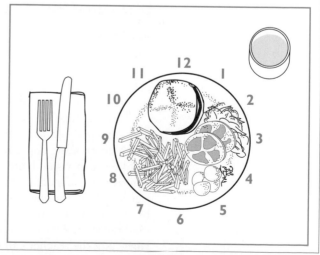

Source: R. Tannebaum. *A Different Way of Seeing.* New York: American Foundation for the Blind, 1988. Reprinted with permission from the American Foundation for the Blind, 11 Penn Plaza, Suite 300, New York, NY 10001. Copyright © 1984.

the child with visual impairment. But with such planning, the student with visual disabilities can perform effectively and truly become a member of the group.

Independence at Home and in the Community Mastering the environment is especially important to children who are blind, for their physical and social independence. The ease with which they move about, find objects and places, and orient themselves to new physical and social situations is crucial in determining their role in peer relationships, the types of vocations and avocations open to them as adults, and their own estimation of themselves.

How do we help children who are blind master the environment? We have to teach them, from a very early age, not to be afraid of new experiences or injury. Sighted children skin their knees, bump their shins, fall from trees, and step in holes. Children who are blind must have the same chance if they are going to learn to control themselves and the environment. This means encouraging risk taking.

Children with visual impairment should be taught to feel the difference in the weight of their forks when they have successfully cornered a few peas and when they haven't. They also should learn a system of marking and organizing clothes for both efficiency and good grooming.

Models—of the classroom, the playground, the child's neighborhood—can help children who are visually impaired understand the relationship of one place or size to another. Models are not a substitute for experience. But they are an extension of experience and a means of drawing perceptual relationships between areas too large to be included at one time in direct experience.

The "Home and Community" box on page 455 lists a number of home and community experiences that are within the easy reach of most children with visual disabilities. The child can even compile such a list. As the child begins to extend his or her repertoire, the list will grow longer and longer so that there is an impressive set of skills and knowledge that have been mastered.

> Involve parents by asking them to provide a model of the child's classroom so the child can learn the relationship of one place to another.

■ Adapting Teaching Strategies

Communicating with Print and Braille

Some students can be instructed in both print and braille. They learn readiness skills and word identification strategies in this style of parallel instruction, and the decision about which channel to emphasize is postponed until the teacher and the school gain experience with the child's learning style.

The language experience approach to reading offers many advantages. It uses students' actual experiences as the basis for reading instruction and is a highly motivating approach for a student. But adaptations have to be made for children with visual handicaps. For example, the class visits a local fire station. Afterward, the student with visual impairment dictates a story about the experience, and the teacher writes down exactly what the student says, using a braillewriter or a special slate and stylus. The student and the teacher then read the story together. They can continue to discuss and elaborate on the story, and the teacher can develop reading strategy lessons using the story as a base—for example, thinking about the firefighters' various activities at the firehouse and when fighting a fire.

Home and Community: Some Early Experiences for Young Children

HOME EXPERIENCES	COMMUNITY EXPERIENCES
▶ Helping prepare a snack or bake cookies ▶ Picking up the morning newspaper ▶ Helping stack dishes in the dishwasher ▶ Helping rake leaves or plant flowers ▶ Picking up clothes or toys ▶ Playing with siblings or friends in the backyard ▶ Calling grandmother and grandfather on the telephone	▶ Playing at the city park with siblings and friends ▶ Splashing in the wading pool at a public swimming pool ▶ Exploring the grocery store and stores at a mall ▶ Visiting a farm with animals and machinery ▶ Eating at a fast-food restaurant and at a more formal restaurant ▶ Visiting a petting zoo ▶ Visiting public places like the post office, fire station, and library

Source. From Alan J. Koenig, Growing into literacy, in M. Cay Holbrook (Ed.), *Children with visual impairments: A parent's guide* (Bethesda, MD: Woodbine House, 1996). Reprinted with permission.

Listening Skills

A child with visual impairment can learn few skills more important than to be able to listen, to learn through the auditory sense. This directed listening begins at birth when the child turns his or her attention to speakers and listens to language

It is important for the schools to provide time and practice for children to learn braille.
(© Susie Fitzhugh)

that describes the child's environment. Directed listening continues in preschool with young children listen to their classmates telling about experiences and describing favorite objects brought from home. The most direct teaching of listening skills occurs in orientation and mobility instruction, in which auditory cues are used for orientation to the environment and for safe travel (Koenig & Holbrook, 2000).

As the child with visual impairments grows older, he or she tends to gather information from audio-tape materials and books. Talking Books become a favorite source of information and pleasure and a number of organizations provide specially prepared tapes for these students. However, the child with visual impairments should be cautioned to not use these auditory aids exclusively. There should be a proper balance between the use of listening skills and the development of literacy skills in braille and/or accessible print.

The use of *live readers* to read aloud mail, memos, bills, textbooks, etc. is another way to develop listening skills. As with other devices or tools, working with the live reader requires practice and effective interaction between the reader and the student. The student can ask the *live reader* to skip around or to read the table of contents or summaries of materials. This lets the listener gain some flexibility over the audio tapes.

Teaching Braille or Print People with profound visual disabilities must develop a series of special communication skills. For children who are blind, using braille is a key skill for communicating with the sighted world.

Braille is a system of touch reading developed in 1829 by Louis Braille, a Frenchman who was blind. The system uses embossed characters in different combinations of six dots arranged in a cell two dots wide and three dots high (see the "Braille Alphabet and Numerals" box on page 457). The symbols are embossed on heavy paper from left to right, and users usually read with both hands, one leading, the other following. Advanced readers may use the second hand to orient themselves to the next line while reading the line above, and they may read as much as one-third of the lower line with the second hand. Punctuation, music, and mathematical and scientific notations are based on the same system. Standard English braille was accepted in 1932 as the system for general use, although many other communication systems have been tried.

One of the problems faced by teachers and administrators is whether the child is a candidate as a print reader or should be taught how to read braille. Such a decision has long-term implications for the student, because it will send him or her down a path of *print reading* or make the focus *braille reading*. The box on candidates for print reading and for braille reading on page 458 lists distinguishing characteristics that will help educators decide which path is appropriate for a given youngster.

For instance, Doris is a 7-year-old with serious visual impairments. Her vision has been assessed at 20/200, but she has shown an ability to deal with print reading, even though slowly. She seems eager to learn to read print and has a stable eye condition (that is, her vision will not deteriorate) and no additional disabilities. In these circumstances, she would be chosen for a program that stresses print reading and that uses all the technology available to help Doris become a print reader.

Recording for the Blind and Dyslexic
www.rfbd.org

National Library Service (NLS) for the Blind and the Physically Handicapped
www.loc.gov/nls

I Braille Alphabet and Numerals

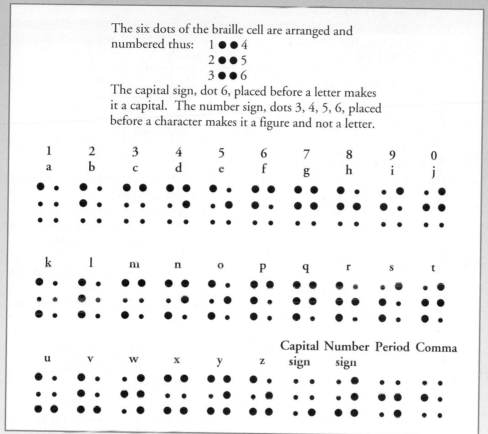

The six dots of the braille cell are arranged and numbered thus:

```
1 ● ● 4
2 ● ● 5
3 ● ● 6
```

The capital sign, dot 6, placed before a letter makes it a capital. The number sign, dots 3, 4, 5, 6, placed before a character makes it a figure and not a letter.

Source: Division for the Blind and Physically Handicapped, Library of Congress, Washington, DC 20542.

If Doris had had an unstable eye condition or was strongly frustrated by trying to read print and had good tactile skills, the decision might well have been to introduce her to braille reading. There are no set rules for such decisions—each one has to be made taking into account the individual characteristics of the child.

In many communities, an uncertain number of itinerant teachers manage a growing caseload of children. These teachers have less and less time to teach braille or to transcribe print to braille for their students. Teachers in some communities have only three hours a week on average to provide direct services to children with visual impairments, and many teachers have even less time. Under such circumstances it is understandable why these children are not able to read rapidly or efficiently (Ferrell & Suvak, 1995). When highly specialized instruction is needed so a youngster can learn other material—whether the child has auditory problems and is trying to learn total communication or has visual problems and is trying to learn braille—it becomes very important for the school to provide sufficient time and practice so the children master these crucial skills at a functional level.

Characteristics of Candidates for Print Reading and Braille Reading Programs

CHARACTERISTICS OF A LIKELY PRINT READER	CHARACTERISTIC OF A LIKELY BRAILLE READER
▶ Uses vision efficiently to complete tasks at near distances	▶ Shows a preference for exploring the environment tactilely
▶ Shows interest in pictures and demonstrates the ability to identify pictures or elements within pictures	▶ Uses the tactile sense efficiently to identify small objects
▶ Identifies his or her name in print or understands that print has meaning	▶ Identifies his or her name in braille or understands that braille has meaning
▶ Uses print to perform other prerequisite reading skills	▶ Uses braille to acquire other prerequisite reading skills
▶ Has a stable eye condition	▶ Has an unstable eye condition or a poor prognosis for retaining the current level of vision in the near future
▶ Has an intact central visual field	▶ Has a reduced or nonfunctional central field to the extent that print reading is expected to be inefficient
▶ Shows steady progress in learning to use his or her vision as necessary to ensure efficient print reading	▶ Shows steady progress in developing the tactile skills necessary for efficient braille reading
▶ Is free of additional disabilities that would interfere with progress in a developmental reading program in print	▶ Is free of additional disabilities that would interfere with progress in a developmental reading program in braille

Source: Adapted from A. J. Koenig & M. C. Holbrook, *Learning media assessment of students with visual impairments: A resource guide for teachers.* (Austin: Texas School for the Blind and Visually Impaired, 1995). Reprinted by permission.

One of the most significant decisions for a student is whether to learn print or braille. It's important to meet with the family to discuss this decision.

Braille, by its very nature, will be read more slowly than print. A reasonably good braille reader will read at a rate of around 100 words per minute. A reasonably good print reader will read at a rate of 250 to 300 words per minute. Thus, the sighted high-school reader will cover three times as much material in the same period of time as a braille reader. (This is not a condemnation of braille; it reflects the differences between visual reading and tactile reading.) Therefore, most blind high school students use recorded books or live readers as a supplement to braille to cover the amount of reading material they are assigned in a regular school (Hatlen, 2003).

It is ironic that in these days of including greater numbers of visually impaired students in the general classroom and curriculum, instructional materials are becoming more elaborate and ever more difficult to use. On a single print textbook page, there are likely to be sidebars, boxes, graphs, pictures, boldfaced words, colored words, words of all different sizes, italicized words, and charts. What was once a simple format consisting of words printed in uninterrupted lines has now become an exciting multimedia production for the sighted student.

Adapting Technology

Often, the biggest stumbling block to using assistive technology is the children's reluctance. Many youngsters are self-conscious about devices that make them look "strange" or "weird." To overcome this self-consciousness, it's important to introduce these tools in a positive way (by playing games, for example) when the children are young.

Technology has given us the capability to transcribe printed language into spoken language and braille. It also allows us to move easily from one form of communication to another, such as transferring braille to print and back again. Obviously, this technology has enormous potential for students with visual impairments and for their teachers:

> Teachers can type a lesson or test and then, using the appropriate hardware or software, convert the material to large print, braille, regular print, or speech, depending upon the needs of the student. The student, on the other hand, could do homework or tests in braille and convert it to print for the teacher. (Todd, 1986, p. 292)

For Listening

Synthetic speech is the production of sound—of phonemes into words—by means of a computer. The process allows us to convert written words into speech so that those with severe and profound visual handicaps can listen to books, newspapers, and even typed letters and manuscripts.

The increasing popularity of talking books—books on tape—is a boon for those with visual disabilities. In addition to commercially made tapes, the Talking Book program produces books on tape and makes them available at no charge to children and adults who are visually impaired.

The Speech Plus Talking Calculator is a hand-held calculator that announces (using a twenty-four-word vocabulary) each entry and the result of each operation. It is a relatively inexpensive device.

There is a wide range of assistive technology devices to help children with visual impairments exchange information with sighted persons. Table 11.5 provides a brief summary of the more common of these devices (Hatlen, 2003).

For Reading and Writing

The rapidly growing use of the computer in the public schools has created yet another dilemma for children with visual impairments. Since many of these youngsters will be in inclusive settings (the general education classroom), how can they stop from falling farther and farther behind their classmates who find it easy to use this new tool? One way to help children with visual impairments is to pay attention to **access technology,** adaptations to a computer's normal operations that allow a student with disabilities to use and benefit from the computer's operations

Children may be reluctant to use machines that can assist persons who are visually impaired.

Access technology refers to adaptation of a regular computer for the student with visual disabilities.

TABLE 11.5
Assistive Technology Devices

Assistive technology device: any item, piece of equipment, or product system, whether acquired commercially off the shelf, modified, or customized, that is used to increase, maintain, or improve functional capabilities of individuals with disabilities (P.L. 100-407, P.L. 101-476). May include low vision aids, bold line paper, braille writers, screen readers, braille printers, communication devices, etc.

Screen reader	Software program that works in conjunction with a speech synthesizer to provide verbalization of everything on the screen, including menus, text, and punctuation.
Screen magnification	Software that focuses on a single portion (1/4, 1/9, 1/16, etc.) of the screen and enlarges it to fill the screen.
Refreshable braille displays	These provide tactile output of information presented on the computer screen. Unlike conventional braille, which is permanently embossed onto paper, refreshable braille displays are mechanical in nature and lift small, rounded plastic pins as needed to form braille characters. The displays contain 20, 40, or 80 braille cells. After the line is read, the user can "refresh" the display to read the next line.
Braille translation software	Translates text and formatting into appropriate braille characters and formatting.
Braille writing equipment	Manual or electronic devices used for creation of paper braille materials.
Closed-circuit television	As an assistive device, it magnifies a printed page through the use of a special television camera with a zoom lens and displays the image on a monitor.
Portable notetakers	Small portable units that employ either a braille or standard keyboard to allow the user to enter information. Text is stored in files that can be read and edited using the built-in speech synthesizer or braille display. The file may be sent to a printer or braille embosser or transferred to a computer.
Braille embosser	A braille printer that embosses computer-generated text as braille on paper.
Scanner	A device that converts an image from a printed page to a computer file. Optical-character-recognition (OCR) software makes the resulting computer file capable of being edited.
Adaptive keyboard	This offers a variety of ways to provide input into a computer through various options in size, layout (i.e., alphabetical order), and complexity.
Augmentative communication device	One that provides speech for people unable to communicate verbally. The device may talk; the user indicates communication through the use of tactile symbols, auditory scanning, large print symbols, and so on.

(Taylor & Murphy-Head, 1996). Examples of such adaptations are listed in the "Examples of Access Technology" box on page 461. In short, a variety of steps can be taken to make sure the child with visual disabilities can participate with classmates in the use of the computer as a key learning tool.

When optical devices are not sufficient, a closed-circuit television (CCTV) system can provide electronic magnification. A video camera directed at an object or symbol projects the image onto a television monitor. CCTVs are costly, but for appropriate users they can be a highly effective means of enlarging and viewing information (Ward, 1996).

Examples of Access Technology

PROBLEM	ACCESS SOLUTION
The student cannot see the screen.	Use a standard desktop publishing program with a variety of fonts and type sizes that are larger or easier to read.
The student cannot hear feedback.	Use plug-in amplified speakers or headphones.
The student has trouble shifting between the screen and the keyboard or desktop.	Position the keyboard on a slant board directly below the monitor.
The student is too heavy-handed, causing the keystrokes to repeat.	Use an alternative keyboard that generally allows the student to control the repeat rate.

Although in the future even more exotic technology may provide help for students with visual impairments, a number of devices are available now. Portable computer devices allow students to take notes and do assignments without the need for a computer in each classroom. Both print and braille copies can be printed from these devices. With additions, they allow the student to listen to synthesized speech. A student can place a book on a scanner and listen to it through a voice-reader computer program. Portable talking dictionaries are within financial reach and a welcome addition, because a braille dictionary can cost over $1,000. It would be good to get these devices into the hands of as many students as possible, because they will allow much more effective use of students' time than was previously possible. See the Houghton Mifflin Teacher Education website for an expanded list of assistive technology equipment.

A student can type on a computer keyboard and have the contents printed in braille on a small braille display.

Houghton Mifflin Teacher Education website
http://education.college.hmco.com/students

■ Transition

Career Education: From School to Work

The transition from school to work is an extremely important aspect of the total educational program. Although there have been attempts to use sheltered workshops, where students produce goods in a protected setting that is publicly subsidized, the newer emphasis is on placement in real job settings whenever possible (Sacks & Bullis, 1988). The secondary school program then becomes a part-time academic and part-time workplace program to give the student a chance to experience employment while still in a supervised setting. The academic program focuses on functional reading and other skills that can enhance the student's chance of success in the workplace.

John, a teenager with a visual disability, was exposed to several jobs and learned a series of generic work skills (such as greeting and conversation

ECOLOGY OF THE CHILD

SCHOOL **Blindness Is Not a Barrier**

Sure but sightless, Timothy Cordes arrived on the campus of the University of Notre Dame four years ago, an 18-year-old freshman from Eldridge, Iowa, who wanted to enroll in the biochemistry program.

Faculty members tried, politely, to dissuade him. Just how, they wondered aloud, could a blind student keep up with the rigorous courses and demanding laboratory work of biochemistry?

Mr. Cordes graduated Sunday from Notre Dame with a degree in biochemistry and a 3.991 grade-point average on a four-point scale. . . . His German shepherd, Electra, led him to the lectern to deliver the valedictory speech as his classmates rose, applauded and yelled his name affectionately.

Mr. Cordes starts medical school in two months, the second blind person ever admitted to a U.S. medical school. He does not plan to practice medicine, preferring research. "I've just always loved science," he said. . . .

Armed with Electra, a high-powered personal computer and a quick wit, Mr. Cordes received the top grade, A, in all his classes save for an A-minus in a Spanish class. Two weeks ago, he earned a black belt in the martial arts tae kwon do and jujitsu.

"He is really a remarkable young man," said Paul Helquist, a Notre Dame biochemistry professor. Mr. Helquist had doubts at first but ultimately recommended Mr. Cordes for medical school. "He is by far the most brilliant student I've ever come across in my 24 years of teaching." . . .

"I don't see myself as some sort of 'Profiles in Courage' story," [Mr. Cordes] said. "If people are inspired by what I've done, that's great, but the truth is that I did it all for me. It was just hard work. It's like getting the black belt. It's not like I just took one long lesson. It was showing up every day and sweating and learning and practicing."

His sophomore-year roommate, Patrick Murowsky, said: "The thing about Tim is that he's fearless and

---

skills). This type of experience should serve John well in whatever occupation he decides to enter.

Case Study: John

John, age 17, has had a visual impairment since birth. Congenital cataracts, which were removed at age 2, left him with light perception in his left eye and usable residual vision in the right eye. John is able to read standard print with a hand-held magnifier or specially prescribed lenses, but his reading rate is slow and extremely labored. John has received the services of a teacher of visually handicapped students throughout his school years, first in an elementary resource room and later from itinerant teachers. John has been mainstreamed into regular education classes since the third grade, even though his skill levels range from fourth grade in math comprehension to eighth grade in spelling. His reading comprehension, organization, and note-taking skills are particularly weak and require constant support, yet his educational program has continued to emphasize academic pursuits.

he just seems to have this faith. Once we were late for a football game and we had to run to the stadium. He had no qualms about running at top speed while I yelled 'jump,' or I would yell 'duck' and he would duck. And we made it. He is simply amazing to be around sometimes."

Mr. Cordes has Leber's disease, a genetic condition that gradually diminished his vision until he was blind at age 14.

When doctors at the University of Iowa first diagnosed the disease when he was age 2, "it was the saddest moment of my life," his mother, Therese, said. She said the doctors told her, "He won't be able to do this, and don't expect him to be able to do this."

"So I went home," she said, "and just ignored everything they said." . . .

The study of biochemistry relies heavily on graphics and diagrams to illustrate complicated molecular structures. Mr. Cordes compensated for his inability to see by asking other students to describe the visual aids or by using his computer to re-create the images in three-dimensional forms on a special screen he could touch. . . .

"Tim has always exceeded people's expectations of him," said Therese Cordes, who, with her husband, Tom, watched him graduate. "He really does inspire me."

Source: From Jon Jeter, Blind student leaps barriers [originally titled "Blind Valedictorian Is Headed to Med School"], *Washington Post,* May 18, 1998. Copyright © 1998 The Washington Post. Reprinted with permission.

WHAT IS THE CONTEXT?

Timothy Cordes graduated from the University of Notre Dame. His next accomplishment was being only the second blind person ever admitted to a U.S. medical school. Tim Cordes asserts there is no mystery to his achievement—he just worked hard. As a child, Tim and his family were told there would be many limitations to what he could do, predictions they ignored.

PIVOTAL ISSUES FOR TEACHERS

- What are some of the ways you can encourage students with visual impairment in your classroom?

- How can you instill in them the confidence that people with visual impairments can achieve their dreams of attending college?

Although John attends his neighborhood high school, he has few friends. He spends much of his leisure time alone and finds interaction with peers difficult and sometimes rather awkward. Encouraged by his VH [vocational high school] teacher, John has begun to participate in the drama club. He is quite verbal and enjoys acting a variety of roles; however, he is easily intimidated when questioned about his visual impairment or difficulty with reading. At home, John is responsible for his personal needs, but does not consistently perform other job tasks around the house. He has repeatedly volunteered to help mow the lawn or prepare meals, but his parents are hesitant to allow him to perform such jobs because of his limited vision. Although John's parents recognize the importance of allowing him to become more independent, they are fearful of his safety and have not allowed him to travel by himself throughout the community or spend his own money as readily as his siblings or same-aged peers.

At a recent IEP meeting, John's VH teacher, along with other team members (orientation and mobility specialist, vocational coordinator, vocational rehabilitation counselor, school psychologist, John, and his parents) discussed future educational and vocational goals for him. As they spoke, it was apparent that John's parents perceived his academic performance much differently from other team members. His parents believed that John was functioning at or above grade level on most academic tasks and felt that he would be able to attend college. Conversely, team members did not recognize John's desire to develop more independent living and travel skills, as well as wanting to secure a job for himself. When questioned about job preference, John seemed interested in working at a radio station or developing his acting skills. At the suggestion of the vocational coordinator, John was asked to participate in a series of community vocational experiences, where he would be able to explore and to learn about a variety of jobs through hands-on experience. Reluctantly, John's parents allowed him to do so.

Instead of full participation in a regular education setting, John now spent half of his school day in a community classroom at a real job site. Assisted by a vocational special education teacher and his VH teacher, John gained exposure to landscape gardening, sorting and packaging, and basic office skills. Each experience lasted approximately three months. In addition, he developed a set of generic work behaviors and social skills (basic greetings and conversational skills through role plays and modeling) that transferred to other settings. In the community classroom environment, time was also spent developing functional math and reading skills that included money management, time management, and completion of job applications. John was expected to travel to work independently in the morning, and back to his local high school in the afternoon. As a result of this initial vocational experience, John's educational program has shifted from a purely academic focus to one that is more functionally based. He will continue to participate in the community classroom program during his final year of high school, while working with his special education teachers and vocational counselors to secure employment after high school. (Kekelis & Sacks, 1988).

■ Family and Lifespan Issues

In the preceding chapters, we have been concerned with what happens to exceptional children after they leave school and try to make their way in the world. After all, educational programs are supposed to prepare students for life in the community. We have the same concerns for children with visual impairments.

As for what happens to children with disabilities after secondary school, and what kind of life adjustment they make as young adults, there is increasing evidence that social adjustment, rather than specific vocational training, is what is central to successful adult adaptation.

In recent years a careful study was made of groups of children who were blind, children who had low vision, and children who were sighted. Sixteen students aged 15–21 were in each group. Extensive questionnaires as to their daily activities and interests were given to students and parents, along with *time diaries* asking the participants to identify their activities in one-hour blocks over a 24-hour period (Sacks, Wolffe, & Tierney, 1998).

This investigation yielded a variety of interesting facts. The majority of sighted students had worked for pay, while only 31 percent of low-vision and

19 percent of blind students did likewise. The majority of the blind and low-vision students reported that they spent their after-school time alone. Many of the students who were visually impaired, particularly those with low vision, required extensive support to succeed academically in inclusive school environments. Adaptive computers and other devices specially designed for such students were not widely used. The students with the visual impairments spent more time on the telephone, participated in more sedentary activities, and were bound to their home by their inability to travel independently, which also affected their vocational opportunities.

The authors of the study concluded that the secondary curriculum for adolescents with visual impairments should include a stronger focus on career development and social skills competencies, and that travel training also seemed advisable.

There is a limited supply of evidence available on this topic, but one longitudinal study (Freeman, Goetz, Richards, & Groenveld, 1991) provided a fifteen-year follow-up study of sixty-nine legally blind persons who were 10 years old at the time of the original investigation. The follow-up data were collected through structured interviews conducted by the first two authors of the study.

The importance of multiple disabilities becomes clear in the results. Of the forty participants in the study whose only disability was visual, 71 percent received a normal psychiatric diagnosis, and 44 percent were employed. However, of the twenty-nine participants with other disabilities, only 24 percent received a normal psychiatric diagnosis, and only 17 percent were employed.

Twenty percent completed secondary school and went no further. Nineteen percent attended a university, and 6 percent graduated. Twenty percent did not complete secondary school, and another 17 percent were always in special classes. Freeman et al. felt that many of these subjects could have been employed, though they were not. Among those with partial sight, there was a strong tendency to try to "pass" as normal, to avoid the presumed stigma of blindness.

Freeman et al. felt that study of the resilience of some children needs to be pursued further—that is, students who appear to persevere against odds to reach a good adaptation. We know little about this topic and thus are unable to provide guidance about how to achieve the state of resilience. Certainly, there is sufficient evidence of good adult adjustment, given the right set of conditions and past experience and preparation.

A Final Word

We need to remember that comparisons of children with visual impairments and sighted children reveal only what *is*, rather than what could be with a more comprehensive intervention program. As Warren reminds us, "In virtually every area of development there are visually impaired children whose developmental progress is at least at the norm for, and at the high end of the distribution for, sighted children" (1994, p. 334). In this area, as in others, individual differences should be used to guide educational strategies, not some general average that may not be applicable to a particular child.

Summary

▶ Children with visual impairments are classified in several ways. Educational classifications rest on the special adaptations necessary to help these children learn.

▶ A visual impairment can hamper the individual's understanding of the world, but such understanding can be enhanced through extending the experiential world of the child with vision impairment.

▶ Hereditary factors are one major cause of visual impairments in young children. Other causes are infectious diseases, injuries, and poisonings.

▶ Today most educators agree that the cumulative experiences of children as they develop affect intelligence. Youngsters with visual impairments lack the integrating experiences that come naturally to sighted children. The challenge for educators is to compensate for this lack of integration through special instructional programs.

▶ One of the byproducts of restricted mobility and limited experience can be a passive orientation to life. Teachers play a critical role in helping students with visual impairments be active and independent.

▶ It is important for parents and teachers to help children with visual impairment develop their skills. It is equally important to let these children do things for themselves and to experience as much as possible the things that sighted children experience.

▶ Inclusion of children with visual impairments has left many such youngsters without the special skills training they need to live independently.

▶ Braille reading is slower than regular reading, which can affect the academic performance of students with profound visual impairments.

▶ Orientation and mobility training are critically important parts of the curriculum for children with visual disabilities. Such services should be available in the public schools.

▶ Technology is improving the means of communication for those with visual impairments. It has also broadened their occupational choices. Keyboarding and word processing are particularly useful skills, and access technology is equally important in today's schools.

▶ One of the important areas of curriculum adaptation is how to modify the standard CORE curriculum (e.g., math, language arts, social studies, science) to take into account the special needs of children with visual impairment.

▶ Another major need is to implement the expanded CORE curriculum. That includes such items as orientation and mobility, independent living skills, uses of assistive technology, and so forth. Very specially trained personnel are needed for this expanded program.

Future Challenges

1. *Will technology become more accessible for students with vision impairment?*

Technology is wonderful—when it is usable. The widespread distribution of technological developments for those with visual disabilities has been impeded by the cost and size of equipment. In the same way, we have to increase accessibility to the computers and word processors that are transforming the academic and work worlds of those with visual disabilities.

2. *Where will the specially trained teachers come from?*

There has always been a thin supply of teachers with expertise in dealing with children with visual impairments. This situation has grown worse because of the many complications and multiple disabilities that are becoming the responsibility of the special education teacher. We are sure to face a major teacher shortage despite the financial help given by the Office of Special Education Programs in the U.S. Department of Education.

Key Terms

access technology   *p. 459*

accommodation   *p. 422*

braille   *p. 456*

case coordinator   *p. 440*

ciliary muscles   *p. 422*

Resources

References of Special Interest

Corn, A., & Koenig, A. (Eds.). (1996). *Foundations of low vision: Clinical and functional perspectives.* New York: American Foundation for the Blind. *This book of eighteen chapters and many different contributors focuses on what low vision really means to the person who lives with it. It stresses the psychological and social implications of low vision and provides up-to-date information on mobility training and the instruction of children with low vision in academic programs.*

Goodman, S., & Wittenstein, S. (Eds.). (2002). *Collaborative assessment.* New York: American Foundation for the Blind. The theme of this book is appropriate assessment of children with visual impairment through a multidisciplinary team, each member bringing his or her own specialty to an overall collaborative assessment. Separate chapters are written by speech-language pathologists, psychologists, orientation and mobility specialists, and others. This professional collaboration is stressed not only in the initial planning for the child but also as continuing through the core curriculum.

Holbrook, M., & Koenig, A. (Eds.). (2000). *Foundations of education: Vol. I. History and theory of teaching children and youths with visual impairments* (2nd ed.). New York: American Foundation for the Blind. *This volume, along with the companion Volume II, provides a solid basis for anyone interested in the education of children with visual impairments. The book focuses on the special developmental issues and problems that children with visual impairments face—challenges that require adaptations of the general education curriculum. Each chapter is prepared by a specialist on the topic being discussed.*

Koenig, A., & Holbrook, M. (Eds.). (2000). *Foundations of education: Vol. II. Instructional strategies for teaching children and youths with visual impairments* (2nd ed.). New York: American Foundation for the Blind Press. *A compilation of chapters by a wide range of specialists details the special curriculum adaptations necessary for children with visual impairments. Its coverage represents the most comprehensive effort to date. Included are chapters on core curriculum subjects such as social studies and mathematics, and a variety of selections on extended core curriculum subjects such as visual efficiency and recreational and leisure skills.*

Poground, R., & Fazzi, D. (Eds.). (2002). *Early focus* (2nd ed.). New York: American Foundation for the Blind. A comprehensive portrait of how early intervention (from birth through age 5) can aid children with visual impairments. Emphasis is placed on family reactions and support. Since these children are denied the incidental learning that children with normal vision pick up automatically, carefully designed experiences must be provided to help children with visual impairments developmentally. Specialists discuss topics such as literacy, social skills, mobility, motor skills, and family support. A valuable addition to the literature on how to use the critical early years to help these children.

Sacks, S., & Silberman, R. (Eds.). (1996). *Educating children with visual impairments with other disabilities.* Baltimore: Paul H. Brookes. *This is an important book because over half of the current population of children with visual impairments also have other disabilities that complicate their educational program. This book, which includes chapters on learning disabilities, orthopedic disabilities, neurological disabilities, and emotional and behavioral problems, discusses how additional disabilities complicate the education of children with visual impairments and what can be done.*

Silberman, R., Bruce, S., & Nelson, C. (2004). *Children with sensory impairments.* Baltimore: Paul H. Brookes. A thorough review of the challenge presented by children with visual impairments. Topics range from definitions to causation to the special techniques and technologies that can present a level playing field for these children in the public schools.

Journals

Journal of Special Education Technology
peabody.vanderbilt.edu/peabody

Journal of Visual Impairment and Blindness
www.afb.org/jvib.asp

RE: view
www.heldref.org

Professional Organizations

American Foundation for the Blind
www.afb.org/afb

Division on Visual Impairment
c/o Council for Exceptional Children
www.cec.sped.org

National Association for Parents of the
Visually Impaired, Inc.
www.napvi.org

National Association for Visually Handicapped
www.navh.org

Association for Education and Rehabilitation of the Blind
and Visually Impaired
www.aerbvi.org

Please visit the book's website at
http://education.college.hmco.com/students for new and
updated information on websites listed here and for the
mailing addresses of the journals and organizations.

Children with
Multiple and
Severe Disabilities

12

▶ How prevalent are multiple and severe disabilities?

▶ What are some types of multiple disabilities?

▶ What adaptations can be made to the environment, the curriculum, and teaching strategies to support inclusion in everyday life?

▶ What types of vocational opportunities are available?

Children with disabilities do not always fit neatly into well-defined categories. There are individual differences among children with hearing, visual, cognitive, and emotional impairments. We also find children who have more than one impairment and children who have severe disabilities. These youngsters are even more heterogeneous than other children with special needs.

The children who are the subject of this chapter have multiple disabilities, and the disabilities are so severe that the child needs some type of support for the rest of his or her life. Such support might include a driver for transportation, a companion to provide assistance in areas of daily living (such as meal preparation or personal hygiene), or a job coach who facilitates working in the community.

Understand that not all individuals who have multiple disabilities have mental retardation. Persons with multiple disabilities vary widely in cognitive abilities. Some have profound mental retardation and will need continuous caregiving to meet their needs. Young men and women with Usher syndrome are deafblind but have normal cognitive abilities. A cognitively gifted child who is spastic may not be able to control muscle movements and may need a sophisticated voice output communication system so that he or she can express his or her thoughts. This individual may need adaptive equipment to be able to type to express his or her thoughts.

Some professionals who work with persons with multiple and severe disabilities do not adhere to a developmental approach. In this chapter, we present the view that the path of normal development, which is a product of genetic-environmental transactions, provides a framework for the selection of age-appropriate instructional activities.

Association for Persons with
Severe Handicaps (TASH)
www.tash.org

A Note About Terminology

In the field of multiple and severe disabilities, major advances have been made in recent years. Specialists in this field hold different opinions about the language to use to describe the individuals they serve. Clearly, throughout this book we favor terminology that reflects a humanistic, "people-first" approach to writing about persons with disabilities—using, for example, the term *individual with cerebral palsy* rather than *cerebral palsy child*.

The professionals in the field of multiple and severe disabilities have been leaders in the efforts to make regular schools accessible and welcoming to all students with disabilities, including those with multiple and severe disabilities. They perceive not only benefits to nondisabled students but enormous value in providing opportunities for students with disabilities to interact, to establish friendships, and to be exposed to a diverse cultural population comprising individuals from different social, economic, and cultural groups (Falvey, 1995; Meyer, Park, Grenot-Scheyer, Schwartz, & Harry, 1998; Sailor, Gee, & Karasoff, 2000). They believe that these positive lifestyle changes will develop not only social skills but academic ones as well, which will aid persons with disabilities in their employment and living settings (Smith & Nelson, 1997).

The trend today is to involve the students in making decisions about themselves, based on their interests and desires. Two terms are used to help students with multiple disabilities make decisions about their own lives: *self-determination* and *self-advocacy*. Self-determination is a broad concept: the extent to which an individual exerts control over his or her life (Brown & Cohen, 1996; Browder & Lohrmann-O'Rourke, 2001). Self-advocacy refers to the extent to which a person can make his or her needs known and is aware of basic rights and of how to use self-advocacy skills to achieve goals (Wood, Karvonen, Test, Browder, & Algozzine, 2004).

■ Definition

Children with multiple and severe disabilities possess such a diverse combination of characteristics that it is difficult to give a succinct statement that includes them all. Probably the most useful definition is the one adopted by the organization most concerned with this group of people and their families: The Association for Persons with Severe Handicaps (TASH). The definition accepted by TASH is as follows:

> Persons with severe handicaps include individuals of all ages who require extensive ongoing support in more than one life activity in order to participate in integrated community settings and to enjoy a quality of life that is available to citizens with fewer or no disabilities. Support may be required for life activities such as mobility, communication, self-care, and learning as necessary for independent living, employment, and self-sufficiency. (Original by Bureau for the Education of the Handicapped, April 1985; revised and adopted by TASH, December 1985, and revised November 1986; see Meyer, Peck, & Brown, 1991, p. 19)

| Many children with severe disabilities have normal intelligence or are gifted.

The term *disability* refers to the state of the individual—that is, persons with vision, hearing, or other impairments. The term *handicapped* refers to environmental conditions that restrict a person with disabilities, such as lack of ramps or elevators for persons who use wheelchairs for mobility. This chapter is concerned with persons who have *multiple and severe disabilities*.

Any definition of individuals with multiple or severe disabilities must be broad, because it would include a very heterogeneous population: for example, persons with psychiatric disorders, deafblindness, and combinations of health, motor, or cognitive impairments (Bigge, 1991b; Fewell & Cone, 1983). Children who have severe retardation generally have other disabilities and are considered to be multiply disabled. However, not all children with multiple disabilities, or even with one severe disability, are mentally retarded. The film *My Left Foot* tells the story of Christy Brown, a severely spastic man with cerebral palsy but without mental retardation. Brown learned to type with one toe and wrote several books (Brown, 1982). It took a long time for those in Brown's environment to realize that he did not have multiple disabilities but one severe disability that almost completely disrupted his functioning. Fortunately, he received specialized assistance that allowed him to express his intelligence.

Generally, children with multiple disabilities have sensory deficits, motor disabilities, health or neurological disorders, or genetic inheritances that interfere with the normal progression of development of cognitive, social, and physical skills.

Children with severe disabilities have physical, cognitive, or emotional problems of an intense nature and require special education programs.
(© Bob Daemmrich/Stock Boston)

■ Prevalence of Multiple and Severe Disabilities

The U.S. Office of Education (2001) categorizes populations of persons with multiple and severe disabilities as follows: multiple, autism, deafblind, and traumatic brain injury. By 2001, 112,993 students in these populations were receiving special education. This chapter includes children who are deafblind and who have multiple disabilities. Autism and TBI are discussed in other chapters in this text.

The trend today is to include children with multiple disabilities in regular school settings, although the separate classroom is still the dominant placement (see Table 12.1).

Severe and multiple disabilities appear equally across racial, ethnic, and economic groups.

The term *severe disabilities,* although not specifically a category in IDEA, refers to individuals who require intensive instruction in the basic skills and self-help that children without disabilities acquire in the first years of life. Thus, severe disabilities are usually found in one or more intellectual, physical, sensory, or social functionings.

TABLE 12.1
Educational Environment

	GENERAL EDUCATION CLASS	RESOURCE ROOM	SEPARATE CLASS	OTHER
Multiple	9.16%	8.68%	61.68%	11.0%
Deafblind	11.11%	11.11%	55.56%	22.0%

In the 1996–1997 school year, IDEA served 104,109 children with multiple disabilities. Hembree (2000) reports that there were 10,198 identified as deafblind, but IDEA reports that only 1,511 were served. Thus, as Baldwin (1993) observed, persons with deafblindness are greatly underreported, and a realistic number would be higher than the IDEA report indicates.

Teachers usually do not have many of these children in general education classes. They may encounter one or two children with physical disabilities or speech or language problems or perhaps a child who is gifted and who has visual and hearing losses. It is generally thought that most of these children require so much specialized intervention that often they are educated either in special education classes in regular schools with a great deal of professional support from an interdisciplinary team or in segregated schools.

Meyer (1991) suggested that students who have multiple disabilities account for only one-half of 1 percent of the total special education population. And only 0.07 percent were considered to have multiple and severe disabilities (Evans, 1991).

■ Causes of Multiple and Severe Disabilities

National Association for Rare Disorders
www.rarediseases.org

A discussion of causes of multiple and severe disabilities could go on at great length, because many conditions cause these problems, although many of these problems are rare. For example, as of the early 1990s, only five children had ever been diagnosed with Leigh disease, which causes widespread damage to the central nervous system, particularly to the brainstem (Behrman, Vaughn, & Nelson, 1987). Most low-incidence disorders—there are more than a thousand (Kopp, 1983)—are not highlighted in this text.

A number of things can cause multiple and severe disabilities: genes passed to the child by one or both parents; a negative influence during pregnancy, such as the mother's use of alcohol or other harmful drugs; or events that occur during birth, such as breech birth (emerging feet first) or anoxia (lack of oxygen during birth). After birth, accidents or child abuse can cause multiple and severe disabilities (Cohen & Warren, 1987). Whatever the cause of the disabilities, keep in mind the following realities about learners with severe and multiple disabilities:

▶ Learning is not only possible but probable.

▶ There are more similarities with their peers without disabilities than there are differences (Falvey & Grenot-Scheyer, 1995, p. 131).

■ Characteristics of Children with Multiple and Severe Disabilities

In this section, we discuss some of the major categories in which the largest numbers of children with multiple and severe disabilities are found, including deafblindness, behavior disturbance, hearing impairment, and mental retardation.

Deafblind Impairment

American Association of the Deaf-Blind
www.tr.wou.edu/dblink/aadb.htm

Helen Keller National Center
www.helenkeller.org/national

IDEA (P.L. 101–476) defines deafblindness as concomitant hearing and visual impairments, the combination of which causes such severe communication and other developmental and educational needs that children with this condition cannot be placed in special education programs solely for those with deafness or with blindness (NICHCY, 2000).

The Helen Keller National Center defines **deafblind** more specifically as someone

(1) with central vision acuity of 20/200 or worse in the better eye with corrective lenses and/or a visual field of 20 degrees or less in the better eye . . . or with a progressive visual loss . . . ; (2) who has either a chronic hearing impairment so severe that most speech cannot be understood . . . ; (3) and for whom the combination of impairments . . . causes extreme difficulty in daily life activities. (Everson, 1995)

The National Technical Assistance Consortium for Children and Young Adults who are Deaf-Blind (NTAC) reports there were 10,940 such individuals in the 2002 count. These individuals were categorized as having low vision in the better eye, being legally blind with light perception only, being totally blind, or having critical visual impairments (Hembree, 2000). Hearing impairments among persons with deafblindness range from mild loss to severe and profound loss. Thus in instructing those identified as deafblind, it is important for the teacher to have full access to the amount of vision or hearing the learner may possess, in order to build an instructional program that utilizes all his or her sensory reception.

It takes a great deal of time, patience, empathy, and repetition to establish the first word (usually a sign) for the child who is deafblind. The goal is to connect a movement made by the child to a sign. The learning process begins with the names of parents (*mama, papa*) or a toy or activity the child likes (*swing*, for example).

If the child is blind, the sign is taught by placing both hands on the child and encouraging the child to respond. Bear in mind that children who can see and hear do not speak until they have heard thousands of words. Children with deafblindness need similar multiple experiences with the movement they make and the sign (adapted from Miles & Riggio, 1999). For children with vision, 75 percent of learning is done visually. Children who are deafblind will need to develop a sense of self and a time concept.

Usher Syndrome

Persons with **Usher syndrome** have progressive sensorimotor deafness, retinitis pigmentosa, and central nervous system defects (Batshaw, 2002). A person with Usher syndrome has a hearing impairment and a vision disability that worsens over time (National Institute on Deafness and Other Communication Disorders [NIDCD], 1999). More than half of the population with deafblindness have this problem, which is an inherited condition. In its extreme form, referred to as Usher's II, the individual is deaf from birth and has severe balance problems. In the second type, children are born with moderate to severe hearing impairments and can perform well in the general education classroom. In the third type, the person has normal hearing that worsens over time, followed by blindness beginning in adolescence. There is no cure for Usher syndrome, but children with this condition can profit from early identification and appropriate technological and educational assistance (NIDCD, 1999).

Early Intervention—Deafblind

The National Technical Assistance Consortium for Children and Young Adults Who Are Deaf-Blind
www.tr.wou.edu/ntac

An infant who is deafblind needs to realize that he or she has needs.

Concern for the infant who is deafblind begins with the family. A major disruption has occurred in the life of this child. It should be met by the family, who will help establish realistic goals for the child and initiate special instructional techniques consistently (Huebner, Prickett, Welch, & Joffee, 1995; Murphy, 1983, p. 21). Visual evaluation and intervention are critical for infants who are deafblind for two main reasons: Efficient vision use is important for learning, and visual functioning can be improved (Michael & Paul, 1995, p. 201).

The first step with any individual, particularly one who has multiple disabilities, is to help that person maintain sufficiently focused attention to realize the following: (1) he or she exists; (2) others exist; (3) he or she has needs; (4) these needs can be met; (5) some of the needs will be met by himself or herself; and (6) some, if not most, of these needs will be met by others (Murphy & Byrne, 1983, p. 355). This is the genetic sequence of the development of the self (Schore, 1994). Many infants who possess deafblind impairments can go beyond point 6 and, as they develop, begin to meet many, if not most, of their own needs.

The key to all development is to begin joint attention; that is, transaction between the caregiver (usually the mother) and the infant (Donnellan, Mirenda, Mesaros, & Fassbinder, 1984, p. 34). With the infant who is deafblind, this joint attention begins through touch. As communication develops through touch, it is augmented by any residual hearing or vision through the

The key to development is the transaction between the child and caregiver.
(© Jeff Greenberg/Photo Edit)

use of hearing aids and glasses or sonic directional devices that give the infant vibrational feedback about the location of objects (Bower, 1989).

Without intervention, infants who are deafblind focus on their own bodies and show little interest in object use. They do little exploration of the environment and resist new stimuli, becoming prone to self-stimulation (Downing, 1995; Taylor, 1988). Recall that some learners who are classified as deafblind have some useful hearing or vision that should be a major part of their instructional programs.

In addition, changes occur as the brain matures, and a child without the ability to see or hear is deprived of normal sensory stimulation that facilitates normal development. Without early intervention to offset these lacks, the changes in the brain are degenerative and abnormal (Sameroff & Haith, 1996). Immediate programming is needed for these children as soon as their condition is diagnosed.

One early intervention approach that has been particularly successful with children who are deafblind is the Van Dijk method. The Van Dijk method is a movement-based approach that considers the sensorimotor experiences to be the foundation of all learning (Writer, 1987, p. 191). The aim is to enhance the quality of the child's interaction with people and objects. Van Dijk proposed that through body contact with others, children who are deafblind learn that they are separate persons, that other people are present in the environment and that they can communicate and have an impact upon their environment through communication. In addition, Van Dijk suggested that children with disabilities need to learn that their movements can affect others, a process he calls *resonance* (Van Dijk, 1986).

Table 12.2 presents guidelines for vocational training. IDEA mandates transitional services, goals, and objectives for the IEP of students who are deafblind. These IEPs should be outcome-oriented process objectives that promote movement from school to postschool activities (Everson, 1995).

The Education Program—Deafblind

When one of the two major systems that bring information to the child is impaired, the special education program emphasizes the unimpaired sense. For the child who is hearing impaired, the visual channel is used to establish a communication system based on signing, finger spelling, picture communication systems, and lip reading. For the child who is visually impaired, the program uses auditory and tactile aids to help compensate for the visual-channel problem. Literacy for the deafblind begins in early childhood and involves the use of language, either print or braille (National Clearing house on Children Who Are Deafblind, 2000). To facilitate literacy skills, have the child observe significant people reading and writing, usually by positioning the child's hands and moving them toward the activity (computer, book, newspaper, pencil and paper) so the child can explore the material. If the child has some vision, allow him or her to view the material as well as feel it. Have the child observe others reading braille. Read stories to the deafblind child, using speech, signing, or touch. Encourage active participation.

In the education of children and adolescents who are deafblind, the focus has changed from grants to multistate centers to allowing states to develop their own programs. The states are now responsible for both the education of

TABLE 12.2
Jobsite Training Guidelines for Individuals Who Are Deafblind

1. Always orient the worker to the setting, materials, and activities.

2. Ensure optimal positioning for efficient use of residual auditory and visual skills.

3. Always use task analyses to test and teach specific and related job skills.

4. Although it is always most desirable to have a worker respond to naturally occurring stimuli, for most individuals who are deafblind and have multiple impairments, it may be more efficient to provide a planned system of prompts and cues.

5. Selection of prompts and cues should consider types of visual and hearing losses, amount and extent of residual hearing and/or vision, age of onset of sensory losses, communication systems, and related disabilities (if any).

6. Prompts and cues include visual or tactual signed instruction, tactual cues, enhanced visual and/or auditory cues, model prompts, physical prompts, large print or braille cues, enlarged photographs, low-vision aids, hearing aids, assistive listening devices, and other assistive technology.

7. Prompts and cues should be defined as permanent or temporary. All temporary cues and prompts should be faded along with the job coach or other employment personnel. Before presenting a temporary cue or prompt, know how you are going to fade it! Before presenting a temporary cue or prompt, ensure that it is site and age appropriate.

8. Choose an instructional format that includes a system of least-to most intrusive prompts and/or time delay combined with whole task instruction, backward chaining, or forward chaining.

9. For individuals who have significant visual impairments or are blind but have some residual hearing, combine auditory prompts with tactual cues and prompts.

10. For individuals who have profound hearing losses or are deaf but have some residual vision, combine signed instruction with model prompts, enlarged visual cues, and physical prompts.

11. For individuals who are profoundly deaf and legally blind, combine tactual instruction and cues with physical (hand-over-hand) prompts.

Source: J. Everson (Ed.), *Supporting young children who are deaf-blind in their communities: A transition planning guide for service providers, families, and friends* (p. 157, Table 7.2) (Baltimore: Paul H. Brookes, 1995). Reprinted with permission of the author.

youngsters with deafblindness impairments and the transition of young adults (ages 21 and older) "from education to employment," including "vocational, independent living, and other post-secondary services" (U.S. Department of Education, 1985, pp. 2–3). These programs have brought comprehensive diagnostic processes and facilities and qualified personnel in contact with children and adolescents who are deaf and blind.

Case Study: Seth

Seth is 19½ years old. He is enrolled in an education-based program for youth in transition to adult life, at a state center for the deaf. His educational and developmental challenges are influenced by deafness, visual impairment, and cognitive delays. These challenges manifest themselves in avenues of communication, social emotional development, mobility and orientation, and overall academic learning. Seth may be characterized as an individual who enjoys being among people but will avoid sustained interaction with individuals. He displays behaviors that suggest pervasive developmental order. Seth is very ritualistic and mandates a schedule that he can depend upon.

Seth is very clear as to his preferences and presents a variety of strengths and abilities. These include going to the movies, walking in the mall, taking photographs, eating at specific restaurants, staying at hotels, visiting his relatives, and collecting light fixtures. He does not enjoy change in his routine or new, unexpected experiences.

The education team has been guided by Seth's parents to develop for him a program that includes a community-based part-time job at a movie theater within a shopping mall in his hometown. Therefore, his school program consists of a combination of direct instruction in activities of daily living; instruction within the local community in appropriate skills in shopping, public transportation, banking, and so forth; and supported part-time work within a preferred environment in his community. His academic abilities are embedded across these activities to ensure generalization of meaningful skills.

Behavior Disturbance and Hearing Impairment

A child with both a hearing loss and behavioral difficulties may have developed the behavioral problems because of the lack of environmental input resulting from the sensory disability.

Nothing inherent in a hearing deficit should create additional social or psychological problems (Schlesinger, 1983, p. 83). Most of the social and psychological problems found in persons with hearing deficits are secondary outgrowths of their lack of hearing in a speech-dominated world. Fredericks and Baldwin (1987) cautioned against diagnosing a person as having more than one disability because an individual may have only one disability with secondary characteristics growing out of the lack of environmental input from the sensory disability.

Unfortunately, many children with hearing impairments have behavior problems. Many researchers believe that the secondary problem can be avoided if intervention is begun early and the strengths of the child are reinforced and communication training begun early (Mencher & Gerber, 1983). Children who are deaf and who have deaf parents tend to have fewer problems than children who are deaf whose parents have normal hearing (Moores, 2000).

Teaching early communication skills to children who are deaf enhances cognitive, language, and social development and is a major step in preventing behavior problems.

Part of the problem for children with hearing losses is that so much of what they cannot hear they can feel vibrationally or see in shadow movements in the environment around them. This causes them to become confused and frustrated and to act out in consequence. Teaching caregivers to look at and explain by gesture, signing, or pointing to the event for the child with hearing impairment can keep some of the challenging behaviors from occurring. The aim of many intervention programs is to teach signing at an early age, so the child who is deaf can communicate with others and therefore not be isolated.

Mental Retardation with Another Disability

A child who has a hearing loss may be classified as having mental retardation because of a lack of appropriate teaching, not a lack of intelligence.

A major problem for children who have mental retardation is the slowness with which they learn or retain what they have learned. When this slowness is combined with other problems, the difficulty of teaching these children is compounded. Many special educators are concerned with the excessive use of the term *dual diagnosis* to classify individuals, particularly those with mental retardation. The term *dual diagnosis* is limited to the combination of mental retardation and behavioral and psychiatric dysfunction (Dykens & Kasari, 1997). In Prader-Willi syndrome, there appears to be a higher frequency of both behaviors than there is in Down syndrome or nonspecific retardation. Thus, assuming that psychiatric issues are a necessary part of retardation is faulty reasoning.

Some children do have more than one disability; an individual with a hearing loss may also possess mental retardation. However, a careful and appropriate assessment of a child with a hearing loss may reveal that the child's poor performance is due to the hearing loss and not to poor cognitive functioning. In other words, the second disability is an outgrowth of the first disability. The child's low score on a standardized test may reflect that he or she is not able to accurately hear spoken language, or that the child uses a sign language but the test was administered orally.

Persons with limited cognitive abilities also tend to be very rule oriented and rigid, applying a rule to all situations rather than being flexible. For example, a person with mental retardation who learns to open a door by pushing it may push all doors, even those that need to be pulled or to have a knob turned.

Teaching strategies that take advantage of the person's rule orientation by teaching rules can be very effective.

A teacher may believe that a person with mental retardation who is not following directions in the classroom is actively resisting the teacher's effort or is emotionally disturbed to the point of being unable to relate to reality. The teacher should investigate, however, whether the child is depressed because of his or her inability to understand instruction. The teacher can ask the parents if the child has poor sleep habits, has a poor appetite, and is generally sad and listless. If so, the child may need to be treated for depression and receive training in social skills to help solve what must be terrible emotional feelings beyond the cognitive understanding of a person with mental retardation (Evans, 1991). The sections that follow discuss the importance of teaching self-determination and self-advocacy to help students gain indepedence. These skills assist in the reduction of depressed states (Wehmeyer, Agran, & Hughes, 1998; Wehmeyer, Field, Doren, Jones, & Mason, 2004).

Mental Retardation and Cerebral Palsy

People tend to assume that children with cerebral palsy are mentally retarded, and a relationship does exist between the two conditions. Whatever genetic or environmental insult damages the motor control centers of the central nervous system sufficiently to cause **cerebral palsy** can cause enough damage to the cerebral cortex to create retardation. But the relationship is not universal. Dorman and Pellegrino (1998) report that only 25 to 30 percent of children with cerebral palsy have lower IQ scores than typically developing children.

Standardized intelligence testing often does not take into account a child's disability.

It is hard to justify a diagnosis of mental retardation in youngsters with cerebral palsy if we are using intelligence tests that are normed on children with adequate speech, language, and motor abilities. Many children with cerebral palsy have expressive problems in both speech and psychomotor areas. Their test results, then, are not necessarily valid. All we can conclude is that when these children are tested with instruments normed on other populations, about half of them show IQ scores below 70 or 80. However, IQ tests have serious limitations in terms of evaluating children with multiple disabilities.

Often the poor speech and spastic movements of children with cerebral palsy give the layperson and the professional the impression that these individuals have mental retardation. Actually, there is little relationship between the degree of physical impairment and intelligence in children with cerebral palsy. A child who is severely spastic may be intellectually gifted; another with mild physical involvement may be severely retarded.

Although IQ tests—the most common instruments used to determine retardation—are inappropriate for those with disabilities in speech and motor areas, the subtest scores on an IQ test can reveal more about a child's strengths than the total or derived score reveals. Thus, we find these subtest scores helpful when we must design an individualized teaching strategy to capitalize on those strengths. Keep in mind that most of the current remedial efforts in special education focus on the children's strengths, not their weaknesses.

To assess adequately whether retardation exists, we need to be sure that whatever test of intelligence yields information on how to provide an intervention

Parents and therapists need to teach children with severe disabilities to turn from their internal world to the outer world of the environment and other people for stimulation.
(© Jerry Howard/Positive Images)

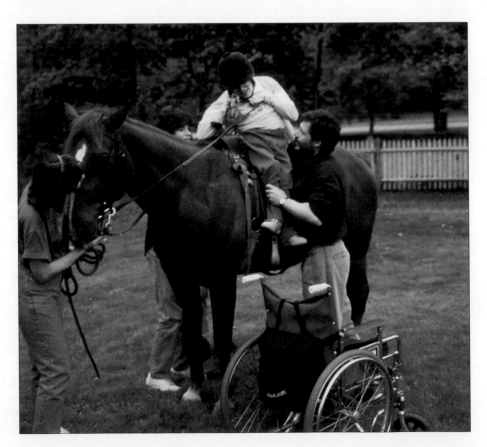

design will lead to an outcome better than the outcome of an intervention design constructed solely on the basis of observation (Evans, 1991, p. 40). IDEA suggests that assessments be "timely, comprehensive, and multidisciplinary" (Section 1435) and include participation of children and youth with disabilities in state and local assessment programs (NICHCY, 1998).

■ Early Intervention—Multiple and Severe Disabilities

| Parents and teachers need to teach these children how to transact with the world.

A critical need of children with multiple and severe disabilities is early intervention, so the parents can provide appropriate and consistent care. Parents and therapists need to help children with severe disabilities recognize that they are persons in an environment and that they can influence the environment. The adults need to teach these children to turn outward from their internal world to the external world of the environment and other people for stimulation. If they do not, these children tend to respond to internal rather than external stimuli and use their genetic capacity for curiosity to explore by manipulating their internal world through body movements. As Murphy (1983) wrote, once children fail to turn outward to the environment, it is almost impossible to get them to respond to the world around them. In addition, the child who responds to his or her internal world is likely to develop self-stimulating behaviors, some of which, such as head banging and eye poking, can be physically, psychologically, and socially damaging to the child and hard to eliminate.

An excellent example of this pattern is described in the work of Fraiberg (1977), who found that infants who are blind and were institutionalized appeared to have mental retardation and developed problematic self-stimulating behaviors. On the other hand, children who are blind and were reared at home and received ample physical stimulation did not develop these behaviors, and most were cognitively normal. Teaching **self-determination skills** to these children has several advantages. It promotes autonomous behavior, develops independence in making choices in leisure and recreational times, and cultivates important safety skills and the ability to make choices effectively (Wehmeyer, Agran, & Hughes, 1998).

| Coping skills need to be reinforced as they emerge.

Considerable evaluation is required to determine the nature of the disability and the kind of intervention needed to help the child function as effectively as possible. Early identification of infants with disabilities is crucial for the maximum development of the child (see Chapter 3). Hearing tests at birth and tests for PKU and thyroid deficiency are some examples. IDEA allows for early evaluation to detect delays or disabilities, as well as providing the comprehensive support parents need when a child is diagnosed as having severe disabilities. These evaluations have to be conducted periodically by an interdisciplinary team to determine if progress is being made and what changes, if any, are needed in the intervention process. Table 12.3 (page 482) shows the types of professionals included on a multidisciplinary team and the services they provide (Rainforth, York, & MacDonald, 1992).

After evaluation, a decision is made about what type of classroom is most appropriate for the child. Some children with multiple and severe disabilities will be placed in the general education classroom. Recently, there has been a movement to have these students served for all or part of their education in

TABLE 12.3
Professional Members of a Multidisciplinary Team

Audiologist: To provide and coordinate services to children with auditory handicaps, including detecting the problem and managing any existing communication handicaps.

Early Childhood Special Educator: To ensure that environments for handicapped infants and preschoolers facilitate children's development of social, motor, communication, self-help, cognitive, and behavioral skills and enhance children's self-concept, sense of competence and control, and independence.

Physician: To assist families in promoting optimal health, growth, and development for their infants and young children by providing health services.

Nurse: To diagnose and treat actual and potential human responses to illness; for infants and preschoolers wih disabilities, this means (1) promoting the highest health and developmental status possible and (2) helping families cope with changes in their lives resulting from the child's disabilities.

Nutritionist: To maximize the health and nutritional status of infants and preschoolers through developmentally appropriate nutrition services within family and community environments.

Occupational Therapist: To promote children's independence, mastery, and sense of self-worth in their physical, emotional, and psychosocial development. Purposeful activity is used to expand the child's functional abilities, such as self-help skills; adaptive behavior and play skills; and sensory, motor, and postural development. These services are designed to help families and other caregivers improve children's functioning in their environment.

Ophthalmologist: To determine the extent of the child's visual capacity.

Physical Therapist: To enhance the sensory motor development, neurobehavioral organization, and cardiopulmonary status of disabled or at-risk infants and preschool children within a family and community context.

Psychologist: To derive a comprehensive picture of child and family functioning and to identify, implement, or evaluate psychological interventions.

Social Worker: To improve the quality of life for infants and toddlers and their families who are served by PL 99-457 through the provision of social work services.

Speech Language Pathologist: To promote children's communications skills in the context of social interactions with peers and family members, in school, and in the community.

Source: From L. Rossetti, *Infant-toddler assessment* (Boston: Little, Brown, 1990). Adapted from the Carolina Institute for Research on Infant Personal Preparation, *Proceedings of a Working Conference* (Unpublished manuscript, revised, 1988). Reprinted with permission.

Two or more appropriate members of a multidisciplinary team are needed for an accurate assessment.

regular schools (U.S. Department of Education, 1999). Schools hire personnel especially prepared to work with and teach these individuals. Most of the specialized classrooms are located in regular schools. There are advocates who insist that all children, regardless of the severity of their disability, be included with their agemates in general education classrooms (Falvey, 1995; Stainback & Stainback, 1996). Many in the field disagree (Kauffman & Hallahan, 1995).

A major question to be considered when planning intervention is how multiple and severe disabilities influence each other and shape the individual's experience of the environment. For example, if a child is disabled both cognitively and physically, his or her academic accomplishments will be less than those of one who has mild retardation and a physical disability. Multiple disabilities are not simple additions of disabilities. They interact with each other and confound the individual's condition (Mencher & Gerber, 1983).

As Mencher and Gerber (1983) suggested, helping to improve the functioning of an individual with a disability begins with identifying and developing the child's assets. Because 93.8 percent of the deafblind population have some residual vision or hearing (Baldwin, 1997), the residuals need to be identified and enhanced to improve the child's functioning. By encouraging the child's assets, the instructional staff hopes to avoid the development of negative challenging behaviors, such as self-stimulation, self-injury, tantrums, and aggression.

A comprehensive system in the community can greatly assist families by providing easy access to needed services (Harbin & West, 1998). The parents also need to be made aware of the supports available in the community (Everson, Burwell, & Killan, 1995).

Consider these five axioms when providing service for children with severe disabilities:

A comprehensive system in the community can greatly assist families by providing easy access to needed services.

▶ They have a right to services that improve their quality of life and maximize their developmental potential.

▶ Early childhood services are effective in improving the quality of life and maximizing developmental potential.

▶ Intervention services that begin earlier in the child's life will be more effective than services that begin later.

▶ Early childhood services that involve families are more effective than those that do not (Westlake & Kaiser, 1991, p. 432).

▶ Including children with disabilities in general education classrooms increases their social skills and interpersonal relationships (Helmstetter, Peck, & Giangreco, 1994).

The aim of special education is to support individuals with disabilities so they can become as independent as possible in the activities of daily life and work and develop the social skills expected by society. For most children with multiple disabilities, achieving those goals requires a long and specialized process, but much has been accomplished in recent years.

■ Identification of Children with Multiple and Severe Disabilities

Most children with multiple and severe disabilities are identified at birth through simple screening techniques. The Apgar scoring system (Apgar & Beck, 1973), described in Chapter 3, is administered at one minute and five minutes after birth. It assesses the child's motor functioning, skin color, heart rate, respiration, and general appearance. The Brazelton Neonatal Behavioral Assessment Scale (Brazelton, 1973) may also be administered to assess the same areas.

(text continues on page 500)

ADAPTATIONS

EDUCATIONAL

CHILDREN WITH MULTIPLE AND SEVERE DISABILITIES

A philosophy of teaching students with multiple and severe disabilities has been evolving from research, experience, and common sense. Today the objective is to reach functional, age-appropriate skills in integrated school and nonschool settings and to base teaching on ongoing, systematic evaluation of the student's progress. The approach has become more age oriented; hence, it is more developmentally oriented. Recall that age appropriateness is defined by what the average individual without disabilities can do at a given age.

Keep in mind that many children with multiple and severe disabilities are cognitively normal; they are capable of mastering the regular curriculum when they receive the necessary supports (augmentative communication devices, motorized wheelchairs, low-vision aids). Here, however, *we focus on students who cannot follow the general education school curriculum and who have not mastered the self-help skills that lead to independence.*

▋ Adapting the Learning Environment

In the past, many children with multiple and severe disabilities were excluded from public schools because they did not fit into ongoing special education programs or because they did not have basic self-care skills such as being toilet trained. Many of these youngsters were assigned to a residential institution for the more severe of their disabilities. For example, a child with both mental retardation and hearing impairment might have been placed in a residential institution serving people with mental retardation or mental illness; often the institution had neither the facilities nor the personnel to provide education for someone with a hearing loss.

Provisions for children with disabilities are different today because of parent involvement and the efforts of the Association for Persons with Severe Handicaps, the Council for Exceptional Children, the National Association for Retarded Citizens, the American Association on Mental Retardation, and other advocacy groups. The Civil Rights Act and the Education for All Handicapped Children Act of 1975 (Public Law 94-142) made it mandatory for public schools to educate all children. Each program should be constructed to be "person centered" rather than "system centered" (Mount, 2000a). **Person-centered programs** identify and develop the interests, desires, and talents of each individual, rather than fitting the person to a preconceived "system-centered" program.

Today, it is recommended that children who have multiple or severe disabilities be placed in educational programs with the following characteristics (Horner & Carr, 1997):

▶ Person-centered

▶ Team-centered

- ▶ Practical and valid
- ▶ Socially valid
- ▶ Oriented toward functional priority
- ▶ Providing active participation
- ▶ Fostering self-determination
- ▶ Individualized

For example, Promoting Learning Through Active Intervention (PLAI) is a program designed to promote communication skills in preschoolers and young children with multiple disabilities. The program includes a teacher's guide and a video tape to help train the child's parents. The core intent of this program is to alert teachers and parents to nonverbal cues and signals on which to build a communication system for the child with multiple disabilities. The video tape, available in English or Spanish, demonstrates the challenges of building an interactive communication system (Klein, Chen, & Haney, 2003).

Students who have multiple and severe disabilities can participate at least partially in most school and nonschool activities, increasing their confidence and their peers' perceptions of them as valuable, productive members of society. (© Gale Zucker)

The present trend is to embed basic skills in a context of age-appropriate activities in inclusive classrooms (Sailor, Gee, & Karasoff, 2000; Bigge, Best, & Heller, 2004).

The procedural safeguards included in IDEA 1997 are extensive. They include parents' rights to timely resolution of complaints, to confidentiality, whether to accept services, to examine records, and to receive written notices in their native language of all their rights (U.S. Department of Education, 1999). In addition, the parents, guardians, or surrogates of each child have the right to share with educators in making decisions that affect the child's education.

These laws and court decisions also have mandated the development of community programs for many children who previously were institutionalized. Brown, Nietupski, and Hamre-Nietupski (1976) advocated very early that "severely handicapped students should be placed in self-contained classes in public schools. . . . They have a right to be visible functioning citizens integrated into the everyday life of complex public communities" (p. 3). This thinking has been expanded to the idea of placing these students in a general education classroom for at least part of the day (Baumgart et al., 1982).

> Students who have severe disabilities should participate in general classroom activities for at least part of the day.

Inclusion in Context

Inclusion is grounded in the social development theory of Bandura (1977); specifically, observation learning and the development of social cognitive skills (Sailor, Gee, & Karasoff, 2000). Successful inclusion requires individualized educational support in addition to placement in a general education class (Harrower, 1999). Harrower (1999) and Snell and Brown (2000) describe three ingredients of successful inclusive classrooms:

► Sophisticated, trained, available support staff

► Collaborative training

► Teacher modification of instructional and social activities

One successful teaching strategy is to prime or prepractice the activity in which the student is to participate. This involves previewing the information or activity with which the student is likely to have difficulty, before actually engaging in the activity. For example, one might take the student verbally through every step of buying his or her lunch in the cafeteria before he or she attempts to do so. Many of these students have difficulty generalizing skills and applying skills they have learned in one setting to another. Mary, a 16-year-old with severe disabilities, has just completed the bed-making program at school. But she cannot make her bed at home or at her grandmother's house because she is not able to generalize the skills across different environments, from school to home and to her grandmother's house.

There are many ways to help youngsters generalize skills. One is to teach the skill in the environment in which the person will use it. This kind of real-world training requires multiple integrated educational settings, both at school and in the community. This training is not classroom based; it is community based. If we want to teach shopping skills, we do not use a pretend store in the classroom. Instead, we go out into the community to grocery stores, department stores, and specialty shops.

TABLE 12.4
Life Skills Across the Grades

STUDENT	DOMESTIC	COMMUNITY	LEISURE	VOCATIONAL
Tim (elementary age)	—Picking up toys —Washing dishes —Making bed —Dressing —Grooming —Practicing eating skills —Practicing toileting skills —Sorting clothes —Vacuuming	—Eating meals in a restaurant —Using restroom in a local restaurant —Putting trash into container —Choosing correct change to ride city bus —Giving the clerk money for an item he wants to purchase —Recognizing and reading pedestrian safety signs —Participating in local scout troop —Going to a neighbor's house for lunch	—Climbing on swing set —Playing board games —Playing tag with neighbors —Tumbling activities —Running —Playing kickball —Playing croquet —Riding bicycles —Playing with age-appropriate toys	—Picking up plate, silverware, and glass after a meal —Returning toys to appropriate storage spaces —Cleaning the room at the end of the day —Working on a task for a designated period (15–30 minutes) —Wiping tables after meals —Following two- to four-step instructions —Answering the telephone —Emptying trash —Taking messages to people
Mary (junior high age)	—Washing clothes —Preparing simple meals (e.g., soup, salad, sandwich) —Keeping bedroom clean —Making snacks —Mowing lawn —Raking leaves —Making grocery lists —Purchasing items from a list —Vacuuming and dusting living room	—Crossing streets safely —Purchasing an item from a department store —Purchasing a meal at a restaurant —Using local transportation system to get to and from recreational facilities —Participating in local scout troop —Going to a neighbor's house for lunch on Saturday	—Playing volleyball —Taking aerobics classes —Playing checkers with a friend —Playing miniature golf —Cycling —Attending high school or local basketball games —Playing softball —Swimming —Attending craft class at city recreation center	—Waxing floors —Cleaning windows —Filling lawn mower with gas —Hanging and bagging clothes —Busing tables —Working for 1–2 hours —Operating machinery (e.g., dishwasher, buffer) —Cleaning sinks, bathtubs, and fixtures —Following a job sequence
Sandy (high school age)	—Cleaning all rooms in place of residence —Developing a weekly budget —Cooking meals —Operating thermostat to regulate heat and air conditioning —Doing yard maintenance —Maintaining personal needs —Caring for and maintaining clothing	—Utilizing bus system to move about the community —Depositing checks into bank account —Using community department stores —Using community restaurants —Using community grocery stores —Using community health facilities (e.g., physician, pharmacist)	—Jogging —Archery —Boating —Watching college basketball games —Playing video games —Playing card games (e.g., Uno) —Attending athletic club swimming class —Gardening —Going on a vacation trip	—Performing required janitorial duties at J.C. Penney —Performing housekeeping duties at Days Inn —Performing groundskeeping duties at college campus —Performing food service at K Street cafeteria —Performing laundry duties at Moon's Laundromat —Performing photocopying at Virginia National Bank headquarters —Performing food-stocking duties at Farm Fresh —Performing clerical duties at electrical company —Performing job duties at company standards

Source: From J. Bigge, S. Best, & K. Heller, *Teaching individuals with physical, health, and multiple disabilities* (4th ed.) (Upper Saddle River, NJ: Merrill-Prentice, 2001). Copyright © 2001. Reprinted with permission of Pearson Education.

Benefits of Inclusion Today, a growing body of literature supports the concept of including these students in public schools and community settings:

▶ They have shown greater academic gains (Wehmeyer & Schwartz, 1998).

▶ Positive changes have been reported in the attitudes of nondisabled individuals toward their peers with severe disabilities at various age levels (Grenot-Scheyer, 1994; Voeltz, 1980; Ryndak & Alper, 2003).

▶ Inclusion has led to improvements in the social and communication skills of children with severe disabilities (Jenkins, Speltz, & Odom, 1985; Newton, Horner, Ard, LeBaron, & Sapperton, 1994; Jackson, Ryndak, & Billingsley, 2000).

▶ Inclusion has improved interaction between students with severe disabilities and their nondisabled agemates (Roberts, Burchinal, & Bailey, 1994; Downing & Eichinger, 2003).

▶ Inclusion facilitates adjustment to community settings as adults (Hasazi, Gordon, & Roe, 1985; Helmstetter, Peck, & Giangreco, 1994).

One of the major findings about including persons with multiple and severe disabilities in general education classrooms is that the participation increases their social and interpersonal skills. They display increased responsiveness to others,

www.inclusion.org

To maximize inclusion for students with severe disabilities, teachers should limit the ratio of students with disabilities to students without disabilities in any setting and use students without disabilities as peer tutors.
(© Spencer Grant)

increased reciprocal interactions, and increased displays of affect toward others (Grenot-Scheyer, 1994). In addition, the inclusion of those with multiple and severe disabilities in general education classrooms has an impact on their peers who do not have disabilities. The latter show increased tolerance for others, increased tolerance for diversity, and growth in their own personal development (Helmstetter, Peck, & Giangreco, 1994).

Whatever the age of the students or the severity of their disabilities, inclusion must provide them with a curriculum that is the most functional and age appropriate possible. Downing (2001) suggested several ways for teachers and administrators to make inclusion work.

> Interacting with students who have severe disabilities teaches tolerance to students who do not have disabilities.

MAKING INCLUSION WORK

► Limit the ratio of students with disabilities to students without disabilities in any setting.

► Highlight your student's strengths. If the student has well-developed gross motor skills but weak fine motor skills, integrate her or him into sports rather than art.

► Provide "extra help" at first to start the process.

► Encourage students with disabilities to dress like their peers. Send home dress tips to parents.

► Use students without disabilities to be peer tutors and friends to the student with disabilities.

► Be positive when talking to other teachers or students about the student with disabilities.

► Arrange the classroom schedule to maximize inclusive opportunities. (Adapted from Guiltinan, 1986, pp. 4–5)

While the inclusion movement has expanded and opened up placement options for students with severe and multiple disabilities, the most significant increase in inclusive placements has occurred for those with milder forms of severe disabilities (Palmer, Fuller, Arora, & Nelson, 2001). The vast majority of students with severe and multiple disabilities are educated in general special education classrooms. For example, when a student cannot walk, talk, or communicate, the parents feel that his or her needs can best be met in a special education classroom. Palmer et al. (2001) suggest that an expanded view of inclusion must consider the type of educational setting that is most appropriate for the student as well as the characteristics and values of his or her family.

■ Adapting Curriculum

Data Collecting

Teachers of students with multiple and severe disabilities collect data on all kinds of things: the number of steps a student making a sandwich completes correctly, the length of time it takes a student to complete a vocational assembly task (such as packaging drill bits), the percentage of community information signs a student reads correctly, the amount of time a student spends on off-task behaviors.

The ongoing collection of data about a student's responses is the core of an educational program.

Wolery, Bailey, and Sugai (1988) suggested several reasons why data collection is necessary:

▶ To pinpoint students' status

▶ To monitor progress and determine the program's effectiveness

▶ To provide feedback to students and parents

▶ To document efforts and demonstrate accountability

This kind of information enables teachers and other service providers to plan programs that meet a student's needs and to make decisions about the student's educational progress.

The teacher takes the individual through as many stages as possible by

▶ Conditionally reinforcing simple responses related to causality, such as picking up a toy or touching someone to signal a need

▶ Interactional coaching, turn taking, imitation of facial expressions, gestures, and sound

▶ Individual teaching at the time of engaging in functional activities

The communication skills taught to persons with multiple and severe disabilities are functional in that they are relevant to the individual's survival and independent functioning in the community as appropriately (societally determined) as possible (Bradley, Ashbaugh, & Blaney, 1994).

The collaborative team might use video tapes of students in natural settings to evaluate a plan for the student.

Structural observation of expressive and receptive language in a typical communication context, which is a familiar and comfortable environment, can reveal the student's level of communication skills (Brown & Snell, 2000). In an ecological inventory of the expectations of a natural environment—for example, a fast-food restaurant—the examiner would determine what behaviors are required in that environment. By combining the ecological inventory with the assessment of the student's strengths and weaknesses and comparing them to the demands of the environment, the teacher and the collaborative team can develop a plan for instruction. Video taping the student in natural settings, without the pressure of instruction, can provide the team with a means of evaluating the instruction and plans for the next phase (Mount, 2000a, pp. 33–40).

Fuchs and Deno (1994) suggested that measurement of students' status and progress must

▶ Be repeated on material of comparable difficulty (to curriculum taught) over time

▶ Incorporate valid indicators of the critical outcomes of instruction

▶ Rely on a data base that permits quantitative and qualitative descriptions of students' performance to assist teachers in adjusting and enhancing their instruction

In addition, commenting about samples of the students' work (portfolio assessment) is an important means of communicating with parents.

Ecological Inventory

To enrich the lives of children with multiple and severe disabilities, it is critical to assess what is available in each child's total environment. An assessment of this nature is called an *ecological inventory*.

A simple ecological inventory would involve the home: persons with whom and objects with which to interact. Such objects include radios, televisions, and computer games (both individual and interactive-social). Beyond the home, the ecological inventory would include the school and other resources and activities available to the child. Among the latter, it is essential to include stores, religious organizations, and recreational facilities. It is also important to identify persons with whom the child can be involved interactively and socially: parents, siblings, other relatives, peers in the neighborhood, members of the family's religious group, clerks in stores, and teachers, staff, and classmates at school.

To improve students' functioning and lives, ecological inventories ought to include a wide array of environments and people. They should identify places in which functional skills can be developed.

Functional Age-Appropriate Skills

The skills taught to students with severe disabilities must be both functional and age appropriate. Functional skills can be used immediately by the student, are necessary in everyday settings, and increase to some extent the student's independence. Folding a sheet of paper in half is not a functional skill; folding clothes is (Campbell, 2000; Kaiser, 2000).

Age appropriate skills are appropriate to the student's chronological age, not mental age. A 16-year-old boy who has severe disabilities is not taught how to solve a four-piece jigsaw puzzle of a dog, although it may correspond to his mental age. Instead, the focus is on activities the boy can carry out to some degree as his nondisabled agemates do—for example, eating in a restaurant, using a neighborhood health club, or operating a television set or personal stereo. If the skills are not age appropriate, they are not likely to be functional. Moreover, age-appropriate skills give students with severe disabilities a measure of social acceptance.

Clearly, some youngsters with severe disabilities cannot do many tasks that their nondisabled agemates can do. Nevertheless, most of them can at least take part in certain activities. Partial participation enables students with disabilities to interact with their nondisabled agemates as much as possible (Falvey, 1995; Sailor, Gee, & Karasoff, 2000).

The standard practice is to teach each step. Take, for example, buying a hamburger: You open the door, stand in line, ask for what you want, pay for it, accept any change, wait until it is served, move from the order line to the reception area, receive the food, take it to the accepted place for eating, and clean up afterward.

Some students with autism and others with severe physical disabilities may be apraxic—that is, they cannot realize what to do when confronted with a situation such as opening a door and will stand in front of the door in confusion. Thus, teaching how to open different types of doors becomes the first step. After each step is mastered, the individual who has multiple and severe disabilities must be taught that the same (or very similar) procedures apply at the pizza parlor, the ice cream store, and so on. Preparation may begin in the classroom, but it also must be taught in the actual community for **generalization** and maintenance to take place (Lehr & Brown, 1996). Rewarding and reinforcing each successfully completed step are very important.

Teaching functional skills that students will use in daily living is an important part of the curriculum.

Generalization of Skills The major problem for the teacher or facilitator of individuals with multiple and severe disabilities is to teach the individual that what he or she has learned can be applied in other settings. Traditionally, skills were taught in the classroom and were not transferred to or used in other settings by these individuals.

To understand the importance of this concept, consider a practical example. Most of us have forgotten how we learned to go to a store or to a fast-food restaurant to buy something. We learned it at some time, however, probably through guided instructions from our parents or by imitating them. Children with multiple and severe disabilities must be taught each step that is necessary to complete what to us might seem to be a simple task. They also must learn that they can apply these steps in other settings. It is not an easy process but one that requires persistence, repetition, and a variety of settings in which to use the skills.

Assessment of Skills Federal regulations about assessing or evaluating the skills of individuals with multiple and severe disabilities are quite clear: The evaluation must be appropriate to the needs of the individual, his or her family, and the recommended potential early intervention program. The regulations are also concerned with cultural and language issues. Any evaluation must be based on the reality of the family's culture and community and on the individual's experience. Most normed tests assume uniform cultural experiences; thus, they are obviously biased against individuals whose life experiences vary from those of the dominant middle class.

Good assessment is the foundation of good instruction. Knowing what a person can do and what he or she needs to learn how to do provides the initial step for instruction. A basic tenet of professional education has been to plan instruction at the level of a child's functioning and then take him or her to the next step. In other words, needs are focused on strengths. Authentic assessments comprise a variety of tasks in which the person generates a response in a real-life situation, rather than choosing a response on a piece of paper (Gage & Falvey, 1995).

Although commercial assessment devices are available, they sometimes fail to meet the individual needs of students with multiple and severe disabilities. Norm-referenced tests are not very helpful for classroom teachers. IQ scores and developmental-age quotients do not give us specific information about what students can and cannot do. **Criterion-referenced tests**—tests that compare students' levels of functioning to a standard of mastery—are more useful. Because children with multiple and severe disabilities are a heterogeneous group, commercial assessment devices must be adjusted to each child's age and type of disabilities, to the teacher's qualifications, and to the characteristics and demands of the school, the community, and the student's home environment.

The assessment of a student's skill must take place in the setting where the student will use the skill.

Alternative Portfolios
www.ihdi.uky.edu/projects/KAP/

Alternative Assessment **Portfolio assessment** is popular with students without disabilities in general education classrooms (Meisels et al., 1994). This technique has also been employed with students with moderate and severe disabilities (Kleinert, Kearns, & Kennedy, 1997). The assessment includes a description of the student's primary mode of communication (oral, sign, alternative, or gesture), weekly schedule, individual projects, and work résumé, and a letter from the student's parents (pp. 90–91). The portfolio is then evaluated as to the student's performance across a variety of activities, interactions, and contexts.

Collaborative Teams Collaborative teams are made up of two or more appropriate professionals (see Table 12.3) who work together to assess students, determine their strengths and needs, and plan systematic activity-based instruction (Snell & Janney, 2000; Snell & Brown, 2000). Members of teams share information from their respective areas of specialization. A well-working team develops common values and agrees to operational ground rules for evaluating themselves and students (Snell & Janney, 2000).

Systematic activity-based instruction is the teaching of skills in the context in which they will be used. Basic academic skills will often be embedded in the skill training. For example, Colin, a young man with cerebral palsy, is being taught how to buy food in the cafeteria. He learns how to maneuver his wheelchair into the line, survey the food, make a selection and take it to the cashier, pay for it, and count his change. Reading the name of the food and its price, knowing whether he has enough money to pay for it, and determining if the change is correct all involve basic academic skills (Hunt, Soto, Maier, & Doering, 2003).

■ Adapting Teaching Strategies

Teaching and Assessing

There are two approaches to teaching children with multiple and severe disabilities. One recognizes that development starts before birth, that it continues rapidly in the first year, and that the individual is more flexible and more easily influenced by environmental input during the early years. The other, newer approach uses knowledge of age-appropriate development to decide what the child will need to know to function in a specific environment and what skills the child already possesses. The teacher then develops strategies to teach the child specific activities that will lead to mastery of a set of functional skills that support independence.

To understand these approaches, it is necessary to understand some of the basics of normal (ordinary) development.

One of the great achievements in human beings is the ability to communicate by using symbols, usually words or signs. A symbol is something that stands for something else—a person, event, attitude, feeling, concept. It usually refers directly to the thing signified; for example, "mama" is mother, usually a specific mother. A gesture is not a symbol unless it is part of a system, such as sign language, in which specific gestures always mean the same thing. Gestures that are not part of a sign language system usually have a variety of meanings. For example, the gesture of pointing can mean "See the dog," "Bring me a toy," or "I want to go outside."

A symbol system grows out of genetically programmed prelinguistic behaviors such as cries, grunts, the social smile, eye contact, and interaction with another followed by babbling; finally, around 12 months of age, a child's oral sounds become words (Bates, 1979; Dromi, 1993). Rowland (1996) states four basic reasons for communicating: to refuse, to obtain, to engage in social interaction, and to provide or seek information. This applies to both the preintentional reflexive-reactive state and the mature intentional communication period. After 12 months of age, the average child proceeds rapidly from one word to the mastery of thousands by age 5, using them in a variety of ways to express logical communications and cognitive functioning.

Both speech and gestures can be part of a communication system. Persons who are most severely cognitively disabled, however, may never learn either speech or a gestural system and have to rely on nonlinguistic systems to communicate their wants and needs (Sternberg, 1991).

At the beginning of the education process, an early intervention teacher does not know how far the individual with multiple disabilities will develop. The prelinguistic system usually begins at birth and definitely begins by 2 months of age for the individual with severe retardation. Therefore, education must begin early to identify the prelinguistic vocalizations and gestures so they can be developed into a communication system and ideally a symbol system consisting of signs or words.

A major problem with children with multiple and severe disabilities is that they tend to lack the natural, genetically programmed inquisitiveness, curiosity, and desire to manipulate objects that come automatically to the average, nondisabled child. The facilitator (teacher or family member) must encourage children with multiple and severe disabilities to learn that they can use their genetically programmed prelinguistic skills and sounds to communicate—that is, they can use a gesture to show, to request, to accept, or to refuse. These simple sensorimotor patterns can help the individual move from internal worlds to the external world (Dunst & Lowe, 1986). Developing these genetically programmed gestures into a communication system enables the individual with severe and profound disabilities to relate to people in his or her environment. The importance of teaching social skills is a major educational goal from infancy to maturity (Gresham, Sugai, & Horwer, 2001; Kolb & Hanley-Maxwell, 2003).

> Some type of communication system needs to be taught to children who otherwise would have difficulty communicating.

Preschool

Most young children with multiple and severe disabilities attend special preschools for half a day or a full day. Mastery of communication skills is usually the major aim of the curriculum. The ability it teaches to recognize the self as a person is also included (recall our discussion of Murphy and Byrne's [1983] six-step developmental sequence earlier in this chapter). The curriculum does not teach isolated skills; it teaches activities and routines that combine functional communication with physical and social needs. In addition, specialized personnel, such as physical, speech, and occupational therapists, will assist by providing appropriate therapies.

A major goal of the preschool is to move the children forward so they will begin to act on the environment by manipulating objects, making requests to satisfy their needs, and exercising their natural curiosity—in other words, learning how to learn. The skills should relate to communication, mobility, social skills, and self-management. The best generalization and maintenance occurs when the skill

▶ Has immediate utility to the individual

▶ Produces something the student wants

▶ Was acquired in the social context where it will be used

▶ Is appropriate for the student's level of development

▶ Is practical and useful

▶ Is adaptable (Goetz, Guess, & Campbell, 1987)

Those characteristics are the guidelines for the development of any skill, from drinking from a cup or eating an apple to working in a fast-food restaurant.

In addition to overcoming the child's disabilities, the teacher or facilitator must overcome two other obstacles: (1) Caregivers usually are less flexible and less permissive than teachers in encouraging creative activity, and they are more intrusive in their interactions with children with multiple and severe disabilities. They tend to do things for the children, such as putting on their coats, instead of teaching them how to do things. This is a less-than-ideal learning strategy (Linden, Kankkunen, & Tjellstrom, 1985). (2) The young child with multiple disabilities is usually less inquisitive, more withdrawn, less active, and less fun than a child without disabilities, and engages in little play with objects. The teacher has to help families learn new strategies and also help the child overcome his or her lack of involvement with the environment. The teacher does so by teaching family members the meaning of their child's gestures and how to be more interactive with their child.

Primary and Secondary School

In elementary school, individuals with multiple and severe disabilities and those with severe retardation are likely to have similar curricula, which are continuations of efforts to teach functional skills that lead to clear communication and independence. If the child has moderate retardation, more complex skills can be taught—skills that are useful, practical, survival oriented, and socially appropriate.

Major efforts are being made to teach these children self determination skills and to help them become more involved in their own decision making (Wehmeyer, Agran, & Hughes, 1998). Self-determination skills include the expression of rights (the ability to say no, ask for favors, and make requests) and the ability to express positive and negative feelings. Some students will have to express their feelings nonverbally or with the help of augmentative or alternative communication systems (Grigal, Nobert, Moon, & Graham, 2003).

Person-centered planning refers to the process of designing programs for individual students rather than attempting to fit them into programs with set expectations (Mount, 2000a). The process first assesses the individual's capacities, strengths, interests, and desires. By building on the strengths and interests, a program can help the individual become as independent as his or her disability will allow, function as an active member of family and community, and participate in recreational activities. The goals of person-centered planning mesh well with the goals of the self-determination movement (Brown & Cohen, 1996; Martin et al., 2003).

The person-centered approach permits the individual to make choices throughout the day (Downing, 1999). For example, he or she can select a snack, choose which music to listen to, decide what job to do, pick a place to sit during lunch, and so on (p. 81). Curriculum adaptations in inclusive settings include adapting what is taught into functional skills for use in daily living, such as counting money or social communication. Motor skills are used in a variety of settings and promoting life skills (Bigge, Best, & Heller, 2001). Partial participation is taking place when the student participates in the same activity as the rest of the class but with special modifications to the activity that adapt it to the student's disabilities.

Skills Needed for Assertiveness

SKILL AREA	DISCRETE SKILLS
Expression of rights	Identifies and articulates rights Identifies and articulates associated responsibilities Discriminates conflicts between rights of individual(s) and groups Identifies and articulates personal beliefs and values Identifies and articulates differences among assertive, nonassertive, and aggressive behaviors Discriminates among statements of wants, needs, opinion, and fact Understands inherent risk factor in assertion
Verbal assertion skills	Expresses rights statement in brief, concise, and direct manner Communicates rights statement in first person Discriminates between and employs refusals and behavior-change requests Communicates opinions and beliefs appropriately Employs appropriate tone of voice Uses intonation and timing effectively Responds appropriately to aggression and persists in assertion
Nonverbal assertion skills	Uses and understands body language Uses gestures and facial expressions appropriately Makes eye contact appropriately Uses appropriate posture and body positioning
Expression of elaborations	Communicates understanding of others' feelings, opinions, or experiences Employs negotiation, compromise, and persuasion skills Modulates voice characteristics to match elaboration
Conversation skills	Practices active listening skills

Source: From M. L. Wehmeyer, M. Agran, & C. Hughes, *Teaching self-determination to students with disabilities: Basic skills for successful transition* (p. 222) (Baltimore: Paul H. Brookes, 1998). Reprinted with permission.

Teachers can directly introduce a skill, discuss it, identify steps, model the skill, rehearse or role-play, and assist the student in generalizing the skill. The box above lists social skill training instructional steps.

A guide for planning inclusive education, *Choosing Options and Accommodation for Children (COACH)*, emphasizes collaborative teamwork with the family as the cornerstone of educational planning (Giangreco, Cloninger, & Iverson, 1998). The manual includes clear statements of goals, activities, and sample forms, including forms for interviews, assessments, and IEPs, and community and school worksheets.

The key elements of the curriculum are to develop throughout elementary, middle, and high school individualized programs that lead to successful transition into the community and adult lifestyles. A teacher trained in alternative instructional strategies is necessary to accomplish these goals.

Communication boards and other augmentative systems have been developed to help the nonvocal student add to and supplement available speech.
(© Bob Daemmrich Photography Inc.)

Teaching Strategies for Nonvocal Students

Many children with severe physical and cognitive disabilities have major communication impairments. They often are unable to use speech functionally. This inability to communicate is one of the most formidable obstacles that children with multiple and severe disabilities face. It prevents them from interacting successfully with their environments and impedes their ability to learn from interactive experiences, things that nondisabled children do readily.

The use of signing, pantomime, and gesture are techniques that can be used with the nonverbal student (Mirenda, 1999). And there are other techniques:

▶ Symbols like the golden arches of McDonald's

▶ Tangible symbols such as objects that feel or sound like what they are used for such as keys to indicate "I want to open a door"

▶ Photographs to represent specific objects or places

▶ Black and white drawings

▶ Textured symbols (Mirenda, 1999, pp. 119–130)

Augmentative and alternative communication devices have been developed to help students who are nonvocal communicate. A simple device is the *communication board,* a piece of cardboard or other stable material on which pictures,

Computers with speech synthesizers produce messages and written text. Custom-made keyboards, touch screens, and the mouse provide students with access to a wide array of curricula.

words, or symbols can be written or attached. Computer screens also can serve as communication devices. These devices are designed not to replace speech but to add to and supplement available speech. With these devices the student can indicate needs, preferences, and responses by pointing to items (direct selection). The student may also look in the direction of an item (scanning), and the teacher recognizes the student's response (Beukelman & Mirenda, 1992).

Technology for Nonvocal Students

Trace Research and Development Center www.trace.wisc.edu

Technological advances have increased the sophistication of augmentative devices. There are wall charts that are battery operated, voice synthesizers in several different languages, and a wide range of devices for computer access. Beukelman and Mirenda (1994) mention that a compact disc containing over sixteen thousand product descriptions can be obtained from Trace Research and Development Center, S-151 Waisman Center, 1500 Highland Avenue, Madison, WI 53705.

■ Adapting Technology

A wide range of software is available to assist the teaching of persons with disabilities.

A national commitment to support and encourage the development of computer technology for use by and with persons with disabilities is contained in IDEA as amended in 1997. The act encourages widespread use of computer technology with persons with disabilities for education, measurement, vocational training, and transition to the world of work (Greenwood, 1994).

Instructional Technology

Computers are becoming standard equipment in classes for children with disabilities. Curriculum software—programs too numerous to mention—is being developed continuously. There are programs designed specifically for individuals with learning, hearing, vision, motor, and cognitive disabilities (see Council for Exceptional Children, 1994).

Assistive Technology

Don Johnston Developmental communication equipment www.donjohnston.com

Some children may need to use head pointers to type. Some can use a single finger to call up software (the curriculum) to read, and they can respond to it with single-finger pressure. Notebook computers, which are the size of a textbook and weigh from seven to eight pounds, are very useful for children with disabilities who possess a communication system (Cary & Sale, 1994).

Electronic communication devices range from single-level, which can produce voice outputs of a message, to multilevel, and handle more than twenty messages. See Table 12.5. The simple devices can be used by the teacher to record a message, and the student can record over the message to reply. The more complicated devices can be programmed and connected to printers or calculators; they can also be used to store lengthy text. (See the appendix in Downing, 1999, for a list of more than twenty communication companies and centers.)

Houghton Mifflin Teacher Education website http://education.college.hmco.com/students

See the Houghton Mifflin Teacher Education website for an expanded list of assistive technology equipment.

TABLE 12.5
Wisconsin Assistive Technology Initiative Assistive Technology Checklist

WRITING	READING, STUDYING, AND MATH

WRITING

Mechanics of Writing
- ❏ Regular pencil/pen
- ❏ Pencil/pen with adaptive grip
- ❏ Adapted paper (e.g., raised line, highlighted lines)
- ❏ Slantboard
- ❏ Use of prewritten words/phrases
- ❏ Templates
- ❏ Portable word processor to keyboard instead of write
- ❏ Computer with word processing software
- ❏ Portable scanner with word processing software
- ❏ Voice recognition software to word process
- ❏ Other:

Computer Access
- ❏ Keyboard w/Easy Access or Access DOS
- ❏ Word prediction, abbreviation/expansion to reduce keystrokes
- ❏ Keyguard
- ❏ Arm support (e.g., Ergo Rest)
- ❏ Track ball/track pad/joystick w/ on-screen keyboard
- ❏ Alternate keyboard (e.g., IntelliKeys, Discover Board, TASH)
- ❏ Mouth stick/Head Master/Tracker w/ on-screen keyboard
- ❏ Switch with Morse code
- ❏ Switch with scanning
- ❏ Voice recognition software
- ❏ Other:

Composing Written Material
- ❏ Word cards/word book/word wall
- ❏ Pocket dictionary/thesaurus
- ❏ Writing templates
- ❏ Electronic/talking electronic dictionary/thesaurus/spell checker (e.g., Franklin Speaking Homework Wiz)
- ❏ Word processing w/ spell checker/grammar checker
- ❏ Talking word processing
- ❏ Abbreviation/expansion
- ❏ Word processing w/ writing supports
- ❏ Multimedia software
- ❏ Voice recognition software
- ❏ Other:

Communication
- ❏ Communication board/book w/pictures/objects/letters/words
- ❏ Eye gaze board/frame
- ❏ Simple voice output device (e.g., BIGmack, Cheap Talk, Voice in a Box, MicroVoice, Talking Picture Frame)
- ❏ Voice output device w/levels (e.g., 6 Level Voice in a Box, Macaw, Digivox)
- ❏ Voice output device w/icon sequencing (e.g., Alpha Talker II, Vanguard, Chatbox)
- ❏ Voice output device w/ dynamic display (e.g., Dynavox, Speaking Dynamically w/ laptop computer/Freestyle)
- ❏ Device w/ speech synthesis for typing (e.g., Cannon Communicator, Link, Write:Out Loud w/ laptop)
- ❏ Other:

READING, STUDYING, AND MATH

Reading
- ❏ Standard text
- ❏ Predictable books
- ❏ Changes in text size, spacing, color, background color
- ❏ Book adapted for page turning (e.g., page flutters. 3-ring binder)
- ❏ Use of pictures/symbols with text (e.g., Picture it, Writing with Symbols 2000)
- ❏ Talking electronic device/software to pronounce challenging words (e.g., Franklin Speaking Homework Wiz, American Heritage Dictionary)
- ❏ Single word scanners (e.g., Seiko Reading Pen)
- ❏ Scanner w/OCR and talking word processor
- ❏ Electronic books
- ❏ Other:

Learning/Studying
- ❏ Print or picture schedule
- ❏ Low-tech aids to find materials (e.g., index tabs, color coded folders)
- ❏ Highlight text (e.g., markers, highlight tape, ruler, etc.)
- ❏ Recorded material (books on tape, taped lectures with number coded index, etc.)
- ❏ Voice output reminders for assignments, steps of task, etc.
- ❏ Electronic organizers
- ❏ Pagers/electronic reminders
- ❏ Single word scanners
- ❏ Hand-held scanners
- ❏ Software for concept development/manipulation of objects (e.g., Blocks in Motion, Toy store)—may use alternate input device, e.g., switch, touch window
- ❏ Software for organization of ideas and studying (e.g., Inspiration, ClarisWorks Outline, PowerPoint)
- ❏ Palm computers
- ❏ Other:

Math
- ❏ Abacus/Math Line
- ❏ Enlarged math worksheets
- ❏ Low tech alternatives for answering
- ❏ Math "Smart Chart"
- ❏ Money calculator and Coinulator
- ❏ Tactile/voice output measuring devices
- ❏ Talking watches/clocks
- ❏ Calculator/calculator with printout
- ❏ Calculator with large keys and/or large display
- ❏ Talking calculator
- ❏ Calculator with special features (e.g., fraction translation)
- ❏ On-screen/scanning calculator.
- ❏ Alternative keyboard (e.g., IntelliKeys)
- ❏ Software with cueing for math computation (may use adapted input methods)
- ❏ Software for manipulation of objects
- ❏ Voice recognition software
- ❏ Other:

Source: From J. Bigge, S. Best, & K. Heller, *Teaching individuals with physical, health, or multiple disabilities* (4th ed.) (Upper Saddle River, NJ: Merrill-Prentice Hall, 2001). Reprinted with permission of Pearson Education.

(*text continues from page 483*)

Some vision defects such as cataracts are easy to spot. However, some hearing defects are difficult to identify and may not be detected until the child is 2 or 3 months of age. For early identification, screening at birth is highly recommended. Most states require mandatory screening at birth in the hospital. Most physical defects can be diagnosed early by observing the infant's lack of normal reflex and body movement. Some physical disabilities may not be diagnosed until late in the first year of life or in some children with disabilities, not until adolescence.

Infants who are premature or of low birth weight (usually both) may have experienced lack of oxygen during the birth process (anoxia), usually as a result of the umbilical cord's being wrapped around the neck or of being breech born (delivery feet first). Such children are monitored carefully, because these types of birth are often associated with disabilities.

Other defects such as some types of spina bifida (see Chapter 13; Batshaw, 1997; Williamson, 1987) can easily be identified from obvious physical deformities. In some types of spina bifida, an opening is present on the spinal cord, and other children who are affected may have enlarged heads from excess spinal fluid in the brain cavity (hydrocephalus). These children have surgery shortly after birth to drain the excess fluid from the brain because if the condition is allowed to continue, it will cause retardation. The process of draining is called *shunting*.

Children with Down syndrome can also be identified, from their flat facial profile and upwardly slanted eyes, as well as from their low Apgar scores (Batshaw & Perret, 1992). Children with Down syndrome may require immediate medical supervision for survival.

Individuals with spina bifida and Down syndrome can suffer from multiple disabilities and must be examined carefully at birth to determine their immediate needs. Children in both groups, however, vary across a wide range of cognitive functioning and will need intensive intervention to help them achieve their highest potential.

■ Transition

From Home and School to Community and Work

The recent emphasis on transitional programming from high school to work and supportive employment (Moon & Inge, 2000) has opened new vistas for persons with multiple and severe disabilities. Persons with multiple and severe disabilities can be empowered to make decisions about their own preferences for work, living arrangements, and leisure activities (Brown & Gothelf, 1996; Brown & Lehr, 1996). Wehmeyer, Agran, and Hughes (1998) suggest that for assertive training for transition, the teacher should include a series of basic elements and activities, which are listed in Table 12.6 on the following pages. Such empowerment suggests moving toward supportive apartments, home-ownership, and cooperative and shared living space (Brown & Gothelf, 1996). The group home may not be the ideal housing model. Some articles indicate a shift from program-centered to person-centered decision making. An important aspect of this perspective is the belief that person-centered programs will improve the mental and physical health of persons with severe disabilities (Newton, Horner, Ard, LeBaron, & Sapperton, 1994; Mount, 2000b; Wehman, 1996).

TABLE 12.6
Transition Support Strategies

SUPPORT STRATEGY	DEFINITION	EXAMPLE
Teach social skills	Teach student social behaviors that facilitate interactions with significant others in a manner considered socially appropriate.	A student initiates conversation with peers without disabilities while at lunch or between classes.
Teach self-management and independence	Teach student self-management skills to enable him or her to perform expected behaviors more independently.	Using pictures of household tasks while cleaning her home, a young woman looks at a picture, performs the task, records completion of the task, and moves on to the next task.
Identify independence objectives	Survey student's environments (e.g., home, community, school, work) through observation and by interviewing student and significant others to identify areas in which performance is not consistent with expectations.	In a restaurant in which a student works, ask the supervisor to identify specific tasks that the student is not performing consistently when serving food.
Assess social acceptance	Assess student's acceptance of everyday performance via evaluations completed by student's teachers, employers, and others and by comparing student's performance to that of peers.	A student compares her evaluation of her attendance at school with her teacher's evaluation.
Identify co-worker, peer, and family support	Identify individuals who may provide supports for a student at home, school, work, or in the community.	Co-workers are identified who may assist a new employee in learning required job skills and who may interact socially with the employee during breaks or lunch.
Identify student's preferences and choices	Identify student's expectations and preferences with respect to daily living and support choice making by observations and interviews with student and other stakeholders; in addition, assess student's choice-making and decision-making skills.	Observe a graduating senior's participation in his or her chosen recreation activity during free time over a 2-week period.
Monitor social acceptance across time	Establish a continuous schedule by which student, teachers, employers, co-workers, and significant others evaluate acceptance of student's performance; use evaluations to identify and discuss discrepancies between observed and expected performance.	A schedule is established in which an employee's job supervisor completes evaluation of employee's social behavior on a weekly basis. Supervisor discusses each evaluation with the employee, including areas that differ from the supervisor's expectations.
Identify environmental support	Identify naturally occurring cues in the student's workplace and other environments that will support him or her in initiating and completing expected and desired behavior.	A man employed in housekeeping in a motel learns to empty wastebaskets when they are overflowing with trash.

(continued)

TABLE 12.6 *(continued)*
Transition Support Strategies

SUPPORT STRATEGY	DEFINITION	EXAMPLE
Match support to student's needs	Match existing support identified to those areas in which student needs support.	An employee fails to take breaks or return back to his or her work station on time. The employee is taught to go on break when co-workers leave their job stations and return to work when co-workers do.
Teach choice making and decision making	Teach the student skills that are necessary to make choices and decisions and to express preferences, and provide opportunities to exercise choice.	A high school sophomore chooses to work in a child care center rather than a fast-food restaurant.

Source: Adapted from M. L. Wehmeyer, M. Agran, & C. Hughes, *Teaching self-determination to students with disabilities: Basic skills for successful transition* (pp. 64–65) (Baltimore: Paul H. Brookes, 1998). Reprinted with permission.

Transition programs from school to adult life aim for lifestyles for those with multiple and severe disabilities that develop their valued participation in the world of work with its routines, its monetary benefits, and its social relationships that build the self-confidence and self-efficacy of the individual (O'Neill, Gothelf, Cohen, Lehman, & Woolf, 1991). To aid in transition, it is useful to interview the family (IDEA 1997 mandates involvement of the family) to ascertain their hopes and expectations for their child and to secure information about family support and transportation. The process should begin as early as when the child is 12 years of age.

Also included in IDEA 1997 is the concept of involving the student in making decisions about his or her future. The focus should be not only on limitations but also on recognition of the individual's skills and areas in which he or she can act independently. This includes becoming as autonomous as possible in all environments, self-regulation, self-evaluation, self-confidence, and ways to reach desired goals (Wehmeyer, Agran, & Hughes, 1998). To be able to accomplish this participation, the individual needs to be taught to move from high school vocational skills development to the community setting in which the work is to take place. This requires a *transition coordinator,* who plans for and assists in the transition (Bellamy, Rhodes, Mank, & Albin, 1988; Falvey, Coot, Bishop, & Grenot-Scheyer, 1989; O'Neill, Gothelf, Cohen, Lehman, & Woolf, 1991).

A transition coordinator assists in the transition from school to work.

Competitive paid employment at or above the minimum wage is still infrequent for persons with multiple and severe disabilities who may need ongoing support to perform in a work setting. Supportive employment is subsidized with government funds to encourage the employment of individuals with multiple and severe disabilities. It is conducted in a variety of settings (for example, fast-food restaurants, supermarkets, parks, and libraries) with additional support provided to include supervision and skills development for the individual.

The goal is to hold a paying job successfully (functional competence) and to live one's own life. Ideally, to support these goals, working side by side with those with multiple and severe disabilities, the nondisabled appreciate them as valued members of society (O'Neill et al., 1991). Public acceptance leads to acceptance of persons with severe disabilities taking part in leisure activities, developing relationships with nondisabled persons, and pursuing interests of their own (O'Neill et al., 1991).

The goal of the transition coordinator is to find age-appropriate settings in the community, prepare the person in that setting, and teach the individual how to function in that setting in accordance with the expectations of nondisabled persons (Falvey, 1989; Kregel, 1994).

An individual transition plan (ITP) is now being developed for each individual in these programs. The ITP requires a great deal of information from the school, the individual, the parents, and the community. Questions to be answered include the following:

Individual Transition Plan

▶ What will the student need to learn before leaving school?

▶ Where will the person live as an adult?

▶ What activities will replace school for recreation?

▶ How will this individual support himself or herself?

▶ What will he or she do in leisure time?

▶ How will this person travel using community transportation?

▶ How will he or she gain access to medical care?

▶ What will be the relationship with his or her family? (adapted from O'Neill et al., 1991)

Naturally, every person with multiple and severe disabilities is different from any other. Such persons have similar but different needs. No one set of treatments can cover everyone adequately. It is clear that the coordinator must have the skill to develop a plan for each person. The teacher or coordinator collects information on the individual to find the most suitable community site, to conduct a task analysis of what will be required at that work site, and then to initiate a prescriptive program to meet these demands. The coordinator will try to match the individual to activities on the basis of the person's preferences.

■ Family and Lifespan Issues

Attempts to normalize the lifestyles of children with multiple and severe disabilities must be followed by the normalization of the lifestyles of adults in the community. Over the past twenty-five years, substantial efforts have been made to create community living and vocational arrangements to provide for these adults and to prevent the institutionalization of youngsters who have been living in the community.

Living Arrangements

Programs for community living include living facilities, vocational and rehabilitation workshops, and recreational services. Coordinated team planning in the community is considered the appropriate manner to support people with disabilities so they can live independently in their community (Bradley, Ashbaugh, & Blaney, 1994).

Major efforts are being made to enable persons with severe and profound disabilities to live and work as independently as they are able (Brown & Gothelf, 1996). The emerging trend emphasizes the involvement of the person with a disability and his or her family in decision making about work, leisure, and living arrangements (Bradley, Ashbaugh, & Blaney 1994; U.S. Department of Education, 1999).

Vocational Opportunities

Another step in the integration of adults with multiple and severe disabilities is providing appropriate vocational opportunities. Various options exist, among them day treatment and day habilitation programs, sheltered workshops, and supportive competitive employment. The Virginia Commonwealth University Rehabilitation and Training Center offers a Web-based certification service for supportive employment opportunities (VCURTC, P.O. Box 842011, Richmond, VA 23284-2011). The center also provides useful material for workplace support. Table 12.7 lists other services that are available.

Day Treatment Programs

The day treatment program is the most restrictive setting for adults with multiple and severe disabilities. These programs are

> designed to provide therapeutic activities for disabled workers whose physical or mental impairment is so severe as to make their productive capacity inconsequential. Therapeutic activities include custodial activities (such as activities that focus on teaching basic living skills) and any purposeful activity so long as work or production is not the main purpose. (U.S. Department of Labor as cited in Bellamy, Rhodes, Bourbeau, & Mank, 1986, p. 260)

The purpose of these centers is to teach necessary life skills. Rather than providing vocational opportunities, the day treatment center provides continuing education.

Day Habilitation Programs

Day habilitation programs are funded by the individual states. They are often based in classrooms, but much of the experience provided takes place in the community. Transportation is furnished by the program. There also are individualized day habilitation programs. In these cases, individuals may volunteer in the community, participate in community recreation, and/or work in their homes with support.

Sheltered Workshops

The **sheltered workshop** provides vocational services to adults with disabilities (Bellamy et al., 1986). The U.S. Department of Labor defines a sheltered workshop as

> a charitable organization or institution conducted not-for-profit, but for the purpose of carrying out a recognized rehabilitation program for handicapped workers, and/or providing such individuals with remunerative employment or other occupational rehabilitating activity of an educational or therapeutic nature. (Bellamy et al., 1986, p. 260)

TABLE 12.7
Vocational Rehabilitation Services

SERVICE	DESCRIPTION OF SERVICE
Evaluation	To determine a person's interests, capabilities, aptitudes, and limitations, and the range of services needed to prepare the individual for employment
Counseling and guidance	To help the person aim for a job in keeping with his or her interests, capabilities, aptitudes, and limitations
Medical and hospital care	To attend, if needed, to mental or physical problems that are obstacles to job preparation
Job training	To provide training that fits the person's needs and that leads to a definite work goal; can include personal adjustment training, prevocational training, vocational training, on-the-job training, and training in a sheltered workshop
Maintenance payments	To cover increases in a person's basic living expenses because of participation in vocational rehabilitation
Transportation	To support and maximize the benefits of other services being received
Services to family members	To help the person achieve the maximum benefit from other services being provided
Interpreter services	To assist the person with visual impairments
Reader services	To assist the person with visual impairments, including note-taking services and orientation and mobility services
Aids and devices	To provide the person with needed aids and devices, such as telecommunication devices, sensory aids, artificial limbs, braces, and wheelchairs
Tools and equipment	To provide the person with tools and equipment needed to perform the job
Recruitment and training services	To provide new work opportunities in public service employment
Job placement	To help the person find a job, taking into consideration the person's abilities and training; includes placement into supported employment
Job follow-up	To help the person make whatever adjustments are needed to succeed at the job into which he or she has been placed
Occupational licenses or permits	To provide the person with the occupational licenses or permits that the law requires a person have before entering an occupation
Other	To provide other services that an individual may need to become employable

Source: L. Kupper (Ed.). (1991). "Options After High School for Youth with Disabilities." *NICHCY Transition Summary,* no. 7, p. 8. Available from the National Information Center for Children and Youth with Disabilities, P.O. Box 1492, Washington, DC 20013.

ECOLOGY OF THE CHILD

SCHOOL   ## A Career Taking Off

Ali Zebari is a senior at Mountlake Terrace High School in Mountlake Terrace, Washington. Ali has osteogenesis imperfecta and uses a motorized wheelchair for mobility. With plans to attend college and an interest in engineering and computer sciences, Ali wanted to get a head start on mapping out his career path and gaining valuable work-related experience.

Ali accessed the Career Center at his high school last year and found out about the School-to-Work Tech Prep Program. Working closely with his career counselor, Ali was able to secure a summer internship last year with Boeing in Everett, Washington. "The reason I wanted this internship is because they work with airplanes and I was very interested in how they make them and make them fly," says Ali. Like other internships, Boeing's Tech Prep program offers planned learning activities and an opportunity to experience work firsthand.

For Ali, the internship gave him an opportunity to practice disclosing his disability and asking for accommodations. This was a positive experience for him and his employer and Ali feels more confident about himself and his self-advocacy skills.

As part of his continuing involvement with Tech Prep, Ali will be returning to Boeing again this summer for a second internship. Through Tech Prep, Ali is earning college credits through this internship. He is off to a good start in his post-secondary education and is gaining highly valuable work experience. He is on the right track to a successful and challenging career.

More information on The School-to-Work Opportunities Act of 1994 can be found at

---

Although the goal of sheltered workshops is to prepare individuals with multiple and severe disabilities to obtain and maintain competitive employment, placement out of the segregated work environment rarely occurs (Bellamy et al., 1986).

Supportive Competitive Employment

> Supportive competitive employment is more inclusive than other vocational opportunities.

Day treatment centers and sheltered workshops violate many of the philosophical tenets of inclusion, supportive employment, and paid employment. The settings are segregated, and they do not fall within the boundaries of normalization, least restrictive environment, or partial participation. These shortcomings have increased the popularity of **supportive competitive employment** training programs. These programs are attractive because both the individual and the public benefit (Bellamy et al., 1988).

Hill and Wehman (1983) presented an analysis of workshop versus competitive employment costs over a four-year period. They followed ninety adults who had moderate or severe disabilities, and they measured many variables, including the number of months each person worked, the number of staff hours needed at each workplace, the income earned, and the cost of operation. After four years, the competitive employment program had saved the public $100,000.

http://www.stw.ed.gov/general/general.htm. Or, contact the School-to-Work coordinator in your local school district for information on available programs.

High School/High Tech is a community-based partnership of parents, educators, rehabilitation professionals, and business representatives. The partnership combines site tours, job shadowing, internships, and mentoring to encourage students with disabilities to pursue careers in the technology industry. The program encourages students to attend college and earn degrees. Contact your State Governor's Committee on Employment of People with Disabilities to find out if there is a High School/High Tech program in your area. High School/High Tech is sponsored by the Office of Disability Employment Policy (ODEP), U.S. Department of Labor (formerly the President's Committee on Employment of People with Disabilities). For more information about ODEP programs, consult the ODEP Web site at http://www.dol.gov/dol/odep/public/pubs/hshtdo/toc.htm or call: (202) 376-6200 (voice); TDD: (202) 376-6205.

Source: From School: A career taking off, *Exceptional Parent*, (July 2001). Reprinted with permission.

WHAT IS THE CONTEXT?

Ali, a senior in high school, has osteogenesis imperfecta and uses a motorized wheelchair. He has completed a summer internship with Boeing, where he worked with airplanes. He gained experience with disclosing his disability and asking for accommodations.

PIVOTAL ISSUES FOR TEACHERS

- How can you encourage students to investigate work and career choices?

- How can students learn to advocate for themselves and create greater self-esteem?

- What internships are available for students with multiple and severe disabilities?

Data that encourage supportive competitive employment and discourage sheltered workshop employment are growing. But determining how to deliver the most effective and efficient vocational opportunities to people with multiple and severe disabilities remains an unsolved problem. Rusch, Chadsey-Rusch, and Johnson (1992, p. 146) described supportive employment approaches.

Approaches to Supportive Employment

▶ *Individual placement model:* The individual is hired by an employer, and a job coach assists the employee, gradually decreasing the amount of support until the employee is able to perform the task without assistance.

▶ *Clustered placement model:* A group of six to eight individuals working for a company receives continuous guidance and supervision from a job coach employed by the company.

▶ *Mobile work crew:* A group works out of a van at several locations in the community under the supervision of a job coach, who provides continuous guidance and direction.

These models offer a range of supervision levels, from independence to continuous supervision. The models allow many individuals with multiple and severe disabilities the opportunity to engage in meaningful work. Currently,

Fewer than 30 percent of people with multiple and severe disabilities are employed.

fewer than 30 percent of the population with multiple and severe disabilities are employed, but it is hoped that this percentage can be greatly increased in the future.

Szymanski (1994) suggested that lifespan considerations for transition should include interventions that

▶ Are designed to be maximally under the control of the individual rather than others

▶ Are designed to facilitate independence or interdependence and autonomy

▶ Use the least intrusive means that are effective

▶ Use the most natural interventions for the particular work environment (pp. 406–407)

The Rehabilitation Research and Training Center at Virginia Commonwealth University is a valuable resource for technical assistance and information on supportive employment. The goal of the center is to "improve supportive employment outcomes for individuals with the most severe disabilities."

Virginia Commonwealth University Rehabilitation Research and Training Center on Workplace Support www.worksupport.com

Impact on the Family

Never underestimate the impact on a family of having a child with severe and multiple disabilities. Some families suffer grief and mourn because they do not have their ideal child. Others show amazing strength in coping with the emotional, physical, and economic demands placed on them.

Involvement in family-focused intervention programs has major effects on the family's concept of its effectiveness (Trivette, Dunst, Boyd, & Hamby, 1995; National Early Childhood Technical Assistance System [NEC-TAS], 2000). Some families face the lifelong challenge of providing assistance to a child with sensory impairments who is in a wheelchair. Consider the needs of a child who uses a wheelchair. One wheelchair will not serve for a lifetime. A child may require larger prostheses as he or she ages. Leg braces will need to be lengthened; wheelchairs will need to be larger; glasses and hearing aids will need to be replaced. From the outset, the family needs expert diagnosis and treatment plans (Turnbull & Turnbull, 2000).

The environmental issues for families that we discussed in Chapter 2 are relevant here. Having a child with severe and multiple disabilities causes added stress. It modifies the family's concept of itself and creates lifetime demands that can be anticipated from infancy. Consider a child with a speech deficit or a child with Down syndrome. For the former, there is a possibility of complete remediation, and the latter may attain nearly normal cognitive functioning, independent living, and supportive employment. Such accomplishments are difficult to predict for children with multiple and severe disabilities.

Intervention will focus on how far the child can progress. Is the child likely to be able to master sign language, control a motorized wheelchair, or use a word processor or a communication board? Some children will be able, and some will not. Those who are can move on to independent living and supportive employment. The others may be their family's responsibility for life. Family resources will be siphoned into child care, equipment, and therapies. The needs of the child with multiple and severe disabilities will absorb large amounts of time that otherwise would be spent in husband-wife interactions or family-peer interactions. Brothers and sisters will be involved in caring for their disabled sibling and lose some of their playtime or peer-interaction time.

These families need expert counseling and a case coordinator who is fully aware of community resources and services. Counseling can assist family members in working through their grief and accepting their child's disabilities.

If the family is headed by a single parent, multiple supports will be needed. A single caregiver may have to seek public assistance to survive economically and provide the therapies and education the child requires. A working parent (usually the mother) may have to give up her career (see Chapter 3). In a two-parent family, if it is an economic necessity for both parents to work, the loss of income will worsen their problems. As we have seen in cases of children with autism, the family may not be able to afford the preferred treatment.

Active and passive rejection of a child may be a serious issue that needs to be addressed. An additional problem is that so much is unknown about some of these disabilities, such as autism. The family may spend enormous amounts of time seeking an accurate diagnosis and placement for the child.

Finding a baby sitter or respite services to allow the family respite or leisure time is a problem. A child with physical and sensory disabilities may need feeding and toileting assistance beyond what a baby sitter is willing to provide. Parents who seek respite care may require the services of a trained specialist for their child with behavior disorders and sensory impairments. Despite the many issues confronting the family, the child with multiple or severe disabilities can gain family members' respect and enjoyment, demonstrate and receive love, have a sense of humor, and relish being a family member. These children do enrich other lives. It takes admirable strength and courage on their part to master their disabilities to the extent possible.

In essence, a family's needs and problems are intensified by a child with multiple and severe disabilities.

Summary

▶ Not all persons with multiple and severe disabilities have mental retardation and many can achieve an adult status of independent living and competitive work.

▶ Some individuals with multiple and severe disabilities possess some degree of mental retardation. These individuals may need supportive employment and supervised living arrangements as adults.

▶ The current effort in the field of multiple and severe disabilities is to begin intervention as soon after birth as the disability has been diagnosed and to provide appropriate treatment, prostheses, family support, and education to assist the individual to develop to his or her full potential. With the advancement of technology, these children can attain higher-level skills. With inclusion, these children are educated in local schools and more and more frequently in general education classrooms, where they can have contact with and make friends with their nondisabled peers.

▶ The current practice in the field of multiple and severe disabilities is to teach the person to perform functional activities in settings in which he or she will use these skills and to enhance self-advocacy and self-determination practices.

Future Challenges

1. How can community participation be increased?

Supportive employment is an attempt to open up workplaces to persons with multiple and severe disabilities. The goal of providing a variety of meaningful work and vocational opportunities that will benefit both individuals with multiple and severe disabilities and their employers has not been fully achieved. Not all workplaces or communities are prepared to accept them.

2. Who pays the high cost of intervention and support?

The costs of intervention and support are high. Persons with multiple and severe disabilities need specialized training from numerous professionals as well as specialized teaching tools and prostheses. They may require lifetime support. Funds for these services are not always readily available.

3. What is the role of technology?

Technology aids or enables but means fewer jobs for those with fewer skills.

4. How can inclusion of people with multiple and severe disabilities be increased?

Key Terms

cerebral palsy   *p. 479*

criterion-referenced tests   *p. 492*

deafblind   *p. 474*

generalization   *p. 491*

person-centered programs   *p. 484*

portfolio assessment   *p. 492*

self-determination skills   *p. 481*

sheltered workshop   *p. 504*

supportive competitive employment   *p. 506*

Usher syndrome   *p. 474*

Resources

References of Special Interest

Bigge, J., Best, S., & Heller, K. (2004). *Teaching individuals with physical, health, or multiple disabilities* (6th ed.). Upper Saddle River, NJ: Merrill-Prentice Hall. A recent edition of a comprehensive work that discusses educational and treatment issues. Practical suggestions and the names of vendors specializing in assistive technology are provided (pp. 226–227)

Bradley, V., Ashbaugh, J., & Blaney, B. (1994). *Creating Individual supports for people with disabilities.* Baltimore: Paul H. Brookes. *This guide helps individuals change community- and state-based agencies to organizations that become community supports for individuals with disabilities.*

Browder, D. (Ed.). (2001). *Curriculum and assessment for students with moderate and severe disabilities.* New York: Guilford Press. A basic orientation for the range of issues confronting the teaching and assessment of disabled students. Includes family-centered planning, communication and leisure skills, academic skills, inclusion, and transition.

Elias, S. (2005). *Special needs trusts.* Berkeley, CA: Nolo Press. *Provides instructions and forms for establishing a trust fund to pay for the needs of individuals with disabilities. A CD-ROM is also available.*

Gerry, M. H., & McWhorter, C. M. (1991). "A comprehensive analysis of federal statutes and programs for persons with severe disabilities." In L. H. Meyer, C. Peck, & L. Brown (Eds.). *Critical issues in the lives of people with severe disabilities,* pp. 521–525. Baltimore: Paul H. Brookes. *This chapter provides a current review of the varied federal statutes regarding persons with severe and multiple disabilities. It also describes some current operating programs.*

Lehr, D. H., & Brown, F. (2000). *Instruction of students with severe disabilities* (5th ed.). Baltimore: Paul H. Brookes. *Twenty leaders in the field discuss in twelve chapters issues of teaching, policy, integration, research, and suggestions for practice. This book presents current thinking on persons with multiple and severe disabilities.*

Masselwhite, C., & King, D. (1997). *Emergent literary success: Merging technologies with whole language for students with disabilities.* Park City, UT: Creative Communications. *A rich guide filled with teaching suggestions on how to include literacy skills (writing, reading, listening, talking, interacting) in daily classroom activities. Numerous suggestions for modifications for students with specific disabilities are included.*

Wehmeyer, M. L., Agran, M., & Hughes, C. (1998). *Teaching self-determination skills to students with disabilities.* Baltimore: Paul H. Brookes. *A broad compendium of ideas and techniques for teaching independence skills to students. The acquisition of these skills will contribute greatly to students' transition.*

Journals

Research and Practice for Persons with Severe Disabilities (formerly *Journal of the Association for Persons with Severe Handicaps [JASH]*)
www.tash.org/publications

Journal of Visual Impairment and Blindness
www.afb.org/jvib.asp

Professional Organizations

The Association for Persons with Severe Disabilities (TASH)
www.tash.org

National Clearinghouse on Children Who Are Deafblind
www.aade.org

National Rehabilitation Information Center
www.naric.com

National Information Center for Children and Youth with Disabilities (NICHCY)
www.nichcy.org

Rehabilitation Research and Training Center
Virginia Commonwealth University
www.worksupport.com

Virginia Commonwealth University Rehabilitation Research and Training Center on Workplace Supports
www.worksupport.com

Please visit the book's website at **http://education.college.hmco.com/students** for new and updated information on websites listed here and for the mailing addresses of the journals and organizations.

13

Children with Physical Disabilities and Health Impairments

FOCUS QUESTIONS

▶ Is every physical disability or health condition a disabling condition?

▶ How does the age at which a child becomes physically disabled affect the child's adjustment to the condition?

▶ What unique problems are faced by children with physical and health disabilities?

▶ Why is it important for the general classroom teacher to discuss a student's condition openly with the student's classmates?

▶ What technology aids children who have physical and health impairments?

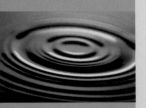

Information and Referral
Resource Network
www.ir-net.com

Infants and young children without disabilities acquire cognitive, language, and social competence by interacting with their physical and social environments (Bower, 1989). They interact by using coordinated motor patterns that are genetically programmed to appear early in life and to assist them in learning what they need to know to adapt to their homes and environments (Bower).

This chapter is concerned with infants and children whose physical disabilities or health impairments interfere with their ability to interact with people and objects in their environment to the extent that they are not able to reach the normal milestones of development that their agemates reach easily. Some of the issues we discuss here you have encountered in other chapters, such as Chapter 12 on children with multiple and severe disabilities. However, only 20 percent of the children with chronic illnesses or physical disabilities have impairments that are classified as severe and profound (Lehr & Noonan, 1989). Because of medical intervention and technology, many of these children are living normal, healthy lives and can function in regular environments. Until now, this has been a relatively small and diverse group. The situation may change, however, as technology helps to save the lives of very small premature infants (below 4 pounds) and as the increase in severe child abuse and neglect causes the population of children with physical disabilities to grow.

■ Definitions

The Individuals with Disabilities Education Act (IDEA) (NICHCY, 1993) includes physical disabilities and health impairments in two categories: *orthopedic impairments* and *other health impairments*. The orthopedic category means "a severe orthopedic impairment that adversely affects a child's educational performance. The term includes impairment caused by congenital anomaly (e.g., club foot, absence of some member, etc.), impairment caused by disease (e.g., poliomyelitis, bone tuberculosis, etc.), and impairment from other causes (e.g., cerebral palsy, amputations, and fractures or burns that cause contractions" (p. 3). The other health impairments are "having limited strength, vitality, or alertness, including heightened alertness to environmental stimuli, that results in limited alertness with respect to the educational environment that (a) is due to a chronic or acute health problem, such as asthma, attention deficit disorder or attention deficit hyperactivity disorder, diabetes, epilepsy, a heart condition, hemophilia, lead poisoning, leukemia, nephritis, rheumatic fever, or sickle cell anemia; and (b) adversely affects a child's educational performance" (Bigge, Best, & Heller, 2001).

The population of children with physical disabilities is heterogeneous. It includes children with many different conditions. Most of these conditions are unrelated. Bigge, Best, and Heller (2001) include the following neurological impairments: cerebral palsy, seizure disorders, neural tube defects, and traumatic brain injury (p. 35).

According to the Individuals with Disabilities Education Act (IDEA), a person is disabled if he or she has a mental or physical impairment that substantially limits participation in one or more life activities. When a child's conditions—whether medical or physical—interfere with his or her ability to take part in routine school or home activities, the child has a physical disability.

Early intervention with a child who has physical disabilities and health impairments can minimize the severity of certain conditions and help the child participate in his or her environment, which in turn helps the child acquire the skills necessary for success in school.

(© Michael D. Sullivan/TexasStock)

When a physical condition interferes with a student's ability to participate in routine activities such as walking to class, the child is physically disabled.

By this definition, a student with an artificial arm who takes part in all school activities, including physical education, is not physically disabled. But when a physical condition leaves a student unable to hold a pencil, walk from class to class, or use conventional toilets—when it interferes with the student's participation in routine school activities—the child is physically disabled. This does not mean that the child cannot learn. But it does place a special responsibility on teachers and therapists to adapt materials and equipment to meet the student's needs and help the student learn to use these adaptations and develop a strong self-concept.

Health impairments—for example, asthma, cystic fibrosis, heart defects, cancer, diabetes, and hemophilia—usually do not interfere with the child's ability to participate in regular classroom activities and do not require curricular adaptations. But these conditions can require medication or special medical treatment and can restrict physical activities and diet. Teachers should familiarize themselves with the student's medical history, first-aid procedures, and any restrictions recommended by the child's physician.

Health impairments don't interfere with regular activities but may require a special diet or medical treatment.

■ Prevalence of Physical Disabilities and Health Impairments

How many children have physical disabilities? The question is difficult to answer because of the way physical disabilities are defined and the way they are reported. Although we could determine the incidence of conditions that can result in physical disabilities, these figures would greatly overestimate the number of children whose participation in routine activities is actually limited by those conditions. The U.S. Department of Education (1999) estimated that about 0.54 percent of all school-age children have physical or health disabilities. This figure includes severely and profoundly disabled children as well as children with milder physical disabilities and health impairments.

For example, about 2 million persons in the United States have epilepsy (NICHCY, 2000). There are approximately 125,000 new cases each year, about 50 percent of which are children and adolescents (NICHCY). Medication can control seizures completely in most of the people with the disorder and reduce the number of seizures in most others. With regular medication, then, most children with epilepsy can participate in the same activities as their friends and classmates. Less than half of the total number of children with epilepsy are considered physically disabled.

This example applies to most other categories of physical and health disorders. Most of these children are not considered physically disabled and function well in regular classes. However, they may need classrooms accessible for wheelchairs or crutches or the support that persons with health impairments need (such as people who know how to clean and regulate oxygen tubes and other lifesaving devices).

Local variations in the classification of disabilities further complicate the process of determining the prevalence of physical disabilities among schoolchildren. For example, one state may classify a large number of students as "other health impaired," and another state may classify similar students as "learning disabled." Or one state may classify students as "multihandicapped," and another may classify similar students according to the primary disabling conditions, such as "orthopedically impaired" (U.S. Department of Education, 1999).

Finally, at the national level there is no specific educational category for children with physical disabilities. The number of children receiving special education and related services during the 1997–1998 school year who were classified as "orthopedically impaired" was 670,502; the figure for "other health impairments" was 191,152; and that for "traumatic brain injury," 11,194 (U.S. Department of Education, 1999). Taken together, the figures probably provide the best estimate of the number of school-age children with physical disabilities. Current figures reveal that only about 3.5 percent of all the children receiving special education and related services (or 0.27 percent of the entire school population) are physically disabled (U.S. Department of Education, 1999).

The low incidence of students with physical disabilities limits the exposure of educators to their special needs. In the course of their careers, special education teachers might work with only a few students with physical disabilities, and these students' disabilities might be very different. Most of these children attend schools in which there is a staff of support personnel (occupational therapists, physical therapists, physicians, nurses, special educators). If a public school does not have the necessary support staff, it may contract for services in special schools.

| During their careers, special education teachers may encounter only a few students with physical disabilities.

■ Causes of Physical Disabilities and Health Impairments

Physically disabling conditions and health impairments can be either congenital or acquired. The cause of a condition and the age at which the condition develops influence the kinds of problems that children with physical disabilities and health impairments face as well as the implications for their teachers.

Congenital Disabilities

Children with congenital conditions are born with physical disabilities or develop them soon after birth. These children do not have the same developmental experiences that other children do. The extent of the differences depends on the type and severity of the condition. At one extreme, some children never sit or walk. At the other extreme, some children with congenital conditions grow up and adapt with the help of prostheses or technical devices. Technology has provided devices and aids, such as head pointers and communication boards, to help these children attain normal growth and development while they try to compensate for their disability (Siegel & Wetherby, 2000).

Acquired Disabilities

Some children progress through normal developmental sequences and experiences and then develop or acquire—through injury or disease—a physically disabling condition. Some of these children are not able to use their preinjury experiences during rehabilitation. For example, a child with a traumatic brain injury may not be able to roll over, sit, or stand up, but remembers how to do it and tries to imitate the process. Most children with physical disabilities stemming from injuries are motivated to regain or replace their former abilities (NICHCY, 2000). When a child loses an ability, however, he or she usually goes through a period of mourning. The ability to adjust to a physical disability caused by injury depends on many factors, including the reactions of others, the importance of the lost abilities to the child's lifestyle, and the child's previously established style of coping (Hill, 1999).

> Not all physical disabilities are genetic. Some are acquired during the prenatal life and others at or after birth.

■ Classification and Characteristics

Children with specific physical and health conditions are classified as physically (or orthopedically) disabled or as health impaired. This section provides an overview of the characteristics of children with common physical disabilities and health impairments (Bigge, Best, & Heller, 2001).

Children with Physical Disabilities

Children with physical disabilities have many different types of conditions. Although there are important differences among these conditions, there are also similarities. Most affect one system of the body in particular: the **neurological system** (the brain, spinal cord, and nerves) or the **musculoskeletal system** (the muscles, bones, and joints).

Clearly, the severity of the disability is a critical variable to consider when determining the amount of help and the kinds of adaptation a student needs. All children with physical disabilities have some limitations in their motor skills. For some, these limitations are severe: They cannot walk or sit independently or use their hands. Their dependence on others for getting around, for eating, and even for toileting can both frustrate and embarrass them. And conditions that affect appearance can increase these youngsters' social discomfort.

Neurological Impairments

The neurological system (often referred to as the *central nervous system*) is made up of the brain, the spinal cord, and a network of nerves that reach all parts of the body. The spinal cord and nerves carry messages between the brain and the rest of the body. Among its other functions, the brain controls muscle movement, and receptors in the muscles and joints send sensory feedback about speed, direction of movement, and body position to the brain.

With a neurological condition such as cerebral palsy, the brain either sends the wrong instructions or interprets feedback incorrectly. In both cases, the result is poorly coordinated movement. With a spinal cord injury or deformity, pathways between the brain and the muscles are interrupted, so messages are transmitted but never received. The result is muscle paralysis and loss of sensation beyond the point where the spinal cord (or nerve) is damaged. Children with these neurological conditions have motor skill deficits that can range from mild incoordination to paralysis from the neck down. The most severely involved children are totally dependent on other people or sophisticated equipment to carry out academic and self-care tasks.

Teachers can help students who have neurological conditions by adapting the learning environment to their needs. But because neurological conditions often affect the brain, teachers must first determine which behaviors the child can and cannot control and whether problems reflect a physical or socio-emotional disability. They also have a responsibility to any exceptional child to create a supportive atmosphere that fosters the child's acceptance by providing classmates with information about the student's condition. An example of a neurological condition is sensory motor dysfunction.

Sensory Motor Dysfunction Sensory integration is the normal neurological process of taking in information from one's body and environment through the senses; of organizing and unifying this information and using it to plan and execute adaptive responses in order to learn and function smoothly in daily life (Kranowitz, 1998). Sensory integration dysfunction is the inability to accurately process information received through the senses, as a result of a neurological inefficiency and brain disorganization (Ayers, 1979). As with other neurological problems, the dysfunction is on a continuum. At one extreme, the child may be hypersensitive; may avoid being touched; may be overreactive to foods, peers, smells, and colors; and emotionally insecure. At the other extreme, the child may be hyposensitive and react to sensations less intensely than children without the dysfunction. The child may also act in uncoordinated and disorganized ways (Kranowitz, 1998).

| Children with neurological problems are often misdiagnosed with behavior problems, ADD/ADHD, and/or a hearing impairment. |

Children with neurological problems are often misdiagnosed as having behavior problems, ADD/ADHD, and/or a hearing impairment. The key is that the child has difficulties in several areas, which may include motor skills, lack of hand preference, failure to relate to peers and cooperate in group play—in essence, a failure to acquire information through the senses and failure to use and organize it as children without the dysfunction are able to do.

Diagnostic instruments have been developed by Ayers (1979) and Williamson and Anzalone (2001). They are usually administered by a trained occupational therapist who will also provide treatment plans for individual therapy and suggestions for school/home treatment and management of routines. Early identification and intervention is highly recommended, as these children can be very difficult to incorporate into the regular routines of preschool or regular classrooms.

Cerebral Palsy **Cerebral palsy** refers to a disorder of movement and posture caused by damage to the motor control centers of the brain (Figure 13.1) (Batshaw, 1997; Pellegrino, 2002; March of Dimes, 1999). *Cerebral* refers to the brain and *palsy* to disorders of movement (NICHCY, 2000). The damage that results in cerebral palsy can occur before birth, during the birth process, or after birth from an accident or injury (a blow to the head, lack of oxygen). The condition affects muscle tone (the degree of tension in the muscles), interferes with voluntary movement and full control of the muscles, and delays gross and fine motor development.

In **spastic (pyramidal) cerebral palsy,** muscle tone is abnormally high (hypertonia) and increases during activity. Muscles and joints are tight or stiff, and movements are limited to affected areas of the body (see Figure 13.1). Some children are *hemiplegic:* Just one side of the body (either left arm and left leg or right arm and right leg) is affected. Others are *diplegic:* Their whole body is involved, but their legs are more severely involved than their arms. Still others are *quadriplegic:* Involvement is equally distributed throughout the body.

United Cerebral Palsy
Association
www.ucp.org

FIGURE 13.1

Regions of the Brain Affected by Various Forms of Cerebral Palsy (The darker the shading, the more severe the involvement)

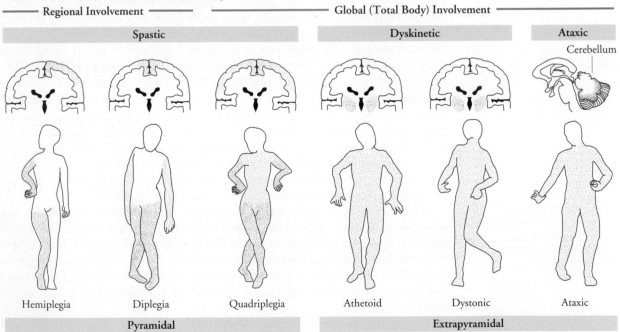

Source: J. P. Dorman & L. Pellegrino, *Caring for children with cerebral palsy: A team approach* (p. 12) (Baltimore: Paul H. Brookes, 1998). Reprinted by permission of the author.

All children with cerebral palsy have problems with posture and movement.

With *spastic quadriplegia,* all four limbs are spastic. The whole torso is involved as well as the mouth, tongue, or pharynx, and other disorders, such as visual and hearing impairment, almost always exist. The child has difficulty controlling movements and usually mental retardation (Pellegrino, 2002; March of Dimes, 1999).

In *dyskinetic cerebral palsy,* tonal abnormalities involve the whole body. The individual's muscle tone is changing constantly, often rigid while he or she is awake and decreased when asleep (Pellegrino, 1997).

Ataxic cerebral palsy is a condition in which voluntary movement involving balance is abnormal. These persons have difficulty controlling their hands and arms, and their gait is unsteady.

Children can have one or a combination of types of cerebral palsy. The form and degree of physical involvement varies from child to child. In addition, the affected areas of the body also vary. A child with *mixed type cerebral palsy* has severe problems with balance and coordination, which affect ambulation.

Additional problems that can be associated with cerebral palsy include learning disabilities, mental retardation, seizures, speech impairments, eating problems, sensory impairments, and joint and bone deformities such as spinal curvatures and contractures (permanently fixed, tight muscles and joints). Scissor or toe walking is common among children with cerebral palsy who are able to walk.

Approximately 40 percent of children with cerebral palsy have normal intelligence; the remainder have mild to severe retardation (Batshaw, 1997). Those classified as hemiplegic, the most common form of cerebral palsy, are most likely to have normal intelligence (Batshaw, 1997). The probability of normal intelligence decreases and the probability of secondary problems increases with the severity of the condition. But most children with cerebral palsy are not severely involved and do not have all or even some of the associated problems. This is an extremely heterogeneous group of children. Each child has unique abilities and needs. Technological advances in recent years have greatly improved the long-term well-being of these children (NICHCY, 2002). They are more like their classmates who do not have a disability than they are different.

Mild or severe seizures can occur in epilepsy.

Epilepsy **Epilepsy** is a disorder that occurs when the brain cells are not working properly (NICHCY, 2000). It is often called a seizure disorder. Epilepsy can occur in one hemisphere of the brain (*partial seizure*) or in both (*generalized seizure*). Some children may experience both types, and this condition is called *mixed seizure disorder.* Generalized seizures include the following types:

Epilepsy Foundation of America
www.epilepsyfoundation.org

▶ *Tonic-clonic seizures.* This is the most common type of seizure and involves major firing of neurons in both hemispheres of the brain. The child generally loses consciousness and falls to the floor. The convulsive seizure usually starts with the eyes turning upward or to one side, a sudden loss of consciousness, and rigidity. This tonic phase usually lasts from 30 seconds to a minute. The clonic phase follows and lasts about 1 to 3 minutes, with jerking of the body, which is then followed by sleep. The clonic phase of the seizure is characterized by jerking of the body, sweating, and incontinence (Weinstein, 2002).

ECOLOGY OF THE CHILD

FAMILY **Grandparents Adopt and Advocate for Levi and Tia**

My husband Dave and I adopted our grandchildren, Levi and Tia, when they were infants. Both children have cerebral palsy. Their mother could no longer care for them, and we decided we couldn't turn them away. They needed us.

By the time we decided to adopt Levi, the bond that had grown between us was very special. We knew we had to become his parents. We also noticed that he wasn't progressing physically as he should have been. But we never let that influence our decision to become his Mom and Dad.

With Tia, who came later, we were equally sure that she needed to be with us and her half-brother Levi. At first it took some getting used to. It wasn't until six months after we met her that she gave us eye contact—much later for people whom she did not know. All she could do was turn from her stomach to her back. She couldn't sit up, and she couldn't even suck from a nipple. I had to use preemie nipples and move them back and forth in her mouth to make the milk come. Since then, we have never looked back.

Though neither child can talk, both Levi, now 11, and Tia, 10, are learning to use communication devices. They can also walk with the aid of a walker. Both children have seizures as well, which are controlled by medication, but that does not stop them from riding their own bikes independently and riding their horse, Rocky, while their Dad leads them. We do not let negative words like "can't" or "never" be used when it has to do with Levi and Tia. They will prove those words wrong almost every time.

In school, aside from Levi's sixth grade home economics class, neither child is currently taking regular education classes. The fight to keep Levi even in his one regular-ed class has been difficult. I want him to mix with the other kids. Everybody likes him, and I don't want him segregated.

During his IEP meetings I have been told quite often that Levi does not have the cognitive abilities to learn things like printing his name or other academic skills. I will not stand for this, however, because I know better. Recently, a children's respite provider and I worked with Levi. By the time he went back to school in the fall, he could print his name, and has since made great progress in all areas. He has advanced past many goals which we were told he would never accomplish. In fact, both Tia and Levi are doing many things that the professionals told us they would never be able to do. So I continue to be vocal and fight for them. My husband stays home with the kids while I go out and do the advocating.

▶ *Absence seizures,* or *primary generalized seizures.* During this seizure, the child has a blank expression, perhaps blinking before becoming unconscious, is unaware of the surroundings, and cannot be awakened. There may also be jerking of the arms. Afterward, the child is not aware of having had the seizure, which lasts less than ten seconds (Weinstein, 2002). This was previously referred to as petit mal.

▶ *Atypical absence seizures.* The onset of this type of seizure is more gradual than that of the absence type, but it lasts longer and creates

I have been told many times that I have unrealistic expectations—that I am in denial. Some even wonder if being a grandparent—not a parent—is an obstacle in advocating and caring for Levi and Tia. But my answer to that is, we adopted Levi and Tia as our own. In our minds, that is enough to make us the parents. They're just our kids, and we see no difference.

Physically there are some challenges to being older than regular parents. Lifting them was difficult, but now they can help me get them on their feet or in and out of the tub. We also have an adapted van, so transporting them is easy.

I know that my children have to be exposed to different things in order to learn. It's the educators who need to move beyond the disabilities and broaden their expectations of these children. Special children have to try so much harder to reach a goal, but they really have more ambition than most people give them credit for. Each one is unique and will learn at different rates, just like regular-ed children learn.

While my husband and I do not expect Levi or Tia to become the President of the United States, we do have great expectations for them. This helps us to work them harder, and we become extremely happy with every bit of progress they make. We know that there will be more to come.

We all know how much more work it is to take care of our special children. The hardest, most heartbreaking thing is how hard we have to fight for every bit of equal rights for them. But we should never give up and never let anyone else give up on them either. The greatest reward in the world is when they accomplish something. It's like the sun just came out. Everything's worth it.

Source: From Marge Clark, Family, friends, and the community. grandparent adoption: The Clark family, *Exceptional Parent* (December 2000): 35–36. Reprinted with permission.

WHAT IS THE CONTEXT?

The article discusses how Marge and Dave Clark adopted their two grandchildren, Levi and Tia. Both children have cerebral palsy. The Clarks persevered in helping them increase their skills by teaching them to write their names, providing them with access to general education, and continuing to advocate for the children in all areas of their lives.

PIVOTAL ISSUES FOR TEACHERS

- What is your view of placing children with severe disabilities in the general education classroom?

- Is this the most beneficial placement for the children? Why or why not?

- As a teacher, what practical things could you do to integrate Levi and Tia into—for example, a writing lesson in your general education classroom?

---

greater confusion. It is more serious because a child who has atypical absence seizures is likely to have other types of seizures as well (Brown, 1997).

▶ *Myclonic and atonic seizures.* Myclonic seizures start with abrupt jerking of the muscles; in infancy they are called *infantile spasms.* Atonic seizures are the opposite of myclonic ones. They are characterized by a sudden loss of muscle tone, falling, and loss of consciousness (Brown, 1997; NICHCY, 2000).

Partial seizures are limited to one hemisphere of the brain. When the individual loses consciousness, they are called *complex partial seizures.* When consciousness is not lost, they are called *simple partial seizures* (Batshaw & Perret, 1992).

Fortunately, once epilepsy is diagnosed, medication can completely control it in 70 to 90 percent of cases. Specific procedures and recommendations of how to deal with the child during a seizure can be found in Ault, Rues, Gruff, and Holovet (2000). Surgery is often recommended for those who do not respond to medication (Freeman & Vining, 1990). Epilepsy does not interfere with performance in school. Most individuals with epilepsy have normal intelligence (Brown, 1997) There are 2 million children and adolescents with epilepsy in the United States (NICHCY, 2000).

> In the United States there are 2 million students with epilepsy.

Neural Tube Defects   The most common type of neural tube defects (defects of the backbone and spinal cord) are *spina bifida, encephalocele,* and *anencephaly* (March of Dimes, 1997).

The most common form of spina bifida is *spina bifida occulta,* which is a small defect or gap on the backbone. The spinal cord and nerves usually are normal (March of Dimes, 1999; NICHCY, 2000). Another form of spina bifida is *meningocele,* which involves a cyst or lump that can be removed surgically; and the person can then develop normally. A more severe form of spina bifida is *myelomeningocele,* in which nerve roots are involved and spinal fluid may leak out of the cord. Surgery is necessary to close the back, and varying degrees of leg paralysis and bladder and bowel problems remain (March of Dimes, 1997).

Encephalocele is a major malformation of the brain resulting in severe retardation. *Anencephaly* is an opening in the brain that usually results in spontaneous abortion or infant death (Brown, 1997; Liptak, 2002).

The cause of spina bifida is considered unknown; however, if women who have given birth to a child with spina bifida or myelomeningocele are given folic acid (a type of vitamin B) before a subsequent pregnancy, they tend not to have another child with neural tube defects. The U.S. Public Health Service recommends that women of childbearing age take 0.4 milligrams of folic acid a day as a preventive measure, because spina bifida occurs in the first 26 to 28 days of pregnancy, usually before a woman is aware of her condition (March of Dimes, 1999).

> Folic acid taken by the mother before pregnancy tends to reduce the chances of spina bifida in the child.

The location and extent of injury to the spinal cord determine the degree of physical involvement and loss of function. Injuries to the upper segments of the spinal cord can leave the individual quadriplegic, with no function in the trunk, arms, or legs. Injuries to lower levels of the spinal cord result in varying degrees of paralysis in the legs (paraplegia). About 80 percent of persons with spina bifida have injury in the lower back, and most can walk with aids (March of Dimes, 1999).

Secondary or medical problems associated with myelomeningocele and spinal cord injury, as with cerebral palsy, include loss of bladder and bowel control (requiring catheterization or surgical intervention) and joint and bone deformities (spinal curvatures and contractures). In addition, children with myelomeningocele typically are hydrocephalic (hydrocephalus is the buildup of cerebrospinal fluid in the skull). A shunt is surgically inserted to drain excess fluid from the brain (Figure 13.2).

> WWW Information relating to spina bifida www.spinalcord.org

FIGURE 13.2
Ventriculoperitoneal Shunt

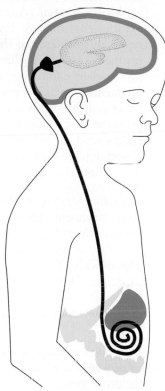

Source: From G. Williamson, *Children with spina bifida: Early intervention and preschool programming* (p. 83, Figure 4.1) (Baltimore: Paul H. Brookes, 1987). Copyright © 1987. Reprinted with the permission of the author.

About 75 percent of children with myelomeningocele have low average intelligence. However, the population is very heterogeneous, and numerous disabilities are related to this disorder. The degree of physical involvement determines the extent to which mobility and performance of daily activities are affected (March of Dimes, 1999).

Spinal cord injuries are caused by car, motorcycle, in-line skating, and diving accidents and by disease. Adolescents older than age 15 and young adults are at the greatest risk for spinal cord injuries because of their active lifestyles and tendency to take risks (Gilgoff, 1983).

Musculoskeletal Conditions

The musculoskeletal system includes the muscles and their supporting framework, the skeleton (Leet, Dorman, & Tosi, 2002). Conditions that affect the musculoskeletal system can result in progressive muscle weakness (muscular dystrophy), inflammation of the joints (arthritis), or loss of various parts of the body (amputation). Severe burns can lead to amputation, damage to muscles, or scars that impede movement. Severe scoliosis (curvature of the spine) can limit movement of the trunk, can cause back pain, and eventually may compress the lungs, heart, and other internal organs. Degenerative conditions include muscular dystrophy and spinal muscular atrophy (Bigge, Best, & Heller, 2001).

Most children with musculoskeletal conditions have normal intellectual abilities (Batshaw & Perret, 1992). They do not necessarily encounter academic difficulties, but their physical limitations and social and emotional adjustment can create educational problems.

Teachers can help students with musculoskeletal conditions by making adjustments for pain or poor endurance and encouraging as much physical activity as possible. They can arrange for a splint to hold a pencil or spoon or for a different faucet handle for a bathroom sink. They can be sensitive to the child's need for help with toileting and make arrangements for someone to respond quickly and competently. And they can encourage classmates to volunteer to help the child with difficult activities.

Muscular Dystrophy Muscular dystrophy is a disease of the muscles that affects movement. The most common form, Duchenne, is a genetic disorder that occurs primarily but not exclusively in boys (Leet, Dormans, and Tosi, 2002). The disease appears at about 2 to 5 years, and by age 12 the child may not be able to walk. The disease gradually weakens the heart and diaphragm, leading to death. Other forms of muscle disorder, such as congenital myopathies, occur less frequently. Other orthopedic and musculoskeletal conditions include curvature of the spine, hip conditions, limb deficiencies, juvenile arthri-

Musculoskeletal conditions affect the muscles and the skeleton. They often severely limit a child's motor skills and can increase the child's social discomfort but usually do not impair intellectual and academic abilities.
(© Alan Careyl/The Image Works)

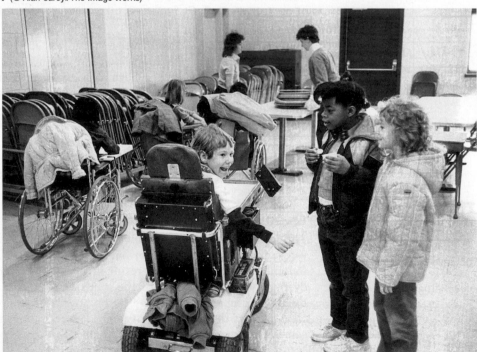

tis, osteogenesis imperfecta, and arthrogryposis (joint contractor and muscle weakness) (Batshaw, 2002; Bigge, Best, & Heller, 2001).

Arthritis **Arthritis** is a group of disorders that involve the joints (Leet, Dorman, & Tosi, 2002). Symptoms include swollen and stiff joints, fever, and pain in the joints during acute flare-ups. Prolonged inflammation can lead to joint deformities, which eventually can affect mobility. Students may require frequent medication or miss school if surgery is needed. There are three forms of juvenile rheumatoid arthritis, and a multidisciplinary team is required to evaluate, identify, and recommend appropriate therapies, medications, exercises, and educational adaptations (Bigge, Best, & Heller, 2001).

Polio Polio was a common disease before the development of vaccines that offset the responsible virus. The virus could invade the brain and cause mild to severe paralysis of the body. There were also milder cases of partial paralysis. The virus is still present, and every child needs to be immunized for protection against this disease (March of Dimes, 1999). Post polio muscle atrophy appears in some individuals who had polio early in life. Muscles that were previously damaged weaken, and in some persons muscles that were not previously affected weaken as well (March of Dimes, 2002).

Tuberculosis

All infants and children should be screened for tuberculosis.

Tuberculosis is a communicable disease usually located in the lungs. Preschool children are most vulnerable to the disease. Symptoms include fatigue, weight loss, coughing, and wheezing (Hill & Davis, 1999, p. 116). Tuberculosis is on the increase, and the American Academy of Pediatrics recommends screening for all infants and children. While contagious, children with tuberculosis should not be in school, but they can return after treatment when they are no longer contagious.

Children with Health Impairments

Children with health impairments require ongoing medical attention. Like physical disabilities, health impairments stem from a wide variety of conditions. Care should be taken to recognize that these children are more similar to their peers than they are different, and efforts should be made to support their needs, rather than focusing solely on the condition (Lehr & McDavid, 1999).

Major health impairments include heart and blood disorders, cystic fibrosis, juvenile diabetes, and childhood cancer (Bigge, Best, & Heller, 2001). Infectious diseases include hepatitis B, HIV, and AIDS (Bigge, Best, & Heller, 2001). School personnel may encounter a child with *osteogenesis imperfecta,* or brittle bone disease, which results in multiple fractures and may be misinterpreted as child abuse. These children usually have normal intelligence, but care must be taken in physical activities to prevent fractures (Bigge, 1991a).

Cardiopulmonary Conditions

The **cardiopulmonary system** includes the heart, blood, and lungs. When a health problem affects the cardiopulmonary system, a child may have problems in breathing (for example, asthma, cystic fibrosis), or the heart may not pump blood properly (heart defects). Some children with these conditions cannot run, climb stairs, or even walk from one part of the school to another. Although it is possible to limit strenuous exercise for these children, simply sitting in school all day takes more energy than some of them can produce. Their inability to take part in normal activities with their agemates can create social problems for these youngsters. Adding to these problems is the high susceptibility of these children to illness. Frequent absences put them at an academic disadvantage in spite of their normal intelligence.

Suggested classroom modifications are listed in Table 13.1. Suggestions for individual children may vary even within a syndrome. Individualized health-care plans should be mandatory. In all cases, the teacher should be given complete information about each child's condition, as well as instructions for appropriate therapies and assistive technologies.

Teachers can help a student with a cardiopulmonary condition by adapting instruction and the learning environment to the child's needs. For example, they can schedule the most important learning activities during the child's period of greatest energy, allow the child to rest at certain intervals, give the child extra time to complete assignments, arrange for locker space close to the classroom, or provide alternatives (and academic waivers) for physical education classes that exceed the child's capabilities.

Asthma **Asthma** is a condition affecting an individual's breathing. It usually has three features: Lungs are swollen, breathing is difficult, and the airways react negatively to a variety of environmental conditions (such as dust, smoke, cold air, and exercise). Asthma may also cause acute constriction of the bronchial tubes (Batshaw & Perret, 1992).

In children, the condition varies from mild to severe. Asthma usually does not pose a major problem for the teachers of children with this condition. Nevertheless, all teachers need to know how to deal with the frequent absences of children with severe asthma and what symptoms indicate that a child is having a severe attack. Teachers who have a child with asthma in their classes need a doctor's suggested plan of medication, a list of symptoms that indicate daily or emergency medical attention, and some indication of the degree to which the child can safely exercise and participate in classroom activities.

Children with asthma need accurate diagnosis and treatment plans from appropriate medical personnel. Medication may be necessary throughout an individual's life, and those who are seriously affected are likely to require emergency treatment from time to time.

Cystic Fibrosis Cystic fibrosis is the most frequently occurring lethal genetic disease in the United States (*Science*, 1990). Children affected with this disorder have severe respiratory and digestive problems. Recently, geneticists have identified the gene accounting for 70 percent of the cases (*Science*). Currently, an experiment is being conducted to determine if the problem can be avoided by supplying normal genes to a child afflicted with this disease. Techniques for screening prospective parents for the lethal gene are being developed (*Science*). It is hoped that in the future, gene treatment can control both cystic fibrosis and muscular dystrophy.

Teachers can help students with cardiopulmonary conditions by scheduling important activities when the child has the most energy.

Health conditions often result in absences, forcing teachers to adjust their instructional plans.

Information relating to cystic fibrosis
www.cff.org

TABLE 13.1
Potential Classroom Modifications and Teacher Skill Requirements

CHRONIC CONDITION	POTENTIAL MODIFICATIONS	SKILLS REQUIRED
Asthma	Avoidance of allergens; participation in physical activity, administration of medication as needed	CPR; recognition of signs and symptoms of respiratory distress and of medication side effects
Congenital heart disease	Participation in physical activity; administration of medication as needed; diet or fluids	CPR; recognition of signs and symptoms of heart failure and medication side effects
Diabetes	Diet; bathroom frequency; availability of snacks and source of sugar; balance of exercise and food	Recognition of signs and symptoms of hypoglycemia (rapid onset) and of hyperglycemia (slow onset)
Leukemia	Participation in physical activity exposure to communicable diseases	Recognition of signs and symptoms of infection and of bleeding
Seizure disorder	Participation in physical activity; environment; administration of medication as needed	Seizure management, recognition of signs and symptoms of distress during and after seizure and of medication side effects
Spina bifida	Participation in physical activity; environment to accommodate mobility and movement; fluids; pressure relief	Recognition of signs and symptoms of shunt blockage, of urinary infections, and of skin breakdowns; use of equipment and mobility devices
Sickle cell anemia	Participation in physical activity; fluids	Recognition of signs and symptoms of impending crisis
Juvenile rheumatoid arthritis	Participation in physical activity; environment (stairs); administration of medication as needed; frequency of movement; classroom activities (writing, carrying books)	Recognition of signs and symptoms of increased inflammation and of broken bones
Hemophilia	Physical activity	Recognition of signs and symptoms of bleeds; management of bleeding (cuts and scrapes)
Cystic fibrosis	Physical activity; administration of medication as needed; diet	Recognition of signs and symptoms of respiratory distress and of medication side effects

Source: Adapted from J. L. Bigge and L. Best (2000). *Teaching Individuals with Physical and Multiple Disabilities.* Upper Saddle River, NJ: Merrill.

Traumatic Brain Injury

Traumatic brain injury is a separate category of disability.

Severe head injury is the most common acquired disorder in the category of traumatic brain injury (TBI) (Michaud, Semel-Concepción, Duhaime, & Lazar, 2002). With more than two million brain injuries occurring annually, it is also the most common cause of accidental death and disabilities (NICLICY, 2003). The results of these injuries may resemble spina bifida, cerebral palsy, or other physical disabilities. TBI can result in cognitive, social, and language deficits as well.

Care must be taken to distinguish between genetic disabilities and those brought on by TBI. In the evaluation of these students, a multidisciplinary team approach is necessary to ensure that the most appropriate education placement and intervention are provided (Keyser-Marcus, Briel, Sherron-Targett, Yasuda, Johnson, & Wehman, 2002). Individual students with TBI may vary in terms of the severity of injury, manifestations of disability, and potential for recovery (Keyser-Marcus et al., 2002).

Acquired Immunodeficiency Syndrome

Acquired immunodeficiency syndrome (AIDS) is a breakdown of the body's immune system caused by the **human immunodeficiency virus (HIV)**. Ninety percent of AIDS cases in children are the result of the virus being transmitted from the infected mother during pregnancy, the birth process, or breast feeding (Rutstein, Conlon, & Batshaw, 1997). About one-third acquire the virus during pregnancy and most of the others during the birth process. A child may also become infected through a transfusion of contaminated blood. HIV is now being treated before birth with some success (http://www.niaid.nih.gov/factsheets/hivinf.htm). It is recommended that infants under one year of age be treated with antiretroviral agents approved by the Food and Drug Administration (Spiegel & Bonwit, 2002). Of the sixteen antiretroviral agents approved by the FDA in 2002, eleven are approved for children.

Among adults, the disease is transmitted through sexual contact, by using contaminated needles to administer drugs intravenously, or through transfusions of infected blood. Adolescents exposed to any of these are as much at risk of contracting the disease as adults.

www CDC National Prevention Information Network (HIV & AIDS) www.cdcnpin.org

Not all children born with HIV develop AIDS. In 1999, incomplete state reports included 224 newborns with AIDS and a total of 6,812 children under 5 with AIDS (Clearing House on Child Neglect Information [CDCNPI], 2001). It has been estimated that more than 10,000 infants are born with HIV, but many do not develop AIDS (National AIDS Clearing House, 2001). AIDS is a serious concern in our society, and communities are still formulating policies on how to work with infants and children who have the infection (including how those children are to be educated).

Professionals must respond to each child individually to best care for his or her health needs and to maximize his or her competencies. Infants need careful diagnosis, and individualized family service plans (IFSPs) must be developed to ensure adequate medical and educational services (Crocker & Porter, 2000).

Cooley's Anemia (Thalassemia) and Sickle Cell Anemia

Cooley's anemia is a blood cell disease of genetic origin; it is most frequently found in persons living in the Mediterranean area or among those of

Mediterranean stock. The child appears healthy at birth but soon becomes listless, has a poor appetite, and contracts frequent infections. Cooley's anemia is treated with frequent blood transfusions. At this time, there is no known cure.

Sickle cell anemia is an inherited blood disease most commonly found among African Americans and Hispanics of Caribbean ancestry. Oxygen-carrying red blood cells usually are round, but in children with sickle cell anemia they are crescent or sickle shaped. The sickle cells are not as flexible as the round cells and can be trapped in body organs. When the red blood cells are trapped, oxygen is not carried through the body, and the resulting shortage of oxygen can leave the child highly vulnerable to infection. Currently, massive doses of penicillin are administered to children with sickle cell anemia to prevent the development of infections. The penicillin dosage continues throughout early childhood until the individual's immune system can fight the infections (summarized from March of Dimes, 1999).

Substance Abuse Causing Disabilities

It is estimated that in 1990, 4.8 million women of childbearing age used illicit drugs (Shriver & Piersal, 1994). This figure does not include the women who used legal drugs such as alcohol and tobacco—30.5 million women consumed alcohol, and 17.4 million used nicotine (Shriver & Piersal).

The media overemphasize the effects of maternal drug use in children born to these women, but some serious disabilities can occur. For example, although research has *not* demonstrated negative effects from prenatal exposure to heroin or marijuana, negative effects have been found in children whose mothers used cocaine or alcohol during pregnancy. The effect of alcohol on the fetus is the most thoroughly researched aspect of prenatal exposure to drugs.

Alcohol The most adverse effects have been observed in the children of mothers who consumed alcohol heavily (more than 8 ounces per day) while they were pregnant. This consumption results in **fetal alcohol syndrome (FAS)** or a milder form, *fetal alcohol effects* (FAE). Many children with FAS have low birth weight and severe feeding problems. The most severe cases of FAS result in facial abnormalities, mental retardation, and challenging behaviors. Those with FAE will have milder forms of intellectual and behavioral impairments, and they usually do not have facial abnormalities (Batshaw & Conlon, 1997; Wunsch, Conlon, & Scheidt, 2002). Both FAS and FAE can present a variety of learning problems and difficulties with social interaction. Children with this condition have disorders in three categories: growth deficiencies, facial malformations, and central nervous system effects in the form of mental retardation and challenging behaviors. These disorders are generally diagnosed in childhood and adolescence. Facial and physical abnormalities may require medical treatment (Batshaw & Perret, 1997; Shriver & Piersal, 1994). Generally, children exposed to alcohol (less than 8 ounces per day) have lower birth weight, decreased height, and smaller heads (Streissgath, 1997). There appears to be a relationship between an expectant mother's binge drinking (five or more drinks per day) and her child's lower cognitive functioning (see Chapter 3).

Children with fetal alcohol effects may have mild intellectual and behavioral impairments.

Cocaine An expectant mother's use of cocaine has been associated with her child's lower birth weight, shorter body length, and smaller head circumference.

The newborn infant exposed to cocaine may show irritability, restlessness, poor feeding, and sleep problems (Batshaw & Conlon, 1997; Wunsch, Conlon, & Scheidt, 2002).

Some studies have found cognitive deficits, challenging behaviors, and lower achievement; however, the results are not the same for all cocaine-exposed children. Cohen and Erwin (1994) found that only one-fourth of their sample of children exposed to cocaine prenatally exhibited problem-causing behavioral characteristics in the classroom. Moreover, half of the sample hardly resembled the cultural stereotype of the drug-exposed child at all (p. 248).

In summary, Shriver and Piersal's (1994) statement merits attention:

> Knowledge that a child has been exposed to drugs prenatally will not automatically qualify the child for early special education, *nor should it.* For example, information that children exposed in utero to crack cocaine will automatically have some type of learning disability, or that children exposed to alcohol will automatically be developmentally delayed, is unsubstantiated by current research. (p. 176, emphasis added; see also Hansen & Ulrey, 1993)

Heroin The most common effects for infants whose mothers use heroin are low birth weight and preterm delivery (Lockhart, 1996; Wunsch, Conlon, & Scheidt, 2002). The infant may have severe withdrawal symptoms, increased blood pressure, and potential nutritional problems. Another issue is that heroin is frequently mixed ("cut") with other substances that can be harmful to the fetus. For example, if the mother's heroin is cut with quinine, serious malformations can occur in the infant, such as deafness (Lockhart).

Marijuana Mothers who use marijuana may have smaller babies in terms of total weight, arm mass, and overall decreased body size (Lockhart, 1996). These infants may be highly irritable and exhibit increased sensitivity to noises in the environment.

Other Health-Related Conditions

Other health-related conditions include chronic and sometimes life-threatening diseases such as cancer (leukemia, malignant tumors), diabetes, and hemophilia. Children with these conditions may require extensive medical treatment or periodic hospitalization. When working with a student who has a serious health disorder, teachers should obtain current information about the child's condition so needed changes can be made in expectations and school activities. Also, teachers should be sensitive to the social and emotional status of the child, keep activities as normal as possible, and provide support.

Children with diabetes or hemophilia may require regular medication or other medical treatment. Teachers working with these children should be knowledgeable about medical procedures needed at school, limitations on activities, and emergency procedures that may be necessary if problems arise (see Table 13.1). It is important for all members of the child's environment (medical, therapist, parents, teachers) to prepare a detailed plan once the child is

Teachers should keep activities as normal as possible and provide support.

After a prolonged absence from school, a child needs a detailed plan for re-entering.

ready to enter or re-enter the school environment following an illness or chronic condition. It should include

developing policies at the school district level to include services, emergency care, steps for managing the child in school, and guidelines for school support personnel (Hill & Davis, 1999). For example, it should include what exercise is recommended, periods of rest and quiet times, and ways of encouraging a positive self-concept (pp. 53–62). Wellness-illness is a continuum, and these plans must be individualized.

Technological Assistance

Children who depend on technological devices to survive are increasingly included in regular and special education classes (Levine, 1996). Most of these children have chronic health or physical disabilities and will require technological assistance for long periods of their lives, although some outgrow the conditions in early childhood and do not require continued mechanical aids for survival.

Technology-dependent children are encouraged to live normal lives, and most of them can acquire academic, social, and language skills at an age-appropriate time (Crocker & Porter, 2000). In 1984, the Supreme Court ruled that technology-dependent children have a right to live at home (instead of in a hospital or nursing facility) and to attend school and have nursing procedures provided for them. It is usually more difficult for a child who develops a chronic condition after birth, as he or she may suffer from depression, lack of independence, and low self-esteem (Hill & Davis, 1999).

In the following sections, we discuss some of the devices that educators may encounter.

Tube Feeding

Some infants are born with or develop problems that prevent them from being able to eat. These children may have poorly developed sucking and swallowing reflexes; the sucking reflex is necessary to pull food into the mouth to be swallowed (Levy & O'Rourke, 2002; Krajicek, Steinke, Hertzdeng, Anastasiow, & Skandel, 2003). They may also have abnormal muscle tone in the lips or tongue, which makes eating difficult or causes vomiting, or they may have a malformed breathing tube and esophagus, which allow food to enter the lungs.

When a child cannot receive enough nutrients through mouth feeding, a tube is inserted into the stomach, and food is fed directly into it. This is called *gastrostomy feeding* (Eicher, 1997; Haynie, Porter, & Palfrey, 1989). As an alternative, the tube may be passed through the nose (nasogastric tube). The nasogastric technique cannot be used for longer than a few months, because the esophagus becomes irritated. Gastrostomy is usually the preferred treatment (Batshaw, 1997). Figure 13.3 illustrates gastrostomy and nasogastric tube feedings.

Intravenous Feeding

In some children, intravenous feeding is administered through a large, deep vein in the neck or chest. Children usually require this procedure if they need

FIGURE 13.3
Gastrostomy and Nasogastric Feeding

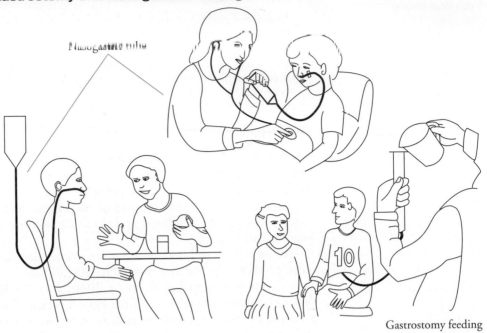

Gastrostomy feeding

long-term care, such as chemotherapy or antibiotic therapy, or if the bowels are incapable of absorbing adequate nutrients (Levy & O'Rourke, 1997).

Catheterization and Colostomy

Catheterization and colostomy are used to remove wastes from the bladder and bowels when the nerves that normally stimulate their removal fail to function properly or a physical disability has damaged the signal area in the bladder or bowels. A child can be taught to insert a tube to remove the urine (catheterization). Colostomy is a surgical procedure in which a doctor inserts a tube that allows waste from the bowels to be collected in a bag attached to the child's abdomen. The child can be taught to empty the pouch that contains the waste. Of course, when the child is an infant, the parents or caretakers have to learn to perform these procedures.

Oxygen-Dependent Children

Premature infants frequently suffer from severe respiratory distress. The therapy of providing oxygen to premature and low-birth-weight infants can cause a thickening and drying of the lung tissue (bronchopulmonary dysplasia), further complicating the problem and prolonging oxygen therapy (Krajicek et al., 2003). Children with cystic fibrosis (a dysfunction of mucous production), severe asthma, and some diseases of the heart also require oxygen therapy.

The most common method of treatment is providing oxygen through a nasal cannula. Other means of delivering oxygen are a nasal mask or, if the nasal passage is blocked, a tracheostomy (a tube inserted into the windpipe through a surgical opening).

Car seats and wheelchairs equipped with respirators and other oxygen-supplying equipment are available. They allow the infant and young child to be transported more easily from home to school or for out-of-home experiences. Parents and personnel who care for or teach these children need specialized training.

Case Study: Alex, a Home Care Success Story

By the end of his first day of life, Alex Hughes had been placed on a respirator and transferred from a community hospital to a neonatal intensive care unit (NICU). He had severe hyaline membrane disease, bronchopulmonary dysplasia, and multiple complications. Within days, Alex was baptized and given last rites.

With intensive care, though, his condition gradually improved. At 9 months he was transferred to Children's Memorial Hospital in Chicago, where he underwent a tracheostomy. At 15 months, the treatment team found a ventilator setting on which Alex was stable, and a joint decision was made to send him home. The alternative was two or three more years of high-tech hospital care. His mother, Ann Hughes, had been living at the hospital and at a nearby Ronald McDonald House; meanwhile, she was eight months pregnant with her second child. Alex's father, Steve, was making regular visits from home, forty miles away.

"We had been thoroughly trained in using the ventilator, but all of a sudden the equipment looked very scary," Ann recalls. They maintained the ventilator, ordered supplies, changed the tracheostomy tube three times a week, and measured oxygen saturation with a pulse oximeter.

They worked closely with nurses and therapists and consulted by telephone with doctors at Children's Memorial and with their own pediatricians, who took responsibility for Alex's general care and reviewed the need for physical, speech, and occupational therapy. "Our pediatricians listened to us and believed what we had to say," Steve says. "They trusted our judgment and our ability to assess Alex's condition."

Alex was gradually weaned from the ventilator and from the need for in-house nursing care. He is now off the ventilator entirely, and the tracheostomy has been closed. At 4½ years of age, he is doing well physically but is still not talking and tends to be withdrawn. He is attending a school for physically and developmentally handicapped youngsters.

"Everything we went through has been worth every second just to have him home," his mother says. "His improvement has been extraordinary." Sister Katie, 2½, is developmentally close to Alex and is his best friend. "She's a good influence," says Ann. "She's better than a therapist" (Goldberg, 1991, pp. 26–32).

Child Abuse

An epidemic of child abuse can be a major cause of some children's disabilities.

Children who suffer from child abuse may acquire disabilities that are not caused by any genetic or birth disorder. Child abuse has become a leading cause of injury and death for children in the United States, outpacing the leader of the

PROFILES

DEVELOPMENTAL

Paolo and Margaritte are two children with physical disabilities. Their developmental profiles in the graph below show that they are like their classmates in many ways but very different in others.

Paolo: Paolo was born with cerebral palsy, a condition that affects his nervous system and makes it hard for him to coordinate his muscles. Although he has average intelligence, he

has never learned to sit by himself or walk. He cannot control the movements of his face and arms. When he tries to speak, he makes grunts and groans instead of words.

For many years, Paolo's doctors and school personnel thought he was mentally retarded. When Paolo was 8, he learned to use an electronic communicating system. He has not stopped "talking" since. He now uses a Touch Talker that is programmed with the alphabet

Profiles of Two Children with Physical Disabilities

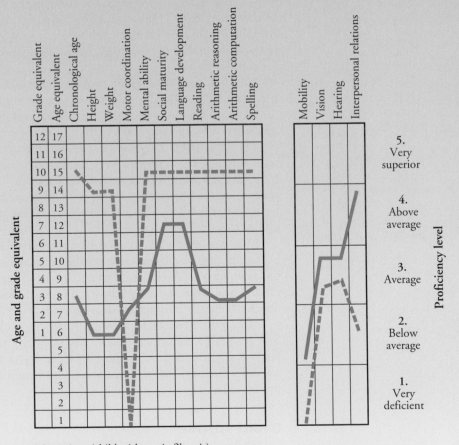

Margaritte (child with cystic fibrosis) ——————
Paolo (child with cerebral palsy) – – – – –

and about a hundred words and phrases. By touching squares on the keyboard, Paolo can construct sentences and "speak," using the device's voice synthesizer. Paolo's communication system is mounted on his wheelchair, so he is never at a loss for words.

Now 15, Paolo attends a regular tenth-grade class at a public high school. His schedule includes weekly occupational and physical therapy classes, which focus on the skills required for using the school bathrooms. These skills include maneuvering the electric wheelchair in and out of the bathroom, transferring to the toilet, and adjusting clothing. In other respects, Paolo is fairly independent. He has several pieces of specially designed equipment, and his therapists are continually looking for new devices to improve his communication and self-care abilities.

After Paolo was introduced to electronic communication systems, he developed a strong interest in computers, a subject he hopes to study in college. His parents and sister are excited about his wanting to go to college and, as usual, will do what they can to help him achieve this goal. They have always been his greatest supporters and have helped him develop an optimistic outlook on life.

Paolo sometimes regrets that he has cerebral palsy. Although he has a couple of close friends, he believes that his appearance, his bulky equipment, and his inability to speak have limited his social relationships. His friends agree that he has a wonderful personality but that it does take a while to get to know him. Paolo looks forward to having girlfriends, getting married, and eventually having a family. He knows he will run into problems but feels confident about overcoming them.

Margaritte: Margaritte is 8 years old. She has cystic fibrosis, a disease that affects many organs in the body, especially the lungs. The disease has left her pale, thin, and short for her age. Her breathing problems have caused her chest to become barrel shaped, which is typical for children with cystic fibrosis. Margaritte has had frequent bouts with pneumonia since she was 3 months old. She is a regular patient at the local hospital, where she has become a favorite with the nurses.

Margaritte is in the third grade. She is a good student, but frequent absences have made it hard for her to keep up. Even when her health is better, she has trouble breathing and wheezes and coughs all day long at school. She is usually tired by lunchtime, so she has a regular appointment with the school nurse. The nurse "claps" Margaritte's chest to loosen the secretions in her lungs, letting her breathe more easily for a while. During lunch and recess, she rests, reads, or works on assignments she has missed. She would like to play with her friends, but their activity exhausts her. She chooses to save her energy for the afternoon.

Margaritte knows that cystic fibrosis is a progressive disease and that she may not live to adulthood. Her teacher has explained the condition to Margaritte's classmates and has always tried to answer their questions honestly. Whenever Margaritte is sick, the class sends letters to her. This gives the students another chance to ask the teacher questions or express their concerns, and it reminds Margaritte that they are her friends and are looking forward to her return.

Note that Paolo's achievement scores are rather consistent whereas Margaritte has a mixed pattern of wide intraindividual differences.

past, childhood accidents. Because they exhibit all the symptoms and disabilities of children with genetic or birth disorders, many of these children are misclassified by health-care workers. For example, Cohen and Warren (1987) found that about one-third of the children in a center for cerebral palsy were victims of child abuse and might or might not have had cerebral palsy before the abuse.

Traumatic brain injuries can result in cognitive, social, and language defects that treatment sometimes reverses.
(© Spencer Grant/Index Stock Imagery)

National Clearinghouse on Child Abuse and Neglect Information
www.nccanch.acf.hhs.gov

There is an epidemic of child abuse in the United States. There has been an increase of a million cases of reported child abuse since 1980, bringing the total to 2 million cases reported in 1987 (Zirpoli, 1990). Reported nationwide in 1999 were 826,000 cases of maltreatment. This is a rate of 11.8 per thousand (National Clearing House on Child Abuse and Neglect, 2000). Many abused children are placed in special education classes because their symptoms and needs are the same as those of children with congenital disabilities.

■ Early Intervention

Early intervention with children who have physical disabilities and health impairments is critical. The expression *early intervention* takes on two meanings in the context of children with physical disabilities and health impairments: It means (1) identifying a disorder at birth and in infancy and (2) identifying an acquired health disorder as soon as it is apparent, which may be in infancy, in early childhood, or later in life.

Early intervention means starting therapy or treatment immediately following diagnosis.

In some children, physical disabilities can be corrected with early medical treatment. In other children, early intervention can minimize the severity of certain physical disabilities and health conditions or prevent the development of additional disabling or medical conditions. For example, children with cerebral palsy who receive physical and occupational therapy may have fewer joint contractures or deformities that could decrease function in later years.

In addition, correct physical management procedures, adaptations, and devices, if implemented by teachers, families, and others, can help the child participate in daily activities at home, at school, and in the community and acquire needed motor and self-care skills to increase independence in preparation for public school placement. The early development of adequate skills also gives children a foundation for increasing interactions in their environments and helps them acquire the cognitive, language, and social skills that are necessary for success in school.

■ Identification of Children with Physical Disabilities and Health Impairments

The identification of children with physical disabilities and health impairments is primarily the responsibility of physicians: pediatricians; neurologists, who specialize in conditions and diseases of the brain, spinal cord, and nervous system; and orthopedists and orthopedic surgeons, who are concerned with muscle function and conditions of the joints and bones. Other specialists involved in identification include physical and occupational therapists.

The identification process involves a medical evaluation, which includes a medical and developmental history (illnesses, medical history of family members, problems during pregnancy and labor, developmental progress), a physical examination, and laboratory tests or other special procedures needed for accurate diagnosis. Comprehensive assessment of a child's performance is an ongoing process mandated by PL 101-476. It provides information to the teacher, therapist, and family concerning what the child can do, what the child does not know now, and what the child needs to learn for the future (Carpignano & Bigge, 1991).

Case Study

Elizabeth is 16 years old. She attends a countywide specialized school for students with significant and complex disabilities. She has cerebral palsy and moderate cognitive impairment that result in her need to use a wheelchair, augmentative communication systems, and personal assistance services. Elizabeth is a pleasant and compliant student who appears cheerful and agreeable most of the time. She seems to enjoy everything she does in school. At home, Elizabeth's parents report, she enjoys watching television, sitting on the front porch during nice days, listening to music with her 9-year-old sister, and going for an occasional ride to the grocery store. Elizabeth has a reliable point and uses a large switch to activate voice messages that her teacher programs into her augmentative device.

Her speech therapist worked with Elizabeth's parents to develop a "TV picture guide" so that Elizabeth can choose which TV show to watch. Additionally, the speech therapist helped Elizabeth's mom use switch interfaces around the house so that Elizabeth can turn on the CD player herself (she also has a picture guide to her CDs), turn lights on and off in her room, and activate the whirlpool in the bathtub by herself.

Elizabeth spends her entire school day within one classroom in her school with eight other students, 14–18 years old, who present similar

(text continues on page 552)

EDUCATIONAL

CHILDREN WITH PHYSICAL DISABILITIES AND HEALTH IMPAIRMENTS

Adapting the Learning Environment

The academic curriculum and academic skills do not necessarily present problems to children with physical disabilities. Children who miss school frequently or for long periods because of illness or surgery, however, may require special attention to catch up. Some children with health problems are unable to last a full day in school, so the teacher must teach the essentials over a shorter period of time or arrange for some home instruction.

Instructional adaptations may be necessary in order for children with physical disabilities to participate fully and benefit from classroom instruction. Teachers can adapt existing instructional materials, modify skill sequences or performance requirements, or use adaptive and assistive devices. And they should work cooperatively with physical and occupational therapists when they have students with physical disabilities. Therapeutic techniques must be integrated into daily programs.

Browder (2001) offers a curriculum-building model to assist the teacher in deciding what to teach. She states that curriculum and assessment are intertwined and recommends an "ecological assessment" process, which is a blend of person-centered planning and behavioral assessment (p. ix). This process emphasizes the need to consider the student in the context of his or her family, community, and culture (Lidz, 2003).

Not all children need the same number or types of adaptations. The necessary adaptations depend on the child's physical capabilities and individual needs. Related services play an important role in four areas of concern: communication, interaction with instructional materials, physical education, and emergency and medical procedures.

Inclusion in Context

IDEA encourages schools to educate students in inclusive settings and to offer the services necessary for students to succeed in that environment. Although changes in reporting methods make it difficult to compare past and current figures, the U.S. Department of Education (1999) reported that more than 93 percent of students with physical disabilities are being educated in public school environments and that the number of students with physical disabilities in public schools is increasing. Minnesota educates 70 percent of these children in general education classes, Vermont 88 percent. Most states use the general education classroom, resource room, and separate class (U.S. Department of Education).

Individualization requires that the learning environments discussed in Chapter 2 be available to students with physical disabilities. This means students are in general education classrooms, resource rooms, special classes, special schools, perhaps at home or in hospitals—according to their needs.

Students with physical disabilities may need to master augmented and alternative forms of communication to complete their schoolwork.
(© Rhoda Sidney/The Image Works)

Students with physical disabilities who have no other learning impairments can achieve their greatest potential in the regular classroom. Here these children have the same learning opportunities and expectations as their peers. If children with physical disabilities are going to learn to live in integrated environments as adults, they must attend regular schools and classes to the greatest extent possible (Brown & Gothelf, 1996). Adjustments, like providing additional space to maneuver a wheelchair, extra time to change classes, or access to a computer terminal, are often the key to enabling a child to participate in a challenging curriculum and in meaningful social interaction.

Some students may need tutoring by a resource room teacher to catch up with the class after a long absence. Others may go to adapted physical education or physical therapy while classmates go to physical education. These services are most effective as integral supports to general education rather than as separate entities. Some students, however, require such extensive adaptation that their needs can be met only in a separate class.

For students without learning impairments, placement in a special class should be temporary, and instruction should be geared toward reducing barriers that prevent participation in regular classes. For example, school personnel determined that Paolo had normal intelligence but could not communicate his needs or complete academic tasks because of severe cerebral palsy. It took approximately two years of intensive training to teach Paolo to use an electronic communication system and to bring him up to grade level in essential reading,

> For students with normal intelligence, instruction should be geared toward full participation in the regular classroom.

Students with physical disabilities but no specific learning impairment require adjustments—space to maneuver a wheelchair, time to change classes, or access to an elevator or computer terminal—before they can successfully participate in the regular school setting. (© Paul Meredith/Getty Images)

spelling, and math skills. During that time, he was assigned to a special class; it was understood, however, that the assignment was temporary. The goal of Paolo's educational program was to integrate him in the regular classroom. His special education teacher arranged for him to visit general education classes during a variety of activities and to have lunch with children his age. When Paolo was finally placed in the regular classroom, he knew his classmates and was prepared to enter the general education curriculum. Also, his classroom teacher understood his needs, and the special education teacher and related services continued to be resources.

Children who are recovering from an acute illness, a serious accident, or surgery may have to continue their school program at home or in the hospital. In some cases, children's hospitals run their own schools. In others, an itinerant teacher maintains contact between homebound or hospitalized students and their regular teachers. Schools also have begun to use closed-circuit television and computers connected via telephone lines to maintain contact with homebound students.

| Some schools use closed-circuit television and computers to stay in contact with students who need to be at home.

Collaboration: The Role of Related Services Collaboration is crucial for inclusive programs and other placements in regular schools (Snell et al., 2000). The collaborative team sets goals, pools its resources, and is mutually cooperative toward common goals. These teams include two or more teachers and the needed therapists. Occupational and physical therapists recently have started working in educational settings, and school nurses are expanding their traditional roles. These professionals support the efforts of teachers in three primary ways:

▶ They provide direct services to students.

▶ They develop IEPs and specific programs in cooperation with the classroom teacher.

▶ They prepare the classroom teacher to carry out or follow through on specific interventions.

For example, Bridgit, a child with myelomeningocele, goes to physical therapy three times a week to work on increasing her walking speed and endurance. The occupational therapist is teaching her to manage her clothing more independently. The therapists report Bridgit's achievements to her teacher and have helped the teacher incorporate their methods into Bridgit's routine trips to the bathroom. As a result, Bridgit practices her walking and dressing skills daily. Although she continues to need help going to the bathroom, trained aides are available to assist her.

Some teachers may be trained to provide direct services generally associated with another discipline. For example, a teacher might teach a child to use a wheelchair. The nurse or therapist assesses the child's needs, determines the proper method of intervention, and then, with the educational team, decides who should carry out the intervention. The decision is based on several factors.

Members of the interdisciplinary team must assist the teacher in the day-to-day work with children who have health impairments and physical disabilities.

DECIDING WHO PROVIDES SERVICES

▶ Who can perform the function legally?

▶ Who has the expertise now?

▶ Who else could learn the necessary skills?

▶ Who is consistently available to teach the task?

▶ When and where does it make sense to teach the task?

▶ How quickly will the child learn to perform the task?

If the classroom teacher is selected to carry out tasks outside his or her expertise, a nurse or therapist provides the teacher with training and ongoing consultation to ensure that the student's needs are being met. Usually, an interdisciplinary support team is needed to provide the range of necessary services.

Just as it may not be appropriate for a teacher to carry out certain related services, it may not be appropriate to carry out all therapy or medical programs in a school setting. Related services as defined in IDEA include developmental, corrective, and other supportive services, such as speech pathology and audiology, psychological services, physical and occupational therapy, recreation, counseling, and transportation (IDEA, PL 105-17, 1997). The courts have ruled that a health service such as clean intermittent catheterization must be provided in school when without it the student would be unable to receive an education in the least restrictive environment. Similarly, a child with cerebral palsy might need occupational therapy to achieve educational goals. In contrast, a child recovering from a broken leg would not be eligible to receive physical therapy in school because the child could remain in the least restrictive environment and make satisfactory educational progress without those services. Medical services that are not educationally relevant, then, remain the legal and financial responsibility of parents and health-care providers.

Collaboration: Emergency and Medical Procedures Teachers, therapists, and other school personnel who work with children who have physical disabilities or health conditions should know about the nature of the child's condition, restrictions on activities, medications, and emergency procedures. School districts should have a policy for handling medical procedures and emergencies. The policy should indicate what to do in case of seizures, severe falls or blows to the head, severe bleeding, fainting, choking, and other emergencies (Ault, Rues, Gruff, & Holovet, 2000). Teachers should have the policy in writing and should know whom to notify first in case of emergency, how to notify them, how to have the rest of the class supervised during the emergency, and how to intervene during the emergency (Bigge & Best, 2000; Hill, 1999). In addition, written records should be maintained, recording the administration of medications and instances of seizures, accidents, or injuries.

Adapting Instructional Materials and Classroom Equipment Many students with physical disabilities have difficulty using common instructional materials and classroom equipment. They can't hold a book or turn pages. They can't use the classroom tape recorder, film projector, or slide projector. Table 13.2 provides suggestions for adaptations:

> Some children with health disabilities require the presence of medical personnel (nurses or pediatricians) on site during the school day.

TABLE 13.2
Instructional Strategies for Students with Traumatic Brain Injuries

▶ Use a multimodal approach (overheads, videos, hands-on activities) when presenting material and instructions for assignments.

▶ Teach compensatory strategies to students and structure choices.

▶ Begin class with review and overview of topics to be covered.

▶ Provide the student with an outline of the material to be presented, to assist in comprehension.

▶ Emphasize main points and key ideas frequently.

▶ Incorporate repetition into instruction.

▶ Provide specific, frequent feedback on student performance and behavior.

▶ Encourage questions.

▶ Break down large assignments into smaller components.

▶ Use task analyses to determine skill acquisition and maintenance.

▶ Ask the student how he or she could improve learning.

▶ Use a variety of open-ended and multiple-choice questions to encourage independent thinking.

▶ Present difficult material in a simplified fashion, using illustrations or diagrams if possible.

▶ Provide the student with cues when appropriate.

Source: Adapted from L. Keyser-Marias, L. Brill, P. Sharon-Targett, S. Yasasa, S. Johnson, & P. Wehman, Enhancing the schooling of students with tramatic brain injury, *Teaching Exceptional Children, 34*(4) (2002): 62–67. Reprinted with permission.

Increasingly, computers and computer programs are accessible with a mouse replacing the keyboard. The pace of technological evolution is so rapid that we cannot predict what will be available in the next few years. More and more interactive materials are becoming available on a daily basis. Inquiries to information networks such as those described in Chapter 12 will be essential for teachers to keep current.

Accessibility of Facilities

Section 504 of the Rehabilitation Act of 1973 laid the groundwork for moving students with physical disabilities to less restrictive environments by requiring that public buildings be accessible to all people. School buildings built after the passage of this legislation should be accessible. Older buildings, however, may require renovations. Minimal renovations might include adding ramps at entrances. Extensive renovations might include installing an elevator in a two-story building and renovating the restrooms in addition to adding ramps. The American National Standards Institute (1980) developed accessibility standards for new facilities; these guidelines also can be used to determine if facilities are accessible for students with impaired mobility.

> Teachers can consider removing or securing rugs so that a student with impaired ambulation won't trip.

MAKING FACILITIES ACCESSIBLE

▶ Walkways should be at least 36 inches wide and have a continuous surface that is not interrupted by steps or abrupt changes of more than one-half inch.

▶ Ramps should be at least 36 inches wide. Indoor and outdoor ramps should have a slope of not more than 1 foot for every 12 feet and 1 foot for every 20 feet, respectively.

> United States Access Board information on physical access of the environment
> www.access-board.gov

▶ Entrances and doorways should be 32 inches wide to allow for easy passage of a wheelchair. The threshold should be beveled and have a maximum edge height of three-quarters of an inch.

▶ An accessible restroom should be available for both males and females on all floors. Stalls should be 60 inches wide and 60 inches deep and have stall doors that swing out to easily accommodate a wheelchair.

Adapting Curriculum

The unique needs of children with physical disabilities demand expansion of the traditional school curriculum into three areas: motor skills and mobility, self-care skills, and social and emotional adjustment.

Section 504 of the Rehabilitation Act of 1973 requires that schools receiving assistance for educational purposes must not discriminate against children with disabilities (deBettencourt, 2002). Such students are to be provided with reasonable accommodations, comparable to those of their peers who do not have disabilities. To be eligible for funding under Section 504, evaluations must be administered to verify the existence of a substantial list of major life activities, such as breathing, walking, seeing, hearing, working, learning, and caring for oneself. Note that these are functional skills, not disability categories like those described in IDEA.

Both IDEA and Section 504 may be applied to students with disabilities. Section 504 does not require an IEP (Individualized Education Program), and students are placed in a regular classroom. Kent (2004) states that Section 504 may be important as a rationale for providing services to students with conditions such as asthma or diabetes.

Motor Skills and Mobility

Motor skills and mobility constitute a critical area of skill development for children with physical disabilities. These skills are necessary to maintain upright postures (sit, stand), perform functional movements (reach, grasp), and move around in the environment. The programming priorities for motor skill development should include developing functional movements and postures that are needed to perform classroom and school activities. Appropriate positioning techniques include the following:

▶ Development of head control and trunk control to maintain an upright sitting posture to perform needed activities throughout the school day (attending and listening, writing, using a computer or communication device, eating)

▶ Development of arm movements and fine motor skills for performance of needed activities throughout the school day (holding a pencil and paper to write, holding a book and turning pages, using keyboards or switches to access a computer or communication device)

▶ Development of standing and balance for assisted ambulation (using braces and crutches)

▶ Development of skills needed to maneuver a wheelchair in the classroom and throughout the school environment (using arms to propel, learning to use an electric wheelchair with a joystick or other control, turning corners and entering doorways, negotiating ramps and curbs, crossing streets)

Physical and occupational therapists assume the primary responsibility for setting goals in motor development and mobility. They must work closely with teachers, other professionals, and parents, however, for the child to meet these goals. Teachers should become familiar with the basic working components of mobility equipment (wheelchairs, braces, crutches, walkers) and report needed repairs or adjustments to the child's therapist. Therapists should provide teachers and others with information related to the child's physical condition, limitations, and abilities.

Classroom teachers and others may be required to learn special techniques to help children perform motor tasks during the school day. Positioning, handling, lifting, and transfer techniques are physical management procedures that teachers and others use to help the student maintain good body alignment in a variety of positions (postures) and perform functional movements and skills in the context of daily activities.

A child with spastic cerebral palsy who constantly leans sideways in the wheelchair will have tremendous difficulty reaching the keyboard on the computer and striking the correct keys or using the mouse. With help from a physical therapist or occupational therapist, the teacher can learn to position the student

Physical and occupational therapists hold primary responsibility for setting a child's goals in motor development and mobility.

WWW American Physical Therapy Association information and resources www.apta.org

in the wheelchair, use a slant board to move the keyboard closer to the child, and relax the child's arms and bring them forward to rest on the keyboard.

Increasingly, children with cerebral palsy are involved in motor skill activities under the guidance of a physical therapist. These activities include swimming, dance, martial arts, horseback riding, and other real-life experiences. The activities prevent atrophy of damaged muscles. Current data indicate that 67 percent of adults with cerebral palsy live independently, a significant increase over previous years (Anastasiow, 2001).

Self-Care Skills

Being able to take care of themselves is another critical area for children with physical disabilities. Self-determination and independence training are very important for these children as well. (See Chapter 12 for a full discussion of these issues.) Self-care skills include eating, toileting, dressing, bathing, and grooming. Students with severe physical involvement may require physical assistance in eating or may have to be fed. Some children need assistive devices or physical help to perform many of these tasks; for example, utensils with built-up or larger handles, special plates and cups, or nonskid mats to stabilize the child's plate.

Students who have health conditions that require medication on a routine basis (injections for diabetes) or a periodic basis (inhalants for asthma) should be taught as early as possible to administer the medication themselves. Teachers or school nurses must monitor the process closely, however, because they ultimately are responsible for seeing that the correct procedures are followed and that appropriate legal permission from parents, guardian, or physicians is secured before any medication is administered.

Social and Emotional Adjustment

Children with physical disabilities sometimes feel powerless. Christie knows that she has leukemia and that she will probably live only a few more months. She is frequently absent from school. She misses her friends when she is away from school, but when she returns, she no longer feels a part of the group. Besides being sick, she is lonely and is keeping to herself more and more. Josh faces an entirely different problem. He is recovering from a traumatic brain injury that has left him using a wheelchair. He is no longer able to do many things for himself, and he has discovered that temper tantrums are an effective way to get people to respond to his needs immediately. It seems that the more people try to help Josh, the more aggressive he becomes.

Although withdrawal and aggression are normal stages in the process, children like Christie and Josh need support and help in accepting and adjusting to their disabling conditions. Christie's and Josh's behavior patterns are similar to those of children who face continuing academic or environmental problems. They have lost control over certain aspects of their lives.

Harvey and Greenway (1984) found that children with physical disabilities have "a lower sense of self-worth, greater anxiety, and a less integrated view of self" than do children without handicaps (p. 280). Orr (1989), however, found children with physical disabilities in several settings who had positive self-concepts. Research shows that people are more likely to accept their physical disability when the environment is supportive (Heinemann & Shontz, 1984),

A major goal of education is to assist children with physical disabilities to achieve and maintain a positive self-concept.

when they achieve some sense of control over their disability, and when they begin to demonstrate new competence. In addition to using the methods described in Chapter 12, teachers can enhance the social and emotional adjustment of children with physical disabilities by increasing the understanding of the disabling condition, emphasizing quality of life, and increasing a sense of control.

Adapting Teaching Strategies

Increasing the Understanding of the Disabling Condition

The teacher of a student with a physical disability should learn as much as possible about the condition—its cause, treatments, prognosis, and educational implications. Then, in cooperation with the child's parents, the teacher should help the child and other students understand relevant aspects of the condition. One of the major functions of organizations like the Epilepsy Foundation of America, the American Cancer Society, the March of Dimes Birth Defects Foundation, and United Cerebral Palsy is to provide information to the public. Many of these organizations offer teaching kits or help in developing educational workshops to increase children's and adults' understanding of a particular condition. Commercial materials are also available to help children learn about a variety of disabilities. School work may need to be modified to conform to the student's ability to function at his or her best (Janney, Snell, & Elliot, 2000).

When teaching children about disabling conditions, help them understand that a physical disability is an individual difference, not something to fear, ridicule, or be ashamed of:

▶ Honestly answer questions about a condition.

▶ Acknowledge and respect the way children (and adults) feel without condoning maladaptive behaviors (teasing, name calling).

▶ Discuss the incidents that can occur at school—an epileptic seizure, an insulin reaction—and ask students to decide how they could help or how they should behave during such an incident.

Emphasizing the Quality of Life

Teachers can help students adjust to physical disabilities by helping them see their disabilities as just one aspect of their lives and of themselves. One elementary school approached this situation by offering a group counseling session, an hour each week, for children with physical disabilities (Williams & Baeker, 1983). One goal of the group was to develop a support system; another was to recognize individual limitations and strengths. Within the general education classroom a teacher might have students list what they like or admire about each of their classmates. This kind of exercise often gets surprising results, and it is a good starting point for illustrating that children have different assets. Although children with physical disabilities must be allowed to talk about their limitations, they also should be encouraged to inventory their abilities, including the ability to help others. A physical disability cannot be ignored, but these children can learn to focus on the more positive aspects of their lives.

Focus on positive characteristics by asking students to list what they like or admire about their classmates.

Finally, teachers can improve the quality of life for a child like Christie by helping classmates show their interest and concern. When Christie is absent, her teacher has the other students send her letters, keeping her informed of the latest activities and reminding her that she is missed. When Christie returns to school, the teacher carefully avoids overprotecting and favoring the child and keeps her involved in as many activities as her condition allows.

Increasing the Sense of Control

Although Josh and Christie cannot control their physical disabilities, they can control many other aspects of their lives. It is revealing to have children with physical disabilities list the aspects of their lives that they believe they cannot control. Josh knew he could no longer move independently, and he thought he was powerless. School personnel worked with Josh and his family to show the child that his temper tantrums were in fact one way to control people and events. They also helped Josh understand how he could achieve the same results in a more constructive way. Josh learned that his family and classmates were happy to help him when necessary and were interested in socializing with him when he took a more positive approach. He found that people understood his frustration and could help him find ways to express that frustration without damaging his relationships with others. Although he still has a severe physical disability, Josh now believes that he can control many aspects of his life.

Encouraging Appropriate Physical Education

Before physical education or planned-play programs begin, the teacher should obtain from the child's physician information related to physical limitations, precautions, and restrictions on physical activities. School personnel should be aware of medical and emergency procedures related to the child's condition. Special adaptations may be needed in physical education programs or for playground activities to accommodate children with physical disabilities or health conditions. Classroom teachers should work closely with physical education teachers to design programs for children with physical disabilities or to include these children in games and playground activities.

Special equipment is available to help students. For example, a lowered basketball hoop can be used for wheelchair basketball, and a bowling ball ramp allows students in wheelchairs to bowl with their classmates. In many cases, all that's needed is a change in rules or procedures. For instance, a child in a wheelchair can play softball or baseball by batting and then having another child run the bases. The child with the disability can coach the runner to either run or stay on base. Students with physical disabilities should participate as fully as possible in physical education, recreational, and play activities. These students can play a major role in helping teachers and school personnel come up with ways to adapt activities for them.

A child in a wheelchair can bat the baseball and coach another child to run the bases.

Driver's Education A driver's license is a major step for teenagers in their quest for independence and maturity. The same holds true for those with physical disabilities. However, while 88 percent of other teenagers acquire their licenses, only 46 percent of teenagers with disabilities acquire them (McGill & Vogtle, 2001).

For the student with disabilities, securing a driver's license is a step toward being perceived as a typical teenager and means the acquisition of additional freedom and independence in being able to engage in activities without parental assistance. In addition, being able to transport oneself increases educational and employment opportunities. Every effort should be made to encourage school systems to include students with physical disabilities in driver's education programs.

Technology

Augmentative and Alternative Communication

Students with physical disabilities who cannot acquire understandable speech or legible writing skills must be provided with augmented and alternative communication systems (Light, Beukelman, & Rejechle, 2003). Some children with cerebral palsy, for example, have severe involvement of the oral muscles used in speech and limited fine motor abilities that hamper their writing skills. Muscular dystrophy or arthritis can leave children so weak that they tire easily when writing. Teachers and parents should work closely with speech therapists in selecting, designing, and implementing augmented and alternative communication devices for children with physical disabilities.

The U.S. Office of Special Education defines *assistive technology device* as follows: "Assistive technology device means any item, piece of equipment, or product system, whether acquired commercially off the shelf, modified or customized, that is used to increase, maintain, or improve the functional capability of children with a disability [Authority 20 U.S.C.—1401-(1)]."

Assistive technology service means "any service that directly assists a child with a disability in the selection, acquisition, and use of an assistive technology device [Authority 20 U.S.C.—1401-(2)]."

Assistive technology devices include the following:

For mobility
▶ Walker

▶ Grab bars and rails

▶ Wheelchair (manual or powered)

▶ Powered scooter

For activities of daily living
▶ Nonskid material

▶ University cuff and strap for holding items in hand

▶ Adaptive eating utensils, dressing equipment, devices for hygiene and cooking

For seating
▶ Nonslip surface on chair

▶ Holster, rolled towel, blocks for feet

Vision
▶ Eyeglasses

▶ Magnifiers

- Large-print books
- Screen magnifiers
- Braille material

Hearing
- Pen and paper
- Computer/portable word processor
- TTY/TDD
- Closed captioning
- Flash alert signals
- Phone amplifier

Recreation
- Toys adapted with Velcro
- Toys with single-switch operation
- Universal cuff to hold crayons
- Arm support
- Electronic aid to operate TV, VCR, etc.
- Computer games

Adapted from the Technology and Media Division (TAM) of the Council for Exceptional Children and the Wisconsin Assistive Technology Initiative.

Speech: Boards and Electronic Devices The most common augmented and alternative methods for speech are communication boards and electronic devices with synthesized speech output.

- Most children use the board or electronic device by pointing with a finger or fist to a word or symbol.
- Children who are not able to point accurately use a hand-held pointer, a head-mounted wand, or a mouthstick.
- Youngsters with limited use of their hands may use their eyes instead, visually focusing on the intended word or letter.

A single switch may be necessary for students who have limited or no use of their hands. The type of switch depends on the child's movement abilities. Numerous commercial switches are available, and many can be made at home. A switch is used with devices that light each possible selection on the board by rows, then columns. When the correct row is lit and the child presses the switch a second time, the correct sentence, phrase, word, or letter is "spoken." Although this method is slower than accessing the device by pointing or use of a keyboard, it does accommodate students with severe physical involvement. Many electronic communication devices can be connected to a computer for word processing or computer-assisted instruction.

Many electronic communication devices can be connected to computers for word processing and computer-assisted instruction.

Houghton Mifflin Teacher Education website http://education.college .hmco.com/students

Supplemental boards or overlays for electronic devices may be needed for academic content areas. For example, a mathematics board contains numbers, mathematics symbols, and words related to current classroom instruction. Other subject boards reflect the content and vocabulary of the specific academic subject (science, social studies, history). These boards should be revised or replaced as classroom content changes throughout the school year.

The provision of augmented and alternative communication devices for students with unintelligible speech is critical (Beukelman & Mirenda, 1998; Flippo, Inge, & Barcus, 1995). Many of these students may be denied placement in a less restrictive environment (resource room or general education classroom) because of their lack of spoken language. Professionals should work cooperatively with speech therapists, parents, and others to select an appropriate device, teach the student how to use it, and help others communicate with the student. (More specific information on the selection, design, and use of communication boards and other electronic devices is found in Chapters 7 and 12.) See the Houghton Mifflin Teacher Education website for an expanded list of assistive technology equipment.

Writing: Aids and Systems A variety of aids and augmented and alternative systems are available for written communication. Students with physical disabilities that cause muscle weakness, involuntary movements, and poor coordination of the fingers and hands may require a writing aid or an alternative system to complete written assignments in school and at home in a near and timely manner.

A critical area of skill development for children with physical disabilities is motor skills and mobility, which are necessary to maintain upright postures, perform functional movements, and move around in the environment.
(© Jerry Speier/Design Conceptions)

ADAPTATIONS FOR WRITING

▶ Hand splints to aid in grasping a crayon or pencil

▶ Special pencil holders

▶ Slant board to support forearms

▶ Clipboard, heavy weight, or masking tape to secure paper while writing

▶ Wide-lined paper (Bigge & Best, 2000)

Computers as Writing Aids Computers are another alternative means for written communication. Word-processing software can be used to complete written assignments. Keyguards are available for most types of computer keyboard. For students who cannot use a standard keyboard because they lack fine motor skills, expanded keyboards with large keys are easier to use. A student with muscular dystrophy might use a miniature keyboard because he or she lacks the range of motion in the arms required to use a standard keyboard, yet has good finger movement within a limited range. Alternative keyboards are placed directly on the student's lap, desk, or lap tray for easy access. Manuel, a wheelchair-using student with advanced muscular dystrophy, has very little strength. However, he can control the computer mouse with two fingers. With the mouse, he can move the cursor on the screen and interact with the computer program, which gives him access to a world of knowledge and games. In this manner, students with severe physical involvement need not be able to use the keyboard. They can use the mouse, which requires far less effort.

Some students find it easier to use the computer mouse instead of a keyboard.

(text continues from page 537)

educational challenges. Her curriculum reflects an array of activities that are age-appropriate. Computers in the classroom have adapted keyboards and switches. Each morning Elizabeth and her classmates develop their daily schedule with the teachers. She attends academic classes along with students from other classes who share the same interests. As Elizabeth loves to cook, she helps out in the school cafeteria every day doing preparation for lunch. She sorts condiments. She also goes to a volunteer job at a nearby college where she delivers mail. People at the college recognize Elizabeth and are warm and friendly to her. The teacher is trying to arrange for Elizabeth to have a snack in the college snack bar with a student.

■ Transition

For all individuals with disabilities, the transition from school to work and independent living presents a range of challenges, such as obtaining a driver to take them to and from work, remodeling an apartment so that all appliances can be reached from a wheelchair, or having a live-in aide with special knowledge of how to deal with various kinds of equipment.

The National Information
Center for Children and Youth
with Disabilities
www.nichcy.org

The National Information Center for Children and Youth with Disabilities (NICHCY, 2000) has prepared a Transition Summary for parents, teachers, and individuals to assist individuals with disabilities in moving into work and independent living. The center indicates that research has demonstrated an enormous qualitative difference in the lives of people with disabilities because of recent legislation leading to changes to assist these individuals throughout the transition process. Postsecondary programs, on-the-job education, internships and apprenticeships, adult education, trade school, and technical schools as well as college and career education are all available with some support (NICHCY).

■ Family and Lifespan Issues

A child with health impairments
may feel conflict between daily
health needs and happiness.

Children with health impairments such as diabetes, cystic fibrosis, AIDS, and cancer face shortened lives. These conditions follow different courses, however, which can present children with tremendous uncertainties. For some children with diabetes, even strict compliance with prescribed medication and diet does not guarantee good health or a normal lifespan, and violations often do not have immediate serious effects. Children with cystic fibrosis face a prognosis that is more certain but also more pessimistic: Few survive into adulthood, although recent treatments are increasing the lifespan of some individuals (*Science,* 1990). Children with advanced cancers face death daily. There are times when a child's death will occur. This is a very difficult time for parents, for the whole collaborative multidisciplinary team, and particularly for the child's classmates. Children's concept of death matures slowly, and they need support to be able to deal with grief following a death. Table 13.3 offers some guidelines for helping a child deal with grief.

Nevertheless, most children want to live as normally as possible. When a child with a terminal illness attempts to participate fully in life's activities, we may consider the child valiant. For a child with a condition like diabetes,

TABLE 13.3
Guidelines for Helping a Child Deal with Grief

1. Encourage children to express their feelings but don't push for too much or require that they do so.
2. Be honest. Answer questions truthfully and express your own emotions honestly.
3. Keep it simple. Discuss death in terms children can understand. Don't give them more information than they can handle at their developmental level.
4. Relate to children at their developmental level. If you're unsure of their level, ask them for their interpretation of what happened.
5. Be patient. Be aware that children may repeat the same questions as they seek reassurance and deal with confusion and fear. Also remember that the length of grieving differs from child to child and may last for some time.
6. Don't preestablish expectations. Each child deals with death differently.
7. Do suggest some ways a child can memorialize the person such as planting a tree in that person's honor, drawing a special picture, or writing something about the person.
8. Accept the child's feelings, perceptions, and reactions. Allow for differences of opinion, doubt, and questions.
9. Refer the child (and perhaps the parents) to other support people or services if necessary.
10. Prepare children for the continuation of their life. Reassure them that they will feel better after a time and that the time differs from person to person. Children should be assured that, in time, they will be able to play and have fun and that doesn't mean they love the person any less.

Source: From C. Thornton & J. Karjewski, Death education for teachers: A refocused concern relative to medically fragile children, *Intervention in School and Clinic, 29* (1993): 31–35. Copyright © 1993 by PRO-ED, Inc. Reprinted with permission.

which has a less certain course, efforts to live normally—eating the same foods as friends and family, strenuous exercise—may violate prescribed care. We may think this child is unaccepting, ambivalent, or noncompliant, but he or she may be experiencing a daily conflict between health needs and happiness. When we recognize the conflict, we can offer more effective support and accommodation (Bradley, Ashbaugh, & Blaney, 1994).

As a child with a terminal illness or progressive condition approaches the point where death becomes a certainty, he or she may face tremendous fear and grief, as may family members, classmates, and school personnel. Teachers must confront their own feelings about death and dying before they can offer support to children and their families.

Parents need to be prepared for lifelong issues that they and their child may face. Table 13.4 offers an overview of these issues.

Policies Against Discrimination

People with physical handicaps face intentional and unintentional discrimination from other people and from the "system." Fear, ignorance, lack of experience, and inflexibility are the most common causes of discrimination. It is

TABLE 13.4
Possible Issues Encountered by Parents at Life Cycle Stages

EARLY CHILDHOOD, AGES 0–5	▶ Obtaining an accurate diagnosis ▶ Informing siblings and relatives ▶ Locating services ▶ Seeking to find meaning in the exceptionality ▶ Clarifying a personal ideology to guide decisions ▶ Addressing issues of stigma ▶ Identifying positive contributions of exceptionality ▶ Setting great expectations
ELEMENTARY SCHOOL, AGES 6–12	▶ Establishing routines to carry out family functions ▶ Adjusting emotionally to educational implications ▶ Clarifying issues of mainstreaming vs. special class placement ▶ Participating in IEP conferences ▶ Locating community resources ▶ Arranging for extracurricular activities
ADOLESCENCE, AGES 12–21	▶ Adjusting emotionally to possible chronicity of exceptionality ▶ Identifying issues of emerging sexuality ▶ Addressing possible peer isolation and rejection ▶ Planning for career/vocational development ▶ Arranging for leisure time activities ▶ Dealing with physical and emotional change of puberty ▶ Planning for postsecondary education
ADULTHOOD, AGES 21 ON	▶ Planning for possible need for guardianship ▶ Addressing the need for appropriate adult residence ▶ Adjusting emotionally to any adult implications of dependency ▶ Addressing the need for socialization opportunities outside the family ▶ Initiating career choice or vocational program

Source: From A. P. Turnbull & H. R. Turnbull, *Families, professionals, and exceptionality: A special partnership,* (2nd ed.) (Upper Saddle River, NJ: Pearson, 1990). Reprinted with permission of Pearson Education.

difficult to reconcile the fact that individuals limited by physical handicaps must also deal with limitations unnecessarily imposed on them by others.

Section 504 of the Rehabilitation Act of 1973 prohibits employers from discriminating against people with handicaps who are otherwise qualified for employment. The act further requires that all agencies receiving federal funds must make their programs and buildings accessible to those with handicaps.

The Americans with Disabilities Act (ADA) (1990) went into effect in 1991. It mandated the removal of many of the obstacles that individuals with disabilities face and an end to intentional or unintentional discrimination. The legislation requires employers to make reasonable efforts to hire people with disabilities. Although it has substantially reduced some types of barriers, violations and other types of discrimination persist. Public information and advocacy are still necessary to increase acceptance and access for people with physical disabilities.

Summary

▶ A physical disability is a condition that interferes with a child's ability to use his or her body; a health impairment is a condition that requires ongoing medical attention. A physical disability or health impairment is not a handicap unless it limits the individual's participation in routine activities.

▶ The cause of the disability or disorder has a large impact on the problems that children with physical disabilities face. Those with congenital conditions tend to make necessary adaptations to those conditions. Children whose disabilities are caused by injury generally go through a period of mourning before they finally accept and adjust to their conditions. Children whose conditions are caused by disease have the same adjustment problems as other physically disabled youngsters but also face uncertainty and the academic pressure that stems from frequent absence.

▶ Children with neurological conditions suffer from motor disabilities ranging from mild incoordination to total paralysis, and intellectual deficiencies sometimes complicate their development. Children with musculoskeletal conditions have motor skill deficits that in severe cases prevent walking or even sitting up. Children with cardiopulmonary conditions have breathing or heart problems that limit their participation in physical activities. Children with chronic life-threatening health conditions may require extensive medical treatment or hospitalization in acute stages.

▶ Children with physical disabilities, like other exceptional children, should be taught in the least restrictive environment. For most of these children, this means the general education classroom with

extra attention in the resource room if needed. Special classes are a means of bringing children with normal intelligence up to grade level and equivalent capabilities and integrating them as quickly as possible into general education classrooms. Homebound or hospital services are essential to the educational program of some children, if only temporarily.

▶ The implementation of the educational program for children with physical disabilities often involves physical therapists, school nurses, and occupational therapists. These specialists and others (speech therapists, parents) should work in close cooperation with the classroom teacher to reinforce skill learning.

▶ Content and instructional adaptations for children with physical disabilities and health impairments may be needed in the areas of communication, use of instructional materials and classroom equipment, physical education, and emergency and medical procedures. The degree of adaptation varies from child to child.

▶ Teachers can facilitate the social and emotional adjustment of their students in several ways: by increasing students' understanding of the condition, by emphasizing the quality of life, and by increasing feelings of self-control.

Future Challenges

1. *To what extent should students with physical and health issues be included in the regular education classroom?*

Professionals and laypeople continue to disagree about the extent to which children with physical disabilities can or should be taught in the general education classroom. Much of the controversy stems from misconceptions and different experiences. In fact, there is no single "right" method. Decisions must be made case by case, based on individual needs, not on a diagnosis or disability. We cannot assume that certain children do not fit or cannot benefit from inclusion unless they prove it.

2. *Will training programs effectively prepare the multidisciplinary team to work together?*

Students with physical disabilities often require an educational team consisting of members from diverse backgrounds. Professionals from traditional medical disciplines may have trouble adjusting to work in educational settings. Different terminology, methods, and philosophies further challenge the planning and implementation of coordinated educational programs. Unfortunately, some training programs do not prepare teachers and other personnel to be effective team members. Individual school programs should work toward developing models of team service delivery that address the educational needs of individual students.

3. *What technological advances are on the horizon, and who will bear the cost?*

More than any group of exceptional children, students with physical handicaps use adaptive equipment and assistive devices. These devices include specially designed spoons, customized wheelchairs, and electronic communication systems. For many people, adaptive equipment means the difference between dependence and independence. With technological advances have come new and better adaptations, but at a cost. School systems, insurance companies, and public assistance programs disagree about who should bear the cost of expensive equipment.

Key Terms

acquired immunodeficiency syndrome (AIDS)   *p. 528*

arthritis   *p. 525*

asthma   *p. 526*

cardiopulmonary system   *p. 525*

cerebral palsy   *p. 518*

epilepsy   *p. 519*

fetal alcohol syndrome (FAS)   *p. 529*

human immunodeficiency virus (HIV)   *p. 528*

musculoskeletal system   *p. 516*

neurological system   *p. 516*

spastic (pyramidal) cerebral palsy   *p. 518*

Resources

References of Special Interest

Batshaw, M., & Perret, Y. (2002). *Children with handicaps: A medical primer* (5th ed.). Baltimore: Paul H. Brookes. *The fifth edition of this exemplary text explains how genetic abnormalities, problems during pregnancy and early infancy, and nutritional deficiencies can cause disabilities. It also describes how these problems affect the nervous and musculoskeletal systems and, in turn, child development. A few physically disabling conditions also are discussed.*

Bigge, J., Best, L., & Heller, K. (2001). *Teaching individuals with physical health and multiple disabilities.* Upper Saddle River, NJ: Prentice Hall. *Detailed examination of problems that students with physical disabilities encounter and important components of education for these students. Chapters focus on assessment, methods of instruction, and components of the curriculum. Throughout the book are many examples of adaptations that minimize the impact of physical disabilities and help students benefit from the educational program.*

Dorman, J. P., & Pellegrino, L. (1998). *Caring for children with cerebral palsy.* Baltimore: Paul H. Brookes. *A comprehensive text emphasizing an interdisciplinary team approach to assessment, management, treatment, and total functioning of persons with cerebral palsy and their families.*

Hill, J. L., & Davis, A. C. (1999). *Meeting the needs of students with special physical and health needs.* Upper Saddle River, NJ: Prentice-Hall. *Richly documented with multiple checklists, diagrams, anatomical drawings of all major body systems, and helpful suggestions for teaching, this highly recommended volume contains a complete description in understandable language of a wide range of physical and health disorders.*

Krajicek, M., Steinke, T., Hertzden, D., Anastasiow, N., & Skandel, S. (2003). *Handbook for the care of infants and toddlers with disabilities and chronic conditions.* Austin, TX: PRO-ED. *This manual is designed to assist day-care and home-care workers in integrating children with physical disabilities and health problems into general education classes.*

March of Dimes (1998–2000). Public health information sheets: *Congenital heart defects: Oral-facial cleft; neurofibromatoses; spina bifida; sickle cell disease; polio and post-polio syndrome; cerebral palsy;* and many others. Available free of charge from March of Dimes, Community Service Department, 1275 Mamaroneck Avenue, White Plains, NY 10605.

Rowley-Kelley, F. L., & Reigel, D. H. (1993). *Teaching students with spina bifida*. Baltimore: Paul H. Brookes. Also, Rosenthal, R., Dukes, B., Cosgrove, S., Rowley-Kelley, F. L., & Simpson, G. (1993). *Teaching students with spina bifida* (video). Baltimore: Paul H. Brookes. *This book and the video can be ordered as a set. The two together provide a comprehensive set of techniques, strategies, and information about positioning for those who work with students with spina bifida.*

Journals

Journal of Applied Behavior Analysis
envmed.rochester.edu/wwwrap/behavior/jaba/jabahme.htm

Journal of the American Physical Therapy Association
www.ptjournal.org

Physical and Occupational Therapy in Pediatrics
www.bubl.ac.uk/journals/soc/paotip

Research and Practice for Persons with Severe Disabilities (formerly *Journal of the Association for Persons with Severe Handicaps [JASH]*)
www.tash.org/publications

Professional Organizations

Brain Injury Association, Inc. (formerly National Head Injury Foundation)
www.biausa.org

Epilepsy Foundation of America (EFA)
www.epilepsyfoundation.org

March of Dimes Birth Defects Foundation
www.modimes.org

National Information Center for Children and Youth with Disabilities (NICHCY)
www.nichcy.org

United Cerebral Palsy Association, Inc.
www.ucp.org

Please visit the book's website at **http://education.college.hmco.com/students** for new and updated information on websites listed here and for the mailing addresses of the journals and organizations.

academic achievement learning disabilities Problems with academic subjects that are due to underlying disorders in information processing.

academic aptitude A combination of general cognitive abilities that measure a student's potential for learning (such as an intelligence test or an IQ score) and achievement within specific content domains. Knowing a student's academic aptitude helps us predict the optimal level of curriculum that will allow him or her to be successful.

access technology Equipment, such as a computer mouse, that allows a student to use a computer program or that adapts the computer for a person with disabilities.

accommodation Changes in the shape of the lens of the eye in order to focus on objects closer than 20 feet.

acquired immunodeficiency syndrome (AIDS) A breakdown of the body's immune system, allowing the body to become vulnerable to a host of fatal infections that it normally is able to ward off.

alpha-fetoprotein test A blood test given to pregnant women to detect fetal disabilities.

American Sign Language (ASL) A manual language used by many people with hearing impairments that meets the universal linguistic standards of spoken English.

amniocentesis A procedure for analyzing the amniotic fluid (a watery liquid in which the embryo is suspended) to discover genetic defects in the unborn child.

Apgar test A screening test administered to an infant at one minute and five minutes after birth.

applied behavioral analysis (ABA) A learning approach that is based on individual analyses of a student's functioning and relies on the learning of behaviors to remediate learning problems.

aptitude-achievement discrepancy A discrepancy between a student's ability (measured on intelligence tests) and academic achievement; a factor in the diagnosis of learning disabilities.

arthritis Inflammation of the joints that causes them to swell and stiffen.

articulation The movement of the mouth and tongue that shapes sound into speech.

Asperger's syndrome A form of autism that features the usual social and behavior problems, but where the cognitive abilities may be average or above.

assessment A process for identifying a child's strengths and weaknesses; it involves five steps: screening, diagnosis, classification, placement, and monitoring or discharge.

assistive technology Tools that enhance the functioning of persons with disabilities.

asthma A condition affecting a person's breathing.

at-risk infant An infant who has a greater chance of displaying developmental delays or cognitive or motor deficits due to a variety of factors.

attention-deficit hyperactivity disorder (ADHD) A disorder that causes children to have difficulty settling down to do a particular task, especially desk work.

audition Thought transformed into words and received by a listener through hearing.

auditory global method A method of teaching deaf students that involves auditory training and makes extensive use of sound amplification to develop listening and speech skills. Also called *acoupedic method, acoustic method, auditory method, aural method,* and *unisensory method.*

augmented and alternative communication A variety of assistive technologies that help an individual communicate. These range from sophisticated voice synthesizers to relatively simple story boards with pictures that indicate words and actions.

authentic assessment Measuring a child's ability by means of an in-class assignment.

behavior modification Techniques designed to change behaviors and to increase the use of socially constructive behaviors.

Braille A system using embossed characters in different combinations of six dots arranged in a cell that allows people with profound visual impairments to read by touch as well as to write by using special aids.

cardiopulmonary system The heart, blood, and lungs.

case coordinator An educator who takes the lead on the child's multidisciplinary team. The coordinator is generally responsible for setting up the meetings, ensuring that all paperwork is completed, and sharing information about students' needs and progress with other team members.

central processing Classification of a stimulus through the use of memory, reasoning, and evaluation; the second step in the information-processing model.

cerebral palsy A condition caused by damage to the motor control centers of the brain before birth, during the birth process, or after birth.

chorionic villus biopsy A test used to detect disabilities in a fetus during the first trimester.

ciliary muscles Muscles that control changes in the shape of the lens so the eye can focus on objects at varying distances.

circle of friends A social contact technique that brings together disabled and nondisabled children to discuss their likes and dislikes under the leadership of a facilitator.

cleft palate Failure of the bone and tissue of the palate (roof of the mouth) to fuse during early prenatal development; often associated with cleft lip.

coercive cycle Describes a situation where the child misbehaves, the adult responds punitively, and the child in anger is driven to misbehave some more creating a downward cycle in relationship.

cognitive strategies See *executive function*.

collaborative team models Two or more teachers planning, instructing, and evaluating the same student. The team may include general education teachers with special education teachers and other professionals.

collateral skills interventions Attempts to improve skills not central to the primary condition in children with autism, such as motor coordination, which may aid the child's social adjustment.

combined method See *total communication method*.

communication The exchange of thoughts, information, feelings, or ideas.

communication disorder An impairment in articulation, fluency, voice, or language.

content acceleration Curriculum modification that moves students through the traditional curriculum at a fast pace.

content enrichment Curriculum modification that expands the material for study, giving students the opportunity for a greater appreciation of a topic.

content novelty Curriculum modification that introduces material that normally would not appear in the general curriculum, to help students who are gifted master important ideas.

content sophistication Curriculum modification that challenges students who are gifted to use higher levels of thinking to understand ideas that average students of the same age find difficult or impossible to understand.

context of the child The combination of forces in the child's environment that impact his or her development. This context includes the child's family, neighborhood, school, community, and even state and country.

continuum of services A range of personnel to provide needed specialized services such as speech, physical, or occupational therapy.

convergence Change in the extrinsic muscles of the eye.

cooperative learning A set of instructional strategies that emphasize the use of groups for teaching students techniques of problem solving and working constructively with others.

cornea The transparent anterior portion of the tough outer coat of the eyeball.

creativity Mental process by which an individual creates new ideas and products or recombines existing ideas and products in a fashion that is novel to him or her.

criterion-referenced test A test designed to measure a child's development in terms of absolute levels of mastery, as opposed to the child's status relative to other children.

cultural reciprocity Understanding the differing values in families from different cultures and the desire to find a meeting place between cultures for the benefit of the child.

culture The attitudes, values, customs, and language that form an identifiable pattern or heritage.

curriculum compacting Content modification that allows students who are gifted to move ahead. It consists of three steps: finding out what the students know, arranging to teach the remaining concepts or skills, and providing a different set of experiences to enrich or advance the students.

deafblind A person who possesses both a severe hearing loss and a severe loss of vision.

developmental disabilities Mental retardation and related conditions (e.g., cerebral palsy) that create a substantial delay in the child's development and require intervention from many professional disciplines.

developmental learning disabilities Problems in processing information—attention problems, memory problems, disorders in thinking and using language. Also called *neuropsychological learning disabilities*.

developmental scales Instruments used to compare an infant's physical, emotional, and intellectual skills to other same-age children's development.

developmental screening A brief assessment of a child's developmental progress to determine if the child is at risk or is delayed.

developmentally appropriate practices Curriculum practices that match the level of development of the child and are presented in ways that children learn (e.g., play).

diagnostic achievement tests Tests help educators understand how a student solves a problem by examining the strategies that he or she uses when learning. Diagnostic assessments help us determine why a child is struggling so that we can offer appropriate support or remediation.

dialect A variant in pronunciation and syntax of a spoken language.

differential diagnosis Pinpointing atypical behavior, explaining it, and distinguishing it from similar problems of other children with disabilities.

differentiated instruction Refers to the changes in teacher strategies and curriculum made necessary by the characteristics of the exceptional child.

divergent thinking The ability to produce many different answers to a question.

Down syndrome A chromosomal abnormality that leads to mild or moderate mental retardation and, at times, a variety of hearing, skeletal, and heart problems.

dyslexia A severe reading disability involving difficulties in understanding the relationship between sounds and letters.

dysphonia A disorder in voice quality.

early childhood intervention Systematic efforts designed to prevent deficits or to improve an existing disability in children between birth and age 5.

ecological model A view of exceptionality that examines the individual in complex interaction with environmental forces and believes that exceptionalities should be remediated by modifying elements in the environment to allow more constructive interactions between the individual and the environment.

ecological variations Changes in the child's environment that modify activities, schedules, and structures to promote opportunities for socialization. For example, a structured play task might require a student with autism to give specific toys to other children and to show them how these toys work.

ecology of the child Those forces surrounding and impacting on the child from family, culture, peers, physical setting, etc.

environmental modification A strategy creating an environment in which the child can succeed.

environmental risks Factors in the life of the child from conception that can interfere with normal development or cause a disability.

epilepsy A group of diseases of the nervous system marked primarily by seizures.

exceptional child A child who differs from the norm in mental characteristics, sensory abilities, communication abilities, social behavior, or physical characteristics to the extent that special education services are required for the child to develop to maximum capacity.

executive function The hypothesized decision-making element that controls reception, central processing, and expression.

extrinsic motivation Motivating students to complete a task by promising a reward.

fading Gradually cutting back on help as a child becomes competent at a task.

family-centered model A model of family dynamics that empowers families to take the lead in determining what is best for their child. This is done through support that focuses on the strengths of the child and family.

family-focused approach Helping parents become more autonomous and less dependent on professionals.

fetal alcohol syndrome Defects in a child as a result of the mother's heavy use of alcohol during her pregnancy.

finger spelling Spelling in the air or in the palm of another person by using a manual alphabet.

flexible pacing Allowing students to move through the school subjects or program at their own pace.

fluency The flow of speech.

Fragile X syndrome A restriction at the end of the X chromosome that may result in mental retardation or learning disabilities.

functional behavioral assessment (FBA) Valuations of behavior that define a behavior, explain why this behavior occurs, describe where and when the behavior is present, and demonstrate how the behavior impacts the child and his or her surroundings. The premise behind FBA is that there is a rational purpose for every behavior and that it is necessary to understand why and how negative or destructive behaviors are triggered in order to reduce them.

generalization The ability to apply a skill learned in one situation to a new one.

genetic counseling A source of information for parents about the likelihood of their having a child with genetically based disabilities.

gifted underachievers Students whose actual performance is low or mediocre despite their outstanding potential. Gifted students underachieve for a variety of personal and circumstantial reasons, including deciding to disengage from school because they find it boring.

grouping Bringing together students of similar abilities or levels of achievement for instruction.

Head Start A federally funded educational preschool program for children living in poverty.

health impairment A condition that requires ongoing medical attention.

home schooling Educating at home. The home-schooling movement involves over a million parents who have chosen to educate their children at home rather than send them to schools. This movement began as a response to parental concerns about appropriate religious instruction, but today many parents home school because they feel their child's needs cannot be met within the traditional school setting.

human immunodeficiency virus (HIV) A virus that breaks down the body's immune system, causing AIDS.

hyperactivity Excessive movement or motor restlessness, generally accompanied by impulsiveness and inattention.

IDEA, Part C The Individuals with Disabilities Act, Part C; the section of the act that deals with infants and toddlers.

inclusion The process of bringing children with exceptionalities into the regular classroom.

individualized education program (IEP) A program written for every student receiving special education; it describes the child's current performance and goals for the school year, the particular special education services to be delivered, and the procedures by which outcomes are to be evaluated.

individualized family services plan (IFSP) An intervention program for young children and their families that identifies their needs and sets forth a program to meet those needs.

interindividual difference A substantial difference among people along key dimensions of development.

intraindividual difference A major variation in the abilities or development of a single child.

intrinsic motivation Motivation that is internal to the student; self-motivation.

iris The colored muscular partition in the eye that expands and contracts to regulate the amount of light admitted through the pupil.

karyotyping A process by which a picture of chromosomal patterns is prepared to identify chromosomal abnormality.

language disorder The impairment or deviant development of comprehension or use (or both) of a spoken, written, or other symbol system.

learned helplessness The belief that nothing one does can prevent negative things from happening.

least restrictive environment The educational setting in which a child with special needs can learn that is as close as possible to the general education classroom.

legally blind An individual who is legally blind can see at 20 feet an object that a person with normal sight can see at 200 feet. The definition of legally blind does not mean completely without vision.

lifespan perspective An attempt to understand the child by knowing the child's past as well as present and projecting what the child will need in the future.

low vision Visual acuity of 20/70 to 20/200. Students with low vision can still benefit from visual learning through the use of various technologies to enhance their sight.

medical model A view of exceptionality that implies a physical condition or disease within the patient.

mental retardation A combination of subnormal intelligence and deficits in adaptive behavior, manifested during the developmental period.

metacognition The ability to think about one's own thinking and monitor its effectiveness.

mixed hearing loss A condition involving problems in the outer ear as well as in the middle or inner ear.

multidisciplinary team A group of professionals who work with children with disabilities to help them achieve their full potential.

musculoskeletal system The muscles, bones, and joints of the body.

neurological system The brain, spinal cord, and nerves.

neuropsychological learning disabilities See *developmental learning disabilities*.

nonverbal disabilities Children who can read and write, but have difficulty with mathematics and/or executive functions.

object permanence The understanding that objects that are not in the visual field still exist.

orientation and mobility (O&M) training Teaching a person with visual loss or with blindness how to move through space.

parent empowerment The expectation that parents will play a major role in decisions about their child's care.

peer tutoring Interactions where one student is teaching another student. This can be a useful technique, but its overuse can cause problems if the students doing the tutoring do not learn new material, and if the self-concept of the students being tutored is diminished because they feel that they are always needing help.

perceptual-motor disabilities Difficulty in understanding or responding to the meaning of pictures or numbers.

performance assessment A measure of the application of knowledge.

person-centered curriculum A curriculum that focuses on the specific strengths and needs of an individual.

person-centered planning A dynamic approach to helping communities respond to the needs of individuals with disabilities. Through this approach, the person with the disability and those who love that person are seen as the primary authorities on how to help the community develop a supportive and responsive environment where the individual can thrive.

pervasive developmental disorders not otherwise specified (PDDNOS) These are autistic-like conditions that do not fulfill all of the diagnostic characteristics for autism, but show strong resemblance in terms of social and communication problems. Increasingly referred to as Autistic Spectrum Disorders reflecting the variations found in these conditions.

phenylketonuria (PKU) A single-gene defect that can produce severe retardation because of the body's inability to break down phenylalanine, which when accumulated at high levels in the brain results in severe damage; can be controlled by a diet restricting phenylalanine.

phonation The production of sound by the vibration of the vocal cords.

phonology The science of speech sounds and the rules that govern how these sounds combine to form words and to convey meaning.

physical disability A condition that interferes with the individual's ability to use his or her body.

portfolio assessment Utilizing samples of students' work to evaluate their progress.

positive reinforcement The application of a positive stimulus immediately following a response.

postlinguistic deafness The loss of hearing after spontaneous speech and language have developed.

prelinguistic deafness The loss of hearing before speech and language have developed; referred to as *deafness*.

prenatal care Monitoring of a pregnancy by the mother and her physician.

problem based learning A problem that encourages the student to define the issue, organize the components, and then solve the problem.

pupil The central opening of the eye through which light enters.

reciprocal teaching A technique in which small groups of students and teachers take turns leading a discussion.

relationship-focused interventions Interventions that help parents develop responsive interactions with their children that build on the social nurturing between the parents and the child. This approach was first developed to support parents of children who have autism.

resonation The process that gives the voice its special characteristics.

resource room An instructional setting to which an exceptional child comes for specific periods of time, usually on a regularly scheduled basis.

respiration Breathing; the process that generates the energy that produces sound.

respite care The services of a trained individual to relieve the primary caregiver of a child with disabilities on a short-term basis.

retina The light-sensitive innermost layer of tissue at the back of the eyeball.

retinopathy of prematurity A disease of the retina in which a mass of scar tissue forms in back of the lens of the eye. Both eyes are usually affected, and it occurs chiefly in infants born prematurely who receive excessive oxygen.

rubella German measles, which in the first three months of pregnancy can cause visual impairment, hearing impairment, mental retardation, and birth defects in the fetus.

scaffolding A strategy in which a teacher models the expected behavior and guides the learning of the student.

self-determination skills A curriculum that teaches a student with disabilities how to make individual decisions and personal choices.

sensory compensation The theory that if one sense avenue is deficient, other senses are automatically strengthened.

serious emotional disturbance (SED) An emotional disturbance that creates unhappiness for the individual and often leads to behaviors that are socially disruptive or self-destructive. To be considered serious, these problems must be persistent and must interfere with life functioning and/or learning.

sheltered workshop A not-for-profit facility providing vocational services to adults with disabilities.

simultaneous method See *total communication method.*

social language learning Language learning through interaction with native speakers.

social learning approach A system designed to develop critical thinking and independent action by students.

sonography The use of sound waves to take a picture of a fetus in its mother's uterus.

spastic (pyramidal) cerebral palsy A form of cerebral palsy marked by tight muscles and stiff movements.

special courses A variety of special secondary-level courses that address students' needs for additional challenges. These advanced classes may include honors, advanced placement, and international baccalaureate opportunities and may carry college credits.

specific learning disabilities Disabilities that may manifest in any academic content area (such as reading, math, and writing). These disabilities lead to problems with learning that often impact a student's school success. The origin of these difficulties is thought to be neurological and is not due to mental retardation, sensory impairments, emotional disturbances, or the lack of opportunities to learn.

speech The systematic oral production of words of a given language.

speech disorder A disorder of articulation (how words are pronounced), voice (how words are vocalized), or fluency (the flow of speech).

speech reading Lip reading; the visual interpretation of spoken communication.

standard achievement tests Tests that measure the student's level of achievement compared with the achievement of students of similar age or grade. Also called *norm-referenced tests.*

standards movement A movement that is based on the premise that all students should be held accountable to a high level of learning. National curriculum standards for various content domains have been set, and most states have adopted these benchmarks to use as student outcome measures. The insistence on one set of high-level outcomes for all students, based on standards, can be problematic for students with severe cognitive disabilities.

student acceleration Passing students through the educational system as quickly as possible.

stuttering A disorder of fluency.

supportive competitive employment An employment strategy that allows individuals to receive support, based on their needs, for job-related skills so that they can eventually be placed in full- or part-time jobs in the competitive employment market. Support options may include job training, assistance with locating employment, and on-site job coaching.

supportive inclusion Inclusion which involves a specialist to assist the general education teacher.

support teacher A teacher who provides direct assistance to the student with disabilities and to their teacher within the regular classroom setting. This support may include assistance with behavior management, focused work with learning activities, therapeutic tutorials, and general assistance with classroom needs to allow the regular classroom teacher time to work with the student with disabilities.

synthetic speech The production of sound—of phonemes into words—by means of a computer.

TASH The Association for Persons with Severe Handicaps.

task analysis A method that breaks down complex tasks into simpler component parts, teaches each of the components separately, then teaches them together; a procedure under which a child receives positive reinforcement for each step or part of the total task as it is completed.

teratogen A substance ingested by the mother that can damage the growth and development of the fetus.

theory of mind A condition where children are unable to put themselves in the place of others in order to understand what they are feeling or thinking. This inability leads to predictable social problems.

total communication method A method of teaching deaf students that combines finger spelling, signs, speech reading, speech, and auditory amplification. Also called *combined method* and *simultaneous method.*

transient adaptation problem A behavior problem that is temporary—for example, one that occurs due to a family problem that is later resolved.

transition services Programs that help exceptional students move from school to the world of work and community.

TTY, TDD, TT Alternative names for a telephone that produces written text.

unisensory method See *auditory global method.*

universal design for learning (UDL) A variety of strategies that give all students access to the curriculum. These strategies include the use of technology to reduce the impact of sensory and learning disabilities, the incorporation of flexible entry points to allow students to begin work at a level that is appropriate to their needs, and the use of multiple instructional approaches to respond to the different learning needs and styles of the students.

Usher syndrome a progressive degeneration of vision and hearing occurring some years after birth.

vicarious learning Learning that occurs to someone who observes how others' behaviors are reinforced; the learner is not an active participant in the event.

visual impairment Any form of visual loss. These visual difficulties can include very moderate (such as the need for glasses) or a complete loss of vision.

voice disorder A variation from accepted norms in voice quality, pitch, or loudness.

wraparound approach An approach to interventions for children with disabilities and their families that offers full support from multiple perspectives across the community. The support is tailored to the family and their needs but may include things like counseling, educational assistance, medical services, and assistance from social services. The purpose is to provide a full-support network to help the child and family move toward success.

REFERENCES

Adams, M., Foorman, B., Lundberg, I., & Beeler, T. (1998). *Phonemic awareness in young children*. Baltimore: Paul H. Brookes.

Administration on Children, Youth and Families. (2001). *Building their futures: How early Head Start programs are enhancing the lives of infants and toddlers of low-income families* (Vols. 1 and 2). Washington, DC: Department of Health and Human Services.

Affleck, G., Tennen, H., & Rowe, J. (1991). *Infants in crisis: How parents cope with newborn intensive care and its aftermath*. New York: Springer-Verlag.

Affleck, J., Madge, S., Adam, A., & Lowenbrau, M. (1988). An integrated classroom versus a research model. *Exceptional Children, 54*, 339–348.

Affleck, J., Madge, S., Adams, A., & Lowenbrau, L. (1998). Integrated classroom versus resource model. *Exceptional Children, 54*, 339–348.

Als, H. (1997). Earliest intervention for preterm infants in the newborn intensive care unit. In M. Guralnick (Ed.), *The effectiveness of early intervention* (pp. 47–76). Baltimore: Paul H. Brookes.

American Association on Mental Retardation. *Frequently asked questions about mental retardation*. Downloaded from http://www.aamr.org/Policies/faq_mental_retardation. html October 5, 2004.

American Association on Mental Retardation. (2002). *Mental retardation: Definition, classification, and systems of supports* (10th ed.). Washington, DC: Author.

American Speech-Language-Hearing Association. (1991). Committee on prevention of speech, language, and hearing problems. *ASHA, 33*(9), Supple. 6.

American Speech-Language-Hearing Association Ad Hoc Committee on Service Delivery in the Schools (1993). Definitions of Communication Disorders and Variations. *ASHA, 35*(Supple. 10), 40–41.

Anastasiow, N. J. (1982). *The adolescent parent*. Baltimore: Paul H. Brookes.

Anastasiow, N. J. (1986). *Development and disability*. Baltimore: Paul H. Brookes.

Anastasiow, N. J. (1996). Psycho-biological theory of affect and self development. In S. Harel & J. Shonkoff (Eds.), *Early childhood intervention* (pp. 111–112). Jerusalem, Israel: JDC-Brookdale Institute.

Anastasiow, N. J., Frankenberg, W., & Fandall, A. (1982). *Identifying the developmentally delayed child*. Baltimore: University Park Press.

Anastasiow, N. J., Hanes, M., & Hanes, M. (1982). *Language patterns in poverty children*. Austin, TX: PRO-ED.

Anastasiow, N., & Nucci, C. (1994). Social, historical, and theoretical foundations of early childhood special education and early intervention. In P. Safford (Ed.), *Early childhood special education*, Vol. 5, *Yearbook in early childhood education* (pp. 7–25). New York: Teachers College Press.

Anderson-Inman, L. (1987). Consistency of performance across classrooms: Instructional materials versus setting as influencing variables. *Journal of Special Education, 21*, 9–29.

Andrews, J. F., & Jodron, J. (1998). Multimedia stories for deaf children. *Teaching exceptional children, 3*(5), 28–33.

Anthony, T., Fazzi, D., Lampert, J., & Pogrund, R. (1992). Movement focus: Orientation and mobility for young blind and visually impaired children. In R. Pogrund, D. Fazzi, & J. Lampert (Eds.), *Early focus: Working with young blind and visually impaired children and their families*. New York: American Foundation for the Blind.

Antia, S. (1982). Social interaction of partially mainstreamed hearing impaired children. *American Annals of the Deaf, 127*, 18–25.

Antia, S., & Levine, L. (2001). Educating deaf and hard of hearing children together. In M. Guralnick (Ed.), Early childhood inclusion (pp. 365–398). Baltimore: Paul H. Brookes.

Apgar, V., & Beck, J. (1973). *Is my baby all right?* New York: Trident Press.

Assistive Technology Consortium. (n.d.). Technology and Media Division (TAM) of the Council for Exceptional Children. CEC, Arlington, VA 22207–5704.

Atkinson, J. (1993). The Cambridge assessment and screening of vision in high risk infants and young children. In N. Anastasiow & S. Harel (Eds.), *The at-risk infant* (pp. 33–46). Baltimore: Paul H. Brookes.

Attwood, T. (1998). *Asperger's syndrome: A guide for parents and professionals*. Philadelphia: Jessica Kingsley.

Ault, M., Rues, J., Graff, J., & Holovet, J. (2000). Special health care needs. In M. Snell & F. Brown (Eds.), *Instruction of students with severe disabilities* (5th ed., pp. 245–290). Upper Saddle River, NJ: Prentice-Hall.

Ayres, A. J. (1979). *Sensory integration and the child*. Los Angeles: Western Psychological Services.

Badian, N. (1988). The prediction of good and poor reading before kindergarten entry: A nine-year follow-up. *Journal of Learning Disabilities, 21*, 98–103, 123.

Badian, N. A. (1983). Dyscalculia and nonverbal disorders of learning. In H. R. Mykelbust (Ed.), *Progress in learning disabilities* (Vol. 5, pp. 235–264). New York: Grune & Stratton.

Bailey, A., Phillips, W., & Rutter, M. (1996). Autism: Towards an integration of clinical, genetic, neurophysiological and neurobiological perspectives. *Child Psychology and Psychiatry, 37*, 89–126.

Bailey, D. (1997). Evaluating the effectiveness of curriculum alternatives and preschoolers. In M. Guralnick (Ed.), *Effectiveness of early intervention*. Baltimore: Brookes.

Bailey, D. (2002). For the development and well-being of all children. *Early Development, 6*(2), 3–4.

Bailey, D. B., Buysee, V., Edmondson, R., & Smith, T. M. (1994). Building family-centered practices in early intervention: A team-based model for change. *Infants and Young Children, 5*(1), 73–82.

Bailey, D. B., Hatton, D. H., & Skinner, M. (1998). Early developmental trajectories of males with fragile X syndrome. *American Journal on Mental Retardation, 103*, 29–39.

Bailey, D. B., Hatton, D. H., Mesibov, G., Ament, N., & Skinner, M. (2000). Early development, temperament, and functional impairment in autism and fragile X syndrome. *Journal of Autism and Developmental Disorders, 30,* 557–667.

Bailey, D., Palsha, S., & Simeonsson, R. (1991). Professional skill and concerns and perceived importance of work families in early intervention. *Exceptional Children, 58*(2), 156–165.

Bailey, D., Skinner, D., Rodríquez, P., Gut, D., & Correa, V. (1999). Awareness, use, and satifaction with services for Latino parents of young children with disabilities. *Exceptional Children, 65*(3), 367–381.

Baker, L., & Brown, A. L. (1984). Metacognitive skills in reading. In P. D. Pearson (Ed.), *Handbook of reading research* (pp. 353–394). New York: Longman.

Baker, S., & Baker, K. (1997). Educating children who are deaf or hard of hearing: Bilingual-bicultural education. *ERIC Digest, 533.*

Baldwin, A. (1987). Undiscovered diamonds. *Journal for the Education of the Gifted, 10*(4), 271–286.

Baldwin, V. (1993). Understanding the deaf-blind population. *Traces, Teaching Research.* Monmouth, OR: Western Oregon State College.

Baldwin, V. (1997). *Annual census report.* Monmouth, OR: National Technical Assistance Consortium, Teaching Research Division.

Bandura, A. (1977). *Social learning theory.* Englewood Cliffs, NJ: Prentice Hall.

Bandura, A. (1989). Human agency in social cognitive theory. *American Psychologist, 44,* 1175–1184.

Banks, J. (1994). *An introduction to multicultural education.* Boston: Allyn & Bacon.

Banks, R., Milagros, R., & Roof, V. (2003). Discovering family ancestry, priorities and resources: Sensitive family information gathering. *Young Exceptional Children, 6*(3), 11–19.

Baron-Cohen, S., Cox, A., Baird, G., Sweettenham, J., Nightingale, N., Morgan, K., Drew, A., & Charman, T. (1996). Psychological markers in the detection of autism in infancy in a large population. *British Journal of Psychiatry, 168,* 1–6.

Barraga, N., & Erin, J. (1992). *Visual handicaps and learning* (3rd ed.). Austin, TX: PRO-ED.

Barrere, I. (2000). Honoring difference. *Young Exceptional Children, 3*(4), 17–26.

Barrows, H. (1988). *The tutorial process.* Carbondale: Southern Illinois School of Medicine.

Bartlett, L. D., Weisenstein, G. R., & Etscheidt, S. (2002). *Successful inclusion for school leaders.* Upper Saddle River, NJ: Pearson Education.

Bateman, D. P., & Linden, M. A. (1998). *Better IEPs: How to develop legally correct and educationally useful programs.* Longmont, CO: Sopris West.

Bates, E. (1979). On the evolution and development of symbols. In E. Bates (Ed.), *The emergence of symbols: Cognition and communication in infancy* (pp. 1–32). New York: Academic Press.

Batshaw, M. (Ed.). (1977). *Children with disabilities.* Baltimore: Brookes.

Batshaw, M. (Ed.). (2002). *Children with disabilities* (5th ed.). Baltimore: Brookes.

Batshaw, M. L. (Ed.). (1997). *Children with disabilities: A medical primer* (3rd ed.). Baltimore: Paul H. Brookes.

Batshaw, M., & Conlon, C. (1997). Substance abuse. In M. Batshaw (Ed.). *Children with disabilities.* Baltimore: Paul H. Brookes.

Batshaw, M., & Perret, Y. (1988). *Children with handicaps: A medical primer* (2nd ed.). Baltimore: Paul H. Brookes.

Batshaw, M., & Perret, Y. (1992). *Children with handicaps: A medical primer* (3rd ed.). Baltimore: Paul H. Brookes.

Batshaw, M. L., & Rose, N. (1997). Birth defects, prenatal-diagnosis and fetal therapy. In M. L. Batshaw (Ed.), *Children with disabilities* (pp. 35–52). Baltimore: Paul H. Brookes.

Baum, S., Renzulli, J., & Hebert, T. (1995). Reversing under-achievement: Creative productivity as a systematic intervention. *Gifted Child Quarterly, 39*(4), 224–235.

Baumeister, A., & Woodley-Zanthos, P. (1996). Prevention: Biological factors. In J. Jacobson & J. Mulick (Eds.), *Manual of diagnostic and professional practice in mental retardation* (pp. 229–242). Washington, DC: American Psychological Association.

Baumgart, D., Brown, L., Pumpian, I., Nisbet, J., Ford, A., Sweet, M., Messina, R., & Schroeder, L. (1982). Principle of partial participation and individualized programs for severely handicapped students. *Journal of the Association for Persons with Severe Handicaps, 7*(2), 17–26.

Bayley, N. (1993). *Bayley scales of infant development* (2nd ed.). San Antonio: Psychological Corporation.

Bebko, J., & Luhaorp, H. (1998). The development of strategy use and metacognitive processing in mental retardation: Some sources of difficulty. In J. Burack, R. Hodapp, & E. Zigler (Eds.) *Handbook of mental retardation and development.* New York: Cambridge University Press.

Beckwith, L. (1988). Intervention with disadvantaged parents of sick preterm infants. *Psychiatry, 5*(1), 242–249.

Behrman, R., Vaughn, V., & Nelson, W. (1987). *Nelson textbook of pediatrics.* Philadelphia: Saunders.

Beirne-Smith, M., Ittenbach, J., & Patton, J. R. (1998). *Mental retardation* (5th ed.). Upper Saddle River, NJ: Merrill. (p. 83).

Beirne-Smith, M., Ittenbach, R., & Patton, J. (2001). *Mental retardation* (6th ed.). Upper Saddle River, NJ: Merrill.

Bellamy, G., Rhodes, L., Mark, D., & Albin, J. (1988). *Supportive employment.* Baltimore: Brookes.

Bellinger, D., Leviton, A., Waternaux, C., Needleman, H., & Rabinowitz, M. (1987). Longitudinal analysis of prenatal and postnatal lead exposure and early cognition. *New England Journal of Medicine, 316,* 1037–1043.

Bellugi, U. (1988). Language development. *The mind* (Vol. 7). New York: WNET, Educational Broadcasting.

Bellugi, U., & Studdert-Kennedy, A. (Eds.). (1984). *Signed and spoken language.* Deerfield Beach, FL: Verlag Chemie.

Bender, W., Clinton, G., Bender, R. (Eds.). (1999). *Violence prevention and reduction in schools.* Austin, TX: Pro-Ed.

Benz, M., Lindstrom, L., & Yoyanoff, P. (2000). Improving graduation and employment outcomes of students with disabilities: Predictive factors and student perspectives. *Exceptional Children, 66,* 509–529.

Berliner, D. C. (1990). What's all the fuss about instructional time? In R. Bromme & N. Ben-Peretz (Eds.), *The nature of time in schools: Theoretical concepts, practitioner perceptions* (pp. 3–35). New York: Teachers College Press.

Bernal, E. (1979). The education of the culturally different gifted. In A. Passow (Ed.), *The gifted and the talented: Their education and development* (Seventy-eighth Yearbook of the National Society for the Study of Education, Part 1). Chicago: University of Chicago Press.

Best, S. (2004). Personal communication.

Beukelman, D., & Mirenda, P. (1992). *Augmentative and alternative communication.* Baltimore: Paul H. Brookes.

Beukelman, D., & Mirenda, P. (2002). *Augmentative and alternative communication.* Baltimore: Brookes.

Bigge, J. (1991a). Instructional adaptations. In J. Bigge (Ed.), *Teaching individuals with physical and multiple disabilities* (3rd ed., pp. 233–256). Columbus, OH: Merrill.

Bigge, J. (1991b). *Teaching individuals with physical and multiple disabilities.* New York: Merrill.

Bigge, J., & Best L. (2000). *Teaching individuals with physical and multiple disabilities.* Upper Saddle River, NJ: Prentice Hall.

Bigge, J., Best, S., & Heller, K. (2001). *Teaching individuals with physical, health, or multiple disabilities* (4th ed.). Upper Saddle River, NJ: Merrill-Prentice Hall.

Bigge, J., Best, S., & Heller, K. (2004). *Teaching individuals with physical, health, or multiple disabilities* (5th ed.). Upper Saddle River, NJ: Merrill-Prentice Hall.

Bishop, D., Bishop, S., Bright, P., James, C., Delany, T., & Talall, P. (1999). Different origins of auditory and psychological processing problems in children with language impairments. *Journal of Speech, Language and Hearing Research, 42*(1), 155–168.

Bishop, D., Carlyon, R., Deeks, J., & Bishop, S. (1999). Auditory temporal impairment: Neither necessary nor sufficient for causing language impairment in children. *Journal of Speech, Language and Hearing Research, 42*(6), 1295–1310.

Blackhurst, A., & Edyburn, D. (2000). A brief history of special education technology. *Special Education Technology Practice, 2,* 21–36.

Blackman, J. A. (1983). *Medical aspects of developmental disabilities in children, birth to three.* Iowa City: The University of Iowa, Division of Developmental Disabilities.

Blackorby, J., & Wagner, M. (1996, March–April). Longitudinal outcomes of youth with disabilities. *Exceptional Children, 62*(5), 399–413.

Blair, B. (2000). Ryan's story: From job placement challenge to employee of the month. *Teaching Exceptional Children,* p. 47.

Blakeslee, S. (1991, September 15). Study ties dyslexia to brain flow affecting vision and other senses. *New York Times,* pp. 1, 10.

Blance, G., Stedal, K., & Smith, V. (1994, Winter). Stuttering: The role of the classroom teacher. *Teaching Exceptional Children, 26*(2), 10–12.

Bloodstein, O. (1995). *A handbook on stuttering* (5th ed.). San Diego: Singular.

Bloom, B. (Ed). (1985). *Developing talent in young people.* New York: Ballentine Books.

Bloom, L. (1991). *Language development from two to three.* New York: Cambridge University Press.

Bloom, L. (2000). Commentary. In G. Hullich, K. Hirsch-Pasek, & R. Golinkoff (Eds.), *Breaking the language barrier: An emergent coalition model of word learning* (pp. 121–135). Monographs of the Society for Research in Child Development, Serial no. 262, 65.

Bloom, L., & Tinker, E. (2001). The intentionality model and language acquisition: Engagement, effort, and the essential tension. Monographs of the Society for Research in Child Development, Serial no. 267, 66.

Bodner-Johnson, B., & Sass-Lehre, M. (2003). *The young deaf or hard of hearing child: A family-centered approach to early education.* Baltimore: Brookes.

Boone, D., & McFarlane, S. (1988). *The voice and voice therapy.* Englewood Cliffs, NJ: Prentice-Hall.

Boothroyd, A. (1988). *Hearing impairments in children.* Washington, DC: Alexander Graham Bell Association for the Deaf.

Botuck, S., & Winsberg, B. (1991). Effects of respite on mothers of school-age and adult children with severe disabilities. *Mental Retardation, 29*(1), 43–47.

Bower, T. G. R. (1989). *The rational infant.* New York: W. H. Freeman.

Bradley, P., Danielson, L., & Hallahan, D. (Eds.). (2002a). *Identification of learning disabilities: Research to practice.* Mahwah, NJ: Erlbaum.

Bradley, R., Danielson, L., & Hallahan, D. (2002b). Specific learning disabilities: Building consensus for identification and classification. In R. Bradley, L. Danielson, & D. Hallahan (Eds.), *Identification of learning disabilities: Research to practice* (pp. 791–804). Mahwah, NJ: Erlbaum.

Bradley, V., Ashbaugh, J., & Blaney, B. (1994). *Creating individual supports for people with developmental disabilities.* Baltimore: Paul H. Brookes.

Brazelton, T. (1973). *Neonatal behavioral assessment scale.* Philadelphia: Lippincott.

Bredekamp, S., & Cupple, C. (Eds.). (1997). *Developmentally appropriate practice in early childhood programs* (rev. ed.). Washington, DC: National Association for the Education of Young Children.

Brennan, P. A., Hall, J., Bor, W., Najman, J. M., & Williams, G. (2003). Integrating biological and social processes in relation to early-onset persistent aggression in boys and girls. *Developmental Psychology, 39,* 309–323.

Breske, S. (1994). Coping vulnerability in children with disabilities. *Teaching Exceptional Children, 27*(1).

Bricker, D. (1993, Spring). A rose by any name. Or is it? *Journal of Early Intervention, 17*(2), 89–96.

Bricker, D., & Cripes, J. (1992). *An activity based approach to early intervention.* Baltimore: Paul H. Brookes.

Briscoe, J., Gatherole, S., & Morland, N. (1998). Short term memory and language outcomes after extreme prematurity at birth. *Journal of Speech, Language and Hearing Research, 41*(3), 654–666.

Bristol, M. G., Gallagher, J., & Schopler, E. (1988). Mothers and fathers of young developmentally disabled and nondisabled boys: Adaptation and spousal support. *Developmental Psychology, 24*(3), 441–451.

Broidy, L. M., Nagin, D. S., Tremblay, R. E., Bates, J. E., Brame, B., Dodge, K. A., Fergusson, D., Horwood, J. L., Loeber, R., Laird, R., Lynam, D. R., Moffitt, T. E., Pettit, G. S., & Vitaro, F. (2003). Developmental trajectories of childhood disruptive behaviors and adolescent delinquency: A six-site, cross-national study. *Developmental Psychology, 39,* 222–245.

Bronfenbrenner, U. (1989). Ecological systems theory. *Annals of Child Development, 6,* 187–249.

Browder, D. (Ed.). (2001). *Curriculum and assessment for students with moderate and severe disabilities.* New York: Guilford Press.

Browder, D., & Lim, L. (2001). Family-centered planning: A multicultural perspective. In D. Browder (Ed.), *Curriculum and assessment for students with moderate and severe disabilities* (pp. 116–147). New York: Guilford Press.

Browder, D., & Lohrmann-O'Rourke, S. (2001). Promoting self-determination in planning and instruction. In D. Browder (Ed.), *Curriculum and assessment for students with moderate and severe disabilities* (pp. 148–179). New York: Guilford Press.

Browder, D., & Wilson, B. (2001). Using ecological assessment in planning for inclusion. In D. Browder (Ed.), *Curriculum and assessment for students with moderate and severe disabilities* (pp. 337–360). New York: Guilford Press.

Brown, C. (1982). *My left foot.* London: Pan.

Brown, E. (1958). *Corridors of light.* Yellow Springs, OH: Antioch.

Brown, F., & Cohen, S. (1996). Self determination and young children. *JASH, 21*(1), 22–30.

Brown, F., & Gothelf, C. (1996). Self determination for all individuals. In D. Lehr and F. Brown (Eds.), *People with disabilities who challenge the system.* Baltimore: Paul H. Brookes.

Brown, F., & Lehr, D. H. (1996). Making activities meaningful for students with severe multiple disabilities. *Teaching Exceptional Children, 25*(4), 12–16.

Brown, F., & Snell, M. (2000). Measurement, analysis and evaluation. In M. Snell & F. Brown (Eds.), *Instruction of students with severe disabilities* (5th ed., pp. 115–172). Upper Saddle River, NJ: Merrill.

Brown, L. (1997). Seizure disorders. In M. L. Batshaw (Ed.), *Children with disabilities* (pp. 553–594). Baltimore: Paul H. Brookes.

Brown, L., Nietupski, J., & Hamre-Nietupski, S. (1976). Criterion of ultimate functioning. In M. Thomas (Ed.), *Hey, don't forget about me* (pp. 14–21). Reston, VA: Council for Exceptional Children.

Bruder, M. A. (1998). A collaborative model to increase the capacity of children's providers to include young children with disabilities. *Journal of Early Intervention, 21*(2), 177–186.

Bruder, M., & Chandler, L. (1996). *Transition.* In S. Odom & M. McLean (Eds.), *Early intervention/early childhood special education.* Austin, TX: PRO-ED.

Bruder, M., & Dunst, C. (2000). Expanding learning opportunities for infants and toddlers in natural environments. *Zero to Three, 20*(3), 34–36.

Bruner, J. (1966). *Toward a theory of instruction.* Cambridge, MA: Belknap Press.

Bryant, D., & Maxwell, D. (1999). The environment and mental retardation. *International Review of Psychology, 11,* 56–67.

Bryden, K. E., Carrey, N. J., & Kutcher, S. P. (2001). Update and recommendations for the use of antipsychotics in early-onset psychoses. *Journal of Child and Adolescent Psychopharmacology, 11,* 113–130.

Buchanan, M., & Cooney, M. (2000). Play at home, play in the classroom, parent/professional partnerships in supporting child play. *Young Exceptional Children, 3*(4), 9–16.

Burchinal, M., Roberts, J., Riggins, R., Zeisel, S., Neebar, E., & Bryant, D. (2000). Relating quality of center-based child care to early cognitive and language development. *Child Development, 71*(2), 339–357.

Bureau of Labor Statistics. (2002). *Women in the labor force: A databook.* Washington, DC: U.S. Department of Labor.

Buysse, V., Skinner, D., & Grant, S. (2001). Towards a definition of quality instruction: Perspectives of parents and practitioners. *Journal of Early Intervention, 24*(2), 146–161.

Cadoret, R. J., Yates, W. R., Troughton, E., Woodworth, G., & Stewart, M. A. (1995). Genetic-environmental interaction in the genesis of aggressivity and conduct disorders. *Archives of General Psychiatry, 52,* 916–924.

Cairns, R. B. (1983). The emergence of developmental psychology. In W. Kessen (Ed.), *Handbook of child psychology: Vol. 1* (4th ed., pp. 41–102). New York: Wiley.

Cairns, R., & Cairns, B. (1994). *Lifeline and risks. Pathways of youth in our time.* New York: Harvester Wheatsheaf.

Calderon, R., & Greenberg, M. (1997). The effectiveness of early intervention for deaf children and children with hearing loss. In M. Guralnick (Ed.), *The effectiveness of early intervention* (pp. 455–482). Baltimore: Paul H. Brookes.

Calderon, R., & Greenberg, M. (2000). Challenge to parents and professionals in promoting socio-emotional development. In P. Spencer, C. Ertling, & M. Marshark (Eds.), *The deaf child in the family and at school* (pp. 275–291). Mahwah, NJ: Erlbaum.

Camarata, S. (1995). A rationale for naturalistic speech intelligibility intervention. In M. Fay, J. Windsor, & S. Warren (Eds.), *Language intervention: Preschool through elementary years* (pp. 63–84). Baltimore: Paul H. Brookes.

Campbell, P. (2000). Promoting participation in natural environments by accommodating motor disabilities. In M. Snell & F. Brown (Eds.). *Instruction of students with severe disabilities* (5th ed., pp 291–330). Upper Saddle River, NJ: Merrill.

Campbell, T., Dollaghan, C., Rockette, H., Paradise, J., Feldman, H., Shriberg, L., Sabo, D., & Kurs-Lasky, M. (2003). Risk factors for speech delay of unknown origin in three-year-old children. *Child Development, 74*(2), 346–357.

Capute, A., & Accardo, P. (Eds.). (1996). *Developmental disabilities in infancy and childhood,* Vols. 1 & 2 (2nd ed.). Baltimore: Paul H. Brookes.

Carney, A., & Moeller, M. (1998). Treatment efficacy: hearing loss in children. *Journal of Speech, Language, and Hearing Research, 41*(1), S61–S84.

Carpignano, J., & Bigge, J. (1991). Assessment. In J. Bigge (Ed.), *Teaching individuals with physical and multiple disabilities* (3rd ed., pp. 230–236). New York: Merrill.

Cary, D., & Sale, P. (1994, Fall). Notebook computers increase communication. *Teaching Exceptional Children, 27*(1), 62–69.

Castellani, J., & Jeffs, T. (2001). Emerging reading and writing strategies using technology. *Teaching Exceptional Children, 33*(5), 6–67.

Castro, G. (1987). Plasticity and the handicapped child: A review of efficacy research. In J. Gallagher & C. Ramey (Eds.), *The malleability of children* (pp. 103–114). Baltimore: Paul H. Brookes.

Catts, H., Fey, M., Zhang, X., & Tomblin, J. (2003). A longitudinal investigation of reading outcomes in children with language impairments. *Journal of Speech-Language-Hearing Research, 45*, 1142–1157.

Cavallero, C., & Haney, M. (1999). *Preschool inclusion.* Baltimore: Paul H. Brookes.

Cawley, J., Hayden, S., Cade, E., Baker-Kroczynski, S. (2002). Including students with disabilities into the general education science classroom. *Exceptional Children, 68*, 423–436.

Center on Human Development and Disability. (2003, Summer). Pediatric cardiology clinic focuses on newborn hearing screening, early diagnosis and intervention. *CHDD Outlook, 14*(3), University of Washington Health Sciences Center, Seattle, WA 98195-7920.

Chalfant, J. (1989). Learning disabilities: Public issues and promising approaches. *American Psychologist, 44*(2), 392–398.

Chomsky, N. (1988). *Language and problems of knowledge.* Cambridge: MIT Press.

Cioffi, J. (1995). Orientation and mobility issues and support strategies for young adults who are deaf-blind. In J. Everson (Ed.), *Supporting young adults who are deaf-blind in their communities.* Baltimore: Paul H. Brookes.

Clark, D. B. (1988). *Dyslexia: Theory and practice of remedial instruction.* Parkton, MD: York Press.

Clark, D., & Uhry, J. (1995). *Dyslexia: Theory and practice of remedial instruction* (2nd ed.). Baltimore: York Press.

Clark, G., & Zimmerman, E. (1998). Nurturing the arts in programs for gifted and talented students. *Phi Delta Kappan, 79*, 746–751.

Class, C. (2003). *Home visitors guidebook* (2nd ed.). Baltimore: Brookes.

Clauss-Ehlers, C. C. C. (2003). Promoting ecologic health resilience for minority youth: Enhancing health care access through the school health center. *Psychology in the Schools, 40*, 265–278.

Clerc, L. (2003). *Information on deafness.* Washington, DC: National Deaf Information Center, Gallaudet University.

Clymer, E. W., & McKee, B. G. (1997). The promise of the World Wide Web and other telecommunication technology within deaf education. *American Annals of the Deaf, 42*(2), 104–106.

Cohen, I. (1995). Behavioral profiles of autistic and nonautistic fragile X males. *Developmental Brain Dysfunction, 8*, 252–269.

Cohen, S. (1998). *Targeting autism.* Berkeley, CA: University of California Press.

Cohen, S., & Erwin, E. (1994). Characteristics of children with prenatal drug exposure being served in special education programs in New York City. *Topics in Early Childhood Education, 14*(2), 232–253.

Cohen, S., & Warren, K. (1987). Preliminary survey of family abuse of children served by United Cerebral Palsy centers. *Developmental Medicine and Child Neurology, 29*, 12–18.

Colangelo, N., Assouline, S., & Gross, M. (2004). *A nation deceived: How schools hold back America's brightest students. The Templeton national report on acceleration.* Iowa City: Bolen & Blank International Center for Gifted Education.

Cole, C., Waldron, N., & Majd, M. (2003). Academic progress of students across inclusive and traditional settings. *Mental Retardation, 42*, 136–144.

Cole, K. (1995). Curriculum model and language facilitation in the pre-school years. In M. Fey & J. Reiche (Eds.), *Communication intervention for school-age children* (pp. 39–60). Baltimore: Paul H. Brookes

Coleman, L. (1985). *Schooling the gifted.* Menlo Park, CA: Addison-Wesley.

Coleman, L. (2002). A shock to study. *Journal of Secondary Gifted Education. 14*, 39–52.

Coleman, L. J. (2003). Gifted-child pedagogy: A meaningful chimera? *Roeper Review, 25*, 163–164.

Coleman, L., & Cross, T. (2001). *Being gifted in school: An introduction to development, guidance, and teaching.* Waco, TX: Prufrock Press.

Coleman, M. R. (2001) Surviving or thriving? *Gifted Child Today, 24*, 56–63.

Coleman, M. R. (2003). The identification of students who are gifted. *ERIC Clearinghouse on Disabilities and Gifted Education, Digest E644*, EDO-EC-03-5.

Coleman, M. R., & Gallagher, J. J. (1992). *State policies for identification of nontraditional gifted students.* Chapel Hill: University of North Carolina, Gifted Education Policy Studies Program.

Collins, B., Gast, D., Ault, M., & Wolery, M. (1991). Small group instruction: Guidelines for teachers of students with moderate to severe handicaps. *Education and Training in Mental Retardation, 26*, 18–32.

Comer, J., Haynes, N., & Joyner, E. (1999). *Child by child: The Comer process for change in education.* New York: Teachers College Press.

Committee for Children (2002). *Second step: A violence prevention curriculum.* Seattle, WA: Author.

Compton, C., & Brandt, F. (n.d.). *Assistive listening devices.* Washington, DC: National Information Center on Deafness.

Conduct Problems Prevention Research Group (1999). Initial impact of the fast-track prevention trial for conduct problems: II. Classroom effects. *Journal of Consulting and Clinical Psychology, 67*(5), 648–657.

Conroy, M., Asmus, J., Ladwig, C., Sellers, J., & Valcante,

G. (2004). The effects of proximity on the classroom behaviors of students with autism in general education settings. *Behavioral Disorders, 29,* 119–129.

Coons, P. (1987). A student helps other dyslexics. *Boston Globe,* June 14.

Copeland, S., Hughes, C., Agron, M., Wehmeyer, M., & Fowley, S. (2002). An intervention package to support high school students with mental retardation in general education classes. *American Journal on Mental Retardation, 107,* 32–45.

Corso, R., Santos, R., & Roof, V. (2002). Honoring diversity in early childhood educational material. *Teaching Exceptional Children, 34*(3), 30–37.

Cosden, M., Brown, C., & Elliott, K. (2002). Development of self-understanding and self-esteem in children and adults with learning disabilities. In B. Wong & M. Donahue (Eds.), *Social dimensions of learning disabilities* (pp. 32–52). Mahwah, NJ: Erlbaum.

Cosmos, C. (2001). Abuse of children with disabilities (1–15). *Today.* Arlington, VA: Council for Exceptional Children.

Cotzin, M., & Dallenbach, K. (1950). "Facial Vision": The role of pitch and loudness in the perceptions of obstacles by the blind. *American Journal of Psychology, 63,* 485–515.

Coughlin, S. (1999). The intersections of genetics, public health and preventive medicines. *American Journal of Preventative Medicine, 16,* 89–90.

Council for Exceptional Children (1994, October–November). *Exceptional Children, 61*(2, Special Issue).

Council for Exceptional Children (1997). Reading difficulties versus disabilities. *Today, 4*(5), pp. 1, 9, 13.

Council for Exceptional Children (2003). Brain research sheds new light on student learning, teaching strategies and disabilities. *Today, 10*(3), pp. 1, 5, 10–11.

Council for Exceptional Children (CEC). (1998). CEC recommended practices: Indicators of quality in programs for infants and young children with special needs. Reston, VA: CEC.

Council for Exceptional Children (CEC). (2003). *Council for Exceptional Children policy manual* (section 4, part 3, p. 137). Washington, DC: Author.

Council for Exceptional Children, The Association for the Gifted (CEC/TAG). (2001, April). *Diversity and developing gifts and talents: A national action plan.* Reston, VA: Council for Exceptional Children.

Cox, M., & Paley, B. (1997). Families as systems. *Annual Review of Psychology, 48,* 243–267.

Cramer, J., & Oshima, T. (1992). Do gifted females attribute their math performance differently than other students? *Journal for the Education of the Gifted, 16*(1), 18–35.

Cramer, S., & Ellis, W. (1996). *Learning disabilities.* Baltimore: Paul H. Brookes.

Crocker, A., & Orr, R. (1996). Social behaviors of children with visual impairments enrolled in preschool programs. *Exceptional Children, 62*(5), 451–462.

Crocker, A., & Porter, S. (2000). Inclusion of young children with complex health care needs. In M. Guralnick (Ed.), *Early childhood inclusion* (pp. 399–412). Baltimore: Paul H. Brookes.

Crockett, J. B. (2002). Special education's role in preparing responsive leaders for inclusive schools. *Remedial and Special Education, 23*(3), 157–168.

Crockett, J. B. (Ed.). (2001). The meaning of science and empirical rigor in the social sciences (special issue). *Behavioral Disorders, 27,* 1–76.

Crockett, J. B. (In press). Taking stock of science in the schoolhouse: Four ideas to foster effective instruction. In J. B. Crockett (Ed.), Supporting science in the schoolhouse: Fostering the delivery of effective instruction in contemporary schools (special issue). *Journal of Learning Disabilities.*

Crockett, J. B., & Kauffman, J. M. (1999). *The least restrictive environment: Its origins and interpretations in special education.* Mahwah, NJ: Lawrence Erlbaum.

Crockett, J., & Kauffman, J. (1998). Classrooms for students with learning disabilities. In B. Wong (Ed.), *Learning about learning disabilities* (2nd ed., pp. 489–525). Orlando, FL: Academic Press.

Cromer, R. (1978). The basis of childhood dysphasia: A linguistic approach. In D. Wyke (Ed.), *Developmental dysphasia.* New York: Wiley.

Cromer, R. (1991). *Language and thought in normal and handicapped children.* Oxford: Basil Blackwook.

Cross, T., Stewart, R., & Coleman, L. (2003). Phenomenology and its implications for gifted students research: Investigating the lebenswelt of academically gifted students attending an elementary magnet school. *Journal for the Education of the Gifted, 24,* 201–230.

Cryer, D. (2003). Defining program quality. In D. Cryer & R. Clifford (Eds.), *Early childhood education and care in the U.S.A.* (pp. 31–46). Baltimore: Brookes.

Cryer, D., & Clifford, R. (Eds.). (2003). *Early childhood education and care in the U.S.A.* Baltimore: Brookes.

Csikszentmihalyi, M. (1990). *Flow.* New York: Harper & Row.

Csikszentmihalyi, M. (1996). *Creativity: Flow and the psychology of discovery and invention.* New York: HarperCollins.

Csikszentmihalyi, M., & Wolfe, R. (2000). New conceptions and research approaches to creativity: Implications of a systems perspective for creativity in education. In K. A. Heller, F. J. Monks, R. J. Sternberg, & R. F. Subotnik (Eds.), *International handbook of giftedness and talent* (2nd ed., pp. 67–80). New York: Elsevier.

Cucase, A., & McFarland, D. (1998). Central auditory processing disorder in children. *Journal of Speech, Language and Hearing Research, 41*(2), 355–373.

Culatta, R., & Goldberg, S. A. (1995). *Stuttering therapy: An integrative approach to theory and practice.* Needham, MA: Allyn & Bacon.

Curtis, S., & Tallal, P. (1991). On the nature of impairment in language in children. In J. Miller (Ed.), *New directions in research on child language disorders* (pp. 189–210). Boston: College-Hill Press.

Dale, P., Price, T., Bishop, D., & Plomin, R. (2003). Outcomes of early language delay. *Journal of Speech, Language, and Hearing Research, 46*(3), 544–560.

Davis, D. (1988). Nutrition in the prevention and reversal of mental retardation. In F. Menolascino & J. Stark (Eds.),

Preventive and curative intervention in mental retardation (pp. 177–222). Baltimore: Paul H. Brookes.

Davis, S. (Ed.). (2003). *A family handbook on future planning.* Silver Spring, MD: The Arc of the United States.

Dawson, G., & Osterling, J. (1997). Early intervention in autism. In M. J. Guralnick (Ed.), *The effectiveness of early intervention* (pp. 307–326). Baltimore: Paul H. Brookes.

De Weerd, J. (1981). Federal programs for the handicapped. *Exceptional Children, 40*(6), 441.

Deafness Research Foundation. (2000). *The Research News, 1*(1).

deBettencourt, L. (2002). Understanding the differences between IDEA and Section 504. *Teaching Exceptional Children, 34*(3), 16–23.

DeFries, J. C., & Alarcon, M. (1996). Genetics of specific reading disability. *Mental Retardation & Developmental Research Review, 2,* 39–47.

Delello, E. (1998). Classroom dynamics and the development of serious emotional disturbance. *Exceptional Children, 64*(4), 479–492.

Deloukas, P., Schuler, G., Gyapay, G., Beasley, E., Soderland, C., & Rodriguez-Tome. (1998). A physical map of 30,000 human genes. *Science, 282,* 744–746.

Delwein, P., Fewell, R., & Pruess, J. (1985). The efficacy of intervention at outreach sites of the program for children with Down syndrome and other developmental delays. *Topics in Early Childhood Special Education, 5*(2), 78–87.

Denckla, M. (1994). Measurement of executive function. In G. Lyon (Ed.), *Frames of reference for the assessment of learning disabilities* (pp. 117–142). Baltimore: Paul H. Brookes.

Deno, L. (1985). Curriculum-based measurement. *Exceptional Children, 52*(2), 219–232.

Deshler, D., Ellis, E., & Lenz, S. (1996). *Teaching adolescents with learning disabilities: Strategies and methods* (2nd ed.). Denver: Love.

Dewey, J. (1998). *How we think.* Boston: Houghton Mifflin.

DiCarlo, C., Banajee, M., & Buras-Stricklin, S. (2000). Embedding augmentative communication within early childhood classrooms. *Young Exceptional Children, 3*(3), 18–26.

Dickens, M., & Cornell, D. (1993). Parent influences on the mathematics of self concept of high ability adolescent girls. *Journal for Education of the Gifted, 17*(1), 53–73.

Dickenson, D., & Tabors, P. (2001). *Beginning literacy with language.* Baltimore: Brookes.

Dickman, G. E. (1996). Learning disabilities and behavior. In S. C. Cramer & W. Ellis (Eds.), *Learning disabilities* (pp. 215–228). Baltimore: Paul H. Brookes.

Dionne, G., Dale, P., Boivin, M., & Plomin, R. (2003). Genetic evidence for bidirectional effects of early lexical and grammatical development. *Child Development, 74*(2), 394–412.

DiPietro, L., Williams, P., & Kaplan, H. (1991). *Alerting and communication devices for hearing impaired people.* Washington, DC: National Information Center on Deafness (NICD), American Speech-Language-Hearing Association, Gallaudet University.

Dodge, K. A., & Pettit, G. S. (2003). A biopsychosocial model of the development of chronic conduct problems in adolescence. *Developmental Psychology 39,* 349–371.

Doig, K., & Werner, E. (2000). The marriage of a traditional lecture-based curriculum and problem-based learning: Are the offspring vigorous? *Medical Teacher, 22,* 173–178.

Donnellan, A. M., Mirenda, P. L., Mesaros, R. A., & Fassbinder, L. (1984). Analyzing the communicative function of aberrant behaviors. *Journal of the Association for Persons with Severe Handicaps, 9,* 201–212.

Donovan, M., & Cross, C. (2002). *Minority students in special and gifted education.* Washington, DC: National Academy Press.

Dore, J. (1986). The development of conversational competence. In R. L. Schiefelbusch (Ed.), *Language competence, assessment and intervention* (pp. 85–96). Boston: Little, Brown.

Dorman, J., & Batshaw, M. L. (1997). Muscles, bones and nerves. In M. L. Batshaw (Ed.), *Children with disabilities* (pp. 315–322). Baltimore: Paul H. Brookes.

Dorman, J., & Pellegrino, L. (1998). *Caring for children with cerebral palsy.* Baltimore: Paul H. Brookes.

Downing, J. (1995). Instructional strategies for learners with dual sensory impairments in integrated settings. In K. Huebner, J. Prickett, T. Welch, & E. Jaffee (Eds.), *Hand in hand* (pp. 141–148). New York: AFT Press.

Downing, J. (1999). *Teaching communication skills to students with severe disabilities.* Baltimore: Paul H. Brookes.

Downing, J., & Eichinger, J. (2003). Creating learning opportunities for students with severe disabilities in inclusive classrooms. *Teaching Exceptional Children, 36*(1), 26–31.

Downing, J., & Perino, P. (2001). *Including students with severe and multiple disabilities in typical classrooms* (2nd ed.). Baltimore: Brookes.

Drasgow, E. (1998). American Sign Language as a pathway to linguistic competence. *Exceptional Children, 64*(3), 329–342.

Drew, C., Hardman, M., & Logan, D. (1996). *Mental retardation: A life cycle approach* (6th ed.). Upper Saddle River, NJ: Prentice Hall.

Dromi, E. (1993). The development of prelinguistic communication: Implications for language evaluation. In N. J. Anastasiow & S. Harel (Eds.), *The at-risk infant* (pp. 19–26). Baltimore: Paul H. Brookes.

Duchnowski, A., Dunlap, G., Berg, K., & Adeigbola, M. (1995). Rethinking the role of families in the education of their children: Policy and clinical issues. In J. B. Paul, D. Evans, & H. Roselli (Eds.), *Restructuring special education* (pp. 105–118). New York: Harcourt Brace Jovanovich.

Dunst, C. J. (1996). Early intervention in the USA. In M. Branbring, A. Beelman, & H. Rauh (Eds.), *Intervention in early childhood* (pp. 157–180). New York: Aldine de Gruyter.

Dunst, C. J. (2001). Participation of young children with disabilities in community learning activities. In M. Guralnick

(Ed.), *Early childhood inclusion: Focus on change* (pp. 307–336). Baltimore: Paul H. Brookes.

Dunst, C. J., & Lowe, L. W. (1986). From reflex to symbol: Describing, explaining, and fostering communication competence. *Augmentative and Alternative Communication, 2*, 11–18.

Dunst, C. J., & Trivette, C. (1997). Early intervention with young at-risk children and their families. In R. Ammerman & M. Hersen (Eds.), *Handbook of prevention and treatment with children and adolescents: Interventions in the real world* (pp. 157–180). New York: John Wiley & Sons.

Dunst, C., Bruder, M., Trivette, C., & McLean, M. (2001). Natural learning opportunities for infants, toddlers, and preschoolers. *Young Exceptional Children, 4*(3), 18–26.

Dunst, C., Herter, S., Shields, H., & Bennis, L. (2001). Mapping community-based natural learning opportunities. *Young Exceptional Children, 4*(4), 16–27.

Dweck, C. S. (2000). Self-theories: Their role in motivation, personality, and social development. *Essays in social psychology*. Philadelphia: Psychology Press, Taylor & Francis Group.

Dweck, C. S., & Leggett, E. L. (1988). A social-cognitive approach to motivation and personality. *Psychological Review, 95*, 256–273.

Dykens, E. M., & Kasari, C. (1997, November). Maladaptive behavior in children with Prader-Willi syndrome, Down syndrome, and nonspecific mental retardation. *American Journal of Mental Retardation, 102*(3), 228–237.

Dyson, L. L. (1993). Response to the presence of a child with disabilities: Parental stress and family functioning over time. *American Journal on Mental Retardation, 98*, 207–218.

Early, D., Pianta, R. C., & Cox, M. J. (1999). Kindergarten teachers and classrooms: A transition context. *Early Education and Development, 10*, 25–46.

Easterbrooks, S. (1999). Improving practice for students with hearing impairments. *Exceptional Children, 65*(4), 537–554.

Eber, L., & Kennan, C. (In press). Collaboration with other agencies: Wrap around and systems of care for children and youth with EBD. In R. Rutherford, M. Quinn, & S. Mather (Eds.), *Handbook of research in behavioral disorders*. New York: Guilford Press.

Eber, L., Nelson, C., & Miles, P. (1997). School-based wraparound for students with emotional and behavioral challenges. *Exceptional Children, 63*(4), 539–555.

Eber, L., Osuch, R., & Redditt, C. (1996). School-based applications of a wraparound process: Early results on service provision and student outcomes. *Journal of Child and Family Studies, 5*, 83–99.

Edwards, J., & Tyskiewicz, E. (1999). Cochlear implants. In J. Stokes (Ed.), *The hearing impaired infant: The first eighteen months* (pp. 129–162). London: Whurr. (Distributed by Paul H. Brookes.)

Ehri, L. (1998). Graphemphoneme knowledge for learning words in English. In J. Metsuda & L. Ehri (Eds.), *Word recognition in beginning reading* (pp. 3–40). Hillsdale, NJ: Erlbaum.

Eicher, P. (1997). Feeding. In M. L. Batshaw (Ed.), *Children with disabilities* (pp. 621–641). Baltimore: Paul H. Brookes.

Elliott, D. S., Hamburg, B. A., & Williams, K. R. (1998). *Violence in American schools*. New York: Cambridge University Press.

Elmquist, D., Morgan, D., & Bolds, P. (1992). Substance use among adolescents with disabilities. *International Journal of the Addictions, 27*, 1475–1183.

Emde, C. (2003). Charting information over time. In J. Brookes-Gunn (Ed.), *Do we believe in magic: What can we expect from early childhood intervention programs* (pp. 3–14). Social Policy Report, Society for Research in Child Development, *18*(1).

English, R. (1995). *Educational audiology across the lifespan*. Baltimore: Paul H. Brookes.

Epstein, C. (1988). New approach to the study of Down syndrome. In F. Menolascino & J. Stark (Eds.), *Preventive and curative intervention in mental retardation* (pp. 35–60). Baltimore: Paul H. Brookes.

ERIC/OSEP Special Project. (2002). Strengthening the third "R": Helping students with disabilities achieve in mathematics. *Research Connections in Special Education, 11*, Arlington, VA (www.ericcec.org).

Erikson, J. (1996). The infant-toddler developmental assessment (IDA). In S. Meisels & E. Fenichel (Eds.), *New visions for the development assessment of infants and young children* (pp. 147–168). Washington, DC: Zero to Three National Center for Infants, Toddlers and Families.

Erikson, J. (2002). From demonstration model into the real world: Some experiences with IDA. *Zero to Three, 21*, 20–28.

Erin, E. (1993). Social participation of young children with visual impairments in specialized and integrated environments. *Journal of Visual Impairment and Blindness, 87*, 138–142.

Erlbaum, B., Vaughn, S., Hughes, M. T., Moody, S., & Schumm, J. (2000). How reading outcomes of students with disabilities are related to instructional grouping formats: A meta-analytic review. In R. Gersten, E. Schiller, & S. Vaughn (Eds.), *Contemporary special education research* (pp. 105–136). Mahwah, NJ: Erlbaum.

Eron, L. (1990). Understanding aggression. *Bulletin of the International Society for Research on Aggression, 12*, 5–9.

Ertling, C., Theman-Preziuso, C., & Benedict, B. (2000). Bilingualism in a deaf family: Finger spelling in early childhood. In P. Spencer, C. Ertling, & M. Marschark (Eds.), *The deaf child in the family and at school* (pp. 41–54). Mahwah, NJ: Erlbaum.

Erwin, E. (1993). Social participation of young children with visual impairments in specialized and integrated environments. *Journal of Visual Impairment and Blindness, 87*, 138–142.

Erwin, E., & Brown, F. (2003). A contextual framework for understanding self-determination in early childhood environment. *Infants and Young Children, 16*(4), 1.

Espinosa, L. (2002). *High-quality preschool*. New Brunswick, NJ: National Center for Early Education Research.

Etscheidt, S., & Bartlett, L. (1999). The IDEA amendments: A four-step approach for determining supplemental aids and services. *Exceptional Children, 65*(2), 163–174.

Evans, G. (2004). The environment of childhood poverty. *American Psychologist, 59,* 77–92.

Evans, I. M. (1991). Testing and diagnosis: A review and evaluation. In L. H. Meyer, C. Peck, & L. Brown (Eds.), *Critical issues in the lives of people with severe disabilities* (pp. 25–44). Baltimore: Paul H. Brookes.

Everson, J. (Ed.). (1995). *Supporting young adults who are deaf-blind in their communities.* Baltimore: Paul H. Brookes.

Everson, J., Burwell, J., & Killan, S. (1995). Working and contributing to one's community. In J. Everson (Ed.), *Supporting young adults who are deaf-blind in their communities* (pp. 131–158). Baltimore: Paul H. Brookes.

Falvey, M. (1988, September). Letters to the editor. *Journal of Visual Impairment and Blindness,* 3–4.

Falvey, M. (1989). *Community-based curriculum* (2nd ed.). Baltimore: Paul H. Brookes.

Falvey, M. A. (Ed.). (1995). *Inclusive and heterogeneous schooling.* Baltimore: Paul H. Brookes.

Falvey, M. A., Coot, J., Bishop, K. D., & Grenot-Scheyer, M. (1989). Educational and curricular adaptations. In S. Stainback, W. Stainback, & M. Forest (Eds.), *Educating all students in the mainstream of regular education.* Baltimore: Paul H. Brookes.

Falvey, M., & Grenot-Scheyer, M. (1995). Instructional strategies. In M. Falvey, (Ed.) *Inclusive and heterogeneous schooling.* Baltimore: Paul H. Brookes.

Farmer, T., & Farmer, E. (1996). The social relationships of students with exceptionalities in mainstream classes: Social networks and homophily. *Exceptional Children, 62,* 431–450.

Farran, D. (2001). Critical periods and early intervention. In D. Bailey, J. Bruer, F. Symons, & J. Lichtman (Eds.), *Experience-dependent modification of the brain and early intervention* (pp. 121–124). Baltimore: Paul H. Brookes.

Favazza, P., La Roe, J., Phillipsen, L., & Kumar, P. (2000). Representing young children with disabilities. *Young Exceptional Children, 3*(3), 2–8.

Feldman, D. (1984). A follow-up of subjects scoring above 180 IQ in Terman's Genetic Studies of Genius. *Exceptional Children, 50,* 518–523.

Fernald, G. (1943). *Remedial techniques in basic school subjects.* New York: McGraw-Hill.

Ferrell, K. (1986). Infancy and early childhood. In G. Scholl (Ed.), *Foundations of education for blind and visually handicapped children and youth.* New York: American Foundation for the Blind.

Ferrell, K., Shaw, A., & Dietz, S. (1998). *Project PRISM: A longitudinal study of developmental patterns of children who are visually impaired.* University of Northern Colorado, Division of Special Education.

Fewell, D., & Cone, J. (1983). Identification and placement of severely handicapped children. In M. Snell (Ed.), *Systematic instruction of the moderately and severely handicapped* (2nd ed.). Columbus, OH: Charles E. Merrill.

Fey, M., Catts, H., & Larrivee, L. (1995). Preparing preschoolers for the academic and social challenges of school. In M. Fey, J. Windsor, & S. Warren (Eds.), *Language intervention: Preschool through the elementary years* (pp. 3–50). Baltimore: Brookes.

Fey, M., Cleave, P., & Long, S. (1997, February). Two models of grammar facilitation in children with language impairments. *Journal of Speech & Hearing Research, 40*(5), 5–19.

Fey, M., Windsor, J., & Warren, S. (Eds.). (1995). *Language intervention: Preschool through elementary years.* Baltimore: Paul H. Brookes.

Field, T. (1989). Interaction coaching for high risk infants and their parents. *Prevention in Human Services, 1,* 8–54.

Field, T. (1998). Massage therapy effects. *American Psychologist, 52*(12), 1270–1281.

Field, T., Hermundez-Reif, M., & Freedman, J. (2004). Stimulation programs for preterm infants. *Social Policy Report, Society for Research in Child Development, 18*(1).

Flannery, D. J., Vazsonyi, A. T., Liau, A. K., Guo, S., Powell, K. E., Atha, H., & Vesterdal, W. (2003). Initial behavior outcomes for the Peace-Builders universal school-based violence prevention program. *Developmental Psychology, 39,* 292–308.

Flavell, J., & Miller, P. (1998). Social cognition. In W. Damon (Ed.), *Handbook of child psychology,* Volume 2: *Cognition, perception and language* (5th ed., pp. 851–898). New York: Wiley.

Flax, J., Realpe-Bonilla, T., Hirsch, L., Brzustowicz, L., Bartlett, C., & Tallal, P. (2003). Specific language impairment in families: Evidence for co occurrence with reading impairments. *Journal of Speech, Language, and Hearing Research, 46,* 530–543.

Fleishner, J. (1994). Diagnosing and assessment of mathematics learning disabilities. In G. Lyon (Ed.), *Frames of reference for the assessment of children with learning disabilities* (pp. 444–458). Baltimore: Paul H. Brookes.

Fletcher, J., & Forman, B. (1994). Issues in definitions and measurement of learning disabilities. In G. Lyon (Ed.), *Frames of reference for the assessment of children with learning disabilities* (pp. 185–202). Baltimore: Paul H. Brookes.

Flippo, K., Inge, J., & Barcus, J. (1995). (Eds.), *Assistive technology.* Baltimore: Paul H. Brookes.

Flynn, J. (1999). Searching for justice: The discovery of IQ gains over time. *American Psychologist, 54*(1), 5–20.

Ford, D. Y. (2002). Racial identity among gifted African American students. In M. Neihart, S. Reis, N. Robinson, & S. Moon (Eds.), *The social and emotional development of gifted children: What do we know?* (pp. 155–164). Waco, TX: Prufrock Press.

Ford, D. Y., & Harris, J. J., III. (1999). *Multicultural gifted education.* New York: Teachers College Press.

Forness, S., & Kavale, K. (1998). Syndromes on the margins of mental retardation: dual diagnosis and balkanization. In A. Hilton & R. Ringlaben (Eds.), *Best and promising practices in developmental disabilities* (pp. 23–32). Austin, TX: PRO-ED.

Forness, S. R., Kavale, K. A., Sweeney, D. P., & Crenshaw, T. M. (1999). The future of research and practice in behavioral disorders: Psychopharmacology and its future implications. *Behavioral Disorders, 24,* 305–318.

Forum. (2003). *Behavioral Disorders, 28,* 197–228.

Fowler, A. (1998). Language in mental retardation: Associations with and dissociations from general cognition. In J. Burack, R. Hodapp, & E. Zigler (Eds.), *Handbook of mental retardation and development* (pp. 290–333). New York: Cambridge University Press.

Fox, J., & Gable, R. (2004). Functional behavioral assessment. In R. Rutherford, M. Quinn, & S. Mather (Eds.), *Handbook of research in behavioral disorders*. New York: Guilford Press.

Fox, L., Hanline, M., Vail, C., & Galant, K. (1994). Developmentally appropriate practices: Applications for young children with disabilities. *Journal of Early Intervention, 18*(3), 243–257.

Fraiberg, S. (1977). *Insights from the blind: Comparative studies of blind and sighted infants.* New York: Basic Books.

Frank Porter Graham Child Development Institute. (2004). Screening newborns for fragile X. *Early Developments, 8,* 11–13.

Fraser, D. (2003). From the playful to the profound: What metaphors tell us about gifted children. *Roeper Review, 25,* 183.

Frasier, M. (1997). The identification of gifted black students: Developing new perspectives. *Journal for the Education of the Gifted, 10*(3), 155–190.

Fredericks, B., & Baldwin, V. (1987). Individuals with sensory impairments: Who are they? How are they educated? In L. Goetz, D. Guess, & K. Stremmel Campbell (Eds.), *Innovative program design for individuals with dual sensory impairments* (pp. 3–14). Baltimore: Paul H. Brookes.

Freeman, J. M., & Vining, E. (1990). Is surgery the answer for childhood epilepsy? *Contemporary Pediatrics, 5*(109), 88–95.

Freeman, R., Goetz, E., Richards, D., & Groenveld, M. (1991). Defiers of negative prediction. A 14-year follow-up study of legally blind children. *Journal of Visual Impairment and Blindness, 85,* 365–370.

Frick, P. J., Cornell, A. H., Bodin, S. D., Dane, H. A., Barry, C. T., & Loney, B. R. (2003). Callous-unemotional and developmental pathways to severe conduct problems. *Developmental Psychology, 39,* 246–260.

Frostig, M., Lefever, W., & Whittesey, J. (1964). *Developmental test of visual perception.* Palo Alto, CA: Consulting Psychological Press.

Fuchs, D., Fuchs, L., Mathes, P., & Lipsey, M. (2000). Reading differences between low-achieving students with and without learning disabilities. In R. Gersten, E. Schiller, & S. Vaughn (Eds.), *Contemporary Special Education Research* (pp. 81–104). Mahwah, NJ: Erlbaum.

Fuchs, D., Fuchs, L., Mathes, P., Lipsey, M., & Roberts, D. (2002). Is earning disabilities just a fancy term for low achievement? In R. Bradley, L. Danielson, & D. Hallahan (Eds.), *Identification of learning disabilities: Research to practice* (pp. 737–761). Mahwah, NJ: Erlbaum.

Fuchs, L., & Deno, E. (1992). Effects of curriculum within curriculum-based measurement. *Exceptional Children, 58,* 232–243.

Fuchs, L., & Deno, S. (1994, September). Must instructionally useful performance assessment be based in the curriculum? *Exceptional Children, 6*(1), 15–24.

Fuchs, L., Fuchs, D., Hamlett, C., Phillips, N., & Bentz, J. (1994). Classroom curriculum-based assessment. *Exceptional Children, 60*(6), 518–537.

Fuchs, S., Fuchs, D., Hamlett, N., Phillips, N., & Korn, K. (1995, August). General educator's specialized adaptation for students with learning disabilities. *Exceptional Children, 61*(5), 440–459.

Fujiura, G., & Yamaki, K. (2000). Trends in demography of childhood poverty and disability. *Exceptional Children, 66,* 187–199.

Furuno, S., O'Reilly, K., Haiako, C., Inatsuka, T., Allman, T., & Zeisloft-Falbey, X. (1979). Hawaii early learning profile (HELP). Palo Alto, CA: Vort Publisher.

Furuno, S. F., O'Reilly, K. A., Hosaka, C. N., Inatsuka, T., & Falb, B. Z. (1993). *Helping babies learn: Developmental profile and activities for infants and toddlers.* Tucson, AZ: Communication Skill Builders, The Psychological Corporation.

Furuno, S., O'Reilly, E., Hosuka, C., Inatsuka, T., Allmant, T., & Zeisloft-Falbey, X. (1979). Hawaii early learning profile (HELP). Palo Alto, CA: Vort Publishers, PO Box 60132.

Gage, S., & Falvey, M. (1995). Strategies to develop appropriate curricula and educational programs. In M. Falvey, *Inclusive and heterogeneous schooling.* Baltimore: Paul H. Brookes.

Gagne, R. (1985). *Conditions of learning.* New York: Holt, Rinehart & Winston.

Gallagher, J. (1985). *Teaching the gifted child* (3rd ed.). Boston: Allyn & Bacon.

Gallagher, J. (1997). We make a difference: No Nobel prizes though. *Journal of Early Intervention, 21,* 88–91.

Gallagher, J. (1998). Planning for young children with disabilities and their families: The evidence from IFSP/IEPs. Frank Porter Graham Center, University of North Carolina at Chapel Hill, Chapel Hill, NC.

Gallagher, J. (2000). The beginnings of federal help for young children with disabilities. *Topics in early childhood special education* (pp. 3–6). Austin, TX: PRO-ED.

Gallagher, J. (2002). Interventions and children with special needs. In A. Cranston-Gingus & E. Taylor, *Rethinking professional issues in special education* (pp. 43–68). Westport, CT: Ablex.

Gallagher, J. (Ed.) (1974). *Windows on Russia.* Washington, DC: U.S. Government Printing Office.

Gallagher, J. J., & Bray, W. (2002). *Project insight: Program evaluation.* Chapel Hill, NC: Frank Porter Graham Child Development Institute.

Gallagher, J. J., & Clifford, R. (2000). The missing support infrastructure in early childhood. *Early Childhood Research and Practice, 2,* 1–24.

Gallagher, J. J., Cook, E., & Shoffner, M. (2003). *Project insight II: Program evaluation.* Chapel Hill, NC: Frank Porter Graham Child Development Institute.

Gallagher, J., & Desimone, L. (1995). Lessons learned from implementation of the IEP: Applications to the IFSP. *Topics in Early Childhood Special Education, 15*(3), 353–378.

Gallagher, J., & Gallagher, S. (1994). *Teaching the gifted child* (4th ed.). Boston: Allyn & Bacon.

Gallagher, J., Harbin, G., Eckland, J., & Clifford, R. (1994). State diversity and policy implementation. In L. Johnson, R. J. Gallagher, & M. L. LaMontagne (Eds.), *Meeting early intervention challenges.* Baltimore: Paul H. Brookes.

Gallagher, S., & Stepien, W. (1996). Content acquisition in

problem based learning: Depth versus breadth in American studies. *Journal for the Education of the Gifted, 19,* 257–275.

Gallaudet Research Institute. (1997). *Annual survey of deaf and hard of hearing children and youth: 1995–1996 school year.* Washington, DC: Gallaudet University.

Gallimore, R., Bernheimer, L., & Weisner, T. (1999). Family life is more than managing crisis: Broadening the agenda of research on families adapting to childhood disability. In R. Gallimore, L. Bernheimer, D. MacMillan, D. Speece, & S. Vaughn (Eds.), *Developmental perspectives on high incidence handicapping conditions papers in honor of Barbara Keogh.* Mahwah, NJ: Erlbaum.

Gannon, J. (1981). *Deaf heritage: A narrative history of deaf America.* Silver Spring, MD: National Association of the Deaf.

Garcia, C., & Magnuson, K. (2000). Cultural difference. In J. Shonloff & S. Meisels (Eds.), *Handbook of early intervention* (pp. 94–114). New York: Cambridge.

Gardner, H. (1985). *Frames of mind: The theory of multiple intelligence.* New York: Basic Books.

Gardner, H. (1998a). The intelligence of leaders. *International Journal of Leadership in Education, 1,* 203–206.

Gardner, H. (1998b). *Multiple intelligences: The theory in practice.* New York: Basic Books.

Gardner, H. (1999). *Intelligence reframed: Multiple intelligences for the twenty-first century.* New York: Basic Books.

Gardner, J., & Bates, P. (1991). Attitudes and attributions on use of microcomputers in school by students who are mentally handicapped. *Education and Training in Mental Retardation, 26,* 98–107.

Garland, A., & Zigler, E. (1999). Emotional and behavioral problems among highly gifted youth. *Roeper Review, 22*(1), 41–44.

Garnett, M. (1996). The structure of language processes: Neurological evidence. In M. Gazzaniga (Ed.), *Cognitive neuroscience* (pp. 881–899). Cambridge, MA: The MIT Press.

Garwood, G., & Sheehan, R. (1989). *Designing a comprehensive early childhood system.* Austin, TX: PRO-ED.

Gately, S. (2004). Developing concept of word: The work of emergent readers. *Teaching Exceptional Children, 36*(6), 17–22.

Ge, X., Conger, R., Cadoret, R., Nedierhiser, J., Yates, W., Troughton, E., & Stewart, M. (1996). The development interface between nature and nurture: A mutual influence model of child antisocial behavior and parent behaviors. *Developmental Psychology, 32*(4), 574–589.

Getman, G. (1965). The visuo-motor complex in the acquisition of learning skills. In B. Straub & J. Hellmuth (Eds.), *Learning disorders* (Vol. 1). Seattle: Special Child Publications.

Getzels, J. (1978). Paradigm and practice: On the impact of basic research in education. In P. Suppes, *Impact of research in education.* Washington, DC: National Academy of Education.

Getzels, J., & Jackson, P. (1962). *Creativity and intelligence.* New York: Wiley.

Giangreco, M., Cloninger, C., & Iverson, V. (1998). *Choosing outcomes and accommodations for children (COACH).* Baltimore: Paul H. Brookes.

Gibb, S., Allred, K., Ingram, C., Young, J., & Egan, W. (1999). Lessons learned from the inclusion of students with emotional and behavioral disorders in one junior high school. *Behavioral Disorders, 24*(2), 122–136.

Gilgoff, I. (1983). Spinal cord injury. In J. Umbreit (Ed.), *Physical disabilities and health impairments: An introduction* (pp. 132–146). Columbus, OH: Charles E. Merrill.

Gillingham, A., & Stillman, S. (1960). *Remedial training for children with specific disabilities in reading, writing, and penmanship.* Cambridge: Educational Publishing Service.

Gleason, B. (Ed.). (1993). *The development of language* (3rd ed.). New York: Macmillan.

Goetz, L., Guess, D., & Campbell, K. (1987). *Innovative programs for individuals with dual sensory impairments.* New York: Grune & Stratton.

Goh, D. S. (2004). *Assessment accommodations for diverse learners.* Boston: Allyn & Bacon.

Goldberg, A. (1991). Children on ventilators: Breathing easier at home. *Contemporary Pediatrics, 7,* 59–79.

Goldberg, A. M. (2000). Transition timeline. Retrieved July 15, 2004, from http://www.nass.org.

Goldberg, D. (1997). Educating children who are deaf or hard of hearing: Auditory-verbal. *ERIC Digest, 552.*

Goldin-Meadow, S. (1998). The resilience of language in humans. In C. Snowden & M. Hanberger (Eds.), *Social influence on vocal development* (pp. 293–311). New York: Cambridge University Press.

Goldstein, B., & Iglesias, A. (2001). The effect on phonological analysis: Evidence from Spanish-speaking children. *American Journal of Speech-Language Pathology, 10*(1), 394–406.

Goodman, S., & Wittenstein, S. (Eds.). (2003). *Collaborative assessment.* New York: American Foundation for the Blind.

Goodrich, G., & Sowell, V. (1996). Low vision: A history in progress. In A. Corn & A. Koenig (Eds.), *Foundations of low vision: Clinical and functional perspective* (pp. 397–414). New York: American Foundation for the Blind.

Gorman, C. (2003, July 28). Why some children struggle so much with reading used to be a mystery; now researchers know what's wrong—and what to do about it. *Time,* 52–59.

Gothelf, C. (1991). Personal communication. New York: Jewish Guild for the Blind.

Gothelf, C., Crimmins, D., Mercer, C., & Finocchiaro, P. (1994, Fall). Teaching choice-making skills to students who are deaf-blind. *Teaching Exceptional Children, 26*(1), 13–15.

Gottesman, M. (1971, June). A comparative study of Piaget's developmental schema of sighted children with that of a group of blind children. *Child Development,* 573–580.

Gottfredson, D. C., Gottfredson, G. D., & Skroban, S. (1993). Can prevention work where it is needed most? *Evaluation Review, 22,* 315–340.

Gottlieb, G. (1997). *Synthesizing nature-nurture: Prenatal roots of instinctive behavior.* Mahwah, NJ: Erlbaum.

Gottlieb, J., Alter, M., & Gottlieb, B. W. (1991). Mainstreaming mentally retarded children. In J. Matson

& J. Mulick (Eds.), *Handbook of mental retardation* (2nd ed., pp. 63–73). New York: Pergamon Press.

Gottlieb, J., Alter, M., Gottlieb, B., & Wisner, J. (1994). Special education in urban America: It's not justifiable for many. *Journal of Special Education, 27,* 453–465.

Grabe, M., & Grabe, C. (2000). *Integrating the Internet for meaningful learning.* Boston: Houghton Mifflin.

Grandin, T. (1988). Teaching tips from a recovered autistic. *Focus on Autistic Behavior, 5,* 1–15.

Grandin, T. (1992). An inside view of autism. In E. Schopler & G. Mesibov (Eds.). *High functioning individuals with autism* (pp. 105–128). New York: Plenium Press.

Grandin, T. (1995). The learning style of people with autism: An autobiography. In K. Quill (Ed.). *Teaching children with autism: Methods to enhance communication and socialization* (pp. 33–52). Albany, NY: Delmar.

Gray, D. B., & Kavanaugh, J. H. (1985). *Biobehavioral measures of learning disabilities.* Parkton, MD: York Press.

Green, R. (1999). Audiological identification and assessment. In J. Stokes (Ed.). *Hearing impaired infants* (pp. 1–38). Baltimore: Paul H. Brookes.

Greenspan, S. (1999). A contextual perspective on adaptive behavior. In R. Schalock (Ed.), *Adaptive behavior and its measurements: Implications for the field of mental retardation* (pp. 15–42). Washington, DC: American Association on Mental Retardation.

Greenwood, C. (1994). Advances in technology-based assessment within special education. *Exceptional Children, 61*(2), 102–104.

Grenot-Scheyer, M. (1994, Winter). The nature of interactions between students with severe disabilities and their friends and acquaintances without disabilities. *The Journal of the Association for Persons with Severe Handicaps, 19*(3).

Greschwind, N. (1985). The biology of dyslexia. In D. B. Gray & J. F. Kavanaugh (Eds.), *Biobehavioral measures of dyslexia* (pp. 1–120). Parkton, MD: York Press.

Gresham, F. (1998). Social skills training: Should we raze, remodel or rebuild? *Behavior Disorders, 24*(1), 19–25.

Gresham, F. (2002). Responsiveness to intervention: An alternative approach to the identification of learning disabilities. In R. Bradley, L. Danielson, & D. Hallahan (Eds.), *Identification of learning disabilities: Research to practice* (pp. 447–457). Mahwah, NJ: Erlbaum.

Gresham, F., Beebe-Frankenberger, M., & Macmillan, D. (1999). A selective review of treatments for children with autism: Description and methodological considerations. *School Psychology Review, 28*(44), 559–575.

Gresham, F. M., Sugai, G., & Horner, R. H. (2001). Interpreting outcomes of social skills training for students with high-incidence disabilities. *Exceptional Children, 67*(3), 331–344.

Grigal, M., Neubert, D., Moon, M., & Graham, S. (2003). Parents' and teachers' views of self-determination for students with disabilities. *Exceptional Children, 70*(1), 97–111.

Grisso, T. (1996). Introduction: An interdisciplinary approach to understanding aggressive behavior in children. In C. F. Ferris & T. Grisso (Eds.), *Understanding aggressive behavior in children.* New York: Annals of the New York Academy of Sciences, Volume 794, p. 6.

Gross, M. (2002). Social and emotional issues for exception-ally intellectually gifted students. In M. Neihart, S. Reis, N. Robinson, & S. Moon (Eds.), *The social and emotional development of gifted children: What do we know?* (pp. 19–30). Waco, TX: Prufrock Press.

Gross, M., & Van Vliet, V. (2003). *Radical acceleration of highly gifted students.* Sydney, Australia: University of South Wales.

Grzywacz, P. (Ed.). (2001). *Students with disabilities and special education* (18th ed.). Birmingham, AL: Oakstone Legal and Business Publishing.

Guiltinan, S. (1986, Fall). How to . . . tips on integration. *SPLASH Flash, 4–5.* (Printed by the Office of Education for Exceptional Children, Kentucky Department of Education.)

Gullo, D. (1992). *Developmentally appropriate teaching in early childhood.* Washington, DC: National Educational Association of America.

Gunter, P. L., & Denny, R. K. (1998). Trends and issues in research regarding academic instruction of students with emotional and behavioral disorders. *Behavioral Disorders, 24,* 44–50.

Guralnick, M. (1998, June). Effectiveness of early intervention: A developmental perspective. *American Journal of Mental Retardation, 102*(4), 319–345.

Guralnick, M. (1999). The nature and meaning of social integration for young children with mild developmental delays in inclusive settings. *Journal of Early Intervention, 22*(1), 70–86.

Guralnick, M. (2000a). Early childhood intervention: Evolution of a system. In M. Wehmeyer & J. Patton (Eds.), *Mental retardation in the 21st century* (pp. 68–79). Austin, TX: PRO-ED.

Guralnick, M. (2000b). *Interdisciplinary clinical assessment of young children with developmental disabilities.* Baltimore: Paul H. Brookes.

Guralnick, M. (2001a). Connection between developmental science and intervention science. *Zero to Three, 21*(5), 24–29.

Guralnick, M. (2001b). A framework for change in early childhood inclusion. In M. Guralnick (Ed.), *Early childhood inclusion: Focus in change* (pp. 3–38). Baltimore: Paul H. Brookes.

Guralnick, M. (Ed.). (1997). *The effectiveness of early intervention.* Baltimore: Paul H. Brookes.

Guralnick, M., & Bricker, D. (1987). The effectiveness of early intervention for children with cognitive and general developmental delays. In M. Guralnick & F. C. Bennett (Eds.), *The effectiveness of early intervention for at-risk and handicapped children* (pp. 115–168). New York: Academic Press.

Guralnick, M., Neville, B., Connor, R., & Hammond, M. (2003). Family factors associated with the peer social competence of young children with mild delays. *American Journal of Mental Retardation, 108,* 272–287.

Guskey, T., Passaro, P., & Wheeler, W. (1997). Mastery learning in the regular classroom: Help for at risk students with learning disabilities. In *Educating exceptional children* (9th ed., pp. 42–45). Guilford, CT: Dushkin Publications.

Gust-Brey, K., & Cross, T. (1999). An examination of the literature based on the suicidal behaviors of academically gifted students. *Roeper Review, 22*(1).

Gutierrez-Clellen, V. (1999). Language choice in intervention with bilingual children. *American Journal of Speech-Language Pathology, 8*(4), 291–302.

Hallahan, D., & Mercer, C. (2002). Learning disabilities: Historical perspective. In R. Bradley, L. Danielson, & D. Hallahan (Eds.), *Identification of learning disabilities: Research to practice* (pp. 1–67). Mahwah, NJ: Erlbaum.

Hallahan, D., & Kauffman, J. (1995). (Eds.), *The illusion of full inclusion.* Austin, TX.: PRO-ED.

Halpern, R. (2000). Early childhood intervention. In J. Shonkoff & S. Meisels (Eds.), *Handbook of early intervention* (pp. 361–386), New York: Cambridge.

Hammer, C. S., & Weiss, A. L. (1999). Guiding language development: How African American mothers and their infants structure play interactions. *Journal of Speech, Language, and Hearing Research, 42,* 1219–1233.

Hammill, D. (2004). What we know about correlates of reading. *Exceptional Children, 70,* 453–468.

Hancock, K., Craig, A., McCready, C., McCaul, A., Costello, D., Campbell, K., & Gilmore, G. (1998). Two-to-six-year controlled trial stuttering outcomes of children. *Journal of Speech, Language and Hearing Research, 41*(6), 1242–1252.

Hanks, J., & Velaski, A. (2003). A cooperative collaboration between speech-language pathology and deaf education. *Teaching Exceptional Children, 36*(4), 58–63.

Hannah, M. E., & Midlarsky, E. (1987). Siblings of the handicapped: Maladjustment and its prevention. *Techniques, 3,* 188–195.

Hansen, R., & Ulrey, G. (1993). Knowns and unknowns in the outcomes of drug-dependent women. In N. J. Anastasiow and S. Harel (Eds.), *The at-risk infant* (pp. 115–126). Baltimore: Paul H. Brookes.

Harbin, G., & West, T. (1998). *Early intervention service delivery models and their impact on children.* Available from Frank Porter Graham Child Development Center, CB #8040, University of North Carolina, Chapel Hill, NC.

Harms, T., & Clifford, R. (1980). *Infant/toddler environmental rating scales.* New York: Teachers College Press.

Harrell, R., & Curry, S. (1987). Services to blind and visually impaired children and adults: Who is responsible? *Journal of Visual Impairment and Blindness,* 368–376.

Harris, S. (1995). Educational strategies in autism. In E. Schopler & G. Mesibov (Eds.), *Learning and cognition in autism* (pp. 293–309). New York: Plentum Press.

Harris, V., & McHale, S. (1989). Family life problems, daily caregiving activities and the psychological well being of mothers of mentally retarded children. *American Journal on Mental Retardation, 94,* 231–239.

Harrison, A., & Coleman, M. R. (2004). *Do you teach some who . . . : An observational reporting procedure to identify gifted behaviors in children.* Chapel Hill, NC: University of North Carolina, Frank Porter Graham Child Development Institute, Project U-STARS PLUS.

Harrower, J. (1999). Educational inclusion of children with severe disabilities. *Journal of Positive Behavior Interventions, 1*(4), 215–230.

Harry, B. (1992). *Cultural diversity, families, and the special education system.* New York: Teachers College Press.

Harry, B. (1997). Application and misapplications of ecological principles in working with families from diverse cultural backgrounds. In J. Paul, M. Churton, W. Morse, A. Duchnowski, B. Epanchin, P. Gross, & R. Smith (Eds.), *Special education practice* (pp. 156–170). Pacific Grove, CA: Brooks/Cole.

Harry, B. (2002). Trends and issues in serving culturally diverse families of children with disabilities. *Journal of Special Education, 36,* 131–138.

Harry, B., Rueda, R., & Kalyanpur, M. (1999). Cultural reciprocity in sociocultural perspective: Adapting the normalization principle for family collaboration. *Exceptional Children, 66*(1), 123–136.

Hart, B., & Risley, T. (1995). *Meaningful differences in the everyday experiences of young children.* Baltimore: Paul H. Brookes.

Hart, B., & Risley, T. (1999). *The social world of children learning to talk.* Baltimore: Brookes.

Harvey, D., & Greenway, A. (1984). The self-concept of physically handicapped children and their non-handicapped siblings: An empirical investigation. *Journal of Child Psychology and Psychiatry, 25,* 273–284.

Hasazi, S., Gordon, L., & Roe, C. (1985). Factors associated with the employment status of handicapped youth exiting high school from 1979 to 1983. *Exceptional Children, 51,* 455–465.

Hasazi, S. B., Furney, K. S., & DeStefano, L. (1999). Implementing the IDEA transition mandates. *Exceptional Children, 65,* 151–164.

Hassan, M. W. (1992). My turn: The making of a miracle. *Newsweek,* January 6, 7.

Hasselbring, T. (1997). The future of special education and the role of technology. In J. Paul, M. Churton, W. Morse, A. Duchnowski, B. Epanchin, P. Osnes, & R. Smith (Eds.), *Special education practice: Applying the knowledge, affirming the values and creating the future* (pp. 118–135). Pacific Grove, CA: Brooks/Cole.

Hatlen, P. (1996). The core curriculum for blind and visually impaired students, including those with additional disabilities. *RE: view, 28*(1), 25–32.

Hatlen, P. (1998). Foreword. In S. Sacks & R. Silberman (Eds.), *Educating students who have visual impairments with other disabilities* (pp. xv–xvi). Baltimore: Paul H. Brookes.

Hatlen, P. (1998). Foreword. In S. Z. Sacks & R. K. Silberman (Eds.), *Educating students who have visual impairments with other disabilities* (pp. xv–xvi). Baltimore: Paul H. Brookes.

Hatlen, P. (2000). Historical perspectives. In A. Koenig & M. Holbrook (Eds.). *Foundations of education: Vol. I. History and theory of teaching children and youths with visual impairments* (2nd ed., pp. 1–54). New York: American Foundation for the Blind Press.

Hatlen, P. (2000). The core curriculum for blind and visually impaired students, including those with additional disabilities. In A. J. Koenig & M. C. Holbrook (Eds.), *Foundations of education* (2nd ed.), Vol. 2, *Instructional strategies for teaching children and youths with visual impairments* (p. 781). New York: AFB Press.

Hatlen, P. (2003). *Impact of literacy on the expanded curriculum.* Paper presented at the Getting in Touch with

Literacy Conference, December 4. Available at http://www.tsvbi.edu/agenda/literacy.htm.

Hatlen, P., & Curry, S. (1987). In support of specialized programs for blind and visually impaired children: The impact of vision loss on learning. *Journal of Visual Impairment and Blindness, 81,* 7–13.

Hatton, D., & Bailey, D. (2001). Fragile X syndrome and autism. In E. Schopler, N. Yirmiya, C. Shulman, & L. Marcus (Eds.), *The research basis for autism intervention* (pp. 75–89). New York: Kluwer Academic/Plenum.

Hatton, D., Bailey, D., Burchinal, M., & Ferrell, K. (1997). Developmental growth curves of preschool children with vision impairments. *Child Development, 68*(5), 788–806.

Hatton, D., Wheeler, A., Skinner, M., Bailey, D., Sullivan, K., Roberts, J., Mirrett, P., & Clark, R. (2004). Adaptive behavior in children with fragile X syndrome. *American Journal of Mental Retardation, 108,* 373–390.

Hatton, D. D., Bailey, D. B., Roberts, J. P., Skinner, M., Mayhew, L., Clark, R. D., Waring, E., & Roberts, J. E. (2000). Early intervention services for young boys with fragile X syndrome. *Journal of Early Intervention, 23,* 235–251.

Hatton, D. D., McWilliam, R. A., & Winton, P. J. (2002). *Infants and toddlers with visual impairments: Suggestions for early interventionists* (Report EDO-EC-02-14). Washington, DC: Office of Educational Research and Improvement (OERI), U.S. Department of Education, ERIC Clearinghouse on Disabilities and Gifted Education Digest E636.

Hawley, R. (1987). School children and drugs: The fancy that has not passed. *Phi Delta Kappan, 68,* K1–K8.

Haynie, M., Porter, S., & Palfrey, J. (1989). *Children assisted by medical technology in educational settings: Guidelines for care.* Boston: Project School Care, Children's Hospital.

Heal, L. W., & Rusch, F. R. (1995). Predicting employment for students who leave special education high school programs. *Exceptional Children, 61,* 472–487.

Heinemann, A., & Shontz, F. (1984). Adjustment following disability: Representative case studies. *Rehabilitation Counseling Bulletin, 28*(1), 3–14.

Heinicke, C. (1993). Factors affecting the efficacy of early family intervention. In N. J. Anastasiow & S. Harel (Eds.), *The at-risk infant* (pp. 91–100). Baltimore: Paul H. Brookes.

Helburn, S. W. (1995). Cost, quality, and child outcomes in child care centers: Key findings and recommendations. *Young Children, 50,* 40–44.

Heller, K., Monks, F., Sternberg, R., & Subotnik, R. (Eds.). (2000). *International handbook of giftedness and talent* (2nd ed.). New York: Elsevier.

Helmstetter, E., Peck, C., & Giangreco, M. (1994, Winter). Outcomes of interaction with peers of moderate and severe disabilities: A statewide survey of high school students. *The Journal of the Association for Persons with Severe Handicaps, 19*(4), 260–276.

Hembree, R. (2000). *National deaf-blind child count summary: December 1, 1999 count.* Monmouth, OR: National Technical Assistance Consortium for Children and Young Adults Who Are Deaf-Blind (NTAC), Teaching Research Division, Western Oregon University.

Henderson, L., & Meisels, S. (1994). Parental involvement in the developmental screening of their young children. *Journal of Early Intervention, 18*(2), 141–154.

Herter, G., Knightly, C., & Steinberg, A. (2002). Hearing: Sound and silences. In M. Batshaw (Ed.), *Children with disabilities* (5th ed., pp. 193–228). Baltimore: Brookes.

Hettleman, K. R. (2003). *The invisible dyslexics: How public school systems in Baltimore and elsewhere discriminate against poor children in the diagnosis and treatment of early reading difficulties.* Baltimore: Abell Foundation.

Hickson, L., Blackman, L., & Reis, E. (1995). *Mental retardation: Foundations of educational programming.* Boston: Allyn & Bacon.

Hill, E. (1992). Instruction in orientation and mobility skill for students with visual handicaps. *Division for the Visually Handicapped Quarterly, 37*(2), 25–26.

Hill, J. L., & Davis, A. (1999). *Meeting the needs of students with special physical and health needs.* Upper Saddle River, NJ: Prentice Hall.

Hill, R. (1999). Genetic features of families under stress. *Journal of the Association for Persons with Severe Handicaps, 8,* 30–38.

Hitchcock, C., Meyer, A., Rose, D., & Jackson, R. (2002). Providing new access to the general curriculum: Universal design for learning. *Teaching Exceptional Children, 32,* 8–17.

Holahan, C., & Sears, R. (1995). *The gifted group in later maturity.* Stanford, CA: Stanford University Press.

Holden-Pitt, R., & Diaz, J. (1998, April). Thirty years of the annual survey of deaf and hard of hearing children and youth. *American Annals of the Deaf, 143*(2), 72–76.

Hollinger, D. (Ed.). (1993). Single sex schooling: *Perspectives from practice and research.* Washington, DC: Office of Education Research and Improvement, U.S. Department of Education.

Horner, R., & Carr, E. (1997). Behavioral support for students with severe disabilities: Functional assessment and comprehensive intervention. *Journal of Special Education, 31*(1), 84–104.

Horowitz, F., & Haritos, C. (1998). The organism and the environment: Implications for understanding mental retardation. In J. Burack, R. Hodapp, & E. Zigler (Eds.), *Handbook of mental retardation and development* (pp. 20–40). New York: Cambridge University Press.

Hosp, J., & Reschly, D. (2004). Disproportionate representation of minority students in special education: Academic, demographic, and economic predictors. *Exceptional Children, 70,* 185–200.

Hua, C. B., & Coleman, M. R. (2002). Preparing twice exceptional students for adult lives: A critical need. *Understanding Our Gifted, 17–19.*

Huebner, K., Prickett, J., Welch, T., & Joffee, E. (Eds.). (1995). *Hand in hand* (Vol. 1). New York: AFB Press.

Huesmann, L. R., Moise-Titus, J., Podolsky, C. L., & Eron, L. D. (2003). Longitudinal relations between children's exposure to TV violence and their aggressive and violent behavior in young adulthood: 1977–1992. *Developmental Psychology, 39,* 201–221.

Hughes, C., Ruhl, K., & Misra, A. (1989). Self-management with behaviorally disordered students in school settings: A promise unfulfilled. *Behavioral Disorders, 14*(4), 250–262.

Hughes, M., Dote-Kwan, J., & Dolendo, J. (1998). A close look at the cognitive play of preschoolers with visual impairments in the home. *Exceptional Children, 64*(4), 451–462.

Hunt, J. (1961). *Intelligence and experience.* New York: Ronald Press.

Hunt, P., Soto, G., Maier, J., & Doering, K. (2003). Collaborative teaming to support students at risk and students with severe disabilities in general education classrooms. *Exceptional Children, 69*(3), 315–332.

Hutchinson, T. A. (1995, Winter). IDEA and the Provence profile-efficient early assessment. *ECO Letter, 4*(1), 11–13.

Huttenlocher, P. (1988). Developmental neurobiology: Current and future challenges. In F. Menolascino & J. Stark (Eds.), *Preventative and curative intervention in mental retardation* (pp. 101–111). Baltimore: Paul H. Brookes.

Hynd, G. (1992). Neurological aspects of dyslexia. *Journal of Learning Disabilities, 25,* 100–113.

Individuals with Disabilities Education Act (IDEA) of 1997, PL 105-17, U.S. Department of Education, Washington, DC.

Infant Health and Development Project. (1990). Enhancing the outcome of low-birth-weight premature infants. *Journal of the American Medical Association, 263*(22), 3035–3042.

Interagency Committee. (1990). *Learning disabilities: A report to Congress.* Washington, DC: U.S. Government Printing Office.

Jackson, L., Ryndak, D. L., & Billingsley, F. (2000). Useful practices in inclusive education: A preliminary view of what experts in moderate to severe disabilities are saying. *Journal of the Association for Persons with Severe Handicaps, 25*(3), 129–141.

Jamieson, J. (1994). Teaching as transaction: Vygotskian perspective on deafness and mother-child interaction. *Exceptional Children, 60*(5), 434–449.

Jamieson, J. (1995, Spring). Interaction between mothers and children who are deaf. *Journal of Early Intervention, 19*(2), 108–117.

Janney, R., Snell, M. E., & Elliot, J. (2000). *Modifying school work.* Baltimore: Paul H. Brookes.

Jenkins, J., & O'Connor, R. (2002). Identification and intervention for young children with reading/learning disabilities. In R. Bradley, L. Danielson, & D. Hallahan (Eds.), *Identification of learning disabilities: Research to practice* (pp. 99–172). Mahwah, NJ: Erlbaum.

Jenkins, J., Speltz, M., & Odom, S. (1985). Integrating normal and handicapped preschoolers: Effects on child development and social interaction. *Exceptional Children, 52*(1), 7–17.

Jensen, E. (1998). *Teaching with the brain in mind.* Alexandria, VA: Association for Supervision and Curriculum Development.

Johnsen, Susan K. (Ed.). (2004). *Identifying gifted students: A practical guide.* Waco, TX: Prufrock Press and Texas Association for the Gifted and Talented.

Johnson, H. C. (1989). Behavior disorders. In F. J. Turner (Ed.), *Child psychopathology: A social work perspective* (pp. 73–140). New York: Free Press.

Johnson, J., Baumgart, D., & Helmsteller, E. (1996). *Augmenting basic communication skills in natural context.* Baltimore: Paul H. Brookes.

Johnson, R., & Johnson, D. (1991). Collaboration and cognition. In: A. Costa (Ed.), *Developing minds: A resource book for teaching thinking* (pp. 298–301). Alexandria, VA: ASCD.

Johnson-Martin, N., Attermeier, S., & Hacker, B. (2004). *Carolina curriculum for preschoolers with special needs.* Baltimore: Paul H. Brookes.

Judge, S. (2001). Integrating technology within early childhood classrooms. *Young Exceptional Children, 5*(2), 20–26.

Jung, L. (2003). National learning opportunities for young exceptional children. *Exceptional Children, 6*(3), 21–26.

Jusczyk, E. W. (1997). *The discovery of spoken language.* Cambridge: MIT Press.

Justice, L., Chow, S., Capellini, C., Flanigan, K., & Colton, S. (2003). Emergent literacy intervention for vulnerable preschoolers: A comparison of two approaches. *American Journal of Speech-Language Pathology, 12*(3), 320–332.

Kagan, S. (1989). The structural approach to cooperative learning. *Educational Leadership, 47*(4), 12–15.

Kaiser, A. (2000). Teaching functional communication skills. In M. Snell & F. Brown (Eds.), *Instruction of students with severe disabilities* (5th ed., pp. 453–492). Upper Saddle River, NJ: Merrill.

Kaiser, A., & Gray, D. (1993). *Enhancing children's research foundation for intervention:* Vol. 2. *Communication and language series.* Baltimore: Paul H. Brookes.

Kaiser, A., & Hancock, T. (2003). Teaching parents new skills to support their young children's development. *Infants and Young Children, 26*(1), 9–21.

Kamps, D., Potucek, J., Dugan, E., Kravitz, T., Gonzales-Lopez, A., Garcia, J., Carnasso, K., Morrison, L., & Kane, L. (2002). Peer training to facilitate social interaction for elementary students with autism and their peers. *Exceptional Children, 68,* 173–188.

Kamps, D. M., & Tankersley, M. (1996). Prevention of behavioral and conduct disorders: Trends and research issues. *Behavioral Disorders, 22,* 41–48.

Kanner, L. (1943). Autistic disturbance of affective contact. *Nervous Child, 2,* 217–250.

Kantrowitz, B., & Underwood, A. (1999, November 22). Dyslexia and the new science of reading. *Newsweek,* 72–78.

Kapperman, G., Heinze, T., & Sticken, J. (2000). Mathematics. In A. J. Koenig & M. C. Holbrook (Eds.), *Foundations of education,* Vol. 2, *Instructional strategies for teaching children and youths with visual impairments* (2nd ed., pp. 370–399). New York: American Foundation for the Blind.

Karnes, F., & Marquart, R. (2000). *Gifted children and legal issues: An update.* Scottsdale, AZ: Gifted Psychology Press.

Kasari, C., & Bauminger, N. (1998). Social and emotional development in children with mental retardation. In J. Burack, R. Hodapp, & E. Zigler (Eds.), *Handbook of mental retardation and development* (pp. 411–433). New York: Cambridge University Press.

Kasari, C., & Freeman, S. (2001). Task-related social behavior in children with Down syndrome. *American Journal of Mental Deficiency, 106,* 253–264.

Katsiyannis, A., Landrum, T. J., Bullock, L. M., & Vinton, L. (1997). Certification requirements for teachers of students with emotional or behavioral disorders: A national survey. *Behavioral Disorders, 22,* 131–140.

Katz, L. (2003). Program content and implementation. In D. Cryer & R. Clifford (Eds.), *Early childhood education and care in the U.S.A.* (pp. 107–118). Baltimore: Brookes.

Kauffman, J. (1994). One size does not fit all. *Beyond Behavior, 5*(3), 13–14.

Kauffman, J., & Hallahan, D. (1995). *The illusion of full inclusion.* Austin, TX: PRO-ED.

Kauffman, J., & Hallahan, D. P. (Eds.). (1995). *Handbook of special education.* Englewood Cliffs, NJ: Prentice-Hall.

Kauffman, J., Brigham, F., & Mock, D. (In press). Historical to contemporary perspectives of the field of behavior disorders. In R. Rutherford, M. Quinn, & S. Mather (Eds.), *Handbook of research in behavioral disorders.* New York: Guilford Press.

Kauffman, J. M. (2001). *Characteristics of emotional and behavioral disorders of children and youth* (7th ed.). Columbus, OH: Merrill.

Kauffman, J. M. (2002). *Education reform: Bright people sometimes say stupid things about education.* Lanham, MD: Scarecrow Education.

Kauffman, J. M. (2003). Reflections on the field. *Behavioral Disorders, 28,* 205–208.

Kauffman, J. M., Mostert, M. P., Trent, S. C., & Hallahan, D. P. (2002). *Managing classroom behavior: A reflective case-based approach.* (3rd ed.). Boston: Allyn & Bacon.

Kavale, K. (2002). Discrepancy models in the identification of learning disabilities. In R. Bradley, L. Danielson, & D. Hallahan (Eds.), *Identification of learning disabilities: Research to practice* (pp. 369–426). Mahwah, NJ: Erlbaum.

Kavale, K., & Forness, S. (2000). Policy decisions in special education. In R. Gersten, E. Schiller, & S. Vaughn. *Contemporary special education research* (pp. 281–326). Mahwah, NJ: Erlbaum.

Kavale, K., Forness, S., & Bender, M. (Eds.). (1988). *Handbook of learning disabilities:* Vol. 1. *Dimensions and diagnoses;* Vol. 2. *Methods and intervention;* Vol. 3. *Programs and practices.* Boston: College-Hill/Little, Brown.

Kavale, K., Mather, S., & Mostert, M. (2004). Social skills training and teaching social behavior to students with emotional and behavioral disorders. In R. Rutherford, M. Quinn, & S. Mather (Eds.), *Handbook of research in behavioral disorders.* New York: Guilford Press.

Kearney, K. (1999). Gifted children and homeschooling: Historical and contemporary perspectives. In S. Cline & K. Hegeman (Eds.), *Gifted education in the twenty-first century,* pp. 175–194. Delray Beach, FL: Winslow Press.

Kekelis, L., & Sacks, S. (1988). Mainstreaming visually impaired children into regular education programs: The effects of visual impairment on children's interactions with peers. In S. Z. Sacks, L. S. Kekelis, & R. J. Gaylord-Ross (Eds.), *The development of social skills by visually impaired children* (pp. 1–42). San Francisco: San Francisco State University.

Kekelis, L. S. (1992). Peer interactions in childhood: The impact of visual impairment. In S. Z. Sacks, L. S. Kekelis, & R. J. Gaylord-Ross (Eds.), *The development of social skills by blind and visually impaired students: Exploratory studies and strategies* (pp. 13–35). New York: American Foundation for the Blind.

Kekelis, L. S., & Sacks, S. Z. (1992). The effects of visual impairment on children's social interactions in regular classroom programs. In S. Z. Sacks, L. S. Kekelis, & R. J. Gaylord-Ross (Eds.), *The development of social skills by blind and visually impaired students: Exploratory studies and strategies* (pp. 59–82). New York: American Foundation for the Blind.

Kelly, L. (1995, February). Processing bottom-up and top-down information by skilled and average deaf readers and implications for whole language learning. *Exceptional Children, 61*(4), 315–334.

Kennedy, C., & Shukla, S. (1995). Social interaction research for people with autism as a set of past, current, and emerging propositions. *Behavior Disorders, 21,* 21–35.

Keogh, B. (1996). Strategies for implementing policy. In S. Cramer & W. Ellis, *Learning disabilities.* Baltimore: Paul H. Brookes.

Keogh, B. K. (2003). *Temperament in the classroom: Understanding individual differences.* Baltimore: Paul H. Brookes.

Kerr, B. (1997). Developing talents in young girls and women. In N. Colangelo & G. Davis (Eds.), *Handbook of gifted education* (pp. 483–497). Boston: Allyn & Bacon.

Kerr, B. A., & Cohn, S. J. (2001). *Smart boys: Talent, manhood, and the search for meaning.* Scottsdale, AZ: Great Potential.

Kerr, M., & Nelson, C. (2002a). *Addressing behavior problems* (4th ed.). Upper Saddle River, NJ: Prentice Hall.

Kerr, M., & Nelson, C. (2002b). *Strategies for managing behavior problems in the classroom* (3rd ed.). Upper Saddle River, NJ: Merrill.

Kettman, J., Klinger, R., Vaughn, S., Schuman, J., Cohen, P., & Forgan, J. (1998, March/April). Inclusion or pull-out: Which do students prefer? *Journal of Learning Disabilities, 31*(2), 148–151.

Keyser-Marcus, L., Briel, L., Sherron-Targett, P., Yasuda, S., Johnson, S., & Wehman, P. (2002). Enhancing the schooling of students with traumatic brain injury. *Teaching Exceptional Children, 34*(4), 62–67.

Kim, A., Vaughn, S., Elbaum, B., Hughes, M., Sloan, C., & Sridhar, D. (2003). Effect of toys on group composition for children with disabilities: A synthesis. *Journal of Early Intervention, 25*(3), 189–205.

Kim-Cohen, J., Moffitt, T., Caspi, A., & Taylor, A. (2004). Genetic and environmental processes in young children's resilience and vulnerability to socioeconomic deprivation. *Child Development, 75*(3), 651–668.

Kingery, P., Coggeshall, M., & Alford, A. (1998). Violence at school: Recent evidence from four national surveys. *Psychology in the Schools, 35,* 247–258.

Kirk, S. (1950). A project for pre-school mentally handicapped children. *American Journal of Mental Deficiency, 55,* 305–310.

Kirk, S. A. (1963). Behavioral diagnosis and remediation of learning disabilities. *Proceedings of the Conference on the Explorations into the Problems of the Perceptually Handicapped Child.* Evanston, IL: Fund for the Perceptually Handicapped Child.

Kirk, S. A., & Kirk, W. D. (1971). *Psycholinguistic learning disabilities* (rev. ed.). Urbana: University of Illinois Press.

Klein, M., Chen, D., & Haney, M. (2003). *Promoting hearing through active intervention.* Baltimore: Brookes.

Kleinert, H., Kearns, J., & Kennedy, S. (1997). Accountability for all students: Kentucky's alternate portfolio assessment for students with moderate and severe cognitive disabilities. *JASH, 22*(2), 88–101.

Kline, F. M., Deshler, D. D., & Schumaker, J. B. (1991). *Implementing learning strategies instruction in class settings, a research perspective: Barriers to strategy instruction.* Mimeo, University of Kansas Institute for Research in Learning Disabilities.

Klingner, J. K., & Vaughn, S. (2002). The changing roles and responsibilities of an LD specialist. *Learning Disabilities Quarterly, 25,* 19–31.

Knight, M. (2003a). A natural history of language. *Contemporary Psychology, 48*(2), 172–173.

Knight, M. (2003b). A natural history of language. *Contemporary Psychology, 48*(3), 306–308.

Knitzer, J., Steinberg, Z., & Fleisch, B. (1990). *At the schoolhouse door.* New York: Bank Street College.

Koegel, R., & Koegel, L. (1995). *Teaching children with autism: Strategies for initiating positive interactions and improving learning opportunities.* Baltimore: Paul H. Brookes.

Koegel, R., Koegel, L., & Carter, C. (1999). Pivotal teaching interactions for children with autism. *School Psychology Review, 28,* 576–594.

Koegel, R., Schriebman, L., Dirlich-Wilhelm, H., Dunlap, G., Robbins, F., & Plienis, A. (1992). Consistent stress predictors in mothers of children with autism. *Journal of Autism and Developmental Disorders, 22,* 205–216.

Koenig, A., & Holbrook, M. (2000). Literacy skills. In A. Koenig & M. Holbrook (Eds.), *Foundations of education:* Vol. II. *Instructional strategies for teaching children and youths with visual impairments* (2nd ed., pp. 264–329). New York: Foundation for the Blind Press.

Koenig, A., & Rex, E. (1996). Instruction of literacy skills to children and youths with low vision. In A. Corn & A. Koenig (Eds.), *Foundations of low vision: Clinical and functional perspective* (pp. 280–305). New York: American Foundation for the Blind.

Koenig, A. J., Holbrook, M. C., Corn, A. L., DePriest, L. B., Erin, J. N., & Presley, I. (2000). Specialized assessments for students with visual impairments. In A. J. Koenig & M. C. Holbrook (Eds.), *Foundations of education,* Vol. 2, *Instructional strategies for teaching children and youths with visual impairments* (2nd ed., pp. 103–172). New York: AFB Press.

Koester, L. S., Karkowski, A., & Traci, M. (1998). How do deaf and hearing mothers regain eye contact when their infants look away? *American Annals of the Deaf, 143*(1), 5–13.

Kolb, B. (1995). *Brain plasticity and behavior.* Mahwah, NJ: Erlbaum.

Kolb, S., & Hanley-Maxwell, S. (2003). Critical social skills for adolescents with high incidence disabilities: Parental perspectives. *Exceptional Children, 69,* 163–180.

Kollins, S. H., Barkley, R. A., & DuPaul, G. J. (2001). Use and management of medications for children diagnosed with attention deficit hyperactivity disorder (ADHD). *Focus on Exceptional Children, 33,* 1–24.

Kolloff, P. (1997). Special residential high schools. In N. Colangelo & G. Davis (Eds.), *Handbook of gifted education* (2nd ed.), pp. 198–206. Boston: Allyn & Bacon.

Kolvin, I., Miller, F. J. W., Scott, D. M., Gazonts, S. K. M., & Fleeting, M. (1990). *Continuities of deprivation? The Newcastle 1000 family study.* Adershot, England: Arcburn Gover.

Konidaris, J. (1997). A sibling's perspective on autism. In D. Cohen & F. Volkman (Eds.), *Handbook of autism and pervasive developmental disorders* (2nd ed., pp. 1021–1031). New York: Wiley.

Koorland, M. A. (1986). Applied behavior analysis and the correction of learning disabilities. In J. K. Torgesen & B. Y. L. Wong (Eds.), *Psychological and educational perspectives on learning disabilities* (pp. 297–326). San Diego: Academic Press.

Kopp, C. (1983). Risk factors in development. In M. M. Haith & J. J. Campos (Eds.), *Handbook of child psychology* (Vol. 2, pp. 1081–1188). New York: Wiley.

Korinek, L., & Polloway, E. (1993). Social skills: Review and implications for instruction for students with mild mental retardation. *Advances in Mental Retardation and Developmental Disabilities, 5,* 71–92.

Kortering, L. J., Braziel, P. M., & Tomkins, J. R. (2002). The challenge of school completion among youths with behavioral disorders: Another side of the story. *Behavioral Disorders, 27,* 142–154.

Krajicek, M., Steinke, T., Hertzdeng, D., Anastasiow, N., & Skandel, S. (Eds.). (1997). *Handbook for the care of infants and toddlers with disabilities and chronic conditions.* Austin, TX: PRO-ED.

Krajicek, M., Steinke, T., Hertzdeng, D., Anastasiow, N., & Skandel, S. (Eds.). (2003). *Instructor's guide for the handbook for the care of infants and toddlers with disabilities and chronic conditions.* Austin, TX: PRO-ED.

Kranowitz, C. S. (1998). *The out-of-sync child: Recognizing and coping with sensory integration dysfunction.* Berkeley, CA: Perigee Books.

Krauss, M. W., Seltzer, M. M., Gordon, R., & Friedman, D. H. (1996). Binding ties: The roles of adult siblings of persons with mental retardation. *Mental Retardation, 34,* 83–93.

Krauss, R., Thurman, K., Brodsky, W., Betancourt, L., Giannetta, J., & Hart, H. (2000). Caregivers' interaction behavior with prenatally cocaine-exposed and nonexposed preschoolers. *Journal of Early Intervention, 23*(1), 62–73.

Kregel, J. (1994, Fall). *Natural support and the job coach: An unnecessary dichotomy.* Richmond: Virginia Commonwealth University, Rehabilitation and Research Training Center.

Lackaye, T. (1997). General education teachers' willingness to and current use of academic interventions for students with learning disabilities. Unpublished dissertation. New York: Columbia University.

Lackaye, T. (2001). *Personal communication.* New York: Hunter College.

Lahm, E. L., & Nickels, B. L. (1999). What do you know? Assistive technology competencies for special educators. *Teaching Exceptional Children, 32,* 56–63.

Lane, H., Hoffmeister, R., & Bahan, B. (1996). *A journey into the deaf-world.* San Diego: Dawn Sign Press.

Lane, K., Gresham, F., & O'Shaughnessy, T. (Eds.). (2002). *Interventions for children with or at risk for emotional and behavioral disorders.* Boston: Allyn & Bacon.

Langlois, L., & Liben, L. (2003). Child care research: An editorial perspective. *Child Development, 74*(4), 469–975.

LaSasso, C. J., & Mobley, R. T. (1996). National survey of reading instruction for deaf and hard of hearing students in the U.S. *The Volta Review, 95*(1), 31–58.

Lathor, S., Cicchetti, D., & Becker, B. (2000). The construct of resilience: A critical evaluation and guidelines for future work. *Child development, 71*(3), 543–562.

Lederberg, A., & Everhart, V. (1998). Communication between deaf children and their hearing mothers. *Journal of Speech, Language, and Hearing Research, 41*(1), 887–899.

Lederer, S. (2002). First vocabulary for specific language impairments: A focused language stimulation approach. *Exceptional Children, 6*(1), 10–17.

Leet, A., Dormans, J., & Tosi, L. (2002). Muscles, bones, and nerves: The body's framework. In M. Batshaw (Ed.), *Children with disabilities* (5th ed., pp. 263–286). Baltimore: Paul H. Brookes.

Leffert, J., Siperstein, G., & Millikan, E. (2000). Understanding social adaptation in children with mental retardation. *Exceptional Children, 66*(4), 530–545.

Lehr, D., & Brown, F. (1996). *People with disabilities who challenge the system.* Baltimore: Paul H. Brookes.

Lehr, D., & McDavid, P. (1999). Opening the door further. *Focus on Exceptional Children, 25*(6), 1–7.

Lehr, D., & Noonan, M. (1989). Issues in the education of students with complex health care needs. In D. Ellis (Ed.), *Sensory impairments in mentally handicapped persons* (pp. 139–160). San Diego: College-Hill Press.

Lejeune, J., Gautier, M., & Turpin, R. (1959). Etudes des chromosomes somatiques de neuf enfants. *C. R. Academie Sic., 248,* 1721–1722.

Lenz, B., Ellis, E. S., & Scanlon, D. (1996). *Teaching learning strategies to adolescents and adults with learning disabilities.* Austin, TX: PRO-ED.

Leonard, L. (1998). *Children with specific language impairments.*

Leonard, L. B. (1993). Intervention approaches for young children with communication disorders. In N. J. Anastasiow & S. Harel (Eds.), *The at-risk infant.* Baltimore: Paul H. Brookes.

Leone, P. (1997). The school as a caring community: Proactive discipline and exceptional children. In J. Paul, M. Churton, W. Morse, A. Duchnowski, B. Epanchin, P. Gross, & R. Smith (Eds.), *Special education practice.* Pacific Grove, CA: Brooks/Cole.

Leone, P., Greenburg, J., Tricket, E., & Spero, E. (1989). A study of the use of cigarettes, alcohol and marijuana by students identified as "seriously emotionally disturbed. *Counterpoint, 9*(3), 6–7.

Leong, S. (1996). Preschool orientation and mobility: A review of the literature. *Journal of Visual Impairment and Blindness, 90,* 145–153.

Lerner, J. (2000). *Learning disabilities* (8th ed.). Boston: Houghton Mifflin.

Lerner, R. M. (1986). *The nature of human plasticity.* New York: Cambridge University Press.

Lesar, S. (1998). Use of assistive technology with young children with disabilities: Current status and learning needs. *Journal of Early Intervention, 21*(2), 146–159.

Lessenberry, B. M., & Rehfeldt, R. A. (2004). Evaluating stress levels of parents of children with disabilities. *Exceptional Children, 70,* 231–244.

Levine, J. (1996, Spring). Including children dependent on ventilators in schools. *Teaching Exceptional Children, 28*(3), 25–29.

Levy, S., & O'Rourke, M. (1997). Technological assistance. In M. L. Batshaw (Ed.), *Children with disabilities* (pp. 687–708). Baltimore: Paul H. Brookes.

Levy, S., & O'Rourke, M. (2002). Technological assistance. In M. Batshaw (Ed.), *Children with disabilities* (pp. 629–646). Baltimore: Brookes.

Lewis, T., & Russo, R. (1998). Educational assessment for students who have visual impairments with other disabilities. In S. Sacks & R. Silberman (Eds.), *Educating students who have visual impairments with other disabilities* (pp. 39–72). Baltimore: Paul H. Brookes.

Lewis, T., & Sugai, G. (1999). Effective behavior support: A systems approach to proactive school wide management. *Focus on Exceptional Children, 31,* 1–24.

Liberman, I. Y., & Liberman, A. M. (1990). Whole language versus code emphasis. *Annals of Dyslexia, 40,* 51–75.

Liberman, I., & Shankweiler, D. (1985). Phonology and the problem of learning to read and write. *Remedial Special Education, 6,* 8–17.

Lidz, C. (2003). Polishing the link between assessment and intervention. *Contemporary Psychology, 48*(6), 837–839.

Liefert, F. (2003). Introduction to visual impairment. In S. Goodman & S. Wittenstein (Eds.), *Collaborative assessment* (pp. 1–22). New York: American Foundation for the Blind.

Light, S., Beukelman, D., & Reichle, B. (2003). *Communicative competence: Who uses AAC.* Baltimore: Brookes.

Lillie, T. (1993). A harder thing than triumph: Roles of fathers of children with disabilities. *Mental Retardation, 31,* 438–443.

Lillo-Martin, D. (1997). In support of the language acquisition device. In Marschark, M., Simple, P., Lillo-Martin, D., Campbell, R., & Everhart, V. (Eds.), *Relations of language and thought.* New York: Oxford University Press.

Linden, G., Kankkunen, A., & Tjellstrom, A. (1985). Multihandicaps and ear formation in hearing impaired children. In G. Mencher & S. Gerber (Eds.), *The multiply handicapped hearing impaired child* (pp. 67–82). New York: Grune & Stratton.

Linder, T. (1993). *Transitional play-based assessment.* Baltimore: Paul H. Brookes.

Linder, T. (1999). *Read, play, and learn.* Baltimore: Brookes.

Liptak, G. (2002). Neural tube defects. In M. Batshaw (Ed.), *Children with disabilities* (5th ed., pp. 467–492). Baltimore: Paul H. Brookes.

Locke, J. (1994). Gradual emergence of developmental language disorders. *Journal of Speech and Hearing Research, 37,* 608–616.

Lockhart, P. C. (1996). Infants of substance-abusing mothers. In A. Capute & P. Accardo (Eds.), *Developmental disabilities in infancy and childhood* (pp. 215–229). Baltimore: Paul H. Brookes.

Loeber, R., & Farrington, D. (Eds.) (1998). *Serious and violent juvenile offenders: Risk factors and successful interventions.* London: Sage.

Lord, C. (1995). Follow-up of two year olds referred for possible autism. *Journal of Child Psychology and Psychiatry, 36,* 1365–1382.

Lord, C. (2001). *Children with autism.* Washington, DC: National Academy of Sciences.

Losen, D. J., & Orfield, G. (Eds.). (2002). *Racial inequity in special education.* Cambridge, MA: Harvard University Press.

Lovaas, O. (1987). Behavioral treatment and normal educational and intellectual functioning in young autistic children. *Journal of Consulting and Clinical Psychology, 55,* 3–9.

Lovaas, O. J. (1993). The development of a treatment project for developmentally disabled and autistic children. *Journal of Applied Behavior Analyses, 26*(4), 617–630.

Lovaas, O., & Buch, G. (1997). Intensive behavioral intervention with young children with autism. In N. Singh, *Prevention and treatment of severe behavior problems.* Pacific Grove, CA: Brooks/Cole Publishers.

Love, J., Harrison, L., Sagi-Schwartz, A., van Ijzendoorn, M., Ross, C., Ungerer, J., Raikes, H., Brady-Smith, C., Boller, K., Brooks-Gunn, J., Constantine, J., Kisker, E., Pausell, D., & Chazen-Cohen, R. (2003). Child care quality matters. *Child Development, 74*(4), 1021–1033.

Love, J. M., Logue, M. E., Trudeau, J. V., & Thayer, K. (1992). *Transitions to kindergarten in American schools.* Portsmouth, NH: U.S. Department of Education, contract LC 88089001.

Loveland, K., & Tunali-Kotoski, B. (1998). Development of adaptive behavior in persons with mental retardation. In J. Burack, R. Hodapp, & E. Zigler (Eds.), *Handbook of mental retardation and development* (pp. 521–541). New York: Cambridge University Press.

Lowenfeld, B. (Ed.). (1973). *The visually handicapped child in school.* New York: Day.

Lowenfeld, B. (1982). In search of better ways. *Education of the Visually Handicapped, 14*(3), 69–77.

Lubinski, D., Webb, R. M., Morelock, M. J., & Benbow, C. P. (2001). Top 1 in 10,000: A 10-year follow-up of the profoundly gifted. *Journal of Applied Psychology, 86,* 718–729.

Luckasson, R., Coulter, D., Polloway, E., Reiss, S., Schaleck, R., Snell, M., Spitalnek, D., & Stark, J. (1992). *Mental retardation: Definition, classification and systems of supports.* Washington, DC: American Association on Mental Retardation.

Luetke-Stahlman, B. (1994). Procedures for socially integrating preschoolers who are hearing, deaf and hard of hearing. *Topics in Early Childhood Special Education, 14*(4), 472–487.

Lundy, S. (2002). *Pathways to competence.* Baltimore: Brookes.

Lynam, D., Moffitt, T. E., & Stouthamer-Loeber, M. (1993). Explaining the relationship between IQ and delinquency: Class, race, test motivation, school failure, or self-control? *Journal of Abnormal Psychology, 102,* 187–196.

Lynas, W. (2000). Communication options. In J. Stokes (Ed.), *The hearing impaired infant: The first eighteen months* (pp. 98–128). London: Whurr. (Distributed by Paul H. Brookes.)

Lyon, G. (Ed.). (1994). *Frames of reference for the assessment of learning disabilities.* Baltimore: Paul H. Brookes.

Lyon, G. (1999). Programmatic research in learning disabilities. In R. Gallimore, L. Bernheimer, D. MacMillan, D. Speece, & S. Vaughn (1999), *Developmental perspectives on children with high incidence disabilities* (pp. 261 271), Mahwah, NJ: Erlbaum.

Lyon, G. R. (1995). Toward a definition of dyslexia. *Annals of Dyslexia, XLV,* 3–27.

Lyon, G. R. (1996). The state of research. In S. Cramer & W. Ellis (Eds.), *Learning disabilities* (pp. 3–64). Baltimore: Paul H. Brookes.

Lytle, R., & Rovins, N. (1997, April). Reforming deaf education. *American Annals of the Deaf, 142*(1), 7–15.

Maag, J., & Howell, K. (1992). Special education and the exclusion of youth with social maladjustments: A cultural-organizational perspective. *Remedial and Special Education, 13*(1), 47–54.

Maccini, P., & Gagnon, J. (2002). Perceptions and application of NCTM standards by special and general education teachers. *Exceptional Children, 68,* 325–344.

Maccoby, E., & Lewis, C. (2003). Less day care or different day care. *Child Development, 74*(4), 1069–1075.

MacDonald, J., & Gillette, Y. (1986). Communicating with persons with severe handicaps: Role of parents and professionals. *Journal of the Association for Persons with Severe Handicaps, 11*(4), 255–265.

MacMillan, D., & Forness, S. (1998). Role of IQ in special education placement decisions: Primary and determination of peripheral and inconsequential. *Remedial and Special Education. 19,* 239–253.

MacMillan, D., Siperstein, G., & Gresham, F. (1996). A challenge to the viability of mild mental retardation as a diagnostic category. *Exceptional Children, 62*(4), 356–372.

MacMillan, D., & Speece, D. (2000). Utility of current diagnostic categories for research and practice. In R. Gallmore, D. MacMillan, D. Spence, & S. Vaughn (Eds.), *Development perspectives on children with high incidence disabilities.* Mahwah, NJ: Erlbaum.

Maddox, R. (2003). Early start: The early entrance program at California State University, Los Angeles. *Gifted Educator Communicator, 34,* 42–49.

Mahaffey, K., Annest, J., Roberts, J., & Murphy, R. (1982). National estimate of blood lead levels: United States, 1976–1980. *New England Journal of Medicine, 307,* 573–579.

Mahoney, G., & Perales, F. (2003). Using relationship-focused intervention to enhance the social-emotional functioning of young children with autism spectrum disorders. *TECSE, 23,* 74–86.

Mahshie, J. (1998). Balloons, penguins and visual displays. *Perspectives, 16(4),* 20–24.

Mainzer, R. W., Deschler, D., Coleman, M. R., Kozleski, E., & Rodriguez-Walling, M. (2003). To ensure the learning of every child with a disability: Report to the Council of Exceptional Children. *Exceptional Children, 35,* 1–12.

Maker, J. (1993). Creativity, intelligence and problem solving: A definition and design for cross-cultural research and measurement related to giftedness. *Gifted Education International, 9,* 68–77.

Mandlawitz, M. (1999). *The impact of the legal system on educational programming for young children with autism spectrum disorder.* Washington, DC: National Research Council Workshop.

Mann, V. A., & Liberman, A. M. (1984). Phonological awareness and verbal short-term memory. *Journal of Learning Disabilities, 17,* 592–599.

March of Dimes Defects Foundation. (1997). *Polio, club foot, cleft palate, cerebral palsy, Marfan syndrome, Cooley syndrome, sickle cell anemia, acondroplasia, thalassemia.* Available from March of Dimes, Community Service Department, 1275 Mamaroneck Avenue, White Plains, NY 10605.

March of Dimes Defects Foundation. (2002). *Hearing loss.* March of Dimes Resource Center, P.O. Box 1657, Wilkes-Barre, PA 18703-1657.

March of Dimes. (1998–2000). Public health information sheets. Community Service Department, 1275 Mamaroneck Ave., White Plains, NY 10605.

March of Dimes. (1999). *Cerebral palsy.* Public health information link, 1275 Mamaroneck Ave., White Plains, NY 10605.

March of Dimes. (2000). *Pre-pregnancy planning; Amniocentesis; Chronionic villus; Biopsy.* Available from March of Dimes, P.O. Box 1657, Wilkes-Barre, PA 18706-1657.

March of Dimes. (2001). *Genetic screening and genetic counseling.* Available from March of Dimes, 1275 Mamaroneck Avenue, White Plains, NY 10605.

March of Dimes. (2002a). *Low birth weight; HIV and AIDS in pregnancy; Chromosomal abnormalities; Teenage pregnancy; Rubella; Cocaine during pregnancy; Newborn screening.* Available from March of Dimes, P.O. Box 1657, Wilkes-Barre, PA 18706-1657.

March of Dimes. (2002b). *Maternal blood screening for Down and neural tube defect; PKU; Toxoplasmosis; RH disease; Preterm birth; Birth defects.* Available from March of Dimes, P.O. Box 1657, Wilkes-Barre, PA 18706-1657.

March of Dimes. (2003). *Ultrasound; Smoking during pregnancy.* Available from March of Dimes, P.O. Box 1657, Wilkes-Barre, PA 18706-1657.

Marschark, M. (2000). Education and development of deaf children. In P. Spencer, C. Erting, & M. Marschark (Eds.), *The deaf child in the family and at school* (pp. 275–291). Mahwah, NJ: Erlbaum.

Marschark, M., & Harris, M. (1996). Success or failure in learning to read. In J. Oakhill & C. Cornoldi (Eds.), *Reading comprehension difficulties* (pp. 279–300). Hillsdale, NJ: Erlbaum.

Marschark, M., Lang, H., & Albertini, J. (2002). *Educating deaf students.* New York: Oxford University Press.

Marschark, M., Simple, P., Lillo-Martin, D., & Everhart, U. (1998). *Language and thought: The view from sign language and deaf children.* New York: Oxford University Press.

Marsh, T., & Cornell, D. (2001). The contribution of student experiences to understanding ethnic differences in high-risk behaviors at school. *Behavior Disorders, 26(2),* 152–163.

Marston, D., Muyskens, P., Lau, M., & Canter, A. (2003). Problem solving model for decision making with high incidence disabilities. *Learning Disabilities Research and Practice, 18(3),* 187–200.

Martin, E. (1995). Case studies of inclusion. *Journal of Special Education, 29(2),* 192–199.

Martin, J., Mithaug, D., Cox, P., Peterson, L., Van Dycke, J., & Cash, M. (2002). Increasing self-determination: Teaching students to plan, work, evaluate, and adjust. *Exceptional Children, 69(4),* 431–449.

Masataka, N. (1996). Perceptions of motherese in a signed language by six-month-old deaf infants. *Developmental Psychology, 32,* 874–879.

Mastropieri, M. A., & Scruggs, T. E. (2001). Promoting inclusion in secondary classrooms. *Learning Disabilities Quarterly, 24,* 265–274.

Mathur, S., Kavale, K., Quinn, M., Forness, S., & Rutherford, R. (1998). Social skill intervention with students with emotional and behavior problems: A quantitative synthesis of single-subject research. *Behavior Disorders, 23(3),* 193–201.

Mauk, G., & White, K. (1995, Winter). Giving children a sound beginning: The promise of universal hearing screening. *Volta Review, 97(1),* 5–32.

Maxwell, N. L., Bellisimo, Y., & Mergendoller, J. (2001). Problem-based learning: Modifying the medical school model for teaching high school economics. *Social Studies, 92,* 73–78.

McCall, R. (1987). Developmental function, individual differences and the plasticity of intelligence. In J. Gallagher & C. Ramey (Eds.), *The malleability of children* (pp. 25–36). Baltimore: Paul H. Brookes.

McCarthy, M. (1994). Inclusion and the law: Recent judicial decisions. *Phi Delta Kappa Research Bulletin,* No. 13.

McCathren, R., Yoder, P., & Warren, S. (1995). The role of directives in early language intervention. *Journal of Early Intervention, 19(2),* 91–101.

McCathren, R., Yoder, P., & Warren, S. (1999). Relationship between prelinguistic vocalization and later expressive vocabulary in young children with developmental delay. *Journal of Speech, Language and Hearing Research, 42*(4), 915–924.

McClearn, G. (1993). Behavioral genetics: The last century and the next. In R. Plomin & G. McClearn (Eds.), *Nature, nurture & psychology* (pp. 27–51). Washington, DC: American Psychological Association.

McCoach, D. B., & Siegle, D. (2003). Factors that differentiate underachieving gifted students from high-achieving gifted students. *Gifted Child Quarterly, 47*, 144–154.

McCombs, K., & Moore, D. (2002). Substance abuse prevention and intervention for students with disabilities: A call to educators. *ERIC Digest,* E627.

McConnell, S. (2000). Interventions to facilitate social interaction for young children with autism: Review of available research and recommendations for educational intervention (paper prepared for National Research Council of the National Academy of Sciences). Minneapolis: University of Minnesota.

McDonnell, L., McLaughlin, M., & Morrison, P. (Eds.). (1997). *Educating one and all: Students with disabilities and standards-based reform.* Washington, DC: National Academy Press.

McGee, G., Feldman, R., & Morrier, M. (1997). Benchmarks of social treatment for children with autism. *Journal of Autism and Developmental Disorders, 27*, 353–364.

McGill, T., & Vogtle, L. (2001). Driver's education for students with physical disabilities. *Exceptional Children, 67*(4), 455–466.

McGregor, D., & Farrenkopf, C. (2000). Recreation and leisure skills. In A. Koenig & M. Holbrook (Eds.). *Foundations of education: Vol. II. Instructional strategies for teaching children and youths with visual impairments* (2nd ed., pp. 653–678). New York: Foundation for the Blind Press.

McGuffin, P., Riley, B., & Plomin, R. (2001). Toward behavioral genomics. *Science, 291,* 1232–1249.

McHale, S., & Gamble, W. (1987). Sibling relationships and adjustment of children with disabled and nondisabled brothers and sisters. *Journal of Children in Contemporary Society, 19*, 131–158.

McLaughlin, J., & Lewis, R. (2001). *Assessing students with special needs* (5th ed.). Upper Saddle River, NJ: Prentice-Hall, Inc.

McLean, L., & Cripe, J. (1997). The effectiveness of early intervention for children with communication disorders. In M. Guralnick (Ed.), *The effectiveness of early intervention* (pp. 349–428). Baltimore: Paul H. Brookes.

McLeskey, J., Lancaster, M., & Grizzle, K. (1995). Learning disabilities and grade retention: A review of issues with recommendations for practice. *Learning Disabilities Research and Practice, 10*(2), 120–128.

McNulty, B., Soper, E., & Smith, D. (1984). *Effectiveness of early childhood special education of handicapped children.* Denver: Colorado State Department of Education.

Meadow, K. (1980). *Deafness and children.* Berkeley: University of California Press.

Meese, R. (1997). Adapting textbooks for children with learning disabilities in mainstreamed classrooms. In *Educating exceptional children* (9th ed., pp. 39–41). Guilford, CT: Dushkin Publications.

Meisels, S. (1987, January). Uses and abuses of developmental screening and school readiness testing. *Young Children,* 4–9.

Meisels, S., Jablon, J., Marsden, D., Dichtelmiller, M., & Dorfman, A. (1994). *The work sampling system* (2nd ed.). Ann Arbor, MI: Rebus Planning Associates.

Meisels, S., Marsden, D., Wiske, M., & Henderson, L. (1997). *The early screening inventory* (rev. ed.). Ann Arbor: University of Michigan.

Meisels, S. J., Bickel, D. D., Nicholson, J., Xue, Y., & Atkins-Burnett, S. (2001). Trusting teachers' judgments: A validity study of a curriculum-embedded performance assessment in kindergarten–grade 3. *American Educational Research Journal, 38*(1), 73–95.

Meisels, S. J., Dombro, A. L., Marsden, D. B., Weston, D. D., & Jewkes, A. (2003). *The ounce scale: An observational assessment for infants, toddlers, and families.* New York: Pearson Early Learning.

Meisels, S. J., Jablon, J. R., Marsden, D. B., Dichtelmiller, M. L., & Dorfman, A. B. (2001). *The work sampling system.* New York: Pearson Early Learning.

Meisels, S. J. & Provence, S. (1989). *Screening and assessment: Guidelines for identifying young disabled and developmentally vulnerable children and their families.* Arlington, VA: Zero to Three/National Center Clinical Infant Program.

Mencher, G., & Gerber, S. (1983). *The multiply handicapped hearing-impaired child.* New York: Grune & Stratton.

Mercer, C. (1992). *Students with learning disabilities* (4th ed.). Columbus, OH: Charles E. Merrill.

Mesibov, G. B. (1999). Are children with autism better off in an autism classroom or multidisability classroom? *Journal of Autism Developmental Disorders, 29*, 429.

Mesibov, G., Schopler, E., & Hearsey, K. (1994). Structured teaching. In E. Schopler & G. Mesibov (Eds.). *Behavioral issues in autism* (pp. 195–207). New York: Plenum Press.

Metz, I. (1991). Albuquerque, New Mexico. In M. Anderson & P. Goldberg (Eds.), *Cultural competence in screening and assessment* (pp. 8–10). National Early Childhood Technical Assistance System. Pacer Center, 4826 Chicago Avenue South, Minneapolis, MN 55417-1095.

Meyer, C., Akamatsu, C., & Stewart, D. (2002). A model for effective practice dialogue with students who are deaf. *Exceptional Children, 68*(4), 485–502.

Meyer, G. (1997). Syndromes of inborn errors of metabolism. In M. L. Batshaw (Ed.), *Children with disabilities.* Baltimore: Paul H. Brookes.

Meyer, L. H. (1991, August). Personal communication.

Meyer, L. H., Park, H. S., Grenot-Scheyer, M., Schwartz, I. S., & Harry, B. (1998). *Making friends: The influence of culture and development.* Baltimore: Paul H. Brookes.

Meyer, L. H., Peck, C. A., & Brown, L. (1991). *Critical issues in the lives of people with severe disabilities.* Baltimore: Paul H. Brookes.

Michael, M., & Paul, P. (1995). Early intervention with deaf-blindness. In S. Huebner, J. Prickett, T. Welch, & E. Jaffee (Eds.). *Hand in hand* (pp. 130–140). New York: AFT Press.

Michaud, L., Semel-Concepcíon, J., Duhaime, A., & Lazar, M. (2002). Traumatic brain injury. In M. Batshaw (Ed.), *Children with disabilities* (5th ed., pp. 525–546). Baltimore: Paul H. Brookes.

Miles, B., & Riggio, M. (1999). *Remarkable conversations: A guide to developing meaningful communication with children and young adults who are deaf/blind.* Watertown, MA: Perkins School for the Blind.

Milian, M. (2000). Multicultural issues. In A. Koenig & M. Holbrook (Eds.). *Foundations of education:* Vol. I. *History and theory of teaching children and youths with visual impairments.* (2nd ed., pp. 197–217). New York: American Foundation for the Blind Press.

Milian, M., & Ferrell, D. (1998). *Preparing special educators to meet the needs of students who are learning English as a second language and are visually impaired: A monograph.* ERIC Document No. Ed426545.

Miller, J., & Paul, R. (1995). *The clinical assessment of language comprehension.* Baltimore: Paul H. Brookes.

Mills, P., Cole, K., Jenkins, J., & Dale, P. (1998). Effects of differing levels of inclusion in preschoolers with disabilities. *Exceptional Children, 65*(1), 79–90.

Mirenda, P. (1999). Augmentative and alternative communication techniques. In J. Downing (Ed.), *Teaching communication skills to students with severe disabilities* (pp. 119–138). Baltimore: Paul H. Brookes.

Mirenda, P., & Erickson, K. (2000). Augmentative communication and literacy. In A. Wetherby & B. Prizant (Eds.), *Autism spectrum disorders* (pp. 333–368). Baltimore: Paul H. Brookes.

Moats, L. G. (1994). Assessment of spelling in learning disabilities. In G. Lyon, *Frames of reference for the assessment of learning disabilities.* Baltimore: Paul H. Brookes.

Moffitt, T. E. (1993a). Adolescence-limited and life-course-persistent antisocial behavior: A developmental taxonomy. *Psychological Review, 100,* 674–701.

Moffitt, T. E., Caspi, A., Rutter, M., & Silva, P. A. (2001). *Sex differences in antisocial behavior: Conduct disorder, delinquency, and violence in the Dunedin longitudinal study.* New York: Cambridge University Press.

Montgomery, J. (2002). Understanding the language difficulties of children with specific language impairments: Does verbal working memory matter? *American Journal of Speech-Language Pathology, 11*(1), 71–91.

Moon, M., & Inge, K. (2000). Vocational preparation and transition. In M. Snell & F. Brown. (Eds.), *Instruction of students with severe disabilities* (5th ed., pp. 591–628). Upper Saddle River, NJ: Merrill.

Moon, T., Brighton, C., & Callahan, C. (2003). State standardized test programs: Friend or foe of gifted education? *Roeper Review, 25,* 49–60.

Moore, D. (1989). *Educating the deaf* (3rd ed.). Boston: Houghton Mifflin.

Moores, D. (1996). *Educating the deaf: Psychology, principles, and practices* (4th ed.). Boston: Houghton Mifflin.

Moores, D. (2000). *Educating the deaf* (5th ed.). Boston: Houghton Mifflin.

Moores, D., Kluwin, T., & Mertens, D. (1985). *High school program for the deaf in metropolitan areas* (Research Monograph No. 3). Washington, DC: Gallaudet Research Institute.

Morelock, M. J., & Feldman, D. H. (1991). Extreme precocity. In N. Colangelo & G. A. Davis (Eds.), *Handbook of gifted education* (pp. 347–364). Boston: Allyn & Bacon.

Morelock, M., & Feldman, D. (1997). High IQ children, extreme precocity and savant syndrome. In N. Colangelo & G. Davis (Eds.), *Handbook of the gifted education* (2nd ed., pp. 439–459). Boston: Allyn & Bacon.

Morris, S. (2002). Promoting social skills among students with non-verbal learning disabilities. *Teaching Exceptional Children, 34*(3), 66–70.

Morrison, R., Sainato, D., Benchaaban, D., & Endo, S. (2002). Increasing play skills of children with autism using activity schedules and correspondence training. *Journal of Early Intervention, 25,* 58–72.

Mount, B. (2000a). *Life building.* New York: Graphic Futures.

Mount, B. (2000b). *Person-centered planning.* New York: Graphic Futures.

MTA Cooperative Group. (1999). A 14-month randomized clinical trial of treatment strategies for attention-deficit/hyperactivity disorder. *Archives of General Psychiatry, 56,* 1073–1086.

Murphy, K. (1983). The educator-therapist with deaf, multiply disabled children: Some essential criteria. In G. Mencher & S. Gerber (Eds.), *The multiply handicapped hearing-impaired child* (pp. 13–16). New York: Grune & Stratton.

Murphy, K., & Byrne, D. (1983). Selection of optimal modalities as avenues of learning in deaf, blind, multiply disabled children. In G. Mencher & S. Gerber (Eds.), *The multiply handicapped hearing-impaired child* (pp. 335–396). New York: Grune & Stratton.

Myklebust, H. (1965). *Development of disorders in written language, 7.* New York: Grune & Stratton.

Naglai, A. (1991). Manhattan, New York. In M. Anderson & P. Goldberg (Eds.), *Cultural competence in screening and assessment* (pp. 14–15). Pacer Center, 4826 Chicago Avenue South, Minneapolis, MN 55417-1095.

Nakamura, K. (1997). *The deaf resource library* (online). Available http://pantheon.yaleeduc/~Nakamura/deaf/

National Clearing House on Child Abuse and Neglect. (2000). Personal communication.

National Early Childhood Technical Assistance System. (2000). *Programs for young children with disabilities under IDEA.* Chapel Hill, NC: Frank Porter Child Development Center, University of North Carolina.

National Information Center for Children and Youth with Disabilities (NICHCY). (1993). *The Individuals with Disabilities Education Act (IDEA).* NICHCY, PO Box 1492, Washington, DC 20013.

National Information Center for Children and Youth with Disabilities (NICHCY). (1997). *Traumatic stuttering and brain injury.* NICHCY, PO Box 1492, Washington, DC 20013.

National Information Center for Children and Youth with Disabilities (NICHCY). (2000a). *Epilepsy.* NICHCY, PO Box 1492, Washington, DC 20013.

National Information Center for Children and Youth with Disabilities (NICHCY). (2000b). *Traumatic brain injury.* NICHCY, PO Box 1492, Washington, DC 20013.

National Information Center for Children and Youth with Disabilities (NICHCY). (2001). *General information about disabilities.* NICHCY, PO Box 1492, Washington, DC 20013.

National Information Center for Children and Youth with Disabilities (NICHCY). (2002). *Cerebral palsy.* NICHCY, PO Box 1492, Washington, DC 20013.

National Information Center for Children and Youth with Disabilities (NICHCY). (2003b). *Spina bifida.* NICHCY, PO Box 1492, Washington, DC 20013.

National Information Center for Children with Disabilities (NICHCY). (1999). *The Individuals with Disabilities Education Act (IDEA) 1998.* NICHCY, PO Box 1492, Washington, DC 20013.

National Information Center for Children with Disabilities (NICHCY). (2003a). *Autism/PDD, cerebral palsy, epilepsy, learning disabilities, traumatic brain injury.* NICHCY, PO Box 1492, Washington, DC 20013.

National Information Center on Children and Youth with Disabilities (NICHCY). (March 1997). *Learning Disabilities.* (Fact Sheet N. 7). Washington, DC: N. Amos.

National Information Center on Children and Youth with Disabilities. (1998). *IDEA 1998.* Available from NICHCY, P.O. Box 1492, Washington, DC.

National Information Center on Children and Youth with Disabilities (NICHCY). (2000). *Epilepsy, cerebral palsy, spina bifida & traumatic brain injury.*

National Information Center on Children and Youth with Disabilities (NICHCY). (2000). *Severe and/or multiple disabilities.* P.O. Box 1492, Washington, DC.

National Information Center on Children and Youth with Disabilities (NICHCY). (2002). *Deafness and hearing loss.* NICHCY, P.O. Box 1492, Washington, DC 20013-1492.

National Information Center on Children and Youth with Disabilities (NICHCY). (2003). *Individuals with Disabilities Education Act.* Washington, DC: National Information Center on Children and Youth with Disabilities, PO Box 1492, Washington, DC 20013-1492.

National Information Center on Children and Youth with Disabilities. (2003). *Speech and language disorders.* NICHCY, P.O. Box 1492, Washington, DC 20013-1492.

National Information Center on Deafness (NICD). (1994). *TTY's, TT's, and TDD's.* Washington, DC: National Information Center on Deafness.

National Information Center on Deafness. (1994). *What are TTY's, TT's, and TDD's?* NICD, Gallaudet University, 800 Florida Ave., N.E., Washington, DC 20002-3695.

National Information Center on Deafness. (1999). *Deafness: A factsheet.* NICD, Gallaudet University, 800 Florida Ave., N.E., Washington, DC 20002-3695.

National Information Center on Deafness. (2000). *Assistive listening devices: A consumer-oriented summary.* NICD, Gallaudet University, 800 Florida Ave., N.E., Washington, DC 20002-3695.

National Information Center on Deafness. (2003). *Deafness: A fact sheet.* Silver Spring, MD: Author.

National Information Center on Deafness and Other Communication Disorders. (1999). *Usher syndrome.* Bethesda, MD: National Information Center on Deafness and Other Communication Disorders.

National Institute for Health. (2003). *Publication No. 93-3611.* Silver Springs, MD: National Institute for Health.

National Institute of Health Consensus Statement. (2000). *Phenylketonuria (PKU): Screening and management.* Washington, DC.

National Institute of Mental Health. (2001). *Blueprint for change: Research on child and adolescent mental health.* Rockville, MD: Author.

National Institute on Deafness and Other Communication Disorders (NIDCD). (1999). *Hearing loss in children: Delayed speech and language.* NIDCD Information Clearinghouse, National Institute of Health, One Communication Avenue, Bethesda, MD 20892-3456.

National Institute on Deafness and Other Communication Disorders (NIDCD). (2000). *Usher syndrome.* Bethesda, MD.

National Organization on Fetal Alcohol Syndrome. (2004). *Teaching students with FAS/FASD.* Retrieved June 1, 2004, from http://www.nofas.org/educator/teaching.aspx.

National Research Council (2002). *Minority students in special and gifted education.* Washington DC: National Academy Press.

National Technical Assistance Consortium (NTAC). (2002). Teaching Research Division, Western State College, Monmouth, OR 97361.

Neidecker, E. (1987). *School programs in speech and language: Organization and management* (2nd ed.). Englewood Cliffs, NJ: Prentice-Hall.

Neihart, M. (1999). The impact of giftedness on psychological well-being: What does the empirical literature say? *Roeper Review, 22*(1), 10–17.

Neihart M. (2002a). Delinquency and Gifted Children. In M. Neihart, S. Reis, N. Robinson, & S. Moon (Eds.), *The social and emotional development of gifted children: What do we know?* (pp. 103–112). Waco, TX: Prufrock Press.

Neihart, M. (2002b). Gifted children and depression. In M. Neihart, S. Reis, N. Robinson, & S. Moon (Eds.), *The social and emotional development of gifted children: What do we know?* (pp. 93–102). Waco, TX: Prufrock Press.

Neihart, M., & Olenchak, F. R. (2002). Creatively gifted children. In M. Neihart, S. Reis, N. Robinson, & S. Moon (Eds.), *The social and emotional development of gifted children: What do we know?* (pp. 165–176). Waco, TX: Prufrock Press.

Neihart, M., Reis, S., Robinson, N., & Moon, S. (Eds.). (2002). *The social and emotional development of gifted children: What do we know?* Waco, TX: Prufrock Press.

Nelson, C., Leone, P., & Rutherford, R. (In press). Youth delinquency: Prevention and intervention research. In R. Rutherford, M. Quinn, & S. Mather (Eds.), *Handbook of research in behavioral disorders.* New York: Guilford Press.

Nelson, C., & Huefner, D. (2003). Young children with autism: Judicial responses to the Lovaas and discrete trial training debates. *Journal of Early Intervention, 26*, 1–19.

Nelson, C. M. (2003). Through a glass darkly: Reflections on our field and its future. *Behavioral Disorders, 28*, 212–216.

Nelson, J., Crabtree, M., Marchand-Martella, N., & Martella, R. (1998). Teaching good behavior in the whole school. *Teaching Exceptional Children, 30*(4), 4–9.

Nelson, K., Camarata, S., Welsh, J., Butskovsky, L., & Camarata, M. (1996, August). Effects of imitative and conversational recasting treatment on the acquisition of grammar in children with specific language impairment and younger language-normal children. *Journal of Speech and Hearing Research, 39*(4), 850–859.

Neumeister, K., & Hebert, T. (2003). Underachievement versus selective achievement: Delving deeper and discovering the difference. *Journal for the Education of the Gifted, 26,* 221–238.

Neuwirth, S. (1994). *Attention deficit hyperactivity disorder.* Washington, DC: National Institutes of Health Publication 94-3572.

Neuwirth, S. (1996). *Attention deficit hyperactivity disorder: Decade of the brain.* Silver Spring, MD: National Institute of Mental Health.

Neuwirth, S. (2002). *Learning disabilities.* Washington, DC: National Institute of Mental Health Publication No. 93-364.

Newman, S., Copple, C., & Bredekamp, S. (2001). *Learning to read and write: Developmentally appropriate practices for young children.* Washington, DC: National Association for the Education of Young Children.

Newton, J., Horner, R., Ard, W., LeBaron, N., & Sapperton, G. (1994). Social aspects and social relationship of individuals with disability. *Mental Retardation, 32*(5), 393–402.

Newton, V., & Stokes, J. (1999). Causes of hearing impairments. In J. Stokes (Ed.), *The hearing impaired infant: The first eighteen months* (pp. 39–54). London: Whurr. (Distributed by Paul H. Brookes.)

Nihira, K., Leland, H., & Lambert, N. (1993a). *AAMR adaptive behavior scale: Residential and community* (2nd ed.). Austin, TX: PRO-ED.

Nolet, V., & McLaughlin, M. J. (2000). *Accessing the general curriculum: Including students with disabilities in standards-based reform.* Thousand Oaks, CA: Corwin.

Northern, J., & Downs, M. (1978). *Hearing in children* (2nd ed.). Baltimore: Williams & Wilkins.

Norvich, R. (1993). Activity based intervention and developmentally appropriate practice: Points of convergence. *Topics in Early Childhood Special Education, 3*(4), 403–417.

Obiakor, F., Grant, P., & Dooley, E. (2002). *Educating all learners: The comprehensive support model.* Springfield, IL: Charles C. Thomas.

O'Brien, M. (1997). *Inclusive child care for infants and toddlers: Meeting individual and special needs.* Baltimore: Paul H. Brookes.

Odom, S., & McLean, M. (1996). *Early intervention/early childhood special education.* Austin, TX: PRO-ED.

Office of Special Education Programs. (2001). *General education teachers' role in special education: A study of personnel needs in special education fact sheet.* Retrieved May 12, 2004, from http://www.spense.org.

Office of Special Education Programs. (2003). *Twenty-fourth annual report to Congress.* Washington, DC: Author.

Ogura, T. (1991). A longitudinal study of the relationship between early language development and play development. *Journal of Child Language, 18,* 273–294.

O'Hara, D., & Levy, J. (1987). Family intervention. In K. Kavale, S. Forness, & M. Bender (Eds.), *Handbook of learning disabilities* (pp. 215–235). Boston: College-Hill/Little, Brown.

Okolo, C., Cavalier, A., Ferretti, R., & MacArthur, C. (2000). Technology literacy and disabilities. A review of the research. In R. Gersten, E. Schiller, & S. Vaughn (Eds.), *Contemporary special education research* (pp. 179–250). Mahwah, NJ: Erlbaum.

Olenchak, F. R., & Reis, S. M. (2002). In M. Neihart, S. Reis, N. Robinson, & S. Moon (Eds.), *The social and emotional development of gifted children: What do we know?* (pp. 177–192). Waco, TX: Prufrock Press.

Olesen, D. (1996). The top ten technologies for the next ten years. In E. Cornish (Ed.), *Exploring your future: Living, learning, and working in the information age* (pp. 67–71). Bethesda, MD: World Future Society.

Oller, D. K. (1985). Infant vocalizations. In S. Harel & N. J. Anastasiow (Eds.), *The at-risk infant* (pp. 323–332). Baltimore: Paul H. Brookes.

Olley, J. (1999). Curriculum for students with autism. *School Psychology Review, 28*(4), 595–604.

O'Neill, J., Gothelf, C., Cohen, S., Lehman, L., & Woolf, S. (1991). *A curricular approach to support the transition to adulthood of adolescents with visual or dual sensory impairments and cognitive disabilities.* Albany: New York State Education Department, Office of Special Education and Rehabilitation Services.

Onslow, M., Costa L., Andrews, C., Harrison, E., & Packman, A. (1996, August). Speech outcomes of a prolonged speech treatment for stuttering. *Journal of Speech and Hearing Research, 39*(4), 734–749.

Orelove, F., Sobrey, D., & Silberman, R. (2004). *Educating children with multiple disabilities* (4th ed.). Baltimore: Brookes.

Orr, D. (1989). *Measurement of self-concept among disabled children.* Unpublished doctoral dissertation, Harvard University, Cambridge, MA.

Orton Dyslexia Research Committee. (1994). Definition of Dyslexia. Baltimore: International Dyslexia Society.

Orton, S. T. (1937). *Reading, writing and speech problems in children.* New York: Norton.

Osher, D., Cartledge, G., Oswald, D., Sutherland, K., Artiles, A., & Coutinho, M. (In press). Issues of cultural and linguistic competency and disproportionate representation. In R. Rutherford, M. Quinn, & S. Mather (Eds.), *Handbook of research in behavioral disorders.* New York: Guilford Press.

Osher, D., Morrison, G. M., & Bailey, W. (2003). Exploring the relationship between students: Mobility and dropout among students with emotional and behavioral disorders. *Journal of Negro Education, 72,* 79–96.

Osher, D., Woodruff, D., & Sims, A. (2002). Schools make a difference: The relationship between education services for African American children and youth and their overrepresentation in the juvenile justice system. In D. Losen (Ed.), *Minority issues in special education* (pp. 93–116). Cambridge, MA: Harvard University, Harvard Education Publishing Group, Civil Rights Project.

Owens, R. (1996). *Language development.* Boston: Allyn & Bacon.

Ozonoff, S., & Cathcart, K. (1998). Effectiveness of a home program intervention for young children with autism. *Journal of Autism and Developmental Disorder, 28,* 25–32.

Pagliaro, C. (1998). Mathematics reform in the education of deaf and hard of hearing students. *American Annals of the Deaf, 143,* 22–28.

Palinscar, A. S., & Brown, D. A. (1986). Interactive teaching to promote independent learning from text. *Reading Teacher, 39,* 771–777.

Palmer, D., Fuller, K., Arora, T., & Nelson, M. (2001). Taking sides: Parent views on inclusion for children with severe disabilities. *Exceptional Children, 67*(4), 467–484.

Panacek, L., & Dunlap, G. (2003). The social lives of children with emotional and behavioral disorders in self-contained classrooms: a descriptive analysis. *Exceptional Children, 69,* 333–348.

Pappas, D. (1985). *Diagnosis and treatment of hearing impairment in children.* San Diego: College-Hill.

Parasnis, I. (Ed.). (1997). *Cultural and language diversity and the deaf experience.* New York: Cambridge University Press.

Parette, H. (1991). The importance of technology in the education and training of persons with mental retardation. *Education and Training in Mental Retardation, 26,* 165–178.

Parette, Jr., H. (1998). Assistive technology effective practices for students with mental retardation and developmental disabilities. In A. Hilton & R. Ringlaben (Eds.), *Best and promising practices in developmental disabilities* (pp. 205–224). Austin, TX: PRO-ED.

Parette, H., & Petch-Hogan, B. (2000). Approaching families. *Teaching Exceptional Children, 33*(2), 4–10.

Park, J., Turnbull, A. P., & Turnbull, H. R. (2002). Impacts of poverty on quality of life in families of children with disabilities. *Exceptional Children, 68,* 151–172.

Parke, B. N. (1989). *Gifted students in regular classrooms.* Boston: Allyn & Bacon.

Patterson, G. R., & Chamberlain, P. (1994). A functional analysis of resistance during parent training therapy. *Clinical Psychology Science and Practice, 1,* 53–70.

Patton, J. R. (1986). *Transition: Curricular implications.* Honolulu: Project Ho-ko-ko, University of Hawaii.

Paul, J., & Epanchin, B. (Eds.). (1986). *Emotional disturbance in children* (3rd ed.). Columbus, OH: Merrill.

Paul, P., & Quigley, S. (1994). *Education and deafness.* White Plains, NY: Longman.

Paul, P., & Quigley, S. (1995). *Education and deafness.* White Plains, NY: Longman.

Paul, R. (1995). *Language disorders from infancy through adolescence.* St. Louis, MO: Mosby.

Paul, R. (1996a, February). Clinical implications of natural history of slow expressive language development. *American Journal of Speech-Language Pathology, 5,* 5–12.

Paul, R. (1996b, Spring). First-second language English literacy. *Volta Review, 98*(2), 5–16.

Pear, R. (1992, January 19). The hard thing about cutting infant mortality is educating mothers. *New York Times,* p. E5.

Pearpoint, J., Forest, M., & O'Brien, J. (1996). MAPs, circles of friends, and PATH: Powerful tools to help build caring communities. In W. C. Stainback & S. B. Stainback (Eds.),

Inclusion: A guide for educators (pp. 67–86). Baltimore: Brookes.

Pellegrino, K. (2002). Cerebral palsy. In M. Bradshaw (Ed.), *Children with disabilities* (pp. 443–466). Baltimore: Brookes.

Pellegrino, L. (1997). Cerebral palsy. In M. L. Batshaw (Ed.), *Children with disabilities* (pp. 499–528). Baltimore: Paul H. Brookes.

Pellegrino, L. (2002). Cerebral palsy. In M. Batshaw (Ed.), *Children with disabilities* (5th ed., pp. 443–466). Baltimore: Paul H. Brookes.

Pennington, B. (1997). *Towards an integrated understanding of dyslexia.* Department of Psychology, Denver University, Denver, CO.

Perkins, D. (1995). *Outsmarting IQ: The emerging science of learnable intelligence.* New York: Free Press.

Perrone, P. (1997). Gifted individuals' career development. In N. Colangelo & G. Davis (Eds.), *Handbook of gifted education* (2nd ed., pp. 398–407). Boston: Allyn & Bacon.

Peterson, N. (1987). Parenting the young handicapped and at-risk child. In N. Peterson (Ed.), *Early intervention for handicapped and at-risk children: An introduction to early childhood special education* (pp. 409–446). Denver, CO: Love.

Petitto, L., & Marentette, P. (1991, March). Babbling in the manual mode: Evidence for the ontogeny of language. *Science, 251,* 1493–1495.

Pianta, R. C., & Cox, M. J. (2002). *The transition to kindergarten: Research, policy, training and practice.* Baltimore: Brookes.

Pianta, R. C., Cox, M. J., Early, D., & Taylor, L. (1999). Kindergarten teachers' practices related to the transition to school: Results of a national survey. *Elementary School Journal, 100,* 71–86.

Pianta, R., & Kraft-Sayre, M. (2003). *Successful kindergarten transition.* Baltimore: Brookes.

Pietrot, L., Williams, P., & Kaplan, H. (1991). *Alternative and communicative devices for hearing impaired people: What's available now.* National Information Center on Deafness, Gallaudet University, 800 Florida Avenue N.E., Washington, DC 20002-3695.

Pinker, S. (1991). Rules of language. *Science, 253,* 530–535.

Plomin, R. (Ed.). (1997). *Nature, nurture and psychology.* Washington, DC: American Psychological Association.

Plomin, R., DeFries, J., & McClearn, G. (1980). *Behavioral genetics: A primer.* San Francisco: Freeman.

Plomin, R., & Petrill, S. (1997). Genetics and intelligence: What's new? *Intelligence, 24*(1), 53–77.

Pogrund, R., & Fazzi, D. (Eds.). (2002). *Early focus* (2nd ed.). New York: American Foundation for the Blind.

Pogrund, R., Fazzi, D., & Lampert, J. (Eds.). (1992). *Early focus: Working with young blind and visually impaired children and their families.* New York: American Foundation for the Blind.

Polsgrove, L. (2003). Reflections on the past and future. *Behavioral Disorders, 28,* 221–226.

Powell, T., & Gallagher, P. (1993). *Brothers and sisters* (2nd ed.). Baltimore: Paul H. Brookes.

Premack, D. (1959). Toward empirical behavior laws: I. Positive reinforcement. *Psychological Review, 66,* 291–333.

Pressley, M., Brown, R., El-Dinary, P. B., & Afflerbach, P. (1995). The comprehension instruction that students need. *Learning Disabilities Research and Practice, 10*(4), 215-224.

Pressley, M. (1990). *Cognitive strategy instruction*. Cambridge, MA: Brookline Press.

Pressley, M., & Woloshyn. V. (1995). *Cognitive strategy instruction that really improves children's academic performance.* (2nd ed.) Cambridge, MA: Brookline Books.

Priasner, C. L. (2003). Attitudes of elementary school principals toward the inclusion of students with disabilities. *Exceptional Children, 69,* 135-146.

Pueschel, S. (1983). The child with Down syndrome. In M. Levine, W. Carey, & R. Gross (Eds.), *Developmental-behavioral pediatrics*. Philadelphia: Saunders.

Pueschel, S. (1991). Ethical considerations related to prenatal diagnosis of fetuses with Down syndrome. *Mental Retardation, 29*(4), 185-190.

Pueschel, S., Scala, P., Weidenman, L., & Bernier, J. (Eds.). (1995). *The special child* (2nd ed.). Baltimore: Paul H. Brookes.

Quigley, S., Jenne, W., & Phillips, S. (1968). *Deaf students in colleges and universities.* Washington, DC: Alexander Graham Bell Association.

Rabinowitz, M., & Glaser, R. (1986). *Cognitive structure and process in highly competent performance*. Pittsburgh, PA: Learning Research and Development Center.

Rainforth, B., York, J., & MacDonald, C. (1992). *Collaborative teams for students with severe disabilities.* Baltimore: Paul H. Brookes.

Rais-Barahmi, K., Short, B., & Batshaw, M. (2002). Premature and small for date babies. In M. Batshaw (Ed.), *Children with disabilities* (5th ed., pp. 85-106). Baltimore: Brookes.

Ramey, C., & Ramey, S. (1998). Early intervention and early experience. *American Psychologist, 53*(2), 109-120.

Ramey, S. L., & Ramey, C. T. (1999). The transition to school for "at-risk" children. In R. C. Pianta & M. J. Cox (Eds.), *The transition to kindergarten* (pp. 217-251). Baltimore: Paul H. Brookes.

Ramsey, E., & Walker, H. (1988). Family management correlates of antisocial behavior among middle school boys. *Behavioral Disorders, 13*(3), 187-201.

Raus-Bahrami, K., Short, B., & Batshaw, M. (2003). Premature and small-for-date babies. In M. Batshaw (Ed.), *Children with disabilities* (5th ed., pp. 85-106). Baltimore: Brookes.

Ray, B. (1997). *Home education across the United States: Family characteristics, student achievement, longitudinal traits.* Purcellville, VA: Home School Legal Defense Association.

Rea, P., McLaughlin, V., & Walther-Thomas, C. (2002). Outcomes for students with learning disabilities in inclusive and pullout programs. *Exceptional Children, 68,* 203-224.

Reichle, J., Beukelman, D., & Light, J. (2002). *Exemplary practices for beginning communicators: Implications for AAC.* Baltimore: Paul H. Brookes.

Reis, D. (2003). Child effects in family systems. In A. C. Crocker & A. Booth (Eds.), *Child influence on family dynamics* (pp. 1-23). Mahwah, NJ: Erlbaum.

Reis, S. M. (2003). Gifted girls, twenty-five years later: Hopes realized and new challenges found. *Roeper Review, 25,* 154-157.

Reis, S., & McCoach, D. (2000). The underachievement of gifted students: What do we know and where do we go? *Gifted Child Quarterly, 44,* 152-170.

Reis, S. M., & McCoach, D. B. (2002). Underachievement in gifted students. In M. Neihart, S. Reis, N. Robinson, & S. Moon (Eds.), *The social and emotional development of gifted children: What do we know?* (pp. 81-92). Waco, TX: Prufrock Press.

Reis, S. M., Burns, D. E., & Renzulli, J. S. (1992). *Curriculum compacting: A process for modifying curriculum for high ability students.* Videotape V921. Storrs, CT: National Research Center on the Gifted and Talented.

Rimm, S. B. (2003). *See Jane win for girls: A smart girl's guide to success.* Minneapolis: Free Spirit.

Rittenhouse, R. (1985). *TTY language in deaf adolescents: A research report.* Normal: Illinois State University.

Rivers, K., Lombardino, L., & Thompson, C. (1996, February). Effects of phonological decoding training on children's word recognition. *American Journal of Speech-Language Pathology, 5*(1).

Roberts, J., Burchinal, M., & Bailey, D. (1994). Communication among preschoolers with and without disabilities in same-age and mixed-age classes. *American Journal of Mental Retardation, 99*(3), 231-249.

Roberts, R., Rule, S., & Innocenti, M. (1998). *Strengthening the family professional partnership in services for young children.* Baltimore: Paul H. Brookes.

Robinson, N. M. (2002). Assessing and advocating for gifted students: Perspectives for school and clinical psychologists. *Senior scholars series.* Storrs, CT: National Research Center on the Gifted and Talented.

Robinson, N., Zigler, E., & Gallagher, J. (2000). Two tails of the normal curve: Similarities and differences in the study of mental retardation and differences in the study of mental retardation and giftedness. *American Psychologist, 55*(112), 1413-1424.

Roeper, A. (2003). The young gifted girl: A contemporary view. *Roeper Review, 25,* 151-153.

Rogoff, B., & Chavajay, P. (1995). What's become of research on the cultural basis of cognitive development? *American Psychologist, 50*(10), 859-877.

Roizen, N. J. (1997). Down syndrome. In M. L. Batshaw (Ed.), *Children with disabilities* (pp. 361-376). Baltimore: Paul H. Brookes.

Rose, D., & Meyer, A. (2002). Teaching every student in the digital age: Universal design for learning. Alexandria, VA: Association for Supervision and Curriculum Development.

Roseberry-McKibbin, C. (1997). Distinguishing language disorders in linguistically and culturally diverse students. *Educating exceptional children* (9th ed., pp. 109-112). Guilford, CT: Dushkin Publications.

Rosenthal-Malik, A., & Bloom, A. (1998). Beyond acquisition: Teaching generalization for students with developmental disabilities. In A. Hilton & R. Ringlaben (Eds.), *Best and promising practices in developmental disabilities* (pp. 139-156). Austin, TX: PRO-ED.

Ross, P. (Ed.). (1993). *National excellence.* Washington, DC: U.S. Department of Education.

Rourke, B. P. (1994). Neuropsychological assessment of children with learning disabilities. In G. Lyon (Ed.), *Frames of reference for the assessment of learning disabilities* (pp. 475–514). Baltimore: Paul H. Brookes.

Rourke, B. P. (Ed.). (1991). *Neuropsychological validation of learning disability subtypes.* New York: Guilford Press.

Rourke, B. P. (Ed.). (1995). *Syndrome of non-verbal learning disabilities.* New York: Guilford.

Rowland, C. (1996). Increasing functional communications. *Journal for Persons with Severe Handicaps, 18,* 161–176.

Rusch, F., Chadsey-Rusch, J. U., & Johnson, T. (1992). Preparing students for employment. In M. Snell (Ed.), *Systemic instruction of persons with severe handicaps* (3rd ed., pp. 471–490). Columbus, OH: Merrill.

Rutherford, R., Quinn, M., & Mathur, S. (2004). *Handbook of research in behavioral disorders.* New York: Guilford Press.

Rutstein, R., Conlon, C., & Batshaw, M. L. (1997). HIV and AIDS. In M. L. Batshaw (Ed.), *Children with disabilities* (pp. 163–181). Baltimore: Paul H. Brookes.

Rutter, M. (1996). Autism research: Prospects and priorities. *Journal of Autism and Developmental Disorders, 26,* 257–275.

Rutter, M. (1997). Nature-nurture integration: The example of antisocial behavior. *American Psychologist, 52,* 390–398.

Rutter, M. (2000). Resilience reconsidered. In J. Shonkoff & S. Meisels (Eds.), *Handbook of early intervention* (pp. 135–159). New York: Cambridge.

Rutter, M. (2003). Commentary: Causal processes leading to antisocial behavior. *Developmental Psychology, 39,* 372–378.

Rutter, M., Giller, H., & Hagell, A. (1998). *Antisocial behavior by young people.* New York: Cambridge University Press.

Rylance, B. J. (1997). Predictors of high school graduation or dropping out for youths with severe emotional disturbance. *Behavioral Disorders, 23,* 5–18.

Ryndak, D., & Alper, S. (2003). *Curriculum and instruction for students with significant disabilities in inclusive settings* (2nd ed.). Boston: Allyn & Bacon.

Sacks, S. (1992). The social development of visually impaired children: A theoretical perspective. In S. Sacks, L. Kekelis, & R. Gaylord-Ross (Eds.), *The development of social skills by blind and visually impaired students* (pp. 3–12). New York: American Foundation for the Blind.

Sacks, S., & Silberman, R. (1998). *Educating students who have visual impairments with other disabilities.* Baltimore: Paul H. Brookes.

Sacks, S., Wolffe, K., & Tierney, D. (1998). Lifestyles of students with visual impairments: Preliminary studies of social networks. *Exceptional Children, 64*(4), 463–478.

Sacks, S. Z. (1998). Education of students who have visual impairments with other disabilities: An overview. In S. Z. Sacks & R. K. Silberman (Eds.), *Educating students who have visual impairments with other disabilities* (pp. 3–38). Baltimore: Paul H. Brookes.

Safford, P., Sargent, M., & Cook, C. (Eds.). (1994). Instructional models in early childhood special education: Origins, issues and trends. In P. Safford (Ed.), *Early childhood special education* (pp. 96–117). New York: Teachers College Press.

Sailor, W., Gee, K., & Karasoff, P. (2000). Inclusion and school restructuring. In M. Snell & F. Brown. (Eds.), *Instruction of students with severe disabilities* (5th ed., pp. 3–30). Upper Saddle River, NJ: Merrill.

Sainato, D., Goldstein, H., & Strain, P. (1992). Effects of self evaluation on preschool children's use of social interaction strategies with their classmates with autism. *Journal of Applied Behavior Analysis, 25,* 127–141.

Sale, P., & Carey, D. (1995). The sociometric status of students with disabilities in a full inclusion school. *Exceptional Children, 62*(1), 6–19.

Salend, S., & Salinas, A. (2003). Language differences or learning difficulties. *Teaching Exceptional Children, 35*(4), 36–43.

Salvia, J., & Ysseldyke, J. (2001). *Assessment* (9th ed.). Boston: Houghton Mifflin.

Salzman, M. (2003). *True notebooks.* New York: Knopf.

Sameroff, A. (1990). Neo-environmental perspectives on developmental theory. In R. Hodapp, J. Burack, & E. Zigler (Eds.), *Issues in the developmental approach to mental retardation.* New York: Cambridge University Press.

Sameroff, A., & Fiese, B. (2000). Transactional regulation. In J. Shonkoff & S. Meisels (Eds.), *Handbook of early intervention* (pp. 135–159). New York: Cambridge.

Sameroff, A., & Haith, M. (Eds.). (1996). *The five to seven shift.* Chicago: University of Chicago Press.

Sandal, S., McLean, M., & Smith, B. DEC recommended practices. Longmount, CO: Sopris Press.

Sasso, G. M., Conroy, M. A., Stichter, J. P., & Fox, J. J. (2001). Slowing down the bandwagon: The misapplication of functional assessment for students with emotional or behavioral disorders. *Behavioral Disorders, 26,* 282–296.

Satz, P., & Morris, R. (1981). Learning disability subtypes: A review. In F. J. Pirozzolo & M. C. Wittock (Eds.), *Neuropsychological and cognitive processes in reading* (pp. 109–141). New York: Academic Press.

Scanlon, D. (2003). Changing LD eligibility—proceed with caution. *CEC Today, 10*(2), 14.

Scarr, S. (1982). Development is internally guided, not determined. *Contemporary Psychology, 27,* 852–853.

Schachter, M., & Demerath, R. (1996). Neuropsychology and mental retardation. In J. Jacobson & J. Mulick (Eds.), *Manual of diagnostic and professional practice in mental retardation* (pp. 165–178). Washington, DC: American Psychological Association.

Schaeffer, C., Petras, H., Ialongo, N., Poduska, J., & Kellam, S. (2003). Modeling growth in boys' aggressive behavior across elementary school: Links to later criminal involvement, conduct disorder, and antisocial personality disorder. *Developmental Psychology, 39,* 1020–1035.

Schaffner, C. B., & Buswell, B. E. (1996). Then critical elements for creating inclusive and effective school communities. In W. C. Stainback & S. B. Stainback (Eds.), *Inclusion: A guide for educators* (pp. 49–65). Baltimore: Paul H. Brookes.

Schalock, R. (1999). The merging of adaptive behavior and intelligence: Implications for the field of mental retardation. In R. Schalock & D. Braddock (Eds.), *Adaptive behavior and its measurement* (pp. 43–59). Washington, DC: American Association of Mental Retardation.

Schalock, R., & Braddock, D. (Eds.) (1999). *Adaptive behavior and its measurement*. Washington, DC: American Association on Mental Retardation.

Schery, T., & O'Connor, L. (1995). Computers as a context for language intervention. In M. Rey, J. Windson, & S. Warren (Eds.), *Language intervention*. Baltimore: Paul H. Brookes.

Schiefelbusch, R. L., Sullivan, J.W., & Ganz, V. K. (1980). Assessing children who are at risk. In S. Harel (Ed.), *The at-risk infant* (pp. 277–284). Amsterdam: Excerpta Medica.

Schimmel, C., Edwards, S., & Prickett, H. (1999). Reading . . .? Uh, I got it. *American Annals of the Deaf, 144*(4), 298–305.

Schlesinger, H. (1983). Early intervention: The prevention of multiple handicaps. In G. Mencher & S. Gerber (Eds.), *The multiply handicapped hearing-impaired child* (pp. 83–116). New York: Grune & Stratton.

Schneider, W. (2000). Giftedness, expertise, and (exceptional) performance: A developmental perspective. In K. A. Heller, F. J. Monks, R. J. Sternberg, & R. F. Subotnik (Eds.), *International handbook of giftedness and talent* (2nd ed., pp. 165–178). New York: Elsevier.

Schonberg, R., & Tifft, C. (2002). Birth defects, prenatal diagnoses and fetal therapy. In M. Batshaw (Ed.), *Children with disabilities* (5th ed., pp. 27–42). Baltimore: Brookes.

Schopler, E., Mesibov, G., & Hearsey, K. (1995). Structured teaching in the TEACCH system. In E. Schopler & G. Mesibov (Eds.), *Learning and cognition in autism* (pp. 243–268). New York: Plenum Press.

Schopler, E., Mesibov, G., & Kunce, L. (Eds.). (1998). *Asperger syndrome of high-functioning autism.* New York: Plenum Press.

Schore, A. (1994). *Affect regulation and the origin of the self.* Hillsdale, NJ: Erlbaum.

Schuler, P. (2002). Perfectionism in gifted children and adolescents. In M. Neihart, S. Reis, N. Robinson, & S. Moon (Eds.), *The social and emotional development of gifted children.* Waco, TX: Prufrock Press.

Schuman, J., Vaughn, S., Haager, D., McDowell, J., Rothstein, L., & Saumell, L. (1995). General education teacher planning: What can students with learning disabilities expect? *Exceptional Children, 61*(4), 335–352.

Schumm, J. S., & Vaughn, S. (1995). Getting ready for inclusion: Is the stage set? *Learning Disabilities Research and Practice, 10*(3), 169–179.

Schumm, J. S., Vaughn, S., Haager, D., McDowell, J., Rothlein, L., & Saumell, L. (1995). General education teacher planning: What can students with learning disabilities expect? *Exceptional Children, 61,* 335–352.

Schweinhart, L., & Weikart, D. (1998, March). Why curriculum matters in early childhood research. *Educational Leadership,* 57–60.

Science (1990, January). To test or not to test, 247(5), 17–18.

Scruggs, T., & Mastropieri, M. (2002, Summer). On babies and bathwater: Addressing the problem of identification and learning disabilities. *Learning Disabilities Quarterly, 25*(3), 148–155.

Scruggs, T., & Mastropieri, M. (2003). Summarizing special education research. *Contemporary Psychology, 48*(2), 248–250.

Seligman, M., & Peterson, C. (1986). A learned helplessness perspective on childhood depression. In M. Rutter, C. Izard, & P. Read (Eds.), *Depression in young people: Developmental and clinical perspectives.* New York: Guilford.

Serna, L., & Patton, J. (1989). Science. In G. Robinson, J. Patton, E. Polloway, & L. Sargent (Eds.), *Best practices in mild mental retardation* (pp. 197–199). Reston, VA: Council for Exceptional Children.

Serry, T., & Blaney, P. (1999). A four-year investigation into phonetic inventory development in young cochlear implant users. *Journal of Speech, Language, and Hearing Research, 42*(1), 887–899.

Shantz, M., & Eberling, K. (1991). Patterns of language related behaviors: Evidence for self-help in acquiring grammar. *Journal of Child Language, 18,* 295–313.

Shapiro, B., Church, R., & Lewis, M. (2002). In M. Batshaw (Ed.), *Children with disabilities* (5th ed., pp. 417–442). Baltimore: Brookes.

Sharp, K. G., & Patasky, V. M. (2002). *The current legal status of inclusion.* Horsham, PA: LRP.

Shaywitz, S., Pugh, K., Jenner, A., Fulbright, R., Fletcher, J., & Gore, J. (2002). The neurobiology of reading and reading disabilities. In M. Kamil, D. Mosenthal, P. Pearson, & R. Barr (Eds.), *Handbook of reading research* (Vol. 3, pp. 229–249). Mahwah, NJ: Erlbaum.

Shonkoff, J. P., & Hauser-Cram, P. (1988). Early intervention for disabled infants and their families. *Pediatrics, 80,* 650–658.

Shonkoff, J., & Meisels, S. (Eds.). (2000). *Handbook of early childhood intervention* (2nd ed.). New York: Cambridge University Press.

Shonkoff, J., & Phillips, D. (Eds.). (2000). *From neurons to neighborhoods.* Washington, DC: National Academy Press.

Shore, B., & Dela'court, M. (1996). Effective curricular and program practices in gifted education and the interface with general education. *Journal of Education of Gifted, 20,* 138–154.

Short, E. J., & Ryan, E. B. (1984). Metacognitive differences between skilled and less skilled readers: Remediating deficits through story grammar and attribution training. *Journal of Educational Psychology, 76*(7), 225–235.

Shriberg, L., & Kwiatowski, J. (1988). A follow-up study of children with phonological disorders of unknown origin. *Journal of Speech and Hearing Disorders, 53*(2), 144–145.

Shriver, M., & Piersal, W. (1994, Summer). The long-term effects of intrauterine drug exposure: Review of recent research and implications for early childhood special education. *Topics in Early Childhood Special Education, 14*(2), 161–183.

Siegel, E., & Wetherby, A. (2000). Nonsymbolic communication. In M. Snell & F. Brown (Eds.), *Instruction of students with severe disabilities* (5th ed., pp. 409–451). Upper Saddle River, NJ: Prentice Hall.

Siegler, R. (Ed.). (1986). *Children's thinking: What develops?* Englewood Cliffs, NJ: Prentice-Hall.

Silberman, R. (2000). Children and youths with visual impairments and other exceptionalities. In A. Koenig & M. Holbrook (Eds.), *Foundations of education: Vol. I. History and theory of teaching children and youths with visual impairments* (2nd ed., pp. 173–198). New York: American Foundation for the Blind Press.

Silberman, R., & Brown, F. (1998). Alternative approaches to assessing students who have visual impairments with other disabilities in classroom and community environments. In S. Sacks & R. Silberman (Eds.), *Educating students who have visual impairments with other disabilities* (pp. 73–98). Baltimore: Paul H. Brookes.

Silberman, R., Bruce, D., & Nelson, S. (2004). Children with severe disabilities. In F. Oreloves, D. Sobery, & R. S. Silberman (Eds.), *Educating children with multiple disabilities*. Baltimore: Brookes.

Silberman, R., Bruce, S., & Nelson, C. (2004). *Children with sensory impairments*. Baltimore: Paul H. Brookes.

Silver, L. B. (1990). Attention-deficit hyperactivity disorder: Is it a learning disability? *Journal of Learning Disabilities, 23,* 394–397.

Silverman, L. (1997). Family counseling with the gifted. In N. Colangelo & G. Davis (Eds.), *Handbook of gifted education* (2nd ed., pp. 382–397). Boston: Allyn & Bacon.

Silverman, L. (1998). The highly gifted. In J. Can-Tassel-Baska (Ed.), *Excellence in educating gifted and talented learners* (pp. 115–128). Denver: Love Publishers.

Silverman, L. K. (2002a). Asynchronous development. In M. Neihart, S. Reis, N. Robinson, & S. Moon (Eds.), *The social and emotional development of gifted children: What do we know?* (pp. 31–40). Waco, TX: Prufrock Press.

Silverman, L. K. (2002b). *Upside-down brilliance: The visual-spatial learner.* Denver, CO: DeLeon.

Simon, H. (1979). Information processing models of cognition. *Annual Review of Psychology, 30,* 363–396.

Simonoff, E., Bolton, P., & Rutter, M. (1998). Genetic perspectives on mental retardation. In J. Burack, R. Hodapp, & E. Zigler (Eds.), *Handbook of mental retardation and development* (pp. 41–79). New York: Cambridge University Press.

Simonton, D. (1999). *Origin of genius: Darwinian perspectives on creativity.* New York: Oxford University Press.

Simpson, R. (2002). Finding effective intervention and personnel preparation practices for students with autism spectrum disorders. *Exceptional Children, 70,* 135–144.

Simpson, R. (2004). *Exceptional Children, 70*(2), 135–144.

Simpson, R. L., Myles, B. S., Walker, B. L., Ormsbee, C. K., & Downing, J. A. (1991). *Programming for aggressive and violent children and youth.* Reston, VA: Council for Exceptional Children.

Skeels, H. M. (1966). Adult status of children with contrasting early life experiences. *Monographs of the Society for Research in Child Development, 31*(3), no. 105.

Skiba, H. N., & Knitzer, J. (1992). Classrooms for emotionally and behaviorally disturbed students: Facing the challenge. *Behavioral Disorders, 17,* 145–156.

Skinner, B. (1953). *Science and human behavior.* New York: Free Press.

Skinner, L., Gillespie, P., & Balkam, L. (1997). Waysiders in America's classrooms. *Technos, 6*(1), 29–31.

Slavin, R. (1988). *Student team learning: An overview and practical guide.* Washington, DC: Natural Education Association.

Smalley, S. (1997). Genetic influences in childhood-onset psychiatric disorders: autism and attention-deficit/hyperactivity disorder. *American Journal of Human Genetics, 60,* 1276–1282.

Smith, A., & Geruschat, D. (1996). Orientation and mobility for children and youth with low vision. In A. Corn & A. Koenig (Eds.), *Foundations of low vision: Clinical and functional perspective* (pp. 306–321). New York: American Foundation for the Blind.

Smith, A., & O'Donnell, L. (1991). *Beyond arms reach: Enhancing distance vision.* Philadelphia: Pennsylvania College of Optometry Press.

Smith, B., & Rapport, M. J. (1999). Early childhood inclusive policy and systems: What we know. In M. Guralnick (Ed.). *Early childhood inclusion: Focus on change* (pp. 49–68). Baltimore: Paul H. Brookes.

Smith, D., & Nelson, J. (1997). Goal setting, self-monitoring, and self-evaluation for students with disabilities. In M. Agran (Ed.), *Student-directed learning* (pp. 80–110). Pacific Grove, CA: Brookes/Cole.

Smith, S., Boone, R., & Higgins, K. (1998). Expanding the writing process to the web. *Teaching Exceptional Children, 30*(5), 5.

Snell, M. (1987). *Systematic instruction of persons with severe handicaps* (3rd ed.). Upper Saddle River, NJ: Merrill Prentice Hall.

Snell, M., & Brown, F. (2000a). Developing and implementing instructional programs. In M. Snell & F. Brown (Eds.), *Instruction of students with severe disabilities* (5th ed., pp. 115–172). Upper Saddle River, NJ: Merrill.

Snell, M., & Brown, F. (2000b). *Instruction of students with severe disabilities* (5th ed.). Upper Saddle River, NJ: Merrill.

Snell, M. E., Burton, C. C., Janney, R., Elliot, J., Colley, K. M., & Raynes, M. (2000). *Collaborative teaming.* Baltimore: Paul H. Brookes.

Snell, M., & Janney, R. (2000). *Collaborative teaming.* Baltimore: Paul H. Brookes.

Snow, C. (1999). Social perspectives on the emergence of language. In B. McWhinney (Ed.), *The emergence of language* (pp. 257–276). Mahwah, NJ: Erlbaum.

Snowling, M. J., & Perrin, D. (1988). Cognitive processes in written language dysfunction. In R. L. Schiefelbusch & L. Lloyd (Eds.), *Language perspectives* (pp. 147–185). Austin, TX: PRO-ED.

Snowman, J., & Biehler, R. (2000). *Pyschology applied to teaching* (9th ed.) Boston: Houghton Mifflin.

Solnit, G., Taylor, M., & Bednarczyk, A. (1992). *Access for all: Integrating deaf, hard of hearing and hearing students.* Washington, DC: Gallaudet University Press.

Southern, W., & Jones, E. (Eds.). (1991). *The academic acceleration of gifted children.* New York: Teachers College Press.

Sparrow, S., & Cicchetti, D. (2003). *Vineland adaptive behavior scales* (Vineland-II). Circle Pines, MN: AGS.

Speece, D., & Keogh, B. (Eds.). (1996). *Research on classroom ecologies: Implications for inclusion of children with learning disabilities.* Mahwah, NJ: Erlbaum.

Spencer, P., Ertling, C., & Marschark, M. (2000). *The deaf child in the family and at school.* Mahwah, NJ: Erlbaum.

Spiegel, H., & Bonwit, A. (2002). HIV infection in children In M. Batshaw (Ed.), *Children with disabilities* (5th ed., pp. 123–139). Baltimore: Paul H. Brookes.

Spillaine, J. P., Reiser, B. J., & Reimber, T. (2002). Policy implementation and cognition: Reframing and refocusing implementation research. *Review of Educational Research, 72,* 387–431.

Spinath, F., Harlaar, N., Ronald, A., & Plomin, R. (2004). Substantial genetic influence on mild mental impairment in early childhood. *American Journal of Mental Retardation, 109,* 34–43.

Sprague, J., & Walker, H. (2000). Early identification and invention for youth with antisocial and violent behavior. *Exceptional Children, 66(3),* 367–379.

Stainback, S., & Stainback, W. (1992). *Curriculum considerations on inclusive classrooms: Facilitating learning for all students.* Baltimore: Paul H. Brookes.

Stainback, S., & Stainback, W. (1996). *Inclusion: A guide to educators.* Baltimore: Paul H. Brookes.

Stanley, J. (1996). The study of mathematically precocious youth. In C. Benbow & D. Lubinski (Eds.), *International talent.* Baltimore: Johns Hopkins University Press.

Stanovich, K. (1986). Cognitive processes and the reading problems of learning disabled children. In J. K. Torgesen & B. Y. L. Wong (Eds.), *Psychological and educational perspectives on learning disabilities* (pp. 85–131). San Diego: Academic Press.

Stanton-Chapman, T., Stanton, D., & Scott, K. (2001). Identification of early risk factors for learning disabilities. *Journal of Early Intervention, 24(3),* 193–206.

Stein, M., Efron, L., Schiff, W., & Glazman, M. (2002). Attention deficits and hyperactivity. In M. Batshaw (Ed.), *Children with disabilities* (5th ed., pp. 389–416). Baltimore: Brookes.

Steinberg, A., & Knightly, C. (1997). Hearing: Sounds and silences. In M. L. Batshaw (Ed.), *Children with disabilities* (pp. 241–274). Baltimore: Paul H. Brookes.

Stephens, T., Blackhurst, A., & Magliocca, L. (1982). *Teaching mainstreamed students.* New York: Wiley.

Sternberg, L. (Ed.). (1991). *Functional communication.* New York: Springer-Verlag.

Sternberg, R. (1991). *The nature of creativity: Contemporary psychological perspectives.* Cambridge, MA: Cambridge University Press.

Sternberg, R. (1997). *Successful intelligence.* New York: Plume.

Sternberg, R. (1998, January). Teaching and assessing for successful intelligence. *School Administrator, 55,* 26–27, 30–31.

Stinson, M., & Foster, S. (2000). Socialization of deaf children and youths in school. In P. Spencer, C. Ertling, & M. Marschark (Eds.), *The deaf child in the family and at school* (pp. 191–209). Mahwah, NJ: Erlbaum.

Stolting, J. C. (1998, September). Acting civil. *Exceptional Parent,* 74.

Stone, C., & Conca, L. (1993). The origin of strategy deficits in children with learning disabilities. In L. J. Meltzer (Ed.), *Strategy assessment and instruction for students with learning disabilities* (pp. 23–60). Austin, TX: PRO-ED.

Stone, P. (1997). Educating children who are deaf or hard of hearing: Auditory-oral. *ERIC Digest, 551.*

Stone, W., Lee, E., Ashford, I., Brissie, J., Hepburn, S., Coonrod, E., & Dphr, H. (1999). Can autism be diagnosed accurately in children under 3 years? *Journal of Child Psychology and Psychiatry, 40,* 219–226.

Strain, P., Kohler, F., & Goldstein, H. (1996). Learning experiences, an alternative program: Peer-mediated interventions for young children with autism. In E. Hibbs & P. Jensen (Eds.), *Psychosocial treatments for child and adolescent disorders: Empirically based strategies for clinical practice* (pp. 573–586). Washington, DC: American Psychological Association.

Strauss, M. (1999). Hearing loss and CMV. *Volta Review, 99(5),* 71–77.

Streissgath, A. (1997). *Fetal alcohol syndrome.* Baltimore: Paul H. Brookes.

Stromswald, K. (1996). The cognitive and aural base of language acquisition. In M. S. Gazzanica (Ed.), *Cognitive neuroscience* (pp. 855–870). Cambridge: MIT Press.

Students with Disabilities and Special Education. (18th ed.). (2001). Birmingham, AL: Oakstone Legal and Business Publishing Co.

Sturomski, N. (1997, July). Inventions for students with learning disabilities. *NICHCY News Digest, 25,* 2–18.

Subotnik, R., Kassan, L., Summers, E., & Wasser, A. (1993). *Genius revisited: High IQ children grow up.* Norwood, NJ: Ablex.

Sugai, G. (2003). Mike is right: Lessons learned from reflections. *Behavioral Disorders, 28,* 217–230.

Supplee, P. (1990). *Reaching the gifted underachiever.* New York: Teachers College Columbia University.

Swanson, E., Harris, K., & Graham, S. (Eds.). (2003). *Handbook of learning disabilities.* New York: Guilford Press.

Swanson, H. (1999). Reading research for students with LD: A meta-analysis of intervention outcomes. *Journal of Learning Disabilities, 32,* 504–532.

Swanson, H. L. (2000). What instruction works for students with learning disabilities. In R. Gersten, E. Schiller, & S. Vaughn (Eds.), *Contemporary special education research* (pp. 1–30). Mahwah, NJ: Erlbaum.

Swanson, L. (1987). Verbal decoding effects on visual short-term memory of learning disabled and normal readers. *Journal of Educational Psychology, 70,* 539–544.

Szymanski, P. (1994). Transition: Life-span considerations for empowerment. *Exceptional Children, 60(5),* 402–410.

Tager-Flushberg, H., & Sullivan, K. (1998). Early language development in children with mental retardation. In J. Burack, R. Hodapp, & E. Zigler (Eds.), *Handbook of mental retardation and development* (pp. 208–239). New York: Cambridge University Press.

Tallal, P., Curtis, S., & Kaplan, S. (1988). The San Diego Longitudinal Study. In N. S. Garber & G. Mincher (Eds.), *International perspectives on communication disorders.* Washington, DC: Gallaudet University Press.

Tallal, P., Galaburda, D., Llinas, R., & Von Euler, C. (1993). *Temporal information processing in the nervous system.* New York: New York Academy of Science.

Tallal, P., Miller, J., Badi, G., Wang, X., Nagarajon, S., Schreiner, C., Jenken, W., & Merzenich, M. (1996, December). Language comprehension in language-learning impaired children improved with acoustically modified speech. *Science, 271,* 81–84.

Tallal, P., Miller, S., & Fitch, R. (1993). Neurological bases of speech: A case for the preeminence of temporal processing. *Annals of New York Academy of Science, 682,* 27–47.

Taylor, B., Miller, E., Lingam, R., Andrews, N., Simmons, A., & Stowe, J. (2002). Measles, mumps, and rubella vaccination and bowel problems or developmental regression in children with autism: population study. *British Medical Journal, 324,* 393–396.

Taylor, R. (1988). Assessment policies and procedures. In L. Sternberg (Ed.), *Educating students with severe or profound handicaps* (pp. 103–118). Austin, TX: PRO-ED.

Taylor, R. (1997). *Assessment of exceptional students* (pp. 510–515). Boston: Allyn & Bacon.

Taylor, R., & Murphy-Head, M. (1996). Access technology with computers for students who have visual impairments with other disabilities. In S. Sacks & R. Silberman (Eds.), *Educating students who have visual impairments with other disabilities* (pp. 469–496). Baltimore: Paul H. Brookes.

Taylor-Green, S., Brown, D., Nelson, L., Longton, J., Gassman, T., Cohen, J., Swartz, J., Homer, R., Sugai, G., & Hall, S. (1997). School-wide behavior support: Starting the year off right. *Journal of Behavior Education, 7,* 99–112.

Telzrow, C., & Bonar, A. (2002). Students with non-verbal learning disabilities. *Teaching Exceptional Children, 34*(6), 8–13.

Terman, L., & Oden, M. (1947). *The gifted child grows up: Twenty-five-year follow-up of a superior group* (Vol. 4). Stanford, CA: Stanford University Press.

Tharp, K., & Gallimore, R. (1988). *Rousing minds to life: Teaching, learning, and schooling in social context.* New York: Cambridge University Press.

Tindal, G., & Marston, D. (1986). Approaches to assessment. In J. K. Torgeson & B. Y. Wong (Eds.), *Psychological and educational perspectives on learning disabilities* (pp. 54–84). San Diego: Academic Press.

Todd, J. (1986). Resources, media, and technology. In G. Scholl (Ed.), *Foundations of education for blind and visually handicapped children and youth.* New York: American Foundation for the Blind.

Tolan, P. H., Gorman-Smith, D., & Henry, D. B. (2003). The developmental ecology of urban males' youth violence. *Developmental Psychology, 39,* 274–291.

Topor, I., Holbrook, M., & Koenig, A. (2000). Creating and nurturing effective educational teams. In A. Koenig & M. Holbrook (Eds.), *Foundations of education:* Vol. II. *Instructional strategies for teaching children and youths with visual impairments* (2nd ed., pp. 3–26). New York: Foundation for the Blind Press.

Torgesen, J. (1994). Issues in the assessment of executive function. In G. Lyon (Ed.), *Frames of reference for the assessment of learning disabilities* (pp. 475–514). Baltimore: Paul H. Brookes.

Torgesen, J. (1999). Reading disabilities. In R. Gallimore, L. Bernheimer, D. MacMillan, D. Speece, & S. Vaughn, (1999). *Developmental perspectives on children with high incidence disabilities* (pp. 157–181). Mahwah, NJ: Erlbaum.

Torgesen, J. (2002). Empirical and theoretical support for direct diagnosis of learning disabilities in assessment of intrinsic processing weakness. In R. Bradley, L. Danielson, & D. Hallahan (Eds.), *Identification of learning disabilities* (pp. 556–622). Mahwah, NJ: Erlbaum.

Torgesen, J., & Wagner, R. (1998). Alternative diagnostic approaches for specific developmental reading disabilities. *Learning Disabilities Research and Practice, 13*(4), 220–232.

Torgesen, J. K., & Wong, B. Y. L. (1986). *Psychological and educational perspectives on learning disabilities.* San Diego: Academic Press.

Torrance, E. (1969). *Creativity.* Belmont, CA: Dimensions Publishing Co.

Torres, I., & Corn, A. (1990). *When you have a visually handicapped child in your classroom: Suggestions for teachers.* New York: American Foundation for the Blind.

Tralli, R., et al. (1996). The Strategies Intervention Model: A model for supported inclusion at the secondary level. *Remedial and Special Education, 17*(4), 204–216.

Traxler, C. (2003). Measuring up to performance standards in reading and mathematics. *Journal of Deaf Studies and Deaf Education, 5,* 332–348.

Treffinger, D., Young, G., Selby, E., & Sheperdson, C. (2002). *Assessing creativity: A guide for educators.* Storrs, CT: National Research Center on the Gifted and Talented.

Tremblay, R., Pagani-Kurtz, L., Masse, L., Vitaro, F., & Pihl, R. (1995). A bimodal preventive intervention for disruptive kindergarten boys: Its impact through mid-adolescence. *Journal of Consulting and Clinical Psychology, 63*(4), 560–568.

Trieber, F. A., & Lahey, B. R. (1983). Toward a behavioral model of academic remediation with learning disabled children. *Journal of Learning Disabilities, 16,* 11–116.

Trivette, C., Dunst, C., Boyd, K., & Hamby, D. (1995). Family oriented program models, helpgiving practices, and parental control appraisals. *Exceptional Children, 62*(3), 237–248.

Trybus, R. (1985). *Today's hearing impaired children and youth: A demographic and academic profile.* Washington, DC: Gallaudet Research Institute.

Tsao, F. M., Huec-Mei, L., & Kull, P. (2004). Speech perception in the second year of life. *Child Development, 75*(4), 1067–1084.

Turkaspa, H. (2002). Social cognition in learning disabilities. In B. Wong & M. Donahue (Eds.), *The social dimensions of learning disabilities* (pp. 11–32). Mahwah, NJ: Erlbaum.

Turnbull, A., & Turnbull, H. (2000). Fostering family-professional partnerships. In M. Snell & F. Brown. (Eds.), *Instruction of students with severe disabilities* (5th ed., pp. 31–66). Upper Saddle River, NJ: Merrill.

Turnbull, A., & Turnbull, H. (2002). From the old to the new paradigm of disabilities and families. In J. Paul, C. Lavely, A. Cranston-Gingras, & E. Taylor (Eds.), *Rethinking professional issues in special education* (pp. 83–118). Westbrook, CT: Ablex.

Turnbull, A., & Turnbull, H. R. (1997). *Families, professionals, and exceptionality: A special partnership* (3rd ed.). Upper Saddle River, NJ: Merrill.

Turnbull, A., Edmonson, H., Griggs, P., Wickham, D., Sailor, W., Freeman, R., Guess, D., Lassen, S., McCart, A., Park, J., Riffel, L., Turnbull, R., & Warren, J. (2002). A blueprint for schoolwide positive behavior support: Implementation of three components. *Exceptional Children, 68*, 377–402.

Turnbull, A., Turnbull, H., Shank, M., & Leal, D. (1995). *Exceptional lives: Special education in today's schools.* Upper Saddle River, NJ: Prentice-Hall.

Tuttle, D., & Tuttle, N. (1996). *Self-esteem and adjusting with blindness* (2nd ed.). Springfield, IL: Charles C Thomas.

Tuttle, D., & Tuttle, N. (2000). Psychosocial needs of children and youths. In M. C. Holbrook & A. J. Koenig (Eds.), *Foundations of education* (2nd ed.), Vol. 1, *History and theory of teaching children and youths with visual impairments* (p. 167). New York: AFB Press.

Twachtman-Cullen, D. (2000). Moveable children with autism spectrum disorders. In A. Wetherby & B. Prizant (Eds.), *Autism spectrum disorders: A transactional developmental perspective* (pp. 225–250). Baltimore: Paul H. Brookes.

Upsur, C. (1990). Early intervention as preventive intervention. In S. Meisels & J. Shonkoff (Eds.), *Handbook of early childhood intervention* (pp. 633–650). New York: Cambridge University Press.

U.S. Department of Education. (1996). *To assure the free appropriate public education of all children with disabilities: Twentieth annual report to Congress on the implementation of the Individuals with Disabilities Education Act.* Washington, DC: Author. ERIC Document Reproduction Service No. ED 424 722.

U.S. Department of Education. (1997). *18th annual report to Congress on the implementation of Public Law 94–142: The Education of All Handicapped Children Act.* Washington, DC: U.S. Government Printing Office.

U.S. Department of Education. (1999a). *The free appropriate public education of children with disabilities.* Washington, DC. www.ed.gov/offices/osers.

U.S. Department of Education. (1999b). *Twenty-first annual report to Congress on the implementation of the Individuals with Disabilities Act.* Washington, DC: U.S. Department of Education.

U.S. Department of Education. (2002). *Fall 1998 elementary and secondary school civil rights compliance report.* Washington, DC: Office for Civil Rights.

U.S. Department of Education. (2003). *Twenty-fourth annual report to Congress: Individuals with Disabilities Education Act.* Washington, DC: Office of Special Education Programs.

Utley, C. A., & Obiakor, F. E. (2001). *Special education, multicultural education, and a school reform: Components of quality education for learners with mild disabilities.* Springfield, IL: Charles C. Thomas.

Vaillant, G., & Milofsky, M. (1980). Natural history of male psychological health. *American Journal of Psychiatry, 137*(11), 1348–1359.

Valdez, K., Williamson, C., & Wagner, M. (1990). *The National Longitudinal Study of special education students.*

Statistical almanac, Vol. 3, *Youth categorized as emotionally disturbed.* Menlo Park, CA: SRI International.

Valletutti, P. J. (1987). Social problems. In K. Kavale, S. Forness, & M. Bender (Eds.), *Handbook of learning disabilities:* Vol. 1. *Dimensions and diagnoses* (pp. 211–226). Boston: College-Hill/Little, Brown.

VanDenBerg, J., & Grealish, E. (1996). Individualized services and supports through the wraparound process: Philosophy and procedures. *Journal of Child and Family Studies, 5*(1), 7–21.

Vanderwood, M., McGrew, K., & Ysseldyke, J. (1998). Why we can't say much about students with disabilities during education reform. *Exceptional Children, 64*(3), 359–370.

Van Dijk, J. (1986). An educational curriculum for deaf-blind multiply handicapped persons. In D. Ellis (Ed.), *Sensory impairments in mentally retarded people* (pp. 375–382). San Diego: College-Hill Press.

Van Tassel-Baska, J. (1998). *Excellence in educating gifted and talented learners* (3rd ed.). Denver: Love Publishing.

Van Tassel-Baska, J. (Ed.). (2004). *Curriculum of gifted and talented students.* Thousand Oaks, CA: Corwin Press.

Vaughn, S., & Elbaum, B. (1999). Self-concept with friendships of students with learning disabilities. In R. Gallimore, L. Bernheimer, D. MacMillan, D. Speece, & S. Vaughn (1999). *Developmental perspectives on children with high incidence disabilities* (pp. 81–110). Mahwah, NJ: Erlbaum.

Vaughn, S., & Fuchs, L. (2003). Redefining learning disabilities as inadequate response to instruction: The promise and potential problem. *Learning Disabilities Research and Practice, 18*(3), 137–146.

Vaughn, S., Gersten, R., & Chard, D. (2000). The underlying message in LD instruction: Research findings from research synthesis. *Exceptional Children, 67*(1), 99–114.

Vaughn, S., Levy, S., Coleman, M., & Bos, C. S. (2002). Reading instruction for students with LD and BED: A synthesis of observation studies. *Journal of Special Education, 36*, 2–13.

Vaughn, S., Linen-Thompson, S., & Hickman, P. (2003). Response to instruction as a means of identifying students with reading/learning disabilities. *Exceptional Children, 69*(1), 391–409.

Vaughn, S., McIntosh, R., & Spencer-Rowe, J. (1991). Peer rejection is a stubborn thing: Increasing peer acceptance of rejected students with learning disabilities. *Learning Disabilities and Practice, 6*, 83–98.

Vellutino, F. (1987, March). Dyslexia. *Scientific American, 256*, 3.

Vigotsky, L. (1978). *Man in society.* Cambridge, MA: Harvard University Press.

Voeltz, L. (1980). Children's attitudes toward handicapped peers. *American Journal of Mental Deficiency, 84*, 455–464.

Volkmar, F. (Ed.). (1998). *Autism and pervasive developmental disorders.* New York: Cambridge University Press.

Wachs, T. (2000). *Necessary but not sufficient.* Washington, DC: American Pyschological Association.

Wagner, M., & Blackorby, J. (1996). Transition from high school to work or college: How special education students fare. In D. Terman, M. Lerner, C. Stevenson, & R. Behrman (Eds.), *The future of children, 6*(1), 4–24.

Wagner, R., Torgesen, J., & Rashutte, C. (1999). Comprehensive test of phonological processing. Austin, TX: PRO-ED.

Walker, H. M., Calvin, G., & Ramsey, E. (1995). *Antisocial behavior in school: Strategies and best practices.* Pacific Grove, CA: Brooks/Cole.

Walker, H. M., Stieber, S., Ramsey, E., & O'Neil, R. E. (1991). Longitudinal prediction of the school achievement, adjustment, and delinquency of antisocial versus at-risk boys. *Remedial and Special Education, 4,* 43–51.

Wallace, T., Anderson A., Bartholomay, T., & Hupp, S. (2002). An ecobehavioral examination of high school classrooms that include students with disabilities. *Exceptional Children, 68,* 345–360.

Wang, P., & Bacon, M. (1997). Language. In M. Batshaw (Ed.), *Children with disabilities* (pp. 275–292). Baltimore: Paul H. Brookes.

Wanzek, J., Bursuck, B., & Dickson, S. (2003). Evaluating the suitability of phonological awareness programs for children who are at risk. *Teaching Exceptional Children, 35*(4), 28–35.

Ward, L., & McCune, S. (2002). The first weeks of life. In M. Batshaw (Ed.), *Children with disabilities* (5th ed., pp. 69–84). Baltimore: Brookes.

Ward, M. J. (1996). Coming of age in the age of self-determination: A historical and personal perspective. In D. J. Sands & M. L. Wehmeyer (Eds.), *Self-determination across the life span: Independence and choice for people with disabilities* (pp. 3–36). Baltimore: Paul H. Brookes.

Warren, D. (1994). *Blindness and children: An individual differences approach.* New York: Cambridge University Press.

Warren, F. (1985). Call them liars who would say all is well. In H. Turnbull & A. Turnbull (Eds.), *Parents speak out: Then and now.* Columbus, OH: Merrill.

Warren, S. (2003). Genes, brains, and behavior: The road ahead (AAMD 2002 presidential address). *Mental Retardation, 40,* 471–476.

Warren, S. F., & Kaiser, A. P. (1988). Research in early childhood language intervention. In S. L. Odom & M. B. Karnes (Eds.), *Research in early childhood special education* (pp. 89–108). Baltimore: Paul H. Brookes.

Waxman, R., Spencer, P., & Poisson, S. (1996, Fall). Interactions between mothers and deaf and hearing children. *Journal of Early Intervention, 20*(4), 341–355.

Wehby, J., Symons, F., & Canale, J. (1998). Teaching practices in classrooms for students with emotional and behavior disorder: Discrepancies between recommendations and observations. *Behavior Disorders, 24*(1), 19–25.

Wehman, P. (1996). *Life beyond the classroom: Transition strategies for young people* (2nd ed.). Baltimore: Paul H. Brookes.

Wehmeyer, M., & Schwartz, M. (1997). Self-determination and positive adult outcomes: A follow-up study of youth with mental retardation or learning disabilities. *Exceptional Children, 63,* 245–255.

Wehmeyer, M., & Schwartz, M. (1998). The relationship between self-determination and quality of life. *Education and Training in Mental Retardation and Developmental Disabilities, 33,* 3–12.

Wehmeyer, M., Agran, M., & Hughes, C. (1998). *Teaching self determination to students with disabilities.* Baltimore: Paul H. Brookes.

Wehmeyer, M., Field, B., Doren, B., Jones, B., & Mason, C. (2004). Self-determination and student involvement in standards-based reform. *Exceptional Children, 70*(4), 413–425.

Weisz, J. (1999). Cognitive performance and learned helplessness in mentally retarded persons. In E. Zigler & D. Bennett-Gates (Eds.), *Personality development in individuals with mental retardation* (pp. 17–46). New York: Cambridge University Press.

Werner, E. (2004). What can we learn about resilience from large-scale longitudinal studies? In S. Goldstein & R. Brooks (Eds.), *Handbook of resilience in children.* New York: Kluwer Academic/Plenum.

Werner, E. E. (2000). Individual differences needs: A thirty-year study of resilient high-risk infants. *Zero to Three, 8,* 1–5.

Werner, E. E., & Smith, R. (2001). *Journeys from childhood to midlife.* Ithaca, NY: Cornell University Press.

Werner, E. E., & Smith, R. S. (1992). *Overcoming the odds.* Ithaca, NY: Cornell University Press.

Wesley, P. W., & Dennis, B. C. (2000). *Inclusive child care: A training series of early childhood professionals* (participant handbook). Chapel Hill: University of North Carolina, Frank Porter Graham Child Development Center, Partnerships for Inclusion.

Westlake, C. P., & Kaiser, A. (1991). Early childhood services for children with severe disabilities: Research, values, policies and practice. In L. Meyer, C. Peck, & L. Brown (Eds.), *Critical issues in the lives of people with severe disabilities* (pp. 429–458). Baltimore: Paul H. Brookes.

White, W., & Renzulli, J. (1987). A forty year follow up of students who attended Leta Hallingworth's school for gifted children. *Roeper Review, 10*(2), 89–94.

Whitmore, J. (1981). *Giftedness, Conflict and Underachievement.* Boston: Allyn & Bacon.

Wiggins, G. (1992, May). Creating tests worth taking. *Educational Leadership,* 26–33.

Will, G. F. (1993). Jon Will's aptitudes. In *The leveling wind.* New York: Viking Penguin.

Williams, D. (1999). The child who stutters: Guidelines for the educator. *Young Exceptional Children, 2*(3), 9–14.

Williams, K., & Baeker, M. (1983). Use of small groups with chronically ill children. *Journal of School Health, 53,* 205–208.

Williamson, G. (1987). *Children with spina bifida.* Baltimore: Paul H. Brookes.

Williamson, G. G., & Anzalone, M. (2001). *Sensory integration and self-regulation in infants and toddlers.* Washington, DC: Zero to Three.

Wilson, B. A. (1999). Inclusion: Empirical guidelines and unanswered questions. *Education and Training in Mental Retardation and Developmental Disabilities, 34,* 119–133.

Wise, B., & Snyder, L. (2002). Clinical judgments in identifying and teaching children with language-based reading difficulties. In R. Bradley, L. Danielson, & D. Hallahan

(Eds.), *Identification of learning disabilities: Research to practice* (pp. 653–692). Mahwah, NJ: Erlbaum.

Wissich, C., & Gardner, J. (2000). Multimedia or not multimedia. *Teaching Exceptional Children, 32*(4), 34–43.

Wolery, M. (1992). Preschoolers with learning disabilities. *Topics in Early Childhood Special Education, 12*(2).

Wolery, M., & Brookfield, J. (1988). Preacademic instruction for handicapped preschool children. *Journal of Applied Behavior Analysis, 25,* 117–126.

Wolery, M., Bailey, D., & Sugai, G. (1988). *Effective teaching: Principles and procedures of applied behavior analysis with exceptional children.* Boston: Allyn & Bacon.

Wolffe, K. (2000). Career education. In A. Koenig & M. Holbrook (Eds.). *Foundations of education: Vol. II. Instructional strategies for teaching children and youths with visual impairments* (2nd ed., pp. 679–719). New York: Foundation for the Blind Press.

Wong, B. (1986). Problems at issue of identification of learning disabled. In J. K. Torgesen & B. Y. L. Wong (Eds.), *Psychological and educational perspectives on learning disabilities* (pp. 3–22). San Diego: Academic Press.

Wong, B. (1999). Metacognition in writing. In R. Gallimore, L. Bernheimer, D. MacMillan, D. Speece, S. Vaughn (1999). *Developmental perspectives on children with high incidence disabilities* (pp. 183–271). Mahwah, NJ: Erlbaum.

Wong, D. (1998). Suit says welfare slights the disabled. *Boston Globe,* August 12, B1, B6.

Wood, L., Lasker, J., Siegel-Causey, E., Beukelman, D., & Ball, L. (1998). An input framework for augmentative and alternative communication. *Augmentative and Alternative Communication, 14,* 261–267.

Wood, L., Rankin, J., & Beukelman, D. (1997, August). Word prompt programs: Current uses and possibilities. *American Journal of Speech-Language Pathology, 6*(3), 57–65.

Wood, M. (1998). Whose job is it anyway? Educational roles in inclusion. *Exceptional Children, 64*(2), 181–195.

Wood, W., Karvonen, M., Test, D., Browder, D., & Algozzine, B. (2004). Promoting student self-determination skills in IEP planning. *Teaching Exceptional Children, 36*(3), 8–16.

Workman, S. (1986). Teachers' verbalizations and the social interactions of blind preschoolers. *Journal of Visual Impairment and Blindness, 80,* 532–534.

Writer, J. (1987). A movement-based approach to the education of students who are sensory impaired/multihandicapped. In L. Goetz, D. Guess, & K. Stremel-Campbell

(Eds.), *Innovative program design for individuals with dual sensory impairments* (pp. 191–224). Baltimore: Paul H. Brookes.

Wunsch, M., Conlon, C., & Scheidt, L. (2002). Substance abuse: A preventable threat to child development. In M. Batshaw (Ed.), *Children with disabilities* (5th ed., pp. 107–122). Baltimore: Brookes.

Yairi, E., Ambrose, N., & Cox, H. (1996, August). Genetics of stuttering: A cultural review. *Journal of Speech and Hearing Research, 39,* 771–784.

Yell, M. L., Rogers, D., & Rogers, E. L. (1998). The legal history of special education. *Remedial and Special Education, 19,* 219–228.

Yirmiya, N., Erel, O., Shaked, M., & Solomonica-Levi, D. (1998). Meta-analysis comparing theory of mind abilities of individuals with autism, individuals with mental retardation, and normally developing individuals. *Psychological Bulletin, 124,* 283–307.

Yoder, P., & Warren, S. (2004). Early predictors of language in children with and without Down syndrome. *American Journal of Mental Retardation, 109,* 285–300.

Zeitlin, S., & Williamson, G. (1994). *Coping in young children.* Baltimore: Paul H. Brookes.

Zigler, E., Finn-Stevenson, M., & Hall, N. (2003). *The first three years and beyond: Brain development and social policy.* New Haven: Yale University Press.

Zigler, E., Kagan, S., & Hall, N. (1996). *Children, families, and government.* New York: Cambridge University Press.

Zigmond, N. (1997). Educating students with disabilities. In J. W. Lloyd, E. Kameeui, & D. Chard (Eds.), *Issues in educating students with disabilities* (pp. 377–390). Mahwah, NJ: Erlbaum.

Zigmond, N., & Baker, J. (1990). Mainstream experiences for learning disabled students. *Exceptional Children, 57,* 176–185.

Zigmond, N., & Baker, J. (1995). Concluding comments: Current and future practice in inclusive schooling. *Journal of Special Education, 29*(2), 245–250.

Zigmond, N., Jenkins, J., Fuchs, L., Deno, S., Fuchs, D., Baker, J., Jenkins, L., & Contino, J. (1995). *Phi Delta Kappan,* 531–540.

Zipprich, M. (1995, January). Teaching web making as a guided planning tool to improve student narrative writing. *Remedial and Special Education, 16*(1), 3–15.

Zirpoli, T. (1990). Physical abuse: Are children with disabilities at greater risk? *Intervention in School and Clinic, 26*(1), 6–12.

AUTHOR/SOURCE INDEX